Land-Mobile Communications Engineering

Land-Mobile Communications Engineering

Edited by
Dennis Bodson
National Communications System

George F. McClure
Martin Marietta Orlando Aerospace

Samuel R. McConoughey
Federal Communications Commission

A volume in the IEEE PRESS Selected Reprint Series,
prepared under the sponsorship of the
IEEE Vehicular Technology Society.

IEEE PRESS

1884 1984
A CENTURY OF ELECTRICAL PROGRESS

The Institute of Electrical and Electronics Engineers, Inc., New York

IEEE PRESS

1983 Editorial Board

IEEE Order Number: PCO1685

Library of Congress Cataloging in Publication Data
Main entry under title:

Land-mobile communications engineering.

(IEEE Press selected reprint series)
Includes index.
1. Mobile communication systems—Addresses, essays,
lectures.   2. Data transmission systems—Addresses, essays,
lectures.   3. Radio, Short wave—Addresses, essays, lectures.   I. Bodson, Dennis.   II. McClure, George F.
III. McConoughey, Samuel R.
TK6570.M6L26   1984   621.3841'65   83-26564
ISBN 0-87942-174-6

Contents

Introduction

BOTH the practicing engineer and the newcomer to the field of mobile communications engineering will find this volume to be of assistance in their work. The material presented covers three separate areas of concern: mobile propagation, mobile data transmission, and communications systems and techniques for use in the 900 MHz band. Experienced engineers will find it convenient to have a single source for many of the standard references they use frequently. Newcomers will benefit from the selection of papers that, taken together, provide an overview of the field, and serve as a tutorial introducing them to the relevant issues and considerations in mobile communications design engineering. The papers presented here first appeared in various publications, including the IEEE TRANSACTIONS ON VEHICULAR TECHNOLOGY, the PROCEEDINGS OF THE IRE, the *Bell System Technical Journal,* and the *Review of Electrical Communication Laboratory.*

The first part of this volume covers mobile propagation over the frequency range from 40 MHz to 1370 MHz. There are 17 papers in this category. The first three papers survey propagation. Bullington presents a series of nomographs that have been found useful in solving radio propagation problems in the very-high-frequency range and above. Okumura *et al.* describe detailed propagation tests for the land-mobile radio service which were carried out at VHF (200 MHz) and UHF (453, 922, 1310, 1430, and 1920 MHz) during various situations over irregular terrain and environmental clutter. Egli presents an analysis of statistical wave propagation information on terrain effects versus frequency, antenna height, polarization, and distance, in expressions with empirical formulas and in the form of nomographs and correction curves amenable for use by the systems engineer. The next eight papers—Nylund, Reudink, Black and Reudink, Shepard, Cox and Leck, Cox (two papers), Young, and Turin *et al.*—discuss mobile radio propagation for mobile-to-mobile stations and mobile-to-base stations. These papers cover the frequency range from 150 MHz to 3700 MHz.

The next two papers address service areas for VHF/UHF land-mobile radio services. Barsis defines the service area of VHF/UHF land-mobile and broadcast stations, and demonstrates geographical and computer methods to determine such areas. Durkin describes a computer program written to predict the effective service area of a transmitter in a VHF or UHF mobile radio network. Following these are two papers by Lee which discuss the effects of the environment on antenna performance. The concluding paper by Nielson discusses coverage by spread-spectrum signals at microwave frequencies.

Part II of this volume focuses on data transmission for mobile communications, and is comprised of six papers. The first paper by Caples *et al.* describes the design and performance of a mobile channel simulator which simulates the ground mobile environment at UHF. Aulin investigates different ways of modeling the digital errors for a mobile radio channel at a comparatively low data rate (1200 bits/s). French presents a method of predicting the loss in error performance in mobile radio data transmission in which the variation in local mean signal level (shadowing) is included as well as fading. Otani *et al.* describe burst error performance encountered in digital land mobile radio channel. Hummels *et al.* present a technique for determining the error-rate performance of a digital communications system in a fading multipath environment. The concluding paper in this section by Karim discusses the transmission of digital data over a Rayleigh fading channel.

There are 13 papers in the third and final part of this volume which cover mobile communications above 800 MHz. The paper by Ito and Matsuzaka presents an overview on how an 800-MHz band land-mobile telephone system is going to be implemented in Tokyo and other cities. Hata *et al.* describe and discuss a procedure for a radio link design of a cellular land-mobile radio system. Rhee presents the results of field measurements in both an urban and rural environment to assess the accuracy of vehicle location at 820 MHz.

The next four papers address diversity techniques and frequency strategy for use in land-mobile radio systems. The papers by Adachi *et al.* and by Adachi address periodic switching diversity techniques. Yee's paper describes the performance of a two-branch equal-gain diversity system as a function of the cross correlation between two received signals from diversity antennas. Hattori and Hirade discuss advantages of providing control channels separate from voice channels in a high-capacity land-mobile telephone system which employs a small zone technique.

Advanced mobile phone service (AMPS) is the topic discussed in the next five papers. Blecher describes the advanced mobile telephone service system, which is an FM cellular radio system. Arredondo *et al.* describe the transmission features of the AMPS system, emphasizing the processing and control techniques designed to deal with the dynamic nature of the mobile radio channel. Ehrlich *et al.* describe the cell-site functional groups, their physical characteristics and design, and

1

the ways they interface with the rest of the AMPS system. Di Piazzo *et al.* discuss the "cellular test bed," which is a comprehensively instrumented field test laboratory supporting the development and evaluation of AMPS. The concluding paper in this group, by Huff, describes the developmental system, the activities which were prerequisite to the major system test phases, and the status of the system as of July 1978.

The final paper in this volume, by Balzano *et al.*, discusses energy deposition in simulated human tissues due to exposure from 800 MHz portable radio transmitters. This information is considered to be important in that a large number of operators are expected to be using equipment at these frequencies. The 800–900 MHz band is very close to the frequencies used for medical diathermy (918 MHz). Diathermy applicators at 918 MHz are well known for efficiently depositing energy deep into human tissue. This fact may create some concern about the exposure of the head of a portable transmitter operator because the radio is held close to the mouth in normal use.

Bringing together material from scattered and sometime difficult to obtain publications, this volume is intended to assist the engineer engaged in system design or applications engineering of mobile communications in the demanding environment posed by frequency bands above 800 MHz, as well as in the more familiar lower frequency bands. To the extent that the practicing land-mobile communications engineer finds this book useful in carrying out a variety of assignments, its purpose will have been fulfilled.

DENNIS BODSON
GEORGE F. MCCLURE
S. R. MCCONOUGHEY
Editors

Part I
Mobile Propagation

Radio Propagation for Vehicular Communications

KENNETH BULLINGTON, FELLOW, IEEE

Abstract—Radio propagation is affected by many factors including the frequency, distance, antenna heights, curvature of the earth, atmospheric conditions, and the presence of hills and buildings. The influence of each of these factors at frequencies above about 30 MHz is discussed with most of the quantitative data being presented in the series of nomograms. By means of three or four of these charts an estimate of the received power and the received field intensity for a given point-to-point radio transmission path ordinarily can be obtained in a minute or less. The theory of propagation over a smooth spherical earth is presented in a simplified form that is made possible by restricting the frequency range to above about 30 MHz where variations in the electrical constants of the earth have only a secondary effect. The empirical methods used in estimating the effects of hills and buildings and of atmospheric refraction are compared with experimental data on shadow losses and on fading ranges.

I. INTRODUCTION

METHODS of calculating ground-wave propagation over a smooth spherical earth have been given by Burrows and Gray and by Norton for all values of distance, frequency, antenna height, and ground constants [1], [2]. These two methods are different in form but they give essentially the same results. Both methods are relatively simple to use at the lower frequencies where grounded antennas are in common use, but their complexity increases as the frequency increases. At frequencies above 30 or 40 MHz, elevated antennas are in common use and the radio path loss between two horizontal antennas tends to be equal to the loss between two vertical antennas. In addition, both types of transmission tend to be independent of the electrical constants of the ground so that considerable simplification is possible. This paper presents a series of nomograms that have been found useful in solving radio propagation problems in the very-high-frequency range and above. These charts are arranged so that radio transmission can be expressed in terms of either the received field intensity or the received power delivered to a matched receiver. The field-intensity concept may be more familiar, but the power-transfer concept becomes more convenient as the frequency is increased.

In addition to the smooth earth theory an approximate method is included for estimating the effects of hills and other obstructions in the radio path. The phenomena of atmospheric

Manuscript received January 3, 1977. This invited paper consists of selections from two earlier papers written by the author. Only minor changes have been made in keeping with uniformity and standardized methods of expressing parameters, e.g., MHz, dBW, and μV/m. The papers are "Radio Propagation at Frequencies Above 30 Megacycles," PROCEEDINGS OF THE IRE, vol. 35, no. 10, pp. 1122-1136, October 1947 (also presented at National Electronics Conference, October 1946), and "Radio Propagation Fundamentals," *Bell System Technical Journal*, vol. 36, no. 3, 593–626, May 1957. Reprinting is by permission of the IEEE, the *Bell System Technical Journal*, and the National Electronics Conference, an activity of National Engineering Consortium, Inc.

The author is with Bell Laboratories, Holmdel, NJ 07733.

refraction (bending away from straight-line propagation), atmospheric ducts (tropospheric propagation), and atmospheric absorption are discussed briefly, but the principal purpose is to provide simplified charts for predicting radio propagation under average weather conditions. It is expected that normally the nomograms will provide the desired answer directly without any additional computation except the addition of the dB values obtained from three or four individual charts. The basic formulas are presented as an aid to understanding the principles involved and as a more accurate method should one be required. This paper does not consider sky-wave propagation although ionospheric reflections may occur at frequencies above 30 MHz and may cause occasional long-distance interference between systems operating on the same frequency.

A convenient starting point for the theory of radio propagation is the condition of two antennas in free space, which is discussed in terms of both received field intensity and received power. Since most radio paths cannot be considered to be free-space paths the next step is to determine the effect of a perfectly flat earth, and this is followed by the effect of the curvature of the earth. After the basic smooth-earth theory is completed there is a discussion of the variations in received power caused by atmospheric conditions and by irregularities on the earth surface, but the methods used in predicting these factors are necessarily less exact than the data for a smooth spherical earth in a uniform atmosphere.

II. FREE-SPACE FIELD

A free-space transmission path is a straight-line path in a vacuum or in an ideal atmosphere and sufficiently removed from all objects that might absorb or reflect radio energy. The free-space field intensity E_0 at a distance d meters from the transmitting antenna is given by

$$E_0 = \frac{\sqrt{30 g_1 P_1}}{d} \text{ V/m} \qquad (1)$$

where P_1 is the radiated power in watts and g_1 is the power-gain ratio of the transmitting antenna. The subscript 1 refers to the transmitter and the subscript 2 will refer to the receiver. For an ideal (isotropic) antenna that radiates power uniformly in all directions $g = 1$. For any balanced antenna in free space (or located more than a quarter-wavelength above the ground) g is the power-gain ratio of the antenna relative to the isotropic antenna. A small doublet or dipole whose overall physical length is short compared with a half-wavelength has a directivity gain of $g = 1.5$ (1.76 dB), and a half-wave dipole has a gain of $g = 1.64$ (2.15 dB) in the direction of maximum radiation. In other directions of transmission the field is reduced in accordance with the free-space antenna pattern obtained from

Reprinted from *IEEE Trans. Veh. Technol.*, vol. VT-26, pp. 295–308, Nov. 1977.

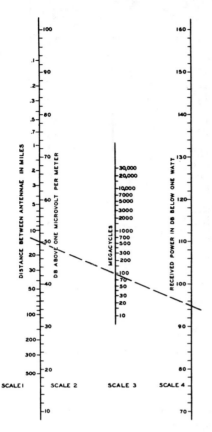

Fig. 1.   Free-space field intensity and received power between half-wave dipoles, 1 W radiated.

theory or measurement. Consequently, the freespace field intensity in a direction perpendicular to a half-wave dipole is

$$E_0 = \sqrt{\frac{30 \times 1.64 P_1}{d}} \sim 7\sqrt{\frac{P_1}{d}}. \qquad (2)$$

This field intensity in μV/m for 1 W of radiated power is shown on scale 2 of Fig. 1 as a function of the distance in miles shown on scale 1. For radiated power of P W the correction factor to apply to the field intensity or power is 10 log P (dB). For example, the free-space field intensity at 100 mi from a half-wave dipole radiating 1 W is 33 dBμV/m (about 45 μV/m). When the radiated power is 50 W (17 dBW) the received field intensity is 33 + 17 = 50 dBμV/m (about 315 μV/m). It will be noted that the field intensity is related to the energy density of the radio wave at the receiving antenna but is independent of the type of the receiving antenna.

The directivity gain of an array of n dipoles (sum of driven and parasitic elements) of optimum design is approximately equal to n times the gain of one dipole although some allowance should be made for antenna power losses. The theoretical power-gain ratio of a horn, paraboloid, or lens antenna whose aperture has an area of B m^2 is $g = 4\pi B/\lambda^2$; however, the effective area is frequently taken as one-half to two-thirds of the actual area of the aperture to account for antenna inefficiencies.

III. RELATION BETWEEN THE RECEIVED POWER AND THE RADIATED POWER

Before discussing the modifications in the free-space field that result from the presence of the earth, it is convenient to show the relation between the received field intensity (which is not necessarily equal to the free-space field intensity) and the power that is available to the receiver. The maximum useful power P_2 that can be delivered to a matched receiver is given by

$$P_2 = \left(\frac{E\lambda}{2\pi}\right)^2 \frac{g_2}{120} \text{ W} \qquad (3)$$

where

E received field intensity in volts per meter,
λ wavelength in meters = $300/F$,
F frequency in megacycles,
g_2 power-gain ratio of the receiving antenna.

This relation between received power and the received field intensity is shown by scales 2-4 in Fig. 1 for a half-wave dipole. For example, the maximum useful power at 100 MHz that can be picked up by a half-wave dipole in a field of 50 dBμV/m is $-$95 dBW.

A general relation for the ratio of the received power to the radiated power obtained from (1) and (3) is

$$\frac{P_2}{P_1} = \left(\frac{\lambda}{4\pi d}\right)^2 g_1 g_2 \left(\frac{E}{E_0}\right)^2. \qquad (4)$$

When both antennas are half-wave dipoles, the power transfer ratio is

$$\frac{P_2}{P_1} = \left(\frac{1.64\lambda}{4\pi d}\right)^2 \left(\frac{E}{E_0}\right)^2 = \left(\frac{0.13\lambda}{d}\right)^2 \left(\frac{E}{E_0}\right)^2 \qquad (4a)$$

and is shown in Fig. 1 for free-space transmission ($E/E_0 = 1$).

When the antennas are horns, paraboloids, or multi-element arrays, a more convenient expression for a ratio of the received power to the radiated power is given by

$$\frac{P_2}{P_1} = \frac{B_1 B_2}{(\lambda d)^2} \left(\frac{E}{E_0}\right)^2 \qquad (4b)$$

where B_1 and B_2 are the effective areas of the transmitting and receiving antennas, respectively. This relation is obtained from (4) by substituting $g = 4\pi B/\lambda^2$ and is shown in Fig. 2 for free-space transmission when $B_1 = B_2$. For example, the free-space loss at 4 GHz between two antennas of 10 ft^2 effective area is about 72 dB for a distance of 30 mi.

IV. TRANSMISSION OVER PLANE EARTH

The presence of the ground modifies the generation and the propagation of the radio waves so that the received field inten-

5

sity is ordinarily less than would be expected in free space. The ground acts as a partial reflector and as a partial absorber, and both of these properties affect the distribution of energy in the region above the earth. The principal effect of plane earth on the propagation of radio waves is indicated by the following equation [4], [5]:

$$E = E_0 [1 + \underbrace{Re^{j\Delta}}_{} + \underbrace{(1 - R)Ae^{j\Delta}}_{} + \cdots].$$

(5)

$$\underset{a)}{} \quad \underset{b)}{} \qquad \underset{c)}{} \qquad \underset{d)}{}$$

where a) is the direct wave, b) is the reflected wave, c) is the surface wave, and d) is the induction field and secondary effects of the ground. R is the reflection coefficient of the ground and is approximately equal to −1 when the angle θ between the reflected ray and the ground is small. The commonly used concept of a *perfectly conducting* earth, for which the reflection coefficient for vertical polarization is +1 for any angle of incidence, may cause some misunderstanding at this point. In practice the principal interest is in low angles, and as the angle θ approaches zero the reflection coefficient approaches −1 for any finite value for the conductivity of the earth, even if it were made of solid copper. The magnitude and phase of the reflection coefficient can be computed from the following equation[1]:

$$R = \frac{\sin \theta - z}{\sin \theta + z}$$

(6)

where

$$z = \sqrt{\epsilon_0 - \cos^2 \theta}/\epsilon_0 \text{ for vertical polarization,}$$

$$z = \sqrt{\epsilon_0 - \cos^2 \theta} \text{ for horizontal polarization,}$$

$$\epsilon_0 = \epsilon - j60\sigma\lambda,$$

---

[1] It will be noted that for vertical polarization this expression agrees with the data given by Burrows and subsequently included in [20], but for horizontal polarization it is the negative of that given in these references. This change was necessary in order to make (5) and (6) independent of polarization. The pseudo-Brewster angle frequently mentioned in the literature occurs when the reflection coefficient is a minimum and is approximately equal to the value of θ for which $\sin \theta = |z|$; this occurs with vertical polarization only, since $z > 1$ for horizontal polarization. The reflection coefficient is sometimes modified by a divergence factor to give a first approximation of the effect of the curvature of the earth, but this additional complication does not seem essential. The effect of the curvature of the earth is discussed in the next section, and for conditions of frequency and antenna height where some interpolation is required the possible variations due to atmospheric conditions are usually greater than the error introduced by the omission of the divergence factor. The measured data on the plane-earth reflection coefficient agrees reasonably well with the theoretical values at frequencies below about 1000 MHz. At higher frequencies the magnitude of the reflection coefficient is sometimes less than 1 presumably due to multiple reflections from the irregularities on the earth's surface. Measured values as low as −0.2 at 10 000 MHz over rolling country have been reported by W. M. Sharpless. The low value of reflection coefficient is not expected to be important for ground-to-ground transmission, but it tends to smooth the lobes that occur in the high-angle radiation, hence, may be important in air-to-ground transmission.

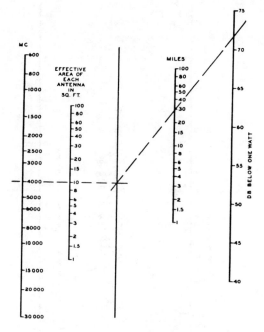

Fig. 2.　Received power in free space between two antennas of equal effective areas, 1 W radiated.

ϵ　dielectric constant of the ground relative to unity in free space,

σ　conducitivity of the ground in mhos per meter,

λ　wavelength in meters,

j　$= \sqrt{-1}$,

$e^{j\Delta}$　$= \cos \Delta + j \sin \Delta$.

The surface-wave attenuation factor A depends upon the frequency, ground constants, and type of polarization. It is never greater than unity and decreases with increasing distance and frequency as indicated by the following approximate equation[2]:

$$A \cong \frac{-1}{1 + j\dfrac{2\pi d}{\lambda}(\sin \theta + z)^2}.$$

(7)

The angle Δ used in (5) is the phase difference in radians resulting from the difference in the length of the direct and reflected rays. It is equal to $4\pi h_1 h_2/\lambda d$ radians when the distance d between antennas is greater than about five times the sum of the two antenna heights h_1 and h_2.

The effect of the ground shown in (5) indicates that ground-wave propagation may be considered to be the sum of three principal terms; namely, the direct wave, the reflected wave, and the surface wave. The first two types correspond to our common experience with visible light, but the surface

---

[2] This approximate expression is sufficiently accurate as long as $A < 0.1$, and it gives the magnitude of A within about 2 dB for all values of A. However, as A approaches unity, the error in phase approaches 180 deg. More accurate values are given by Norton, where in his nomenclature $A = f(P, B)e^{i\phi}$.

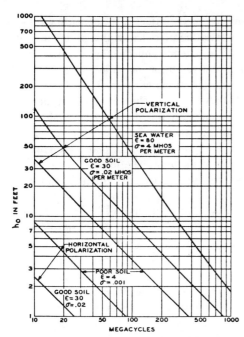

Fig. 3. Minimum effective height.

wave is less familiar. Since the earth is not a perfect reflector some energy is transmitted into the ground and is absorbed. As this energy enters the ground it sets up ground currents, which is another way of saying that the distribution of the electromagnetic field in the region near the surface of the earth is distorted relative to what it would have been over an ideal perfectly reflecting surface. The surface wave is defined as the vertical electric field for vertical polarization, or the horizontal electric field for horizontal polarization that is associated with these ground currents.[3]

The practical importance of the surface wave is limited to a region above the ground of about one wavelength over land or five to ten wavelengths over sea water since for greater heights the sum of the direct and reflected waves is larger in magnitude. Thus the surface wave is the principal component of the total ground wave at frequencies less than a few megahertz, but it is of secondary importance in the very high-frequency range (30 to 300 MHz) and it usually can be neglected at frequencies above 300 MHz.

A physical picture of the various components of the ground wave can be obtained from (5), but an equivalent expression which is more convenient for this discussion, is

$$\frac{E}{E_0} = 2 \sin \frac{\Delta}{2} + j[(1 + R) + (1 - R)A] e^{j(\Delta/2)}. \qquad (8)$$

When the angle $\Delta = 4\pi h_1 h_2/\lambda d$ is greater than about 0.5 radian the terms inside the brackets (which include the surface

wave) are usually negligible, and a sufficiently accurate approximation is given by

$$\frac{E}{E_0} = 2 \sin \frac{2\pi h_1 h_2}{\lambda d}. \qquad (8a)$$

In this case, the principal effect of the ground is to produce interference fringes or lobes so that the field intensity, at a given distance and for a given frequency, oscillates around the free-space field as either antenna height is increased.

When the angle Δ is less than about 0.5 rad the receiving antenna is below the maximum of the first lobe, and the surface wave may be important. A sufficiently accurate approximation for this condition is[4]

$$\left| \frac{E}{E_0} \right| = \left| \frac{4\pi h_1' h_2'}{\lambda d} \right|. \qquad (8b)$$

In this equation $h' = h + jh_0$ where h is the actual antenna height and $h_0 = \lambda/2\pi z$ has been designated as the minimum effective antenna height. The magnitude of the minimum effective height $|h_0|$ is shown in Fig. 3 for sea water and for "good" and "poor" soil. "Good" soil corresponds roughly to clay, loam, marsh, or swamp while "poor" soil means rocky or sandy ground.

The surface wave is controlling for antenna heights less than the minimum effective height, and in this region the received field or power is not affected appreciably by changes in the antenna height. For antenna heights that are greater than the minimum effective height, the received field or power is increased approximately 6 dB every time the antenna height is doubled until free-space transmission is reached. It is ordinarily sufficiently accurate to assume that h' is equal to the actual antenna height or the minimum effective antenna height, whichever is the larger.

The ratio of the received power to the radiated power for transmission over plane earth is obtained by substituting (8b) into (4), resulting in

$$\frac{P_2}{P_1} = \left(\frac{\lambda}{4\pi d} \right)^2 g_1 g_2 \left(\frac{4\pi h_1' h_2'}{\lambda d} \right)^2 = \left(\frac{h_1' h_2'}{d^2} \right)^2 g_1 g_2. \qquad (9)$$

This relation is independent of frequency and is shown in Figure 4 for half-wave dipoles ($g = 1.64$). A line through the two

---

[3] Another component of the electric field associated with the ground currents is in the direction of propagation. It accounts for the success of the wave antenna at lower frequencies, but it is always smaller in magnitude than the surface wave as defined above. The components of the electric vector in three mutually perpendicular coordinates are given by Norton.

[4] This approximate expression is obtained from (8) by assuming

$$\sin \theta = \frac{h_1 + h_2}{d} \ll z \qquad (a)$$

$$\sin \frac{2\pi h_1 h_2}{\lambda d} = \frac{2\pi h_1 h_2}{\lambda d} \qquad (b)$$

$$A = \frac{\lambda}{j 2\pi d z^2}. \qquad (c)$$

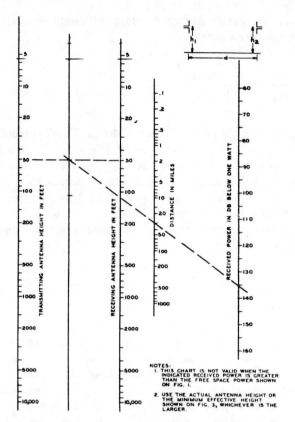

Fig. 4. Received power over plane earth between half-wave dipoles, 1 W radiated.

scales of antenna height determines the point on the unlabeled scale between them, and a second line through this point and the distance scale determines the received power for 1 W radiated. When the received field intensity is desired, the power indicated on Fig. 4 can be transferred to scale 4 of Fig. 1, and a line through the frequency on scale 3 indicates the received field intensity on scale 2. The results shown in Fig. 4 are valid as long as the value of received power indicated is lower than shown in Fig. 1 for free-space transmission. When this condition is not met, it means that the angle Δ is too large for (8b) to be accurate, and that the received field intensity or power oscillates around the free-space value as indicated by (8a).

As an example, consider a 250-W 30-MHz transmitter with both transmitting and receiving dipoles mounted 50 ft above the ground and separated by a distance of 30 mi over plane earth. The transmission loss is shown in Fig. 4 to be 135.5 dB. Since 250W is 24 dBW, the received power is 24 − 135.5 = −111.5 dBW. (The free-space power transfer shown in Fig. 1 indicates a received power of 24 − 91 = −67 dBW, so Fig. 4 is controlling.) The received field intensity can be obtained from Fig. 1, which shows that a received power of −111.5 dBW corresponds to a received field intensity of about 23 dBuV/m at a frequency of 30 MHz. Should one antenna be only 10 ft above "good" soil, rather than 50 ft, the minimum effective height of 30 ft shown in Fig. 3 should be used on one of the height scales in Fig. 4 in determining the transmission loss. It will be noted that this example assumes a perfectly flat earth. The curvature of the earth introduces an additional loss of about 4 dB, as discussed in the next section.

In addition to the effect of plane earth on the propagation of radio waves, the presence of the ground may affect the impedance of an antenna and thereby may have an effect on the generation and reception of radio waves. This effect usually can be neglected at frequencies above 30 MHz except where whip antennas are used. The impedance in the presence of the ground oscillates around the free-space value, but the variations are unimportant as long as the center of the antenna is more than a quarter-wavelength above the ground. A convenient method of showing the effect of the change in impedance of a balanced antenna near the ground is to replace the directivity gain g in the preceding formulas by the arbitrary factor of $g' = g/r$ where r is the ratio of the input resistance in the presence of the ground to the input resistance of the same antenna in free space. This assumes an impedance match between the antenna and the transmitting equipment with proper tuning to balance out any reactance.

For horizontal dipoles less than a quarter-wavelength above the ground the ratio r is less than unity. It approaches zero as the antenna approaches a perfectly conducting earth, but in practice it does not reach zero at zero height because of the finite conductivity of the earth. The wave antenna and the top-loaded antenna frequently used at lower frequencies are sometimes called horizontal antennas, but since they are used to radiate or receive vertically polarized waves they are not horizontal antennas in the sense used here.

For vertical half-wave dipoles the factor r is approximately equal to unity since the height of the center of the antenna can never be less than a quarter-wavelength above the ground. For very short vertical dipoles, however, the ratio r is greater than unity, and it approaches a value of $r = 2$ for antennas very near to the ground. This means that, whereas a short vertical dipole whose total length $2l$ is small compared with the wavelength that has an input radiation resistance of $80(\pi l/\lambda)^2$ Ω in free space, it has a resistance of $160(\pi l/\lambda)^2$ Ω near the ground.

Correct results for a vertical whip antenna working against a perfectly counterpoise are obtained by using $r = 2$. This means that a vertical whip antenna of length l is 3 dB less efficient than a dipole of length $2l$ (located more than a quarter-wavelength above the ground) for either transmitting or receiving. The poorer efficiency at the receiver is not important when external noise is controlling.

V. FADING PHENOMENA

Variations in signal level with time are caused by changing atmospheric conditions. The severity of the fading usually increases as either the frequency or path length increases. Fading cannot be predicted accurately, but it is important to distinguish between two general types: (1) inverse bending and (2) multipath effects. The latter includes the fading caused by interference between direct and ground reflected waves as well as interference between two or more separate paths in the atmosphere. Ordinarily, fading is a temporary diversion of energy to some other than the desired location.

The path of a radio wave is not a straight line except for the ideal case of a uniform atmosphere. The transmission path

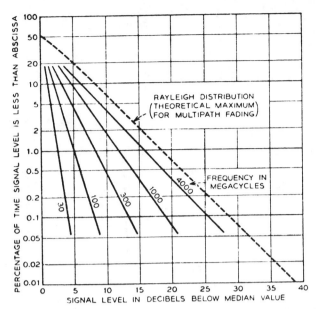

Fig. 5. Typical fading characteristics in the worst month on 30 to 40 mile line-of-sight paths with 50 to 100 ft clearance.

may be bent up or down depending on atmospheric conditions. This bending may either increase or decrease the effective path clearance and inverse bending may have the effect of transforming a line of sight path into an obstructed one. This type of fading may last for several hours. The frequency of its occurrence and its depth can be reduced by increasing the path clearance, particularly in the middle of the path.

Severe fading may occur over water or on other smooth paths because the phase difference between the direct and reflected rays varies with atmospheric conditions. The result is that the two rays sometimes add and sometimes tend to cancel. This type of fading can be minimized, if the terrain permits, by locating one end of the circuit high while the other end is very low. In this way the point of reflection is placed near the low antenna and the phase difference between direct and reflected rays is kept relatively steady.

Most of the fading that occurs on "rough" paths with adequate clearance is the result of interference between two or more rays traveling slightly different routes in the atmosphere. This multipath type of fading is relatively independent of path clearance, and its extreme condition approaches the Rayleigh distribution. In the Rayleigh distribution, the probability that the instantaneous value of the field is greater than the value R is $\exp[-(R/R_0)^2]$ where R_0 is the rms value.

Representative values of fading on a path with adequate clearance are shown in Fig. 5. After the multipath fading has reached the Rayleigh distribution, a further increase in either distance or frequency increases the number of fades of a given depth, but it decreases the duration so that the product is the constant indicated by the Rayleigh distribution.

VI. TROPOSPHERIC TRANSMISSION BEYOND LINE OF SIGHT

A basic characteristic of electromagnetic waves is that the energy is propagated in a direction perpendicular to the sur-face of uniform phase. Radio waves travel in a straight line only as long as the phase front is plane and is infinite in extent.

Energy can be transmitted beyond the horizon by three principal methods: reflection, refraction, and diffraction. Reflection and refraction are associated with either sudden or gradual changes in the direction of the phase front, while diffraction is an edge effect that occurs because the phase surface is not infinite. When the resulting phase front at the receiving antenna is irregular in either amplitude or position, the distinctions between reflection, refraction, and diffraction tend to break down. In this case the energy is said to be scattered. Scattering is frequently pictured as a result of irregular reflections although irregular refraction plus diffraction may be equally important.

The following paragraphs describe first the theories of refraction and of diffraction over a smooth sphere and a knife edge. This is followed by empirical data derived from experimental results on the transmission to points far beyond the horizon, on the effects of hills and trees, and on fading phenomena.

Refraction

The dielectric constant of the atmosphere normally decreases gradually with increasing altitude. The result is that the velocity of transmission increases with the height above the ground, and on the average the radio energy is bent or refracted toward the earth. As long as the change in dielectric constant is linear with height, the net effect of refraction is the same as if the radio waves continued to travel in a straight line but over an earth whose modified radius is

$$ka = \frac{a}{1 + \dfrac{a}{2}\dfrac{d\epsilon}{dh}} \qquad (10)$$

where

a	true radius of earth,
$d\epsilon/dh$	rate of change of dielectric constant with height.

Under certain atmospheric conditions the dielectric constant may increase ($0 < k < 1$) over a reasonable height, thereby causing the radio waves in this region to bend away from the earth. Since the earth's radius is about 2.1×10^7 ft (6.4×10^6 m), a decrease in dielectric constant of only 2.4×10^{-8}/ft (7.9×10^{-8}/m) of height results in a value of $k = 4/3$, which is commonly assumed to be a good average value [6]. When the dielectric constant decreases about four times as rapidly (or by about 10^{-7} per foot (3.3×10^{-7}/m of height), the value of $k = \infty$. Under such a condition, as far as radio propagation is concerned, the earth can then be considered flat, since any ray that starts parallel to the earth will remain parallel.

When the dielectric constant decreases more rapidly than 10^{-7}/ft (3.3×10^{-7}/m) of height, radio waves that are radiated parallel to or at an angle above the earth's surface may be bent downward sufficiently to be reflected from the earth. After reflection the ray is again bent toward the earth, and the path of a typical ray is similar to the path of a bouncing tennis ball. The radio energy appears to be trapped in a duct or waveguide between the earth and the maximum height of the radio path. This phenomenon is variously known as trapping, duct transmission, anomalous propagation, or guided propagation [7], [8]. It will be noted that in this case the path of a typical guided wave is similar in form to the path of sky waves, which are lower frequency waves trapped between the earth and the ionosphere. However, there is little or no similarity between the virtual heights, the critical frequencies, or the causes of refraction in the two cases.

Duct transmission is important because it can cause long distance interference with another station operating on the same frequency; however, it does not occur often enough nor can its occurrence be predicted with enough accuracy to make it useful for radio services requiring high reliability.

Diffraction over a Smooth Spherical Earth and Ridges

Radio waves are also transmitted around the earth by the phenomenon of diffraction. Diffractions is a fundamental property of wave motion, and in optics it is the correction to apply to geometrical optics (ray theory) to obtain the more accurate wave optics. In other words, all shadows are somewhat "fuzzy" on the edges, and the transition from "light" to "dark" areas is gradual rather than infinitely sharp. Our common experience is that light travels in straight lines and that shadows are sharp, but this is only because the diffraction effects for these very short wavelengths are too small to be noticed without the aid of special laboratory equipment. The order of magnitude of the diffraction at radio frequencies may be obtained by recalling that a 1000-MHz radio wave has about the same wavelength as a 1000-Hz sound wave in air so that these two types of waves may be expected to bend around absorbing obstacles with approximately equal facility.

The effect of diffraction around the earth's curvature is to make possible transmission beyond the line-of-sight. The magnitude of the loss caused by the obstruction increases as either the distance or the frequency is increased, and it depends to some extent on the antenna height [1]. The loss resulting from the curvature of the earth is indicated by Fig. 6 as long as neither antenna is higher than the limiting value shown at the top of the chart. This loss is in addition to the transmission loss over plane earth obtained from Fig. 4.

When either antenna is as much as twice as high as the limiting value shown in Fig. 6, this method of correcting for the curvature of the earth indicates a loss that is too great by about 2 dB with the error increasing as the antenna height increases. An alternate method of determining the effect of the earth's curvature is given by Fig. 7. The latter method is approximately correct for any antenna height, but it is theoretically limited in distance to points at or beyond the line-of-sight assuming that the curved earth is the only obstruction. Fig. 7 gives the loss relative to free-space transmission (and hence is used with Fig. 1) as a function of three distances: d_1 is the distance to the horizon from the lower antenna, d_2 is the distance to the horizon from the higher antenna, and d_3 is the distance beyond the line-of-sight. In other words, the total distance between antennas is $d = d_1 + d_2 + d_3$. The dis-

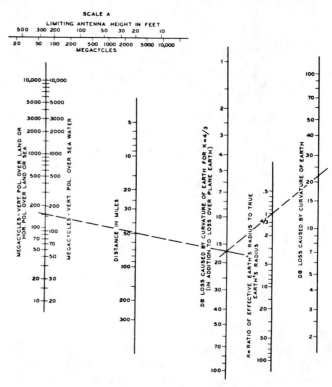

Fig. 6. Diffraction loss caused by curvature of the earth assuming neither antenna height is higher than shown on scale A.

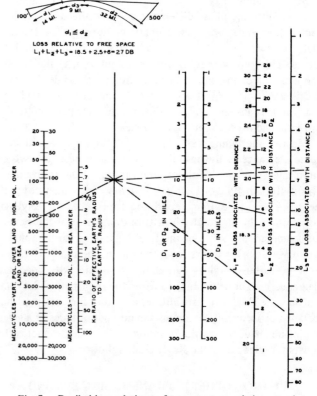

Fig. 7. Decibel loss relative to free-space transmission at points beyond line-of-sight over a smooth earth.

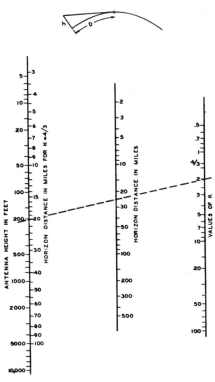

Fig. 8.   Distance to horizon.

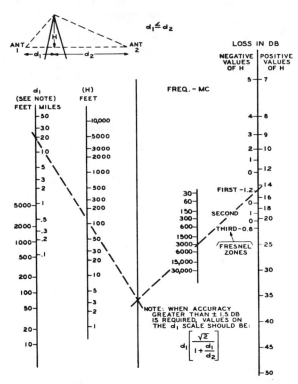

Fig. 9.   Knife-edge diffraction loss relative to free space.

tance to the horizon over smooth earth is shown in Fig. 8 and is given by

$$d_{1,2} = \sqrt{2kah_{1,2}} \qquad (11)$$

where $h_{1,2}$ is the appropriate antenna height and ka is the effective earth's radius.

The preceding discussion assumes that the earth is a perfectly smooth sphere, and the results are critically dependent on a smooth surface and a uniform atmosphere. The modification in these results caused by the presence of hills, trees, and buildings is difficult or impossible to compute, but the order of magnitude of these effects may be obtained from a perfectly absorbing knife edge.

The diffraction of plane waves over a knife edge or screen causes a shadow loss whose magnitude is shown in Fig. 9 The height of the obstruction H is measured from the line joining the two antennas to the top of the ridge. It will be noted that the shadow loss approaches 6 dB as H approaches 0 (grazing incidence), and that it increases with increasing positive values of H. When the direct ray clears the obstruction H is negative, and the shadow loss approaches 0 dB in an oscillatory manner as the clearance is increased. In other words, a substantial clearance is required over line-of-sight paths in order to obtain "free-space" transmission. The knife edge diffraction calculation is substantially independent of polarization as long as the distance from the edge is more than a few wavelengths.

At grazing incidence the expected loss over a ridge is 6 dB, (Fig. 9) while over a smooth sperical earth Fig. 7 indicates a loss of about 20 dB. More accurate results in the vicinity of

the horizon can be obtained by expressing radio transmission in terms of path clearance measured in Fresnel zones as shown in Fig. 10. In this representation the plane earth theory and the ridge diffraction can be represented by single lines, but the smooth sphere theory requires a family of curves with a parameter M that depends primarily on antenna heights and frequency. The big difference in the losses predicted by diffraction around a perfect sphere and by diffraction over a knife edge indicates that diffraction losses depend critically on the assumed type of profile. A suitable solution for the intermediate problem of diffraction over a rough earth has not yet been obtained.

The problem of two or more knife-edge obstructions between the transmitting and receiving antennas such as shown in Fig. 11(a) has not been solved rigorously. However, graphical integration indicates that the shadow loss for this case is equivalent within 2 or 3 dB to the shadow loss for the knife edge represented by the height of the triangle composed of a line joining the two antennas and a line from each antenna through the top of the peak that blocks the line-of-sight from that antenna.

Thus far it has been assumed that the transmission between the two antennas would be approximately the same as in free space if the obstacles could be removed. This assumption is usually valid only at centimeter wavelengths, and at lower frequencies it is necessary to include the effects of waves reflected from the ground. This results in four paths, namely, MOQ, MOQ' $M'OQ$, and $M'OQ'$ shown in Fig. 11(b) for a single obstruction. Each of these paths is similar in form to the single path illustrated by Figure 11(a). The sum of the field intensi-

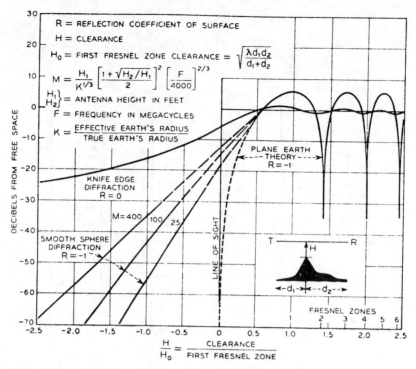

Fig. 10.   Transmission loss versus clearance.

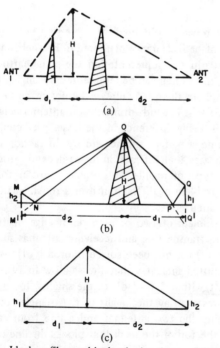

Fig. 11.   Ideal profiles used in developing theory of diffraction over hills.

ties over these four paths, considering both magnitude and phase, is given by the following equation:

$$\left|\frac{E}{E_0}\right| = S_1\left[1 - \frac{S_2}{S_1}e^{-j(\Delta+b)} - \frac{S_3}{S_1}e^{-j(\Delta+c)} + \frac{S_4}{S_1}e^{-j(b+c)}\right]$$

(12)

where

E received field intensity,
E_0 free-space field intensity,
S_1 magnitude of the shadow loss over path MOQ,
S_2 magnitude of the shadow loss over path MOQ',
S_3 Magnitude of the shadow loss over path $M'OQ$,
S_4 Magnitude of the shadow loss over path $M'OQ'$,
Δ $=4\pi h_1 h_2/\lambda(d_1 + d_2)$ radians,
b approximately equal to $4\pi h_2 H/\lambda d_2$ rad,
c approximately equal to $4\pi h_1 H/\lambda d_1$ rad.

This equation assumes that the reflection coefficient is -1 and that the actual antenna heights are greater than the minimum effective antenna height h_0. This means that the surface wave is neglected, and the equation fails when either antenna height approaches zero. The angles b and c are phase angles associated with the diffraction phenomena, and the approximate values given above assume that H is greater than h_1 or h_2. This assumption permits the shadow losses to be averaged so that $S_1 = S_2 = S_3 = S_4 = S$. After several algebraic manipulations (12) can be reduced to

$$\left|\frac{E}{E_0}\right| = 2(2S)\left|\sin\frac{\Delta}{2}\cos\frac{b-c}{2}\right.$$

$$\left. + j\left(\sin^2\frac{b+c}{4} - \sin^2\frac{b-c}{4}\right)e^{j(\Delta/2)}\right|$$

(13)

where S is the average shadow loss for the four paths. This means that the shadow triangle should be drawn from a point

12

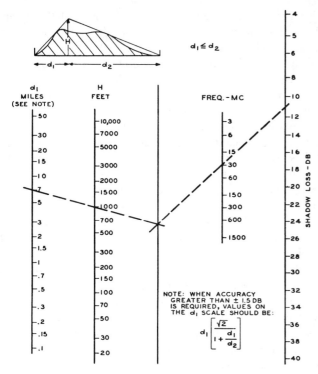

Fig. 12. Shadow loss relative to smooth earth.

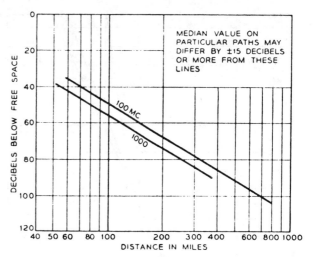

Fig. 13. Beyond-horizon transmission; median signal level versus distance.

midway between the location of the actual antenna and the image antenna as shown in Fig. 11(c). For small values of H this equation is approximately equal to

$$\left| \frac{E}{E_0} \right| = 2(2S) \sin \frac{\Delta}{2}. \tag{14}$$

Since the field intensity over plane earth (assuming that the antenna heights are greater than the minimum effective height h_0) is $2E_0 \sin \Delta/2$, the first-order effect of the hill is to add a loss of 20 log $2S$ which is shown by the nomogram in Fig. 12. The complete expression given in (12) indicates that, under favorable conditions, the field intensity behind sharp ridges may be greater than over plane earth. This result has been found experimentally in a few cases, but the correlation between theory and experiment is not complete. In general, the field intensity predicted by either (12) or (13) tends to be too high; that is, shadow losses rather than gains occur on most of the paths on which measured data are available. The less-approximate expression given in (14) agrees more closely with experimental data, is more conservative, and is easier to use. Consequently, it is usually assumed that the effect of obstructions to line-of-sight transmission (at least in the 30- to 150-MHz range) is to introduce the loss shown in Fig. 12 in addition to the normal loss over smooth earth for the antenna heights and distances involved. Measured results on a large number of paths in the 30- to 150-MHz range indicate that about 50 percent of the paths are within 5 or 6 dB of the values predicted on this basis. The correlation on 10 percent of the paths is no better than 10 to 12 dB, and an occasional path may differ by 20 dB.

VII. EXPERIMENTAL DATA FAR BEYOND THE HORIZON

Most of the experimental data at points far beyond the horizon fall in between the theoretical curves for diffraction over a smooth sphere and for diffraction over a knife edge obstruction. Various theories have been advanced to explain these effects, but none has been reduced to a simple form for every day use [9]. The explanation most commonly accepted is that energy is reflected or scattered from turbulent air masses in the volume of air that is enclosed by the intersection of the beamwidths of the transmitting and receiving antennas [10].

The variation in the long term median signals with distance has been derived from experimental results and is shown in Fig. 13 for two frequencies [11]. The ordinate is in decibels below the signal that would have been expected at the same distance in free space with the same power and the same antennas. The strongest signals are obtained by pointing the antennas at the horizon along the great circle route. The values shown in Fig. 13 are essentially annual averages taken from a large number of paths, and substantial variations are to be expected with terrain, climate, and season as well as from day to day fading.

Antenna sites with sufficient clearance so that the horizon is several miles away will on the average provide a higher median signal (less loss) than shown in Fig. 13. Conversely, sites for which the antenna must be pointed upward to clear the horizon will ordinarily result in appreciably more loss than shown in Fig. 13. In many cases the effects of path length and angles to the horizon can be combined by plotting the experimental results as a function of the angle between the lines drawn tangent to the horizon from the transmitting and receiving sites [12].

When the path profile consists of a single sharp obstruction that can be seen from both terminals, the signal level may approach the value predicted by the knife edge diffraction theory [13]. While several interesting and unusual cases have been recorded, the knife edge or "obstacle gain" theory is not applicable to the typical but only to the exceptional paths.

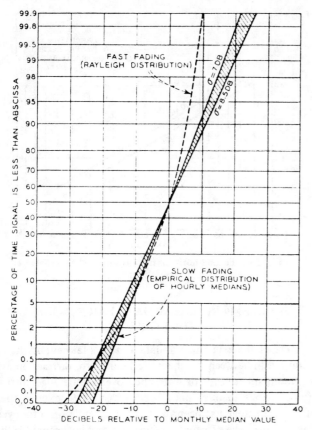

Fig. 14. Typical fading characteristics at points far beyond horizon.

gain antenna, and perhaps 6 to 8 dB for a 50-dB antenna. These extra losses vary with time, but the variations seem to be uncorrelated with the actual signal level.

The bandwidth that can be used on a single radio carrier is frequently limited by the selective fading caused by multipath or echo effects. Echoes are not troublesome as long as the echo time delays are very short compared with one cycle of the highest baseband frequency. The probability of long delayed echoes can be reduced (and the rate of fast fading can be decreased) by the use of narrow beam antennas both within and beyond the horizon [13], [15]. Useful bandwidths of several megahertz appear to be feasible with the antennas that are needed to provide adequate signal-to-noise margins. Successful tests of television and of multichannel telephone transmission have been reported on a 188-mi path at 5 000 MHz [16].

The effects of fast fading can be reduced substantially by the use of either frequency or space diversity. The frequency or space separation required for diversity varies with time and with the degree of correlation that can be tolerated. A horizontal (or vertical) separation of about 100 wavelengths is ordinarily adequate for space diversity on 100- to 200-mi paths. The corresponding figure for the required frequency separation for adequate diversity seems likely to be more than 20 MHz.

VIII. EFFECTS OF NEARBY HILLS—PARTICULARLY ON SHORT PATHS

The experimental results on the effects of hills indicate that the shadow losses increase with the frequency and with the roughness of the terrain [17]. An empirical summary of the available data is shown in Fig. 15. The roughness of the terrain is represented by the height H shown on the profile at the top of the chart. This height is the difference in elevation between the bottom of the valley and the elevation necessary to obtain line-of-sight from the transmitting antenna. The right-hand scale in Fig. 15 indicates the additional loss above the expected over plane earth. Both the median loss and the difference between the median and the 10 percent values are shown. For example, with variations in terrain of 500 ft, the estimated median shadow loss at 450 MHz is about 20 dB, and the shadow loss exceeded in only 10 percent of the possible locations between points A and B is about 20 + 15 = 35 dB. It will be recognized that this analysis is based on large-scale variations in field intensity and does not include the standing-wave effects which sometimes cause the field intensity to vary considerably within a few feet.

IX. EFFECTS OF BUILDINGS AND TREES

The shadow losses resulting from buildings and trees follow somewhat different laws from those caused by hills. Buildings may be more transparent to radio waves than the solid earth, and there is ordinarily much more back scatter in the city than in the open country. Both of these factors tend to reduce the shadow losses caused by the buildings, but on the other hand

As in the case of line-of-sight transmission the fading of radio signals beyond the horizon can be divided into fast fading and slow fading. The fast fading is caused by multipath transmission in the atmosphere, and for a given size antenna the rate of fading increases as either the frequency or the distance is increased. This type of fading is much faster than the maximum fast fading observed on line-of-sight paths, but the two are similar in principle. The magnitude of the fades is described by the Rayleigh distribution.

Slow fading means variations in average signal level over a period of hours or days, and it is greater on beyond horizon paths than on line-of-sight paths. This type of fading is almost independent of frequency and seems to be associated with changes in the average refraction of the atmosphere. At distances of 150 to 200 mi the variations in hourly median value around the annual median seem to follow a normal probability law in decibels with a standard deviation of about 8 dB. Typical fading distributions are shown in Fig. 14. The median signals levels are higher in warm humid climates than in cold dry climates, and seasonal variations of as much as ±10 dB or more from the annual median have been observed [14].

Since the scattered signals arrive with considerable phase irregularities in the plane of the receiving antenna, narrow-beamed (high gain) antennas do not yield power outputs proportional to their theoretical area gains. This effect has sometimes been called loss in antenna gain but it is a propagation effect and not an antenna effect. On 150- to 200-mi paths this loss in received power may amount to 1 or 2 dB for a 40-dB

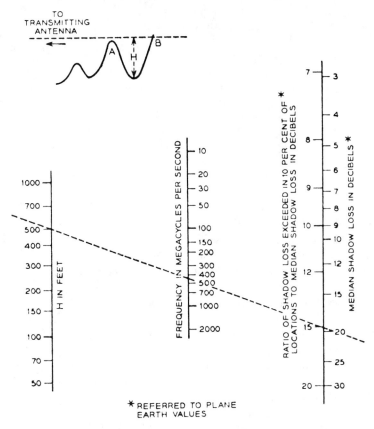

Fig. 15. Estimated distribution of shadow losses.

the angles of diffraction over or around the buildings are usually greater than for natural terrain. In other words, the artificial canyons caused by buildings are considerably narrower than natural valleys, and this factor tends to increase the loss resulting from the presence of buildings. The available quantitative data on the effects of buildings are confined primarily to New York City. These data indicate that in the range of 40 to 450 Mhz there is no significant change with frequency, or at least the variation with frequency is somewhat less than that noted in the case of hills [18]. The median field intensity at street level for random locations in Manhattan (New York City) is about 25 dB below the corresponding plane earth value. The corresponding values for the 10 percent and 90 percent points are about 15 and 35 dB, respectively. Typical values of attenuation through a brick wall are from 2 to 5 dB at 30 MHz and 10 to 40 dB at 3000 MHz depending on whether the wall is dry or wet. Consequently, most buildings are rather opaque at frequencies of the order of thousands of megahertz.

When an antenna is surrounded by moderately thick trees and below tree-top level, the average loss at 30 MHz resulting from the trees is usually 2 or 3 dB for vertical polarization and is negligible with horizontal polarization. However, large and rapid variations in the received field intensity may exist within a small area, resulting from the standing-wave pattern set up by reflections from trees located at a distance of several wavelengths from the antenna. Consequently, several nearby locations should be investigated for best results. At 100 MHz the average loss from surrounding trees may be 5 to 10 dB for ver-

tical polarization and 2 or 3 dB for horizontal polarization. The tree losses continue to increase as the frequency increases, and above 300 to 500 MHz they tend to be independent of the type of polarization. Above 1000 MHz trees that are thick enough to block vision are roughly equivalent to a solid obstruction of the same overall size.

X. MINIMUM ALLOWABLE INPUT POWER

The effective use of the preceding data for estimating the received power requires a knowledge of the power levels needed for satisfactory operation since the principal interest is in the signal-to-noise ratio. The signal level required at the input to the receiver depends on several factors including the noise introduced by the receiver (called first-circuit or set noise), the type and magnitude of any external noise, the type of modulation, and the desired signal-to-noise ratio. A complete discussion of these factors is beyond the scope of this paper, but the fundamental limitations are listed below in order to show the order of magnitude. The theoretical minimum noise level is that set by the thermal agitation of the electrons, and its root-mean-square power in dBW is −204 dB plus 10 log (bandwidth) where (bandwidth) is approximately equal to twice the audio (or video) bandwidth [19]. The set noise of a typical receiver may be 5 to 15 dB higher than the theoretical minimum noise. The lower values in this range of "excess" noise are more likely to be met in the VHF range while the higher values are more probable in the SHF range. This means that the set noise in a 3000-Hz audio band

TABLE I
FIGURES TO USE

Type of Terrain	Both Antennas Lower in Height than Shown on Fig. 6	One or Both Antenna Heights Higher than Shown on Fig. 6	
		Within Line-of-Sight	Beyond Line-of-Sight
Plane earth	Fig. 4 or 1	Figs. 4 or 1 or 2	Figs. 1 or 2 and 7
Smooth earth	Figs. 4 and 6	Figs. 4 or 1 or 2	Figs. 1 or 2
Irregular terrain	Figs. 4, 6, 7 and 12	Figs. 4 and 12 or 1 or 2 and 9	Figs. 1 or 2, 7 and 12

may be −151 to −161 dBW. Measured data indicate that the carrier power needs to be 12 to 20 dB higher than the noise power to provide an average signal-to-noise ratio that is sufficient for moderate intelligibility. This assumes that the modulation level has been adjusted so that most of the peaks of speech power can be transmitted without causing overmodulation in the transmitter. It follows that the required input power for a single-channel voice circuit is of the order of −140 dBW, which is roughly equivalent to 1 μV across a 70 Ω input resistance. This limiting input power is approximately correct (within 3 or 4 dB) for both amplitude and frequency modulation since the radio-frequency signal-to-noise ratio must be above that required for marginal operation before the use of frequency modulation can provide appreciable improvement in the audio signal-to-noise ratio.

The input power must be greater than −140 dBW when circuits of above marginal quality or greater bandwidth are desired and when external noise rather than set noise is controlling. Man-made noise is frequently controlling at 30 MHz, but is less serious at 150 MHz. Above 500 MHz set noise is almost always controlling. For circuits requiring a high degree of reliability a margin should also be included for the fading range to be expected during adverse weather conditions.

XI. SUMMARY AND EXAMPLES

In any given radio propagation problem some of the factors described above are important, while others can be neglected. Table I indicates the figures that apply to any given situation.

Whenever Fig. 4 is used, reference should be made to Figs. 1 and 3 as a check on its proper use. When Fig. 12 is used in determining the effects of hills, the profile is usually drawn on rectangular coordinates (neglecting the earth's curvature), and the shadow triangle is drawn to the base of the antenna halfway between the antenna and its image). Curved coordinates are sometimes used, but they are not necessary since the loss caused by the curvature of the earth is either negligible or has already been considered in Figs. 6 or 7. Fig. 9 is used for determining the first-zone clearance and for estimating the shadow losses when the transmission without the obstruction is expected to be the same as in free space. In the latter case, the shadow triangle is drawn from the actual antennas, and curved coordinates are useful since the curvature of the earth should be included in the profile.. Various examples of the use of these figures have been given during the discussion of each individual chart, but further examples may help to illustrate the

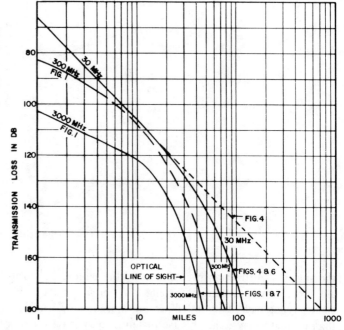

Fig. 16. Transmission over smooth earth at 30, 300, and 3000 MHz; half-wave dipoles at 250 and 30 ft.

relations between the various figures. Assume a transmitting dipole located 250 ft above the ground and a receiving dipole on a 30 ft mast. The estimated transmission losses at 30, 300, and 3000 MHz over smooth earth are shown in Fig. 16 for $k = 4/3$ for various distances between these two dipoles. The solid lines indicate values obtained from the figures, and the dashed lines show the region where some interpolation is required.

The received power depends on the radiated power and the antenna-gain characteristics as well as on the transmission loss between dipoles. A typical 30-MHz transmitter may radiate 250 W so that at a distance of 30 mi the received power is 10 log 250 − 129 = −105 dBW. (The value of 129 dB is obtained from Fig. 16.) Similarly, a 300-MHz transmitter may radiate 50 W from a 5-dB gain antenna, and when a 5-dB gain receiving antenna is used the estimated received power at 30 mi is 10 log 50 + 5 + 5 − 137 = −110 dBW. At 3000 MHz the radiated power may be 0.1 W and antenna gains of 28 dB each are not uncommon, so the received power at 30 miles is 10 log 0.1 + 28 + 28 − 152 = −106 dBW. (The values of radiated power used in this example are not the maximum continuous-wave powers that can be obtained but the down-

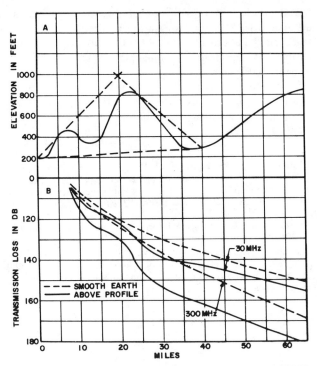

Fig. 17. Transmission loss over irregular terrain at 30 and 300 MHz;
half-wave dipoles of 250 and 30 ft.

TABLE II
SHADOW-LOSS COMPUTATIONS

Miles from Transmitter	H (feet)	d_1 (miles)	Shadow Loss in dB Obtained from Fig. 12	
			30 MHz	300 MHz
12.5	200	4.5	3.5	9
20	70	6.5	2	4
25	310	4.5	5.5	13
35	750	14.5	7	16
40	760	20	6	14
50	610	18	5	12
60	490	16.5	4.5	11

ward trend with increasing frequency is a characteristic of the available tubes.)

Over irregular terrain it is assumed that the shadow loss based on knife-edge diffraction theory is to be added to the transmission loss obtained from smooth-earth theory. The computation of shadow losses for the profile shown in Fig. 17 (a) is given in Table II.

The estimated transmission loss for 30 and 3000 MHz including the shadow loss from Table II is shown by the solid lines on Fig. 17(b), while the dashed lines are the corresponding values over smooth earth taken from Fig. 17. Super-

imposed on these average values will be unpredictable variations of ±6 to 10 dB resulting from the effects of trees and buildings and from profile irregularities that were smooth out in drawing the profile shown in Fig. 17(a).

REFERENCES

[1] C. W. Burrows and M. C. Gray, "The Effect of the earth's curvature on ground wave propagation," in *Proc. I.R.E.*, vol. 29, pp. 16–24, Jan. 1941.

[2] K. A. Norton, "The calculation of ground-wave field intensities over a finitely conducting spherical earth," in *Proc. I.R.E.*, vol. 29, pp. 623–639. Dec. 1941.

[3] E. W. Allen, "Very-high frequency and ultra-high frequency signal ranges as limited by noise and co-channel interference," in *Proc. I.R.E.*, vol. 35, pp. 128–136, Feb. 1947.

[4] C. R. Burrows, "Radio propagation over plane earth-field strength curves, *Bell Syst. Tech. J.*, vol. 16, pp. 45–75, Jan. 1937.

[5] K. A. Norton, "The propagation of radio waves over the surface of the earth and in the upper atmosphere, Part II, in *Proc. I.R.E.*, vol. 25, pp. 1203–1236, Sept. 1937.

[6] J. C. Schelleng, C. R. Burrows, and E. G. Ferrell, "Ultra-Short Wave Propagation," *Bell Syst. Tech. J.*, vol. 12, pp. 125–161, April 1933.

[7] MIT Radiation Laboratory Series, L. N. Ridenour, Editor-in-Chief, Volume 13, *Propagation of Short Radio Waves*, D. E. Kerr, Ed., New York: McGraw Hill, 1951.

[8] Summary Technical Report of the Committee on Propagation, National Defense Research Committee, Volume 1, Historical and Technical survey. Volume 2, Wave Propagation Experiments. Volume 3, Propagation of Radio Waves. Stephen S. Attwood, Ed., Washington, D.C., 1946.

[9] K. Bullington, "Characteristics of beyond-horizon radio transmission," in *Proc. I.R.E.*, vol. 43, p. 1175, Oct. 1955.

[10] W. E. Gordon, "Radio scattering in the troposphere," in *Proc. I.R.E.*, vol. 43, p. 23, Jan. 1955.

[11] K. Bullington, "Radio transmission beyond the horizon in the 40- to 4,000 MC band, in *Proc. I.R.E.*, vol. 41, pp. 132–135, Jan. 1953.

[12] K. A. Norton, P. L. Rice, and L. E. Vogler, "The use of angular distance in estimating transmission loss and fading range for propagation through a turbulent atmosphere over irregular terrain," in *Proc. I.R.E.*, vol. 43, pp. 1488–1526, Oct. 1955.

[13] F. H. Dickson, J. J. Egli, J. W. Herbstreit, and G. S. Wickizer, Large reductions of VHF transmission loss and fading by presence of mountain obstacle in beyond line-of-sight paths," in *Proc. I.R.E.*, vol. 41, pp. 967–969, Aug. 1953.

[14] K. Bullington, W. J. Inkster, and A. L. Durkee, "Results of propagation tests at 505 MC and 4090 MC on beyond-horizon path," in *Proc. I.R.E.*, vol. 43, pp. 1306–1316, Oct. 1955.

[15] H. G. Booker and J. T. deBetterncourt, "Theory of radio transmission by tropospheric scattering using very narrow beams," in *Proc. I.R.E.*, vol. 43, pp. 281–290, Mar. 1955.

[16] W. H. Tidd, "Demonstration of bandwidth capabilities of beyond-horizon tropospheric radio propagation," in *Proc. I.R.E.*, vol. 43, pp. 1297–1299, Oct. 1955.

[17] K. Bullington, "Radio propagation variations at VHF and UHF," in *Proc. I.R.E.*, vol. 38, pp. 27–32, Jan. 1950.

[18] W. R. Young, "Comparison of mobile radio transmission at 150, 450, 900 and 3700 MC, *Bell Syst. Tech. J.*, vol. 31, pp. 1068–1085, Nov. 1952.

[19] Harald T. Friis, "Noise figures of radio receivers," in *Proc. I.R.E.*, vol. 32, 419–422, July 1944.

[20] Terman, *Radio Engineer's Handbook*, 1st ed., p. 699.

Comments on "Radio Propagation for Vehicular Communications"

A. H. BADGER, MEMBER, IEEE

In reference to the November issue of IEEE TRANSACTIONS ON VEHICULAR TECHNOLOGY, I am elated to see a publication with such valuable and comprehensive information on the subject of radio wave propagation. This is the type of material many of us in the Vehicular Technology Society would like to see more often.

In the above paper,[1] there is a typographical error that needs correcting. Equation (2) on page 296 should have read

$$E_0 = \frac{\sqrt{30 \times 1.64\, P_1}}{d} \sim 7\, \frac{\sqrt{P_1}}{d}. \tag{2}$$

This article is a rewrite[2] of another article by the same author entitled "Radio Propagation at Frequenceis above 30 Megacycles" published in the PROCEEDINGS OF THE IRE in October 1947. Interestingly enough, this same equation appears wrong in that article.

I often use Mr. Bullington's work for reference and have admired his clear and concise presentations and his excellent nomographs. I wish we had more writers like him in the engineering field.

Manuscript received February 13, 1978.

The author is with the General Engineering Department, The Cincinnati Gas and Electric Company, P.O. Box 960, Cincinnati, OH 45201.

[1] K. Bullington, *IEEE Trans. Veh. Technol.*, vol. VT-26, no. 4, pp. 295–308, Nov. 1977.

[2] For complete publication information see the first footnote on page 295 of the above reference.

Guest Editor's Note: Thank you for your letter pointing out the error in the expression for free space field intensity. This typographical error had been known to exist in Bullington's 1947 article and somehow was repeated.

Reprinted from *IEEE Trans. Veh. Technol.*, vol. VT-27, p. 158, Aug. 1978.

18

Field Strength and Its Variability in VHF and UHF Land-Mobile Radio Service

Yoshihisa OKUMURA, Eiji OHMORI,
Tomihiko KAWANO, and **Kaneharu FUKUDA**

Detailed propagation tests for land-mobile radio service were carried out at VHF (200 MHz) and UHF bands (453, 922, 1310, 1430, 1920 MHz) over various situations of irregular terrain and of environmental clutter. The results analyzed statistically are described for distance and frequency dependences of median field strength, location variabilities and antenna height gain factors for the base and the vehicular station, in urban, suburban and open areas over quasi-smooth terrain.

The correction factors corresponding to respective terrain parameters for irregular terrain, such as rolling-hill terrain, isolated mountain area, general sloped terrain, and mixed land-sea path are discussed.

As a result, a method is presented for predicting the field strength and service area for a given terrain of the land-mobile radio system, over the frequency ranges of 150 to 2000 MHz, for distances of 1 to 100 km, and for base station effective antenna heights of 30 to 1000 m.

The results of comparison of predicted field strength with measured data published in another paper suggests that a reasonable degree of accuracy is obtainable.

1 Introduction

VHF or UHF band mobile radios, especially for land use, have attracted attention as a means of police communication or as a prerequisite to full functioning of reporting services or traffic control by taxi companies. Indeed, there is every indication of their rapid growth as a new type of communication in the near future. Compared with the well-known propagation characteristics on the fixed radio syctem, that on the land-mobile service is burdened with peculiar complications. They are:

(i) The antenna height of a mobile body (mobile radio car) with which communication is held is very low—usually no more than 1 ~3m above ground.

(ii) Between the base station and the mobile radio cars or between such cars themselves, an ever changing, infinitely large number of propagation paths are formed due to movement from place to plce.

(iii) That causes the clearance of the propagation paths to be lost, while the field strength, hindered by the terrain irregularities and other obstacles, suffers great attenuation and location variability all the time,

In the meanwhile, sufficient test data has been reported on propagation characteristics connected with VHF and UHF band TV broadcasts, closely resembling those with land-mobile radio communication. This data has too many unknown elements to be applicable to the land-mobile radio be cause of peculiarities cited above.

For example, the propagation curves prepared by CCIR,[1] TASO,[2] and others are mainly intended for TV broadcasts with the antenna height fixed at 10m, but do not account for determining characteristics of antennas lower than that or for attenuatton due

Reprinted with permission from *Rev. Elec. Commun. Lab.*, vol. 16, pp. 825–873, Sept.–Oct. 1968.

to various terrain irregularities. On the other hand, for the land-mobile radio itself, some information such as propagation curve presented by J. J. Egli[3] and propagation test data reported by W. E. Young[4] is available; and, quite recently, CCIR has made a report on correction factor data[5] for antennas 3~10 m high. All these, however are not detailed enough to apply to this country where terrain is complicated and irregular.

In order, therefore, to obtain fundamental data for the design of land-mobile radios by clarifying the yet-unknown propagation characteristics, and to assure the possibility of introducing new frequency bands which will be much in demand, two series of experiments—one in 1962 and the other in 1965— were performed over the whole district of Kanto, inclusive of the heart of Tokyo. Four frequency bands were selected between 450 MHz~2000 MHz. All sorts of characteristics on attenuation and variation of the field strength were brough to light, both for quasi-smooth terrain and for hilly, mountainous, or otherwise irregular terrain full of obstructions.

Experimental reaults in UHF bands were added to the formerly obtained results[6] in a VHF band (200 MHz)—making up the land-mobile radio propagation design charts in the frequency ranges of 150~2000 MHz, transmission (base station) antenna heights of 30~1000 m, and distances of 1~100 km— the autors have found a method of predicting with fair exactitude the field strength for vaious sorts of terrain irregularities and environmental clutter.

This report is presented in the hope it will be of some use, and any criticisms will be greatly appreciated.

2 Outline of Propagation Tests Performed

2.1 Selection of Mobile Courses

(1) *First Series of Tests*
Time: November 1962~January 1963.
Topographicallv simple and flat areas were selected for these tests. Quasi-smooth terrains (the definition follows), which contained as many built-up cities as possible within a distance of 100 km were chosen and the transmission (base station) attennas were variable up to near 1000 m.
The mobile courses ran over the Kanto plains area, including the heart of Tokyo.

Care was taken to give two or more mobile courses for each base station, for a compara-

Table 1 (a) PATH CONDITION AND MOBILE COURSE IN FIRST PROPAGATION TEST

Transmitting Base Station	Trans. Ant. Height h_{ts}/h_{tg} (m)	Name of Mobile Course	Direction of Trans. Ant. Beam	Average Ground Level Over Course h_{ga}(m)	Effective Trans. Ant. Height h_{te}(m)	Situation of Path Terrain
Top of Mt. Tsukuba	848/35	Tachikawa	SW 50°	20	828	Quari-smooth terrain, urban, suburban, open area
		Tokyo	SW 30°	25	823	
Halfway of Mt. Tsukuba	239/6	Tachikawa	SW 50°	20	219	
		Tokyo	SW 30°	25	214	
Upper Floor of Tokyo Tower	246/228	Mito	NE 42.5°	10	236	
		Kumagaya	NW 24°	25	221	
Lower Floor of Tokyo Tower	156/138	Mito	NE 42.5°	10	146	
Marunouchi Tokyo	63/60	Soka		3	60	Nikko-Road
		Funabashi	In the city	3	60	Keiyo-Road
		Asaka	of Tokyo	33	30	Kawagoe-Road
		Tamakawa		33	30	Tamakawa Road

tive study of attenuation and variations differing from one another according to the courses to be followed. Table 1 (a) shows particulars about such courses, base stations, propagation path situations, etc.

(2) *Second Series of Tests*
Time: March~June 1965.
This set of tests was carried out to make the results of the first series of tests more exact, aiming further at explaining the characteristics of lower base station antennas and some peculiarities concerning hilly, mountainous, or otherwise irregular terrain as well as investigating the interference characteristics of the waves. The mobile courses selected are shown in Table 1(b).

Figures 1(a) and (b) are roughly-drawn

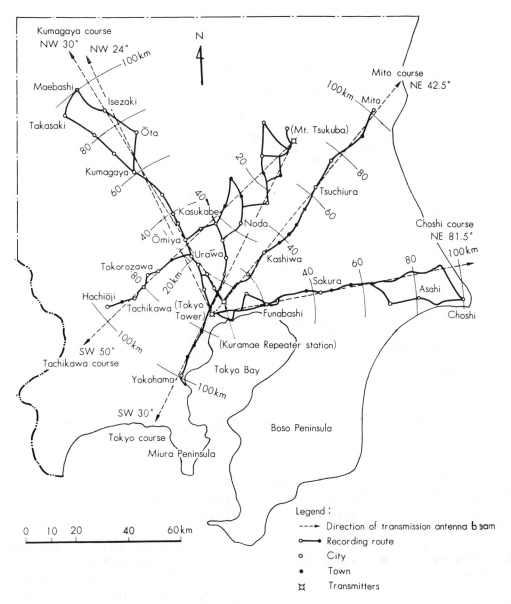

Fig. 1(a)—Map of Kanto District in Japan showing radials and mobile-recording routes over quasi-smooth terrain.

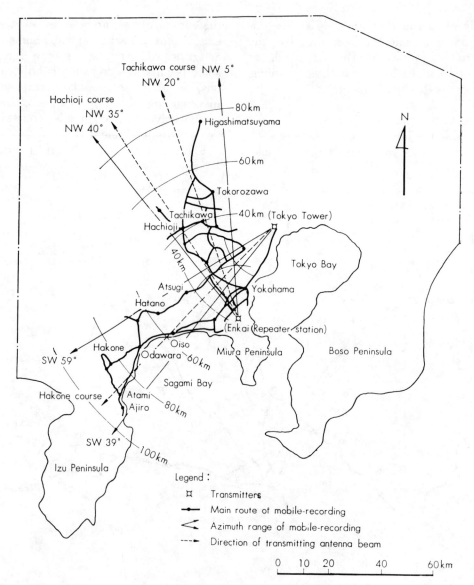

Fig. 1(b)—Map showing radials and mobil-recording routes over hilly and mountainous terrain.

maps of the Kanto district representing the mobile courses shown in Tables 1(a) and (b) respectively. The principal recording routes (built-up cities) are also indicated on them.

2.2 Frequencies; Parameters of Equipment used

The following frequencies were selected to find how they affect various characteristics;

also to see if there was any possibility of developing new frequency bands:

First tests: 453 MHz, 922 MHz, 1310 MHz, 1920 MHz.

Second tests: 453 MHz, 922 MHz, 1317 MHz, 1430 MHz.

The vertically polarized wave was in use for all frequencies. Table 2 shows parameters of measurement with respect to the transmitter power, transmitting and receiving

Table 1 (b)   PATH CONDITION AND MOBILE COURSE IN SECOND PROPAGATION TEST

Transmitting Base Station	Trans. Ant. Height. h_{ts}/h_{tg} (m)	Name of Mobile Course	Direction of Trans. Ant. Beam	Average Ground Level Over Course h_{qa}(m)	Effective Trans. Height h_{te}(m)	Situation of Path Terrain
Lower Floor of Tokyo Tower	150/132	Mito	NE 42.5°	10	140	Quasi-smooth terrain
		Choshi	NE 81.5°	5	145	
		Hakone	SW 45°	30	120	Hilly and mountainous terrain
Kuramae Relay Station	62/59	Mito	NE 42.5°	10	52	Quasi-smooth terrain
		Kumagaya	NW 30°	20	42	
Enkai Relay Station	163/9	Hachioji	NW 35°	55	108	Hilly and mountainous terrain
		Tachikawa	NW 20°	55	108	

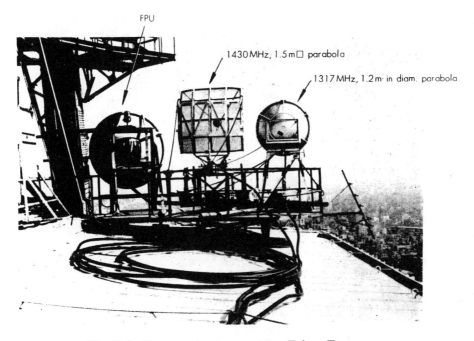

Fig. 2(a)—Transmitting antennas at Tokyo Tower.

antenna type and gain, etc., for all frequencies.

Figures 2(a) and (b) are photographs of the transmitting antennas installed at Tokyo Tower and Enkai transmitting base station, respectively.

2.3 Mobile Field Strength Measuremet

(*1*) *Vehicular Station Antenna Height*
The receiving annennas for all frequencies 3m high above ground, were installed at both sides on top of the mobile radio van, as shown in Fig. 3, to take normal measurements. Simultaneously with it, since most

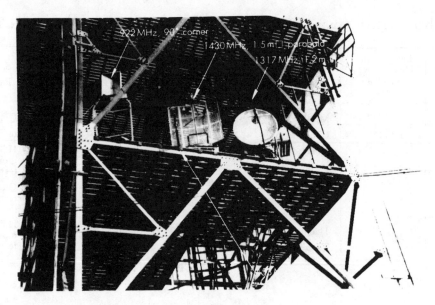

Fig. 2(b)—Transmitting antennas at Enkai base station.

Table 2   PARAMETERS OF MEASUREMENT

Frequency MHz	Transmitter Power	Transmitting Antenna	Gain / Type	Receiving Antenna	Gain / Type
453	150 W	5-element Yagi	11.3 dB	Omni-directional unipole antenna	1.5 dB
922	60 W	90° Corner	11.5 dB	"	1.5 dB
1317	150 kW Pulse	1.2 m in diam. parabola	22.0 dB	"	1.5 dB
1430	30 W	1.5 m parabola	26.3 dB	"	1.5 dB
1920	60 W	Horn	19.0 dB	"	1.5 dB

Note: Antenna gain is the value referred to the isotropic.

mobile radio cars have antennas lower than that, measurement was also taken with 1.5 m high antennas for a comparative study of vehicular station antenna height gain factors.

(2) Data Recording

The input signals from the antennas of the mobile measurement van, were led into their respective field strength meters classified by frequencies, and the outputs therefrom recorded simultaneously, parallel and continuously, by a 4-pen recorder; if necessary, a magnetic tape recorder was made use of at the same time. The variation of received field strength produced by terrain irregularities and environmental clutter, was, as a rule, continuously put on record while traveling.

Special notice was taken of the variation of the median and the instantaneous signal level, with suitable adjustment made to the traveling and the recording paper speed. In

Fig. 3—Mobile field strength measurement van.

normal mobile recording, the variation of the median level due to terrain irregularities and environmental clutter was given more importance; and the traveling speed and the recording paper speed averaged 30 km/hr and 5 mm/sec respectively. In the case of instantaneous level variation, the method of sampling recording for a small sector of 50 m or so, was resorted to when passing through some prominent terrain irregularities and environmental clutter areas. The traveling speed and the recording paper speed this time averaged 15 km/hr and 250 mm/sec, respectively. The recorder pen action was so planned that it might exactly follow speedy variation caused by frequencies and so that the envelope in instantaneous variation might perfectly be separated. The minimum input level recordable was -125 dBm (-12 dBμ) for all frequencies, and the recorder scope was almost lineally 50 dB.

(3) Obtaining Data
The transmitting antennas beam was not wide enough for higher frequency bands, so the measurement car excluded regions where the corrected ratio of antenna directional characteristics became indistinct. Also, with-

in about 10 km, like the built-up areas in the heart of Tokyo, horizontal omni-directional antennas were used for transmission as occasion demanded.

The field strength of the signal received by a mobile measurement car differs with the car running parallel to the direction of the incoming wave (along the path) or perpendicular to it (across the path). Therefore, in obtaining data, the measurement cars traveled on the roads not only in the direction of the main recording routes shown in Fig. 1, but in all directions, especially in the central parts of cities and towns.

2.4 Expressing Propagation Characteristics

Some propagation curves hitherto published were not definitive, because they took in all sorts of elements of terrain irregularities and environmental clutter haphazardly so were not very useful for estimating field strength or service area adapted to the real situation.

It might be better to refer here to the manner of terrain feature classification, and to treatment and expression of various data observed in performing this study.

(1) Classification and Definition of Terrain Features

There are an infinite variety of terrain features on this earth. But our basic idea is that the "quasi-smooth terrain" should be the standard of analysis and expression of propagation characteristics.

By the "quasi-smooth terrain" is meant a flat terrain where, judging from the propagation path terrain profile (drawn from a map on the scale of 1 : 50,000), the undulation height is about 20 m or less with gentle ups and downs and, moreover, the average level of ground does not differ much (not more than 20 m). The Kanto plains meet these requirements on the whole.

Other terrains are difined as "irregular" and are divided into "rolling hilly terrain,"* "isolated mountain," "general sloping terrain," and "mixed landsea path."

Besides the classification of terrains, the following are definitions of the path and the terrain parameters, as well as the differentiation method used here.

(a) Base Station Effective Antenna Height

To obtain a field strength suitable for any existing terrain, it is necessary to define the antenna height of the base station. In the terrain profile shown in Fig. 4, let the average level of ground within 3 to 15 km (or less if the entire distance does not exceed 15 km) from the base station antenna be h_{ga}, the base station antenna height be h_{ts} above

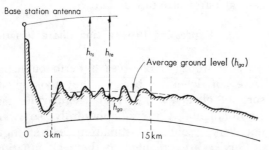

Fig. 4—Definition of effective transmitting antenna height (h_{te}).

---

* Mountainous terrain determination method involves correction for the rolling hilly terrain.

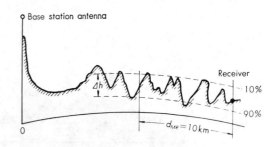

Fig. 5—Definition of the parameter (Δh, "terrain undulation height") for rolling hilly terrain.

sea level; then the effective transmitting antenna height will be defined as $h_{ts} - h_{ga} = h_{te}$. The antenna height gain factor will be examined at this height.

(b) Terrain Undulation Height (Rolling Hilly Terrain Parameter Δh)

Almost all propagation paths have irregular undulations. In a rolling hilly terrain, the "terrain undulation height Δh" expressing the degree of irregularities, may be found from Fig. 5 equal to the difference between 10% and 90% of the terrain undulation height (as the profile shows) within a distance of 10 km from the receiving point to the transmitting point.

This manner of determining terrain parameters may apply to a mountainous area where there are several mountains which affect the receiving point by multiple diffraction, but not to a simple sloped terrain or where there is only one undulation.

(c) Isolated Mountain Ridge and Path Parameter

When the propagation path has a single mountain in the way and there is nothing else to interfere with the receive signal except the obstacles in the neighborhood, the mountain is defined as an "isolated mountain." Such a mountain is presumed to be approximate to a knife edge, when the VHF and UHF band are in use.

Figure 6(a) shows the path parameter of an isolated ridge whose height h is measured from the average ground level.

Figure 6(b) shows a model of an isolated ridge where attenuation is calculated from a

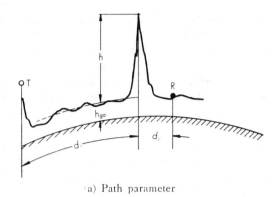

(a) Path parameter

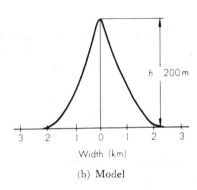

(b) Model

Fig. 6—The model and geometrical parameter of isolated ridge.

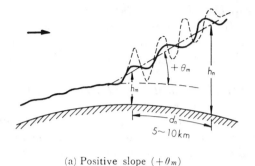

(a) Positive slope $(+\theta_m)$

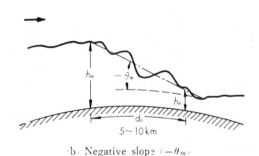

(b) Negative slope $(-\theta_m)$

Fig. 7—Definition of average angle of general terrain slope.

standard height $h=200$ m. Proportional attenuations may be obtained by conversion for other heights.

(d) Average General Slope Angle of Terrain (θ_m)

When terrain, whether flat or undulated, slopes over a distance of at least 5 to 10 km, the terrain parameter in terms of the average angle of general slope θ_m may be expressed, as is shown in Fig. 7, by

$$\theta_m = \frac{h_n - h_m}{d_n}$$

where, if $h_n > h_m$ (uphill), the slope angle is positivive $(+\theta_m)$ and if $h_n < h_m$ (downhill), it is negative $(-\theta_m)$.

(e) Distance Parameter for Mixed Land-Sea Path.

Where there is an expanse of sea or lake in the propagation path, three different cases are presumable. Figure 8 shows where the

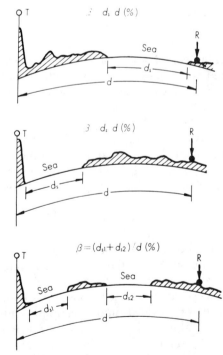

Fig. 8—Definition of distance parameter (β) for mixed land-sea path.

exapanse of water is (a) near the mobile radio car, (b) near the base station, and (c) midway between. Thus three distance parameters usable as terrain parameters may be obtained.

(2) *Classification and Definition of Environmental Clutter*

Whether in a quasi-smooth or an irregular terrain, buildings and trees near the mobile radio car antennas affect the received field strength in diverse ways, according sort and condition of such buildings and trees. In fact, such obstacles in all individual areas classified into minute groups in pursuit of propagation characteristics, would be of little practical use, because that would only make finding the mobile radio field strength in a given area more difficult. Instead, let the ground obstacles be examined in the following three groups classified according to the degree of congesting and shielding:

(a) Open Area

In which are classed an open space where there are no obstacles like tall trees or buildings in the propagation path and a plot of land which is cleared of anything 300 to 400 m ahead, as, for instance, farm-land, rice-field, open fields etc.

(b) Suburban Area

This comprises a village or highway scattered with trees and houses—the area having some obstacles near the moblile radio car, but still not very congested.

(c) Urban Area

This is a built-up city or large town crowded with large buildings and two-or-more-storied houses, or in a larger village closely interspersed with houses and thickly-grown tall trees.

(3) *Treatment of Data*; *Method of Expression*

All the received field strength data recorded throughout by the mobile van were treated statistically. That is, for each of the classified areas defined above, the entire distance was divided into "sampling interval" 1 to 1.5 km each, and readings taken the so-called "small-sector medians" at intervals of about 20 m. Thus was found the cumulative distribution in that sampling interv—alone of

the objects of analysis. And to the attenuation of the field strength due to terrain irregularities and environment clutters, was given the median value of the distribution curve described above (or the sampling-interval median); also to the location variability was given the variation range (e.g., the standard deviation) of the distribution. In expressing the field strengths affected in various ways by terrains and other obstacles, the standand was determined by the urban field strength median in a quasi-smooth terrain (called the "basic median field strength" or simply "basic median"). Then followed the steps to obtain the difference between this standard and the median actually measured for each of the above-classified terrain features, that is to say, the correction factor, positive or negative. And these correction factors were obtained by determining the relation with respective terrain paramerers.

The reason the value for urban area paths was selected as the standard instead of the value (more usually turned to account) under simpler conditions as, for instance, in open or suburban area paths, is explained here. It has been known from experiment that, of all the classified terrains and obstacles, it is in fact in the suburban area that the field strength suffers the most multifarious variations, especially when the receiving antenna height is low. Also, in Japan, there are few areas virtually satisfying the open area conditions; and if any, they ara narrow. The urban area, on the contrary, is best-situated in definitely judging the effects of obstacles, and has conveniences of getting more data in comparatively a small space. The highest degree of accuracy may be expected of the standard value it provides.

3 Propagation Characteristics on Quasi-Smooth Terrain

3.1 Field Strength Variation while Traveling

In land-mobile radio service the vehicular antenna height is extremely low. While the car is in motion, an infinite number of propagation paths are formed between itself and the base station; and its received field strength is subject to multifarious location variations, which are caused by the obstacles coming up one after another in and around the path or by the standing waves due to the inteference of multi-path waves. The following is an outline of how the field strength varies:

(a) There is, in a large swelling variation of the average field strength level, overlapping each other, a deep instantaneous variation of quick periodic motion, due to the changes in terrain irregularities and environmental clutter.

(b) The average field strength level (sampling-interval median), when viewed from the

median attenuation relative to free space, has the largest value in the urban area followed by suburban and open area. For instance, even within the same distance, when the car moves from an open area into an urban area, there occurs a change of as large as 20 to 30 dB. The dynamic range of changes in a 20 km radius are amounts to no less than 50 to 60 dB according to the existing obstacles.

(c) Since, behind the obstacles, the overlapped field strength level variation reffered to in (a) crosses the standing waves due to the multi-path diffracted or the multi-path reflected waves, the variation depth becomes very large—almost equal to the Rayleigh distribution. The speed of variation increases

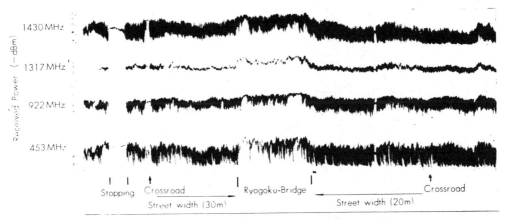

(a) Field strength on 42.5° NE radial from Tokyo Tower. (Urban across path, $d \doteq 6.5$ km)

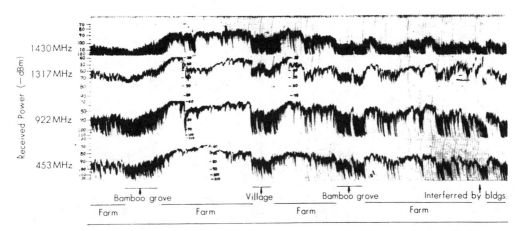

(b) Field strength on the Atsugi-road from Enkai station. (Rural, oblique path, $d \doteq 25$ km)

Fig. 9—Examples of amplitude recording of the received field strength.

in proportion to the product of the frequency of the radio wave and the traveling speed. So a position change of only a few meters by the car, will produce a sharp change of 10 to 20 dB in the field strength.

Figure 9 shows examples of amplitude recording of the received field strength, indicating how it undergoes variation at frequencies of 453 MHz, 922 MHz, 1,317 MHz (pulse), and 1,430 MHz. Figure 9(a) is the record made on an oblique course in an urban area (crowded with 3 to 5-storied buildings and other houses) near Ryogoku, about 6.5 km from Tokyo Tower base station. No marked changes in the average levels can be seen for all frequencies, except that on Ryogoku Bridge there is a rise of about 10 to 15 dB.

Figure 9(b) is the record made on the Atsugi Road, about 25 km from Enkai base station, while traveling obliquely in the direction of the incoming signal. The average level of variation while traveling is very large —within about 25 dB, as this is a suburban area where various obstacles are mixed together on both sides of the road, like farm lands, groups of houses, buildings, etc.

Thus the manner in which the field strengh changes while traveling is vague and uncertain. It may therefore be understood that, in land-mobile radio service, it is more practical to obtain in a statistical manner the attenuation at sampling intervals based on roughly-classified obstacles according to their nature and situation, than to pursue the value in each individual spot.

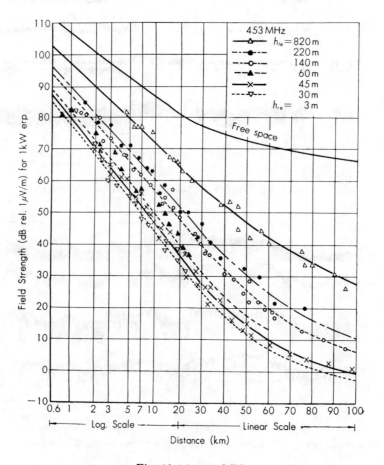

Fig. 10 (a) 453 MHz

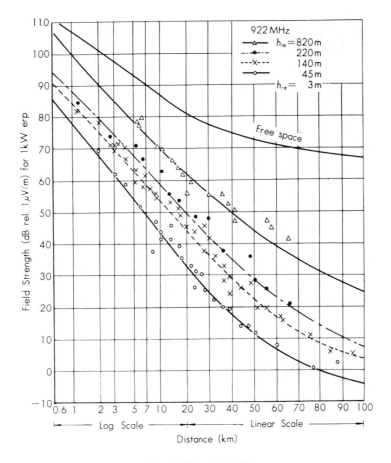

Fig. 10 (b) 922 MHz

3.2 Field Strength Attenuation Characteristics with 3 m High Receiving Antenna

3.2.1 Distance and Frequency Dependence of Field Strength in Urban Area

(1) Median Field Strength vs. Distance Curves at Various Frequencies

Figures 10 (a) to (e) represent the median field strength (dB rel. $1\mu V/m$ for 1 kW e.r.p.) versus distance data, measured in urban areas at 453 MHz, 922 MHz, 1,317 MHz, 1,430 MHz, and 1,920 MHz. In this experiment on quasi-smooth terrain, the transmitting antennas are of five different heights ranging from 62 to 848 m above sea level, but their effective heights (h_{te}) on the average are 820 m, 220 m, 140 m, 60 m, 45 m, and 30 m, though there may be differences of some few meters according to the course. Measurement data was analyzed on the basis of these effective antenna heights. Also the measured values in relation to the distances are shown plotted with averages of the medians of sampling-intervals, each of approximately the same distance, situated in the same urban area. These measured values mean nothing but the averaged values for various directions—along-the-path, across-the-path, etc.,—of traveling in the urban area. The median field strength thus obtained in the quasi-smooth terrain urban area, tends to show a comparatively smooth change with distance, for each base station antenna height and for each frequency. The curves in Fig. 10 are so drawn as to show this smooth change. Now let various charactertstics be investigat-

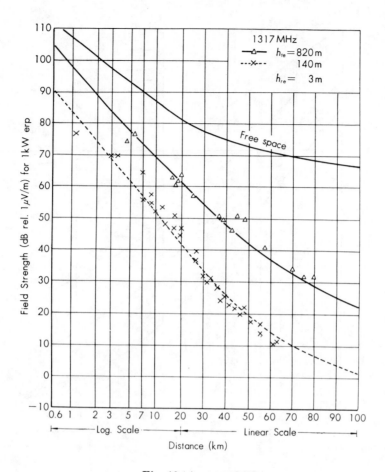

Fig. 10 (c) 1,317 MHz

ed on the basis of these smoothed curves.

(2) Distance Dependence of Median Field Strength in Urban Area

The distance dependence of the field strength is one of the fundamental problems of propagation. From the measured data shown in Fig. 10, this distance dependence develops somewhat different tendency according to the frequency and the effective antenna height of the base station. Figure 11 shows the distance dependence in terms of the median attenuation relative to free space, when the base station antenna effective height $h_{te}=140$ m and the frequencies are 453 MHz, 922 MHz, 1,430 MHz, and 1,920 MHz. The median attenuation goes on to increase within distance of about 15 km, by about the distance to the one half-th power ($A \propto d^n$, $n \doteqdot 1/2$, where A;

median attenuation, d: distance). For over 15 km, a sudden increase follows, but within 40 to 100 km it remains a constant rate, showing $n \doteqdot 2.3$. The distance dependence represented in the relation of the median field strength (E_m) to the base station antenna effective height (h_{te}), will give n ($E_m \propto d^{-n}$) as is shown in Fig. 12. When the distance is less than 15 km, the value of n becomes smaller as h_{te} grows higher (Curve A); and when 40 km $< d <$ 100 km, the maximum value of $n (n \doteqdot 3.3)$ appears in the neighborhood of $h_{te} \doteqdot 200$ m, while n decreases when $h_{te} \doteqdot 70$ m or less (Curve B). It may be said also that, with a low h_{te}, the field strength lapse rate is small (or the long-distance dependence is gentle); and in a middle distance (where 15 km $< d <$ 40 km), n takes on intermediate value between Curve A and Curve B in Fig.

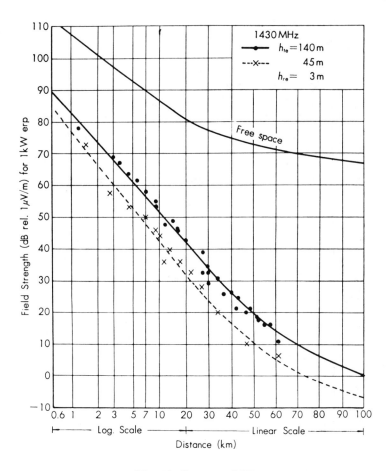

Fig. 10 (d) 1,430 MHz

12. Unless the distance is broken into small divisions, however, n does not remain constant.

(3) Frequency Dependence of Median Field Strength in Urban Area

On a quasi-smooth terrain the field strength attenuation is largest in the urban area, and it increases as the frequency becomes higher. Figure 13 shows the frequeney dependence of median attenuation relative to free space in an urban area, at $h_{te}=140$ m for example, where the value for 453 MHz is taken as the standard. This dependence in terms of the field strength lapse rate relative to frequency $(E_m \propto f^{-n})$, is shown by the curves for n in Fig. 14. The values of n vary according to the frequency band and distance; let the frequency bands—100~500 MHz, 500~1,000 MHz, 1,000~2,000 MHz—be taken, then the higher the frequency the larger the value of n; it also grows large as the distance increases.

In J. J. Egli's prediction curves[3] which incorporate some terrain factors into plane earth calculation, the characteristic shows a constant value of $n=0(E_m \propto f^{-n})$ for the whole range of 40~1,000 MHz and it differs to a considerable degree compared with the values of n in Fig. 14. Figure 15 shows the prediction curves depending on distance and frequency, which represent the median attenuation relative to free space (called the "basic median attenuation") in a quasi-smooth terrain urban area, where the base station effective antenna height $h_{te}=200$ m and that of the mobile radio car $h_{re}=3$ m. These curves, from which the basic median field strength is predictable, derive themselves from the curves (in Fig.

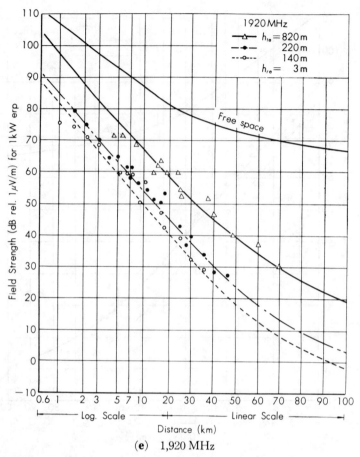

(e) 1,920 MHz

Fig. 10—Examples of median field strength data in urban area for various effective antenna heights (453 MHz).

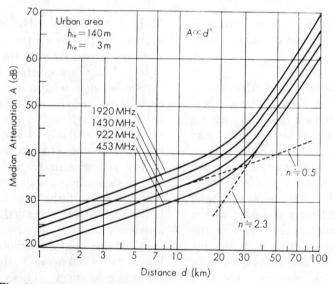

Fig. 11—Example in distance dependence of median field strength attenuation in urban area.

34

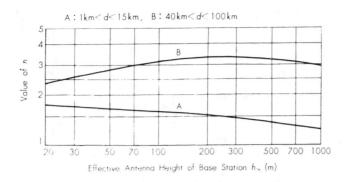

Fig. 12—Distance dependence of median field strength in urban area ($E_m \propto d^{-n}$).

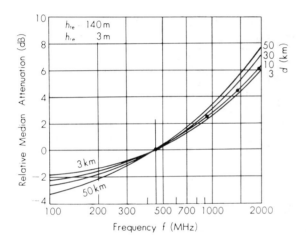

Fig. 13—Example of frequency dependence of median attenuation relative to free space in urban area.

10) which, plotted with distance as a parameter, denote the median field strength data measured at different frequencies, with reference to the base station effective antenna height and the median attenuation relative to free space, by interpolating $h_{te} = 200$ m. For the VHF band, the results[6] from an experiment formerly made at 200 MHz are also employed.

3.2.2 Median Attenuation in Urban Area in Relation to Vertical Angle of Arrival

The field strength median attenuation in highly built-up urban area, depends on such variables as the mean height of the buildings,

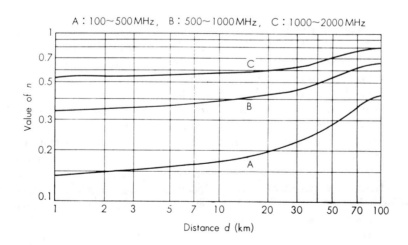

Fig. 14—Frequency dependence of median field strength in urban area ($E_m \propto f^{-n}$).

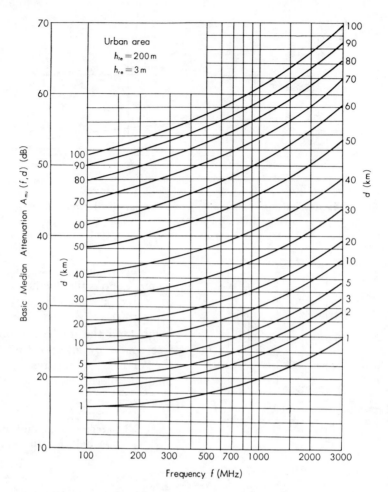

Fig. 15—Prediction curve for basic median attenuation relative to free space in urban area over quasi-smooth terrain, referred to $h_{te}=200$ m, $h_{re}=3$ m.

mean width of the streets, vertical angle of arrival of the signal from the base station antenna, and also the direction of travel with regard to the direction of the incoming signal. The relation to the vertical angle of arrival (that is, the elevation angle the base station antenna forms with the mobile radio car) is also connected with the base station antenna height and the distance. In examining this problem, reference will have to be made to the results of an experiment[7] recently conducted in Italy.

The Italian experiment states that the vartically polarized waves (146 MHz, 475 MHz) transmitted from the mobile radio car

equipped with an antenna 2 m high, were received at several points, to find the relation of the vertical angle of arrival to the median attenuation relative to free space, each traveling interval being 500 to 1,000 m on various streets with different kinds of buildings. Curve A in Fig. 16 represents the result based on a vertical angle of arrival $(\alpha^\circ)=4^\circ$. The distance range is not indicated in this experiment; but it may probably have been within 2 to 3 km. Curve B in Fig. 16 shows the result from our own data within this range.

Curve B relates to the case where the distance was made variable while the base

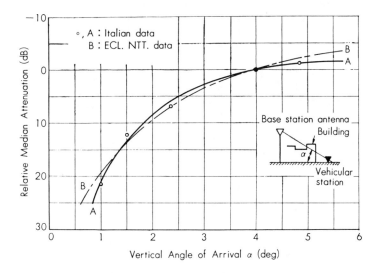

Fig. 16—Dependence of the additional attenuation on the vertical angle of arrival (attenuations are referred to 4°).

station antenna height kept constant, and it well corresponds with the Italian Curve A.

3.2.3 Difference of Median Attenuation due to Orientation of Urban Street

Generally, the received field strength changes according to how the road on which the car travels is oriented with regard to the direction of the signal. Especially in urban areas, clear disparity in median attenuation presents itself, according to whether the course is parallel (along the path) or perpendicular (across the path) to the direction of the signal; the width of the road, too, has more or less effect upon it. Figure 17 shows, in mean values, how along-the-path median attenuation differs from across-the-path median attenuation in the urban area, in respect of various distances and frequencies. Note that the larger the distance the smaller the difference. The median attenuation differences at 453 MHz averages 9 dB for 10 km and 6.5 dB for 50 km. As there is not much difference due to frequencies, from the "basic median" the prediction curves for the along-the-path and the across-the-path correction factor, are obtainable as shown in Fig. 18.

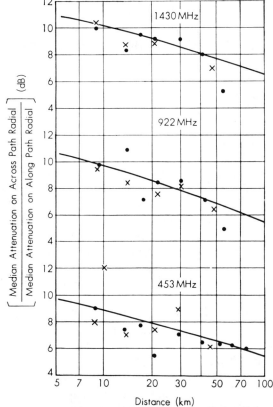

● h_{te} = 140 m Mito course from Tokyo Tower
× h_{te} = 42 m Kumagaya course from Kuramae

Fig. 17—Difference of attenuation in urban area due to the orientation of the street with respect to the radius starting from the base station.

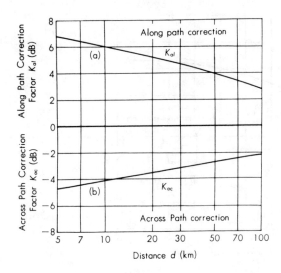

Fig. 18—Prediction curves for along and across path correction factor in urban areas.

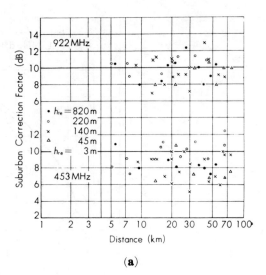

(a)

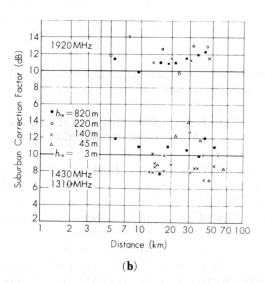

(b)

Fig. 19—Difference of median in urban and suburban area.

3.2.4 Medinn Attenuation in Suburban Area (Suburban Correction Factor)

In suburban areas, the degree of congestion and shielding due to obstacles is slighter than in urban areas; and there the median field strength is usually high. Not specifically drawing the distance dependence curves of field strength for suburban areas, the authors tried to obtain the "suburban correction factor," which is the difference between the median attenuation (or median field strength) in the urban area and that in the suburban area. Figure 19 shows this correction factor by frequencies measured at various distances. There seems to be no great difference arising from the distance and base station antenna height. Therefore, supposing that the correction factor in constant for the whole distance, its mean frequency dependence indicates 8.5 dB at 453 MHz, 10 dB at 922 MHz, and 12 dB at 1,920 MHz. In the light of this suburban area correction factor frequency dependence, connected with the urban median attenuation frequency dependence (shown in Fig. 15), it may be seen that, in the suburban area, the field strength within the frequency band 400 to 1,000 MHz yields no more difference than 1 dB. This is also the case with the CCIR propagation curves.[1] From this result of measurement come the prediction curve representing the suburban correction factor frequency dependence shown in Fig. 20.

3.2.5 Attenuation in Open Area (Open Area Correction Factor)

The spaces that satisfy the conditions of open area are not to be found in too long sampling intervals. Stressing the check of

38

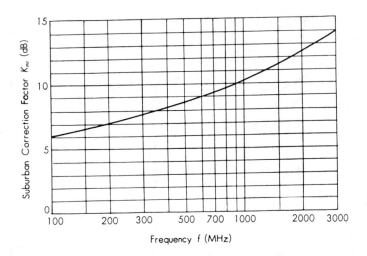

Fig. 20—Prediction curve for "suburban correction factor" as a function of the frequency.

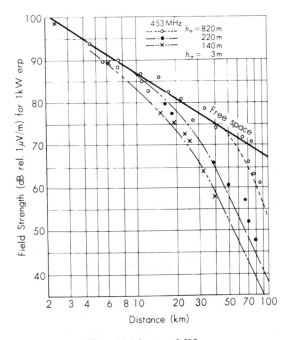

Fig. 21 (a) 453 MHz

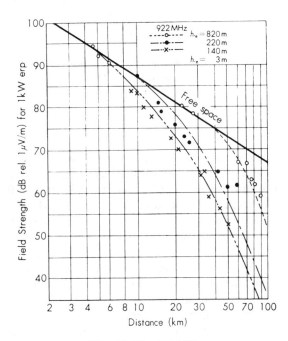

Fig. 21 (b) 922 MHz

received signal levels, propagation experiments obtained the quasi-maximum of field strength for analysis.

Figures 21(a) to (c) show the quasi-maximum of field strength plotted as a function of the distance. The curves represent its smoothed values. Attenuation begins to ap-

pear at about 5 km from the base station whose effective antenna height $h_{te} = 140$ meters. A sudden increase in attenuation may be discerned for distances more than that.

When the quasi-minimum attenuation relative to free space that depends on the distance, is compared with the urban area

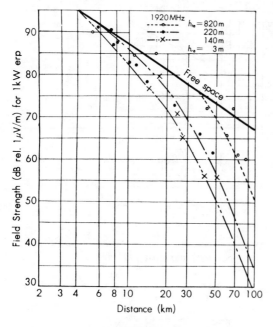

(c) 1920 MHz

Fig. 21—Examples of field strength (quasi-maximum) data in "open area" for various effective antenna height of base station.

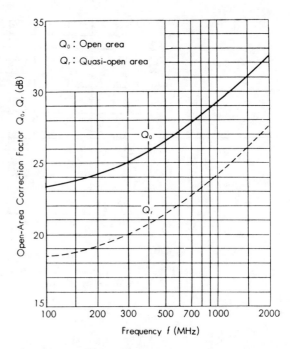

Fig. 22—Prediction curves of "open-area correction factor" as a function of the frequency.

median attenuation (the effective antenna height of the base station being the same), the differences are: 26 dB at 453 MHz, 29 dB at 922 MHz, and 32 dB at 1,920 MHz— all remaining constant on the whole regardless of the distance.

Curve Q_0 in Fig. 22 is the prediction curve of the correction factor, which is represented with the difference between the quasi-maximum of field strength in an ideal open area and the median field strength in an urban area (or "basic median"). But when the corrected field strength becomes higher than the free space value, in cases where the base station with a high antenna is in a short distance, the free space value should be taken. As referred to above, the spaces in which Curve Q_0 must be corrected are very scarce—only such particular places as midway between the open and the suburban area (tentatively called the "quasi-open area"). And in such an area the median field strength may be smaller by about

5 dB than the quasi-maximum strength in an open area. Curve Q_r in Fig. 22 is the prediction curve of the correction factor in a quasi-open area represented in the same way as that for Q_0. By this correction, the open area field strength remains nearly constant for all frequencies, as in a suburban area.

3.3 Relation between Antenna Height and Field Strength (Antenna Height Gain Factor)

While the base station antenna height is usually more than scores of meters, the vehicular station antenna is no higher than 1 to 3 m above ground. There are naturally functional differences between the two, which must be considered separately.

3.3.1 Base Station Antenna Height Gain Factor

According to the definition of base station antenna height (h_{te}) given for our experi-

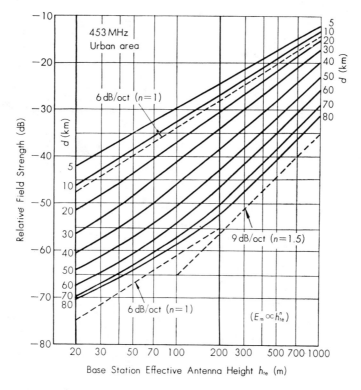

Fig. 23—Dependence of base station effective antenna height on median field strength in urban area.

ments, it may have six different heights— 820 m, 220 m, 140 m, 60 m, 45 m, and 30 m. So let the gain factors be examined from the test results on each of them.

Figure 23 shows, at 453 MHz for example, the depeneence of the relative median field strength (or the reciprocal of the median attenuation) on the urban base station effective antenna height (found from the smoothed curves relating to measured distance dependence given in Fig. 10). The distance, as a parameter, is shown as 5~80 km. When the effective antenna height is 30~1,000 m and the distance is in the neighborhood of 10 km, the field strength tends to be linear uniformly at 6 dB/oct ($n=1$, $E \propto h_{te}^n$). It rises to 9 dB/oct ($n=1.5$) or thereabout with a high antenna at a long distance, it falls, with a low antenna, below 6 dB/oct, not necessarily showing a linear trend. This comes gradually when the base station antenna is low and the transmission path covers a long distance.

The tendency desribed above is the same with other frequencies. On the basis of all this, the prediction curves (shown in Fig. 24) have been obtained for the base station antenna height gain factor, with h_{te} fixed at 200 meters. These curves serve to predict the "basic median field strength."

3.3.2 Vehicular Station Antenna Height Gain Factor

(1) Relative Gain Factor for 1.5 m and 3 m

Figure 25 shows, for various frequencies and base station effective antenna heights, the differences of the medians in one and the same urban sampling interval measured, with a 3 m- and a 1.5 m high vehicular station antenna made exchangeable. There are slight fluctuations in the measured values; but they show no remarkable changes with respect to the distance and base station ef-

41

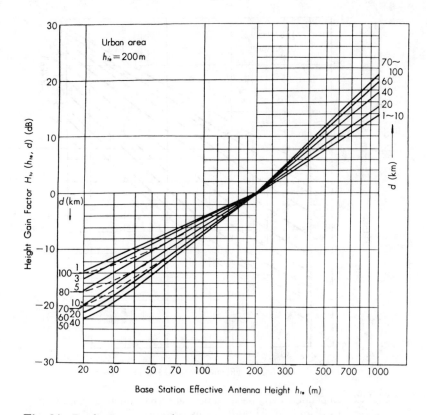

Fig. 24—Prediction curves for base station antenna height gain factor referred to $h_{te}=200\,\mathrm{m}$, as a function of distance.

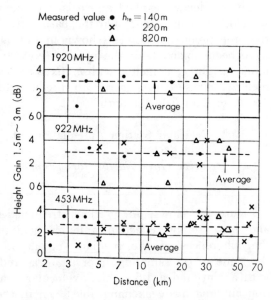

Fig. 25—Measured values of 1.5 m to 3 m height-gain of vehicle in urban area.

ective antenna height. On the average, the height gain is 3 dB for all frequencies as shown by the broken lines in Fig. 25.

It follows that the vehicular station antenna height gain factor for a height of 3 m or less, is supposed to be 3 dB/oct ($n=1/2$, $E\propto h_{re}^{n}$).

(2) Gain Factor for Height above 3 m

The vehicular station antenna height for land-mobile radio service may not usually be more than $3\sim4\,\mathrm{m}$. However, the recently-developed super-highways in large cities, mostly 10 m or so above ground, have induced the authors to make an investigation on the antenn again factor for heights more than 3 m.

As a supplement to our propagation experiments, the results of measurement made at several fixed points are shown in Fig. 29. It may be known that the higher the frequency the larger the height gain, which

42

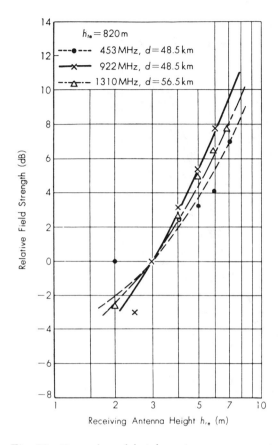

Fig. 26—Examples of height gain measurement of receiving antenna in urban area.

tends to be 6 to 8 dB/oct ($n=1\sim1.3$, $E\propto h_{re}{}^{n}$). As measured values are not ample enough to find the final gain factor, some more data will be referred to for further examination.

According to the height patterns measured by the NHK Technical Laboratory[8] at eight medium and small cities at frequencies of 87 MHz, 176 MHz, and 670 MHz, with the antenna height ranning from 4 to 10 m, the points of inflection appear in the neighborhood of 4 to 6 m; and there is a sharp linear inclination for more heights up to 10 meters.

The appearance of the points of inflection is probably related to the average height of the houses in Japanese cities being 5 m; and for heights more than that, the shielding effect of the houses becomes smaller. So the height patterns are presumed to take considerably different forms according to the average height of houses and buildings in a city. That is, in a built-up residential area (large city) where the building height averages more than 15 m, the points of inflection would move up to more than 10 m in the pattern curves, showing $n<1$ ($E\propto_{re}{}^{n}$) between $3\sim10$ meters.

In this connection, the following data[9] on the relative gain factor for heights of 10 m and 3 m, are recently reported by CCIR:

Frequency band	Suburban area	Large city
450~1000 MHz (Band IV, V)	6~7 dB ($n\doteq0.7$) (dependent on Δh)	4~5 dB ($n\doteq0.5$)
30~250 MHz Band III	7 dB ($n\doteq0.78$)	4~6 dB ($n\doteq0.5$)

There is another report of the measurement[10] taken in the heart of Tokyo, recently issued by the NHK Technical Laboratory confirming that the value is about 6 ~7 dB.

The prediction curves for vehicular antenna height gain factors in a medium-small and a large city, in cases where the antenna height is variable from 1 to 10 m (standard 3 m), if drawn on the basis of all the foregoing data obtained, would be as shown in Fig. 27. These curves will be of use for the prediction of the basic median field strength, and also for the conversion of antenna height gains needed for a comparative study of other propagation curves.

4 Propagation Characteristics on Irregular Terrain

4.1 Correction Factor of Field Strength on Rolling Hilly Terrain

The terrain parameters are to relate the degree of terrain irregularities with the field strength. Where the vehicular antenna height is no more than a few meters, there are several ways to decide them; and the most representative ones so far published are: the CCIR,[11] TASO,[12] and Thiessen[13] method. They are mostly intended for 10 m high TV receiving antennas and have their merits and

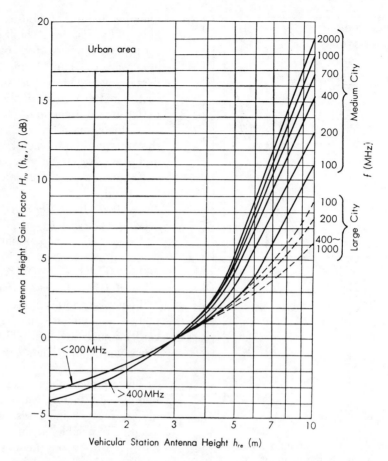

Fig. 27—Prediction curves for vehicular antenna height gain factor in urban area.

demerits, because some are not very clear in description; others are strict in description but must go through complicated processes.

If the receiving antenna is fairly high (more than 10 m), the strict description has enough meaning of its own; but where the vehicular antenna is as low as 1 to 3 m and the field strength suffers a change of more than 10 dB under the influence of houses and trees near it, the description will have to loss the bulk of its meaning.

To find, therefore, a correction factor for field strength in a sampling interval for mobile radio service with as much ease and promptitude as possible, let this method of deciding terrain parameters be based on the following:

(i) To obtain the terrain undulation height Δh following the definition given in Section

2.4, (1), (b), and the method suggested in Fig. 5. This coincides with the description of the CCIR method, but the interval originally intended is 10 km ahead of the receiving point.

(ii) To apply this Δh to undulations of more than a few in number. It is replaced by another parameter (average angle of general slope θ_m), when the place is a simple general sloped terrain.

(iii) To resort, in addition, to a measure of fine correction, when the vehicle happens to be on top or at the bottom of an undulation, in order to find a proper relation between Δh and the correction factor. This means that the correction for the rolling hilly terrain is subjected to treatment from two sides—the sampling interval median and the fine correction adapted to the terrain undulations—which is suggested by F. H. Wise.[14]

(1) Sampling Interval Correction Median on Rolling Hilly Terrain

The data used for this analysis are taken from those measured by a mobile radio car while traveling on Tama rolling hilly terrain, the signals mostly transmitted from the Enkai base station. The values of Δh may be found from the profiles drawn for each azimuth angle of 1° relative to the traveling region. The additional median attenuation was analyzed with the difference between the

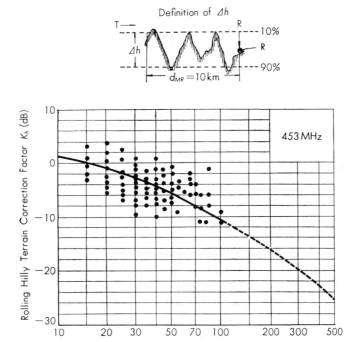

Fig. 28(a) 453 MHz

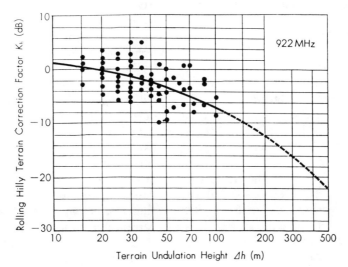

Fig. 28(b) 922 MHz

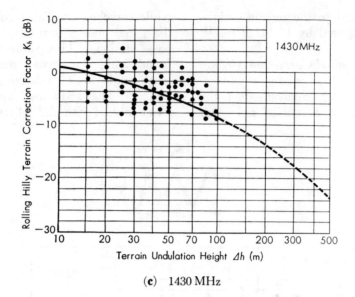

(c)   1430 MHz

Fig. 28—Measured values and prediction curve for "rolling hilly terrain corretion factor."

two values—the sampling interval median of field strength in the rolling hilly terrain and the median field strength (or basic median) for a distance equal to the aforesaid interval in the quasi-smooth terrain urban area (the base station effective antenna height being kept the same), and then this value was represented as a function of the undulation height Δh.

Figures 28(a) to (c) explain how Δh is related to the additional median attenuation (or rolling hilly terrain correction factor), respectively, at 453 MHz, 922 MHz, and 1,430 MHz. The correction factor relative to Δh is seen fluctuating conspicuously for all frequencies, becoming larger as Δh increases. The full-line cuves are smoothed curves for the factor. As no measured values of Δh above 100 m are available, the curves representing them are drawn with refrence to the CCIR curves.

The characteristics tend to be the same with each of the three frequencies; but the correction factor dependence on Δh at 922 MHz, at region of a large Δh, is found to be about 3 dB smaller than that for 453 MHz, and a point midway between the factors for 1,430 MH.

(2) Fine Correction Factor on Rolling Hilly Terrain

The correction factor dealt with in the precediug section (1) relates to the sampling interval median taken while the mobile van is just rising up from the bottom of an undulation.

If, on a rolling hilly terrain, the mobile van draws very near an undulation, the attenuation rises far above the correction factor referred to in the preceding section. On a course rather close to the top of the undulation, it falls below the factor, with the field strength ascending in the meantime.

The analysis that follows is concerned with the fine correction factor (that is, the factor adjusting once again the correction factor referred to in the preceding section), while the mobile van is traveling on a road lying at bottom or on top of an undulation. Figure 29 shows a maximum of changes ($\pm$dB) from the correction factor referred to in the preceding section, or the rolling hilly terrain fine correction factor as a function of the terrain undulation height Δh. The schematic diagram appearing above the curve is to give an idea of the field strength variation correction relative to the terrain profile.

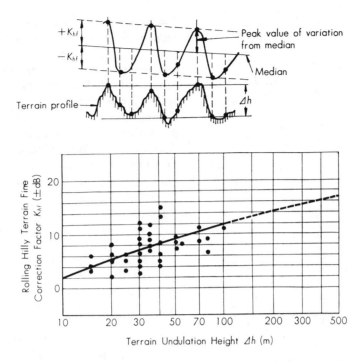

Fig. 29—Measured values and prediction curve for "rolling hilly terrain fine correction factor."

In a position at the bottom of the undulation which is on the side of the base station or on a road lying within 100 m from the side of the undulation, it would be well to correct the correction factor $(-K_h)$ of Fig. 28 first and $(-K_{hf})$ of Fig. 29 next; while, on top of the undulation, the sum of the two factors $(K_{hf}-K_h)$ would have to be corrected.

(3) Vehicular Station Antenna Height Gain Factor on Rolling Hilly Terrain

In the same way as for an urban area (Fig. 25), Fig. 30 shows the vehicular antenna height gain factor relative to the frequency and distance on a rolling hilly terrain, in other words, the differences of the medians in one and the same sampling interval measured, with the antenna height made changeable from 3 m to 1.5 m. Some fluctuations can be seen in the measured values, but there seems to be no distinct variation with respect to the distance. On the average, the gain factor is found to be 2.8 dB at 453 MHz, 3.3 dB at 922 MHz, and 3.3 dB at 1,430 MHz,

showing no great difference among them. Hence estimation of the antenna height gain factor for heights below 3 m on a rolling hilly terrain to be 3 dB/oct.

4.2 Correction Factor for Isolated Mountain

Where the propagation path makes its way through mountains rising one above another, the rolling hilly terrain correction factor would in most cases be capable of prediction. But if there is an isolated mountain ridge like a knife edge, it must be dealt with differently. There are several ways of treatment intended for 10 m high TV receiving antennas suggested so far.

Originally, the calculated value of knife-edge diffraction is to indicate a loss relative to the free space value. When the receiving antenna is low, even though the ridge top is in a free space range against the base station, the received field strength behind the ridge usually suffers more loss than the

47

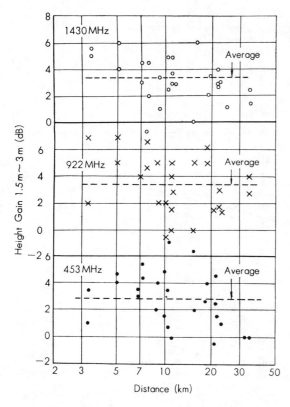

Fig. 30—Measuured values of 1.5 m to 3 m height-gain of vehicular station in rolling hilly terrain.

free space value minus the knife-edge diffraction loss.

Goldsmith[15] and Epstein,[16] in their treatment of this point, both introduce Norton's theoretical values and experimental factors as expressing the additional loss. Wise,[14] on the other hand, tries to obtain the value of field strength without resorting to this action, but acts promptly by deducting the correction factor relative to the basic CCIR curves. This may be said to be a simple method in a practical sense.

This paper likewise puts more stress on methods of practical use. So the basic idea is to find the correction factor relative to the basic median, by using an adequate terrain parameter, following substantially the Wise method.

Figure 31 shows, when the freqency band is 450～900 MHz and the isolated ridge height

$h = 100 \sim 350$ m, the deviation of the measured median field strength from the basic median, with the ridge height correction factor normalized at $h = 200$ m, for each of the distance ranges $10 \sim 20$ km, $20 \sim 40$ m, and $50 \sim 70$ km, against the distance from the ridge top d_2. Curves A, B, and C represent smoothed prediction curves for the respective mean distances. In normalizing the ridge heights, measured correction factors (in dB) were multiplied by α by means of the following empirical formula:

$$\alpha = 0.07 \sqrt{h}, \qquad h: \text{(meters)}. \qquad (1)$$

This conversion factor is given in Fig. 32.

From the findings above, it may be seen that the field strength becomes higher than the basic median on the ridge top, the correction factor approximates 0 in a position a little way down the top (back distance $d_2 < 1$ km), and the attenuation shows its maximum most probably at the base of the ridge where $d_2 \doteq 2$ km or so.

Now examine the method where by the isolated ridge correction factor (Fig. 31) depends on the back distance d_2, comparing with the knife-edge diffraction calculation.

Curve B in Fig. 33 represents Curve B at $d_1 = 30$ km in Fig. 31 just as it is, while Curve K shows the calculated value of knife-edge diffraction loss for d_2 at 450 MHz, $h = 200$ m, $d_1 = 30$ km. The two curves are drawn so as to show their correlation by causing 0 dB graduation (for Curve B) on the left and 20 dB graduation (for Curve K) on the right to come on the same level, assuming that the terrain factor of the basic median (like experimental factors referred to before) is 20 dB. In examining these curves together, a comparatively well-coincided tendency may be seen so far as $d_2 > 2$ km; but the loss on Curve K in increases if $d_2 < 2$ km, because of the fact that the isolated ridge model has a thickness while the knife-edge model has none, thus bringing about, as a matter of course, a difference between the two curves. Furthermore, the magnitude of knife-edge diffraction loss is practically independent of d_1 as long as h is constant, and does not

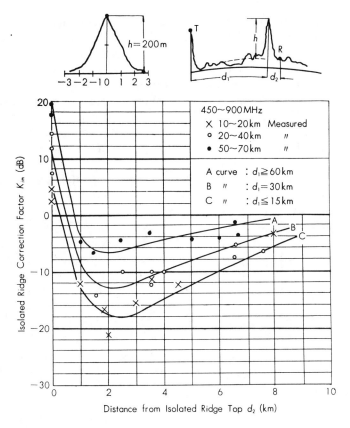

Fig. 31—Measured values and prediction curves for "isolated
ridge correction factor" normalized at ridge height
of $h=200$m. For other ridge height, the conversion
factor should be multiplied by factor of α shown
in Fig. 32.

suffer any more than 1 dB even change with a change of $15\sim60$ km in d_1. Take, for instance, Curve C at $d_1=15$ km and Curve A at $d_1=60$ km in Fig. 31 for the purpose of comparison. Although the tendencies relative to d_2 are very much alike, the relation between the two curves in their absolute value, differs according to the terrain factors relative to distances. It may be asserted then that, supposing there is a growth of terrain factors (or attenuation of the basic median referred to the free space value) in proportion to the distance, the correlation between Curves A, B, and C in Fig. 31 would again be formed here, if the correction factors obtainable from Curve K be arranged according to distances. This correlation might be taken

as reasonable, aside from some minute differences in the absolute values of the curves in Fig. 31.

4.3 Correction Factor for General Slope of Terrain

In this section will be sought the relation of tne average angle of general slope on terrain θ_m to the correction factors in conformity to the definition given in Section 2.4, (1), (d).

Figure 34 shows, where the terrain is sloped for a distance of at least 5 to 10 km, the deviation of the measured median field strength from the basic median—or the slope terrain correction factor—in relation to the average angle of slope θ_m (in milliradian).

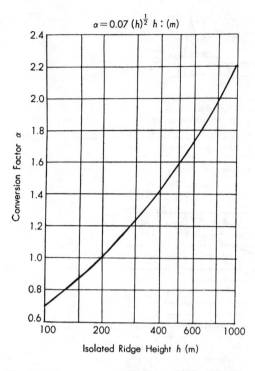

$$a = 0.07 (h)^{\frac{1}{2}} \quad h:(m)$$

Fig. 32—Conversion factor to be multiplied to the value of Fig. 31, when ridge height $h \neq 200$ m.

The correction factor varies with the distance.

The curves are prediction curves drawn for some different distances; and curves for distances other than those may be obtained by interpolating the values of the known curves. Also, for the sloped rolling hilly terrain, the correction treated in Section 4.1 as well as this correction for general slope of terrain, will be made.

4.4 Correction Factor for Mixed Land-Sea Path

Where there is an expanse of sea or lake in the propagation path, the field strength is generally higher than on land only. There is an empirical method[17] of prediction in England which is based on experiments conducted on the North Sea.

This method may be convenient for the prediction of factors between one point and the other; but a large number of such factors will have to be managed in a very troublesome way, where there are various base station antennas propagating waves over a wide range of area, as in the case of mobile radio service.

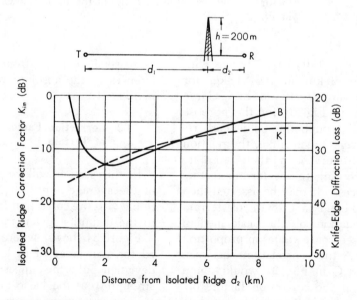

Fig. 33—Relation between the curves of Fig. 31 and of knife-edge diffraction loss. (450 MHz)

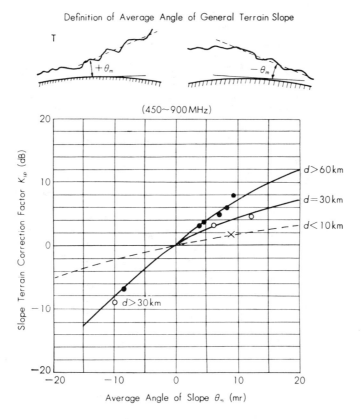

Fig. 34—Measured value and prediction curves for "slope terrain correction factor."

From a practical point of view, this method will turn to finding the relation between the distance parameter of mixed land-sea path (β), which is defined in Section 2.4, (1), (e), and a value called the correction factor for mixed land-sea path, that is, the deviation of the measured median field strength from the basic median.

Figure 35 shows the measured values for this correction factor as the distance varies and also as the expanse of water is near the vehicular or the base station. The degree of field strength rise (correction factor) is larger if the water adjoins the vehicular station (lower diagram (A)) than if it adjoins the base station (pper diagram (B)), depending further on the distance. The full and the broken lines represent the prediction curves for (A) and (B), respectively. For distances other than indicated, curves may

be obtained by interpolation. If the water is in the middle of the path (β to be found from Fig. 8(c)), the intermediate valnes of the full and broken line values will answer very well.

5 Location Variability

Among the propagation characteristics for land-mobile radios, location variability comes next in importance to attenuation, which has been described so far.

Let location variability be considered from the viewpoint of variations in the median level for a sampling interval on the one hand, and in the instantaneous level for a small sector in the same interval on the other.

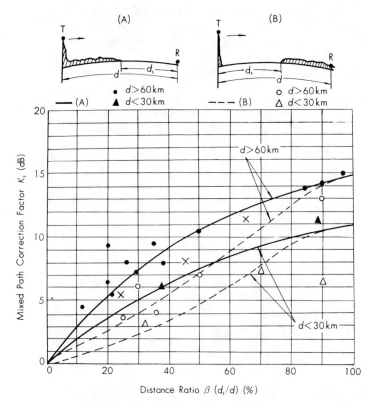

× When the sea lies in the middle of the path.

Fig. 35—Measured values and prediction curves for "mixed path correction factor."

5.1 Distribution Form of Field Strength

5.1.1 Distribution of Instantaneous Field Strength in Small Sector

As stated before, the variation in the instantaneous field strength level experienced by a mobile van station, is due to the fact that it crosses with such rapidity the standing waves which result from the multi-path reflected and diffracted waves. The form of distribution, as seen from its model, conforming to the Rayleigh distribution in this case, will be examined according to the situation of the existing obstacles.

Figure 36 shows, with its respective 50% values meeting together, the distribution of instantaneous field strength for a small sector of about 50 m, in an urban (a) and a forest (b) area, respectively, at different frequencies.

The curves are seen gathering along the Rayleigh distribution theoretical curves. It may be assumed that the variation speed increases but its depth (or the from of distribution) does not change in proportion to the speed of the mobile radio car.

Meanwhile, in a suburban area where obstacles present themselves intermittingly, rises often occur in the field strength; so the form of distribution tends to turn upward at its higher level side, resembling rather more the log-normal distribution than the Rayleigh distribution, and the standard deviation is about $\sigma = 6 \sim 7$ dB on the average.

5.1.2 Distribution of Small Sector Median in Sampling Interval

Even in an urban area where the obstacles are of similar kinds, the small sector median

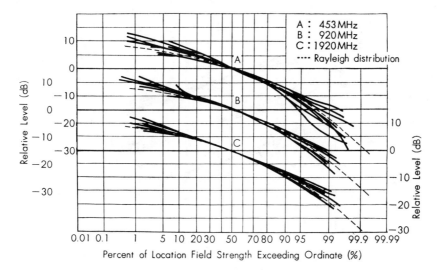

(a) In urban area ($h_{te}=220$ m, $h_{re}=3$ m)

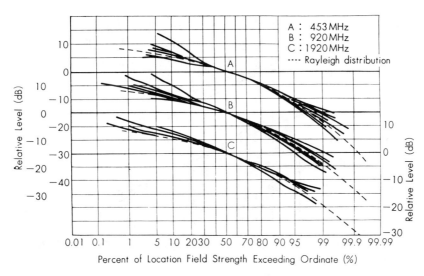

(b) In forest or behind forest ($h_{te}=820$ m, $h_{re}=3$ m)

Fig. 36—Examples of instantaneous field strength distribution in small-sector.

of instantaneous field strength referred to will change to a considerable degree, if the area or interval becomes wide.

Figure 37(a) shows an example of the cumulative distribution of median field strength for a small sector (about 20 m) in an urban sampling interval (1~1.5 km) at different frequencies. Here the curves mostly approximate the log-normal distribution.

Figure 37(b) shows a similar example of the distribution in a suburban area. The curves do not necessarily conform to the log-normal distribution influenced by obstacles, but they might, on the whole, be said to resemble it; and the standard deviation is usually larger than in an urban area.

On the basis of the foregoing description about the distribution form, consider how to

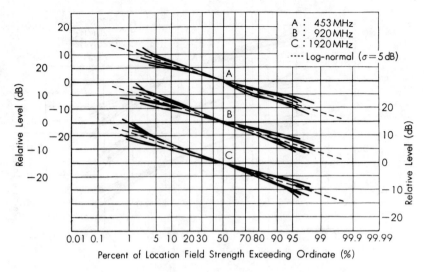

(a) In urban area (h_{te}=220 m, h_{re}=3 m)

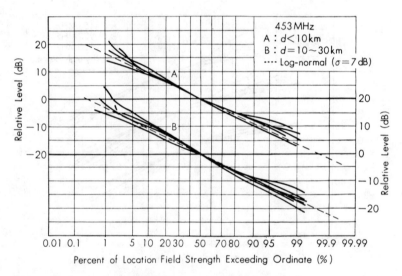

(b) In suburban area (h_{te}=60 m, h_{re}=3 m)

Fig. 37—Examples of distribution of small-sector median field in
sampling inteval (1~1.5 km).

predict lacation variability.

5.2 Prediction of Location Variability

5.2.1 Prediction of Median Field Strength Location Variability

Figure 38 shows the measured mean values of standard deviation (σ) of small sector

median field strength variation in an urban sampling interval, for classified distances of 1~3 km, 3~5 km, 20~30 km, and 70~80 km. The mean values of σ are not very closely connected with the base station antenna height or distance, but they become slightly larger at high frequencies.

The values of σ in a suburban and a rolling hilly terrain area, as may be known from

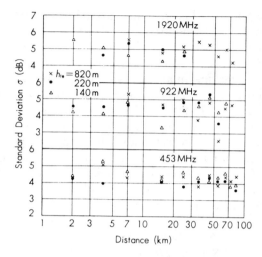

Fig. 38—Measured mean values of standard deviation of small-sector median field strength variation in urban area sampling interval (1~1.5 km).

Figs. 37 (a) and (b), are much larger than those for an urban area—about $\sigma \doteqdot 7$ dB—tending to grow large as the frequency increases.

For a wider region in which various obstacles peculiar to urban and suburban areas exist in a mixed condition, the small sector median distribution does not always take the log-normal distribution form according to how such obstacles are mixed, but is approximate to it if the obstacles are uniformly mixed.

In determining the extent of land for which location variability is to be used in the design of the land mobile service the size of interval or area traveled by the mobile radio car in a period of time taken for one telephone call, may become the accepted standard. With a mean holding time of one call to be 3 to 4 min, the travel speed of the car 60 km/hr, then the interval would come to 3~4 km and the area 2 km in radius.

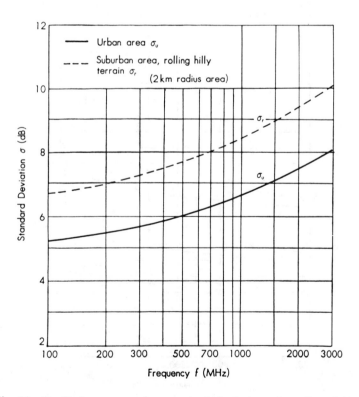

Fig. 39—Prediction curves for standard deviation of median field strength variation in urban, suburban and rolling hilly terrain.

The standard deviation σ of the median variability in an urban area in this respect, will be larger than that shown in Fig. 38. Figure 39 shows the prediction curves for standard deviations in urban, suburban, and rolling hilly terrain areas, each 2 km in radius.

5.2.2 Prediction of Instantaneous Field Strength Location Variability

(1) Prediction in Urban Area

The instantaneous variation of field strength in an urban small sector can be brougut near the Rayleigh distribution of such small-sector medians near the log-normal distribution which has standard deviation σ_u (in Fig.

39) in it. The overall variability, therefore, may be found from the theoretical composition of the two distribution functions. Figure 40 shows the prediction curves (in solid lines) for the instantaneous variation depths from the median field strength (V_{di}, 50~90%, 50~95%, 50~99% in depth) obtained from this composite distribution. Again the equivalent standard deviation where the composite distribution is nearly equal to the log-normal distribution (this is possible because of the large value of σ_u, if its small percentage is negligible) is expressed by σ_u in Fig. 40.

(2) Prodiction in Suburban Area and Rolling Hilly Terrain Area

The instantaneous variation of field strength

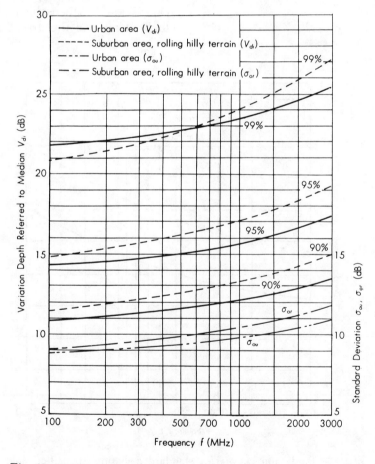

Fig. 40—Prediction curves for instantaneous variation depth from median field strength and standard deviation.

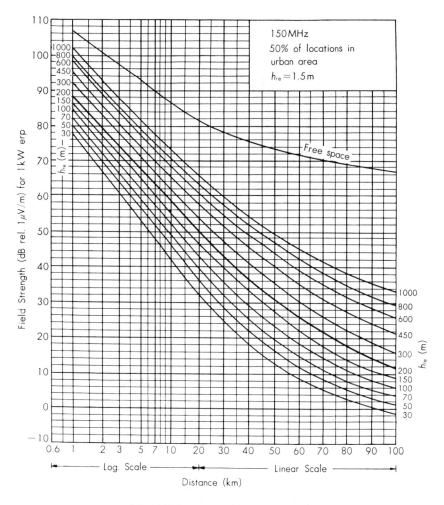

Fig. 41(a)   150 MHz Band

in a suburban and a rolling hill terrain area small sector, can, on the whole, approximate the log-normal distribution (where $\sigma = 6$ B); and the distribution of such small sector medians to the long-normal distribution which has the standard deviation expressed by Curve σ_r in Fig. 39. From the composition of these two distributiohs may be found the overall distribution of instantaneous field strength in the area under examination.

Curve σ_r in Fig. 40 is the prediction curve for the standard deviation of this overall distriburion; and the curves in broken lines are for obtaining the variation depth $V_{d i}$.

6   Prediction of Field Strength; Comparison between Predicted and Measured Values

By making use of the various results and prediction curves so far examined, it is possible to obtain the field strength and its variability peculiar to areas of all sorts of terrain irregularities and environmental clutter usually met with.

6.1   Prediction Procedures

In this method of prediction, to obtain the basic median field strength in a qnasi-smooth terrain urban area is the starting

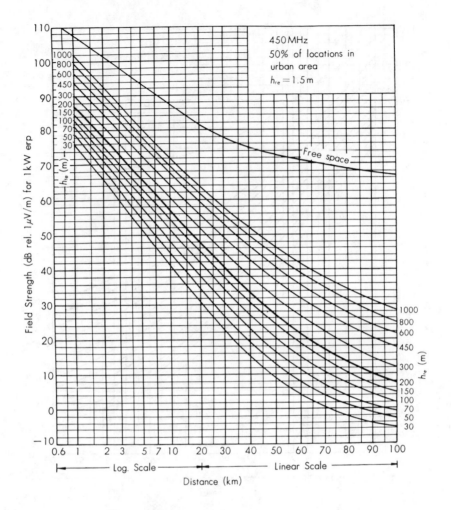

Fig. 41(b) 450 MHz Band

point. The prediction curves representing values for all those terrains and obstacles, are obtainable by adjusting the correction factors for the respective terrain parameters.

6.1.1 Prediction of Basic Median Field Strength (Curves)

The following equation (for addition and subtraction in dB) and curves are used for the prediction of the basic field strength median (curve) which is to be made the standard of prediction procedures:

$$E_{mu}=E_{fs}-A_{mu}(f,d)+H_{tu}(h_{te},d)$$

$$+H_{ru}(h_{re},f) \qquad (2)$$

where

E_{mu} : The median field strength (dB rel. $1\mu V/m$) for a quasi-smooth terrain urban area under a given condition of transmission.

E_{fs} : The free-space field strength (dB real. $1\mu V/m$) for a given condition of transmission.

$A_{mu}(f,d)$: The median attenuation relative to free space (basic median attenuation, dB) in an urban area, where the base station effective antenna height $h_{te}=$ 200 m, vehicular station antenna height

58

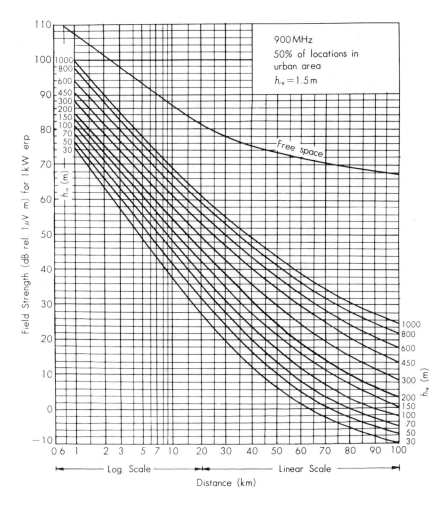

Fig. 41(c) 900 MHz Band

(above ground) $h_{re}=3$ m, expressed as a function of frequency and distance by the curves in Fig. 15.

$H_{tu}(h_{te}, d)$: The base station antenna height gain factor (dB) relating to $h_{te}=200$ m, expressed by the curves in Fig. 24 as a function of distance.

$H_{ru}(h_{re}, f)$: The vehicular station antenna height gain factor (dB) relating to $h_{re}=3$ m, expressed by the curves in Fig. 27 as a function of frequency.

Figures 41(a) to (d) show, respectively, at 150 MHz, 450 MHz, 900 MHz, and 1,500 MHz, the basic median field strength curves for the base station effective antenna height $h_{te}=30$, 50, 70, 100, 150, 200, 300, 450, 600, 800,

and 1,000 m, when the effective radiation power $P_{erp}=1$kW, and the vehicular station antenna height $h_{re}=1.5$ m.

6.1.2 Drawing Field Strength Contour Curves over a Service Area

The procedures to follow in drawing the field strength contour curves around a base station are given below:

(1) Draw a terrain profile for eaeh proper azimuth angle, in order to obtain the base station effective antenna height h_{te} and terrain parameters of all sorts. (See Figs. 4 to 8.)

(2) Draw on a map, with the site of the

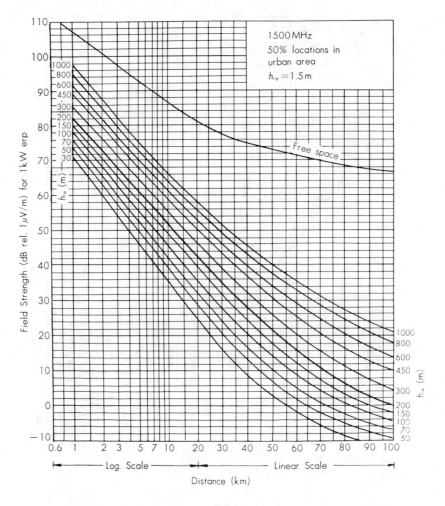

Fis. 41(d) 1500 MHz Band

Fig. 41—Prediction curves of "basic median field strength" (in urban area over the quasi-smooth terrain).

base station as their center and having regard to the height h_{te} fixed in (1), a certain number of basic median concentric circles (together with entry of their respective values), at intervals of metric lengths corresponding to 5 dB of the basic median field strength found from Section 6.1.1.

(3) Amend the basic median concentric circles according to the irregular terrain situation (quasi-smooth terrain excepted) and environmental clutter surroundings, by modifying the distances which correspond to the correction factors cited below:

(a) "Correction to the orientation of an urban area street"—correction factor ($+K_{al}$ dB) represented by Curve (a) in Fig. 18, if there are a large number of along-the-path streets in the area; and factor ($+K_{ac}$ dB) represented by Curve (b) in Fig. 18, if there are plenty of across-the-path streets.

(b) "Correction for a suburban area"—correction factor ($+K_{mr}$ dB) shown in Fig. 20, if the area abounds in suburban features.

(c) "Correction for an open area"—the correction factors ($+Q_0$, or $+Q_r$ dB) shown in Fig. 22 in the open area on a quasi-smooth terrain, according to the degree of shielding.

(d) "Correction for a slope terrain"—correction factor ($+K_{sp}$ dB) shown in Fig. 34 in an area where the ground is sloped up or down for a distance of at least $5 \sim 10$ km.

(e) "Correction for a mixed land-see path" —correction factor ($+K_s$ dB) represented by Curve (A) or (B) in Fig. 35, where there is an expanse of sea or lake in the propagation path.

(f) "Correction for a rolling hilly terrain" —correction factor ($+K_h$ dB) in Fig. 28 on an undulating hilly terrain.

(g) "Fine correction for a rolling hilly terrain"—fine correction factor ($\pm K_{hf}$ dB) in Fig. 29, where there are many roads running

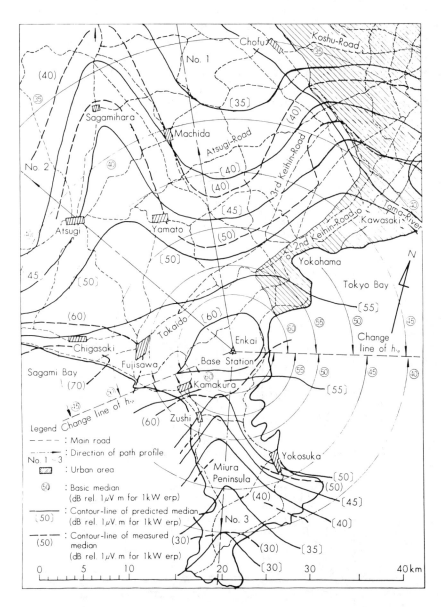

Fig. 42—Comparison of contour line for predicted median field strength with that of measured median in broad area. (Base station : Enkai, $f = 450$ MHz)

on the tops or bottoms of hills.

(h) "Correction for an isolated ridge"—correction factor ($+K_{im}$ dB) shown in Figs. 31 and 32, on top of or behind a ridge that lies in the propagation path. This correction is made when the ridge resembles the model shown in the upper left-hand margin of Fig. 31; but the maximum value of correction show in the same diagram would probably appear at the foot of the ridge, when its breadth is different from that of the model.

6.2 Comparison between Prediction Values and Measured of Field Strength

In this section a comparison will be made between the field strength vs. distance curves

obtainable from the diagrams and predication methods cited in the preceding section on the one hand, and representative propagation curves hitherto reported on the other, in order that the reliability of the propagation design data suggested by this paper may be confirmed.

(1) *Example of A Given Broad Area*

Figure 42 shows a comparison between the measured and the predicted curves of the equifield strength for that part of the Kanto district which includes the Miura peninsula and the Tama highlly zone, with the base station (microwave relay station) established at Enkai. The frequency used is 450 MHz and the base station antenna height is 183 m

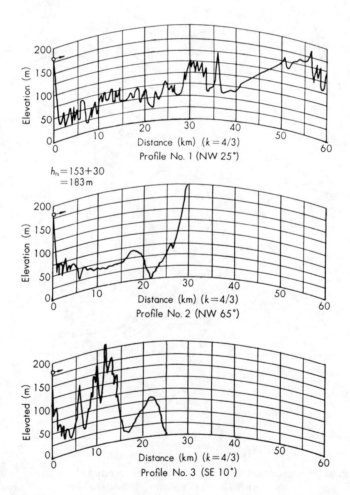

Fig. 43—Path profile on representative direction from Enkai base station.

above sea level. The equifield strength measured is drawn from the data collected by vehicular stations while running on the principal roads; and the prediction curves follow the method mentioned in Section 6.1.2. Figure 43 shows the representative path profiles in this area along three different directions from the base station, as indicated in Fig. 42 as No. 1~No. 3. They suggest that this area may be divided into two parts—the base station effective antenna height for one is 133 m and for the other it is 83 meters. The prediction equifield strength curves in Fig. 42 are drawn according to this distinction; only the rolling hilly part of the area dispenses with the process of fine correction referred to in Fig. 29. From the above, it may be conjectured that the predicted and the measured curves are in substantial agreement.

(2) *Example of A Given Terrain Profile*

Figure 44 shows a comparison between the measured field strength for the sampling in-

terval on the propagation path whose profile is given in the lower diagram, and the prediction curves obtained by following the procedure of Section 6.1.2. The measured and the prediction curve are seen to correspond fairly well with each other.

(3) *Comparisom of Prediction Curves with Measured Values by Other Institutions*

The measurement data taken up for this comparison collected by other institutions, are partly intended for TV broadcasting. Where the receiving antenna is high, prediction is made through correction by means of the curves in Fig. 27.

The principal test data furnished are from the NHK Technical Laboratory,[8] Bell Telephone Laboratories,[4] and RCA.[18] Figures 45 to 47 show some of the results of comparison of these data. The frequencies and transmitting and receiving effective antenna heights are indicated in each diagram.

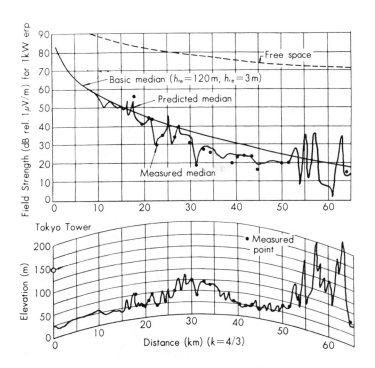

Ffg. 44—Comparison of measured and predicted median field strength on 55° SW radial from Tokyo Tower. ($h_{te}=120$m, $h_{re}=3$m, 453 MHz)

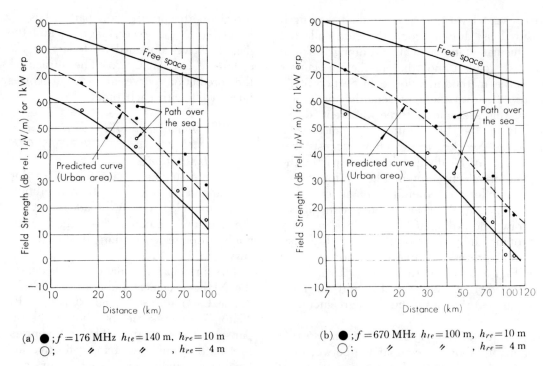

(a) ● ; $f = 176$ MHz $h_{te} = 140$ m, $h_{re} = 10$ m
　　○ ; 〃　　〃　, $h_{re} = 4$ m

(b) ● ; $f = 670$ MHz $h_{te} = 100$ m, $h_{re} = 10$ m
　　○ : 〃　　〃　, $h_{re} = 4$ m

Fig. 45—Comparisons of NHK's data with predicted median field strength curves (urban area).

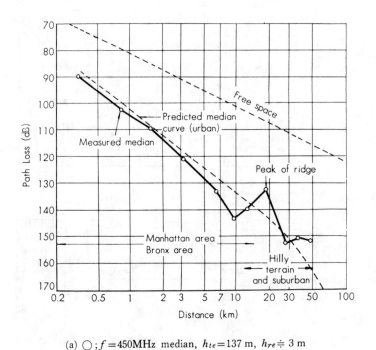

(a) ○ ; $f = 450$MHz median, $h_{te} = 137$ m, $h_{re} \doteqdot 3$ m

Fig. 46

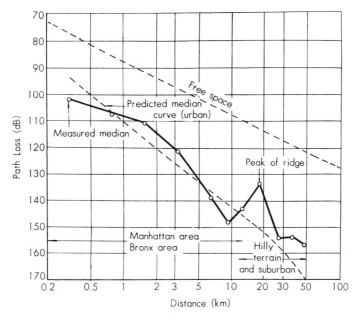

(b) ○; $f = 900$ MHz Median, $h_{te} = 137$ m, $h_{re} \fallingdotseq 3$ m

Fig. 46—Comparisons of Bell Laboratories' data with predicted median field strength curves.

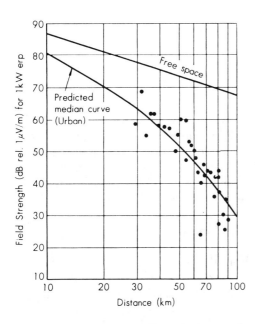

Fig. 47—Comparison of RCA's data with predicted median field strength curve.

The NHK data (Fig. 45) is connected with medium and small cities, showing the median of the measurements taken at about twenty fixed points per city. With the exception of the cities where there are land-sea paths, the distane characteristics tend to be almost the same as those for the prediction curves. The Bell data (Fig. 46) provide us with two medians—one of short-distance values measured at the lofty-building area of Manhattan, and the other of those measured along several directions for a distance of 10 km or more, at suburban and hilly terrain areas. As nothing is known about the suburban and hilly terrain irregularities and environmental clutter along the whole route, correction is impossible to make on the values; but, judging from the urban prediction curves, there is a general agreement on distance characteristics between the measured values and prediction curves.

The RCA data in Fig. 47 show the results for a comparatively smooth terrain area. Here again, there is also a fair agreement.

(4) Comparison between Representative

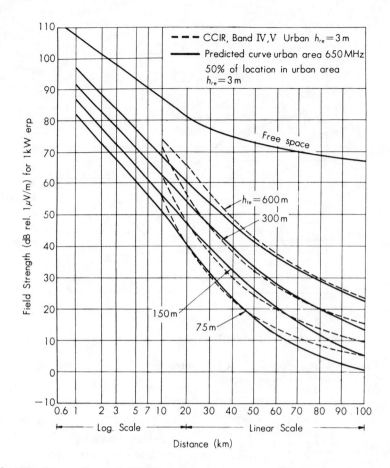

Fig. 48—Comparison of CCIR propagation curves with predicted curves.

Propapation Curves and Prediction Curves.

Considering the importance of land-mobile radio service, CCIR has recently reported[5] the antenna height (3m) gain correction factor in urban and suburban areas found from the former propagation curves (Rec. 370-1). As a representative case, let the urban field strength curves obtainable therefrom be taken up and compared with the prediction curves.

The curves in broken lines in Fig. 48 represent the propagation curves in the urban area for a 3 m high vehicular station antenna, drawn on correcting the curves of Rec. 370-1 by means of the correction factors for Band IV and V shown in Rep. 239-1. Those in solid lines represent the prediction curves at 650 MHz, or the center frequency of Band IV and V 450~1,000 MHz. Here a batter agreement exists for a distance of 20~60km;

but, where the distance is below 20 km, or where the antenna is low and the distance is 60 km or more, the CCIR curves result in rise above the prediction curves, so that further study would be necessary with respect, especially, to long-distance characteristics.

7 Conclusion

For the description given so far, various characteristics about VHF and UHF land-mobile radio service, hitherto ambiguous in this as well as foreign countries, have become clarified; and simple and practical methods of drawing prediction curves been established for obtaining the field strength which is open to much-complicated location variability. This has also made it practical in land-mobile radio service to connect circuit reliability with site location, suggesting a guiding principle to the development of new frequency bands in the future. However, the intricacy of propagation characteristics has not entirely been elucidated by this paper. Also, the test data on correction factors for irregular terrains cannot be said to be sufficient. In order to solve these problems, there is no other way than to rely upon future research.

In concluding this paper, the authors wish to express their sincere thanks to Mr. T. Kamiya, formerly Director of Transmission System Development Division, Mr. F. Iwai, formerly Staff Engineer (now in Fujitsu Co., Ltd.), Dr. T. Masuda, formerly Chief of Radio Transmission Section, Dr. T. Morinaga, Chief of Mobile Radio Section for their deep understanding and invaluable guidance; and also to other persons who shared this study for their efforts in conducting the experiments.

References

(1) CCIR; Rec. 370-1, Oslo, 1966, II, p. 24.
(2) P. L. Rice: Troposheric Fields and their Long-Term Variability as Reported by TASO, *Proc. IRE.*, **48**, 6, p. 1021, June 1960.
(3) J. J. Egli; Radio Propagation above 40 MC over Irregular Terrain, *Proc. IRE.*, **45**, 10, p. 1383, Oct. 1957.
(4) W. E. Young: Comparison of Mobile Radio Transmission at 150, 450, 900 and 37000 MC, *BSTJ.*, 31, 6, p. 1008, Nov. 1952.
(5) CCIR: Rep. 239-1, Oslo, 1966, **II**, p. 125.
(6) E. Shimizu and T. Morinaga, et al.; Propagation Tests of Frequencies for VHF Mobile Radio, *Report of E.C.L.*, NTT, **5**, 1, p. 13, Jan. 1957.
(7) CCIR Doc.; Resuls of Propation Measurements in Large Cities, Doc. V/99-E, p. 21, Jan. 1966 (Italy).
(8) I. Murakami and E. Sugiyama, et al.: Screening Effect of Medium-Sized and Small Cities on UHF and VHF Propagation, *NHK Tech. Journ.*, **13**, 2, p. 12, Mar. 1961.
(9) CCIR: Rep. 239-1. Oslo, 1966, **II**, p. 123.
(10) A. Kinase and K. Suga: Influence of Buit-up City Situation on Propagation Characteristics of UHF Band, *NHK Tech. Journ.*, **19**, 6, 1967.
(11) CCIR: Rec. 370-1, Olso, 1966, **II**, p. 25.
(12) A. Lagron; Forecasting Television Service Field, *Proc. IRE.*, **48**, 6, p. 1009, June, 1960.
(13) CCIR, Doc.; Correction Factor for the Frequency Band, I-V, Doc. V/28-E, p. 22, 1965, (P. P. of Poland).
(14) F. H. Wise: The Influence of Propagation Factors on UHF Television Broadcasting, *Telev. Soc. Journ.*, **10**, 11, p. 330, Nov. 1964.
(15) T. T. Goldsmith, et al.: A Field Survey of Television Channel 5 Propagation of New York Metropolitan Area, *Proc. IRE.*, **37**, 5, p. 556, May 1949.
(16) T. Esptein et al.; An Experimental Study of Wave Propagation at 850 MC, *Prock. IRE.*, **41**, 5, p. 595, May, 1953.
(17) E. Sofer, et al.; Tropospheric Radio Wave Propagation over Mixed Land and Sea Paths., *Proc. IEE.*, **113**, 8, p. 1291, Aug. 1966.
(18) D. W. Peterson: Comparative Studyof Low-VHF, High-VHF and UHF Television Broadcasting in the New York City Area, *RCA Rev.*, **24**, 1, p. 57, Mar., 1963.

Radio Propagation Above 40 MC Over Irregular Terrain*

Summary—Radio transmissions in the vhf and uhf frequency region over land areas always contend with the irregularities of the terrain and the presence thereon of dispersed quantities of trees, buildings, and other man-made structures, or wave propagation incumbrances. The determination of path attenuation is not easily satisfied by simple, curved, or plane earth calculations. However, quantitative wave propagation data are available in varying degrees which take into account conditions experienced by fixed-to-fixed and fixed-to-moving transmissions over irregular terrain. This available statistical wave propagation information on terrain effects vs frequency, antenna height, polarization, and distance is analyzed, expressed by empirical formulas, and presented in the form of nomographs and correction curves amenable for use by the systems engineer.

INTRODUCTION

RADIO transmissions above 40 mc more often than not take place over irregular terrain so that the ordinary method of calculating propagation attenuation over plane earth, curved earth, and simple diffraction edges becomes unsatisfactory. As one moves about in irregular terrain in a vehicle, the received signal is characterized by a slow variation dependent on the major features of the terrain and on distance, and by a

fast variation about the median in a small sector which is independent of the transmission distance but is dependent on the speed of the vehicle and on the frequency of the transmission.

In the practical sense, the systems engineer is interested in knowing how well his equipment will be able to service an area, or how well his equipment will cover many areas in a very large area. Some of these areas may typify curved earth while other areas may be highly mountainous; all others will be in between these areas in terms of surface irregularity.

This irregular terrain has dotted on it, trees, buildings, and other man-made wave propagation encumbrances. If one could run the entire gamut of terrain conditions in a statistical manner and arrive at the transmission loss which would have to be designed into a system at a given frequency to provide the desired coverage, it would appear that such information would be invaluable to the systems engineer.

Fortunately, such data have been collected and studied by the Federal Communications Commission for use in connection with their studies of the vhf and uhf television allocation problems, and by others in connection with mobile service.

* Original manuscript received by the IRE, February 5, 1957; revised manuscript received, June 7, 1957.
† U.S. Army Signal Eng. Labs., Fort Monmouth, N. J.

Reprinted from *Proc. IRE*, vol. 45, pp. 1383–1391, Oct. 1957.

The majority of the terrain data,[1] on which the following material will be derived, are based on survey data taken by commercial organizations in various parts of the country including New York, N. Y.; Washington, D. C.; Cleveland, and Toledo, Ohio; Harrisburg, Easton, Reading, Pittsburgh, and Scranton, Pa.; Kansas City, Mo.; Cedar Rapids, Iowa; San Francisco, Calif.; Bridgeport, Conn.; Nashville, Tenn.; Fort Wayne, Ind.; Richmond and Norfolk, Va.; and Newark, N. J. In each of these locations, a number of radials were investigated. In all, over the uhf range, 288 to 910 mc, 804 miles on 63 radials are represented in the data. The method of measurement, while not the same at all locations, falls into three categories: continuous mobile recording sampling every 0.2 mile, spot measurements properly weighted so as to be considered unbiased, and clusters of measurements. In the vhf region, 50 to 250 mc, approximately 1400 measurements, consisting of continuous data analyzed over 1-mile and 2-mile sectors, are included in the data.

In discussing service area, we will be concerned with expressing the percentage of locations one could expect to cover statistically at a predescribed distance. Thus, if one arbitrarily divides a 10-mile circle into 100 equal parts with each division represented by a point (location) and superimposes this configuration on the statistically derived landscape represented by the data, then 10 per cent coverage would mean that 10 of the points (locations) would receive satisfactory or better transmissions, while at the balance of the points reception would not be possible. Likewise, when considering 90 per cent coverage, 90 of the 100 points would receive transmissions while the balance would have no reception.

Actually, in dividing the circle into 100 locations, it was assumed that these locations represented the median value of signals in the immediate vicinity of the location, since one finds that in the immediate vicinity of a given location, say a few hundred feet, there will be fine variations in received field strength.

TERRAIN-FREQUENCY, DISTANCE DEPENDENCE

The theoretical plane earth field strength expression is given by

$$E = \frac{h_t h_r f}{95 d^2} \sqrt{P_t}$$

where

E = field intensity in microvolts per meter
h_t = transmitting antenna height in feet
h_r = receiving antenna height in feet

[1] H. Fine, "UHF Propagation Within Line of Sight," FCC, TRR Rep. No. 2.4.12; June 1, 1951. Contains material taken from K. A. Norton, M. Schulkin, and R. S. Kirby, "Ground Wave Propagation Over Irregular Terrain at Frequencies Above 50 MC," Ref. C, Rep. of the Ad Hoc Committee of the FCC for the Evaluation of the Radio Propagation Factors Concerning the Television and Frequency Modulation Broadcasting Services in the Frequency Range Between 50 and 250 MC; June 6, 1949.

f = transmission frequency in megacycles
d = distance from transmitter in miles
P_t = effective radiated power in watts.

Eq. (1) is limited to those geographical areas which are similar to plane earth, such as relatively short overwater and very flat barren land paths. Even in these areas man has erected bridges, Texas towers, billboards, and so forth, which alter considerably the propagation characteristics as expressed by the theoretical plane earth formula.

While the theoretical received field strength increases with frequency, all other constraints being the same, it is important to note that the voltage across the input to a receiver will be the same at all frequencies when the receiving antenna is a half-wave dipole. However, if the antenna at the higher frequency is constructed so that it presents an effective area equal to that of the half-wave dipole at the lower frequency, then this increased field strength at the higher frequency will be realized as increased voltage at the input to the receiver.

The measured field strength data[1] over irregular terrain were compared with what one could expect over plane earth rather than curved earth, since the best median field strength data fit for distances up to 30 to 40 miles shows that the inverse distance squared trend for plane earth is better than the curved earth field, at least for low antenna heights. Beyond 30 miles to 40 miles the data are sufficiently meager as to be unworthy of analysis as a representative quantity of data. Therefore, the median field at a given frequency can be described by the theoretical plane earth field intensity, less the median deviation therefrom. This median deviation data from the theoretical plane earth field, called terrain factor, is shown in Fig. 1. The straight line on this figure very nearly passes through all the FCC data, and it will be noted that the deviation from the plane earth field strength varies inversely with the frequency and is independent of distance. The intersection of this line with the theoretical plane earth field strength is at 40 mc, so that the variation with frequency is with respect to this frequency.

With this statistical information, (1) becomes empirically for the median field at the 50 percentile locations, E_{50}, independent of frequency

$$E_{50} = \frac{40 h_t h_r}{95 d^2} \sqrt{P_t}. \tag{2}$$

This E_{50} field strength may be obtained quickly from the nomograph, Fig. 2.

The theoretical plane earth received power between half-wave dipoles (3) is independent of frequency.

$$P_r = 0.345 \left(\frac{h_t h_r}{d^2} \right)^2 P_t \times 10^{-14}. \tag{3}$$

Making use of the power law variation with frequency for the median deviation from the theoretical plane

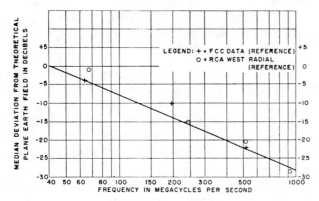

Fig. 1—Median terrain factor for fixed-to-vehicular or mobile service.

earth field, Fig. 1, (3) becomes empirically,

$$P_{50} = 0.345 \left(\frac{h_t h_r}{d^2}\right)^2 \left(\frac{40}{f}\right)^2 P_t \times 10^{-14}. \qquad (4)$$

Eqs. (2) and (4) show that nature, by interposing terrain features, has essentially placed in juxtaposition the frequency dependence of the field strength and received power above 40 mc over plane earth. Thus, while the theoretical received field strength over plane earth increases with frequency, the median received field intensity above 40 mc over irregular terrain is independent of frequency, and while the theoretical received power between half-wave dipole antennas is independent of frequency, over irregular terrain the median received power above 40 mc varies inversely as the frequency squared.

For the purpose of the systems engineer, in making irregular terrain calculations it is preferable to use the plane earth received power (3) shown in nomographic form in Fig. 2, in its theoretical form because field strength, median value statistically derived, and received power theoretically derived are, at this point of exploration of irregular terrain propagation, independent of frequency.

It is interesting to note that if one determines from diffraction theory the depth of hills[2] which will result in the median loss of Fig. 1, the statistical irregular terrain can be conceived as hills with a depth of about 500 feet. It is also interesting to note that the New York west radial terrain over which data are available[3] has an irregular depression of about 500 feet, 12 miles in extent and distance from the transmitter. Most of the data were accumulated in this portion of the radial, and the median values below plane earth theory are shown in Fig. 1 as the composite for the entire radial.

At this point in the paper it will be well to assume a rather simple problem and use it as a means of exemplifying the development of the material to be presented.

[2] K. Bullington, "Radio propagation variations at vhf and uhf," PROC. IRE, vol. 38, pp. 27–32; January, 1950.
[3] G. G. Brown, J. Epstein, and D. W. Peterson, "Comparative propagation measurements; television transmitters at 67.25, 288, 510 and 910 megacycles," *RCA Rev.*, vol. 9, pp. 171–201; June, 1948.

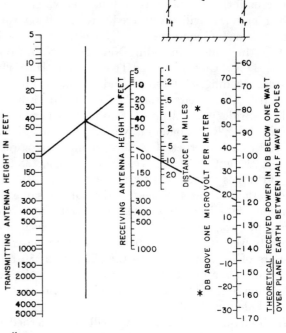

*50 PERCENTILE LOCATION MEDIAN FIELD STRENGTH.

Fig. 2—Received power over plane earth and 50 per cent location median field strength—one watt radiated.

Assume:

Transmission frequency, 150 mc
Dipole antennas, half-wave
Transmitting antenna height, 100 feet
Receiving antenna height, 10 feet
Service range, 10 miles
Service to 90 per cent of locations at 10 miles
50 kc IF bandwidth
Suburban noise
No transmission line losses.

Required: Transmitter power output.

The theoretical received power in db below one watt will be from Fig. 2, 119 dbw. The field strength at 50 per cent of the locations, Fig. 2, will be 17.5 db above one microvolt per meter, one watt radiated.

TERRAIN-FREQUENCY DEPENDENCE

If one explores the data[1] in terms of the distribution of received field strength over irregular terrain, one finds that the over-all terrain distribution when plotted in decibels above the theoretical plane earth attenuation, is log-normally distributed. Thus, on probability paper, the terrain distribution will appear linear and may be described by its median value and standard deviation, Fig. 3. The terrain distribution of field intensity in the vhf band, taken at a center frequency of 127.5 mc appears to have an over-all standard deviation of 8.3 db, while the terrain distribution of field intensity in the uhf region centered around 510 mc, appears to have an over-all standard deviation of 11.6 db. Of course, the median deviation from theoretical plane earth field is

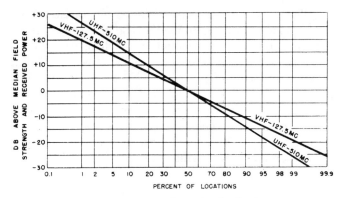

Fig. 3—VHF and uhf terrain distribution.

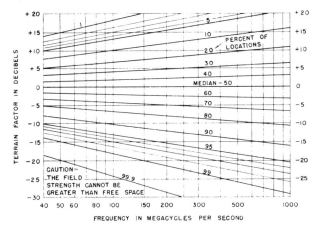

Fig. 4—Fixed-to-vehicular or mobile service field
strength terrain factor.

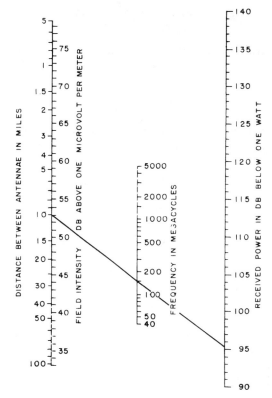

Fig. 5—Free space—one watt radiated between half-wave dipoles.

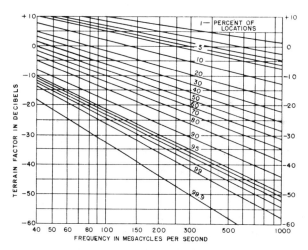

Fig. 6—Received power terrain factor for fixed-to-
vehicular or mobile service.

displaced 12 db by the terrain factor for the two frequencies, Fig. 1. From this standard deviation data, Fig. 4 has been prepared which permits the determination of the correction factor to the E_{50} field strength when the received field strength to other than the 50 percentile location is desired. For example, as previously determined, E_{50} was 17.5 db above one microvolt per meter. Applying the terrain correction factor of -11.5 db for the 90 percentile location results in a median received field strength at the 90 percentile location of 6 db above one microvolt per meter, one watt radiated. This value of field strength does not exceed the free space value for 10 miles of 53 db above one microvolt per meter obtained from Fig. 5. Under conditions of greatly increased antenna heights and/or service to a small percentile of locations, the calculated field strength could exceed the free space field. If such is the case, the free space field should be used. It is interesting to note that while the median field strength (2) and terrain factor for 50 per cent of the locations (Fig. 4), are independent of frequency, for percentages of locations less than 50, the field strength increases with frequency, and for $E_{2.3}$ the field strength varies as $f^{1/2}$. Likewise for percentages of locations greater than 50, the field strength decreases with frequency and for $E_{97.7}$ varies inversely as $f^{1/2}$.

Likewise, Fig. 6 has been prepared to reflect the cor-

rection factor to the theoretical plane earth received power imposed by irregular terrain. The P_{50} value follows an inverse frequency squared relation as per (4), at $P_{97.7}$ an inverse frequency cubed relation, and at $P_{2.3}$ an inverse frequency relation. As previously determined, the theoretical received power is -119 dbw. The terrain correction factor for the 90 percentile location at 150 mc is -23 db, and the received power at this location will be -142 dbw, or the half-wave dipole-to-half-wave-dipole path attenuation for this degree of service is 142 db. The free space received power is -95.4 dbw from Fig. 3 which exceeds that for the 90 percentile location.

TERRAIN-TRANSMITTING ANTENNA HEIGHT DEPENDENCE

The transmitting antenna height, used in conjunction with the data[1] is defined as the height above the median, 2–10 mile terrain level. This rule has not proven as reliable as one might expect, since it does not take into account the terrain within 2 miles or beyond 10 miles. For purposes of this report the effective height of the antenna will be the height of the antenna above plane earth. In actual practice the transmitting antenna heights could be taken as the effective height above local terrain. For all practical purposes, the data confirmed that the received field strength increased linearly with transmitting antenna height. Transmitter height-gain tests made around the New York area[4] seem to indicate that in poor service locations the effect of transmitting antenna height increase is somewhat less than one would theoretically predict. In median or 50 percentile locations the height gain would approximate the theoretical expected height gain, and for good service locations the height gain would be somewhat more than the theoretical. For purposes of this paper, the formulas and nomographs reflect a linear high gain for transmitting antenna height.

TERRAIN-RECEIVING ANTENNA HEIGHT DEPENDENCE

Receiving antenna height is the effective height above local terrain. The data do not appear to support any clear-cut variation of field strength with change in receiving antenna height. For receiving antennas which clear surrounding terrain features, the height gain appears to be linear. For receiving antennas which do not clear the surrounding terrain features, no orderly pattern is discernible. However, test results analyzed statistically,[1] show that in the 6 to 30 feet category, the field strength appears to support a square-root height gain variation. Above 30 feet, the height gain is linear. This variation is reflected in the nomograph of Fig. 2.

In practice, when using low antenna heights, as pointed out in the New York tests,[4] the dependence of field strength upon receiving antenna height is quite variable. When locating in a given area, within the confines of available antenna height, the maximum field strength should be found.

TERRAIN FADING

Both the vhf and uhf studies indicate that the time fading is much smaller for the distances involved than the terrain variation, and may be neglected as a power balance factor in equipment design. In the fear of being misunderstood, suppose equipment is designed for vehicular operation to cover 90 per cent of the locations, at 10 miles from the transmitter. Based on statistical terrain data, the variation in median signal throughout the terrain is far in excess of what the long-time fading would be between two fixed locations. However, fading becomes important for fixed service work. A subscriber land-based for an extended period of time in a poor location, marginal signal, might well compensate for the long-time fading which will ensue by moving to the optimum spot in the small area in which he is to be located, and also by having means for elevating his antenna, which can now be changed to a directional antenna, to the optimum height within the height-raising capability of his antenna system. These two expedients should compensate for time fading and be reflected in a highly reliable transmission circuit.

TERRAIN-ANTENNA POLARIZATION

Theoretically, over plane earth at antenna heights greater than a wavelength and for small angles between the direct and reflected rays, as is the case for irregular terrain transmissions, polarization has negligible effect on the behavior of radio waves above 40 mc. Experimental evidence[5,6] over irregular terrain of the received characteristics of polarized waves appears in general to verify the above. While it appears that vertical polarization is somewhat better directly behind hills or deep in the shadow area, horizontally polarized waves afford better reception in back of, but away from, the deep shadows of hills. In wooded areas, the attenuation is less for horizontally polarized transmissions than for vertically polarized transmissions below 300 to 500 mc. In total, little difference can be detected in the average propagation characteristics.

There is one exception to the latter statement and it concerns propagation using antenna heights less than one wavelength. In this case the ground wave is dominant and theoretically vertical polarization provides an apparent height gain over horizontal polarization.[7] This effect is shown in Fig. 7 and pertains only to vertical polarization since for horizontal polarization the effective height is essentially the actual height at frequencies above 40 mc. As shown in Fig. 7, the effective height also depends on the conductivity of the soil over which the transmission will be effective. Unfortunately, as far as the author knows, terrain-statistical data are lacking on the propagation effects resulting from the use of very low vertically polarized antenna heights in the lower vhf region. Until such time as this theoretical information can be placed in dispute statistically by tests, it is

[4] J. Epstein and D. W. Peterson, "An experimental study of wave propagation at 850 mc," PROC. IRE, vol. 41, pp. 595–611; May, 1953.

[5] J. S. McPetrie and J. A. Saxton, "An experimental investigation of the propagation of radiation having wavelengths of 2 and 3 meters," *J. IEE*, vol. 87, pp. 146–153; August, 1940.

[6] J. A. Saxton and B. N. Harden, "Ground-wave field-strength surveys at 100 and 600 mc/s," *Proc. IEE*, vol. 101, part 3, pp. 215–221; July, 1954.

[7] K. Bullington, "Radio propagation at frequencies above 30 megacycles," PROC. IRE, vol. 35, pp. 1122–1136; October, 1947.

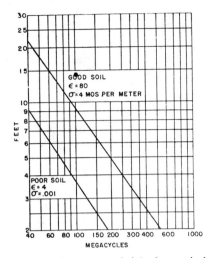

Fig. 7—Minimum effective antenna height for vertical polarization.

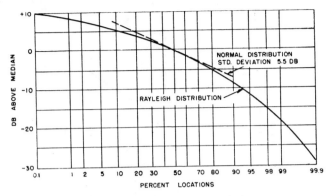

Fig. 8—Terrain-small sector variation.

proposed that when vertically polarized transmissions are under consideration, Fig. 7 be used in finalizing the effective height of low antennas.

In our problem at 150 mc with an antenna height of 10 feet it can be seen from Fig. 7 that even with vertical polarization this height is also the effective height. If the problem had been one of transmission at 40 mc, then in using Fig. 2 the height would have remained the same for poor soil conditions, but would have to be taken as 23 feet over good soil conditions.

Terrain-Small Sector Field Strength Variation

As noted earlier, there is a fine amplitude variation about the median in a small distance or area which is independent of the distance from the radiation source. Some studies indicate that these fine variations of field strength have a normal distribution[1] which appears to be independent of frequency with a standard deviation of 5.5 db. Other studies,[8] indicate a Rayleigh distribution, Fig. 8. The latter appears more likely because the studies which indicate a normal distribution were taken over distances which perhaps exceeded the small sector variation. However the Rayleigh type fading may only occur and be applicable in areas replete with buildings, etc. In open areas the distribution may be log-normal over a small sector. Between the 10 and 90 per cent values of these distributions there is very little difference in the two distributions. The amplitude distribution is the same at all frequencies indicating that the range of constructive and destructive phase interference or standing wave effects is complete. However, the number of constructive and destructive interferences increases in a given distance or area with frequency.

Tests[9] conducted in the Phoenix, Ariz. area indicate that the average vehicle travel between these fine signal minima is one wavelength in free space, while in the direction away from or toward the radiation, the distance between signal minima is the free space half-wave distance. With this information, in vehicular service the small sector amplitude fluctuations in received carrier level will increase in rapidity with frequency and the speed of the vehicle, or

$$A = \frac{v}{\lambda/2}, \text{ and in practical terms, } A = 0.003 \, fv \quad (5)$$

where A is the average amplitude fluctuation rate in cps, f is the radio carrier frequency in mc, and v is the velocity of the vehicle in the direction of transmission in miles per hour. For ready use, (5) has been prepared in the form of a nomograph, Fig. 9. It shows, for example, that at 150 mc the received field in a vehicle traveling at 40 miles per hour in the direction of transmission would have an average fluctuation rate of 18 cps. For vehicular service, this is the rate which would have to be considered in the design of age circuitry with the audio or intelligence pass band designed above this frequency.

The small sector variations at 90 mc[10] appear to be small in open flat country and much greater in built-up areas as might be expected. The variations in built-up and treed areas appear greater for vertically polarized transmissions than for horizontally polarized transmissions.

Another characteristic of these variations which one would expect is that the higher the frequency, the steeper the fall and rise in field strength. In general, the variations appear to be deeper with the time between rise and fall smaller. Maximum envelopes occurring during a test[9] are shown in Fig. 10. At 15 db down, the "outage time" on 459 mc may be in the order of a few milliseconds at vehicle speeds of 40 miles per hour with perhaps no noticeable effect on speech transmissions, whereas at 156 mc the outage time at this level could cause the loss of voice information.

Unfortunately, data were not found which would permit an expression either quantitatively or qualitatively as to the useful distribution or design point criteria of

[8] W. R. Youug, Jr., "Mobile radio transmission compared at 150 to 3700 mc," *Bell Sys. Tech. J.*, vol. 31, pp. 1068–1085; November, 1952.

[9] C. F. Meyer and D. Soule, "Field Strength Study," Motorola, Inc.; February, 1956. Work performed under Signal Corps Contract DA-36-039-sc-64737.

[10] H. L. Kirke, R. A. Rowden, and G. I. Ross, "A vhf field-strength survey on 90 mc/s," *Proc. IEE*, vol. 98, part 3, pp. 343–359; September, 1951.

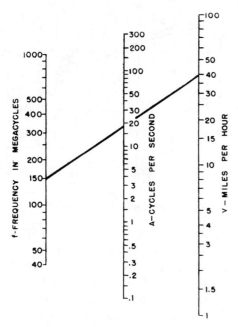

Fig. 9—Fluctuations in vehicles.

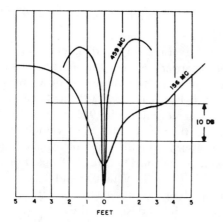

Fig. 10—Maximum small sector variation.

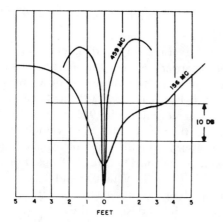

Fig. 11—Echoes in vehicles from a fixed transmission.

these small sector field strength variations. It may well be, at least for the present, that equipment should be designed to the median value of these find grain variations for the percentage of locations service desired.

TERRAIN-WIDE MODULATION BANDWIDTH EFFECTS

The field strength variations discussed so far have been those taken over a very narrow bandwidth of the transmission frequency. On wide-band systems distortion effects may be introduced resulting from propagation via more than one path. These distortions may cause cross talk in multichannel voice systems, or shadows in television reception. This subject will be touched on lightly because not very much statistical data are available nor is literature available on the effects of multipath propagation on various types of modulation. The severity of multipath distortion[11] ap-

pears qualitatively to be independent of frequency and wave polarization, at least within the frequency range of 60 to 3300 mc. The consequences of multipath propagation are not serious for fixed transmission conditions, yet may be very serious in moving situations. For fixed service, movements of the receiving antenna either horizontally or vertically for a distance in the order of a few wavelengths ordinarily cleans up multipath distorted patterns in television reception. More multipath distortion appears in highly built-up and mountainous areas where large off-path reflecting surfaces are present. Directive antennas greatly reduce multipath effects,[11] which means that for equal antenna apertures, the use of the higher frequencies will result in less multipath distortion.

The only good statistical results, unfortunately unrelated to all of the terrain data made use of herein and therefore not representative of all the conditions on which this paper is based, are based on tests in the New York area,[12] where one encounters considerable, and perhaps the worst, multipath propagation conditions. In order to understand the difficulties one may encounter in engineering vehicular wide band systems, the New York data,[12] have been altered (Fig. 11) to reflect the number of echoes per second for a vehicle speed of one mile per hour vs delay of these echoes with amplitudes between 0 and 6 db less than the strongest received signal. Thus a remote television transmitter installed in a vehicle patroling New York at 30 miles per hour would present to the fixed television receiver a picture with thirty, 0- to 6-db echoes per second having $\frac{1}{4}$-μsec delay, 9 shadows per second having 3-μsec delay, and so forth. Besides this ghosting of the picture that is taking place, the synchronous circuit of the television receiver is in essence flip-flopping from the direct signal path amplitude to

[11] D. W. Peterson, "Army Television Problems Phase II Tasks 1 and 2 Final Report," January, 1956, RCA. Work performed under a Signal Corps Contract No. DA-36-039-sc-64438.

[12] W. R. Young, Jr. and L. Y. Lacy, "Echoes in transmission at 450 megacycles from land-to-car radio units," PROC. IRE, vol. 38, pp. 255–258; March, 1950.

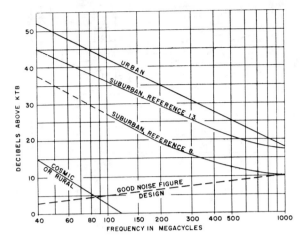

Fig. 12—Median indigenous noise.

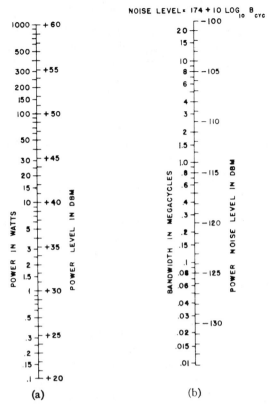

Fig. 13—(a) Conversion of power to dbm. (b) Conversion of bandwidth to thermal noise level.

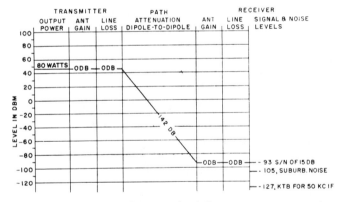

Fig. 14—Power level diagram.

the multipath signal amplitude when the ghost signal is the stronger of the two.

INDIGENOUS NOISE

While the relationship between received signal and frequency over irregular terrain has been covered pretty well, another important power balance factor in systems design is the establishment of the noise level of the receiver, or the signal required to assure satisfactory communication. Noise in the frequency range above 40 mc is mainly caused by man-made noise. The general classifications are rural, suburban or small town, and urban noise. Cosmic noise is still present up to 100 mc. Collectively this noise can be termed indigenous noise.

The extent to which this indigenous noise acts upon a receiver is shown in Fig. 12. Two curves have been drawn for suburban noise since the material for these curves have been drawn from two separate references.[8,13] The lower suburban noise curve is representative of the median indigenous noise experienced in areas suburban to New York, with extrapolated data shown by the dotted portion of the curve. The urban noise data taken from these same two references dovetailed into the same curve. The dotted curve represents the noise figure of a currently well-designed receiver and is shown only to give the figure perspective. The indigenous noise can be referenced with respect to the thermal noise, ktb, of a receiver and is shown in Fig. 12 as the correction factor which must be applied to ktb level, Fig. 13(b).

The difficulty in the use of these curves lies in just what level of noise should be applied in systems design work. Unfortunately indigenous noise data were not collected along with the field strength data. If this had been done a distribution of the magnitude of noise over the areas in which the field strength data were taken would have been available. It would appear that equipment designed for general use should at least consider the lower suburban curve of Fig. 11 with the thought

that in urban areas advantage might be taken of the height-gain in these areas.

PROBLEM SOLUTION

The entire problem is reviewed in Fig. 14 in the form of a power level diagram. Working the level diagram from the ktb level of −127 dbm obtained from Fig. 13(b), for a 50 kc IF, suburban noise and not noise figure plus approximately 12 db, establishes the lowest rf signal, −93 dbm, for an acceptable signal-to-noise ratio. Assuming no transmission line losses to the two dipole antennas and with the path attenuation loss over 10 miles of irregular terrain to the 90 percentile location of 142 db, one arrives at a required transmitter power of 49 dbm or 80 watts, Fig. 13(a).

[13] Federal Telephone and Radio Corp., "Reference Data for Radio Engineers," 3rd ed., p. 442; 1949.

Vehicular-to-Vehicular Transmissions

The entire discussion thus far has dealt with the subject of fixed-to-vehicular, or fixed-to-mobile transmissions over irregular terrain. It is in these subjects that data exist, while in the field of vehicular-to-vehicular transmission good statistical data are nonexistent, at least to the knowledge of the writer.

If one makes the reasonable assumption that the terrain factor will not change whether we deal with the moving-to-moving, fixed-to-fixed, or fixed-to-moving situations, then the median signal received by a vehicle in motion from another vehicle in motion is precisely that given in Fig. 4. However, by statistical theory,[14] it would appear that the standard deviation would be the square root of the sum of the variances of two fixed-to-moving distributions which in this type of transmission can be considered of the same magnitude. Thus the standard deviation for vehicular-to-vehicular transmission is the $\sqrt{2}$ times the standard deviation for the fixed-to-vehicular transmission. This is in essence the correction factor which must be applied to Fig. 6, in order to obtain the vehicular-to-vehicular received power terrain factor shown in Fig. 15. If the given problem were a vehicular-to-vehicular system, fictitiously assuming antenna heights were maintained for this service, the path attenuation at 10 miles to the 90 percentile location would be 119 db, from Fig. 2, plus 32.5 db, from Fig. 15, or 151.5 db compared to a path attenuation of 142 db derived earlier in this paper for the fixed-to-vehicular or mobile transmission. The transmitter power level of 49 dbm, on Fig. 14, must be raised to 58.5 dbm or 700 watts for vehicular-to-vehicular equivalent service.

Remarks

The statistical method of handling propagation over irregular terrain can be used in frequency assignment studies to determine the number of rf channels which should be designed into equipment for cochannel and adjacent channel field service. It has important usage in vulnerability studies of mutual interference, intentional and unintentional jamming, and countermeasures. It also appears to have application in spectrum allocation studies.

Of course the burning question of how well a particular piece of equipment will act in a given environment

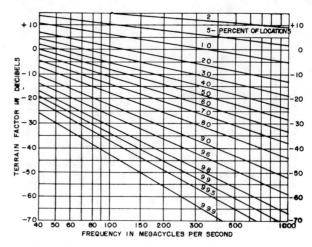

Fig. 15—Vehicular-to-vehicular received power terrain factor.

is difficult to answer. If the terrain is less irregular than the statistical irregular terrain, then better than predicted performance should result. On the other hand, in terrain more irregular than the statistical, a poorer performance should result. However, field operational procedures should be developed which permit a rapid evaluation of the service coverage from a given location. A possible technique for rapid evaluation is one based on a system utilizing the "ground clutter" pattern seen on the radar (PPI) scope.[15]

Conclusion

This paper is considered a modest start in the direction of supplying irregular terrain propagation information applicable to systems engineering. The author encourages constructive criticism or the supply of data which may be beneficial for deriving better statistical data. For example, much data are required on frequencies above 1000 mc; the nature of the fine variations and their effects upon types of modulation; propagation data on vehicular-to-vehicular transmissions; good statistical small sector variation data; and so forth.

Acknowledgment

The author wishes to express his gratitude to all those referenced authors who have made this paper possible by their efforts in collecting propagation data.

[14] A. Hald, "Statistical Theory with Engineering Applications," John Wiley and Sons, New York, N. Y.; 1952.

[15] R. E. Lacy and C. E. Sharp, "Radar-type propagation survey experiments for communication systems," 1956 IRE Convention Record, part 1, pp. 20–27.

CHARACTERISTICS OF SMALL-AREA SIGNAL FADING ON MOBILE CIRCUITS IN THE 150 MHz BAND

H. W. Nylund
Bell Telephone Laboratories, Incorporated
Holmdel, New Jersey

ABSTRACT

Transmission on mobile radio circuits is often affected by "standing-wave breakup" resulting from spatial variations in rf signal amplitude, which to the moving mobile unit appear as rapid fades. Measurements made in the 150 mHz band confirm previous reports that within any small area such signal variations tend to follow the Rayleigh distribution. Statistical distributions have also been determined for the depths and widths of fades, in several different environments where fading was severe; rural, suburban and urban situations were found to produce rather similar results in these respects. Some information is also given on the relation between median signal and circuit quality for speech, under fading conditions.

1. Introduction

When a mobile radio base station transmits to a mobile set in a moving car it is sometimes possible for the car to travel several hundred feet or yards without encountering any variations of over a few dB in the received signal. This however is rather exceptional and usually occurs only if the car with the mobile set is in a clear area where there are few buildings or trees nearby. When operating on city streets or tree-bordered roads it is much more common to find received signals varying by 10, 20 or more dB within a few car-lengths of travel. These fluctuations of course are caused by multipath propagation involving reflections from buildings or other objects; some aspects have been analyzed in References 1, 2, 3, and 6.

It has sometimes been thought that the character of this rapid fading is not predictable, and that where it occurs such characteristics as the depth or the width of fades will vary markedly from one place to another. This paper reports the results of a study that was made some time ago to check these ideas. To do this it was decided to avoid transmission effects caused by variations in major topographical factors, and to deliberately limit the study to small areas that exhibited severe and rapid fading.

2. Measurement Conditions and Methods

RF signals at 152.6 mHz were sent from a base transmitter and received in a car driven along several test courses, each 450' long. The car had a quarter-wave rooftop whip antenna, and was equipped with a special receiver and a paper-chart recorder so that received signal amplitudes could be recorded with a range of over 40 dB and a chart speed of about 1" per second. Distance marks from a speedometer connection were also recorded on the chart. Most of the data herein discussed were obtained by analysis of these chart records; a few speech transmission tests were also made on one of the 450' courses, and for these a standard mobile telephone set was used in the car. Unless otherwise noted all runs were made with a car speed of about 10 mph.

It is essential to note that the objective of this work was not to determine the likelihood of encountering fading, but rather to get an understanding of how the signal behaves when it does fade. Therefore the test courses were not picked at random but were selected as ones which showed severe fading combined with a fairly uniform average signal level. As a result the courses used were all on streets or roads bordered by reflecting objects such as buildings or trees, and each course was laid out so that within its 450' length it avoided intersecting streets, large variations in directions or marked changes in the density and character of nearby objects.

Table I lists information about the test courses and the transmission paths involved in the eight runs herein discussed. For the first three runs the test courses were in suburban or rural areas, while the last five used courses on New York City streets. As a matter of incidental interest the third column of Table I shows how far the actual median received signals fell below the values computed from the transmitted ERP and theoretical path losses. In these computations, the fixed antenna height was measured from adjacent ground level,* and the path losses were computed on a smooth earth basis by the methods of Reference 4, with no allowances for shadow losses. The spread, from 10 or 11 dB in the first three runs to 34 to 42 dB in the last five, is partly attributable to the greater shadow losses caused by big buildings in New York, and also to an obstructed base antenna location used for the New York tests.

3. Distribution of Received Signal Amplitudes

Two samples from the chart records of received signal in Runs one and four are shown in Figure 1. They exhibit the common pattern of broad rounded maxima separated by much sharper fades of varying depths.

---

*The half-wave dipole antenna was about 80' above local ground level for the first three runs, and at 205' height for the others.

Reprinted from *IEEE Trans. Veh. Technol.*, vol. VT-17, pp. 24–30, Oct. 1968.

The chart for each 450' run was first analyzed by reading off signal amplitudes at 200 equally-spaced points and plotting a cumulative distribution curve on Rayleigh probability graph paper. In such a plot a true Raleigh distribution will follow a straight line as illustrated by the dashed line on Figure 2. The actual curves for the eight runs, when plotted with respect to their median values, all fell within the two envelope curves shown on Figure 2. Further, it was not possible to find any characteristic difference between the two groups of curves, for the rural-suburban Runs one to three and for the big-city Runs four to eight; in each group some curves tended toward the maximum-slope envelope, and some toward the minimum slope. This confirms the fact, first reported in Reference 1, that the distribution of signal amplitudes in a small area will usually show a fairly close approximation to the Rayleigh law.

It will be noted that in a true Rayleigh distribution the 1 percent and 99 percent points are separated by 26.6 dB. Earlier studies have indicated that if the received signal is measured at a large number of widely separated points all equidistant from a base transmitter, the spread of values will be much greater than this. Reference 1 shows that in the New York area such measurements gave a spread of some 36 to 52 dB between the 1 percent and 99 percent points. The difference between this and the Rayleigh distribution is attributable to the fact that large changes in the mobile unit's position alter the shadowing losses of building masses, hills, etc., and these alterations are superimposed upon the fading variations found in each small area.

4. Depths of Fades

Figure 2 does not tell anything about the frequency of occurrence of fades of various depths, and so the chart records were also analyzed with this point in mind. Each signal minimum found below the median line on the chart was counted as a fade, and fade depths were measured in dB below the median. An averaged cumulative distribution curve for the eight runs is shown in Figure 3, which also indicates the range of values taken from individual smoothed curves for each run. As shown, 50 percent of the fades were at least 9 dB deep on the average, or slightly over 10 dB deep in the extreme run; the deepest fades ranged from 24 to 35 dB in different runs, with an average just under 30 dB.

Some run-by-run statistics are listed in Table II. Inspection of this table and Figure 3 shows a rather surprisingly small range of characteristic differences between the suburban and the big-city situations. Noting that Table II lists only those fades that fell below the median signal for each run, it is interesting to observe (from the last column) that such fades occurred at an average rate of roughly one per wavelength of car travel. Of course if the

signal dips that stayed above the median had also been counted as "fades" the rate would have been higher; probably approaching two "fades" per wavelength.

The writer's associate Mr. W. C. Jakes Jr. has pointed out that the theoretical rate of occurrence for fades of various depths may be computed by methods found in Reference 7. The relationships used in plotting Figure 3 of reference 7 may be recast in the form:

$$R = \sqrt{2\pi} \ \frac{Vx}{\lambda} \ e^{-x^2}$$

In this expression R is the number of fades per second, for fades of depth $\geq x$. The fade depth x is normalized with respect to the rms value of the signal, which is 1.6 dB above the median; i.e., a fade 20 dB below rms or 18.4 dB below median corresponds to $x = 0.1$. V is the car speed in feet/second and λ the wavelength in feet. Theoretical fading rate computations on this basis can be translated into "percent of fades" terms as used in Figure 3 of this paper, and will be found to give points lying some 2 to 4 dB to the right of the experimental curve. The reason for this small but relatively constant difference is at present unknown.

5. Width of Fades

In addition to the depth of fades it is sometimes of interest to know their spatial extent or width, since this (together with the car speed) determines their time duration to a moving car. For this purpose a line was drawn on each chart record at 10 dB below the median signal value. For each fade extending lower, a measurement was made of the distance the car had moved while the signal trace remained below the 10 dB line, and this distance was noted as a 10 dB fade width.

Cumulative distribution curves were drawn for each run from these measurements, and Figure 4 shows, on a logarithmic probability scale, a curve averaged from these individual plots. The ranges of values from the different plots are also indicated on Figure 4, and Table III gives some additional run-by-run data.

These fade widths exhibit considerably more variation than the fade depths, with a range from 1.5' to 6' for the widest fade observed in each run. However, Table III indicates no characteristic difference between the first three (suburban) and the last five (big-city) runs. If the tests had been extended into different kinds of areas with less cluttered surroundings, other experience suggests that this parameter - fade width - would have been the first to depart from the pattern here depicted, and might have shown substantial increases.

For fades of 20 dB or greater depth there were not enough data to permit plotting width distribution curves; however, the following results applying to these fades may be of interest. The number of such fades ranged from eight to twelve with an average of 9.8 per run. The widest such fade varied from 0.2' to 1', average 0.5'; and the median width of fades at the 20 dB depth ranged from 0.13' to 0.28', average 0.2'.

6. Speech Transmission Tests

Some speech transmission tests were made on the test course of Runs one and two, using in the car a standard IMTS narrowband FM mobile set with receiver sensitivity giving 20 dB tone-to-noise ratio at -139 dBw of rf input. The car was repeatedly driven over the test course at 10 mph, and voice transmissions received from the base station were recorded on a tape recorder.

For each trip over the test course the rf power output of the FM base transmitter was adjusted to a different value by means of attenuators; and since the median received signal had been determined for one value of output power, an appropriate median signal amplitude could be assigned to each one of the speech records.

These records of speech received in the moving car were later played back and their quality judged by several observers. While their judgments varied over a considerable range, some averaged results may be of interest. A median received signal of -137 dBw gave what is sometimes called a "Merit 3" circuit, judged to be readable but with some missed words and phrases that would have required occasional repetition, and with quite annoying noise from the fading break-up effect. A "Merit 4" circuit, judged to require no repetitions and with noise noticeable but not seriously annoying, required a median signal of -125 dBw. Thinking that car speed might be an important factor these tests were later repeated with the car traveling at 25 mph; the averaged results were found to differ by only 1 or 2 dB, a negligible change in view of the nature of the test.

Since mobile radio usage does not always involve a moving car, another talking test was made in which the median signal over the course was adjusted to a rather low level of -142 dBw, and the car was stopped at various points to observe the quality of reception. It was not difficult to find maximum-field spots at which reception was nearly as good as the Merit 4 described above; and when the car was nudged into one of the deeper fades none of the speech was intelligible.

The above of course illustrates one of the reasons why it is difficult to define the coverage range of a mobile system. It has one value for a moving car; a much lower value for a car stopped in what happens to be an unfavorable location; and still another - the maximum - for the user who is willing to hunt for and stop in an advantageous spot.

7. Conclusions

The results of this study indicate that where severe fading is found on mobile radio circuits involving a moving car, what might be called the fine-grained structure of the varying signal is relatively independent of the nature of the car's surroundings and can be described - in statistical terms - with enough accuracy to be useful in some system design and analysis problems.

While these results were obtained in the 150 mHz band, there is reason to believe that they are also applicable - or can be adjusted for application - at higher or lower frequencies. The spatial variation of signal amplitudes would be expected to approximate the Rayleigh distribution at any frequency, and Reference 5 indicates that a reasonably close correspondence to this pattern has been found at 836 and 11,200 mHz.

The fade width distribution of Figure 4 would, for use at other frequencies, need to have its abscissa scale adjusted in proportion to the wavelength involved. For instance, the median width of 10 dB fades - 0.55' at 152 mHz from Figure 4 - would be expected to become about 0.1' at 836 mHz. For comparison, Figure 7 of Reference 5 gives data on the average time duration of fades measured at 836 mHz with a car speed of 30 mph. This shows about 3.5 milliseconds time duration for 10 dB fades; and if this duration is translated into equivalent car travel it corresponds to a fade width of 0.15', which does not differ too widely from the 0.1' projected above.

In regard to the depths of fades it seems likely that the distribution of Figure 3 would apply relatively unchanged at other frequencies, while the rate of occurrence of fades as taken from Table II would vary in proportion to frequency. It is hoped that someone will find an opportunity to check these latter points.

8. Acknowledgment

Thanks are due to the writer's associates Messrs. A. Rudoff, F. C. Henneberg and J. Franzblau, who did all of the experimental work and much of the data reduction and analysis.

REFERENCES

1. "Comparison of Mobile Radio Transmission at 150, 450, 900 and 3700 mc," by W. R. Young, Jr., Bell System Technical Journal, November, 1952.

2. "Echoes in Transmission at 450 mc from Land to Car Radio Units" by W. R. Young, Jr. and L. Y. Lacy; IRE Proceedings, March, 1950.

3. "A Model for Mobile Radio fading due to Building Reflections: Theoretical and Experimental Fading Waveform Power Spectra", by J. F. Ossanna, Jr.; Bell System Technical Journal, November, 1964.

4. "Radio Propagation Fundamentals" by Kenneth Bullington, Bell System Technical Journal, May, 1957.

5. "Comparison of Mobile Radio Transmission at UHF and X Band" by W. C. Jakes, Jr. and D. O. Reudink; Conference Record of IEEE Vehicular Group Annual Conference, December, 1966.

6. "A Statistical Theory of Mobile Radio Reception" by R. H. Clarke, Bell System Technical Journal, July-August 1968.

7. "Statistical Analysis of the Level Crossings and Duration of Fades of the Signal from an Energy Density Mobile Radio Antenna", by W. C. Y. Lee, Bell System Technical Journal, February, 1967.

TABLE I

TRANSMISSION PATHS AND
TEST COURSES

Run No.	Path Length Miles	Median Received Signal in DB Relative to Computed Value	Test Course
1	2.9	-11	Summit, N.J. Residential street, houses and scattered trees
2	2.9	-11	Later repeat of Run 1, following slightly different track on same street
3	3.0	-10	Gillette, N.J. Country road bordered by moderately heavy tree growth
4	1.2	-36	3rd Ave.
5	1.0	-34	4th Ave. New York City streets,
6	1.1	-34	14th St. with buildings mostly
7	0.9	-37	24th St. 4 to 12 stories high
8	1.1	-42	27th St.

TABLE II

FADE DEPTHS

Run No.	Depth of Fade in DB at Indicated Percent Points			Depth of Deepest Fade DB	Total Number of Fades
	10%	50%	90%		
1	20.0	8.5	2.8	24	78
2	21.0	9.5	2.5	35	69
3	24.6	10.2	2.8	34	72
4	21.3	9.0	1.8	27	72
5	21.7	9.0	2.2	32	61
6	20.0	9.4	2.8	29	71
7	21.0	8.1	1.0	29	74
8	22.2	8.1	2.8	28	84
Averages	21.5	9.0	2.3	29.8	72.6

TABLE III

FADE* WIDTHS

Run No.	Width of Fade* in Feet at Indicated Percent Points			Width of Widest Fade* Feet	Number of Fades*
	10%	50%	90%		
1	0.9	.49	.27	2.0	30
2	1.0	.55	.34	2.0	31
3	1.5	.68	.42	3.0	37
4	1.6	.63	.34	3.0	33
5	2.5	.58	.24	6.0	31
6	1.5	.59	.28	3.0	34
7	1.0	.49	.31	1.7	31
8	0.8	.42	.21	1.5	34
Averages	1.35	.55	.30	2.8	32.6

*Note: Considering only fades of depth $\geq$ 10 DB below the median signal for the 450' run. Fade widths measured at 10 DB below median.

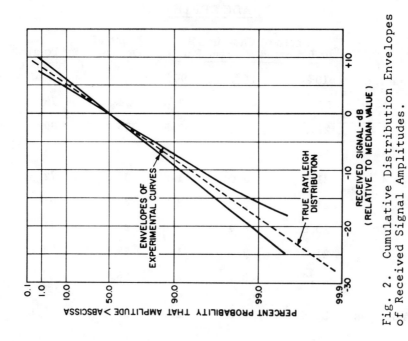

Fig. 2. Cumulative Distribution Envelopes of Received Signal Amplitudes.

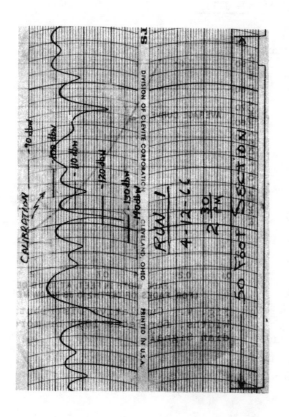
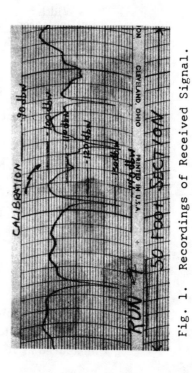

Fig. 1. Recordings of Received Signal.

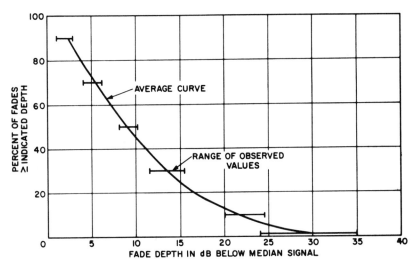

Fig. 3. Cumulative Distribution of Fade Depths.

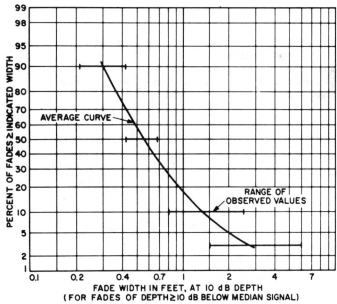

Fig. 4. Cumulative Distribution of Fade Widths, for Fades 10dB or more Below Median Signal.

Properties of Mobile Radio Propagation Above 400 MHz

DOUGLAS O. REUDINK, MEMBER, IEEE

Abstract—This paper begins with a discussion of multipath interference. The spatial description of the field impinging upon a mobile radio antenna is derived and the power spectrum and other properties of the signal envelope are considered. Next, large scale variations of the average signal are discussed. Measurements of observed attenuation on mobile paths over both smooth and irregular terrain are summarized. The paper concludes with a discussion of methods of predicting the area of coverage from a base station.

I. INTRODUCTION

THIS PAPER reviews mobile radio transmission in the frequency ranges above 400 MHz. The emphasis is entirely on CW propagation and the results should thus be applied only to relatively narrow-band systems (<100-kHz channels, for example). The rapid and extreme amplitude fluctuations of the mobile signal are discussed in Section II. The next section first considers factors that affect transmission such as diffraction, rain, and the atmosphere. Then observed attenuation on mobile radio paths are summarized. In Section IV methods are given for predicting field strength.

Manuscript received December 6, 1973; revised July 5, 1974. This paper was presented at the 24th IEEE Vehicular Technology Conference, Cleveland, Ohio, December 4–5, 1973.

The author is with Bell Telephone Laboratories, Inc., Crawford Hill Laboratory, Holmdel, N. J. 07733.

II. SHORT TERM FADING

One readily accessible property of the signal transmitted over a mobile radio propagation path is the amplitude variation of its envelope as the position of the mobile terminal is moved. This information is generally presented in the form of time recordings of the signal level; with uniform vehicle motion there is, of course, a 1:1 correspondence between distance measured on the recording and distance traveled in the street. A typical recording [1] is shown in Fig. 1 for a run made at 836 MHz in a suburban environment. The occasional deep fades and quasi-periodic occurrence of minima are clearly evident in the expanded section of the record.

Recordings such as these made by many workers in the field over the frequency range from 50 MHz to 11 200 MHz have shown that the envelope of the mobile radio signal is Rayleigh distributed [2]–[5] when measured over distances of a few tens of wavelengths where the mean signal is sensibly constant. This suggests the assumption [6], reasonable on physical grounds, that at any point the received field is made up of a number of horizontally traveling plane waves with random amplitudes and angles of arrival for different locations. The phases of the waves are uniformly distributed from zero to 2π. The amplitudes and phases are assumed to be statistically independent.

Reprinted from *IEEE Trans. Veh. Technol.*, vol. VT-23, pp. 143–159, Nov. 1974.

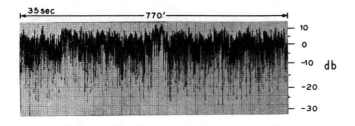

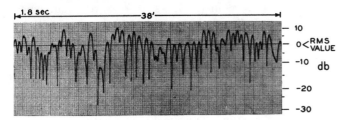

Fig. 1. Typical received signal variations at 836 MHz measured at mobile speed of 15 mi/h records taken on same street with different recording speeds.

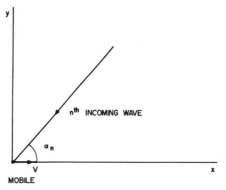

Fig. 2. Typical component wave incident on mobile receiver.

A diagram of this simple model is shown in Fig. 2, with plane waves from stationary scatterers incident on a mobile traveling in the x direction with velocity v. The xy plane is assumed to be horizontal. The vehicle motion introduces a Doppler shift in every wave

$$\omega_n = \beta v \cos \alpha_n \qquad (2.1)$$

where $\beta = 2\pi/\lambda$, λ equals wavelength of the transmitted carrier frequency. If the transmitted signal is vertically polarized the E-field seen at the mobile can thus be written

$$E_z = E_0 \sum_{n=1}^{N} C_n \cos(\omega_c t + \theta_n) \qquad (2.2)$$

where

$$\theta_n = \omega_n t + \phi_n \qquad (2.3)$$

and ω_c is the carrier frequency of the transmitted signal, $E_0 C_n$ is the (real) amplitude of the nth wave in the E_z field. The ϕ_n are random phase angles uniformly distributed from 0 to 2π. Furthermore, the C_n are normalized so that the ensemble average

$$\sum_{n=1}^{N} C_n^2 = 1.$$

We note from (2.1) that the Doppler shift is bounded by the values $\pm\beta v$, which, in general, will be very much less than the carrier frequency. For example, for $f_c = \omega_c/2\pi = 1000$ MHz, $v = 96$ km/h (60 mi/h)

$$\frac{1}{2\pi} \beta v = \frac{v}{\lambda} = 90 \text{ Hz}. \qquad (2.4)$$

The field component may thus be described as narrow-band random processes. Furthermore, as a consequence of the central limit theorem, for large values of N they are approximately Gaussian random processes, and the considerable body of literature devoted to such processes may be utilized. It must be kept in mind that this is still an approximation; for example, (2.2) implies that the mean

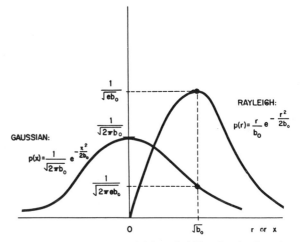

Fig. 3. Gaussian and Rayleigh probability density functions.

signal power is constant with time, whereas it actually undergoes slow variations as the mobile moves distances of hundreds of feet. Nevertheless, the Gaussian model is successful in predicting the measured statistics of the signal to good accuracy in most cases over the ranges of interest for the variables involved, thus its use is justified. In Section III we shall consider in detail the large-scale variations of this average.

Following Rice [7] we can express E_Z as

$$E_z = T_c(t) \cos \omega_c t - T_s(t) \sin \omega_c t \qquad (2.5)$$

where

$$T_c(t) = E_0 \sum_{n=1}^{N} C_n \cos(\omega_n t + \phi_n) \qquad (2.6)$$

$$T_s(t) = E_0 \sum_{n=1}^{N} C_n \sin(\omega_n t + \phi_n) \qquad (2.7)$$

are Gaussian random processes, corresponding to the in-phase and quadrature components of E_z, respectively. We denote by T_c and T_s the random variables corresponding to $T_c(t)$ and $T_s(t)$ for fixed t. They have zero mean and equal variance

$$\langle T_c^2 \rangle = \langle T_s^2 \rangle = \frac{E_0^2}{2} = \langle |E_Z|^2 \rangle. \qquad (2.8)$$

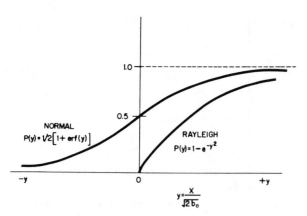

Fig. 4. Normal and Rayleigh cumulative distributions.

The brackets indicate an ensemble average over the ϕ_n and C_n. T_c and T_s are also uncorrelated (and therefore independent)

$$\langle T_c T_s \rangle = 0. \quad (2.9)$$

Since T_c and T_s are Gaussian, they have probability densities of the form

$$p(x) = \frac{1}{(2\pi b_0)^{1/2}} \exp\left(-\frac{x^2}{2b_0}\right) \quad (2.10)$$

where $b_0 = E_0^2/2$ = mean power, and $x = T_c$ or T_s.

The envelope of E_Z is given by

$$r = (T_c^2 + T_s^2)^{1/2} \quad (2.11)$$

and Rice [7] has shown that the probability density of r is

$$p(r) = \begin{cases} \dfrac{r}{b_0} \exp\left(-\dfrac{r^2}{2b_0}\right), & r \geq 0 \\ \\ 0, & r < 0 \end{cases} \quad (2.12)$$

which is the Rayleigh density formula. The Gaussian and Rayleigh densities are shown in Fig. 3 for illustration.

The cumulative distribution functions of T_c (or T_s) are also of interest

$$P[x \leq X] = \int_{-\infty}^{X} p(x)\,dx = \frac{1}{2}\left[1 + \text{erf}\left(\frac{X}{(2b_0)^{1/2}}\right)\right] \quad (2.13)$$

where the error function is defined by

$$\text{erf}(y) = \frac{2}{\pi^{1/2}} \int_0^y \exp(-t^2)\,dt. \quad (2.14)$$

Similarly for the envelope

$$P[r \leq R] = \int_{-\infty}^{R} p(r)\,dr = 1 - \exp\left(-\frac{R}{2b_0}\right). \quad (2.15)$$

These distribution functions are illustrated in Fig. 4.

RF Power Spectrum

From the viewpoint of an observer on the mobile unit, the signal received from a CW transmission as the mobile moves with constant velocity may be represented as a carrier whose phase and amplitude are randomly varying, with an effective bandwidth corresponding to twice the maximum Doppler shift of βV. Many of the statistical properties of this random process can be determined from its moments, which, in turn are most easily obtained from the power spectrum [6].

We assume that the field may be represented by the sum of N waves, as in (2.2). As $N \to \infty$ we would expect to find that the incident power included in an angle between α and $\alpha + d\alpha$ would approach a continuous, instead of discrete, distribution. Let us denote by $p(\alpha)\,d\alpha$ the fraction of the total incoming power within $d\alpha$ of the angle α, and also assume that the receiving antenna is directive in the horizontal plane with power gain pattern $G(\alpha)$. The differential variation of received power with angle is then $b_0 G(\alpha) p(\alpha)\,d\alpha$; we equate this to the differential variation of received power with frequency by noting the relationship between frequency and angle of (2.2)

$$f(\alpha) = f_m \cos \alpha + f_c \quad (2.16)$$

where $f_m = \beta v/2\pi = v/\lambda$, the maximum Doppler shift. Since $f(\alpha) = f(-\alpha)$, the differential variation of power with frequency may be expressed

$$S(f)\,|df| = b_0[p(\alpha)G(\alpha) + p(-\alpha)G(-\alpha)]\,|d\alpha|. \quad (2.17)$$

However,

$$|df| = f_m |-\sin\alpha\,d\alpha| = [f_m^2 - (f - f_c)^2]^{1/2}\,|d\alpha|$$

thus

$$S(f) = \frac{b_0}{[f_m^2 - (f - f_c)^2]^{1/2}}[p(\alpha)G(\alpha) + p(-\alpha)G(-\alpha)] \quad (2.18)$$

where

$$\alpha = \cos^{-1}\left(\frac{f - f_c}{f_m}\right) \quad \text{and} \quad S(f) = 0, \quad \text{if } |f - f_c| > f_m.$$

We assume the transmitted signal is vertically polarized. The electric field will then be in the z direction and may be sensed by a vertical whip antenna on the mobile, with $G(\alpha) = 1$. Substituting in (2.18), the power spectrum of the electric field is

$$S_{E_z}(f) = \frac{b_0}{[f_m^2 - (f - f_c)^2]^{1/2}}[p(\alpha) + p(-\alpha)]. \quad (2.19)$$

The simplest assumption for the distribution of power with arrival angle α is a uniform distribution

$$p(\alpha) = \frac{1}{2\pi}, \quad -\pi \leq \alpha \leq \pi. \quad (2.20)$$

Assuming no additional antenna directivity, the power spectrum is

$$S_{E_z}(f) = \frac{2b_0}{\omega_m}\left[1 - \left(\frac{f - f_c}{f_m}\right)^2\right]^{-1/2}. \quad (2.21)$$

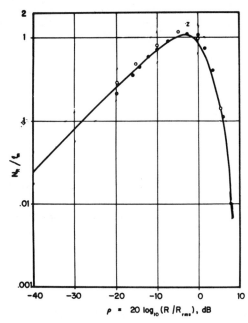

Fig. 5. Normalized level crossing rates of envelope. Measured values: ○—11 215 MHz, ●—836 MHz (E_z).

From the relations between correlations and power spectra the moments can also be obtained [6]

$$b_n = (2\pi)^n \int_{f_c-f_m}^{f_c+f_m} S(f)(f-f_c)^n \, df. \qquad (2.22)$$

Level Crossing Rates

As illustrated in Fig. 1 the signal envelope experiences very deep fades only occasionally; the shallower the fade the more frequently it is likely to occur. A quantitative expression of this property is the level crossing rate N_R, which is defined as the expected rate at which the envelope crosses a specified signal level R in the positive direction. In general, it is given by [7]

$$N_R = \int_0^\infty \dot{r} p(R,\dot{r}) \, d\dot{r} \qquad (2.23)$$

where the dot indicates the time derivative and $p(R,\dot{r})$ is the joint density function of r and $\dot{r}$ at $r = R$. Rice [7] gives the joint density function in the four random variables $r, \dot{r}, \theta, \dot{\theta}$ of a Gaussian process

$$p(r,\dot{r},\theta,\dot{\theta}) = \frac{r^2}{4\pi^2 b_0 b_2} \exp\left[-\frac{1}{2}\left(\frac{r^2}{b_0} + \frac{\dot{r}^2}{b_2} + \frac{r^2\dot{\theta}^2}{b_2}\right)\right] \quad (2.24)$$

where $\tan \theta = -T_s/T_c$. Integrating this expression over θ from 0 to 2π and $\dot{\theta}$ from $-\infty$ to $+\infty$ we get

$$p(r,\dot{r}) = \underbrace{\frac{\dot{r}}{b_0} \exp\left(-\frac{r^2}{2b_0}\right)}_{p(r)} \underbrace{\frac{1}{(2\pi b_2)^{1/2}} \exp\left(-\frac{\dot{r}^2}{2b_2}\right)}_{p(\dot{r})} \quad (2.25)$$

since $p(r,\dot{r}) = p(r)p(\dot{r})$, r and $\dot{r}$ are independent and uncorrelated. Substituting (2.25) into (2.23) we get the

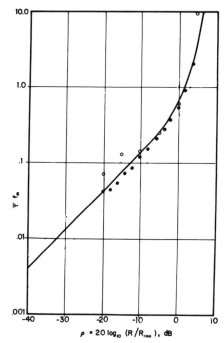

Fig. 6. Normalized durations of fade of envelope. Measured values: ○—11 215 MHz, ●—836 MHz (E_z).

level crossing rate

$$N_R = \frac{p(R)}{(2\pi b_2)^{1/2}} \int_0^\infty \dot{r} \exp\left(-\frac{\dot{r}^2}{2b_2}\right) dr = \left(\frac{b_2}{b_0}\right)^{1/2} \rho \exp\left(-\rho^2\right)$$

$$(2.26)$$

where

$$\rho = R/(\langle r^2 \rangle)^{1/2} = R/(2b_0)^{1/2} = R/R_{\text{rms}}. \quad (2.27)$$

Substituting the appropriate values of the moments b_0 and b_2 we get the expressions for the level crossing rate

$$E_z: N_R = (2\pi)^{1/2} f_m \rho \exp\left(-\rho^2\right). \qquad (2.28)$$

This expression is plotted in Fig. 5 along with some measured values [1]. The rms level of E_z is crossed at a rate of 0.915 f_m; for example: at $f = 1000$ MHz and $V = 96$ km/h, $f_m = 90$ Hz, thus $N_R = 82/\text{s}$ at $\rho = 0$ dB. Lower signal levels are crossed less frequently, as shown by the curves. The maximum level crossing rate occurs at $\rho = -3$ dB.

Duration of Fades

The average duration of fades below $r = R$ is also of interest. Let τ_i be the duration of the ith fade. Then the probability that $r \leq R$ for a total time interval of length T is

$$P[r \leq R] = \frac{1}{T} \sum \tau_i. \qquad (2.29)$$

The average fade duration is

$$\bar{\tau} = \frac{1}{TN_R} \sum \tau_i = \frac{1}{N_R} P[r \leq R]. \qquad (2.30)$$

Since

$$P[r \leq R] = \int_0^R p(r)\, dr = 1 - \exp\ (-\rho^2). \quad (2.31)$$

Then

$$\bar{\tau} = \left(\frac{\pi b_0}{b_2}\right)^{1/2} \frac{1}{\rho} \left[\exp\ (\rho^2) - 1\right]. \quad (2.32)$$

Substituting the appropriate values of the moments

$$E_z : \bar{\tau} = \frac{\exp\ (\rho^2) - 1}{\rho f_m (2\pi)^{1/2}}. \quad (2.33)$$

This expression is plotted in Fig. 6 along with some measured values [1].

III. LARGE SCALE VARIATIONS OF THE AVERAGE SIGNAL

The principal methods by which energy is transmitted to a mobile, namely, reflection and diffraction are often indistinguishable, thus it is convenient to lump the losses together and call them scatter (or shadow) losses. In Section II it was shown that this scattering gives rise to fields whose amplitudes are Rayleigh distributed in space and the Rayleigh model led to very powerful results. In this section it is shown that while the "local statistics" may be Rayleigh, the "local mean" varies because of the terrain and the effects of other obstacles. We shall begin by reviewing briefly the more deterministic factors that influence propagation and conclude with a look at the statistical nature of signal strength.

Free Space Transmission Formula

The power received by an antenna separated from a radiating antenna is given by a simple formula, provided there are no objects in the region which absorb or reflect energy. This free space transmission formula [8] depends upon the inverse square of the antenna separation distance d and is given by

$$P_0 = P_t \left(\frac{\lambda}{4\pi d}\right)^2 g_b g_m \quad (3.1)$$

where

P_0 received power,
P_t transmitted power,
λ wavelength,
g_b power gain of the base station antenna,
g_m power gain of the mobile station antenna.

Thus the received radiated power decreases 6 dB for each doubling of the distance. On first inspection, one might conclude that higher frequencies might be unsuitable for mobile communications because the transmission loss increases with the square of the frequency. However, this usually can be compensated for by increased antenna gain. In mobile communications, it is often desirable to have antennas whose patterns are omnidirect'onal in the azimuthal plane, thus the increase in gain is required in

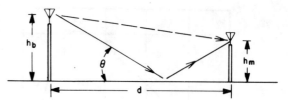

Fig. 7. Propagation paths over plane earth.

the elevation plane. In the limit of the higher microwave frequencies, this additional gain may become impractical to realize for effective communications between an elevated base station and a mobile.

Knowing the propagation characteristics over a smooth conducting flat earth provides a starting point for estimating the effects of propagation over actual paths. Analytical results for propagation over a plane earth have been derived by Norton [9]–[11] and simplified by Bullington [12], [13]. For base station and mobile antennas elevated heights h_b and h_m, respectively, above ground as shown in Fig. 7 the power received is

$$P_r = 4 P_0 \sin^2 \frac{2\pi h_b h_m}{\lambda d} \quad (3.2)$$

where P_0 is the expected power over a free space path. In most mobile radio applications, except very near the base station antenna, $\sin (\Delta/2) \approx \Delta/2$, thus the transmission over a plane earth is given by the approximation

$$P_r = P_t g_b g_m \left(\frac{h_b h_m}{d^2}\right)^2 \quad (3.3)$$

yielding an inverse fourth power relationship of received power with distance from the base station antenna. However, at the higher microwave frequencies the assumption of a plane earth may no longer be valid due to surface irregularities. A measure of the surface "roughness," which provides an indication of the range of validity of (3.2), is given by the Rayleigh criterion, which is

$$C = \frac{4\pi\sigma\theta}{\lambda} \quad (3.4)$$

where σ is the standard deviation of the surface irregularities relative to the mean height of the surface, λ is the wavelength, and θ is the angle of incidence measured in radians from the horizontal. Experimental evidence shows that for $C < 0.1$, specular reflection results and the surface may be considered smooth. Surfaces are considered "rough" for values of C exceeding 10 and under these conditions the reflected wave is very small in amplitude. Bullington [12] has found experimentally that most practical paths at microwave frequencies are relatively "rough" with reflection coefficients in the range of 0.2–0.4.

Knife Edge Diffraction

Very often in the mobile ratio environment a line-of-sight path to the base station is obscured by obstructions

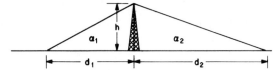

Fig. 8. Geometry for propagation over knife edge.

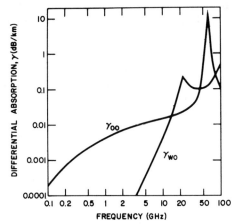

Fig. 9. Signal attenuation from oxygen and water vapor in atmosphere.

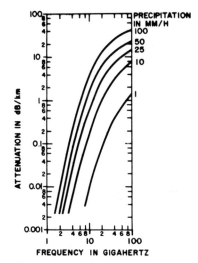

Fig. 10. Signal attenuation for various rainfall rates.

such as hills, trees, and buildings. When the shadowing is caused by a single object such as a hill, it is instructive to treat the object as a diffracting knife edge to estimate the amount of signal attenuation. The exact solution to the problem of diffraction over a knife edge is well known and is discussed in many textbooks ([14], for example).

For most microwave mobile radio applications several assumptions can be made to simplify the calculations. Consider an infinite completely absorbing (rough) half-plane which divides space into two parts as in Fig. 8. When the distances d_1 and d_2 from the half-plane to the transmitting antenna and the receiving antenna are large compared to the height h, and h itself is large compared with the wavelength λ, i.e.,

$$d_1, d_2 \gg h \gg \lambda \qquad (3.5)$$

then the diffracted power can be given by the expression

$$P = P_0 \frac{1}{2\pi^2 h^2}. \qquad (3.6)$$

This result can be considered independent of polarization as long as the conditions of (3.5) are met. In cases where the earth's curvature has an effect there can be up to four paths. A simplified method of computing knife edge diffraction for such cases is treated by Anderson and Trolese [15]. Closer agreement with data over measured paths has been obtained by calculations, which better describe the geometry of the diffracting obstacle [16]–[18].

Effects of Rain and the Atmosphere

Microwave mobile radio signals are attenuated by the presence of rain, snow, and fog. Losses depend upon the frequency and upon the amounts of moisture in the path. At the higher microwave frequencies, frequency selective absorption results because of the presence of oxygen and water vapor in the atmosphere [19]. The first peak in the absorption due to water vapor occurs around 24 GHz, while for oxygen the first peak occurs at about 60 GHz as shown in Fig. 9.

The attenuation due to rain has been studied experimentally [20] by a number of workers. Fig. 10 provides an estimate of the attenuating effect of rainfall as a function of frequency for several rainfall rates. It should be noted that very heavy rain showers are usually isolated and not large in extent. Nevertheless, at frequencies above 10 GHz the effects of rain cannot be neglected.

Signal attenuation over actual mobile radio paths result from a complicated dependence upon the environment, and the formulas derived here apply only in the special cases where the propagation paths can be clearly described. In the remainder of this section we will concentrate our attention on propagation effects over irregular terrain.

Propagation Over Irregular Terrain

Some classification of the environment is also necessary since signal attenuation varies depending upon the type of objects that obstruct the path. Rather than attempt to precisely define many types of environments and then describe propagation characteristics for each we will restrict our definitions of environment to three types:

open areas—areas where there are very few obstacles such as tall trees or buildings in the path, for instance, farm land or open fields;
suburban areas—areas with houses, small buildings and trees, often near the mobile unit;
urban areas—areas which are heavily built up with tall buildings and multistory residences.

Extensive measurements of radio transmission loss over various terrains in unpopulated areas have been made in the frequency ranges from 20 to 10 000 MHz by workers

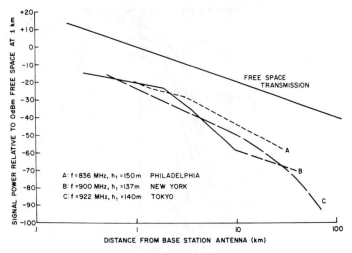

Fig. 11. Examples of transmission loss with distance.

attenuation relative to free space leads one to hope that signal strength parameters in different cities will likewise exhibit consistent traits.

For antenna separation distances between 1 km and 15 km the attenuation of median signal power with distance changes from nearly an inverse fourth power decrease for very low base station antenna heights to a rate only slightly faster than the free space decrease for extremely high base station antennas. For antenna separation distances greater than 40 km, the signal attenuation is very rapid. Fig. 12 shows predictions derived by Okumura [5] for the basic median signal attenuation relative to free space in a quasi-smooth urban areas as it varies with both distance and frequency. These curves provide the starting point for predicting signal attenuation, which will be discussed in Section IV. The curves assume a base station antenna height of 200 m and a mobile antenna height of 3 m. Adjustments to these basic curves for different base station antenna heights and mobile antenna heights are considered in the paragraphs that follow next.

Effect of Base Station Antenna Height

Okumura [5] has found that the variation of received field strength with distance and antenna height remains essentially the same for all frequencies in the range from 200 to 2000 MHz. For antenna separation distances less than 10 km the received power varies very nearly proportional to the square of the base station antenna height (6 dB per octave). For very high base station antennas and for large separation distances (greater than 30 km) the received power tends to be proportional to the cube of the height of the base station antenna (9 dB per octave). Fig. 13 is a set of prediction curves that give the change in received power (often called the height-gain factor) realized by varying the base station antenna height. The curves are plotted for various antenna separation distances and predict the median received power relative to a 200-m base station antenna and a 3-m mobile antenna. They may be used for frequencies in the range 200 to 2000 MHz.

Effect of Mobile Antenna Height

For obvious reasons mobile antenna heights are generally limited to no more than 4 m. For a large range of frequencies and for several base station antenna heights Okumura observed a height-gain advantage of 3 dB for a 3-m high mobile antenna compared to a 1.5-m high mobile antenna. For special cases where antenna height can be above 5 m the height-gain factor depends upon the frequency and the environment. In a medium sized city where the transmitting frequency is 2000 MHz the height-gain factor may be as much as 14 dB per octave, while for a very large city and a transmitting frequency under 1000 MHz the height-gain factor may be as little as 4 dB per octave for antennas above 5 m. Prediction curves for the vehicle height-gain factor in urban areas are given in Fig. 14.

at the Institute for Telecommunications Sciences, and this data has been tabulated in several ESSA reports [21]–[23]. Mobile radio measurements in urban and suburban areas in the microwave region have been made by a number of workers [1]–[5], [24]–[28]. To date, the most extensive work in the field has been reported by Okumura *et al.* [5]. We will rely heavily upon their results to generate prediction curves that are provided in the latter portion of this paper.

Field Strength Variation in Urban Areas

Within the urban environment the received field strength is found to vary with the base station and mobile antenna heights, transmitting frequency, the distance from the transmitter, and the width and orientation of the streets. The median field strengths in a quasi-smooth urban area show a relatively continuous change with frequency, antenna height, and distance, while other effects appear less simply related.

Distance and Frequency Dependence

One of the fundamental problems in the study of radio propagation is to describe the manner in which the signal strength attenuates as the receiving unit moves away from a transmitting base station. Obviously the signal level will fluctuate markedly (even when the Rayleigh fading is averaged out) since building heights, street widths, and terrain features are not constant. However, if we consider for a moment the behavior of the median values of the received signals, we find that there is a general trend for the signal levels to decrease more rapidly the further the mobile is separated from the base station. Fig. 11 is a plot of the received signal power versus distance as measured by independent workers in three different cities—New York [2], Philadelphia [24], and Tokyo [5]. All the measurements were made at approximately 900 MHz from relatively high base station locations. This remarkably consistent trend of both the falloff of the median signal value with distance and the excess

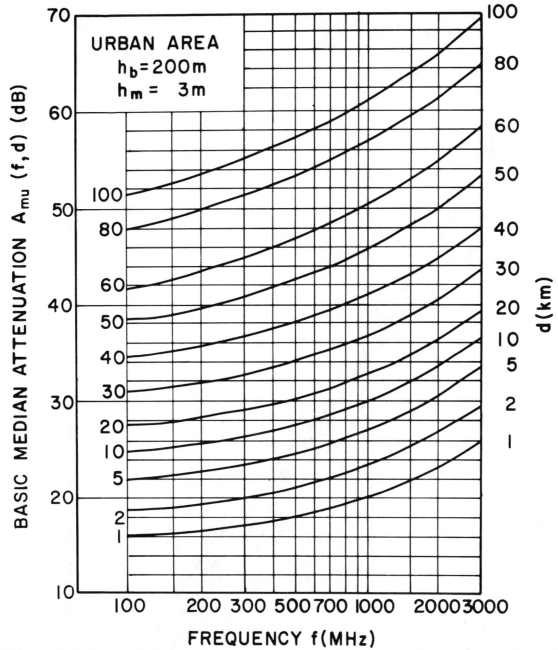

Fig. 12. Prediction curve for basic median attenuation relative to free space in urban area over quasi-smooth terrain referred to $h_b = 200$ m, $h_m = 3$ m.

Correction Factor for Suburban and Open Areas

Suburban areas are generally characterized by lower buildings and generally less congestion of obstacles than in cities. Consequently, one should expect that radio signals would propagate better in such environments. Okumura has found that there is practically no change in the difference between urban and suburban median attenuation (suburban correction factor) with changes in base station antenna height or with separation distances between the base and mobile antennas. The suburban propagation does depend somewhat on the frequency and increases to some extent at the higher frequencies. A plot of the suburban correction factor is shown by the solid curve in Fig. 15 for frequencies in the range of 100 to 3000 MHz. Recent data shows a 10-dB difference between urban and suburban values of the median received signal strength at a frequency of 11 200 MHz, slightly less than that extrapolated in Fig. 15. Open areas, which occur rather infrequently, tend to have significantly better propagation paths than urban and suburban areas and typical received signal strengths run nearly 20 dB greater for the same antenna height and separation distances. The upper curve shown in Fig. 15 provides a correction in dB that may be added directly to the prediction values for the urban case. Rural areas or areas with only slightly built up sections have median signal strength somewhere between the two curves.

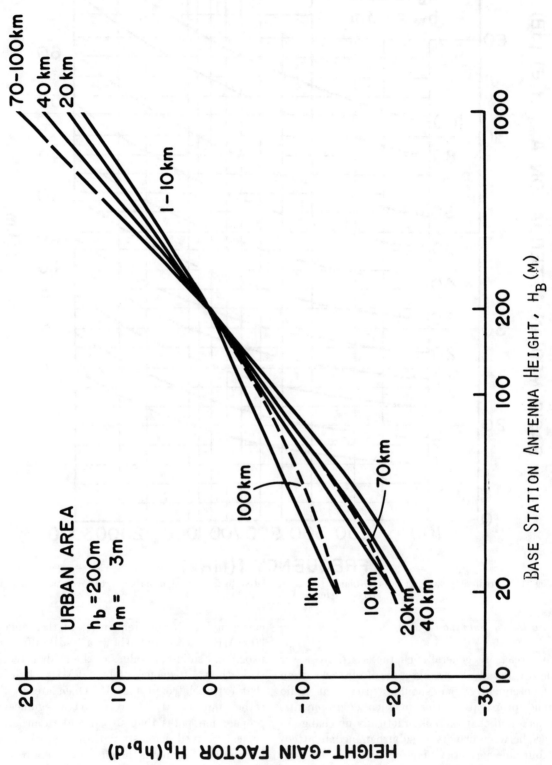

BASE STATION ANTENNA HEIGHT, H_B (M)

HEIGHT-GAIN FACTOR $H_b(h_b, d)$

URBAN AREA
$h_b = 200$ m
$h_m = 3$ m

70-100km
40 km
20 km
1-10km

100km
70km
1km
10km
20km
40km

Fig. 13. Prediction curves for base station height gain factor referred to $h_b = 200$ m.

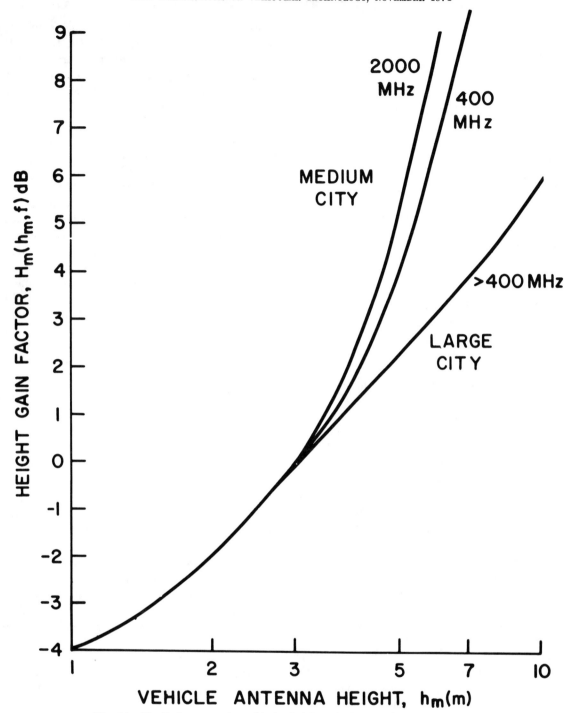

Fig. 14.   Prediction curve for vehicular height gain factor referred to $h_m = 3$ m.

Effects of Street Orientation

It has been observed that radio signals in urban areas tend to be channeled by the buildings so that the strongest paths are not necessarily the direct paths diffracted over the edge of nearby obstructing buildings, but are found to be from directions parallel to the streets. Streets that run radially or approximately radially from the base station are most strongly affected by this channeling phenomena. This causes the median received signal strength to differ by as much as 20 dB at locations nearby the transmitter [24].

The distribution of the signal paths in the horizontal plane as seen from the mobile vehicle in an urban area is strongly affected by the street and building layout. Tests [27] in New York City indicate that the signals arriving parallel to the direction of the street are typically 10 to 20 dB higher than waves arriving at other angles. These tests were carried out at 11.2 GHz by scanning with a highly directive antenna (beamwidth of 5°) at various locations in the city.

Effects of Foliage

There are a great many factors that affect propagation behind obstacles such as a grove of trees. Precise estimates of attenuation are difficult because tree heights are not uniform; also, the type, shape, density, and distribution

93

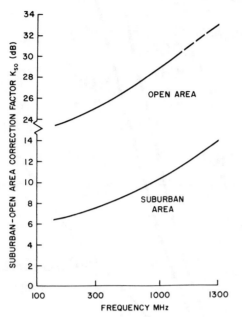

Fig. 15. Prediction curves for suburban and open area correction factor K_{so}.

of the trees influence the propagation. In addition, the density of the foliage depends upon the season of the year. However, some success has been obtained by treating trees as diffracting obstacles with an average effective height.

An experimental study of propagation behind a grove of live oak and hackberry trees in Texas for several frequencies has been reported by Lagrone *et al.* [29]. At frequencies from about 0.5 to 3 GHz and for distances greater than about five times the tree height, the measurements were in good agreement with the theoretical predictions of diffraction over an ideal knife edge, assuming distances and heights the same as those in the measurements. At shorter distances some propagation takes place through the trees, which acts to reduce the effective height of the diffracting edge and at the same time increases the apparent distance from the diffracting edge to the antenna.

Measurements at 836 MHz and 11.2 GHz were made, which compared the signal strength measured on the same streets in summer and in winter in suburban Holmdel, N. J. [30]. At the UHF frequency the average received signal strength in the summer when the trees were in full leaf was roughly 10 dB lower than for the corresponding locations in later winter. At X band frequencies the losses during the summer appear to be greater in the areas where the signal levels were previously low.

Signal Attenuation in Tunnels

It is well known that frequencies in the VHF region commonly used for mobile communications are severely attenuated in tunnel structures [31]. Only by using special antennas are these frequencies usable in long (over 300-m) tunnels. However, at microwave frequencies tunnels are effective guiding or channeling mechanisms and can offer significant improvement over VHF for communications.

A test [32] was performed in the center tube of the

Lincoln Tunnel (3000 m long), which connects midtown Manhattan to New Jersey under the Hudson River. The inside of the tunnel is roughly rectangular in cross section with a height of 4 m and a width of 8 m. Seven test frequencies roughly an octave apart were used to make signal attenuation measurements.

The average loss of signal strength in dB against the antenna separation for the seven frequencies is plotted in Fig. 16. For convenience in plotting the data an arbitrary reference level of 0 dB at 300-m antenna separation was chosen. It is worth noting that the 153- and 300-MHz attenuation rates are nearly straight lines implying that the signal attenuation has an exponential relationship to the separation. At 153 MHz the loss is extremely high (in excess of 40 dB in 300 m, where at 300 MHz the rate of attenuation is of the order of 20 dB in 300 m. At higher frequencies a simple exponential attenuation rate is not evident. For the major portion of the length of the tunnel the received signal level at 900 MHz has an inverse fourth power dependence upon the antenna separation, while at 2400 MHz the loss has an inverse or square dependence. At frequencies above 2400 MHz, dependence of the signal strength with antenna separation is less than the free space path loss (throughout most of the length of the tunnel). Roughly, the attenuation rates appear to be only 2–4 dB in 300 m for frequencies in the 2400 to 11 000 MHz range.

Effects of Irregular Terrain

The traditional approach of predicting attenuation from propagation over irregular terrain has been to approximate the problem to one that is solvable in closed form. This is usually done by solving problems dealing with smooth regular boundaries such as planes or cylinders [33]–[42]. To some extent propagation over more complicated obstacles can be determined by constructing models and performing laboratory experiments at optical frequencies or frequencies in the millimeter wavelength region [43]–[45].

A computer program has been published by Longley and Rice [46] that predicts the long term median radio transmission loss over irregular terrain. The method predicts median values of attenuation relative to the transmission loss in free space and requires the following: the transmission frequency, the antenna separation, the height of the transmitting and receiving antennas, the mean surface refractivity, the conductivity and dielectric constant of the earth, polarization, and a description of the terrain. This program was based upon thousands of measurements and compares well with measured data [47].

The computer method of Longley and Rice provides both point-to-point and area predictions which agree well with the experiment, but a description of the calculation of the many parameters used in their method would be rather lengthy. The reader is referred to their work for precise calculations. We shall adopt a somewhat less accurate method in which we obtain correction factors

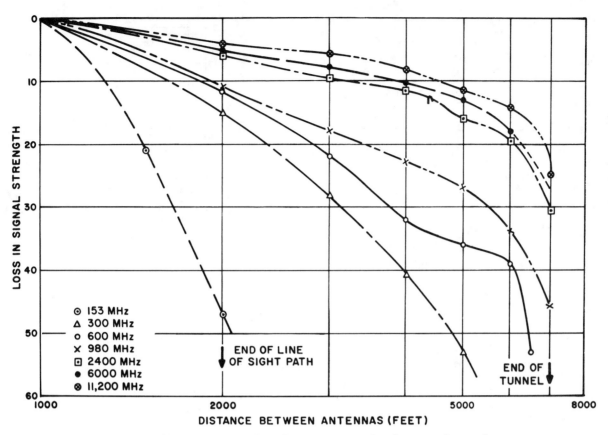

Fig. 16. Signal loss versus log of antenna separation for seven frequencies.

to our basic median curves (Figs. 12–14) for various terrain effects.

Correction Factors for Undulating, Sloping, and Land-Sea Terrain

An approximate prediction curve for undulating terrain is given in Fig. 17, which is based upon work reported by the CCIR [19] and Okumura [5]. This estimates the correction factor to the basic median attenuation curves obtained previously for quasi-smooth urban terrain. More exact predictions would probably have some dependence upon frequency and on antenna separation distance. If the location of the vehicle is known to be near the top of the undulation the correction factor in Fig. 17 can be ignored. On the other hand, if the location is near the bottom of the undulation, the attenuation is higher and is indicated on the lower curve in Fig. 17.

In cases where the median height of the ground is gently sloping for distances of the order of 5 km, a correction factor may be applied. Let us define the average slope θ_m measured in milliradians as illustrated in Fig. 18. Depending upon the antenna separation distance d, the terrain slope correction factor K_{sp} is given in Fig. 19 in terms of the average slope θ_m. (It should be noted that these curves are based upon rather scant amounts of data and should be considered as estimates applying in the frequency range of 450 to 900 MHz.)

Usually on propagation paths where there is an expanse of water between the transmitting and receiving stations the received signal strength tends to be higher than for cases where the path is only over land. The change in signal strength depends upon the antenna separation distance and whether the water lies closer to the mobile receiver or the base station transmitter, or somewhere in between. Let us define a ratio β, which represents the fraction of the path that consists of propagation over water. Two path geometries and the definition of β are illustrated in Fig. 20. It has been observed that when the latter portion of the path from the base station antenna to the mobile antenna is over water, the signal strength is typically 3 dB higher than for cases where the latter portion of the base mobile path is over land. Prediction curves for mixed land-sea paths have been obtained experimentally by Okumura [5] as shown in Fig. 20, which provides correction factors in terms of the percentage of the path over water.

Statistical Distribution of the Local-Mean Signal

Thus far we have obtained results based primarily upon experimental evidence, which has provided us with the behavior of median signal levels obtained by averaging received signals over a distance of 10 to 20 m. Smooth curves were obtained relating the variation of the median received signal with distance, base station antenna height, and frequency in urban, suburban, and rural areas. Consistent but less accurate predictions were found for dependence on street orientation, isolated ridges, rolling hills, and land-sea paths. Considerably less data is avail-

95

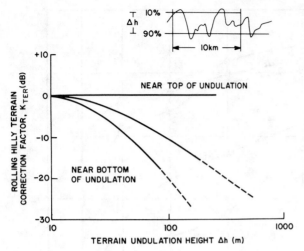

Fig. 17. Rolling hilly terrain correction factor K_{ter}.

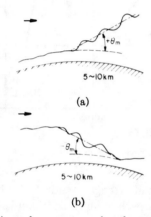

Fig. 18. Definition of average angle of general terrain slope. (a) Positive slope $(+\theta_m)$. (b) Negative slope $(-\theta_m)$.

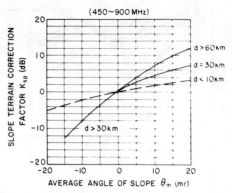

Fig. 19. Measured value and prediction curves for "slope terrain correction factor" K_{sp}.

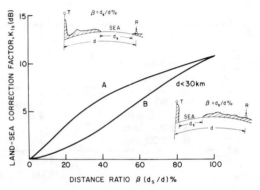

Fig. 20. Prediction curves for land-sea correction factor K_{ls}.

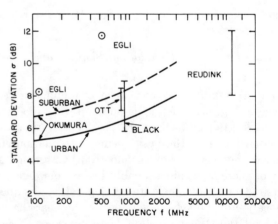

Fig. 21. Prediction curves for standard deviation of median field strength variation in urban, suburban, and rolling hilly terrain.

able that describes the fluctuations of the received signal about the median value. The dependence of the signal distribution upon the parameters mentioned requires a good deal more investigation before definitive results are available.

One consistent result that has been observed is that the distribution of the received signals at fixed base and mobile antenna heights, frequency, and separation distance from the base station within the same environment class (urban, for example) have very nearly a normal distribution when the distribution is plotted for the received signal measured in dB. Such a probability distribution is often referred to as log-normal [48]. Also the excess path loss, that is, the difference (in dB) between the computed value of the received signal strength in free space (3.1) and the actual measured value of the local mean received signal has been observed to be log-normally distributed.

Fig. 21 is a prediction curve for the standard deviation σ of the log-normal distribution, which describes the variation of the median signal strength values in suburban areas as given by Okumura [5]. The data spreads at 850 MHz are from Black [24] and Ott [26]; at 11.2 GHz the data is from Reudink [25]. The data points at 127 and 510 MHz are from the work of Egli [49].

IV. PREDICTION OF FIELD STRENGTH

In order to predict the median power received by a mobile unit from a base station antenna in a basic urban environment we may use the following equation (all quantities in dB):

$$P_p = P_0 - A_m(f,d) + H_b(h_b,d) + H_m(h_m,f) \quad (4.1)$$

where

P_p value of the predicted received power;

P_0 power received for free space transmission (3.1);

$A_m(f,d)$ median attenuation relative to free space in an urban area where the effective base station antenna height h_b is 200 m and the vehicle antenna height h_m is 3 m; these values are expressed as a function of distance and frequency and can be obtained from the curves of Fig. 12;

$H_b(h_b,d)$ base station height-gain factor expressed in dB relative to a 200-m high base station antenna in an urban area; this function is dependent upon distance and has been plotted in Fig. 13;

$H_m(h_m,f)$ is the vehicle station height-gain factor expressed in dB relative to a 3-m high vehicle station antenna in an urban area; this factor is dependent upon frequency and has been plotted in Fig. 14.

If the particular propagation path happens to be over a different environment type or involve terrain that is not "quasi-smooth" we may amend our prediction formula for P_p by adding one or more of the correction factors that were described in earlier portions of the chapter. Thus the "corrected" predicted received power P_c is

$$P_c = P_p + K_{so} + K_{ter} + K_{sp} + K_{ls} \qquad (4.2)$$

where

K_{so} "correction factor for suburban and open terrain," which is plotted in Fig. 15;

K_{ter} "correction factor for rolling hilly terrain," which may be obtained from Fig. 17;

K_{sp} "correction factor for sloping terrain," which is obtained from the curve in Fig. 19;

K_{ls} "land-sea correction factor," which provides a correction to the signal attenuation when there is an expanse of water in the propagation path; a description of this correction factor and a prediction curve is given in Fig. 20.

In addition to these correction factors there are other factors such as isolated mountain ridges, street orientation relative to the base station, the presence or absence of foliage, effects of the atmosphere, and in the case of undulating terrain the position of the vehicle relative to the median height. These additional effects together with the fact that the correction factors and indeed the basic transmission factors A_m, H_b, and H_m are average values based upon empirical data should indicate that discrepancies between measured and predicted values are still possible. It is reassuring to point out, however, that these prediction curves, which are essentially the same as those of Okumura, have been compared to measured data with a great deal of success [5]. This was done over a variety of environments, antenna heights and separation, and for a number of frequencies.

Determination of Signal Coverage in a Small Area

Let us assume that the local mean signal strength in an area at a fixed radius from a particular base station antenna is log-normally distributed. Let the local mean (that is, the signal strength averaged over the Rayleigh fading) in dB be expressed by the normal variable x with mean $\bar{x}$ (measured in dBm for example) and standard deviation σ (dB). To avoid confusion, recall that $\bar{x}$ is the median value found previously from (4.1). As we have seen, $\bar{x}$ depends upon the distance r from the base station as well as several other parameters. Let x_0 be the receiver "threshold." We shall determine the fraction of the locations (at $r = R$) wherein a mobile would experience a received signal above "threshold." The "threshold" value chosen need not be the receiver noise threshold, but may be any value that provides an acceptable signal under Rayleigh fading conditions. The probability density of x is

$$p(x) = \frac{1}{\sigma(2\pi)^{1/2}} \exp\left[\frac{-(x-\bar{x})^2}{2\sigma^2}\right]. \qquad (4.3)$$

The probability that x exceeds the threshold x_0 is

$$P_{x_0}(R) = P(x \geq x_0) = \int_{x_0}^{\infty} p(x)\, dx$$

$$= \tfrac{1}{2} + \tfrac{1}{2}\,\mathrm{erf}\left(\frac{x_0 - \bar{x}}{\sigma\sqrt{2}}\right). \qquad (4.4)$$

If we have measured or theoretical values for $\bar{x}$ and for σ in the area of interest we can determine the percent of the area for which the average signal strength exceeds x_0. For example, at a radius where the median and hence the mean of the log-normal signal strength is -100 dBm ($\bar{x} = -100$ dBm at some particular separation distance R and for some radiated power) assume our system threshold happens to be -110 dBm, then if we assume $\sigma = 10$ dB we have

$$P_{x_0}(R) = \tfrac{1}{2} + \tfrac{1}{2}\,\mathrm{erf}\,\frac{1}{\sqrt{2}} = 0.84.$$

Determination of the Coverage Area from a Base Station

It is also of interest to determine the percent of locations *within* a circle of radius R in which the received signal strength from a radiating base station antenna exceeds a particular threshold value. Let us define the fraction of useful service area F_u as that area, within a circle of radius R, for which the signal strength received by a mobile antenna exceeds a given threshold x_0. If P_{x_0} is the probability that the received signal x exceeds x_0 in an incremental area dA, then

$$F_u = \int P_{x_0}\, dA. \qquad (4.5)$$

In a real-life situation one would probably be required to break the integration into small areas in which P_{x_0} can be estimated and then sum over all such areas. For purposes of illustration let us assume that the behavior of the mean value of the signal strength $\bar{x}$ follows an r^{-n} law. Thus

$$\bar{x} = \alpha - 10n \log_{10}\frac{r}{R} \qquad (4.6)$$

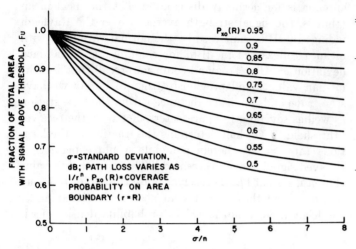

Fig. 22. Fraction of total area with signal above threshold F_u.

TABLE I

Distance (km)	P_0 (dBm)	A_m (dB)	H_b (dB)	H_m (dB)	P_p (dBm)
2	−47	−23	−4	−2	−76
5	−55	−27	−5	−2	−89
10	−61	−30	−5	−2	−98
15	−65	−31	−6	−2	−104
20	−67	−33	−6	−2	−108
25	−69	−35	−6	−2	−112
30	−71	−37	−6	−2	116
40	−73	−41	−7	−2	123
50	−75	−50	−7	−2	134

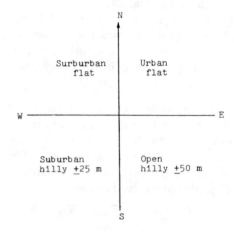

Fig. 23. Environment surrounding base station.

where α, expressed in dB, is a constant determined from the transmitter power, antenna heights and gains, etc. Then

$$P_{x_0} = \tfrac{1}{2} - \tfrac{1}{2} \operatorname{erf} \frac{x_0 - \alpha + 10n \log r/R}{\sigma\sqrt{2}} . \quad (4.7)$$

Then letting $a = (x_0 - \alpha)/\sigma\sqrt{2}$ and $b = 10n \log_{10} e/\sigma\sqrt{2}$ we get

$$F_u = \frac{\pi R^2}{2} + \int_0^R e \operatorname{erf} \left(a - b \ln \frac{r}{R} \right) dr. \quad (4.8)$$

The integral can be evaluated by substituting $t = a - b \ln (r/R)$, so that

$$F_u = \frac{\pi R^2}{2} + \frac{\pi R^2 \exp (2a/b)}{b} \int_a^\infty \exp \left(-\frac{2t}{b} \right) \operatorname{erf} (t) \, dt. \quad (4.9)$$

From [50, p. 6, #1]

$$F_u = \frac{R^2}{2} \left\{ 1 + \operatorname{erf} (a) + \exp \left(\frac{2ab + 1}{b^2} \right) \right.$$

$$\left. \cdot \left[1 - \operatorname{erf} \frac{ab + 1}{b} \right] \right\}. \quad (4.10)$$

For example let us choose α such that $\bar{x} = x_0$ at $r = R$, then $a = 0$ and

$$F_u = R^2 \left\{ \tfrac{1}{2} + \exp \left(\frac{1}{b^2} \right) \left[1 - \operatorname{erf} \left(\frac{1}{b} \right) \right] \right\}. \quad (4.11)$$

Let us further assume that $n = 3$ and $\sigma = 9$, then $F_u = 0.71$, or about 71 percent of the area within a circle of radius R has signal above threshold when 1/2 the locations on the circumference have a signal above threshold.

For the case where the propagation follows a power law, the important parameter is σ/n. Fig. 22 is a plot of the fraction of the area within a circle of radius R, which has a received signal above a threshold for various fractions of coverage on the circle.

V. AN EXAMPLE

Suppose that as a young entrepreneur you have decided to go into the radio controlled pizza delivery business. You received a license to operate at a frequency of 1.0 GHz transmitting 10 W into a 10-dB gain antenna from the top of your home office, the Leaning Tower of Pizza, located in suburban LaPimento. Since it is essential that your product be delivered promptly and orders received correctly, you want to estimate the regions where there is reliable radio coverage.

Looking at a terrain map you determine that your effective base station height is 100 m above the surrounding terrain. The pizza trucks have 2-dB gain dipole antennas 2 m above the ground. With this information you go to (4.1) and calculate basic predictions of received signal power. Table I gives some representative values of P_p for various distances.

Suppose that the environment around the base station can be described as shown in Fig. 23.

The values calculated in Table I apply directly to the NE section but for the remaining areas you need to apply the correction factors of (4.2). For the other areas you add correction factors to P_p to obtain

$$P_c: \quad \mathrm{NW} = P_p + K_{so} = P_p + 10$$

$$P_c: \quad \mathrm{SW} = P_p + K_{so} + K_{ter} = P_p + 10 - 4.$$

$$P_c: \quad \mathrm{SE} = P_p + K_{so} + K_{ter} = P_p + 29 - 7.$$

With Table I and the corrected values for P_p we can plot contours of equal signal strength as shown in Fig. 24.

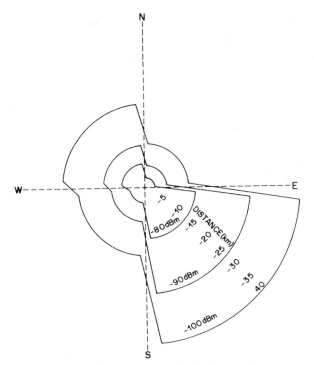

Fig. 24. Contours of equal signal strength.

Now you look at Fig. 1 and determine subjectively that you want your minimum signal for reliable communications to be 10 dB above the rms of the Rayleigh fluctuations. If the radio receivers have 7-dB noise figures and transmit FM in a 50-kHz bandwidth, then the minimum signal desired is

kTB	−127 dBm.
noise figure	+7 dB
FM threshold	10 dB
subjective threshold	10 dB
minimum signal	−100 dBm.

Thus you obtain the radius (different in each quadrant) at which half the locations can be expected to have signal strengths above −100 dBm and half below this value.

We can carry this example another step to determine the radii, say where 90 percent of the locations have signals above −100 dBm. To do this we go to Fig. 19 to find σ and then invert (4.4) to find the extra margin in signal strength required to get 90 percent coverage instead of 50 percent. Choosing 6.5 and 8.5 dB for σ for the urban and suburban areas, respectively, we then have from (4.4)

urban:

$$0.9 = 0.5 + 0.5 \, \mathrm{erf}\left[\frac{100 - x}{6.5\sqrt{2}}\right]$$

$$x = -91.5 \text{ dBm}$$

suburban:

$$0.9 = 0.5 - 0.5 \, \mathrm{erf}\left[\frac{100 - x}{8.5\sqrt{2}}\right]$$

$$x = -89 \text{ dBm.}$$

Referring to the coverage contours of Fig. 23 we find the radii where the signal strengths are −89 dBm and −91.5 dBm. On these radii we expect the signal strength to be above our −100 dBm threshold 90 percent of the time.

VI. CONCLUSIONS

Experiments have verified that the Rayleigh model is excellent for predicting short-term fading. Based on this model, RF power spectra, level crossing rates, duration of fades, and other statistical parameters can be accurately predicted. Likewise, the effects on propagation of certain geometric obstacles, rain, and the atmosphere are well known. However, attempts to determine propagation over terrain that is cluttered with trees, buildings, hills and valleys, and a variety of other obstructions are necessarily less successful. This paper has shown that the local mean value of received signal strength is a relatively continuous function of frequency, antenna heights, and distance. Further, it was shown that correction factors can account for building density, rolling hilly terrain, sloping terrain, and land-sea paths. Finally, it was shown that variations in the local-mean signal strength have a log-normal distribution. Using this as a model, we can predict the expected coverage from a base station for a large range of antenna heights and frequencies and for many types of terrain.

ACKNOWLEDGMENT

I would like to thank W. C. Jakes, Jr. for allowing me to use material that will be used in his forthcoming book, *Microwave Mobile Communications*.

REFERENCES

[1] W. C. Jakes, Jr. and D. O. Reudink, "Comparison of mobile radio transmission at UHF and X band," *IEEE Trans. Veh. Technol.*, VT–16, pp. 10–14, Oct. 1967.
[2] W. R. Young, Jr., "Comparison of mobile radio transmission at 150, 450, 900, and 3700 MHz," Bell Syst. Tech. J., vol. 31, pp. 1068–1085, Nov. 1952.
[3] P. M. Trifonov, V. N. Budko, and V. S. Zotov, "Structure of USW field strength spatial fluctuations in a city," *Trans. Telecomm. Radio Eng.*, vol. 9, pp. 26–30, Feb. 1964.
[4] H. W. Nyland, "Characteristics of small-area signal fading on mobile circuits in the 150 MHz band," *IEEE Trans. Veh. Technol.*, vol. VT–17, pp. 24–30, Oct. 1968.
[5] Y. Okumura *et al.*, "Field strength and its variability in VHF and UHF land-mobile radio service," *Rev. Elec. Commun. Lab.*, 16, pp. 825–873, Sept. 1968.
[6] M. J. Gans, "A power-spectral theory of propagation in the mobile-radio environment," *IEEE Trans. Veh. Technol.*, vol. VT–21, pp. 27–38, Feb. 1972.
[7] S. O. Rice, "Mathematical analysis of random noise," *Bell Syst. Tech. J.*, vol. 23, pp. 282–332, July 1944; vol. 24, pp. 46–156, Jan. 1945, and S. O. Rice, "Statistical properties of a sine wave plus random noise," *Bell Syst. Tech. J.*, vol. 27, pp. 109–157, Jan. 1948.
[8] H. T. Friis, "A note on a simple transmission formula," *Proc. IRE*, vol. 34, pp. 254–256, May, 1946.
[9] K. A. Norton, "The propagation of radio waves over the surface of the earth in the upper atmosphere, Part I," *Proc. IRE*, vol. 24, pp. 1367–1387, Oct. 1936.
[10] ——, "The propagation of radio waves over the surface of the earth in the upper atmosphere, Part II," *Proc. IRE*, vol. 25, pp. 1203–1236, Sept. 1937.
[11] ——, "The calculation of ground wave field intensity over a finitely conducting spherical earth," *Proc. IRE*, vol. 29, pp. 623–639, Dec. 1941.

[12] K. Bullington, "Radio propagation at frequencies above 30 megacycles," *Proc. IRE*, vol. 35, pp. 1122–1136, Oct. 1947.
[13] ——, "Radio propagation fundamentals," *Bell Syst. Tech. J.* vol. 36, p. 593, May 1957.
[14] D. S. Jones, *The Theory of Electro-magnetism*, New York: McMillian 1964, ch. 9.
[15] L. J. Anderson and L. G. Trolese, "Simplified method for computing knife edge defraction in the shadow region," *IRE Trans. Antennas Propagat.*, vol. AP-6, pp. 281–286, July 1958.
[16] N. P. Bachynski and M. G. Kingsmill, "Effect of obstacle profile on knife-edge diffraction," *IRE Trans. Antennas Propagat.*, vol. 10, pp. 201–205, Mar. 1962.
[17] G. Millington, "A Note on diffraction round a sphere or cylinder," *Marconi Rev.*, vol. 23, p. 170, 1960.
[18] H. T. Dougherty and L. J. Maloney, "Application of diffraction by convex surfaces to irregular terrain situations," *Radio Phone*, vol. 68B, no. 2, Feb. 1964.
[19] CCIR Rep. 370-1, Oslo, 1966, II.
[20] D. C. Hogg, "Statistics on attenuation of microwaves by intense rain," *Bell Syst. Tech. J.*, vol. 48, no. 9, Nov. 1969.
[21] P. L. McQuate, J. M. Harman, and A. P. Barsis, "Tabulations of propagation data over irregular terrain in the 230 to 9200 MHz frequency range, part 1: Gun Barrel Hull receiver site," ESSA Tech. Rep. ERL65–ITS52, Mar. 1968.
[22] P. L. McQuate, J. M. Harman, M. E. Johnson, and A. P. Barsis, "Tabulations of the propagation data over irregular terrain in the 230 to 9200 MHz frequency range, part 2: Fritz Peal receiver site," ESSA Tech. Rep. ERL65–ITS58-2, Dec. 1968.
[23] P. L. McQuate, J. M. Harman, M. E. McClamaham, and A. P. Barsis, "Tabulations of propagation data over irregular terrain in the 230 to 9200 MHz frequency range, part 3: North Table Mountain-Golden," ESSA Technical Report ERL65–ITS58-3, July, 1970.
[24] D. M. Black and D. O. Reudink, "Some characteristics of mobile radio propagation at 836 MHz in the Philadelphia area," *IEEE Trans. Veh. Technol.*, vol. VT–21, pp. 45–51, May 1972.
[25] D. O. Reudink, "Comparison of radio transmission at X-band frequencies in suburban and urban areas," *IEEE Trans. Antennas Propagat.*, vol. AP–20, pp. 470–473, July 1972.
[26] G. D. Ott, "Data processing summary and path loss statistics for Philadelphia HCMTS measurements program," unpublished.
[27] D. O. Reudink, "Preliminary investigation of mobile radio transmission at X-band in an urban area," presented at the 1967 Fall URSI Meeting at Ann Arbor, Mich.
[28] W. C. Y. Lee and R. H. Brandt, "The elevation angle of mobile radio signal arrival," *IEEE Trans. Veh. Technol.*, vol. VT–22, pp. 110–113, Nov. 1973.
[29] A. H. LaGrone and C. W. Chapman, "Some propagation characteristics of high UHF signals in the immediate vicinity of trees," *IRE Trans. Antennas Propagat.*, vol. 9, pp. 487–491, Sept. 1961.
[30] D. O. Reudink and M. F. Wazowicz, "Some propagation experiments relating foliage loss and defraction loss at X-band at UNF frequency," *IEEE Trans. Veh. Technol.*, vol. VT–22, pp. 114–122, Nov. 1973.
[31] R. A. Farmer and N. H. Shepherd, "Guided radiation.... the key to tunnel talking," *IEEE Trans. Veh. Commun.*, vol. VC–14, pp. 93–102, Mar 1965
[32] D. O. Reudink, "Mobile radio propagation in tunnels," *IEEE Vehicular Technology Group Conf.*, San Francisco, Calif., Dec. 2–4, 1968.
[33] S. O. Rice, "Diffraction of plane radio waves by prarbolic cylinder," *Bell Syst. Tech. J.*, 33(2), 417–504, (1954).
[34] J. R. Wait and A. M. Conda, "Diffraction of Electromagnetic Waves by Smooth Obstacles for Grazing Angles," *J. Res. Nat. Bur. Stand.*, vol. 63D, pp. 181–197, 1959.
[35] J. C. Schelleng, C. R. Burrows, and E. B. Ferrell, "Ultra shortwave propagation," *Proc. IRE*, vol. 21, pp. 427–463, 1933.
[36] H. Selvidge, "Diffraction Measurements at Ultra-High frequencies," *Proc. IRE*, vol. 29, pp. 10–16, Jan. 1941.
[37] T. B. A. Senior, "The diffraction of a dipole field by a perfectly conduction half-plane," *Quart. J. Mech. Appl. Math.*, vol. 6, pp. 101–114, 1953.
[38] D. E. Kerr, *Propagation of Short Radio Waves*. New York: McGraw-Hill, p. 728, 1951.
[39] H. T. Dougherty and L. J. Maloney, Application of diffraction by convex surfaces to irregular terrain situations." *Radio Sci.*, vol. 68D 284–305, 1964.
[40] G. Millington, "A note on diffraction round a sphere or cylinder," *Marconi Rev.*, vol. 23, pp. 170–182, 1960.
[41] M. H. L. Pryce, "The diffraction of radio waves by the curvature of the earth," *Advances Phys.*, vol. 2, pp. 67–95, 1953.
[42] J. R. Wait and A. M. Conda, "Pattern of an antenna on a curved lossy surface," *IRE Trans. Antennas Propagat.*, vol. AP–6, pp. 187–188, Oct. 1958; and vol. AP–8, p. 628, Nov. 1960.
[43] K. Hacking, "UHF propagation over rounded hills," *Proc. Inst. Elec. Eng.*, vol. 117, Mar. 1970.
[44] M. P. Bachynski, "Scale model investigations of electromagnetic wave propagation over natural obstacles," *RCA Rev.*, vol. 25, pp. 105–44, 1963.
[45] K. Hacking, "Optical diffraction experiments simulating propagation over hills at UHF," in *Inst. Elect. Eng., London, Conf. Pub. #48*, 1968.
[46] A. G. Longley and P. L. Rice, "Prediction of tropospheric radio transmission loss over irregular terrain, a computer method–1968," ESSA Research Laboratories ERL79–ITS67. (U.S. Government Printing Office, Washington, D.C.), 1968.
[47] A. G. Longley and R. K. Reasoner, "Comparison of propagation measurements with predicted values in the 20 to 10,000 MHz range," ESSA Tech. Rep. ERL148–ITS97, Jan. 1970.
[48] J. Aitchison and J. A. C. Brown, *Lognormal Distribution With Special Reference to Its Uses in Economics*. Cambridge, England: Cambridge University Press. 1957.
[49] J. Egli, "Radio propagation above 40 MC over irregular terrain," *Proc. IRE*, vol. 45, pp. 1383–1391, Oct. 1957.
[50] Ng, W. Edward and Murray Geller, "A Table of Integrals of the Error Functions," *J. Res. Nat. Bur. Stand.*, vol. 73B, Jan.–Mar. 1969.

Some Characteristics of Mobile Radio Propagation at 836 MHz in the Philadelphia Area

DONALD M. BLACK, SENIOR MEMBER, IEEE, AND DOUGLAS O. REUDINK, MEMBER, IEEE

Abstract—Mobile radio propagation tests were carried out at 836 MHz from a base station in downtown Philadelphia, Pa., to a mobile which traveled on the city streets. It was found that the median signal power tends to fall off as R^{-3} for distances greater than 1 to 2 mi from the base station antenna. The mean received-signal level was found to be approximately log-normally distributed with a standard deviation varying from 5 to 10 dB, where the higher values were observed close to the base station.

INTRODUCTION

THE USE of a band of frequencies in the 850-MHz region has been suggested as a possibility for the expansion of the present crowded mobile radio spectrum. In order to determine whether this frequency region might be suitable for mobile communications some propagation tests were carried out in the Philadelphia, Pa., area. Continuous field strength recordings were made of the signal received by a mobile unit as it moved about in various areas out to distances of 5 mi from the base station transmitter. The transmitting base station was operated at a frequency of 836.6 MHz and was located 500 ft above the street level in downtown Philadelphia.

A preliminary study of the mobile radio propagation in the Philadelphia area was reported previously [1],[2], but these results were aimed primarily at demonstrating a four-branch predetection FM diversity mobile radio receiver. This paper details more extensive signal strength measurements made in the downtown area of Philadelphia.

TEST AREAS

From the transmitter located on the top of the PSFS Building near City Hall, the area covered by the test runs in the mobile van was the southwest quadrant of the city as measured from City Hall and extending about 3 mi in both directions. Two sections were studied in detail which consisted of a smaller area extending about 1 mi west and 1 mi south of the City Hall, where the test data were examined in fine detail, and a larger area extending 1 mi west and 3 mi south, where the data were examined in slightly less detail. By fine detail it is meant that the mobile test data were examined for each street in the area, whereas in the larger area only every other street was examined. Test data were also taken on diverse test runs out to distances of 5 mi from the base station transmitter. These data runs and the areas of detailed study are indicated in Fig. 1.

Manuscript received May 4, 1971; revised December 23, 1971. This paper was presented at the 1970 IEEE Vehicular Technology Conference, Washington, D.C., December 2–4.

The authors are with the Crawford Hill Laboratory, Bell Telephone Laboratories, Inc., Holmdel, N.J. 07733.

TEST EQUIPMENT AND PROCEDURES

The recording of the received signal at microwave frequencies in mobile radio transmission poses some severe problems due to the deep and rapid fading which occurs as the vehicle moves through randomly scattering media. Some type of logarithmic receiver capable of compressing large amplitude variations of input signal to small changes in output voltage suitable for recording on magnetic tape is required. The receiver must also have a frequency response wide enough to be able to follow the extremely rapid changes in signal amplitude which are encountered at 836 MHz. Such a receiver was used in these tests in which an IF amplifier with the cascaded stages progressively limited as the input amplitude was increased. In this amplifier the portion of the transfer characteristic of each stage has a nonlinear region where the output is approximately proportional to the logarithm of the input. The output from each stage is individually detected and summed at a common point to produce an overall transfer characteristic over the expected range of input amplitudes.

In other respects the receiving equipment was of a type normally used for this frequency range. A one-quarter wavelength vertical whip antenna was mounted on the ground plane on the roof of the van and was used to detect the signal from the transmitter. A low-noise (5-dB noise figure) RF amplifier and mixer unit together with a very stable crystal oscillator converted the signal to a 30-MHz IF. The output of the receiver was connected to a multichannel FM magnetic tape recorder. One channel recorded the signal strength data while a second simultaneously recorded the running commentary made by a person in the van regarding the calibration data and the actual location of the van, including the moment of crossing each street intersection. A third channel recorded a marker tone which was geared to one of the wheels of the vehicle so that a "beep" occurred for every 50 ft of travel of the vehicle. This information made it possible to correlate signal strength with location in fine detail. Prior to each test run a receiver calibration was made by feeding a fixed frequency source through the calibrated attenuator into the receiving unit. The van was usually driven at night during light traffic conditions and the speed maintained was as close to 15 mi/h as possible.

DATA REDUCTION

The data recorded on the magnetic tape was played back in the laboratory and transcribed on paper tape with a pen recorder. The signal level was recorded on one channel including the calibration data preceding and following each run. The

Reprinted from *IEEE Trans. Veh. Technol.*, vol. VT-21, pp. 45–51, May 1972.

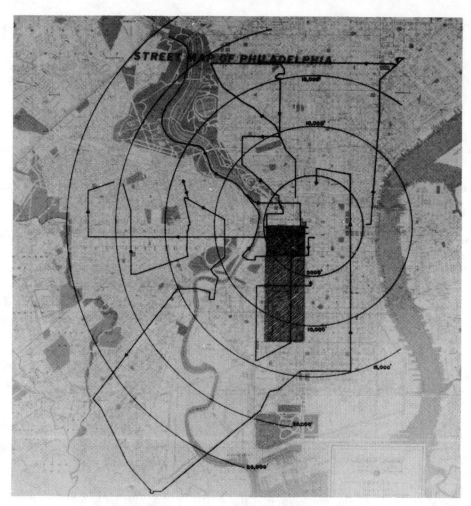

Fig. 1. Data runs at 836 MHz in Philadelphia, Pa.

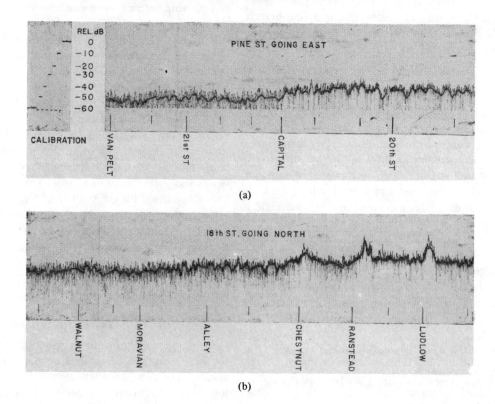

(a)

(b)

Fig. 2. Typical signal level recordings showing 100-ft sampling markers.

50-ft distance marker pulses were recorded on a second channel. The operator who transcribed the tape listened to the running commentary on the magnetic tape and transcribed by hand onto the paper tape at the proper time the information regarding the date, time, place, and start of the run, the names of the streets over which the run took place, and especially the exact moment of crossing each street intersection. This latter information established the correlation between the signal strength and the exact location. Other calibration information was also noted by hand on the paper tape.

The data transcribed on the paper tape showed the variation of signal level along the various streets, including the sharp fading. In order to obtain an approximation to the rms value of the signal level without fading, a line was drawn by eye on the recording of the signal level to approximate this value. This line was not drawn through the peak value of the signal but through the points about 2 dB or so below the peaks.

Using the calibration recorded on the tape the values of the average signal level were read off corresponding to each street intersection, and at points spaced 100 ft apart as determined by the distance markers shown on the tape. This data was tabulated for the various streets in the area of interest.

Fig. 2 is an example of the signal level recordings which were transferred from the magnetic tape to a pen recorder. Fig. 2(a) shows data from a section of Pine Street where the signal level was very low due to the shadowing effect of tall buildings. The gradual improvement going from Van Pelt Street to 20th Street can be seen, and the calibration scale to the left gives an indication of the magnitude of this gradual change. Fig. 2(b) illustrates the peaking up of signal level at some street intersections, such as Chestnut, Ranstead, and Ludlow Streets, as the vehicle was traveling along 18th Street. The same calibration scale applies to this chart. The correlation between the signal peaks and the exact position of the vehicle depends upon the time that the oral announcement was made. The 100-ft distance markers are indicated, and variations in spacing on the chart are due to changes in vehicle speed.

SIGNAL STRENGTH MODEL

Smaller Area Model

The approximate region covered in the fine-detail test area as viewed from the base station transmitter is seen in Fig. 3. There are several buildings greater than 10 stories in height within this area. Occasionally, one can see directly to the street below, but most often the line-of-sight path is obscured. A cardboard model like an egg crate was constructed to correspond in size with sections of the street map to give a visual picture of the variation in received signal strength within the area under study. Each street had a perpendicular strip of cardboard on which was plotted the signal level on a scale of 10 dB/in. The strip was then cut and glued together with other sections to form a three-dimensional pattern of the area. Fig. 4 is the view of the field strength model as seen from behind the transmitter which is indicated by the black vertical strip. This view shows the signal level variation along the streets looking in a southwest direction from the transmitter location. Some items of interest should be noted: 1) the generally good signal level along the wide streets such as Market Street and Broad Street, 2) variations of 20 dB or more along such streets near the transmitter due to shadowing effects of the tall buildings

Fig. 3. Approximate region covered in smaller area model.

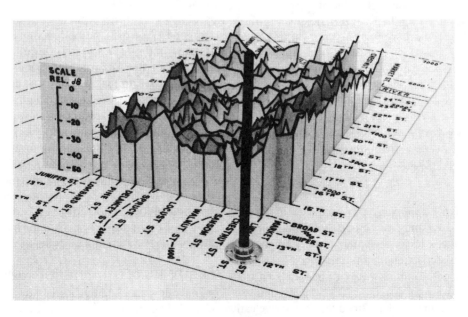

Fig. 4. Model of fine-detail test area.

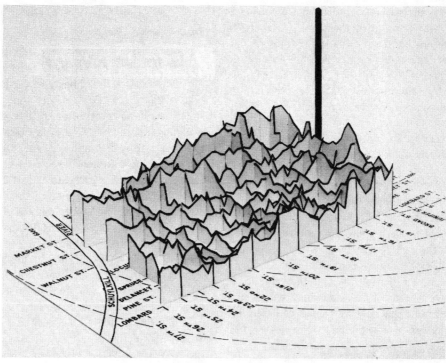

Fig. 5. Model of fine-detail test area.

Fig. 6. Approximate region covered in larger area model.

near the transmitter, and 3) the general rise in signal level near the river as the signal path approaches line-of-sight conditions.

Fig. 5 is a view from the south of the area looking in a northeast direction. There are four principal points in this figure: 1) the variation of signal along Lombard Street is shown very well, including the sharp dips in the generally high level near Broad Street as well as the one or two broad sections of low signal, 2) a depressed signal area near 22nd Street extends all the way from Walnut Street to Lombard Street, 3) peaking up of signal level at the street intersections can be seen quite well at several points in this view, and 4) the increase of signal level approaching the river is clearly shown.

Larger Area Model

An indication of the approximate area covered in the test runs from the larger area study can be obtained from the photo in Fig. 6, which is a view looking in approximately a southwest direction from the base station transmitter. Fig. 7 is a view of the field strength model from East Broad Street looking from the transmitter in a westerly direction. The principal points of this view are that the signal level on Broad Street is very clearly shown and that there are several streets near Snyder Avenue

where the signal level has held up better than that near the transmitter.

Fig. 8 is a view of the model from the western side looking toward the transmitter in an easterly direction. Note the following: 1) the variation along 23rd Street is very clearly shown, 2) the depressed area near 22nd and Spruce Streets is seen to be small in comparison with the whole area, and 3) the variations along the north-south and east-west streets show up quite well for the entire area.

COMPARATIVE RESULTS

A histogram of the received-signal strength was prepared from the data samples used to construct the models. Fig. 9(a) is a histogram of the received-signal strength taken in the smaller model. The distribution function obtained from these data is shown in Fig. 9(b), where the logarithm of the signal strength is plotted on normal probability paper.

One can see from Figs. 7 and 8 that there is considerably less severe variation in signal strength on the larger area model than on the smaller area model shown in Figs. 4 and 5. Much more of this area is now out of the central portion of the city and the buildings are more uniform. The histogram of the data used for constructing this larger model is shown in Fig. 10(a). As one might expect, the standard deviation is less than that of the smaller area model, as can be seen from the distribution function plotted in Fig. 10(b). Also, the signal strength data tend to be a better fit to a log-normal distribution than do the measurements taken in the smaller area.

FURTHER RESULTS OF THE DIVERSE LOCATION DATA

Prediction of the fall-off signal power with distance has been given by Okumura *et al.* [3], and these predictions agree well with our data samples. Fig. 11 is a plot of the data sampled

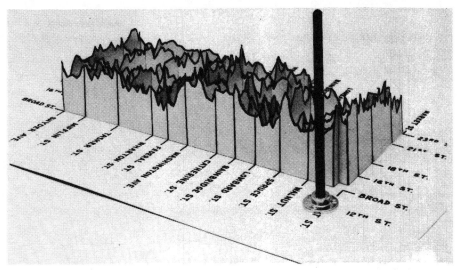

Fig. 7. Model of larger test area.

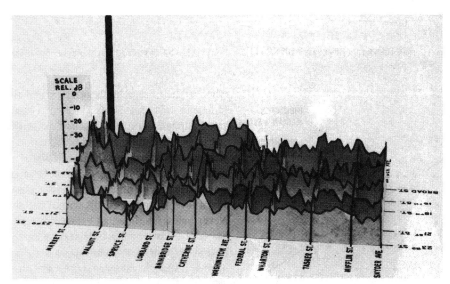

Fig. 8. Model of larger test area.

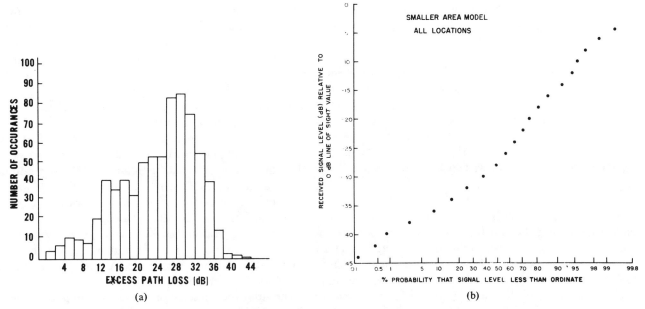

(a)

(b)

Fig. 9 (a) Histogram of excess path loss in 1 × 1-mi grid. (b) Distribution of excess path loss.

105

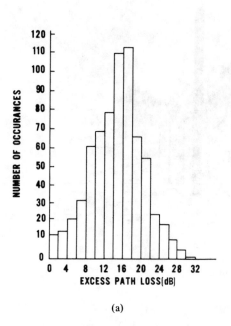

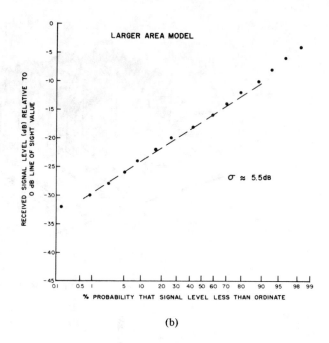

(a)

(b)

Fig. 10. (a) Histogram of excess path loss in 1 × 3-mi grid. (b) Distribution of excess path loss.

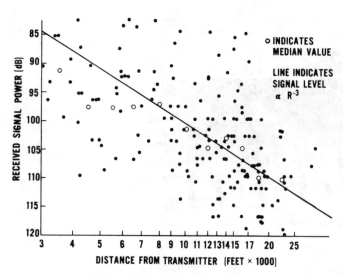

Fig. 11. Signal variation with distance.

at diverse locations, represented by the solid dots. The median signal levels are plotted as open circles. At locations beyond 2 mi distant from the base station transmitter the median values tend to follow an inverse R^3 relation. An examination of the distribution of signal strengths about the median level value again show the variation of signal strengths to be roughly log-normal with a standard deviation of approximately 7.5 dB.

SUMMARY AND CONCLUSIONS

From a large-area study it was found that in most locations there is no line-of-sight path from the mobile to the base station. In such cases the mean received-signal strength (here the mean is a local mean averaged over several wavelengths) tends to be 5–25 dB lower than would be received over the same free-space distance. Furthermore, the received signal fluctuates about this mean value following a Rayleigh distribution. Even

when a line-of-sight path exists, signal fluctuations occur, but fading in this case is less severe. Changes in the local mean value depend upon factors such as terrain, width of the street, size of nearby buildings, and base station antenna height. Cases were observed where the mean signal remained constant to within a few decibels for distances as great as a mile along a single street, yet other examples occurred where the average signal level dropped 20 dB within the distance of a city block. Nevertheless, the median value of received signals tends to follow a R^{-3} law for this base station antenna height. The distribution of the local mean appears to be roughly log-normal, having its mean value near 24 dB below an equivalent free-space path and a standard deviation of about 7–8 dB.

A significant difference in signal strength was observed between radial and cross streets. Even at a distance of 3 mi from the base station, the signals received on radial and nearly radial streets were usually 10 dB or more greater than the signals received on the corresponding cross streets.

Several general conclusions can be drawn from looking at the cardboard models in regard to the signal level variations in a city. First, the signal propagates better down a wide street than down a narrow one. Second, on cross streets the level peaks up at street intersections and drops down in the middle of a block. Third, there are sharper and deeper dips in signal level close to the transmitter than there are farther away. Fourth, a large tall building in line with the transmitter produces a shadowing effect and may blank out a large area.

A typical sharp dip in level along a wide street near the transmitter is about 20 dB, and along a narrow street may be 35 dB. A typical dip in the middle of the block would be 10 dB. At a distance of about 2 mi the dips in signal level are only 5–10 dB over a wide area. A shadowing effect due to buildings may produce a dip of 45 dB only 1 mi from the transmitter and cause all of an area of 2 or 3 square blocks to be 15–20 dB lower than normal.

IEEE TRANSACTIONS ON VEHICULAR TECHNOLOGY, VOL. VT-21, NO. 2, MAY 1972

The variation in signal strength appears to be more severe close to the transmitter than farther away. For distances less than 3000 ft from the base station the distribution of signal strengths measured in dBm appear to have a log-normal distribution with a standard deviation of 9 dB, whereas in a section of the city where the building heights are more uniform, the measured standard deviation was found to be only about 5.5 dB.

REFERENCES

[1] D. O. Reudink and A. J. Rustako, Jr., "Mobile signal strength measurements at 900 MHz in an urban area," in *Conf. Rec., 1969 IEEE Int. Conf. Communications* (Abstr. Informal Papers), p. 5.

[2] ——, "Performance of a four-branch predetection FM mobile microwave receiver in an urban area," in *Conf. Rec., 1969 IEEE Int. Conf. Communications* (Abstr. Informal Papers), p. 5.

[3] Y. Okumura, E. Ohmori, T. Kawano, and K. Fukuda, "Field strength and its variability in VHF and UHF land-mobile radio service," *Rev. Elec. Commun. Lab.*, vol. 16, pp. 825–873, Sept.–Oct., 1968.

Radio Wave Loss Deviation and
Shadow Loss at 900 MHz

NEAL H. SHEPHERD, FELLOW, IEEE

Abstract– Radio wave propagation between base and mobile stations is normally described as being Rayleigh distributed due to multipath radio wave combining. When the number of radio wave paths are limited the variation in received signal amplitude frequently follows a more general case given by a Weibull distribution. A significant portion of the Weibull distribution is defined as the transmission loss deviation. Other definitions have been included with the object of standardizing methods of measuring and reporting propagation data. Data will be presented showing loss deviation between 3 and 30 dB. Shadow loss over hills and around buildings are usually assumed to be knife-edge or rounded knife-edge. Shadow loss based on these assumptions is generally found to be less than the true measured value. Data will be presented comparing calculated shadow loss with measured value.

INTRODUCTION

THE NEED for standardization of propagation parameters and methods of measurement is apparent from a search of the literature. Bullington [1], based on theoretical analysis, presented data in the form of transmission loss between $\lambda/2$ dipoles. The International Radio Consultative Committee (CCIR) [2], Okumura [3] and the Federal Communications Commission (FCC) [4] provide propagation in the form of field strength (dBu) for 1 kW effective radiated power (ERP). Barsis [6] and the National Bureau of Standards (NBS) [5] prefer to use basic transmission loss (dB between isotropic antennas). Field strength and percent time parameters show a boradcast practice influence, and isotropic antennas are indigenous to point-to-point service. The use of different parameters leads to either confusion or time-consuming conversion when necessary comparisons are made.

Other differences can be found in both the methods of measurement and analysis of data. Most of the FCC, NBS, and CCIR data are based on point-to-point measurements as generally used in the broadcast services. Okumura [3] and Young [7] relied on signal amplitude distribution taken from either a fixed distance or time interval with the measurement vehicle in motion. Young noted that a signal amplitude distribution when taken over a small area of less than 1000 ft tended to follow a Rayleigh distribution.

The land-mobile services need a set of propagation curves that are based on appropriate type measurements and given in terms of those parameters which most closely fit its system requirements. The preferred parameters for land-mobile propagation curves will be defined.

Manuscript received June 12, 1976; revised July 5, 1977. This paper was originally presented at the 26th Annual IEEE Vehicular Conference, Washington, DC, March 25, 1976.

The author is with the Department of Mobile Radio Products, General Electric Company, Lynchburg, VA 24502.

Transmission Loss

Transmission loss (TL) is the ratio of the effective radiated power of a radiating antenna to the power received at the termination of the receiving antenna minus the gain of the two antennas relative to half-wave dipoles. This ratio is expressed in decibels as follows:

$$TL = 10 \log \frac{P_1}{P_2} - G_x - G_r \qquad (1)$$

where

P_1	effective radiated power,
P_2	received power,
G_x	gain of transmitting antenna in decibels relative to a half-wave dipole,
G_r	gain of receiving antenna in decibels relative to a half-wave dipole.

Since land-mobile antennas for base and mobile stations are specified according to the standard method, in terms of gain relative to a half-wave dipole, it is most convenient to specify transmission loss in the same manner. Loss expressed in other units, such as in relation to field strength or isotropic antennas, always requires some conversion factor.

Sector

A sector describes the bounds of a large number (at least four per wavelength) of transmission loss measurement locations. It is usually along the straight path of a vehicle while traveling a short distance, but it can be a small area where terrain permits. Sectors are identified by types corresponding to the distance traveled, e.g., 20, 200, or 2000 m in length, which can be along a straight path or within a defined boundary. The three types of sectors are used to compare antenna gains, propagation measurements on roads, and propagation measurements in specific geographical areas, respectively.

Transmission Loss Distribution

Transmission loss distribution (TLD) is the percentage of TL measurements made in a specified sector that are less than a given value. Data points are plotted for the percent of locations where the TL is less than ordinate. The TLD for a given sector is, in general, time independent and should therefore be expressed in terms of percent locations only:

$$TLD = P(TL \leqslant \text{level } x/\text{a given sector}). \qquad (2)$$

Reprinted from *IEEE Trans. Veh. Technol.*, vol. VT-26, pp. 309–313, Nov. 1977.

Median Transmission Loss

Median transmission loss (MTL) is the loss corresponding to 50 percent of locations of the TLD.

Loss Deviation

The loss deviation (LD) is the decibel difference in attenuation between the 50 percent and 90 percent locations on the TLD. In general, it is assumed that the LD will take on a value of 8.2 dB corresponding to a Rayleigh distribution; however, it has been found to have a range of values between 3 and 30 dB.

Median Transmission Loss Distribution

Median transmission loss distribution (MTLD) is the percentage of MTL's for a specified path distance that are less than a given value. The 50 percent value of the MTLD forms the basis for propagation curves for a specified terrain. The standard deviation for the MTLD is a measure of the variation that can be expected for different types of terrain.

Method of Measuring (TLD)

The equipment for measuring the TLD is illustrated in Fig. 1. The signal amplitude sampler and totalizing unit (SASTU) is calibrated by a signal generator set to the lowest signal level of measurement, usually −149 dBW, to which the first SASTU channel is adjusted to respond. The SASTU response is accomplished by a tunnel diode level detector, which is sampled by an internal clock or a pulse train generated by the movement of a vehicle. When in motion in a vehicle each level is sampled about 50 times/m. At the end of 1000, 10 000, or 100 000 samples the printer is initiated. Eight SASTU channels are used with each in order and calibrated to respond to a higher signal level usually in 6 dB steps. The resulting data output of the printer, when divided by the total number of samples, gives the fraction of locations the measured signal level exceeds the level setting for a respective SASTU channel.

The SASTU and printer is faster and more accurate than other types of recording systems in use. The maximum vehicle speed exceeds the posted limits, and an individual level detector will respond on a 0.2 dB change in signal level.

Application of TLD

The amplitude variation of a 900-MHz received signal at a receiver in motion is presented in the form of a TLD as shown in Fig. 2. Only six data points of a possible eight available for the SASTU and printer are shown on each TLD. The other two data points are generally of least interest since they are produced by the higher signal levels. Of main interest is that portion of the TLD between the 50 percent and the 99 percent. Each TLD illustrated tends to follow a straight line where plotted on Weibull distribution graph paper. The Weibull distribution is a more general distribution of which the Rayleigh is a specific case. Also shown in Fig. 2 is a Rayleigh distribution for comparison, since it is generally used as a model for the TLD. The loss deviation, as defined above, can be calculated by using the following:

$$LD = \frac{1.884(X_1 - X_2)}{\ln \cdot \ln (1/P1) - \ln \cdot \ln (1/P2)} \quad (3)$$

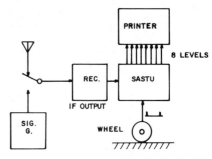

Fig. 1. Equipment for measuring transmission loss distributions.

where

P_n percent/100,
X_n TL at P_n.

Since the LD does not always remain constant over completion amplitude range of the TLD, it is usually calculated by using two data points near 50 percent. The MTL can be calculated from the following:

$$MTL = X_1 + \frac{[.367 + \ln \cdot \ln (1/P1)] \; LD}{1.884} \quad (4)$$

$$MTL = X_1 + \frac{[X_1 - X_2] \, [.367 + \ln \cdot \ln (1/P1)]}{\ln \cdot \ln (1/P1) - \ln \cdot \ln (1/P2)}. \quad (5)$$

Diffraction Loss at 900 MHz

Diffraction or shadow loss caused by buildings and hills increase the 50 percent value of the MTLD and also its standard deviation. The increase in the 50 percent value is usally referred to as the terrain roughness factor [4] and a standard deviation associated with general geographical features, e.g., urban, suburban, and rolling hills. The generally accepted correction for the terrain roughness factor is based on a Δh (meters) measured between 10 and 90 percent of the terrain variation. Although this approach to terrain roughness has provided some improvements in propagation predictions, it needs further changes to reduce possible errors. The choice of parameters for a new terrain roughness factor is based on the knife-edge diffraction loss as illustrated in Fig. 3. The transmission loss relative to free-space is given by [2] the approximation

$$\alpha = 13 + 20 \log V (\text{dB}) \quad (6)$$

where

$$V = h\sqrt{2/\lambda d}, \qquad \text{for } V > 1. \quad (7)$$

Substitution into (6) and simplifying gives

$$\alpha = -8.76 + 20 \log h + 10 \log f - 10 \log d \quad (8)$$

where

h height of obstruction in meters,
d distance to obstruction in meters,
f frequency (MHz).

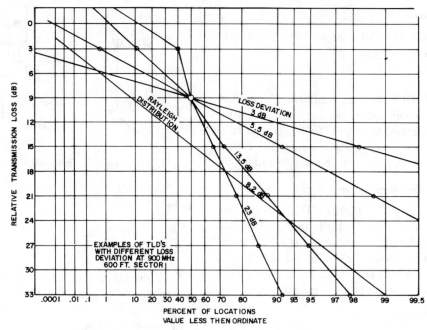

Fig. 2.   Typical transmission loss distributions at 900 MHz for
200-m sectors.

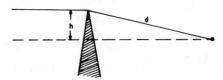

Fig. 3.   Geometry for propagation over knife-edge.

For 900 MHz

$$\alpha = 20.8 + 20 \log h - 10 \log d$$

$$\alpha = 20.8 + 10 \log (h^2/d). \qquad (9)$$

The factor h^2/d should be used in place of the usual Δh since it can be used for calculating attenuation.

Equation (9) is illustrated by Fig. 4. The example given shows that for a distance of 450 m and a hill height of 20 m the attenuation is 20 dB at 900 MHz. Also included are a number of measurement points indicating that (9) underestimates the losses for $h^2/d > 0.2$.

Terrain Roughness Transmission Loss

Several different approaches, each yielding different results, are given for determining terrain roughness transmission loss as illustrated in Fig. 5. Bullington [9], the oldest available data, appears to be in between Longley and Rice [8], and FCC [4], and CCIR [2] data. For comparison, a calculated curve is shown assuming a constant $h^2/d = 10$. The calculation was made by assuming different hill heights and a constant h^2/d. For each hill height the average of a number of TLD's was determined from a number of sectors between each two hills. The experimental data shown in Fig. 4 indicates that the loss for hills increases rapidly where $h^2/d > 0.2$. Thus from the four imperical curves shown it appears that Bullington should be preferred until more complete experimental data is available.

Diffraction Loss Around Buildings

Diffraction loss around a single isolated building assuming a transmission path around both sides, substituting $W = 2h$, $D = d$ into (8), and subtracting 3 dB for two paths gives

$$\alpha = -17.8 + 20 \log W - 10 \log D + 10 \log f \qquad (10)$$

where

W width of building (m),
D distance to building (m).

For 900 MHz this reduces to

$$\alpha = 11.8 + 20 \log W - \log D$$

$$\alpha = 11.8 + 10 \log (W^2/d). \qquad (11)$$

Diffraction loss is only significant where the building is isolated from other buildings or reflecting surfaces which can fill in behind the shadowed area.

Measurements made in Dallas on a single isolated building gave a median attenuation of 47 dB compared to a calculated value based on (10) of 28 dB. This indicates that the knife-edge theory underestimates shadow loss for an isolated building. For other locations in Dallas where many tall and short buildings were mixed together the median loss was only 5 dB. A standard deviation of the MTLD of 5 dB measured for downtown Dallas was also significantly lower than measurements were in less cluttered areas.

Reflections

Reflections from large buildings or hills can be represented by radiated signals with generally narrow beamwidths and multiple lobes. Both the main beam and lobes can frequently equal or exceed the direct path from the transmitter antenna.

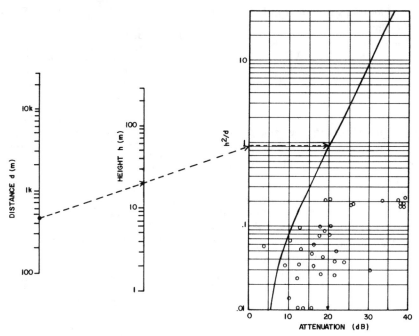

Fig. 4.   Knife-edge transmission loss at 900 MHz.

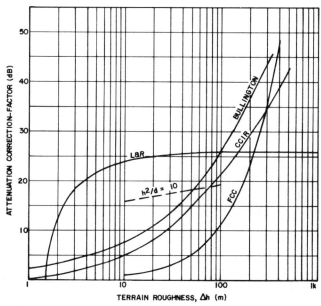

Fig. 5.   Attenuation correction factor for 50 percent of locations at 900 MHz.

When the direct path and reflected paths are nearly equal the TLD has a large LD as illustrated by 13.5 and 23 dB in Fig. 2. Also shown for comparison is the Raleigh distribution. When the reflected path exceeds the direct path the LD can decrease to low values as indicated for curves of 3 and 4.5 dB. As more reflected signals are added from other objects the LD continues to increase or decrease dependent on whether the resultant signal is smaller or larger than the direct path, respectively. The equivalent half-wave dipole gain [10] of a reflector is given by the following:

$$G = \left(\frac{2.44\pi A \sin \theta}{\lambda^2} \right)^2 \qquad (12)$$

where

A area of reflector (m^2),

θ angle of incident,

and the free space less [1] between half-wave dipole is shown by the following:

$$L = \left(\frac{13\lambda}{d} \right)^2 \qquad (13)$$

where d = the distance between antennas (m).

Combining (12) and (13) to make the amplitude of the signal by the direct path equal to that of the reflected path gives

$$d_1 = \frac{fA \sin \theta}{300} \qquad (14)$$

where

f frequency (MHz),

d_1 distance to reflector (m).

for 900 MHz

$$d = 3A \sin \theta \qquad (15)$$

and for a typical $\theta = 42°$

$$d = 2A, \qquad A - 0.5d. \qquad (16)$$

Any time a reflector has an area in square meters that is numerically equal to at least 1/2 the distance to the reflector, it can be expected that the TL and LD will have large variations. The type of variations to be expected and their actual geographical location cannot be accurately predicted and in general must be measured.

111

Two typical examples of locations measured in Dallas at a range of 8 mi gave the following results.

MTL (dB)	LD (dB)
93	3
168	17

The 50 percent value of the MTLD for the same distance was 132 dB, which is about the average of the above maximum and minimum. The average LD is 10 dB, which is 2 dB greater than a Rayleigh distributed TLD.

For many of the buildings in downtown Dallas, it has been estimated that the reflected path can exceed the direct path for distances between the transmitting antenna and the building up to 20 km (12 mi). Measurements made at a distance of 16 mi did confirm a strong influence of reflections from buildings although the variations in MTL were not near as great as shown above.

REFERENCES

[1] K. Bullington, "Radio propagation at frequencies above 30 megacycles," in *Proc. IRE*, vol. 35, no. 10, p. 1122, Oct. 1947.
[2] C.C.I.R., Recommendation 370-2.
[3] Y. Okumura, *et al.*, "Field strength and its variability in VHF, UHF land-mobile radio service," *Rev. Elec. Commun. Lab.*, vol. 16, pp. 825–873, Sept. 1968.
[4] FCC, Report no. R-6602, Sept. 7, 1966.
[5] NBS, Report 8296, July 7, 1964.
[6] A. P. Barsis, "Radio wave propagation over irregular terrain in the 76-9200 MHz frequency range," *IEEE Trans. Veh. Technol.*, vol. VT-20 no. 2, August 1971.
[7] W. R. Young, Jr., "Comparison of mobile radio transmission at 150, 450, 900, and 3700 MHz," *Bell Syst. Tech. J.*, vol. 31, pp. 1068–1085, Nov. 1952.
[8] A. G. Longley and R. L. Rice, "Prediction of tropospheric radio transmission loss over irregular terrain," ERL79-ITS67, July 1968.
[9] K. Bullington, "Radio propagation variations at VHF and UHF," in *Proc. IRE*, vol. 38, no. 1, p. 27, Jan. 1950.
[10] A. Alvira and I. T. Corbell, "Microwave system parameters for reliable communications," *AIEE Trans. (Power App. Syst)*, no. 21, pp. 1100–1107, Dec. 1955.

Correction to "Radio Wave Loss Deviation and Shadow Loss at 900 MHz"

NEAL H. SHEPHERD, FELLOW, IEEE

In the above paper,[1] on page 309, (1) should have read

$$TL = 10 \log \frac{P_1}{P_2} + Gr. \tag{1}$$

The author wishes to thank George Hagn of SRI International for pointing out this error.

Manuscript received April 19, 1978.
The author is with the Department of Mobile Radio Products, General Electric Company, Lynchburg, VA 24502.
[1] N. Shepherd, *IEEE Trans. Veh. Technol.*, vol. VT-26, no. 4, pp. 309–313, Nov. 1977.

Reprinted from *IEEE Trans. Veh. Technol.*, vol. VT-27, p. 158, Aug. 1978.

Correlation Bandwidth and Delay Spread Multipath Propagation Statistics for 910-MHz Urban Mobile Radio Channels

DONALD C. COX, SENIOR MEMBER, IEEE, AND ROBERT P. LECK

Abstract—Distributions of delay spread and correlation bandwidth at 0.9 and 0.5 correlation for Gaussian wide-sense stationary uncorrelated scattering (GWSSUS) channels associated with 100 small-scale areas at different locations within a 2 × 2.5 km region of New York City are presented. For delay spread the maximum value observed was $3\frac{1}{2}$ μs and 10 percent of the areas exceeded $2\frac{1}{2}$ μs; for correlation bandwidth at 0.9 correlation the minimum was 20 kHz and 10 percent of the areas were less than 30 kHz; for correlation bandwidth at 0.5 correlation the minimum was 55 kHz and 10 percent of the areas were less than 130 kHz. The region is representative of the heavily built-up areas of many large cities in the United States.

I. INTRODUCTION

SOME STATISTICS of time-domain representations of multipath propagation at 910 MHz in an urban mobile-radio environment have been described recently [1], [2]. For some applications, these time-domain descriptions are convenient, but in other cases frequency-domain descriptions, such as frequency-correlation functions of the complex transfer function and correlation bandwidths, are more useful. Since the time- and frequency-domain descriptions are related through Fourier transforms, frequency-domain descriptions can be obtained directly from the time-domain measurements [3].

The statistics of the dispersive mobile radio channel are usually quasi-stationary for vehicle travel distances on the order of 5 to 30 m (small scale) but become grossly nonstationary for distances greater than 20 to 150 m [1], [2] (large scale). Small-scale medium fluctuations are dominated by the random phase addition of many signals that have nearly equal path delays. The large-scale changes are caused by the different reflecting structures (buildings, etc.) that contribute to the received power in different regions. Because of the gross nonstationarity throughout large regions, a two-step statistical model of the medium is appropriate. The first step is to model the different small-scale stationary channels and find channel parameters which are related to radio system performance. The Gaussian wide-sense stationary uncorrelated scattering channel (GWSSUS) [4], [5] was shown to be a reasonable model [2] for the urban mobile radio channel over bandwidths up to 10 MHz since: 1)

Paper approved by the Associate Editor for Radio Communication of the IEEE Communications Society for publication without oral presentation. Manuscript received December 18, 1974.

The authors are with Bell Laboratories, Holmdel, N. J. 07733.

as a vehicle moves along streets over small-scale distances the envelopes of the fluctuating signals at fixed time delays are usually Rayleigh distributed [2], suggesting complex Gaussian processes; 2) the fluctuations at different delays separated by more than a resolution cell (0.1 μs) are usually uncorrelated since the RF power spectra at different delays are grossly different [2], [6]; and 3) averages of received power at fixed delays are reasonably stationary for small-scale distances [2] (5–30 m). The GWSSUS channel is a model for a multipath channel made up of independent point scatterers. Therefore, it physically describes mobile radio propagation paths quite well too. Time-domain channel parameters that limit a radio system performance are average excess delay d and delay spread s. In the frequency domain, correlation bandwidth B_c at a correlation of c is a performance-limiting parameter related to s. These are defined in detail later.

This paper, which emphasizes the second step of the modeling process, presents statistical distributions of correlation bandwidth at 0.5 and 0.9 correlations and the related delay spread for many small-scale areas at different locations within a large region of a city. Since these statistics are nearly useless without a description of the characteristics (building heights, street widths, etc. [1]) of the region to which they are applicable, the paper includes a description of the region. This part of New York City is representative of the heavily built-up downtown areas of many large cities in the United States.

II. THE MEASUREMENTS

The measurements were made with a wide-band measuring system described in detail in [7]. The system uses the correlation properties of pseudorandom shift-register sequences. The probing signal is not a pulse but the results are equivalent to measurements made using short RF pulses.

Briefly, a 910-MHz carrier, stable to a few parts in 10^{-10}, is phase-reversal modulated by a pseudorandom shift register sequence (9-bit register and 10-MHz clock). This signal was transmitted from a vertically polarized colinear antenna array which is omnidirectional in azimuth and has an 18° beamwidth in elevation (±9° from horizontal). The transmitting antenna was located 120 m above the street on top of the American Telephone and Telegraph Building at 195 Broadway, New York City.

Reprinted from *IEEE Trans. Commun.*, vol. COM-23, pp. 1271–1280, Nov. 1975.

Fig. 1.   Map of experimental area on Manhattan Island, New York City.

This transmitting site is marked with a T on the map of lower Manhattan Island in Fig. 1.

The signal was received with an omnidirectional $\frac{1}{4}$ wavelength vertical antenna on the roof of a $2\frac{1}{2}$ m high mobile van driven along the city streets. In the Rake-like [7], [8] receiver, the received signal is correlated with a replica of the transmitted signal in two quadrature correlators whose amplitude outputs in time represent amplitude versus time delay for the low-pass quadrature components $I(\tau)$ and $Q(\tau)$ of the band-limited bandpass impulse response of the propagation path [3].

The range of delays included in one impulse response (the delay window) is 15 μs. This 15-μs window can be moved anywhere within an absolute delay range of 0 to 51.1 μs (511 bits $\times$ 0.1 μs/bit) which corresponds to path delays of 0 to about 15 km. The squared envelope

of the complex impulse response, $p(\tau) = I^2(\tau) + Q^2(\tau)$, is the same power delay profile $p(\tau)$ which would be received if a triangular pulse with base width of 0.2 μs and a repetition rate of 20 kHz were transmitted through all equipment filters and the propagation medium and detected with a square law detector [7]. The delay resolution of the equipment is about 0.1 μs (10-MHz bandwidth RF signal).

Data including complex impulse response components, synchronizing pulses, vehicle speed, etc., were recorded on an analog tape recorder in the mobile vehicle while it was driven at 1.4 m/s along the streets marked in bold letters in Fig. 1. These data were then sampled and stored on digital tape for computer processing. Data shown later are from the approximately $2 \times 2\frac{1}{2}$ km region which ranges from 1.5 to 3.5 km from the transmitter. Table I

TABLE I
STREET CHARACTERISTICS

Street	Canyon Width (m)	Building Height (Stories)	Building Concentration	Street Orientation	Distance (km)
Grand	11	5–10	Solid	Circumferential	1.5
Watt	15	2–10	70 Percent Solid	Circumferential	1.5
Broome	17	5–10	Solid	Circumferential	1.5
Lafayette				Radial	1.5–2.5
Houston	32	2–10	70 Percent Solid	Oblique	2.5
Clarkson	15	5–10	50 Percent Solid	Circumferential	2.5
Carmine	17	2–5	Solid	Oblique	2.5
Bleeker	13	3–10	Solid	Circumferential	2.5
Bowery	30	2–5	90 Percent Solid	Oblique	2–2.5
West 14th	25	5–20	Solid	Circumferential	3.5
Ave. of Americas	23	5	80 Percent Solid	Radial	2

summarizes the significant characteristics of the streets. Street widths are from building front to building front (the "canyon" width) and orientations are with respect to a radial from the street to the transmitter. Even the streets that did not have solid building fronts were generally shielded from the transmitter by buildings along adjacent streets. Data sets were taken from small areas that were either in street intersections (the solid rectangles along oblique and circumferential streets and the solid triangles along radial streets in Fig. 1) or in regions between intersections (midblocks indicated by solid circles and + marks in Fig. 1). About 60 percent of the data are from midblock areas and 40 percent from intersections. Except for the buildings the ground is essentially level throughout the measuring area. Photos looking into the measuring area from near the transmitter are in [1].

Individual complex impulse responses were taken every 10 cm along the streets (for examples see [2] or [7]). For the areas chosen for analysis individual power delay profiles $p_i(\tau_k)$ were computed from the samples of the low-pass quadrature impulse response components $I_i(\tau_k)$ and $Q_i(\tau_k)$ by

$$p_i(\tau_k) = I_i{}^2(\tau_k) + Q_i{}^2(\tau_k), \qquad (1)$$

where i orders the set of profiles along the street and k orders the delay samples of each profile. A specified delay τ_k is the same propagation delay from transmitter to receiver for all profiles from a given area because the delay references for both transmitter and receiver were derived from stable clocks.

Average power delay profiles $P_m(\tau_k)$ were computed for 50 consecutive individual profiles from each of the areas m. A 50-profile average is a time-domain description of the GWSSUS communications channel that exists between the base station and the 5-m long street area. The average power delay profile is a bandlimited estimate of Bello's $\overline{g^*(t,\tau)g(t,\tau)}$ for the time-varying medium [4], [5] that occurs when a car moves down the street. Specifically

$$P_m(\tau_k) = \frac{1}{50} \sum_{i=1}^{50} p_i(\tau_k) = \langle |h_m(\tau_k)|^2 \rangle_i \qquad (2)$$

where $h_m(\tau_k)$ is the band-limited bandpass impulse response discussed later and in [3] and m distinguishes the dif-

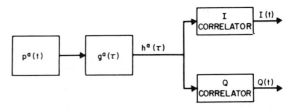

Fig. 2.   Linear system representation of the multipath propagation measurement.

ferent small areas (5-m long street segments) within the $2 \times 2\frac{1}{2}$ km region.

III. TIME-DOMAIN AND FREQUENCY-DOMAIN RELATIONSHIPS

A derivation of the relationships between the time domain measurements and the frequency domain radio channel descriptions is in [3]. Briefly, the measurements described in the preceding section can be modeled by the linear system illustrated in Fig. 2 where $g^a(\tau)$ is the impulse response of the random multipath propagation medium between base station and mobile vehicle and $p^a(t)$ is the real band-limited probing signal. The probe contains both the characteristics of the transmitted carrier ω_0, phase-reversal modulated by the pseudorandom shift-register sequence $s(t)$, and the band-limiting effects of transmitter and receiver filters. In bandpass representation [3]–[5],

$$p^a(t) = 2 \, \mathrm{Re} \, [p^*(t) \exp (j\omega_0 t)]$$
$$= 2p_x(t) \cos (\omega_0 t) + 2p_y(t) \sin (\omega_0 t)$$
$$g^a(\tau) = 2 \, \mathrm{Re} \, [g^*(\tau) \exp (j\omega_0 \tau)]$$
$$= 2g_x(\tau) \cos (\omega_0 \tau) + 2g_y(\tau) \sin (\omega_0 \tau) \qquad (3)$$

where * denotes complex conjugate. The complex envelopes $p(t)$ and $g(\tau)$ comprise the pairs of quadrature components $p_x(\tau)$, $p_y(\tau)$ and $g_x(\tau)$, $g_y(\tau)$, respectively, and

$$p(t) = p_x(t) + jp_y(t)$$
$$g(\tau) = g_x(\tau) + jg_y(\tau). \qquad (4)$$

If $b(\tau)$ is the complex envelope of the impulse response of the transmitter and receiver bandpass filters in cascade then $p(\cdot) = b(\cdot) \star R_s(\cdot)$ where

$$R_s(\tau) = \frac{1}{T} \int_0^t s(t)s(t-\tau)\,dt$$

is the autocorrelation function for the shift register sequence $s(t)$, and $\star$ denotes convolution.

The receiver correlator outputs $I(\tau)$ and $Q(\tau)$ are the quadrature components of the band-limited complex bandpass impulse response envelope $h(\tau)$, where

$$h^a(\cdot) = p^a(\cdot) \star g^a(\cdot)$$
$$h(\cdot) = p(\cdot) \star g(\cdot) \tag{5}$$

and $p^a(t)$ is the band-limited approximation to an impulsive probing signal. That is

$$I(\tau) = \mathrm{Re}\,[p(\cdot) \star g(\cdot)] = \mathrm{Re}\,[h(\tau)]$$

and

$$Q(\tau) = \mathrm{Im}\,[p(\cdot) \star g(\cdot)] = \mathrm{Im}\,[h(\tau)]. \tag{6}$$

The squared envelope of $h(\tau)$ is an individual power delay profile, described in the previous section,

$$|h(\tau)|^2 = I^2(\tau) + Q^2(\tau) \tag{7}$$

and an average power delay profile $P(\tau)$ is then

$$P(\tau) = \langle |h(\tau)|^2 \rangle$$
$$= \langle |p(\cdot) \star g(\cdot)|^2 \rangle$$
$$= \langle I^2(\tau) + Q^2(\tau) \rangle, \tag{8}$$

a band-limited estimate of the average impulse response envelope $\langle |g(\tau)|^2 \rangle$ of the random medium [4], [5]. The brackets $\langle\ \rangle$ indicate averaging over an ensemble of locations chosen uniformly in distance along a street.

A frequency-domain representation of the random multipath propagation medium equivalent to the impulse response $g^a(\tau)$ is the complex transfer function $G^a(\omega)$. These are related by the Fourier transform

$$G^a(\omega) = \int_{-\infty}^{\infty} g^a(\tau) \exp(-j\omega\tau)\,d\tau. \tag{9}$$

Also, for the complex envelope of the bandpass representation,

$$G(\omega) = \int_{-\infty}^{\infty} g(\tau) \exp(-j\omega\tau)\,d\tau. \tag{10}$$

The Fourier transform of $R_s(\tau)$ is the power spectrum of the shift-register sequence $s(t)$ (see [7]). Thus $P(\omega)$, the Fourier transform of $p(t)$, is the filtered complex power spectrum of the probe,

$$P(\omega) = \int_{-\infty}^{\infty} p(t) \exp(-j\omega t)\,dt. \tag{11}$$

A frequency-domain equivalent of the average impulse response is the magnitude of the correlation function of the complex transfer function $|R_G{}^a(\omega)| = |\langle G^a(\omega+q)G^{*a}(q)\rangle|$. It is readily shown [3], [9] that $\langle |h(\tau)|^2 \rangle$ and $R_G{}^a(\omega)$ are related by the Fourier transform

$$\left| \int_{-\infty}^{\infty} \langle |h(\tau)^2| \rangle \exp(-j\omega\tau)\,d\tau \right| = (1/4\pi)\,|R_G{}^a(\omega)|$$
$$\cdot \left| \int_{-\infty}^{\infty} p^a(\omega+q)P^{*a}(q)\,dq \right| \tag{12}$$

if $G^a(q)$ is a random process which is stationary in the frequency variable q. The term

$$\left| \int_{-\infty}^{\infty} p^a(\omega+q)P^{*a}(q)\,dq \right|$$

is the correlation function of the power spectrum of the probe including all filters. This function readily can be obtained by running the transmitter and receiver back-to-back with only a single path of approximately 0 delay (relative to the probe width of 0.1 μs) between them. For this case $g_s{}^a(\tau) = \delta(\tau)$, $G_s{}^a(\omega) = 1$, and

$$\left| \int_{-\infty}^{\infty} \langle |h_s(\tau)|^2 \rangle \exp(-j\omega\tau)\,d\tau \right| = (1/4\pi)$$
$$\cdot \left| \int_{-\infty}^{\infty} P^a(\omega+q)P^{*a}(q)\,dq \right|. \tag{13}$$

Thus, at least for values of frequency separation for which the transform of the measured $\langle |h(\tau)|^2 \rangle$ is significantly greater than the measurement signal-to-noise ratio, the transform can be adjusted for the finite bandwidth of the probe by dividing it by the transform of the back-to-back $\langle |h_s(\tau)|\rangle^2$. It is obvious that for correlation values down to 0.5 the adjustment is very accurate for any reasonable-measurement signal-to-noise ratio.

If the width of $|P^a(\omega)|$ is significantly larger than the width of $|R_G{}^a(\omega)|$, i.e., the probe pulse width is narrow compared to the width of the impulse response, then good estimates of these quantities are obtained from the measured $h_i(\tau)$.

IV. EXPERIMENTAL RESULTS

Fig. 3(a) is an average power delay profile from Broome Street between Lafayette and Crosby. This profile is typical of profiles with moderate values of delay spread and correlation bandwidth as defined later. The profile was taken along the street in the foreground of Fig. 3(c). The transmitter was to the left looking in the direction the photo was taken. This street is typical of the 10 to 20 m wide streets with up to 10-story buildings listed in Table I. The 0 excess delay in this and all other profiles is at the delay of the first signal arrival. For Fig. 3(a), 0 excess delay is 4.7-μs absolute delay from the transmitter to the receiver.[1] The dotted curve that is nearly the same as the solid average profile curve is the standard deviation of the power fluctuations at each fixed delay relative to the peak of the average profile. For a Rayleigh distribution of the fluctuations, the mean and standard deviation

---

[1] The range marks in Fig. 1 are there to show approximate relationships in the measuring region. The map distances are only approximate.

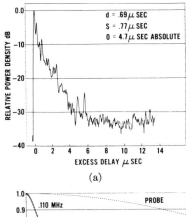

(a)

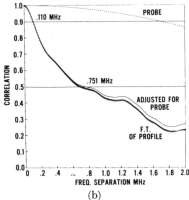

(b)

(c)

Fig. 3.   (a) Average power delay profile for Broome Street between Lafayette and Crosby. (b) Magnitudes of frequency correlation functions for Broome Street between Lafayette and Crosby. (c) Broome Street looking west toward the intersection of Broome and Lafayette Streets.

curves should coincide. The closeness of the two curves for most of the experimental plots indicates that the complex Gaussian (Rayleigh envelope) process is a good model for these channels.

A measure of the width of an average power delay profile that is relevant in assessing the impact on communication system performance is delay spread [4], [10], [12] s_m, defined as the square root of the second central moment of a profile m. In terms of the measured quantities,

$$s_m \triangleq \left[\sum_{k=1}^{725} (\tau_k - d_m - \tau_A)^2 P_m(\tau_k) / \sum_{k=1}^{725} P_m(\tau_k) \right]^{1/2}$$

where k ranges over 14.5 μs of the 15-μs measuring window, $\tau_{k+1} - \tau_k = 0.02$ μs, and d_m is the average excess delay, the first moment of the profile with respect to the first arrival delay τ_A, defined as

$$d_m \triangleq \frac{\sum_{k=1}^{725} \tau_k P_m(\tau_k)}{\sum_{k=1}^{725} P_m(\tau_k)} - \tau_A.$$

Communication system performance limitations caused by multipath propagation are not very sensitive to the shape of the power delay profiles but are quite sensitive to s_m [10], [12]. The average excess delay is the average delay measuring error that would occur in a narrow-band CW ranging system operating over the channel represented by the average power delay profile [11]. Statistics of delay and delay spread are presented in [1].

The curve through the 0's in Fig. 3(b) is the first 2 MHz of the magnitude of the Fourier transform of the average power-delay profile in Fig. 3(a). This function is the magnitude of the frequency-correlation function of the fluctuations in the complex-transfer function of this medium including the probe effects,

$$| R_{G^a}(\omega) | \cdot \left| \int_{-\infty}^{\infty} P^a(\omega + q) P^{*a}(q) \, dq \right|.$$

It is equivalent to the magnitude of the correlation between the complex envelopes of two CW signals separated in frequency by the amount shown on the horizontal axis and sent through the same medium, including the transmitter and the receiver filters.

The dashed curve is the magnitude of the Fourier transform of the probing pulse alone,

$$\left| \int_{-\infty}^{\infty} P^a(\omega + q) P^{*a}(q) \, dq \right|$$

obtained by transforming the power-delay profile for the equipment running back-to-back including all filters but no multipath. The solid curve represents the medium effects after the experimental curve has been adjusted for the effects of the probe. This adjustment is done by dividing the ordinate value of the experimental curve by the ordinate value of the probe spectrum at the same frequency separation since the correlation function for the measurement is the product of the probe spectrum and the correlation function of the transfer function of the medium alone (see the preceding section). It is readily apparent that the probe effects are not significant, i.e., the probe pulse has a wide enough bandwidth, and the resolution is adequate. In the absence of noise, this procedure could be carried out at all frequency separations, and the inverse transform taken to yield the power-delay profile for the medium alone. Noise always prevents this from being accomplished in a practical experimental situation.

The correlation bandwidth B_c at a correlation c is a frequency domain parameter that is relevant in assessing the impact of multipath propagation on communication system performance [10], [12]. (B_c is sometimes called coherence bandwidth.) Statistics are presented later for B_c at correlation levels of 0.9 and 0.5 taken from the frequency correlation functions with the probe effects removed as in the solid curve on Fig. 3(b).

The noise level of the average power delay profiles is always more than 30 dB below the peak level of the profiles. Thus, to insure that noise did not contribute in the calculation of s_m, d_m, and the Fourier transforms, $P_m(\tau_k)$ was set to 0 for all $P_m(\tau_k) < \max(P_m(\tau_k))/1000$. That is, $P_m(\tau_k)$ was truncated 30 dB below the maximum profile value $\max(P_m(\tau_k))$. Of course, in the calculations, the values of $P_m(\tau_k)$ are relative power levels, not levels expressed in decibels.

Fig. 4 is a scatter plot of delay spread versus correlation bandwidth at 0.9 correlation for 100 different small areas (5 m street segments), that is, 100 different GWSSUS channels, within the $2 \times 2\frac{1}{2}$ km region in Fig. 1. They represent 5000 individual complex impulse responses or 7 250 000 individual data samples. Two of the 100 points do not appear on the figure because of excessively large values of $B_{0.9}$. If all profiles and correlation functions had the same shape, the data points would lie along a straight line. The scatter in the points show the phenomena observed in the profiles and correlation functions. Some profiles and correlation functions, Fig. 3 for example, exhibit a relatively smooth decrease in scattered power with increasing excess delay and a relatively smooth decrease in correlation with increasing frequency while others, Figs. 6 and 9 for example, have quite "spikey" profiles with corresponding oscillatory behavior in the correlation function. Smooth decreases are more often associated with low to moderate s and large $B_{0.9}$ while large values of s and small $B_{0.9}$ are usually produced by one or more intense reflections (spikes in the profile) at large excess delays (see Fig. 6). However, the data points do indicate the strong correlation between s and $B_{0.9}$ which is expected since they are parameters related through the Fourier transform. The dashed line at $B_{0.9} = 90/s$ is the least-square fit line to the logarithm of the points. ($B_{0.9}$ proportional to $1/s$ would be expected if all profiles were of similar shape.) The points on the scatter plot have been identified with distance from the transmitter as indicated in the key. The letters indicate points with locations indicated in Table II. The data points on Fig. 4 connected by light lines (either straight or with kinks) indicate data from small areas that are either within the same midblock or within the same intersection, the small areas are separated between 10 and 30 m apart. The light lines connecting the data points were drawn to avoid the unrelated data points so the line positions are not significant. One is tempted to claim a significant distance dependence for s and $B_{0.9}$ but we believe that the observed differences in values for the different locations are caused predominantly by differences in the street characteristics rather than by distance from the trans-

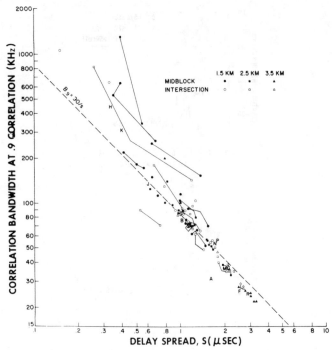

Fig. 4. Scatter plot of correlation bandwidth at 0.9 correlation versus delay spread.

TABLE II
LETTERED POINT LOCATIONS

Lettered Points	Location
A	Intersection of Lafayette and Prince
B	Intersection of Lafayette and Broome
C	Intersection of Lafayette and Canal
D	Intersection of Lafayette and Pearl
E	Lafayette Between Howard and Canal
F	Intersection of Bowery and Prince
G	Bowery Between Houston and Prince
H	Intersection of Ave. of Americas and Charlton
J	Intersection of Ave. of Americas and King
K	Ave. of Americas Between Charlton and King
L	Intersection of Bowery and Stanton
M	Intersection of Bowery and Houston
N	Broadway Between Reade and Chambers
P	Broadway Between Reade and Chambers
Q	Intersection of Broadway and Reade
R	Intersection of Bowery and Spring
S	Intersection of Ave. of Americas and Spring

mitter. For example, 14th Street at 3.5 km radius has the tallest buildings and is a wide street whereas, in contrast, all the streets at 1.5 km radius are narrow and have 5–10 story buildings (see Table I).

Fig. 5 is a similar scatter plot for s versus $B_{0.5}$. There are 24 points out of the set of 100 missing from Fig. 5 because they had excessive values of $B_{0.5}$ and large values of correlation are not usually of interest. The larger scatter of points indicates a lower correlation between s and $B_{0.5}$. The comments to Fig. 4 are appropriate, in general, to this figure also. The line $B_{0.5} = 490/s^{1.3}$ is the least-squares fit line to the logarithm of the points on the figure.

Examples of average power delay profiles and frequency correlation functions distributed through the data set are illustrated in Figs. 6–9. Symbols, etc., for these figures

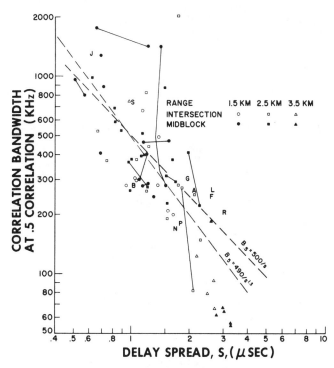

Fig. 5. Scatter plot of correlation bandwidth at 0.5 correlation versus delay spread.

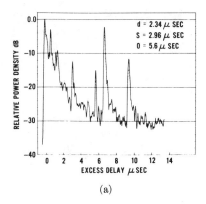

(a)

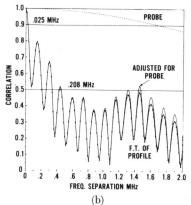

(b)

(c)

Fig. 6. (a) Average power delay profile for the intersection of Bowery and Spring Streets. (b) Magnitude of frequency correlation functions for the intersection of Bowery and Spring Streets. (c) Looking south on Bowery near Houston Street.

are the same as Fig. 3. The profile in Fig. 6(a) and corresponding correlation function in Fig. 6(b) are from the areas designated with the letter R in Table II and the figures. This area is an example with large s and small $B_{0.9}$ that does not come from 14th Street 3.5 km from the transmitter. It serves to illustrate that such extreme cases are not the result of a unique situation but do occur elsewhere. (Areas with $s > 2$ μs also were found at the lower end of Manhattan [2].) Fig. 6(c) is a photo looking south on Bowery into the area where data for Fig. 6(a) and (b) were taken. The transmitter was to the right.

Fig. 7(a) and (b) are from an area with small s and large $B_{0.9}$. This area, in the foreground of Fig. 7(c), is relatively free from multipath propagation. The transmitter was to the left.

Figs. 8(a) and (b) and 9(a) and (b) have values of s and $B_{0.9}$ intermediate between those of Fig. 3 and of Figs. 6 and 7. They are both from small areas on Houston Street but they have quite different characteristics in their average power delay profiles and frequency correlation functions and have significantly different values of s, 1.2 and 2.1 μs, and $B_{0.9}$, 70 and 35 kHz. Fig. 8 is an example that has a delayed path with less attenuation than the minimum delay path and a smoothly decreasing frequency correlation function. Fig. 9 has a relatively long delayed path with nearly the same attenuation as the minimum delay path. The corresponding frequency correlation function has the large amplitude oscillatory behavior that would be expected for such a channel with two dominant paths. This oscillation also points out the hazards involved in measuring correlation functions in this type of medium by transmitting CW signals, varying their frequency separation, and measuring correlation between the envelopes or complex envelopes. It seems

that the risk of missing the first minimum in the correlation function would be high. The areas for Figs. 8 and 9 are both along the street in Fig. 8(c); the Fig. 8 area is in the foreground and the Fig. 9 area is about 2 blocks further down the street.

Fig. 10 is a delay spread histogram for the 100 areas. Again, the midblock and intersection data for the circumferential streets at 1.5, 2.5, and 3.5 km from the transmitter and the lettered points (Table II) have been tagged as indicated in the key. Figs. 11 and 12 are similar histograms for $B_{0.9}$ and $B_{0.5}$. From these histograms it is evident that the largest values of s and smallest values of $B_{0.9}$ and $B_{0.5}$ are contributed by areas along Bowery and along a 3.5 km radius along 14th Street. These large

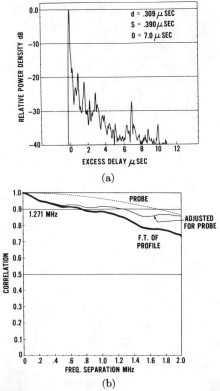

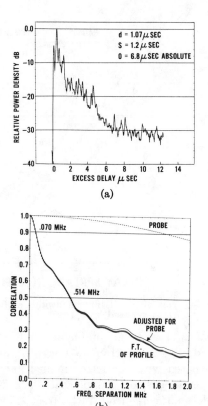

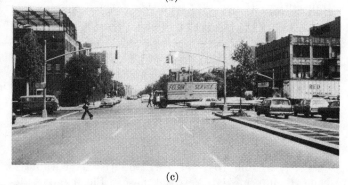

Fig. 7. (a) Average power delay profile for Carmine Street between 7th Avenue and Bedford Street. (b) Magnitude of frequency correlation functions for Carmine Street between 7th Avenue and Bedford Street. (c) Carmine Street looking west toward the intersection of Carmine and Bedford Streets.

Fig. 8. (a) Average power delay profile for Houston Street between Mott and Mulberry Streets. (b) Magnitude of frequency correlation functions for Houston Street between Mott and Mulberry Streets. (c) Houston Street looking west towards the intersection of Houston and Mott Streets.

value "tails" of the distributions, that fluctuate because of the small number of samples, are quite sensitive to the number of samples from these areas. These large values are also the ones that significantly limit system performance. The restrictions placed on system design by the "tails" of these distributions definitely must be considered but fine design lines should not be drawn because of the small-sample-size fluctuations. It should be noted that large values of s and small values of B_c are not unique to those areas. Values of s in the Wall Street area [2] (south of the transmitter) were up to 2.5 μs. In suburban areas [3], [7] values of s up to 2 μs, of $B_{0.9}$ down to 40 kHz, and of $B_{0.5}$ down to 90 kHz were observed.

Fig. 13 is the cumulative distribution for the delay spread data in Fig. 10. A log normal distribution on these coordinates is a straight line. At this time there is no theoretical basis for predicting the shape of the delay spread distribution but a log-normal law often is followed over long intervals over which nonstationarity exists in the small-area statistics [13]. (The set of data points actually fit a square root-normal distribution very closely but there is no reason to think this is anything but fortuitous.) There is some suggestion of saturation of the distribution for large delay spreads ($s > 3$ μs). This may be a result of insufficient measuring window width for some of the large delay spread profiles [1]. If this were

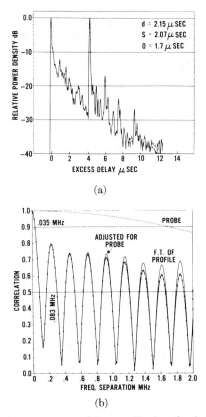

(a)

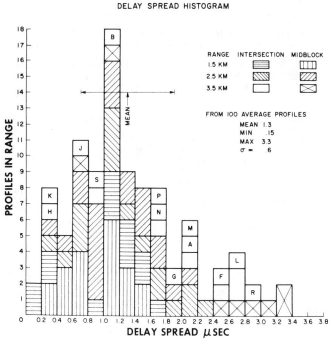

(b)

Fig. 9. (a) Average power delay profile for the intersection of Houston and Lafayette Streets. (b) Magnitude of frequency correlation function for the intersection of Houston and Lafayette Streets.

DELAY SPREAD HISTOGRAM

Fig. 10. Delay spread histogram.

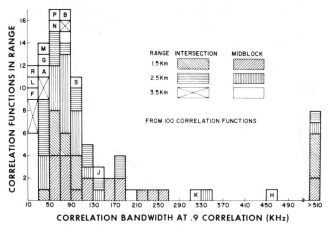

Fig. 11. Histogram of correlation bandwidth at 0.9 correlation.

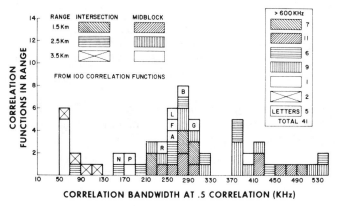

Fig. 12. Histogram of correlation bandwidth at 0.5 correlation.

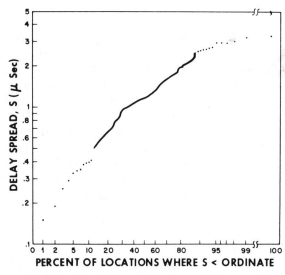

Fig. 13. Cumulative distribution of delay spread.

the case, the extreme tails (<5 percent of the data) of the distribution may have even larger s than indicated. From the distribution 10 percent of the areas have $s >$ 2.5 μs and 50 percent have $s >$ 1.2 μs. To try to determine the percentage or delay spread to any more precision is unreasonable because of small sample fluctuations.

Fig. 14 is the corresponding cumulative distribution for $B_{0.9}$. This distribution does not appear to be log-normal. The suggestion of possible saturation due to insufficient window width again appears at the small bandwidth end of the distribution. From the distribution 10 percent of the areas have $B_{0.9} <$ 30 kHz and 50 percent have $B_{0.9} <$ 70 kHz.

Delay spread and correlation bandwidth have significant impact on communications systems performance as mentioned in the introduction. Limitations on the

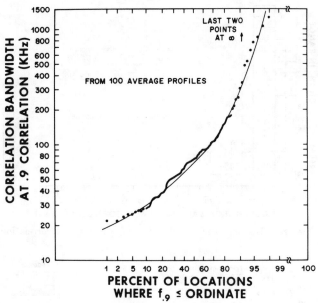

Fig. 14. Cumulative distribution of correlation bandwidth at 0.9 correlation.

From 100 average profiles (label in figure)

LAST TWO POINTS AT ∞ ↑ (label in figure)

CORRELATION BANDWIDTH AT .9 CORRELATION (KHz) (vertical axis)

PERCENT OF LOCATIONS WHERE f_9 ≤ ORDINATE (horizontal axis)

irreducible error rate for digital transmission over non-equalized channels, on distortion in FM systems, and on diversity system performance can be determined from Figs. 13 or 14 using analytical results in [5], [10], [12], and [13] or many others in the open literature.

V. CONCLUSIONS

For 100 small areas in a 2×2.5 km region in New York City, the statistics of the 910-MHz GWSSUS channels range up to $3\frac{1}{2}$ μs for delay spread s, range down to 20 kHz for correlation bandwidth at 0.9 correlation $B_{0.9}$, and down to 55 kHz for correlation bandwidth at 0.5 correlation $B_{0.5}$. Of more concern from the standpoint of system design are the extremes of the distributions where over 10 percent of the areas (GWSSUS channels) exhibit $s > 2\frac{1}{2}$ μs, $B_{0.9} < 30$ kHz, and $B_{0.5} < 130$ kHz. This .region contains wide and narrow streets with low and high buildings and is representative of the heavily built-up downtown areas of many large cities in the United States. Limitations on system performance, such as the irreducible error rate for digital transmission over nonequalized channels, distortion in FM systems, and diversity system performance, can be determined from the distributions presented in this paper using analytical results available in the open literature.

ACKNOWLEDGMENT

The authors would like to thank W. E. Legg, A. J. Rustako, R. R. Murray, and C. O. Stevens for their help in taking the data in New York City and D. Vitello for making the computer plots.

REFERENCES

[1] D. C. Cox and R. P. Leck, "Distribution of multipath delay spread and average excess delay for 910-MHz urban mobile radio paths," *IEEE Trans. Antennas Propagat.*, vol. AP-23, pp. 206–213, Mar. 1975.
[2] D. C. Cox, "910 MHz urban mobile radio propagation: Multipath characteristics in New York City," *IEEE Trans. Commun.*, vol. COM-21, pp. 1188–1194, Nov. 1973.
[3] ——, "Time and frequency domain characterizations of multipath propagation at 910 MHz in a suburban mobile radio environment," *Radio Sci.*, pp. 1069–1077, Dec. 1972.
[4] P. A. Bello, "Characterization of randomly time-variant linear channels," *IEEE Trans. Commun. Syst.*, vol. CS-11, pp. 360–393, Dec. 1963.
[5] P. A. Bello and B. D. Nelin, "The effect of frequency selective fading on intermodulation distortion and subcarrier phase stability in frequency modulation systems," *IEEE Trans. Commun. Syst.*, vol. CS-12, pp. 87–101, Mar. 1964.
[6] D. C. Cox, "A measured delay–Doppler scattering function for multipath propagation at 910 MHz in an urban mobile radio environment," *Proc. IEEE* (Lett.), vol. 61, pp. 479–480, Apr. 1973.
[7] ——, "Delay Doppler characteristics of multipath propagation at 910 MHz in a suburban mobile radio environment," *IEEE Trans. Antennas Propagat.*, vol. AP-20, pp. 625–635, Sept. 1972.
[8] B. B. Barrow, L. G. Abraham, W. M. Cowan, Jr., and R. M. Gallant, "Indirect atmospheric measurements utilizing Rake tropospheric scatter techniques—Part I: The Rake tropospheric scatter technique," *Proc. IEEE*, vol. 57, pp. 537–551, Apr. 1969.
[9] H. E. Rowe and D. T. Young, "Transmission distortion in multimode random waveguides," *IEEE Trans. Microwave Theory Tech.*, vol. MTT-20, pp. 349–365, June 1972.
[10] W. C. Jakes, Ed., *Microwave Mobile Communications.* New York: Wiley, 1974.
[11] J. S. Engel, "Effects of multipath transmission on the measured propagation delay of an FM signal," *IEEE Trans. Veh. Technol.*, vol. VT-18, pp. 44–52, May 1969.
[12] M. J. Gans, "A power-spectral theory of propagation in the mobile-radio environment," *IEEE Trans. Veh. Technol.*, vol. VT-21, pp. 27–38, Feb. 1972.
[13] M. Schwartz, W. R. Bennett, and S. Stein, *Communication Systems and Techniques.* New York: McGraw-Hill, 1966, p. 384.

910 MHz Urban Mobile Radio Propagation: Multipath Characteristics in New York City

DONALD C. COX, SENIOR MEMBER, IEEE

Abstract—Small scale statistics of multipath propagation in a heavily built-up urban mobile radio environment are presented. The statistics cover vehicle travel distances on the order of 30 m along streets. Measuring equipment time delay resolution is about 0.1 μs. In some locations, paths with significant amplitudes are observed with excess delays of 9 to 10 μs. The delay spreads ($\sqrt{\text{second central moment of power delay profile}}$) in this environment are on the order of 2 μs. Often the signal at fixed delays has a Rayleigh-distributed amplitude but large departures from the Rayleigh distribution also occur. From the measurements it appears reasonable to model the urban mobile radio channel as a Gaussian quasi-wide-sense stationary uncorrelated scattering channel within a bandwidth of 10 MHz and for intervals along the street of up to 30 m.

I. INTRODUCTION

THE characteristics of radio propagation between base stations and mobile vehicles place some of the most fundamental constraints on mobile communication systems. The main features of propagation in the urban mobile radio environment are shadowing of the direct or line-of-sight propagation path by intervening buildings and multipath due to scatter or reflection from buildings surrounding the vehicle [1]–[4]. Vehicle motion produces different Doppler shifts on scatter paths arriving at the vehicle from different angles. The time delays and Doppler shifts associated with the multipath propagation can be measured directly by probing the medium with wide bandwidth pulse or pulse-like transmission.

This paper describes some measured characteristics of multipath propagation at 910 MHz in New York City. The data presented describe the "local" statistics of multipath propagation which cover mobile vehicle travel distances on the order of 30 m. Sets of detailed local statistics such as these for heavily built-up urban areas have not been reported previously in the literature.

II. THE MEASUREMENTS

The measurements were made with a wide-band measuring system that used the correlation properties of pseudorandom shift-register sequences. The system is not a pulse system but the measurements are equivalent to measurements made using short RF pulses. The instrumentation is described in detail in [1].

Manuscript received September 6, 1972.
The author is with Bell Laboratories, Holmdel, N.J. 07733.

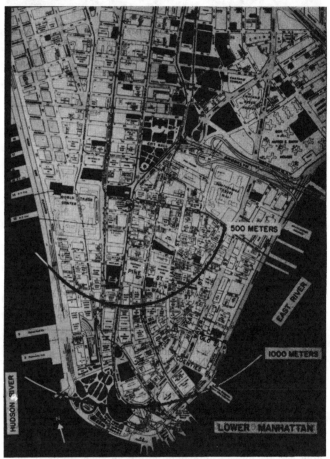

Fig. 1. Map of experimental area on lower Manhattan Island, New York City.

Briefly, a 910 MHz carrier is phase reversal modulated by a pseudorandom shift register sequence and transmitted from an omnidirectional base-station antenna with an elevation beamwidth of about 18°. For these measurements the antenna was located on top of the 120-m high American Telephone and Telegraph building at 195 Broadway, New York City. The transmitter site is marked with an Ⓧ on the map in Fig. 1. Even though by most standards this is a tall building, it is located in an area where many of the buildings surrounding it are considerably taller. Fig. 2 was taken from the building roof near the transmitting antenna looking toward the financial district (Wall Street, etc.) in the general direction of the streets where the data shown later were taken. It is obvious

Reprinted from *IEEE Trans. Commun.*, vol. COM-21, pp. 1188–1194, Nov. 1973.

Fig. 2. Picture looking towards experimental area in financial district from near the transmitting antenna.

from the picture that the transmitter building is tall relative to the streets but not tall relative to its surroundings.

The receiver is installed in a mobile vehicle (medium size modified Cortez self-propelled mobile home about $2\frac{1}{2}$ meters high) and connected to an omnidirectional $\frac{1}{4}$ wavelength vertical antenna on the roof. The signal received in the vehicle is correlated with a replica of the transmitted signal in two quadrature correlators. The two correlator amplitude outputs in time represent amplitude versus time delay for the low-pass quadrature components, $I(\tau)$ and $Q(\tau)$, of bandpass impulse responses of the propagation path [2]. Since transmitter and receiver logic are both driven from precision frequency standards, the absolute delay reference provided by the synchronizing pulse can be maintained to better than 0.05 μs for a few hours. The range of delays included in one impulse response (the delay window) is 15 μs. This 15 μs window can be moved anywhere within an absolute delay range of 0 to 51.1 μs, which corresponds to path delays of 0 to about 15 Km. The squared envelope of the complex impulse response, $p(\tau) = I^2(\tau) + Q^2(\tau)$, is the same power delay profile $p(\tau)$ which would be received if a triangular pulse with base width of 0.2 μs and a repetition rate of 20 kHz were transmitted through all equipment filters and the propagation medium and detected with a square law detector [1]. The delay resolution of the equipment is about 0.1 μs (10 MHz bandwidth RF signal).

Data that includes complex impulse response components, synchronizing pulses, vehicle speed, etc., were recorded on an analog tape recroder in the mobile vehicle while it was driven at 1.4 m/s along streets on lower Manhattan Island, New York City. These data were then sampled, digitized, and stored on a magnetic disc for computer processing. Data shown later are

from Pine Street between Pearl and Williams Streets and from Water Street between Coenties Slip and Old Slip (see Fig. 1). Both street locations have many tall buildings between the transmitting antenna and them, that is, they are behind the tall buildings visible in Fig. 2. Direction of vehicle travel is indicated by the arrows on Fig. 1.

Pine Street is very narrow (10 m between buildings on opposite sides of street) and the tall buildings on both sides form a deep canyon. Water Street is considerably wider (25 m between buildings) but there are many more tall buildings between it and the transmitter. The small-scale statistical data from these streets are representative of data from such heavily built-up areas. The overall average delay spreads obtained probably represent an upper bound on multipath propagation in such an area.

Measurements were made between midnight and about 5:00 A.M. local time when traffic density was low. The most severe scattering centers (longest delays and strongest scattering) are the tall buildings and elevated roadways and these obviously are not affected by traffic. Cars and trucks on the street generally produce only minor multipath effects since they have a relatively small cross section and are also shielded from the transmitting antenna by the large structures. This has been verified in the daytime in heavy traffic. With the receiving vehicle stationary and traffic moving the major features on the power delay profiles remain fixed in delay and amplitude.

Individual Envelope Delay Profiles

The individual envelope delay profiles are plots of received "pulse" (receiver correlation function) amplitude as a function of path delay referred to a fixed absolute delay reference, that is, they are the envelope of the bandpass impulse response of the propagation medium [1], [2] or $\sqrt{p(\tau)}$ where $p(\tau)$ was briefly discussed earlier.

Fig. 3(a) is an envelope delay profile for a line-of-sight path relatively free of multipath propagation. (Data for this profile were taken in a suburban area free of buildings, etc.) It illustrates the equipment resolution and delay window. Fig. 3(b), (c), and (d) are profiles from different locations in New York City, as labeled. The horizontal scales are excess propagation delay in μs from the minimum delay propagation path. The vertical scales are linear in amplitude (voltage). These three profiles are selected bad examples that occur relatively infrequently over relatively short intervals of street. They are not unique however. Note that the paths with long excess delays are of almost equal strength compared to the paths with nearly minimum delay. This is largely due to "fading" of the shorter delay paths at these locations.

Fig. 4 contains three sequences of individual envelope delay profiles taken within a 30 m interval along Pine Street. The profiles in each sequence were taken every 10 cm along the street. Since the delay reference for the measuring system is determined by stable clocks at both the receiver and transmitter and not by triggering on the received signal, the delay measurements are absolute. For the profiles in Fig. 4 the absolute delay to the first arriving "pulse" (the minimum de-

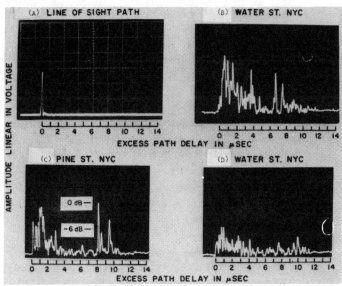

Fig. 3. Individual envelope delay profiles.

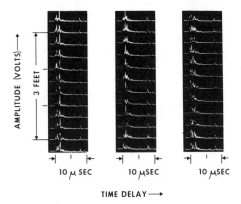

Fig. 4. Three sequences of individual envelope delay profiles from Pine Street.

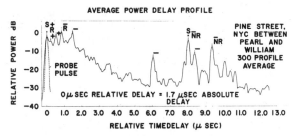

Fig. 5. Average power delay profile from Pine Street.

These profiles can be described by several parameters. The center of gravity or first moment of the profile with respect to the first arrival delay is a measure of the average excess delay D_e. Average excess delay is calculated by

$$D_e \triangleq \frac{\sum_{k=1}^{M} \tau_k P(\tau_k)}{\sum_{k=1}^{M} P(\tau_k)} - \tau_A,$$

where M is the index of the last sample along the delay axis which has a significant amplitude and $k = 1$ is a point before the minimum arrival delay τ_A at which the profile amplitude is insignificant. The locations of $k = 1$ and M are chosen so that moving the $k = 1$ point to smaller delay values or moving the last sample to larger delay values does not affect the value of D_e. Average excess delay is related to the average ranging error that would occur in narrowband CW phase ranging systems [5].

The square root of the second central moment is one possible measure of the delay spread S or width of a power delay profile. It is calculated

$$S \triangleq \sqrt{\frac{\sum_{k=1}^{M} (\tau_k - D_e)^2 P(\tau_k)}{\sum_{k=1}^{M} P(\tau_k)}},$$

where the parameters are as defined previously. Other measures of width, such as delay between outer -3 dB or -10 dB points are also useful from some profiles. Delay spread sets limits on many communication system performance parameters, as indicated in [1].

Fig. 5 is an average power delay profile from Pine Street, New York City. The horizontal axis is excess delay with the zero set at approximately the minimum delay path which is an absolute delay of 1.7 μs. This profile is the average of 300 consecutive individual profiles, including those in Fig. 4, covering about 30 m of travel along the street. The vertical scale is linear in dB relative to the maximum. The total power received from paths with excess delay less than 1.5 μs is much greater than that from paths with excess delays of 8 to 10 μs. Thus the effects of these extreme paths will not be as great on the average as would be the case for nearly equal received powers at 0 and 9 μs excess delays. This fact is further illustrated by the delay spread of 2.5 μs for this profile (see

lay path) is 1.7 μs. Note that the paths near the minimum delay path exhibit deep and rapid fading, indicating the existence of multiple propagation paths within the 0.1 μs resolution of the measurement. For some profiles the strongest path is the minimum delay path but for many others it is a path with excess delay of up to about 1.5 μs. The paths with excess delays of 8 to 9 μs are relatively stable.

Average Power Delay Profiles

Sampled individual power delay profiles $p_i(\tau_k)$ were computed by $p_i(\tau_k) = I_i^2(\tau_k) + Q_i^2(\tau_k)$ where the i orders the set of profiles along the street and k orders the delay samples of each profile. A specified delay τ_k is the same propagation delay from transmitter to receiver for all profiles of a given profile set. The profiles shown in the previous figures were plots of individual $p_i(\tau)$ for various values of i.

An average power delay profile $P(\tau_k)$ for a set of N consecutive individual profiles is then computed as

$$P(\tau_k) = \frac{1}{N} \sum_{i=1}^{N} p_i(t_k) = \langle |h(\tau_k)|^2 \rangle i,$$

where $h(\tau_k)$ is the bandpass impulse response discussed in [2].

TABLE I

Profile Location	Average Excess Delay (μs)	Average Absolute Delay (μs)	Minimum Absolute Delay (μs)	Delay Spread S (μs)	Profile Width −3 dB (μs)	Profile Width −10 dB (μs)	Number of Profiles Averaged
Pine Street	1.9	3.6	1.7	2.53	1.5	9.6	300
Water Street, 1	1.6	4.3	2.7	1.95	0.14	3.3	270
Water Street, 2	2.4	5.3	2.9	2.19	0.8	7.4	270

Table I). (Two discrete equal strength paths with excess delays of 0 and 9 μs would have a delay spread of 4.5 μs.)

The average power delay profile in Fig. 6 is an average of 270 consecutive individual profiles covering a 27 m interval along Water Street. The excess delay axis 0 is at an absolute delay of 2.72 μs.

Table I summarizes the characteristics of the profiles in Figs. 5 and 6 along with another one from a nearby location, 2, on Water Street. Absolute delay is calibrated to about ±0.1 μs.

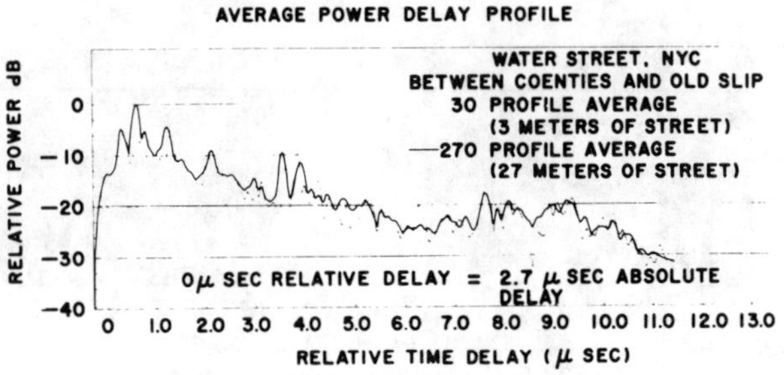

Cumulative Distribution of Signal Level at Fixed Delays

The amplitude at fixed delays for a series of individual envelope delay profiles, such as in Fig. 4, is observed to fluctuate (to fade) from profile to profile. This fading was also observed in profiles taken at 910 MHz in suburban areas [1] and in urban areas at 450 MHz with wider (1/2 μs) probing pulses [3] and is attributed to unresolved multiple propagation paths. The actual distributions of signal level at several fixed delays for the 300 profiles whose average profile is Fig. 5 are plotted in Fig. 7. The solid straight line in Fig. 7 is for a Rayleigh distribution. The distributions for the signals at 0 μs and 0.82 μs approximate a Rayleigh distribution within about 2 dB over a 30 dB range. The paths with excess delays of 8.02 and 9.34 μs are relatively stable with total amplitude fluctuation of less than 15 dB (less than 10 dB at 9.34 μs). On Fig. 5 the symbols ○, ●, □, and ■ and the letters R or NR refer the data at the indicated delays to the distributions on Fig. 7. The R and NR indicate Rayleigh and non-Rayleigh distributed signal fluctuations, respectively. The row of open squares at 99.67 percent on Fig. 7 are quantization effects due to the small finite sample (299 samples out of 300 is 99.67 percent).

Doppler Spectra at Fixed Delays

Scattered signals arriving at the measuring vehicle will be Doppler shifted by different amounts depending on the angle that the arrival path makes with the direction of vehicle travel [8]. When the Doppler shift is expressed in units of cycles/m of vehicle travel, it is not dependent on actual vehicle velocity. (Conversion to units of Hz requires only multiplication by vehicle velocity in m/s.) Signals arriving from scatters directly ahead of the vehicle will be shifted higher in frequency (positive) by the maximum amount 1/λ where λ is the wavelength of the signal; those directly behind will be shifted negatively by the same amount.

Since the equipment used in this experiment uses quadrature coherent detection and stable frequency references, the RF carrier Doppler shifts associated with various scatter paths can

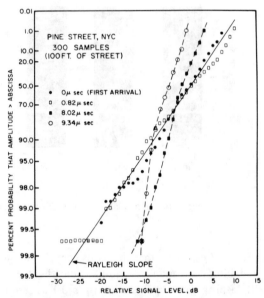

Fig. 6. Average power delay profile from Water Street.

Fig. 7. Cumulative signal level distributions at fixed delays from Pine Street.

be measured. This Doppler shift information is useful in communication system analysis and for further resolving the multipath structure of the media, since paths having nearly the same time delay can be separated if they arrive from different angles. For example, if an adaptive equalizer were built to equalize the multipath on a mobile radio channel for wideband digital data, the bandwidth of the data signal and the spread in time delays of the paths would determine the number of taps required on the equalizer but the Doppler shifts associated with the paths determine the rate at which the tap gains must be adjusted, i.e., the equalization rate required.

Fig. 8(a) is the RF Doppler spectrum of the signal at the fixed excess delay of 0 μs for the 30 m of street represented in Fig. 5. It was obtained by complex Fourier transforming the measured $I_i(\tau)$ and $Q_i(\tau)$ samples at 0 μs delay for $i = 1$ to 300 after they had been multiplied by a Hamming window to reduce spectrum sidelobes. The lower horizontal scale is fre-

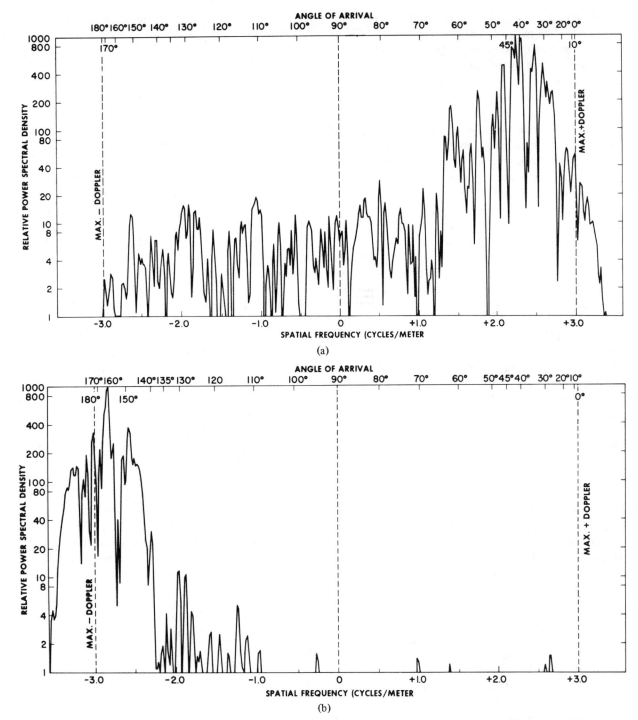

Fig. 8. (a) RF Doppler spectrum at 0 μs excess delay on Pine Street. (b) RF Doppler spectrum at 8.02 μs excess delay on Pine Street.

quency offset from center frequency (910 MHz) in cycles/m of travel. The approximate maximum possible plus and minus shifts are indicated by the vertical dashed lines. The vertical scale is a logarithmic relative power scale. Since the Doppler frequency shift is proportional to the cosine of the angle of arrival of the incoming wave referred to the direction of vehicle travel, the frequency scale can be converted to an angle of arrival scale. This angle of arrival scale is the upper horizontal scale on the figure. The angle specifies a cone only so it is not possible to differentiate between paths arriving from the

right or left. Noise and spurious responses are about 30 dB below the spectral maximum. Hamming window sidelobes are about 40 dB below the maximum. Vehicle velocity could not be held constant within the spectrum resolution of the sample and the equipment frequency stability. The general "multiple peaked" nature of the overall spectral peaks is due to discontinuities in measuring vehicle velocity which result from irregularities in the street surface.

Fig. 8(b) is the equivalent RF Doppler spectrum at 8.02 μs delay. The relative power scale is referred to the same level as

Fig. 8(a). At 8.02 μs the average received power is about 2.3 dB below the average received power at 0 μs (see Fig. 5) but the maximum value of the two spectra [Fig. 8(a) and (b)] are nearly the same. These observations are not inconsistent because there is a significant amount of power spread out over a relatively large frequency range at 0 excess delay but at 8.02 μs the power is very concentrated in frequency. The total power integrated over the entire Doppler range can be greater then even though the maxima are equal. Spectra at other delays have different maximum values. Independent accurate measurement of vehicle velocity, recorded simultaneously with the data, indicate that changes of velocity on the order of that required to produce the broadening of one peak into the jagged series of peaks near the maximum negative Doppler shift in Fig. 8(b) did occur during the data run.

On Fig. 5, the letter S above the profile at 0 and 8 μs indicates the position of these spectra on the delay profile. The associated + and – indicate the direction (+ is up in frequency) of the frequency shift of the strongest peak in the Doppler spectrum at that delay. The + and – signs and arrows at other delays on Fig. 5 indicate the direction of shift of the strongest peak for spectra not included in this paper.

It is interesting to speculate on the sources of reflection or scatter that produce the dominant features on a power profile, taking into account the map (Fig. 1), knowledge of the environment, and the RF Doppler spectra. For example, at excess delays of 0 to about 0.5 μs in Fig. 5 most of the energy arrives from ahead of the vehicle (+ Doppler shift). This energy is "forward" scattered or reflected from buildings ahead of the vehicle. The weakness of the signal at 0 excess delay, the severe shadowing of the vehicle on Pine Street, and the fact that the measured absolute delay appears slightly greater than the map distance to the street suggest that this minimum delay path is also due to reflection from a building ahead of and very close to the vehicle. Most of the energy from 0.8 μs on out in excess delay comes from directly behind the vehicle (approximately maximum negative Doppler shift). This is consistent with the fact that the end of Pine Street is blocked off by buildings at Broadway so that single reflection paths with excess delays greater than 0.7 μs are not possible from ahead of the vehicle. Backscatter from buildings between the vehicle and the East River accounts for the paths between 0.5 and 1.5 μs. A single reflection path from structures along the East River first occurs at about 1.5 μs excess delay. Thus, the decrease in scattered power from 1.5 μs to about 8 μs is caused by the East River open area. Note also that even if Pine Street were not blocked off at Broadway, this decrease of scattered power would probably occur because the Hudson River open area would start at about 2.0 μs. Paths in the 2 to 6 μs region are probably due to multiple reflections. The strong paths near 8 μs excess delay correspond to the first reflections from the "leading edge" of Brooklyn. The near maximum negative Doppler shift indicates that the energy reflected from Brooklyn is traveling straight down the street from behind the vehicle. Paths with greater than 8 μs excess delay result from tall structures further along the waterfront or back from the water in Brooklyn. The relatively strong path at 6 μs does not cor-respond to any known structure in the East River. It could be caused by a ship but is more likely due to multiple reflections.

III. CONCLUSIONS

Small scale statistics of multipath propagation at 910 MHz in a heavily built-up area have been presented. In some locations paths with significant amplitudes are observed with excess delays of 9 to 10 μs. The delay spreads ($\sqrt{}$second central moment of power delay profile) for these areas are 2 to $2\frac{1}{2}$ μs. For excess delays up to 1 or 2 μs considerable energy arrives, via paths at different angles to the vehicle, which cannot be resolved by the 0.1 μs resolution probe. This results in envelope fading at fixed excess delays as the vehicle moves along a street. The fading is approximately Rayleigh distributed. Although the inference is not unique [6] the Rayleigh-distributed envelope suggests modeling of the process as a Gaussian random process. Correlation of the fading envelope at different excess delays has not been computed but visual inspection of sequences of individual envelope delay profiles suggests that the correlation is very low. Also, the Doppler spectra at different delays are quite different. All Doppler spectra cutoff abruptly at spatial frequencies of $\pm 1/\lambda$. Thus, from the results of the delay and Doppler measurements it appears reasonable to model the urban mobile radio channel as a Gaussian quasi-wide-sense stationary uncorrelated scattering channel [7], at least within a bandwidth of 10 MHz and for intervals along a street of up to 30 m. Usually for intervals of over 50 to 100 m of travel along a street the multipath scattering process becomes grossly nonstationary as dominant scatterers and shadowing features (buildings, etc.) change. It appears that joint distributions of average received power and delay spread for a collection of average power delay profiles would be useful in computing system performance on a statistical basis over a large area.

ACKNOWLEDGMENT

The author would like to thank W. E. Legg, A. J. Rustako, R. M. Murray, and C. O. Stevens for their help in taking the data in New York City and W. E. Legg for his help in the data reduction.

REFERENCES

[1] D. C. Cox, "Delay Doppler characteristics of multipath propagation at 910 MHz in a suburban mobile radio environment," *IEEE Trans. Antennas Propagat.*, vol. AP-20, pp. 625–635, Sept. 1972.
[2] ——, "Time and frequency domain characterizations of multipath propagation at 910 MHz in a suburban mobile radio environment," *Radio Sci.*, Dec. 1972.
[3] W. R. Young, Jr. and L. Y. Lacy, "Echoes in transmission at 450 megacycles from land-to-car radio units," *Proc. IRE*, vol. 38, pp. 255–258, Mar. 1950.
[4] G. L. Turin, F. D. Clapp, T. L. Johnston, S. B. Fine, and D. Lavry, "A statistical model of urban multipath propagation," *IEEE Trans. Veh. Technol.*, vol. VT-21, pp. 1–9, Feb. 1972.
[5] J. S. Engel, "Effects of multipath transmission on the measured propagation delay of an FM signal," *IEEE Trans. Veh. Technol.*, vol. VT-18, pp. 44–52, May 1969.
[6] S. H. Lin, "The cumulative amplitude distributions of fading signals," presented at the U.S. Nat. Comm. of URSI 1971 Spring

Meeting, Apr. 8-10, 1971, Washington, D.C., paper 2-3, Commission II.

[7] P. A. Bello, "Characterization of randomly time-variant linear channels," *IEEE Trans. Commun. Syst.*, vol. CS-11, pp. 360-393, Dec. 1963.

P. A. Bello and B. D. Nelin, "Optimization of subchannel data rate in FDM-SSB transmission over selectively fading media," *IEEE Trans. Commun. Syst.*, vol. CS-12, pp. 46-53, Mar. 1964.

[8] D. C. Cox, "A measured delay-Doppler scattering function for multipath propagation at 910 MHz in an urban mobile radio environment," *Proc. IEEE* (Lett.), vol. 61, pp. 479-480, Apr. 1973.

Multipath Delay Spread and Path Loss Correlation for 910-MHz Urban Mobile Radio Propagation

DONALD C. COX, SENIOR MEMBER, IEEE

Abstract—Performance of some mobile radio systems is limited both by multipath delay spread and average path loss. This paper presents data indicating a low correlation between delay spread and path loss at 910 MHz for 100 small areas within a $2 \times 2\frac{1}{2}$-km region. Some small areas with low path loss have large delay spread. The region extends from 1.5 to 3.5 km from a base station on a 120-m high building in New York City. The region is representative of heavily built-up downtown districts of many large U.S. cities.

I. INTRODUCTION

PREVIOUS papers [1], [2] have presented statistics of time delay spreads for multipath propagation at 910 MHz in the urban mobile environment. This delay spread S affects radio system performance [3]. For example, S limits the irreducible error rate at a specified bit rate for digital transmission or limits the minimum distortion at a specified index for frequency modulation. However, because of the ever-present additive system noise and the economic limits on transmitter power, average path loss L also severely limits system performance because it affects signal-to-noise ratio. Therefore, the correlation between S and L is needed for evaluating the overall performance of some mobile radio systems. For example, if

Manuscript received March 3, 1977. This paper was presented at the Symposium on Microwave Mobile Communications, Boulder, CO, September 29, 1976.

The author is with the Crawford Hill Laboratory, Bell Laboratories, Holmdel, NJ 07733.

some small areas within a large region had large S but small L, the fraction of the region having performance less than a specified objective could be greater than it would be if all areas with large S also had large L. The data presented in this paper show examples of areas with large S that also have small L. Overall the correlation between S and L is low.

II. THE EXPERIMENT AND CHANNEL MODEL

The measurements were made with a wide-band measuring system [4] which uses the correlation properties of pseudo-random shift-register sequences. The probing signal is not a pulse, but the results are equivalent to measurements made using short RF pulses.

Briefly, a 910-MHz carrier stable to a few parts in 10^{-10} is phase reversal modulated by a pseudo-random shift register sequence (9-b register and 10-MHz clock). This signal was transmitted from a vertically polarized collinear antenna array which is omnidirectional in azimuth and has an $18°$ beamwidth in elevation ($\pm 9°$ from horizontal). The transmitting antenna was located 120 m above the street on top of the American Telephone and Telegraph building at 195 Broadway, New York City. This transmitting site was marked with a ⓣon the map of lower Manhattan Island in Fig. 1.

The signal was received with an omnidirectional 1/4 wavelength vertical antenna on the roof of a $2\frac{1}{2}$-m high mobile van driven along the city streets. In the RAKE like receiver [4] the

Reprinted from *IEEE Trans. Veh. Technol.*, vol. VT-26, pp. 340–344, Nov. 1977.

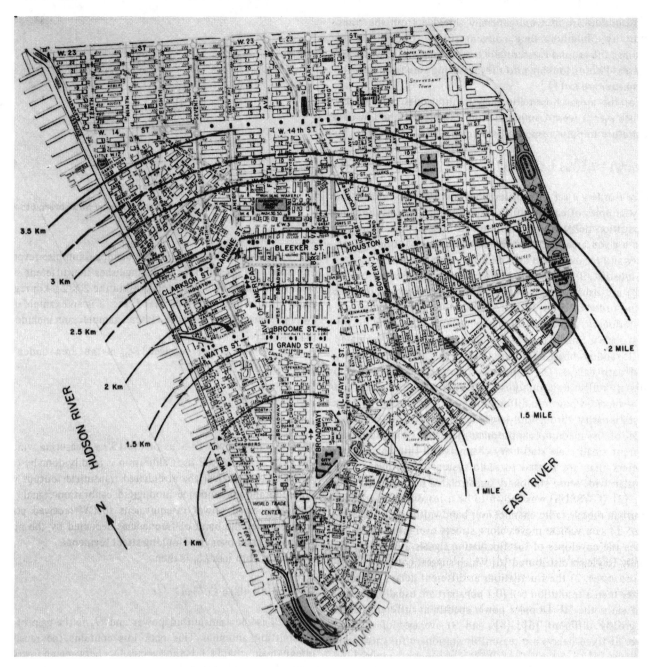

Fig. 1. Map of experimental area on Manhattan Island,
New York City.

received signal is correlated with a replica of the transmitted signal in two quadrature correlators. The correlator outputs represent amplitude versus time delay for the low-pass quadrature components $I(\tau)$ and $Q(\tau)$ of the band-limited bandpass impulse response of the propagation path [2], [5]. A 15 μs delay window for the measurement can be moved anywhere within the delay ambiguity range of 0 to 51.1 μs (511-b sequence $\times$ 0.1 μs/b). The squared envelope of the complex impulse response $p(\tau) = I^2(\tau) + Q^2(\tau)$ is the same power delay profile $p(\tau)$, which would be received if a triangular pulse with a base width of 0.2 μs and a repetition rate of 20 kHz were transmitted through all equipment filters and the propagation medium and detected with a square law detector [4]. The

delay resolution of the equipment is about 0.1 μs (10-MHz band-width RF signal).

Measurements were taken in a 2 $\times$ 2$\frac{1}{2}$-km region ranging from 1.5 to 3.5 km from the transmitter. Data sets were taken from small areas that were either in street intersections (the solid rectangles along oblique and circumferential streets and the solid triangles along radial streets in Fig. 1) or in regions between intersections (midblocks indicated by solid circles and + marks in Fig. 1). Individual complex impulse responses were taken every 10 cm along the streets (for examples see [4] or [6]). About 60 percent of the data are from midblock areas and 40 percent from intersections. Street characteristics are described in [1] and [2]. Even the streets that did not have solid building fronts were generally shielded from the transmitter by buildings along adjacent streets. Except for the buildings the ground is essentially level throughout the measuring area. Photos looking into the measuring area from near the transmitter are in [1].

For the areas chosen for analysis, individual power delay profiles $p_i(\tau_k)$ were computed from samples of the low-pass quadrature impulse response components $I_i(\tau_k)$ and $Q_i(\tau_k)$ by

$$p_i(\tau_k) = I_i^2(\tau_k) + Q_i^2(\tau_k) \qquad (1)$$

where i orders a set of profiles along a street and k orders the delay samples of each profile. A specified delay τ_k is the same propagation delay from transmitter to receiver for all profiles from a given area because the delay references for both transmitter and receiver were derived from stable clocks.

Statistics of the mobile radio channels represented by the $p_i(\tau_k)$ are usually quasi-stationary for vehicle travel distances on the order of 5 to 30 m (small scale) but become grossly nonstationary for distances greater than 20 to 150 m [6] (large scale). Small scale medium fluctuations are dominated by the random phase addition of many signals that have nearly equal path delays. The large scale changes are caused by the different reflecting structures (building, etc.) that contribute to the received power in different regions. Because of the gross nonstationarity throughout large regions a two-step statistical model of the medium is appropriate. The first step is to model different small scale stationary channels and find channel parameters that are related to radio system performance. The Gaussian wide-sense stationary uncorrelated scattering channel [7], [3] (GWSSUS) was shown to be a reasonable model for the urban mobile radio channel over bandwidths up to 10 MHz since: 1) as a vehicle moves along streets over small scale distances the envelopes of the fluctuating signals at fixed τ_k are usually Rayleigh distributed [6] which suggest complex Gaussian processes; 2) the fluctuations at different delays separated greater than a resolution cell (0.1 μs) apart are usually uncorrelated since the RF Doppler power spectra at different delays are grossly different [6], [8]; and 3) averages of received power at fixed delays are reasonably stationary for small scale distances [6] (5–30 m). The GWSSUS channel is a model for a multipath channel made up of independent point scatterers, so physically it describes mobile radio propagation paths quite well too. A time domain channel parameter that limits radio system performance is delay spread S defined later.

As a first step in computing S for small scale areas with quasi-stationary statistics, average power delay profiles $P_m(\tau_k)$ were computed for 50 consecutive individual profiles $p_i(\tau_k)$ from each of the areas m. A 50 profile average is a time domain description of the GWSSUS communications channel that exists between the base station and the 5-m long street area. The average power delay profile or delay power spectrum is a band-limited estimate of Bello's $\overline{g^*(t, \tau)g(t, \tau)}$ for the time varying medium [7] that occurs when a car moves down the street. Specifically,

$$P_m(\tau_k) = \frac{1}{50} \sum_{i=1}^{50} p_i(\tau_k) = \langle |h_m(\tau_k)|^2 \rangle_i \qquad (2)$$

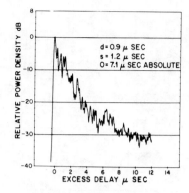

Fig. 2. Average power delay profile for Bleeker St. between 6th Ave. and McDougal St.

where $h_m(\tau_k)$ is the band-limited bandpass impulse response discussed in [2] and [5], m distinguishes the different small areas (5-m long street segments) within the $2 \times 2\frac{1}{2}$-km region, and $\langle \cdot \rangle_i$ indicates an average over i. Fig. 2 is an example of an average power delay profile. Other examples are included in [1] and [2].

The average power received $\overline{P}_m$ is the area under the profile or

$$\overline{P}_m = \sum_{k=1}^{725} P_m(\tau_k) \qquad (3)$$

where k ranges over 14.5 μs of the 15 μs measuring window and $\tau_{k+1} - \tau_k = 0.02$ μs. Calibration is readily done by comparing in the receiver the attenuated transmitter output with a pseudorandom sequence modulated calibration signal. The average received power is equivalent to CW received power averaged over the band of frequencies occupied by the probe ($\approx$10 MHz) and over the 5-m long street segments.

Average path loss L_m is then

$$L_m = [10 \log_{10} P_t/\overline{P}_m] + G_t \qquad (4)$$

where P_t is the transmitted power and G_t is the gain of the transmitting antenna. This path loss contains the receiving antenna gain, that is, it is the average loss between an isotropic base station antenna and the $\lambda/4$ antenna on the mobile van. The transmitting antenna uniformly illuminates (within $\pm\frac{1}{2}$ dB) the $2 \times 2\frac{1}{2}$-km receiving region and all of the buildings, etc., that could produce significant multipath. Therefore, it is reasonable to remove the transmitting antenna gain from the path loss data. The receiving antenna, however, is imbedded deep within the canyons formed by the buildings lining the streets (see [1] and [2] for pictures) so received signals may arrive from any angle. The gain of the receiving antenna is not constant with angle so it is not legitimate[1] to attempt to remove it from the measurement by adding a fixed value.

Delay spread S_m defined as the square root of the second central moment (i.e., the rms width) of a profile m is a meas-

---

[1] The transmitting antenna gain was removed from the path loss data so that it could be applied to other similar cases using equivalent base station antennas with different gains. It is not obvious how to account for different mobile antennas.

ure of profile width that is relevant to communication system performance [3], [7], [9]. Performance limitations caused by multipath propagation are not very sensitive to the shape of the power delay profiles but are quite sensitive to S_m [3], [9]. In terms of measured quantities

$$S_m \triangleq \left(\left[\sum_{k=1}^{725} (\tau_k - d_m - \tau_A)^2 P_m(\tau_k) \right] \Big/ \bar{P}_m \right)^{1/2}$$

where d_m is the average excess delay [1], the first moment of the profile with respect to the first arrival delay τ_A is defined as

$$d_m \triangleq \left[\sum_{k=1}^{725} \tau_k P_m(\tau_k) / \bar{P}_m \right] - \tau_A .$$

The average excess delay is the average delay measuring error that would occur in a narrowband CW ranging system operating over the channel represented by the average power delay profile. Statistics of delay and delay spread are presented in [1].

The noise level of the average power delay profiles is always more than 30 dB below the peak level of the profiles. Thus to insure that noise did not contribute in the calculation of S_m and $\bar{P}_m$, $P_m(\tau_k)$ was set to 0 for all $P_m(\tau_k) < [\max(P_m(\tau_k))] / 1000$. That is, $P_m(\tau_k)$ was truncated 30 dB below the maximum profile value $\max(P_m(\tau_k))$. Of course in the calculations the values of $P_m(\tau_k)$ are power levels, not levels expressed in decibels.

III. THE DATA

The data presented are from average power delay profiles for 100 different small areas (5-m street segments), that is, 100 different GWSSUS channels within the $2 \times 2\frac{1}{2}$-km region in Fig. 1.

Fig. 3 is a scatter plot of delay spread S versus path loss L. The correlation coefficient[2] for these data points is a low -0.4 indicating some trend for delay spread to increase with decreasing path loss. There are, however, several areas with large delay spread and relatively low to moderate loss. The points on the scatter plot have been identified with distance from the transmitter as indicated in the key. The letters indicate points along radial streets and are identified in [1] and [2]. The data points on Fig. 3 connected by light lines (either straight or with kinks) indicate data from small areas that are either within the same midblock or within the same intersection with the small areas separated between 10 and 30 m apart. The light lines connecting the data points were drawn to avoid the unrelated data points so the line positions are not significant.

[2] Correlation coefficient is defined as

$$\left[\sum_m (L_m - \bar{L})(S_m - \bar{S}) \right] \Big/ \left[\sum_m (L_m - \bar{L})^2 \right]^{1/2} \left[\sum_m (S_m - \bar{S})^2 \right]^{1/2}$$

where m ranges over the $m = 100$ areas, $\bar{L} = (1/M) \, \Sigma_m \, L_m$ and $\bar{S} = (1/M) \, \Sigma_m \, S_m$.

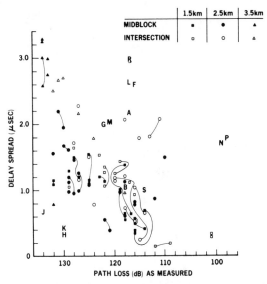

Fig. 3. Scatter plot of delay spread versus measured path loss between isotropic base station antenna and quarter-wave vertical on mobile van.

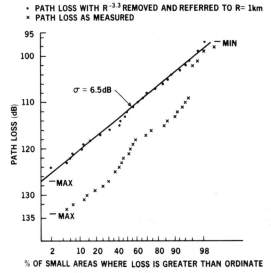

Fig. 4. Cumulative distribution of path loss.

Fig. 4 shows cumulative distributions of L for the 100 small areas. A Gaussian (normal) distribution is a straight line on the plot. The X are the loss as measured with no correction for distance from the transmitter. A linear least squares regression shows an $R^{-3.3}$ dependence of path loss on distance from the transmitter R. This is well within the spread of distance dependences, 3-4, measured by others [3]. Removal of $R^{-3.3}$ and referral of the data to $R = 1$ km yields the · data points which are an excellent fit to a lognormal distribution with a median excess loss of 20 dB over the free space loss between isotropic antennas[3] and a standard deviation σ of 6.5 dB. These median and σ values again are within the range of measurements of others but, like the distance dependence, fall on the low side. Since the receiver to transmitter distance is small (<4 km), the transmitter height is large (120 m), and the

[3] Recall that path loss for Figs. 2-4 is between an isotropic base station antenna and $\lambda/4$ vertical on the mobile.

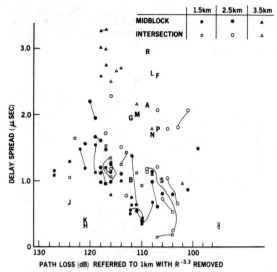

Fig. 5. Scatter plot of delay spread versus path loss referred to 1 km with $R^{-3.3}$ removed.

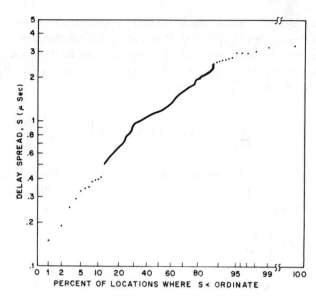

Fig. 6. Cumulative distribution of delay spread.

region is relatively homogeneous (see [1] and [2]) with no open areas, the values of parameters such as distance dependence, median excess loss, and σ are expected to fall on the low side. Thus this set of data and this region are representative of the general urban mobile radio environment and are not just a special case.

Fig. 5 is a replot of the data in Fig. 2 with the $R^{-3.3}$ distance dependence removed from the path loss. With this deterministic variation removed, the correlation coefficient for L and S is only -0.2 or essentially uncorrelated.[4] Also, the number of areas with large S but small to moderate L is significantly increased. Symbols for Figs. 2 and 4 are the same.

A linear least squares regression of S with R shows S proportional to $0.6R$. The correlation coefficient for S with R is <0.5. This slight trend may be a characteristic of this particular region since the areas surrounded by the tallest buildings are farthest from the base station [1]. Removal of the $0.6R$ trend from S leaves the S remainder correlated with path loss (with $R^{-3.3}$ removed) with a correlation coefficient of $+0.26$ or still essentially uncorrelated.

Fig. 6 is the distribution of delay spread for the 100 small areas. In Fig. 6 the S values do not have the $0.6R$ trend removed; they are the same S values as those plotted in Figs. 3 and 5. A Gaussian distribution would be a straight line on the coordinates in Fig. 6. The dots on the tails of the distribution are the contributions of individual areas. The solid line represents the merger of dots where they are close together.

IV. CONCLUSIONS

Delay spread and path loss were measured for 100 small areas along streets within a $2 \times 2\frac{1}{2}$-km region in New York City. The areas ranged from 1.5 to 3.5 km from the base station. The region is representative of the heavily built-up

downtown districts of many large U.S. cities. Correlation between delay spread and measured average path loss is a low -0.4; however, removal of a distance dependence of $R^{-3.3}$ from the path loss reduces the correlation to -0.2, which is essentially uncorrelated. Some areas that have low path loss have large delay spread. Therefore, the performance of some mobile radio systems will be limited by delay spread in some areas but by path loss in other areas. The assessment of overall performance in these systems will require consideration of both delay spread and signal-to-noise (loss) limitations using methods available in the literature [3], [7], [9].

V. ACKNOWLEDGMENTS

I wish to thank W. E. Legg, A. J. Rustako, Jr., R. R. Murray, and C. O. Stevens for their help in taking the data in New York City, and R. P. Leck for help in processing the data.

REFERENCES

[1] D. C. Cox and R. P. Leck, "Distributions of multipath delay spread and average excess delay for 910 MHz urban mobile radio paths," *IEEE Trans. Antennas Propagat.*, vol. AP-23, pp. 206-213, Mar. 1975.

[2] D. C. Cox and R. P. Leck, "Correlation bandwidth and delay spread multipath propagation statistics for 910 MHz urban mobile radio channels," *IEEE Trans. Commun.*, vol. COM-23, pp. 1271-1280, Nov. 1975.

[3] W. C. Jakes, Ed., *Microwave Mobile Communications*, New York: Wiley.

[4] D. C. Cox, "Delay-doppler characteristics of multipath propagation at 910 MHz in a suburban mobile radio environment," *IEEE Trans. Antennas Propagat.*, vol. AP-10, p. 625-635, Sept. 1972.

[5] D. C. Cox, "Time and frequency domain characterizations of multipath propagation at 910 MHz in a suburban mobile radio environment," *Radio Sci.*, pp. 1069-1077, Dec. 1972.

[6] D. C. Cox, "910 MHz urban mobile radio propagation: multipath characteristics in New York City," *IEEE Trans. Commun.*, vol. COM-21, pp. 1188-1194, Nov. 1973.

[7] P. A. Bello, "Characterization of randomly time-variant linear channels," *IEEE Trans. Commun. Syst.*, vol. CS-11, no. 4, pp. 360-393, Dec. 1963.

[8] D. C. Cox, "A measured delay-doppler scattering function for multipath propagation at 910 MHz in an urban mobile radio environment," in *Proc. IEEE*, vol. 61, pp. 479-393, Apr. 1973.

[9] M. J. Gans, "A power-spectral theory of propagation in a Mobile Radio Environment," *IEEE Trans. Veh. Technol.*, vol. VT-21, pp. 27-38, Feb. 1972.

---

[4] The correlation of path loss with delay spread is not uniquely related to system performance since different communication systems have different nonlinear dependences on path loss and delay spread. The scatter plots are included to allow the use of the actual data in studying specific systems without having to relay on the particular independence of the functions of delay spread and path loss illustrated here.

Comparison of Mobile Radio Transmission at 150, 450, 900, and 3700 Mc

By W. RAE YOUNG, JR.

(Manuscript received August 22, 1952)

Based on a series of experiments, a comparison is made of the transmission performance of 150, 450, 900, and 3700 mc in a mobile radiotelephone type of service. This comparison indicates that 450 mc is superior transmission-wise to the presently used 150-mc band in urban and suburban areas. In fact a broad optimum in performance falls in the neighborhood of 500 mc. It is concluded that this range of frequencies would be well suited for providing coverage to meet the large scale needs which are anticipated in and around metropolitan areas. Although higher frequencies are less desirable, the tests indicate that 900 mc is somewhat to be favored over 150 mc from a transmission standpoint if full use is made of the possible antenna gain.

Above this frequency, transmission performance falls off even assuming the maximum practical antenna gain. Transmission at 3700 mc suffers an additional impairment in that the fluctuations in received carrier level occur at an audible rate as the mobile unit moves at normal speeds. It is concluded that while transmission above roughly 1000 mc for these services is not impossible, it would be decidedly more difficult to employ these frequencies satisfactorily.

INTRODUCTION

From the beginning of mobile radiotelephone services offered by the Telephone Companies, both "general" and "private-line" types, it has been apparent that the number of channel frequencies then allocated for these uses would not be sufficient to meet the service needs in the near future.

The bulk of these needs will be for service in urban and suburban areas, where business activities are concentrated. These areas are now served on a few individual FM channels in the vicinity of 150 mc. However, a larger number of channels, needed to meet anticipated demands and to develop a more efficient system, are not to be found in the 150 mc region. This space is already allocated fully and permanently to a variety of other services. In fact, this situation extends up to about 400 mc. The larger number of channels for these services apparently will have to be found, therefore, above 400 mc.

However, it is essential to know whether these higher frequencies would be suitable for urban mobile telephone service, or whether there exists an upper limit to the suitable frequencies. In order to answer these questions, a series of tests has been made to compare the adequacy of coverage that could be provided at several representative higher frequencies. These tests were conducted in and around New York City. This location is considered to be typical of the larger metropolitan areas.

THE PROBLEM OF EVALUATION

It became apparent early in the tests that it would neither be practical nor accurate to compare service results for the different frequencies by the method of determining the coverage at the various frequencies, and then comparing these. This would have required, among other things, that "coverage" be defined precisely and then measured accurately in order to determine the differences with the desired accuracy.

Instead, it was recognized that commercial coverage is at present considered to extend into areas wherein a small percentage of the locations will have less than commercial grade of transmission. This might be ten per cent, for example. It was further recognized that, while there existed a trend of performance with frequency, comparative tests at any one location showed variations from that trend. Thus, even if transmitter powers were adjusted so as to offset the transmission effects of that trend, performance at any location would not be equal at all frequencies. But while one frequency might give relatively poor transmission in one location, it might give good transmission at another location, etc. Thus, while the locations of poor transmission were found to be different at the various frequencies, the number of such locations would be the same at all frequencies, provided the trend had been offset by adjustment of transmitter power.

Viewing the problem in this way, it was sufficient to test at enough locations in representative territory to establish this trend in a statistical manner.

Other problems in evaluating differences in suitability of different frequencies lay in how to take into account differences in practical antenna gains and differences in frequency stability. These will be discussed in the next sections.

Reprinted with permission from *Bell Syst. Tech. J.*, vol. 31, pp. 1068–1085, Nov. 1952.

Transmitter power required to achieve the same service result at various frequencies has been derived by taking into account the changes of path loss with frequency and also the changes of signal required with frequency. Fig. 3 shows the amounts of power that are required in order to achieve the same coverage in all cases as is now obtained at 150 mc with 250 watts of land transmitter power radiated from a dipole. As shown, the use of an antenna having some gain can appreciably lower the land transmitter power that is required. The mobile transmitter power is much less than required of a land transmitter due to the assumption that there are six land receivers located appropriately in the coverage area, rather than just one.

It is apparent from Fig. 3 that the required transmitter power is a minimum in both directions of transmission at around 500 mc. It is also apparent that above this point the required transmitter power increases rapidly with frequency.

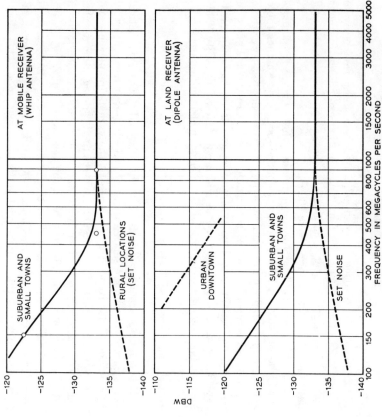

Fig. 2—Median value of signal required to over-ride noise.

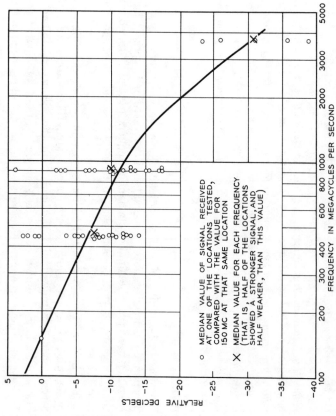

○ MEDIAN VALUE OF SIGNAL RECEIVED AT ONE OF THE LOCATIONS TESTED, COMPARED WITH THE VALUE FOR 150 MC AT THAT SAME LOCATION

✕ MEDIAN VALUE FOR EACH FREQUENCY (THAT IS, HALF OF THE LOCATIONS SHOWED A STRONGER SIGNAL, AND HALF WEAKER, THAN THIS VALUE)

Fig. 1—Median values of received signal power at suburban locations. (Assumes the same power at all frequencies radiated from a dipole and received on a quarter-wave whip.)

OVER-ALL RESULTS

The results of many measurements of path loss between a land radio transmitter and a mobile receiver establish a trend of loss increasing with frequency. This is illustrated in Fig. 1 by the "crosses" which show the strengths of the received signal at higher frequencies as compared with those at 150 mc. The derivation of the values given by the crosses will be discussed in a later section. In the other direction of transmission it appears justified, based upon reciprocal relationships, to assume that path losses from mobile transmitter to land receiver will follow the same trend.

However, although the received signal is seen to decrease with frequency, the amount of received signal which is required to produce satisfactory communication also changes with frequency. The median level of signal required at a mobile or land receiver at various frequencies to override RF noise is given in Fig. 2. The dots here represent the average of many measurements.

Use of gain antennas for the land receivers would result in still further lowering the required mobile transmitter power. This is not shown on Fig. 3 because the amount of reduction cannot be accurately stated on the basis of present knowledge. It appears certain that the reduction will be at least equal to the antenna gain, and may be appreciably more than this, as indicated later.

The system modulation and pass-band were assumed in the above discussion to be the same at all frequencies. This would not be realistic if the tolerance allowed for frequency instability were a fixed percentage of operating frequency. It may be justified, however, because the necessity for frequency economy and for best transmission performance demands better percentage stability at higher frequencies.

A spot check of transmission, observing circuit merits by listening, has been made to determine the validity of the above results in a very general way. Land transmitter powers were adjusted so that the equivalent dipole power at 450 mc was 3 db less than at 150, and power at 900 mc was 1 db less than at 150 mc. This approximates the powers shown on the "dipole" curve of Fig. 3. The map of Fig. 4 shows the results of this test. While the comparison of circuit merits generally shows a preferred frequency at any given location, the performance appears to be about equal when all locations are considered.

TEST EQUIPMENT ARRANGEMENTS

Tests of transmission outward from the land transmitting station were made on signals radiated from antennas on the roof of the Long Lines Building, 32 Avenue of the Americas, New York City. These antennas were 450 feet above ground. One of the existing Mobile Service transmitters served for the 150-mc tests. Special experimental transmitters were set up for the 450, 900, and 3700-mc tests. All were capable of frequency modulation.

The mobile unit was a station wagon equipped to receive and measure signals at the various frequencies. The receiving equipment was arranged for rapid conversion from 150 to 450 to 900 mc. The bandwidth (about 50 kc) and system modulation (±10 kc) were identical at all three frequencies (equal to the existing standards at 150 mc). The 3700-mc tests were handled separately. It was not possible to employ the same bandwidth and deviation, but this does not invalidate the comparison of signal propagation at the various frequencies.

A most useful tool in making these measurements was a device known as a "Level Distribution Recorder", or simply "LDR". This was built

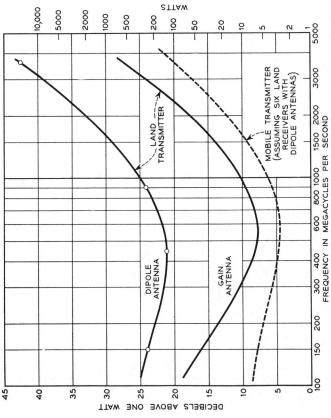

Fig. 3—Transmitter power at antenna input required for urban and suburban coverage. (Mobile antennas are assumed to be quarter-wave ships.)

A word of explanation is needed at this point about the gain antennas which were assumed in one of the curves of Fig. 3. These are antennas which tend to concentrate radiation toward the horizon in all directions. Limits for the amount of gain were based upon the considerations (1) that a set of radiating elements greater than about 50 feet in extent would be impractical to build for this service, and (2) that the vertical width of the beam should not be less than about 2 degrees in order that valleys and hilltops will be covered. The amounts of gain possible within these limits are as follows:

Frequency mc.	Gain-db
150	8
450	13
900	15
3700	15

The mobile antennas were assumed to be quarter-wave whips or the equivalent.

especially for these tests and is similar to its forerunners which have been used in the past for measuring atmospheric static noise. The LDR, in combination with a calibrated radio receiver, is capable of taking as many as twenty instantaneous samples of radio signal strength per second, sorting the samples by amplitude, and rendering information on a "batch" of samples from which a statistical distribution curve can be plotted. The LDR was also used for measuring the statistical distribution of audio noise in the output of the radio receiver. The LDR was, in this case, associated with a special converter whose characteristics resemble those of a 2B noise measuring set.

No arrangements were made for measuring radio propagation from mobile unit to a land receiver. It was felt that the comparison by frequencies would be substantially the same as in the outward direction of transmission. It does not follow, however, that the background electrical noise, against which an r-f signal must compete, will be the same at mobile and land receivers. Strength of r-f signal required at land receivers for satisfactory transmission was measured at several typical locations.

RECEIVED R-F SIGNAL STRENGTHS AND PATH LOSSES

The first factor in evaluating mobile radio transmission is the strength of the r-f signal which is received. This is inversely related to the loss in the r-f path. The mobile units of a mobile system are either moving around or, if stationary, are located at random. Since the effects of the many geographical features, buildings, and the like, which influence propagation can combine differently for different locations of a car, even where the locations are only a fraction of a wavelength apart, the only meaningful measure of signal strength is a statistical one. Such statistical answers were obtained by making and recording many instantaneous samples of field strength with the aid of the LDR, mentioned above.

It is of interest to note that whenever the sample measurements were confined to a relatively small area, say 500 to 1000 feet or less in extent, the amplitude distribution of these samples tended strongly to follow along the particular curve known as a Rayleigh distribution. Such a curve and a typical set of experimental points are shown in Fig. 5. The same distribution was obtained at all of the frequencies tested, including 3700 mc. The rapidity of signal fluctuation, as the car moved, was proportional to frequency, but this does not affect amplitude distribution. Such a distribution could have been predicted if it had been postulated that the transmitted signal reached the car antenna by many paths having a random loss and phase relationship. It is thus inferred that in general the signal reaches a car by many simultaneous paths.

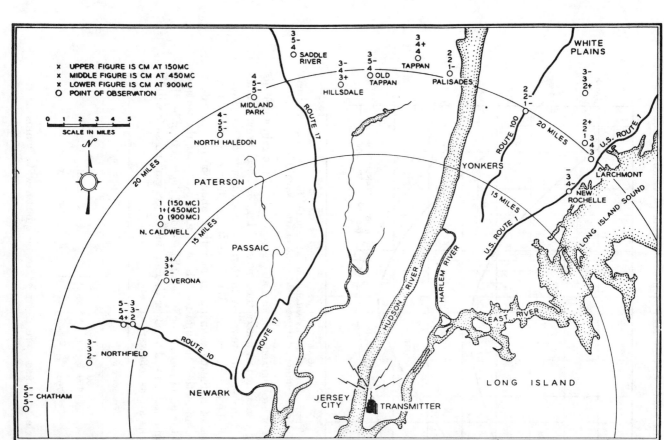

Fig. 4—Circuit merit observations in New York suburbs. Radiated transmitter power was as follows: At 150 mc, 250 watts to a dipole; at 450 mc, the equivalent of 125 watts to a dipole; and at 900 mc, the equivalent of 200 watts to a dipole. Circuit merit grades are as follows: 0—Undetectable; 1—Hopeless, signal unintelligible; 2—Poor, signal understood with much repetition; 3—Fair (commercial); 4—Good, impairment noticeable but not objectionable; and 5—Excellent, no discernible impairment.

ten miles the data are the result of tests in Manhattan and the Bronx. For each distance a test course was laid out approximately following a circle with that distance as a radius. The data for ten miles and greater distances were obtained on two series of tests along radials from the land transmitter, one of which followed Route 1 through New Rochelle, N. Y., and the other followed Route 10 toward Dover, N. J. For reference, a curve has been given on each of these figures which shows the computed loss based upon the assumption of smooth earth.

A curve labeled "1 per cent" means that in one per cent of the sample measurements the loss was less than that indicated on the ordinate. The meaning of the labels on the other curves is similar. The curve labeled "50 per cent" is, of course, the median.

It will be apparent that the assumption of smooth earth is not applicable to the area tested. The data for median losses are in the order of 30 db greater than the value computed over smooth earth. This additional loss may be thought of as a "shadow" loss arising from the presence of many buildings and structures.

The distribution of losses given in these three curves is wider than the Rayleigh distribution of Fig. 5. This is because the data for each

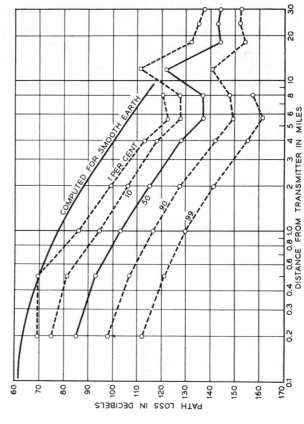

Fig. 6—Measured path loss at 150 mc in Manhattan and the Bronx and suburbs. (Note: Data for 10 miles and greater were taken on Route 1 toward New Rochelle and on Route 10 toward Dover.)

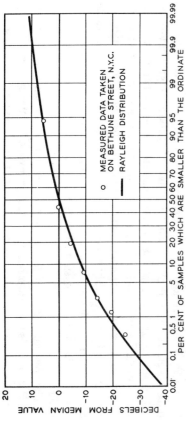

Fig. 5—Typical distribution of test samples of r-f signal strength taken over a small area.

With the shape of the distribution known, only one other value need be given in order to specify the propagation to such a small area. This might be the median, the average, the rms, or any single point on the curve. The one used most often here is the median, that is, the value which is larger than 50 per cent of the samples and smaller than the other 50 per cent. Measurement of the median value by this statistical method was found to be accurately reproducible, and therefore is presumed to be reliable. Successive batches of 200 samples each, all covering the same test area, yielded median values which differed not more than 0.5 db when none of the conditions changed; i.e., transmitter power, antenna gain, and receiver calibration remained the same. This accuracy may seem surprising when it is realized that individual samples differ frequently by 10 db, and often as much as 30 to 40 db.

It was presumed at the outset of the tests that the different frequencies would exhibit different propagation trends with distance. For this reason the samples have been grouped by distance. In presenting these results, it was convenient to express the measurements of received RF signal in terms of path losses. By this it is meant the loss between the input to a dipole antenna at the transmitter and the output of a whip antenna on the test car. These path losses will have, of course, the same distribution as the received r-f signal.

The results of the path loss measurements are given in Figs. 6, 7, and 8 for 150, 450, and 900 mc respectively. These values represent the loss between the input to a half-wave dipole antenna at one end of the path and the output of a quarter-wave whip at the other end. They are shown here as a function of distance from the land station. For distances under

ently much greater than the similarity between the median value and the value computed over smooth earth for any given frequency.

It was not possible to get complete enough data to plot a curve for 3700 mc similar to the ones mentioned above. The test setup at this frequency was limited by transmitter power and receiver sensitivity. Only those locations for which path loss was relatively low could be tested. A comparison of results at these locations is given in Figure 10. The curves labeled "1 mi.", "2 mi.", and "4 mi." for Manhattan are the median values obtained along test routes which followed circles of 1, 2 and 4 miles radius from the transmitters. The other curves refer to selected small areas at greater distances on the Hutchison River Parkway and New Jersey Route 10, as indicated. Although the data at 3700 mc not extensive, the trend with frequency seems clear.

More specific data for path losses measured along the routes toward Dover and New Rochelle are given in Fig. 11. Each value plotted here is the median of about 200 samples taken in a small area, at the distance indicated. The strong effect of the First and Second Orange mountains at fourteen and sixteen miles on the Dover route is of interest.

The coverage desired in these mobile telephone systems extends into suburban locations. It follows that a comparison of coverage by the

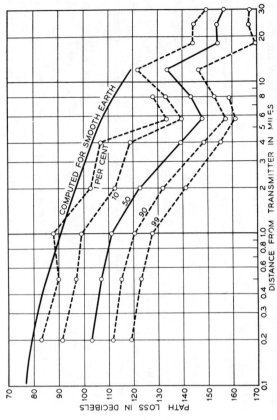

Fig. 8—Measured path loss at 900 mc in Manhattan and the Bronx and suburbs. (Note: Data for 10 miles and greater were taken on Route 1 toward New Rochelle and on Route 10 toward Dover.)

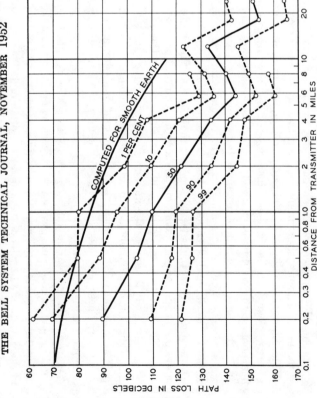

Fig. 7—Measured path loss at 450 mc in Manhattan and the Bronx and suburbs. (Note: Data for 10 miles and greater were taken on Route 1 toward New Rochelle and on Route 10 toward Dover.)

distance are a summation over many different locations rather than a set of samples covering one location.

The data for ten miles and further from the transmitter were taken on routes through suburban areas. The losses at twelve miles appear to be less than the average trend indicated by the curves. This is because data taken at the top of the First Orange Mountain weigh heavily at this distance. It is of interest to note that the losses at distances of ten miles and over are 6 to 10 db less than might have been predicted from the trend at smaller distances, where the measurements were made in city areas. This probably reflects the fact that there is a considerable difference in the character of the surroundings, such as height and number of buildings in the suburban territory as compared with the city itself.

The median curves of loss have been replotted for three frequencies on Fig. 9. This permits a better comparison with frequency. Except very close to the transmitter, the performance at the various frequencies seems to differ by an essentially constant number of db, while exhibiting the same trend with distance. The similarity between frequencies is appar-

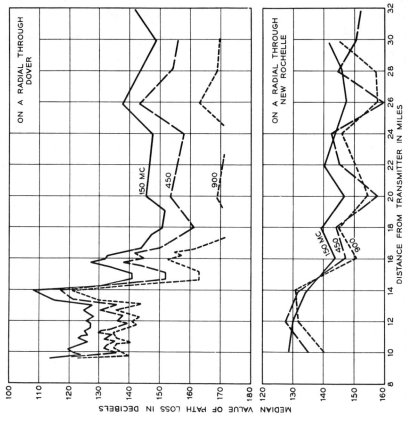

Fig. 11—Median r-f path losses along selected routes. (a) On a radial through Dover. (b) On a radial through New Rochelle.

comparison of frequencies is different at different locations. The "crosses" are the median values of these points, so placed that there are as many points above as below. The points for 3700 mc are taken from the data of Fig. 1. The crosses of Fig. 1 are considered to be the most reliable all-around comparison of propagation at the different frequencies.

RELATION OF SPEECH-NOISE RATIOS TO R-F SIGNAL POWER

Speech-to-noise ratios were measured at all of the test locations by the use of the level distribution recorder as described earlier. During the course of any given test the audio noise from the receiver varied considerably and these variations were recorded on the LDR. It was found by correlation between subjective observations of circuit merit and the

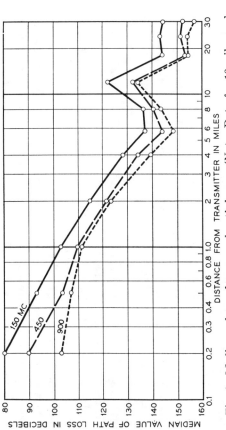

Fig. 9—Median values of measured path losses. (Note: Data for 10 miles and greater were taken on Route 1 toward New Rochelle and on Route 10 toward Dover.)

various frequencies should be based upon measurements taken in the suburbs. The data from the New Rochelle and Dover series have been used as a basis for the points and the curve given in Figure 1. Each of the circle points shows the path loss at a given frequency relative to that at 150 mc for a particular location. Their spread indicates that the

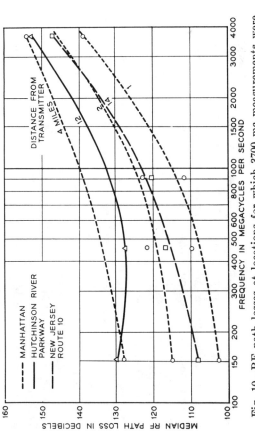

Fig. 10—RF path losses at locations for which 3700 mc measurements were made.

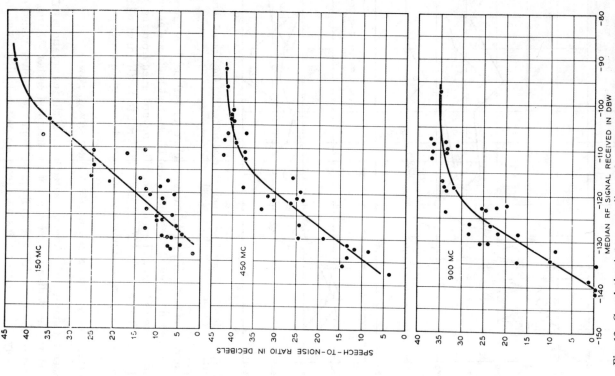

Fig. 12—Correlation between median values of speech-to-noise ratio and r-f signal strength in suburban locations. (Note: Each point represents the speech-to-noise ratio and the r-f signal received at one location. (a) 150 mc. (b) 450 mc. (c) 900 mc.

median value of noise that the latter is equivalent in noise effect to a steady random noise of the same value. In the FM receiver, the level of speech is essentially not affected by the strength of RF signal and so a measurement of the output noise is directly related to the speech-to-noise ratio. The speech-to-noise ratios given here are computed from noise measurements by assuming that speech of −14 vu level is applied to the system at a point where one milliwatt of 1,000 cycles tone would produce a 10-kc frequency deviation. The strength of the speech signal at the receiver output is expressed in the same units as are used for the noise.

As might have been expected the median speech-to-noise ratios correlate strongly with the amounts of r-f signal received at the various locations. This correlation has been evaluated in order that the most likely relationship between speech-to-noise ratio and received r-f signal may be known for the different frequencies. These are shown in Fig. 12, where each circle represents the median speech-to-noise value measured at one test location plotted against the median r-f signal received at that location. The solid lines have been drawn in to show the trend. The bending at the top of the curve is inconsequential. It only represents the limit imposed in the test setup by tube microphonic noise, vibrator noise, etc. The curves show, for example, that in order to produce a commercial grade of transmission, which requires a 12 db speech-to-noise ratio, the median r-f signal must be 122.5 db below one watt at 150 mc. The data given in Fig. 12 pertain only to the suburban locations. Measurements in Manhattan have not been included, even though they indicate that larger signals are required, because the limit of system coverage is to be found in the suburbs. The data on the solid curves of Fig. 12 have been used to derive the curve of Fig. 2 which plots the value of r-f signal required at the mobile receiver for a commercial grade of transmission. The dotted curve of Fig. 2, which shows the median signal required in locations where noise picked up by the antenna is less than set noise, is based on the assumption of an 8 db noise figure for a practical 150-mc receiver, 11 db at 450 mc, and 12 db at 900 mc and higher.

Measurements have been made of the effect of noise picked up by the antenna at land receiver stations. These are expressed here in terms of the carrier strength required for just-commercial grade of transmission (12 db speech-to-noise ratio) as compared with the value required when there is no antenna noise and only receiver noise is present. These comparison measurements were made by injecting a steady carrier into the receiver with an antenna connected normally, and again with a dummy antenna connected. Although these tests were made with a steady rather than randomly varying signal, it is felt that the comparative results will apply to the random signal case as well.

Tests were made at 150, 450 and 900 mc, at four locations of interest, and with dipole and 7 db gain antennas. Not all combinations were tested, but enough to permit some interesting comparisons. The locations tested were as follows:

A: On the Long Lines building, a 27-story building in downtown Manhattan.

B: On the Graybar-Varick building, a 16-story building in downtown Manhattan.

C: On the telephone building which houses the Melrose exchange, a 7-story building in the center of the Bronx.

D: On the 3-story telephone exchange building in Lynbrook, Long Island.

Table I describes the generally prevailing noise situation at these locations. Higher noise was encountered occasionally at some of the sites, due in at least one case to operation of elevators in the building. However, these occasions were so brief and infrequent that the general background of noise is considered to be a better value to use in estimating systems performance.

The trend toward lower site noise at higher frequencies, already noted for mobile installations, is seen to apply to land receivers as well.

These data bring out another interesting and significant fact. Where noise collected by a dipole antenna is discernible over set noise, the noise collected by the 7 db gain antenna at the same site is, surprisingly, less. This means that the gain antenna picks up *less* noise power than a dipole. Since it picks up 7 db more signal from a distant car, a gain antenna thus provides a double improvement in transmission at those sites for which ambient noise is controlling.

An explanation of this behavior may be surmised if it is assumed that the sources of noise are numerous and are scattered around at street level (motor vehicles, mostly). The overall noise received is a sum of contributions from all sources, weighted for distance and the receiving antenna pattern. A gain antenna of the type considered here tends to ignore the strong nearby noise sources because they are below the antenna beam. The sources, which are nearly enough in the beam to count, are also further away and are attenuated by distance.

The amount of data given in Table I does not seem sufficient to warrant stating a firm figure as to the amount of improvement obtainable from a gain antenna. However, substantial improvement at 150 mc is indicated, and this might have the effect of bringing the value of mobile transmitter power required at 150 mc down to the value required at 450 mc, assuming gain antennas in both cases.

ACKNOWLEDGMENTS

A number of people participated at one time or another in setting up and carrying through these tests. It is not possible to name them all, but the principal participants were R. L. Robbins, R. C. Shaw, W. Strack, D. K. White, and F. J. Henneberg. The program was supervised by D. Mitchell. The special radio equipment required was designed and furnished by W. E. Reichle and his group.

TABLE I—R-F Signal Input to Receiver for 12 db Speech-to-Noise Ratio (Given in db Above That Needed to Override Set Noise*)

Station	Frequency	Antenna	
		Dipole	7-db Gain
A	150 mc	10	0.5
	450	1	1.5
	900	—	—
B	150	12	—
	450	4	—
	900	0	—
C	150	11	2.5
	450	1	1
	900	1	—
D	150	5	4
	450	0	0
	900	0	—

* Noise figures in the test receivers were 9, 12 and 12 db for 150, 450, and 900 mc, respectively.

A Statistical Model of Urban Multipath Propagation

GEORGE L. TURIN, FELLOW, IEEE, FRED D. CLAPP, SENIOR MEMBER, IEEE,
TOM L. JOHNSTON, STEPHEN B. FINE, MEMBER, IEEE, AND DAN LAVRY

Abstract– An urban multipath propagation experiment, involving the simultaneous transmission from a fixed site of 100-ns pulses at 488, 1280, and 2920 MHz and their reception at a mobile van, is described. A statistical analysis of the data in the resulting multipath responses is given and used as a basis for a statistical model of urban multipath propagation.

INTRODUCTION

THE URBAN radio-propagation medium has traditionally been used almost exclusively for voice communication. More recently, digital-data links have come into use, and within the next few years vehicle-location systems using active radiolocation techniques will no doubt make their appearance. In connection with the design of systems for these latter uses, it is more important than ever that a detailed model of urban radio propagation, based on thorough measurements, be established.

Most experimental data on urban radio propagation have been obtained by CW techniques and are of the form of fading distributions at particular frequencies. These data may be useful in predicting the behavior of narrow-band (e.g., voice) systems, but are of little value for analysis and design of wideband systems, such as some forms of radiolocation systems, which may utilize as much as 10 MHz of bandwidth.

During an extensive institutional and technical study of urban automatic vehicle monitoring (AVM) systems [1], it became apparent that the appropriate way to study the technical characteristics of urban radiolocation would be first to perform extensive propagation experiments from which a complete statistical model of the urban propagation medium could be constructed, and then to simulate the medium and various radiolocation systems on a digital computer. This technique would have the value of avoiding a multiplicity of costly hardware tests of ad hoc systems and of allowing precisely controlled simulation experiments to achieve valid comparisons of systems. The results of our propagation experiments are described here. The use of the resulting propagation model in the simulation of urban locator systems is described in a companion paper [2].

Manuscript received February 3, 1971; revised August 14, 1971. This work was supported by the U.S. Department of Housing and Urban Development under Grant H-1030, Project DC-D6-1.
G. L. Turin and F. D. Clapp are with the University of California, Berkeley, Calif., and Teknekron, Inc., Berkeley, Calif.
T. L. Johnston is with Teknekron, Inc., Berkeley, Calif.
S. B. Fine was with Teknekron, Inc., Berkeley, Calif. He is now with the Technische Hogeschool, Delft, The Netherlands.
D. Lavry was with Teknekron, Inc., Berkeley, Calif. He is now with Digital Telephone Systems, Inc., San Rafael, Calif.

In modeling the propagation medium, we pictured it as a linear filter, and sought to obtain as complete statistics as possible about the behavior of the impulse response of this filter. The only pertinent experimental data available prior to those we obtained seem to have been those of Young and Lacy [3], which Schmid [4] used in constructing a rudimentary statistical propagation model. (We shall comment later on one facet of Schmid's model.) However, the Young–Lacy data are sketchily presented and are deficient from the point of view of radiolocation system simulation since they lack absolute time-of-arrival information. More specifically, the Young–Lacy data, which are in the form of photographs of the video-detected response of the medium to an RF pulse, were obtained by triggering an oscilloscope with the video response itself. There is thus no indication whether the first discernible path in the video response is a line-of-sight path or a "reflected" path having additional delay. On the other hand, absolute timing information is the essence of radiolocation. In constructing an adequate multipath model, then, the statistics of the excess delays of paths beyond line-of-sight delay are essential. Our approach in obtaining the necessary statistics was to use stable, frequently synchronized and calibrated atomic clocks at the transmitter and receiver ends of the experimental link for the purpose of providing both ends of the link with a common time origin.

PRELIMINARY MULTIPATH MODEL

In order to design the multipath propagation experiment, it was necessary to have a mathematical model in mind [5]. For this preliminary purpose, we drew on a model which has been used most successfully in describing long-distance multipath propagation via the ionosphere or troposphere [6]. In this model, we suppose that the propagation medium acts as a linear filter with the property that, if Re $\{s(t)e^{i\omega_0 t}\}$, $t\in (-\infty,\infty)$ is sent, where $s(\cdot)$ is a complex-valued low-pass waveform and ω_0 is the carrier frequency, then Re $\{\rho(t)e^{i\omega_0 t}\}$, $t\in (-\infty,\infty)$, is received, where

$$\rho(t) = \sum_{k=0}^{\infty} a_k s(t - t_k) e^{i\theta_k} + n(t). \qquad (1)$$

The propagation medium is then described by the set of path variables

$$\{a_1, a_2, a_3, \cdots, t_1, t_2, t_3, \cdots, \theta_1, \theta_2, \theta_3, \cdots\} = \{a_k, t_k, \theta_k\}_0^{\infty}$$

and the (complex-valued) low-pass additive noise $n(\cdot)$. The noise—at least at the frequencies with which we are concerned —is well modeled as Gaussian, and was of no special interest to

Reprinted from *IEEE Trans. Veh. Technol.*, vol. VT-21, pp. 1–9, Feb. 1972.

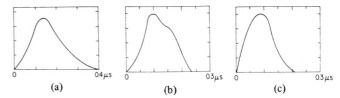

Fig. 1. Transmitted pulse shapes. (a) 488 MHz. (b) 1280 MHz. (c) 2920 MHz.

us. On the other hand, the statistical behavior of the path variables was the major concern of the experiment.

There is no difficulty in assuming *a priori* that the carrier phases $\{\theta_k\}_0^\infty$ of the various paths are mutually independent random variables which are uniformly distributed over $(0, 2\pi]$. This follows from the fact that the carrier phase is critically sensitive to path length, changing by the order of 2π rad as the path length changes by a wavelength (of inches or feet at the frequencies of interest to us). Thus, if one considers, for example, a fixed transmitter and a mobile receiver, and imagines an ensemble of receiver sites spread geographically over hundreds or thousands of wavelengths, then it is clear that the geometry of a single path with modulation delay t_k will lead to a uniform distribution of phase θ_k for that path, while the geometrical relationship between separate paths with modulation delays t_j and t_k will lead to a uniform joint distribution of pairs of phases θ_j and θ_k, i.e., independence of θ_j and θ_k. This *a priori* statistical model for the θ_k seems so irrefutable that we did not deem it necessary to go to the considerable expense of testing it. The statistics of the sequences of path delays $\{t_k\}_0^\infty$ and strengths $\{a_k\}_0^\infty$, on the other hand, were not so obvious *a priori*.

A reasonable conjecture for the t_k is that they form a Poisson sequence [6]. More precisely, if one always lets t_0 be the line-of-sight delay, then one may conjecture that the sequence of excess delays $\{t_k - t_0\}_1^\infty$ of the retarded paths is a Poisson sequence on $(0, \infty)$. (We exclude the line-of-sight path from this hypothesis since its excess delay, i.e., zero, is not a random variable.) This means that, if one ignores their ordering, the excess delays are independent identically distributed random variables taking values in $(0, \infty)$, the probability of any one of them occurring in the infinitesimal interval $(t, t + dt)$ being $p(t)dt$, where $p(t)$ is the so-called mean arrival rate at time t.

The literature [4], [7], [8] bearing on the statistics of the path strengths $\{a_k\}_0^\infty$ indicates that over local geographical areas (perhaps a hundred wavelengths or so in dimension), the path strengths have Rayleigh or Rice distributions, while over larger areas the strengths are log-normally distributed, the change from one distribution to the other apparently being due to the spatial inhomogeneity of the terrain. This result may also be deduced from the literature on long-distance point-to-point communication [9], [10], [11], which shows that short-term fading tends to be Rayleigh or Rice distributed, while long-term fading tends to be log-normally distributed. In this case, the equivalent of spatial inhomogeneity is temporal nonstationarity.

There seems to be no prior literature on the joint distribution of strengths of different paths. One conjecture is that they are independent [5], [6], but in view of the observation that paths often tend to fade together, this conjecture seems oversimplified. Again, nothing was known *a priori* about the relationship, if any, between $t_k - t_0$ and a_k. One conjecture is that delay and strength are independent [6], but it is more likely that the distribution of a_k depends upon $t_k - t_0$. The main purpose of the experiment that will be described was to derive detailed statistics about the path parameters $\{t_k - t_0\}_1^\infty$ and $\{a_k\}_0^\infty$.

OUTLINE OF THE EXPERIMENT

In order to measure the statistics of the path variables, we transmitted from a fixed site, essentially simultaneously, narrow pulses at each of the three frequencies 488, 1280, and 2920 MHz. The pulses all had half-power widths of about 100 ns, with shapes as shown in Fig. 1. (The radiated powers of the pulses are given later.) A mobile receiving van was equipped with receivers at all three frequencies, the video outputs of which were connected to a three-trace oscilloscope with a camera attached. Because of the large dynamic range expected of the received signals, the receivers all were equipped with logarithmic IF amplifiers with 60-dB dynamic range.

Since timing measurements with respect to line-of-sight delay were an essential part of the experiment, it was necessary to provide the transmitter and receiver with accurate clocks which could be depended upon to run synchronously. For this purpose, rubidium frequency standards were used. At the beginning of a set of experimental runs, these could be physically brought together and synchronized in frequency and time precisely enough so that when separated they would drift apart by only 10–20 ns/h. A subsidiary remote calibration procedure was developed in order that the effects of even this small rate of drift could be corrected. The effect of the synchronization and calibration procedures was such that the effective timing error between the transmitter's and receiver's clocks was rarely more than about 25 ns.

A typical experimental run proceeded as follows. The clocks were synchronized and the transmitter clock connected so as to pulse the transmitters once per second. The receiver clock was connected so as to trigger the oscilloscope traces once per second at a time τ s after the transmitters were pulsed, where τ was set to be slightly less than the smallest line-of-sight delay expected in the reception area. The oscilloscope, whose traces were adjusted to be 10 μs long, thus presented up to 10 μs worth of the video-detected response of the multipath medium, starting at the line-of-sight path (if it existed), simultaneously at the three frequencies. This trace length was quite adequate to record virtually all readable paths.

Four types of reception area were investigated. Three of these were in the East Bay region of the San Francisco Bay area, and the fourth in San Francisco, Calif., itself. Each area was large enough to disqualify its classification as "local" in the sense given in the preceding section. On the other hand, each was chosen to be small enough so that signal strength variations over the area were primarily due to the area's structural characteristics rather than to fluctuations in slant range between transmitter and receiver. A gross description of the areas' topographies follows.

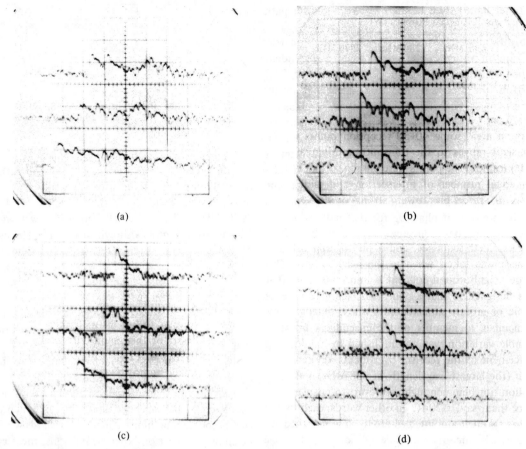

Fig. 2. Examples of multipath profiles: vertical scale—35 dB/major division; horizontal scale—1 μs/major division; top trace—2920 MHz; middle trace—1280 MHz; bottom trace—488 MHz. (a) Area A. (b) Area B. (c) Area C. (d) Area D.

Area A: Transmitters were on the 120-ft-high roof of the Hall of Justice building in San Francisco, about 1 mi from the high-rise financial district of San Francisco, with a clear line of sight to this dense cluster of buildings over intervening low-rise roof tops. The financial-district reception area consisted of densely packed skyscrapers (up to about 50 stories high) and narrow streets, with the singular property that at no point could the transmitting antennas be seen from street level. This area is typical of the worst propagation environment one could expect in a modern metropolis, with the possible exception of midtown Manhattan, New York.

Area B: Transmitters were on the roof of the University of California Space Sciences Laboratory, at an altitude of about 1300 ft in the Berkeley hills, commanding a clear view of almost the entire East Bay region. The reception area was in downtown Oakland, Calif., about 5.5 mi from the transmitters. The reception area was characterized by sparsely clustered skyscrapers, up to about 40 stories, interspersed with 2–3 story metal-frame buildings. Transmitting antennas could be seen from many street-level points in the area. This area is typical of the downtown district of a medium-size city, such as Boston, Mass., Cincinnati, Ohio, etc., or of the fringe of the business area of a larger metropolis.

Area C: Transmitters were on the roof of the University of California Space Sciences Laboratory. The reception area was in downtown Berkeley, about 1.5 mi from the transmitters. The reception area was characterized by a few 10–20-story

buildings, many 2–5-story metal-frame buildings, and some small 1–2-story wood-frame buildings. Transmitting antennas could be seen from many points in the area. The area is typical of the downtown area of a small-to-medium-size town.

Area D: Transmitters were on the roof of the University of California Space Sciences Laboratory. The reception area was in part of the foothills of residential Berkeley, about 1.5 mi from the transmitters. The reception area was characterized by 1–2-story wood-frame houses, trees, supermarkets, etc. This is typical of the private-residence suburbs of most towns and cities.

It is to be noted that both the San Francisco and East Bay transmitting sites were elevated and isolated from their surroundings. Thus one may hypothesize that the reflections which cause the multipath phenomenon will be concentrated almost entirely in the environs of the mobile (receiving) station. This hypothesis will be discussed further.

The effective radiated powers differed for the two transmitting sites, the peak radiated powers being given in Table I. The transmitting-antenna characteristics were as follows: 1) 488 MHz—half-wave vertically polarized dipole (2.15-dB gain at horizon); 2) 1280 MHz—effectively a quarter-wave vertically polarized monopole below a ground plane (5.15-dB gain at horizon); 3) 2920 MHz—23° × 23° vertically polarized horn (17-dB gain on axis). All receiving antennas were effectively quarter-wave vertically polarized monopoles above a ground plane.

146

TABLE I
PEAK RADIATED POWERS (W)

	488 MHz	1280 MHz	2920 MHz
East Bay	390	2760	206
San Francisco	650	3240	1160

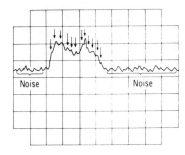

Fig. 3. Peaks and inflection points of multipath profile.

In each reception area, some 40–50 reception points were sited and their slant ranges to the transmitting antennas accurately (± 25 ft) found. The points were chosen so that there were about an equal number of intersection and midblock points, there was no *a priori* bias toward strong- or weak-signal sites, and the points could be sequenced in a route.

In an experimental run, the points in an area were run through in a prescribed sequence, and a photograph of the oscilloscope traces was taken when in the neighborhood of each point. The neighborhood concept is important, for the experiment was designed so that a point was meant to represent an ensemble of grossly similar points whose details vary slightly from member to member of the ensemble. In this case, the ensemble variation was accomplished by randomly varying the placement of the receiver over many wavelengths from run to run (the largest wavelength, at 488 MHz, is about 2 ft), the variation not being enough, however, to change the slant range more than, say, ± 20 ft. In other words, each time a photograph was taken at a point, a photograph was obtained which was grossly similar to other photographs at that point, but differed from them in fine detail.

Enough runs were made in an area so as to accumulate about 1000 frames of data. Thus, if the area consists of 50 points, each visited 20 times, one has the equivalent of 1000 points of a similar but larger area whose points are grouped into 50 groups of 20 similarity ensembles. Four frames of data are shown in Fig. 2. These are better than average, having high signal-to-noise ratios and sharp leading edges—features which are not always present. The differences in the times of occurrence of the leading edges on the three channels are due to different equipment delays, the effects of which were calibrated out in the data-reduction procedure.

DATA-REDUCTION PROCEDURE

Once the photographs were taken, they were reduced on an optical scanning-table as follows. Each trace was reduced to a sequence of words on an IBM card, each word giving the x and y scanning-table coordinates of a peak or inflection point of the signal component of the trace. (Typical points which were read on the scanning table are shown by arrows in Fig. 3.) The scanning-table coordinates of a data point were converted to excess-delay–amplitude coordinates[1] by computer, and the sequence of such coordinate pairs was identified with the $\{t_k - t_0, a_k\}_0^\infty$ sequence of the model.

In order to understand this method of data reduction, in which peaks and inflection points were read, it is necessary to

realize that by virtue of the nonzero pulsewidths of the transmitted pulses, two paths whose delays differ by less than 200–300 ns will not show up as distinct pulses on the trace; rather, they will combine in the RF portion of the receiver and the envelope of their phasor sum will be observed. Thus the inflection point on the leading edge of the signal in Fig. 3, while not a distinct peak, clearly is due to a somewhat attenuated first path. Similarly, many signal humps have double peaks, which we attributed to two distinct paths.

The weaknesses of this method are easily cited. First, it is not necessarily true that two closely spaced paths will combine into a two-peaked hump—there may be only one peak, or even three peaks. Furthermore, it is usually not true that even if there are only two peaks, the coordinates of their maxima will correspond exactly to the excess-delay–amplitude coordinates of the two paths. However, we expected that the deleterious effects of our method would result in only a slight blurring of the statistics we obtained, an expectation which seems to have been borne out by the results obtained in our simulation studies [2].

Having obtained the excess-delay-amplitude sequence for each trace, these were computer edited for errors and then analyzed by computer in order to obtain the following statistical results for each of the areas A, B, C, and D.

1) We found the probability that at least one path will occupy the excess-range[2] interval from $(n - \frac{1}{2}) \times 100$ ft to $(n + \frac{1}{2}) \times 100$ ft, for $n = -4, \cdots, -1, 0, 1, \cdots, 70$. This was obtained by counting all paths in the data for an area which have excess ranges in the given interval, and dividing by the number of frames analyzed. It was assumed from the characteristics of the equipment and the scanning table that two or more paths falling into the same 100-ft interval on the same trace would not be distinguished, so that for all practical purposes "at least one path" means "exactly one path."

2) We found the probability distribution of the number of paths lying in the interval from −450 ft to $(5n + \frac{1}{2}) \times 100$ ft, for $n = -1, 0, 1, \cdots, 13$. This was obtained by counting the number of frames which have 0, 1, 2, $\cdots$ paths in the given interval and then dividing by the number of frames analyzed.

3) The probability that there will be no path (above noise level) was determined. This was obtained by counting the

---

[1] Since the slant range to each reception point was known, the line-of-sight delay was known, and the excess delay was therefore computable.

[2] The excess range is the excess delay times the velocity of light. Negative excess-range intervals were included so as to allow for timing errors in the experiment.

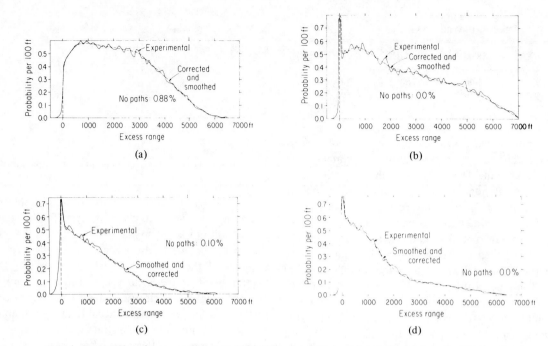

Fig. 4. Probability-of-occupancy curves; 1280 MHz. (a) Area A. (b) Area B. (c) Area C. (d) Area D.

number of frames in which no signal could be discerned and dividing by the total number of frames.

4) The probability density distribution of the excess range of paths 1-10, counting from the first discernible path, was computed.

5) We determined the strength distribution of all paths falling in excess-range interval $(n - \frac{1}{2}) \times 100$ ft to $(n + \frac{1}{2}) \times 100$ ft, for $n = 0, \cdots, 70$. This was obtained in cumulative form by counting all peaks (and inflection points) in the interval whose strength exceeded $-100, -96, -92, \cdots, -32, -28$ dBm.

6) Scatter diagrams of the logarithmic strengths of paths 1 and 2 and of paths 2 and 3, and the associated correlation coefficients, were found.

The statistical data of 1) and 2) were used to test the hypothesis that the sequence $\{t_k - t_0\}_1^\infty$ is a Poisson sequence. Item 3), which is in fact contained also in 2), indicates the extent of geographical coverage of the transmission. The set of data 4) is incidental, as described later. Finally, items 5) and 6) were used to find the distribution of path strengths and to test for the dependence of the strengths of different paths.

RESULTS

A full report on all the statistical data obtained from our propagation experiment is given in [1]. Since the results for the three frequencies were very similar (with a minor exception noted later), we shall summarize here only the data extracted from the 1280-MHz experiment.

As mentioned, the sets of statistical data 1) and 2) in the preceding section are concerned with the verification of the Poisson hypothesis of the preliminary multipath model, viz., that the sequence $\{t_k - t_0\}_1^\infty$ of excess delays forms a Poisson sequence with, perhaps, a time-varying mean arrival rate. Specifically, if the Poisson hypothesis is valid, the probabilities of

occupancy described in item 1) will give the mean arrival rate,[3] while the path-number distributions described in item 2) will be Poisson distributions governed by this mean arrival rate.

Fig. 4 (a), (b), (c), and (d) gives the probabilities of occupancy for reception areas A, B, C, and D, respectively, at 1280 MHz. These probabilities are given in the form of curves, the value of a curve at a given excess range being the probability that there will be a path within ± 50 ft of that excess range. The jagged curves in the figure connect the measured values of probability, which were computed at integral multiples of 100 ft. A smooth curve (broken line) has been passed through each of the jagged curves in order to remove the effects of statistical fluctuations. The smooth curve has also been given a higher value at zero excess range to compensate for the spurious (due to measuremental error) nonzero probabilities at negative excess ranges, which are removed. We note that the relative lack of nonzero probabilities at negative excess ranges attests to the accuracy of the clock calibration methods used.

The most notable feature of the probability-of-occupancy curves is the behavior around the origin. In areas B, C, and D, line-of-sight paths are highly probable, as one intuitively expects. In area A, again as is intuitively reasonable, line-of-sight paths are highly improbable. Furthermore, in areas A and B, large excess delays are more probable than in areas C and D, where few large reflecting objects are available.

We note in passing that our probability-of-occupancy curves seem to contradict a basic conclusion drawn by Schmid [4] from his propagation model, at least as it applies to urban environments. Schmid shows theoretical probability-of-occu-

---

[3] More precisely, if q is the probability that exactly one path falls in excess-range interval $(n - 1/2) \times 100$ ft to $(n + 1/2) \times 100$ ft, then the mean arrival rate at excess delay $t = 100n/c$ is approximately $p(t) = cq/100$, where $c = 9.83514 \times 10^8$ ft/s is the velocity of light.

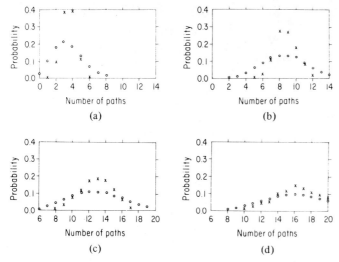

Fig. 5. Some examples of path-number distributions; area B, 1280 MHz. (a) Excess-range interval (–450', 550'), λ = 3.55. (b) Excess-range interval (–450', 1550'), λ = 8.82. (c) Excess-range interval (–450', 2550'), λ = 12.83. (d) Excess-range interval (–450', 3550'), λ = 16.34.

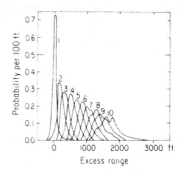

Fig. 6. Probability densities of first ten paths; area B, 1280 MHz.

pancy curves for urban propagation which have widths which increase monotonically with distance between transmitter and receiver. The curves in Fig. 4, however, show no such relationship. (Recall that the transmitter–receiver distance is roughly 1 mi in Fig. 4 (a), 5.5 mi in Fig. 4 (b), and 1.5 mi in Fig. 4 (c) and (d).) In fact, our results seem to show that the multipath spread: (i.e., the width of the probability-of-occupancy curve) depends almost totally on the local environment of the receiver, as we have previously hypothesized. This conclusion is further supported by some phase-ranging tests performed in Chicago, Ill. [12], in which the phase-ranging error (which is heavily dependent on the multipath spread) showed no correlation with the transmitter–receiver distance.

In Fig. 4 (a)–(d), the probability that no path will be seen [item 3) on the list of reduced data] is also inserted. None is excessively high.

In Fig. 5 (a)–(d), a typical set of path-number distributions, derived from the 1280-MHz data for area B, is given. Recall that in computing these, the excess-range axis was divided into intervals whose lengths were multiples of 500 ft, with the left-hand endpoint at –450 ft:[4] the first interval ran from –450 to +50 ft, the second from –450 to 550 ft, the third from –450 to 1050 ft, etc. For each such interval, the distribution of the number of paths occurring in that interval was computed. Four of these are given by the points marked X in Fig. 5.

Now, for each of the excess-range intervals just discussed, the sum λ of the computed probabilities of occupancy (see Fig. 4 (b)) for all the 100-ft quantiles in this interval was computed. Recall that the probability of occupancy for a 100-ft quantile is, for all practical purposes, the probability

that one and only one path falls in that quantile. Then, if $\{t_k - t_0\}_0^\infty$ were a Poisson sequence, λ would be the Poisson parameter, i.e., the mean number of paths within the interval.

Of course, $\{t_k - t_0\}_0^\infty$ cannot strictly be a Poisson sequence, since the first member of the sequence $t_0 - t_0$–i.e., the excess delay of the line-of-sight path–is always zero. Nonetheless, when λ ≫ 1, the effect of the line-of-sight path should be small. Thus, to test our Poisson hypothesis concerning the excess-delay sequence–i.e., $\{t_k - t_0\}_1^\infty$, which excludes the line-of-sight path–we plotted the theoretical Poisson distributions for the computed values of λ. These are shown by the points marked ○ in Fig. 5. One sees that the fit between the Poisson distributions and the empirical distributions in the typical example given in Fig. 5 is, in general, not bad. When λ is small, the mean of the empirical distributions tends to be about one unit too high, as expected because of the effect of the line-of-sight path. Furthermore, for small λ, the empirical distributions tend to be slightly more clustered around their means than a Poisson sequence would dictate; the cause for this is not clear, but it may reflect a tendency of the near-line-of-sight paths to arrive in groups. As λ increases, the fit between the empirical and Poisson distributions improves, which implies that later paths in the sequence tend to be more accurately modeled by the Poisson hypothesis.

The final set of path delay statistics, viz., the probability density distributions of the excess ranges of paths 1-10, is given in Fig. 6 for 1280 MHz in area B. These distributions are of subsidiary interest, but their shapes tend to confirm the quasi-Poisson nature of the path arrival times.

Having summarized items 1)-4) in the list of experimental results, there remain the final two items, which are concerned with path-strength statistics of the multipath model. Succinctly, it was found that a_k has a log-normal distribution (i.e., log a_k is normally distributed) with mean and standard deviation dependent on t_k,[5] while a_j and a_k, $j \neq k$, proved to be

---

[4] Each interval thus included both the line-of-sight path and the small number of other (probably line-of-sight) paths which were erroneously determined to have negative excess delays. The path-number statistics thus developed bear only indirectly on the Poisson hypothesis concerning the retarded path sequence $\{t_k - t_0\}_1^\infty$; see the discussion which follows.

[5] The reasoning leading to this conclusion is slightly subtle. The empirical distribution of item 5) is the strength distribution of all paths with a given excess range, regardless of the path index k. On the other hand, the multipath model calls for the strength distribution of only the kth path, given that the kth path has a prescribed excess range $c(t_k - t_0)$. We have identified these two distributions on the intuitive supposition that, if a path has a specified excess range, the numerical place it occupies in a path sequence cannot have a bearing on its strength distribution.

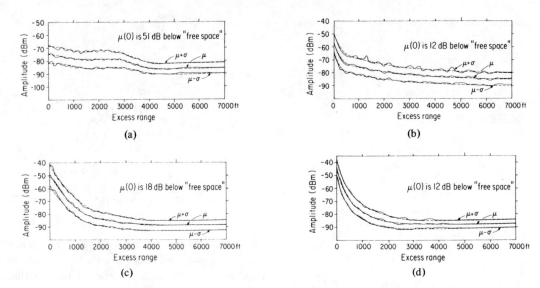

Fig. 7. Means and standard deviations of logarithmic paths strengths; 1280 MHz. (a) Area A. (b) Area B. (c) Area C. (d) Area D.

highly linearly dependent, at least in the cases $j = 1, k = 2$ and $j = 2, k = 3$. As we have seen, the log-normality of the strength distributions is consistent with the literature, for each of the reception areas (A, B, C, and D) used was much too large to be called "local" in the sense previously discussed.

We conclude this discussion of our experimental results by describing in detail the path-strength statistics. The means μ and standard deviations σ of the empirical log-normal strength distributions are given as functions of excess range for areas A, B, C, and D in Fig. 7 (a), (b), (c), and (d), respectively, for the 1280-MHz experiment. Again, the jagged curves are plotted to connect the experimental points, determined for each 100-ft excess-range interval (or group of intervals if they had to be grouped to obtain a statistically valid sample). Smooth curves (broken lines) have been drawn through these empirical curves.

As with the curves of Fig. 4, the behavior of the curves of Fig. 7 around zero excess range is meaningful. In areas B, C, and D, taken in that order, the mean strengths of paths near the line of sight stand out increasingly strongly. In area A, on the other hand, the line-of-sight mean path strength is not substantially above the mean path strength of reflected paths.

Notice that the mean-strength curves approach asymptotes at approximately -85 dBm as the excess range increases. This asymptotic behavior is the effect of noise masking of the signal peaks. In explanation of this effect, we note that the rms video noise level was about -95 dBm, and noise peaks in the range -85 to -90 dBm were not uncommon. Thus signal peaks much below -90 dBm were often undetected, the result being to bias the mean signal strength upward. Therefore, the asymptotic portion of the curves should be interpreted only as indicating that paths with the corresponding excess ranges are often masked by the noise.

It is instructive to compare the mean strength $\mu(0)$ of the line-of-sight path with the theoretically expected strength of signals arriving over a path of the same length in free space. In order to compute the free-space strength, one must start with the peak radiated powers given in Table I and correct for

TABLE II
LOGARITHMIC PATH-STRENGTH CORRELATION COEFFICIENTS

Area	A	B	C	D
Paths 1 and 2	0.512	0.560	0.270	0.290
Paths 2 and 3	0.625	0.488	0.577	0.660

transmitting antenna gain, $1/r^2$ and $1/f^2$ space loss, receiving-antenna gain and efficiency, and receiver-cable losses. Upon making these calculations, one obtains the theoretical free-space-path received powers given in Fig. 7 in reference to $\mu(0)$. In San Francisco, the line-of-sight mean strength is of the order of 50 dB below free space, while in the East Bay, it is of the order of 10–20 dB below free space.

The final statistical results [item 6)] concern path-strength dependences. These dependences were evaluated by plotting scatter diagrams of first- and second-path strengths and of second- and third-path strengths. The scatter diagrams all showed a linear dependence between logarithmic strengths, i.e., each was composed of points well clustered around a straight line. Typical correlation coefficients ran from 0.4 to 0.6. More particularly, we obtained, at 1280 MHz, the coefficients given in Table II.

Scatter diagrams and correlation coefficients among other pairs of paths were not computed, but one may conjecture that the linear dependence among logarithmic path strengths will prove to be the rule upon further study.

As mentioned previously, the results of the experiments at 488 and 2920 MHz were very similar to those given before for 1280 MHz, the only major difference occurring in the 488-MHz probability-of-occupancy curve for area A. This curve differs from that in Fig. 4 (a) in its behavior at the origin. More particularly, at 488 MHz, paths with excess ranges from 0 to 1000 ft are just as probable as longer paths, rather than less probable; this effect is probably due to the greater ease with which 488-MHz waves can diffract around buildings.

REVISED MULTIPATH MODEL

On the basis of the experimental results just presented, it is clear that the preliminary multipath model given at the outset needs some revision and refining. One model which seems to fit the preceding experimental results well is the following. Suppose Re $\{s(t)e^{i\omega_0 t}\}$, $t \in (-\infty, \infty)$, is sent. Then Re $\{\rho(t)e^{i\omega_0 t}\}$, $t \in (-\infty, \infty)$, is received, where

$$\rho(t) = \sum_{k=0}^{\infty} S^{f_k} a_k s(t - t_k)e^{i\theta_k} + n(t) \qquad (2)$$

where $n(\cdot)$ is low-pass complex-valued white Gaussian noise; $20 \log_{10} a_k$ is normal with mean μ_k and variance σ_k^2; $20 \log_{10} S$ is normal with mean μ and variance σ^2; θ_k is uniformly distributed over $(0, 2\pi]$; $\{t_k - t_0\}_1^{\infty}$ is a modified[6] Poisson sequence with mean arrival rate determined by the empirical probability-of-occupancy curves; all the a_k, θ_k, and S are independent; and the $\{f_k\}_0^{\infty}$ are to be empirically determined.

Note that the kth path strength in (2), now denoted $S^{f_k} a_k$, is log normal as required, viz.,

$$20 \log_{10} S^{f_k} a_k = f_k (20 \log_{10} S) + 20 \log_{10} a_k$$

is normal with mean $f_k \mu + \mu_k$ and variance $f_k^2 \sigma^2 + \sigma_k^2$. Furthermore, the logarithmic path strengths are linearly dependent, as required: all of them contain linearly the common random variable $20 \log_{10} S$, the correlation being

$$\lambda_{jk} = \frac{f_j f_k \sigma^2}{\sqrt{(f_k^2 \sigma^2 + \sigma_k^2)(f_j^2 \sigma^2 + \sigma_j^2)}}, \qquad j \neq k. \qquad (3)$$

In order to validate the new model fully, it would, among other things, be necessary to compute λ_{jk} from the experimental data for every j and k, $j \neq k$. (We have only done this for $j = 1$, $k = 2$ and $j = 2$, $k = 3$.) Thus there are $N(N-1)/2$ distinct values of λ_{jk} for N paths, while there are only Nf_k to adjust. In order for the adjustment of the f_k to be possible, it would thus be necessary for the matrix of the λ_{jk} to have a special form, e.g., constant ($\lambda_{jk} = \lambda$, all $j \neq k$) or Toeplitz ($\lambda_{jk} = \lambda^{|j-k|}$, all $j \neq k$). This is not unlikely, but must be investigated further.[7]

[6] We have seen that the Poisson hypothesis concerning the excess-delay sequence $\{t_k - t_0\}_1^{\infty}$ is essentially correct for later members of the sequence, but is somewhat in error for initial members, and we have noted that this may reflect a tendency of initial paths to arrive in groups. In modeling this grouping tendency, one possibility is that the Poisson sequence be modified as follows. Initially, at t_0, the mean arrival rate is as derived from Fig. 4 (see footnote 3). Whenever there is an event—i.e., a path occurs—the mean arrival rate is increased by a factor K for the next Δ s, K and Δ being parameters to be chosen, perhaps as functions of t_k. When $K = 1$ or $\Delta = 0$, the process reverts to a standard Poisson sequence. Otherwise, the incidence of a path increases the probability that there will be another path within the next Δ s. This modified Poisson sequence was used successfully in some of the simulations described in [2]. Other modifications are also possible.

[7] It may be, of course, that a model which posits a single common variable $20 \log_{10} S$ in all logarithmic path strengths is too simple and that a more general linear transformation of independent variables will be needed to model the observed data adequately.

One attractive possibility envisages that S is a common path attenuation of all paths, so that $f_k = 1$, for all k. (This interpretation would account for our physical observation that paths often tend to fade in unison as the receiver is moved.) We have already seen (Fig. 7) that the path-strength standard deviation is almost constant with $t_k - t_0$, decreasing slowly from about 6-8 dB at $t_k - t_0 = 0$ to about 4-5 dB at $t_k - t_0 = 5$-7 μs. If we set $\sigma^2 = \sigma_0^2$, then λ_{jk} has the following characteristics:

1) when $t_j - t_0 \simeq t_k - t_0 \simeq 0$, then $\lambda_{jk} \simeq 0.5$ (we saw this experimentally for $j = 1$, $k = 2$ and $j = 2$, $k = 3$);
2) when $t_j - t_0 \simeq t_k - t_0 \simeq 5$-7 μs, then $\lambda_{jk} \simeq 0.6$;
3) when $t_j - t_0 \simeq 0$ and $t_k - t_0 \simeq 5$-7 μs, then $\lambda_{jk} \simeq 0.4$.

Another possibility is that f_k decreases from 1 to 0 as t_k increases, so that (again, with $\sigma^2 = \sigma_0^2$) λ_{jk} for paths with small excess delay is approximately 0.5, and λ_{jk} for paths of which at least one has large excess delay is approximately zero.

The performance of AVM systems of the radiolocation type depends most heavily on the strong initial paths having small excess delay. Therefore, in simulating such a system, any of a large variety of choices of f_k and σ, including the two just proposed, should be satisfactory. Indeed, in the companion paper on AVM simulation [2], we have used $f_k = 1$, for all k, and $\sigma = 2$-3 dB, and the resulting simulations reproduce experimental AVM system behavior almost exactly.

SUMMARY

We have experimentally derived a viable model for urban multipath propagation, which has proven itself in certain simulation experiments on AVM systems [2]. Clearly, the model will also be valuable for simulation studies of voice and digital-data systems which must operate in an urban environment.

Although the model is sufficiently refined to be useful, further refinement may be possible by a more elaborate analysis of the raw data. For example: the validity of the representation of the kth path strength as $S^{f_k} a_k$ should be studied and further refinements made, if necessary; if the path-strength model in (2) is valid, the sequence of f_k should be determined from the empirical data; the modification of the Poisson process discussed in footnote 6 should be further analyzed, along with other possible modifications, to obtain a better understanding of the non-Poisson nature of the initial path delays; and spatial correlations of the multipath variables should be determined to enable more accurate simulation of systems in which vehicle motion plays a part. These further refinements are implicit in our 55 000 cards of data, but must await further analysis for their discovery.

ACKNOWLEDGMENT

The authors are grateful to the Space Sciences Laboratory of the University of California, Berkeley, and to the City and County of San Francisco, Calif., for providing the transmission sites, and to the University of California Department of Physics for making the optical scanning table available.

REFERENCES

[1] "Urban vehicle monitoring: technology, economics and public policy," prepared by the Inst. Public Administration, Washington, D.C., and Teknekron, Inc., Berkeley, Calif., for the U.S. Dep. Housing and Urban Development under Grant H-1030, Final Rep. (See, in particular, "Vol. II: technical analysis" and "Vol. II-A: technical appendices," Oct. 31, 1970.)

[2] G. L. Turin, W. S. Jewell, and T. L. Johnston, "Simulation of urban vehicle-monitoring systems," *IEEE Trans. Veh. Technol.*, this issue, pp. 9–16.

[3] W. R. Young, Jr., and L. Y. Lacy, "Echoes in transmission at 450 megacycles from land-to-car radio units," *Proc. IRE*, vol. 38, pp. 255–258, Mar. 1950.

[4] H. F. Schmid, "A prediction model for multipath propagation of pulse signals at VHF and UHF over irregular terrain," *IEEE Trans. Antennas Propagat.*, vol. AP-18, pp. 253–258, Mar. 1970.

[5] G. L. Turin, "Simulation of urban locator systems—a preliminary report," in *Proc. 3rd Hawaiian Int. Conf. System Sciences*, pt. 2, pp. 809–812, 1970.

[6] ——, "Communication through noisy, random-multipath channels," *IRE Nat. Conv. Rec.*, pt. 4, pp. 154–166, 1956.

[7] R. H. Clarke, "A statistical theory of mobile-radio reception," *Bell Syst. Tech. J.*, vol. 47, pp. 957–1000, July–Aug. 1968.

[8] J. J. Egli, "Radio propagation above 40 mc over irregular terrain," *Proc. IRE*, vol. 45, pp. 1383–1391, Oct. 1957.

[9] D. K. Bailey, R. Bateman, and R. C. Kirby, "Radio transmission at VHF by scattering and other processes in the lower ionosphere," *Proc. IRE*, vol. 43, pp. 1181–1230, Oct. 1955.

[10] K. Bullington, W. J. Inkster, and A. L. Durkee, "Results of propagation tests at 505 mc and 4090 mc on beyond-horizon paths," *Proc. IRE*, vol. 43, pp. 1306–1316, Oct. 1955.

[11] J. H. Chisholm, P. A. Portmann, J. T. de Bettancourt, and J. F. Roche, "Investigations of angular scattering and multipath properties of tropospheric propagation of short radio waves beyond the horizon," *Proc. IRE*, vol. 43, pp. 1317–1335, Oct. 1955.

[12] "Chicago phase-ranging tests and conclusions," Raytheon Co., Wayland, Mass., June 1968. "Public urban locator service (PULSE)--background and conference proceedings," Clearinghouse for Federal Scientific and Technical Information, Springfield, Va., Document PB 180 116, Oct. 24, 1968, p. 164.

Determination of Service Area for VHF/UHF Land Mobile and Broadcast Operations Over Irregular Terrain

ALBRECHT P. BARSIS

Abstract—In this paper we define the service area of VHF/UHF land mobile and broadcast stations and demonstrate graphical and computer methods to determine and present such areas as a function of known equipment parameters and of a propagation model derived largely from an extensive measurement program over irregular terrain.

I. Introduction

LIMITATIONS in the amount of available electrospace, coupled with continuously increasing demands for frequencies to provide expanded or new services to users, make it mandatory to reexamine current definitions of service area for a given facility, or a given system, and to devise new or improved methods for defining and determining what constitutes useful service. Clearly, a number of technical as well as economic and sociological factors must enter into such definitions, although they may not have been explicitly identified. Apart from sociological and partly economic factors, such as, establishing the need for a particular service within a given area, any attempt to utilize the available electrospace in an efficient manner requires knowledge of several technical parameters that are based partly on equipment performance considerations, and partly on propagation; i.e., the effects of the propagation medium on the information transmitted between two points on or near the earth's surface.

In the most general case one would first establish the need for a given type of communication service using social and economic considerations. The technical feasibility of such a service would then be investigated by comparing *available* ratios of wanted signal power to the sum of unwanted signal powers (including noise) with the ratios *required* for satisfactory operation in accordance with some predetermined criteria or standards.[1] The required ratios are functions of equipment design and performance characteristics, as well as fine-scale fading characteristics; usually they may be assumed to be known or predetermined. Available ratios are primarily functions of environmental effects on the propagation of electromagnetic waves, although they are also dependent on operating parameters, such as, transmitter power, antenna height, antenna size, circuit losses, and the receiver noise figure. In this paper we will assume that the required ratios are known; thus the emphasis will be on the determination of service area on the basis of the statistical distributions of available ratios. The

operations or systems discussed here—generally in the frequency range between about 50 and 1000 MHz—may be best described with the aid of statistical techniques; a purely deterministic method for calculating transmission loss is usually not practical because of various random effects of atmospheric and terrain parameters.

Both VHF/UHF broadcast and land mobile systems are treated in this study because service requirements and propagation effects are quite similar. Furthermore, the Federal Communications Commission has recently authorized the sharing of UHF-TV channels by land mobile operations under quite rigorously specified conditions. Broadcasting consists of providing signals to arbitrary locations in a given area from one central transmitting antenna. Land mobile operations consist largely of two-way communications between a centrally located base station and mobile units at arbitrary locations, although communications between individual mobile units at arbitrary locations may also be required. The common elements for both types of services, which distinguish them from fixed point-to-point communication links, are 1) the arbitrariness of at least one of the link terminal locations, and 2) the impracticality of using deterministic methods for defining transmission loss over irregular terrain in such cases.

In what follows we will first define location variability and service area. Next we will provide source information for required propagation and system performance parameters. Finally the calculation methods for service area determination will be demonstrated using simple examples. Effects of correlation between signals from desired and undesired sources will be discussed in the Appendix.

II. Location Variability and Service Area

Variability of transmission loss when a receiving antenna is moved from point to point in irregular terrain has been amply demonstrated by measurements on FM and TV broadcast stations [1], [2]. More recently, an extensive measurement program of transmission loss[2] and its variability over irregular terrain has been conducted by the Institute for Telecommunication Sciences (ITS) for various defense agencies. Results have been summarized in [3] and have also been used as

---

Manuscript received July 13, 1971; revised June 26, 1972.

The author is with the Office of Telecommunications, Institute for Telecommunications Sciences, Boulder, Colo. 80302.

[1] This process is usually iterative with a general *a priori* knowledge of propagation effects mandatory for the first step.

[2] Transmission loss or path loss varies inversely with field strength or signal level. If all these quantities are expressed in decibels, additive constants depending on the system parameters can be defined to make conversions between transmission loss (in decibels), field strength (in decibels relative to a reference value), and received signal (power) levels in dBW or dBm. These terms are, therefore, used interchangeably in this paper.

Reprinted from *IEEE Trans. Veh. Technol.*, vol. VT-22, pp. 21–29, May 1973.

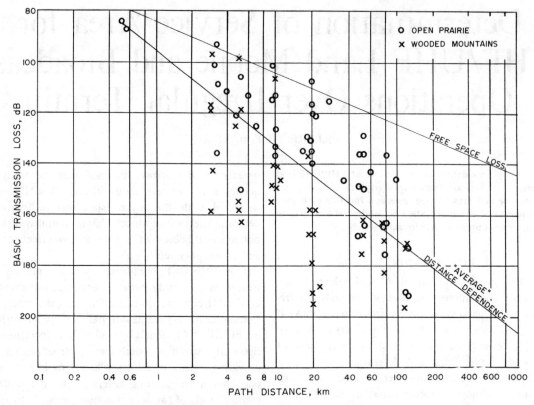

Fig. 1. Example of propagation measurements over irregular terrain at 410 MHz. Antenna heights 6.6 and 3 m above ground.

a basis for a new propagation model for calculating reference transmission loss at VHF and UHF as a function of terrain and atmospheric parameters [4], [5]. In fact, location (or point-to-point) variability of transmission loss over irregular terrain is so great that, at least for service fields at distances less than about 80 km (50 statute miles), time variations can usually be considered to be second-order effects and neglected. An example of location variability of basic transmission loss at 410 MHz is shown in Fig. 1 for antenna heights of 6.6 m and 3 m above ground, where two different terrain types (denoted by circles and crosses, respectively) are represented. The range of values obtained for a given path distance is quite substantial and amounts to more than 30 dB even in the relatively smooth and open terrain represented by the circles.

The required grade of service for broadcasting or land mobile applications can, as a first estimate, be easily defined by a minimum required signal-to-noise ratio in the presence of noise or by a minimum required ratio of wanted-to-unwanted signals when interfering signals other than noise are present. Neglecting time variations of signals as well as of noise, signal levels in irregular terrain still vary spatially as was demonstrated, and it is not always useful or practical to define unique "contours" of signal levels within which a required grade of service can be obtained. In any given area there may be some locations where the signal-to-noise ratio exceeds the required value during a given time fraction, and others where it does not. This is demonstrated in Fig. 2, where each black dot represents a location element receiving the required grade of service or better. Close to the transmitter the black dots predominate, and almost 100 percent of the area receives service. However,

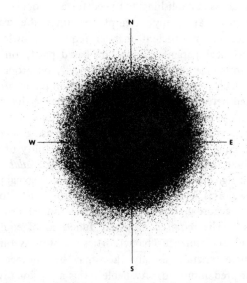

Fig. 2. Concept of service provided by land mobile or television broadcast station.

the appreciable number of locations at larger distances, which receive service, will also contribute to the total "service area" for a broadcast or land mobile station. A useful measure of such a service area would then be the total area A, in black in Fig. 2, which can be defined as

$$A = \int P \, dA \qquad (1)$$

where P is the probability of service for the incremental area dA. The integral in (1) may be approximated by summing a large number of terms $P_i A_i$, where A_i denotes the ith small area A_i within which P_i is the probability of service [6], as follows:

$$A = \sum_{i=1}^{n} P_i A_i. \qquad (2)$$

The size of the individual areas A_i will in practice depend on the characteristics of the terrain. If they are too large, large-scale inhomogeneities may be included that would negate the statistical approach used. In general, the A_i will be smaller in hilly or mountainous terrain than in smooth open terrain. The choice of the size and number of the A_i for any particular application will be determined by the extent of the total area under investigation and by the homogeneity of the terrain within the service area.

A graphical method for utilizing the distribution of received power levels within an incremental area A_i first proposed by Kirby [6] will be demonstrated in Section IV using a simple example. Computer procedures may be required in more complicated situations. Appropriate programs, as outlined in Section V, are already available at ITS.

III. PROPAGATION AND SYSTEM PARAMETERS

Early analyses of propagation data over irregular terrain, as quoted, for example, by Egli [7], have suggested that the distribution of signal levels expressed in decibels within any not-too-small area is approximately normal. Thus a median (equal to the mean for a normal distribution) and a standard deviation for each A_i can be utilized in the computation methods and models. This is also applicable to data from circular arcs or segments around a fixed terminal location. It appears that distance and antenna height are more important for derivation of the median field strength within a segment or a similar area than for the derivation of a standard deviation. Examples of recent measurement results presented in the form of cumulative distributions for various propagation path parameters are shown by Barsis [3] and Barsis, Johnson, and Miles [8].

On the basis of such data and earlier measurement results, Longley and Rice [4] have developed a model and computer method to calculate median transmission loss values as a function of terrain irregularity, carrier frequency, antenna heights above ground, and general criteria regarding the siting of path terminals with respect to foreground characteristics and elevation angles to the horizons. This is an "area" prediction, since it does not require knowledge of a detailed terrain profile and derived parameters for each path. It is particularly useful for broadcast and land mobile applications where a great number of potential propagation paths are involved.

Older methods were based on more detailed knowledge of propagation path and atmospheric parameters derived largely from specific terrain profiles between the actual terminal locations and with correction terms or factors added, which were based on applicable data samples. The resulting models were often used as a basis for nomographs and standard propagation curves. Examples are found in Bullington [9], Egli [7], Rice, Longley, Norton, and Barsis [10], and in the International Radio Consultive Committee recommendations [11]. These

"point-to-point" methods, although adapted for computer use and including other refinements, are not particularly suitable for land mobile and broadcast applications because of the large amount of detailed terrain profile information required. However, the choice between the "point-to-point" and the "area" methods will largely depend on the particular application.

The preceding discussion referred only to models and calculation methods for median transmission loss values in irregular terrain. Estimates of the standard deviation σ_{LA} characterizing the location variability are quoted by Egli [7], as an example. Based on measurements at frequencies between 20 and 100 MHz, Hufford and Montgomery,[3] as well as Longley and Rice [4], have provided estimates of σ_{LA} as a function of frequency and terrain parameters, respectively. Egli's work [7], which was based on data available at that time, suggests values of 8.3 dB for 127.5 MHz and 11.6 dB for 510 MHz independent of path distance. The expression in Longley and Rice [4] results in values of 9–10 dB for σ_{LA} except for very smooth terrain, and further studies have shown that these estimates also apply to frequencies up to 1000 MHz.[4] However, a more comprehensive variance analysis using more recent measurements, in addition to the earlier data, should be conducted in order to develop more general expressions including their confidence limits as a function of terrain characteristics, path distance, antenna heights, siting, terrain clutter, and carrier frequency values up to perhaps 10 GHz.

System performance parameters such as the required signal levels, or desired-to-undesired signal, and desired-signal-to-noise ratios have been defined in the FCC rules [12] and in the work of the Television Allocation Study Organization (TASO) (see, as an example, [1]). Equivalent data for various land mobile applications are unfortunately not available, and this constitutes a serious obstacle to comprehensive analyses. Some work was done more recently in conjunction with studies of sharing possibilities between television broadcast and land mobile operations [13].

For the example in the next section that illustrates procedures, we will use the Longley–Rice "area" prediction method for median field strength values and a standard deviation of 10 dB characterizing the location variability in irregular terrain. Assumptions will be made regarding minimum required signal levels and signal-to-noise ratios.

IV. EXAMPLE OF SERVICE AREA DETERMINATION

In cases where the terrain within a potential circular service area is sufficiently uniform—either as a whole or within a finite number of sectors, relatively simple graphical methods can be used. As an example, assume the system parameters as given in Table I. For simplicity it is assumed that external noise contributions are negligible compared to internal receiver noise. The line- and related system losses are for both system terminals.

In accordance with the Longley–Rice propagation model [4], we characterize the terrain by an interdecile range of terrain heights above and below arbitrary profiles within the

---

[3] Unpublished National Bureau of Standards Report (1966).
[4] Private communication by Ms. A. G. Longley.

155

TABLE I
EXAMPLE SYSTEM PARAMETERS

Operating frequency	460 MHz
Base station antenna height	100 ft above ground
Base station antenna gain	6 dB above isotropic
Base station transmitter power	100 W
Total line and related system losses	3 dB
Mobile station antenna height	6 ft above ground
Mobile station antenna gain	0 dB relative to isotropic
Predetection noise bandwidth	20 kHz
Receiver noise figure	10 dB
Minimum usable predetection signal-to-noise ratio	15 dB

area at any distance, that receive signals corresponding to a given maximum basic transmission loss value. For the assumptions used, the curves are straight lines on this type of graph paper. As an example, the maximum permissible value of 159 dB basic transmission loss is not exceeded at 83 percent of the locations at a path distance of 20 mi. For any specific system, the basic transmission loss scale in decibels can be translated into a scale of received field strength or received power levels by addition or subtraction of appropriate constants expressed in decibels (relative to a reference level such as 1 W).

The percentage or fraction of locations, for which the 159 dB maximum permissible transmission loss value is not exceeded, is determined for the various distances from Fig. 3, and these fractions are multiplied by each corresponding distance and plotted on linear graph paper such as Fig. 4 as ordinates with distance as the abscissa. The points are connected by a smooth curve, and the area under this curve—easily determined by counting grid squares or with the aid of a planimeter—is a measure of the area receiving service as defined earlier. The area under the 45° straight line is of course a measure of the total area out to a given distance. For the relation between abscissa and ordinate scale in Fig. 4, the total area A_0 to a distance (radius) d is expressed by

$$A_0 = \frac{2\pi}{n} \cdot \frac{d^2}{2} \tag{3}$$

where n is the number of sectors into which a circular area is divided. Therefore, the total area served A_s is related to the area measured under the curve A_Δ by

$$A_s = \frac{2\pi}{n} A_\Delta. \tag{4}$$

potential area. In the example, this parameter Δh is assumed to be 250 ft, corresponding to moderately rolling terrain. We further assume that receiver terminal locations are completely arbitrary, so that effective antenna heights will, on the average, not be greater than the physical heights above ground; thus no advantage is gained because of "good" siting.

The equipment performance parameters just listed define a maximum permissible value of basic transmission loss for satisfactory performance using methods such as those described in [14]. In the present example, the minimum required receiver input power is found to be –136 dBW, and the corresponding maximum permissible basic transmission loss value is 159 dB. The propagation model, on the other hand, provides median basic transmission loss values as a function of path distance, and the location variability is characterized by a standard deviation σ_{LA} = 10 dB, on the basis of the discussion in the preceding section.

Cumulative distributions of basic transmission loss can then be drawn on log-normal graph paper for various distances, as in Fig. 3. From this graph we can read directly or determine by interpolation the percentage of locations, within a small

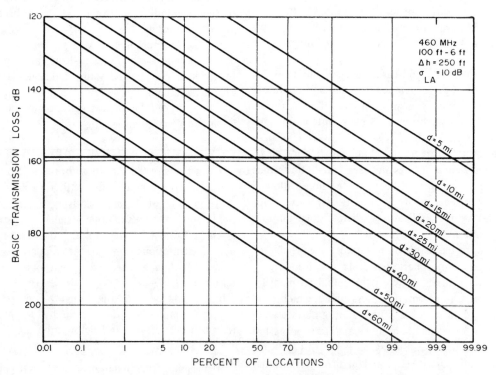

Fig. 3. Cumulative distributions of basic transmission loss for σ_{LA} = 10 dB.

156

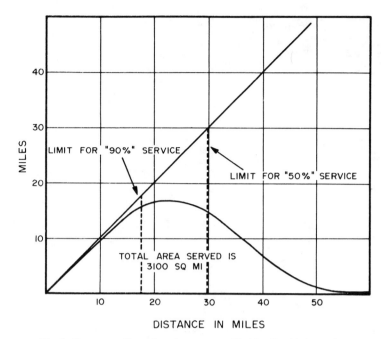

Fig. 4. Representation of service area provided by fixed base station.

For the example, the total area served is 3100 mi² if the graph is taken to be representative of a circular potential service area. Fig. 4 demonstrates quite clearly the appropriateness of the analogy depicted in Fig. 1, i.e., within 15 mi of the transmitter a very large percentage of the area receives service and beyond 30 mi the percentage decreases quite rapidly. Although there is some service even at distances greater than 45 mi, the percentage becomes practically negligible.

The ratio of each ordinate value on the curve to the corresponding value on the 45° line is the percentage of locations served within an incremental area at the distance given by the abscissa. It is easily seen that, for the example, approximately 30 mi corresponds to the distance at which one-half of the points within each *incremental* area receive service, and that a similar "90 percent" value would lie at 17.5 mi. These abscissa values are also indicated in Fig. 4. If, for administrative convenience, it is desirable to define "contours" or sections of contours about a fixed base station, it could be done by using these or similar percentage values. However, it must be understood that such contours do not necessarily correspond to specific field strength or transmission loss values.

V. COMPUTER METHODS

The example in the preceding section illustrates a situation that lends itself quite easily to simple graphical methods. However, such methods are usable only under somewhat restrictive assumptions, such as, the requirement of determining the service from a base station in relatively uniform terrain and limitations to service by noise alone. In the case of service limitations due to interference from other stations, the required signal power level would not be constant over a potential service area, since the level of the *unwanted* signal power also varies generally independent of the variations in the desired signal power. Service is then provided where a

TABLE II
DEFINITION OF SYMBOLS IN GRAPHIC REPRESENTATIONS

Symbol	Fraction of Incremental Area Served
0	<0.025
1	0.075–0.125
2	0.175–0.225
–	.
–	.
9	0.875–0.925
A	0.9375–0.9625
B	0.975–0.985
C	0.9875–0.9925
*	>0.999

fixed ratio between the two powers is exceeded. For such applications a computer method providing graphic printouts for easier visualization of the results was developed by D. R. Ewing of the Office of Telecommunications.[5]

The computer method essentially calculates the service probabilities P_i in (2), performs the required summations, and prints out results in the form of tables and graphs. The use of this method here is merely demonstrated by means of a simple example, since more complicated assumptions would not add very much to the objectives of this paper. The model used here is implicitly based on uniform terrain and assumes that field strength and location variability decrease monotonically with distance from the transmitter. However, the location variability reaches a minimum value at about 60 mi from the transmitter and remains constant for larger distances.

We want to determine: a) the effect of an interfering land mobile station on the service area of a commercial television broadcast station on channel 6 (82–88 MHz) if the land mobile station is operating within this band, and b) the mutual interference effect between identical land mobile operations.

[5] Private communication.

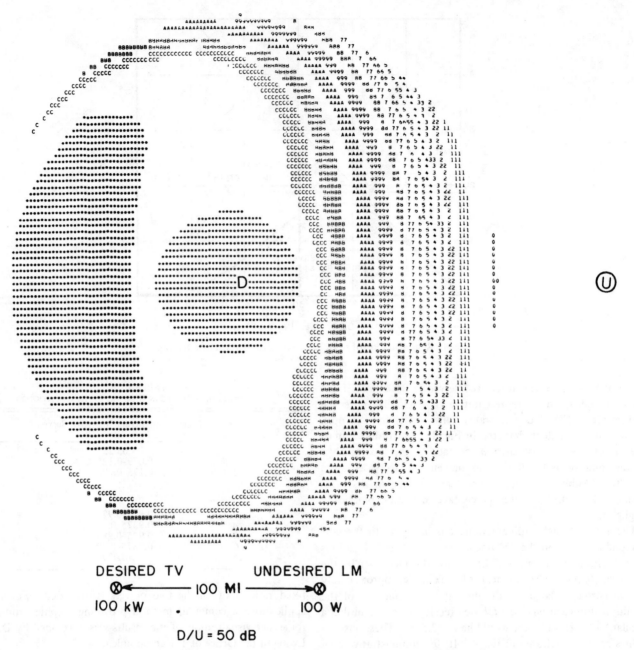

DESIRED TV   UNDESIRED LM

100 kW   ←— 100 MI —→   100 W

D/U = 50 dB

Fig. 5. Interference relations between television and land mobile stations.

We assume that the commercial television broadcast station on channel 6 has an effective antenna height of 1000 ft above average terrain and operates with 100 kW effective radiated power. The Federal Communications Commission Rules [12] specify a potential "Grade B" service area of 70-mi radius for such an operation (under the assumption that the terrain is homogeneous within this area). We now locate an interfering land mobile base station 100 mi from the television transmitter with an effective radiated power of 100 W and 100 ft effective antenna height under the same assumptions regarding terrain irregularity and homogeneity. Its narrow-band signal is radiated in a specific slot within the channel 6 bandwidth so that a minimum ratio of 50 dB between the desired television signal and the undesired land mobile signal is required to assure unimpaired television reception within the potential service area of the television station.

For simplicity, the time variability of both signals has been neglected in this example, although distances in excess of 100 mi are involved. In practical applications one would choose an appropriate value of time availability and correct the transmission loss values accordingly [4], [10]. It is also assumed that no spatial correlation exists between the location variability of the two signals; i.e., changes in the level of one of the signals are independent of changes in the level of the other when the receiving location is moved. Possible effects of spatial correlation of the signal levels will be discussed in the Appendix.

Under the assumptions given, the total service area of the television broadcast station within a 70-mi radius is 15 390 mi^2 if no interfering signal is present. With the presence of the land mobile station the area within this radius receiving satisfactory television service is reduced by 11.3 percent to

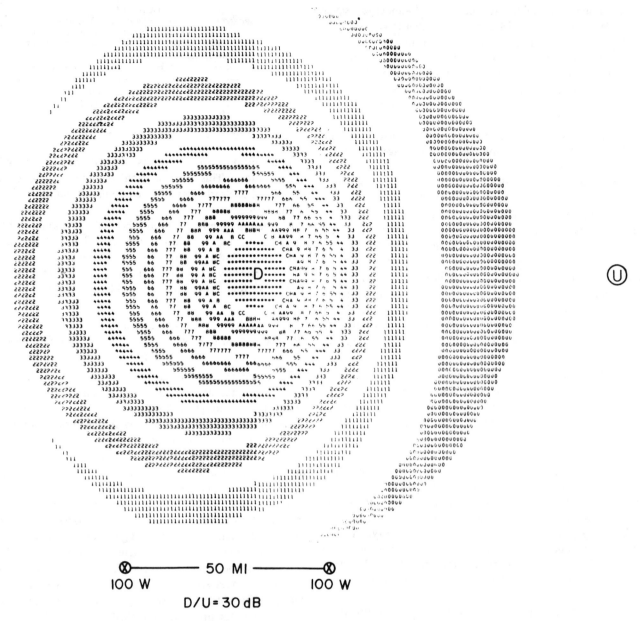

Fig. 6. Interference relations between two land mobile stations of equal power.

13 650 mi². The graphic computer printout for this situation is shown in Fig. 5. Here the desired (television) broadcast station is denoted by D and the location of the undesired land mobile station by U. Each of the other symbols in the printout represents a 1 × 5/3-mi rectangle with an area of 5/3 mi². These are the incremental areas for which the percentages receiving service are summed up to obtain the results given. The symbols denote the fraction of each incremental area served, and are listed in Table II.

Intermediate values (such as 0.125–0.175, or 0.925–0.9375) are suppressed in the printout in order to provide a clearer picture. Similarly, the symbols in the vicinity of D, the desired station location, are omitted. Thus the viewer is able to recognize effects of changing parameters by the shifts in the pattern.

The interpretation of the symbols is as follows. The symbol A, as an example, means that within the 5/3 mi² represented by it, a fraction of this area, amounting to a value between 0.9375 and 0.9625, receives satisfactory service as previously defined from the television broadcast station in the presence of the land mobile operation for the various parameters and other assumptions stated. It should be noted that the graphical presentation exaggerates somewhat the effects of interference, since the "scale" of percentage values, as in any statistical presentation, is expanded for values greater than 90 percent or the corresponding fraction 0.9. Thus, for the simple configuration represented, most of the area is characterized by the symbols *, A, B, and C, denoting service in excess of 90 percent; only in the direction toward the interfering station do the symbols denoting lower service probability appear. Such representations can become more complex when correlation is assumed, and quite unexpected configurations or "patterns" may result.

The second example deals with interference between two land mobile stations of equal power and antenna height (100 W and 100 ft, respectively) that are separated by 50 mi. Here

159

the minimum acceptable ratio of desired-to-undesired signal power is taken to be 30 dB, and the potential service area of a single land mobile station not limited by interference is assumed to have a radius of 36 mi. Using the same model for median transmission loss and spatial transmission loss variability and assuming no correlation between the signals, the computer method shows that the potential service area is reduced from 4072 to 1050 mi^2—a reduction of 74.2 percent. The situation is depicted graphically in Fig. 6 with the same symbols as in Fig. 5, except that the scale is changed. In Fig. 6 each symbol represents a $\frac{1}{2} \times \frac{5}{6}$ mi rectangle with an area of $\frac{5}{12}$ mi^2. Note also that the nominal service area is severely restricted by the presence of the second station.

The computer method provides a rapid means for determining the effects of parameter changes on the service area. As an example, the ratio D_W, expressed in decibels, between the effective radiated power of the desired (TV broadcast) station and the undesired (land mobile) station in the first example is quite critical. Computer runs were made for somewhat changed assumptions, corresponding to a 50-mi separation between the stations and a 40-mi radius for the potential service area (without interference) of the desired station. Table III shows the results for various values of D_W.

One may incorporate various socioeconomic parameters directly into the computer program if such parameters can be associated with the area increments used in the calculations. As an example, the Enumeration Districts or the Standard Location Areas (SLA) previously defined by the U.S. Census Bureau [15] may be used as the area increments in the program to obtain service estimates directly in terms of population. It is only necessary to define for each such increment the median basic transmission loss from the desired and undesired station and the appropriate value for the standard deviation σ_{LA} characterizing the location variability. Assuming uniform population distribution over each increment, the total number of people served can thus be estimated. Other statistics, such as, the number of dwelling units can be used in a similar manner.

The computer method also permits inclusion of effects of directional antenna patterns for the emissions involved and the combination of man-made or other noise with undesired signals. Similarly, the interfering effects from several discrete sources can be combined in the program. Norton and Fine [16], as an example, have shown how the distribution of an undesired signal, varying with location, can be convoluted with constant noise power.

VI. Concluding Summary

In this paper we have shown how the total service provided by a land mobile or broadcast station operating at VHF/UHF over irregular terrain can be determined using available information on the spatial distribution of field strength or transmission loss. Graphic and computer methods have been demonstrated using simple examples.

We must emphasize that this paper has addressed itself only to one of several aspects of the problem: one of the necessary assumptions is the *definition* of what constitutes acceptable service for any particular application and the translation of

TABLE III
PERCENTAGE OF AREAS SERVED FOR VARIOUS RATIOS
OF EFFECTIVE RADIATED POWER

Power Ratio, D_W (dB)	Percent of Potential Area Served
30	89.2
20	71.8
10	45.8
0	21.9

that definition into parameters, such as wanted-to-unwanted signal ratios. This consideration must be investigated separately and is clearly related to equipment technology and user requirements.

Detailed programming approaches will vary widely with the applications and with computer capabilities. Therefore, we have not included descriptions, flow diagrams, or listings of the programs used at ITS for the examples in Section V of this paper, but these can be made available on request.

Appendix
Relations Between Signal Levels and the Effects of Correlation

The discussion in the main body of this paper has shown that service area determination at frequencies in the 50–1000-MHz range in irregular terrain requires a knowledge of the mean and variance of desired as well as undesired signal levels. Further, it cannot always be assumed that the location variability of various signals is independent; i.e., increases and decreases in the power of two signals arriving from sources at different directions may be correlated to some degree, if the receiving location is changed. As an example, consider a receiving location within a small grove of trees: if it is moved into more open surroundings, signal levels originating from most directions are likely to increase. However, in general, correlation coefficients between signal level variations with location changes will be relatively small, and values significantly different from zero will occur only rarely [17], [18].

The computer programs described in Section V permit the insertion of either fixed correlation coefficients between variations in the desired and the undesired signals, or of any desired functional dependence of such correlation coefficients on the angles between the directions of arrival of two signals, or on other geometrical parameters. Calculations have also shown that for the case of interference from a land mobile station to a television broadcast service area (large ratio between desired and undesired signal powers) the effects of correlation are small, and even extreme assumptions (such as values of ±1) change only by small amounts the percentage of area served. For interference between two land mobile stations operating with equal power the effects are somewhat larger.

The following derivation may be helpful in summarizing the mathematical relationship between signal levels including the effects of correlation.

Let the received power level values of the two signals be expressed in decibels relative to an arbitrary reference level, and represented by D_i and U_i, respectively; and let their power ratio, also in decibels, be R_i. Then

$$R_i = D_i - U_i \qquad (1)$$

and for n locations in the area under consideration, the means, M_D and M_U, of the sample values D_i and U_i are

$$M_D = \frac{1}{n} \sum_{i=1}^{n} D_i \qquad (2)$$

and

$$M_U = \frac{1}{n} \sum_{i=1}^{n} U_i . \qquad (3)$$

It is easily seen that $M_R = M_D - M_U$ is independent of the correlation coefficient r_{DU} between variations in the desired and undesired signal levels, since it does not enter in the determination of the means. However, the variance s_R^2 of the power ratio R_i is given by

$$s_R^2 = s_D^2 + s_U^2 - 2 s_D s_U r_{DU} \qquad (4)$$

where

$$s_D^2 = \frac{1}{n-1} \left[\sum_{i=1}^{n} D_i^2 - \frac{\left(\sum_{i=1}^{n} D_i \right)^2}{n} \right] \qquad (5)$$

$$s_U^2 = \frac{1}{n-1} \left[\sum_{i=1}^{n} U_i^2 - \frac{\left(\sum_{i=1}^{n} U_i \right)^2}{n} \right] \qquad (6)$$

and

$$r_{DU} = \frac{n \sum_{i=1}^{n} D_i U_i - \sum_{i=1}^{n} D_i \sum_{i=1}^{n} U_i}{\sqrt{\left[n \sum_{i=1}^{n} D_i^2 - \left(\sum_{i=1}^{n} D_i \right)^2 \right] \left[n \sum_{i=1}^{n} U_i^2 - \left(\sum_{i=1}^{n} U_i \right)^2 \right]}} . \qquad (7)$$

Substitution into (4) of various values for the standard deviations s_D and s_U, with assumptions for the correlation coefficient r_{DU}, will result in the magnitude of the standard deviation s_R of the desired-to-undesired signal ratio (expressed in decibels) for each specific case. As an example, a value for $r_{DU} = +1$ will result in

$$s_R = s_D - s_U . \qquad (8)$$

If now the two standard deviations s_D and s_U are equal, the standard deviation s_R characterizing the variability of the desired-to-undesired signal ratio R is zero. This means that in such a special case the ratio is constant over the entire area for which the assumptions $s_D = s_U$ and $r_{DU} = 1$ are valid.

ACKNOWLEDGMENT

The author wishes to acknowledge the contributions by D. R. Ewing in developing the computer program, and by G. D. Gierhart and M. J. Miles in deriving the propagation model used in the example in Section V. The author is also grateful to Dr. G. A. Hufford, G. W. Haydon, and R. S. Kirby for their review and suggestions.

REFERENCES

[1] G. R. Town, "The television allocations study organization—a summary of its objectives, organization and accomplishments," *Proc. IRE*, vol. 48, pp. 993–999, June 1960.

[2] R. S. Kirby, H. T. Dougherty, and P. L. McQuate, "VHF propagation measurements in the Rocky Mountain region," *IRE Trans. Veh. Commun.*, vol. VC-6, pp. 13–19, July 1956.

[3] A. P. Barsis, "Radio wave propagation over irregular terrain in the 76- to 9200-MHz frequency range," *IEEE Trans. Veh. Technol.*, vol. VT-20, pp. 41–62, Aug. 1971.

[4] A. G. Longley and P. L. Rice, "Prediction of tropospheric transmission loss over irregular terrain—a computer method—1968," Environmental Science Services Administration Tech. Rep. ERL 79–ITS 67, U.S. Government Printing Office, Washington, D.C., 1968.

[5] A. G. Longley and P. L. Rice, "Prediction of tropospheric transmission loss over irregular terrain," in *AGARD Conf. Proc.*, no. 70, vol. CP-70-71, NATO-AGARD, Neuilly-sur-Seine, France, Feb. 1971.

[6] R. S. Kirby, "Measurement of service area for television broadcasting," *IRE Trans. Broadcast Transm. Syst.*, vol. PGBTS-7, pp. 23–30, Feb. 1957.

[7] J. J. Egli, "Radio propagation above 40 Mc over irregular terrain," *Proc. IRE*, vol. 45, pp. 1383–1391, Oct. 1957.

[8] A. P. Barsis, M. E. Johnson, and M. J. Miles, "Analysis of propagation measurements over irregular terrain in the 76- to 9200–MHz range," Environmental Science Services Administration Tech. Rep. ERL 114–ITS 82, U.S. Government Printing Office, Washington, D.C., 1969.

[9] K. Bullington, "Radio propagation at frequencies above 30 megacycles," *Proc. IRE*, vol. 35, pp. 1122–1136, Oct. 1947.

[10] P. L. Rice, A. G. Longley, K. A. Norton, and A. P. Barsis, "Transmission loss predictions for tropospheric communication circuits (vol. 1 and 2)," Nat. Bur. Stand., Tech. Note 101, U.S. Government Printing Office, Washington, D.C., 1967.

[11] *Documents of the 11th Plenary Assembly, International Radio Consultive Committee, 1966 Part 1: Radio Relay Systems*, vol. IV. Geneva: International Telecommunications Union, 1967.

[12] Federal Communications Commission, Rules and Regulations, Subpart E–Television Broadcast Stations, U.S. Government Printing Office, Washington, D.C., 1968.

[13] Committee for Testing Sharing of VHF TV Channels by the Land Mobile Radio Service, Final Rep., Federal Communications Commission, 1969.

[14] A. P. Barsis, K. A. Norton, and P. L. Rice, "Predicting the performance of tropospheric telecommunication links, singly and in tandem," *IRE Trans. Commun. Syst.*, vol. CS-10, pp. 2–22, Mar. 1962.

[15] U.S. Bureau of the Census, "Population within 50 miles of selected points," Geographic Reps. vol. GE-10, U.S. Government Printing Office, Washington, D.C., 1963.

[16] K. A. Norton and H. Fine, "A study of methods for efficient allocation of radio frequencies to broadcast services operating in the range above 50 Mc," Nat. Bur. Stand., Rep. CRPL-4-5, 1949.

[17] M. J. Miles, "The effect of irregular terrain and atmosphere on correlation between transmission loss values," Environmental Science Services Administration Tech. Rep. ERL 84–ITS 69, U.S. Government Printing Office, Washington, D.C., 1968.

[18] R. E. Skerjanec, "A note on measured spatial correlation coefficients between VHF signals received in irregular terrain," Environmental Science Services Administration Tech. Memo. ERLTM-ITS 197, Inst. for Telecommun. Sci., Boulder, Colo. 1969.

Computer Prediction of Service Areas for VHF and UHF Land Mobile Radio Services

J. DURKIN

Abstract— A computer program written to predict the effective service area of a transmitter in a VHF or UHF mobile radio network is described. The computed results enable field strength contours to be determined, and hence provide more useful information than is possible by reference to standard statistical curves. Present manual methods of calculating the attenuation to be expected over transmission paths rely on the laborious extraction of essential ground profile information along the path joining the transmitter to the receiver. This difficulty may be overcome by using a topographical data base in a computerized method of service area prediction. With this scheme each data base entry represents the effective terrain height above sea level within each 0.5-km square. A high-speed computer can access the necessary information from the data base to reconstruct a close approximation of the radio path profile. The reconstructed profile is then processed to calculate the transmission loss. These computations are repeated for numerous points throughout the area and enable field strength contours to be deduced. The propagation model described forms part of a fully automated frequency assignment procedure for the private land mobile radio services in operation in the Directorate of Radio Technology, Home Office, UK.

I. INTRODUCTION

THE UK land mobile services are currently expanding at the rate of 10 percent per annum and will continue to expand as new applications of mobile radio are introduced. At the present time there are approximately 16 000 base stations using the 800 channels available in the VHF and UHF bands. The demand for mobile radio systems is greatest in the larger conurbations, and more sophisticated techniques to assess potential interference are required.

The prediction of the area of coverage and the potential interference of a radio transmitter is of vital importance in the planning of any mobile radio communication network. Methods for calculating the attenuation to be expected over transmission paths in point-to-point links have been well developed at both UHF and VHF. Many authors have developed nomograms and charts to permit calculation of expected field strengths from a given transmitter at chosen receiver locations. These calculation aids rely on the laborious extraction of essential ground profile information along the radial joining the transmitter to the receiver.

The prediction of area coverage of a transmitter appears to have received limited attention. This is primarily due to the difficulty of handling area topographical data and to the immense computational task of evaluating field strengths at a large enough number of receiver locations to permit field strengths contours to be determined. However, the modern digital computer with its vast storage capability and speed of calculation has now made area field strength prediction possible.

This paper describes a computer program written to calculate the theoretical field strength contours from a specified transmitter to an accuracy and resolution adequate for VHF and UHF mobile radio network applications. The program executes two main computational tasks. Firstly, from stored geographical data, the ground profile along a radial from the transmitter to a chosen receiver location is reconstructed. Secondly, the path attenuation to be expected along this profile is evaluated. These computations are repeated for a large number of points along 72 equally spaced radials from the transmitter to enable field strength contours to be deduced.

II. GROUND PROFILE RECONSTRUCTION

The data storage requirement, computation time, resolution, and accuracy of the program depend on the following

Manuscript received March 15, 1977; revised August 8, 1977.

The author is with the Land Mobile Services Branch, Home Office, Waterloo Road, London SE1 8UA, England.

Reprinted from *IEEE Trans. Veh. Technol.*, vol. VT-26, pp. 323–327, Nov. 1977.

factors:

    a) the density and form of geographical data to be extracted from the proposed service area;

    b) the number of radials along which the transmission loss has to be calculated (using a large number of radials will improve the accuracy but leads to excessive computation time);

    c) the interval along the radial at which calculations of signal strength are determined (since the terrain database contains a reading every 0.5-km square, it was decided to estimate the transmission loss every 0.5 km along each discrete radial from the transmitter).

For the above reasons considerable attention was given to the problem of ground profile reconstruction and the number of computations required to achieve a reasonable degree of accuracy.

A. Storage of Geographical Data

For use in the United Kingdon, the Ordnance Survey $2\frac{1}{2}$ in/1 m (1:25 000) maps have been divided into 0.5-km squares [1]. A representative height has been deduced from the maps to represent the terrain height over each 0.5-km square. This work, involving the examination of some 1 760 000 squares, was carried out by a specialized contractor using comprehensive error detecting methods. Various procedures for the assignment of a height to each of the 0.5-km squares were compared from the point of view of the preservation of the fidelity of the essentail topographic features of the ground profile in the reconstruction process. Comprehensive details have been shown by Edwards and Durkin [1] and Durkin [4] regarding the data format and data base organization.

B. Interpolation for Profile Reconstruction

For a specified transmitter site and each chosen receiver location it is necessary to reconstruct the intervening ground profile from the stored geographical data so that the expected path attenuation can be calculated. The computer program was written to evaluate points on the profile by means of an interpolation routine described in this section and record them in the form of the $2 \times (n + 1)$ matrix; the maximum value of n was set at 200 which represented 200-half-km intervals

$$D = \begin{bmatrix} d_0 & h_0 \\ d_1 & h_1 \\ d_2 & h_2 \\ \cdot & \cdot \\ \cdot & \cdot \\ \cdot & \cdot \\ d_n & h_n \end{bmatrix}. \tag{1}$$

The first column is a list of distances (see nomenclature list) measured from the transmitter such that

$$d_n - d_{n-1} = 0.5 \text{ km}, \tag{2}$$

and the second column is a list of the corresponding calculated heights of the ground profile. The matrix is arranged such that

$$d_{m-1} < d < d_m + 1. \tag{3}$$

The following diagram shows a typical transmission path TR overlaid on the matrix A of stored heights.

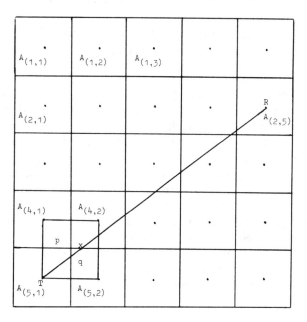

$$\sum_{r=1}^{2} \sum_{s=1}^{2} (h_{rs}, P_r Q_s) \tag{4}$$

where using Lagranges method for interpolation and the related difference formula

$$P_1 = 1 - p \quad\quad P_2 = p \quad\quad Q_1 = 1 - q \quad\quad Q_2 = q \tag{5}$$

gives the expression for the interpolation height as

$$h_x = h_{5,1}(1 - p)(1 - q) + h_{5,2}(1 - p)q + h_{4,1}(1 - q)p + h_{4,2}pq. \tag{6}$$

Thus h_x and 0.5 km became the second entires in the matrix D as given in (1). The computer then steps another half kilometer, and repeats the procedure until it reaches a maximum distance of 100 km from the base station.

Using the above method of storing terrain heights and using the interpolation techniques to derive a path profile enables the attenuation calculations to be reduced to that of the attenuation along a series of equally spaced radials emanating from the base station. In view of the computation time and storage requirements it was decided to use 72 transmission radials spaced at 5 deg intervals around the base station. This gave a compromise between the desired accuracy and the computation time. Also, by interpolating at regular 0.5-km intervals along each transmission radial, the computer programs were simplified and provided adequate resolution and accuracy as the original topographical data base had at height recordings every 0.5-km interval. However, the computer interpolated profiles were compared with profiles extracted from the original maps, and this showed that no significant topographical features had been lost in the interpolation process. This method of interpolation was compared to the method of linear interpolation as in [1] given by Edwards and Durkin, and no significant differences were apparent.

III. TRANSMISSION PATH ATTENUATION CALCULATIONS

The previous sections have shown that the service area prediction can be reduced to the calculation of the expected attenuation along a series of transmission paths. With this simplification it is possible to make use of well-established techniques which have been successfully applied to point-to-point link calculations. In the USA in recent years, various extensive programs of measurements have been undertaken at VHF over irregular terrain using low-antenna heights and some of the results have been used by the Environmental Science Services Administration (ESSA) to develop a computer method for estimating transmission loss over irregular terrain. This section will describe a modified application of the ESSA method [3] and its adaption to include the use of CCIR smooth-earth propagation curves.

A. Path Parameters

The type of paths encountered will be considered either optical (i.e., when the base station and mobile station antennae are mutually visible or when the angle of diffraction θ is less or equal to zero), or non-optical, whose transmission path is obstructed (i.e., when the angular distance θ is greater than zero (Fig 1)). In both cases the effective base station antenna height is evaluated from the expression

$$h_{eb} = h_b + K \exp\left(-2h_b/\Delta h(d)\right) \qquad (7)$$

[3, p. 11] where

h_{eb} effective antenna height;
h_b actual antenna height;
K = 50 for values of $h_b \geqslant 100$ m;
K = 10 for values of $h_b \leqslant 10$ m;
$\Delta h(d)$ interdecile range of terrain heights above and below a straight line fitted to elevations above sea level.

For values of h_b between 10 m and 100 m the value of K is determined by linear interpolation. The total path loss between the base station transmitter and the mobile receiver is determined as follows:

$$\text{total path loss} = \text{free space loss} + L_{50,50} \qquad (8)$$

[3, p. 14] where $L_{50,50}$ represents the smooth earth loss not exceeded at 50 percent of locations for 50 percent of the time on the $L_{50,50}$ contours.

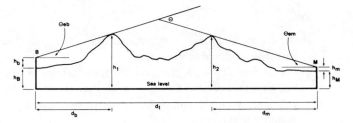

Fig. 1.   Geometry of nonoptical radio path.

In (8) the free space loss takes into account the base station transmitter power and the gain of its antenna relative to a dipole. In determining this loss, dipoles have been taken as the reference antennae for both the base station and the mobile. The received signal power is calculated from

received signal power

$$= 32 + 20 \log(f) + 20 \log(d) - 10 \log(p) - \text{antenna gain},$$

$$(9)$$

where

f frequency in megahertz,
d length of transmission path (kms),
P base station power in watts.

$L_{50,50}$ is now computed depending on the type of radio path.

B. Optical or Line-of-Sight Paths

A transmission path is considered line of sight if the diffraction angle (θ) is less than zero. This condition is detected by computing the vertical distance between the actual height of the terrain and the height at that point of the straight line between the transmitter and receiver aerials. If a positive value is obtained at any point along the radial then the path is deemed not in line of sight. For line-of-sight paths

$$L_{50,50} = A_r.$$

A_r is defined as the diffraction loss assuming a smooth earth and is obtained from either Fig. 2, 3, or 4 depending on the frequency and effective base station antenna height. These curves are stored in the computer as simple reference tables, are derived from the CCIR Atlas [5] containing theoretical propagation curves for a smooth earth, and assume a mobile station height of 2 m. The total path loss is

$$\text{total path loss} = \text{free space loss} + A_r. \qquad (10)$$

C. Non-Line-of-Sight Paths

Fig. 1 illustrates a typical nonoptical path likely to be associated with a specific transmission radial. The total angular distance θ is given by

$$\theta = \theta_{eb} + \theta_{em}$$

where θ_{eb} and θ_{em} are as shown in Fig. 1.

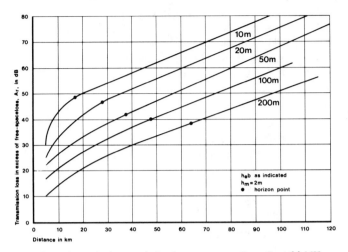

Fig. 2.   Theoretical transmission loss over smooth earth at 80 MHz.

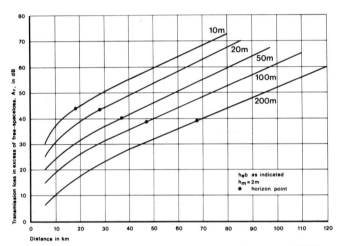

Fig. 3.   Theoretical transmission loss over smooth earth at 160 MHz.

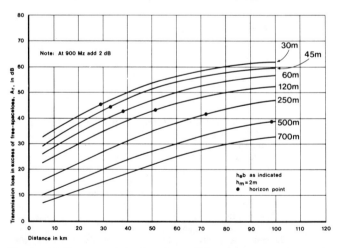

Fig. 4.   Median transmission loss due to diffraction over quasi-smooth earth in rural areas (frequency 460 MHz).

In determining $L_{50,50}$ for nonoptical paths it is first necessary to derive A_r as given in Section III-B, and add to this a weighted average of the diffraction loss A_k over a single or double knife edge as applicable, i.e.,

$$L_{50,50} = (1-w)A_k + wA_r \qquad (11)$$

[3, p. 17, (13)]. w is an empirical weighting factor defined by

$$w = \left\{ 1 + 0.1 \left[\frac{\Delta h(d)}{\lambda} \left(\sqrt{\frac{2h_{eb} + 10}{2h_b + 10}} \right. \right. \right.$$

$$\left. \left. \left. + \frac{a\theta + db + dm}{d_t} \right) \right] \frac{1}{2} \right\} - 1 \qquad (12)$$

[3, annex 3, 3.23]. The derivation of A_k is as follows. Having determined the effective height of the base station, it is then necessary to determine the effective aerial height of the mobile station h_{em}, where

$$h_{em} = 2 + 10 \exp\left(-4/\Delta h(d)\right). \qquad (13)$$

Using (7) and (13), d_{Ls} is computed as

$$d_{Ls} = \sqrt{17 h_{eb}} + \sqrt{17 h_{em}} \qquad (14)$$

where d_{Ls} is the sum of the base station and mobile horizon distances. Having evaluated d_{Ls}, it is now possible to obtain a value for d_z which is used to evaluate the variables V_b and V_m

$$\text{if } d_t \leqslant d_{Ls}, \qquad \text{then } d_z = d_{Ls}$$

$$\text{if } d_t > d_{Ls}, \qquad \text{then } d_z = d_t + 0.5(72250000/f)^{1/3}.$$

Having computed the variable d_z, the variables V_b and V_m are calculated to determine the diffraction loss A_k:

$$V_b = 1.2915.\theta.\sqrt{fd_b(d_z - d_b - d_m)/(d_t - d_m)} \qquad (15)$$

[3, annex 3, 3.26(a)] and

$$V_m = 1.2915.\theta.\sqrt{fd_m(d_z - d_b - d_m)/(d_t - d_b)}. \qquad (16)$$

[3, annex 3, 3.26(c)]. A_k is now computed depending on the values of the variables V_b and V_m [3], annex 3, 3.27 (a)]. (i) If $V_b \leqslant 2.4$ and $V_m \leqslant 2.4$, then

$$A_k = 12.04 + 9.11(V_b + V_m) - 1.27(V_b)^2 - 1.27(V_m)^2. \qquad (17)$$

(ii) If $V_b \leqslant 2.4$ and $V_m > 2.4$, then

$$A_k = 19 + 9.11 V_b - 1.27(V_b)^2 + 20 \log V_m. \qquad (18)$$

(iii) If $V_b > 2.4$ and $V_m \leqslant 2.4$, then

$$A_k = 19 + 20 \log V_b + 9.11 V_m - 1.27(V_m)^2. \qquad (19)$$

(iv) If $V_b > 2.4$ and $V_m > 2.4$, then

$$A_k = 26 + 20 \log (V_b V_m). \qquad (20)$$

Having determined A_k and the weighting factor w, $L_{50,50}$ is computed from (11) and the total transmission loss evaluated by adding the free space loss, i.e.,

$$\text{total loss} = \text{free space loss} + (1-w)A_k + wA_r. \qquad (21)$$

D. Summary of Transmission Loss Calculations

With the development of the transmission loss routines, it was possible to compare the attenuations predicted for an actual profile and its reconstructed counterpart. Examples were chosen to include profiles which were line-of-sight and non-line-of-sight, and in each case the comparisons showed a difference of less than 3 dB. The labor involved in making such comparisons prevented a sufficient number of differences being obtained for statistical conclusions to be drawn. The effect of the earth curvature was also incorporated into the computer program. The radius of the earth was taken to be 4/3 of its true value to allow for atmospheric refraction of the transmitted wave. However, for the relatively short transmission paths (less that 20 km), this correction was found to have negligible influence, but it had a significant effect on the longer transmission radials. It is also possible to include a correction for absorption of the transmitted wave over irregular terrain. Saxton [6] has given an empirical relationship for this additional loss as a function of frequency for "average" irregular terrain; however, at a frequency of 85 MHz used for the experimental verification of the computer program, this correction is negligible. At higher frequencies, however, this additional correction can be readily incorporated. It should be noted that multipath propagation is not included in the present algorithms, but as improved information on the effect of multipath propagation becomes available the algorithms can be improved.

IV. EXPERIMENTAL VERIFICATION

In order to evaluate the accuracy of the computer program, its performance in predicting the area of coverage for an actual mobile radio installation was investigated. A preliminary study of the accuracy of this new method has been made by comparing the predicted values of signal strength set up by a 85 MHz transmitter at Barkway, Hertfordshire, UK, with the values measured along the computed -136 dBW signal strength contour.

The computer program was run with the appropriate engineering parameters to predict the geographical location of the -136 dBW (corresponds to 12 dB SINAD for a receiver input of 0.7 uV emf) signal strength contour on each of the 72 radials surrounding the base station. In addition, the computer printed out the signal strength level at 0.5-km intervals along each radial up to a maximum distance of 100 km. Practical measurements were made on the transmitter using a test vehicle incorporating a half-wavelength receiving dipole. Test receiver locations were always taken to be on a road, as this is the normal siting for mobile radio working, but otherwise were selected at random. A total of 270 readings was recorded; about half the readings were at locations within line of sight of the transmitter, with the remainder being in shadow. By expressing in decibels the ratio of actual measurements to those predicted by the computer, samples of the estimation error process were obtained. The standard deviation of the errors settled down to a value less than 10 dB.

NOMENCLATURE

D Height distance matrix.
$A(i,j)$ Matrix of stored terrain heights.
a Effective radius of the earth in kilometers.
A_k Total diffraction loss in decibels (dB).
A_r Smooth earth diffraction loss in decibels (dB).
$L_{50,50}$ Loss not exceeded at 50 percent locations for 50 percent of the time.
d Length of transmission path in kilometers.
d_b Distance of the base station from the radio horizon.
d_m Distance of the mobile station from the radio horizon.
d_{Ls} Sum of the base station and mobile station horizon distances.
d_z Variable used in determining V_b and V_m.
f Frequency of the radio wave in megahertz.
h_{eb} Effective height in meters of the base station antenna.
h_{em} Effective height in meters of the mobile station antenna.
h_b Height above ground level (meters) of the base station antenna.
h_m Height above ground level (meters) of the mobile station antenna.
h_B Height of the base station above sea level (m).
h_M Height of the mobile station above sea level (m).
K Factor used to determine the effective height of the antenna.
V_B, V_M Parameters used to determine A_k, the diffraction loss.
$\Delta h(d)$ Difference in height (meters) exceeded by 10 percent and 90 percent of terrain along a given transmission path.
θ Angular distance (radius) for a nonoptical path.
θ_{eb} Horizon elevation as seen by the base station antenna.
θ_{em} Horizon elevation as seen by the mobile station antenna.
λ Wavelength in meters.
P Base station transmitter power in watts [ERP].

REFERENCES

[1] R. Edwards and J. Durkin, "Computer prediction of service areas for VHF mobile radio networks," *Proc. IEE (London)*, vol. 116, no. 9, pp. 1493–1500, 1969.
[2] C. E. Dadson, J. Durkin, and R. E. Martin, "Computer prediction of field strength in the planning of radio systems," *IEEE Trans. Veh. Technol.*, vol. VT-24, no. 1, Feb. 1975.
[3] A. G. Longley and P. L. Rice, "Prediction of tropospheric radio transmission loss over irregular terrain, a computer method," ESSA Tech. Rep., ERL -79-ITS 67, Institute for Telecommunications Sciences, Boulder, CO.
[4] J. Durkin, "A Study of Computer Methods in Mobile Radio Planning," Ph.D. thesis, Victoria University of Manchester, Sept 1969.
[5] Atlas of Ground-Wave Propagation Curves for Frequencies between 30 MHz and 300 MHz. CCIR Resolution no. 11, Geneva, 1955.
[6] J. A. Saxton, "Basic ground-wave propagation characteristics in the frequency band 50–800 Mc/s," in *Proc. IEE*, vol. 101, pt. III, pp. 211–224, 1954.

Mobile Radio Signal Correlation Versus Antenna Height and Spacing

WILLIAM C. Y. LEE, MEMBER, IEEE

Abstract—In mobile radio communications, a given correlation value between two signals received at a base station can be achieved by adjusting the antenna spacing and height; this has been experimentally verified [1], [2]. From this fact, a parameter η, defined as

$$\eta = \frac{\text{antenna height}}{\text{antenna spacing}}$$

is proposed as a measure of correlation for design purposes. Data from field experiments using horizontally spaced, vertically polarized base-station antennas have been analyzed in terms of η and are presented here. These data provide an upper bound correlation coefficient for any antenna separation and height. The upper bound value can be directly applied in system design.

I. INTRODUCTION

RHEE'S and Zysman's data [1] and Lee's [2] data experimentally verify the fact that adjusting both antenna heights and spacings at a base station can achieve a given decorrelation value between two signals. From this fact, a new design parameter η is defined as

$$\eta = \frac{\text{antenna height}}{\text{antenna spacing}}.$$

The parameter η is useful in selecting an antenna placement which achieves a desired signal decorrelation. To illustrate the use of the new parameter η, we first choose only a few data points from [1] and plot them in Fig. 1. The transmission paths for obtaining those data are approximately 3 mi from a broadside configuration of the two base-station antennas as sketched in the figure. For each one of three base-station antenna separations (3.4λ, 6.6λ, and 10λ) and a given antenna height (the height for the case we choose is 41.7λ), three areas I, J, and K indicated in the figure are the locations where the data were obtained. Hence, for each of three η (12.26, 6.32, and 4.17) there are three points shown in the figure corresponding to the measured correlation coefficients in each of three locations I, J, and K.

In Fig. 2, we just add more data points to the data already shown in Fig. 1. One set of data is from Rhee's and Zysman's paper [1] and another set from Lee's paper [3] for the broadside orientation of horizontally spaced vertically polarized base-station antennas.[1] The antenna configuration for these data is the same as shown in Fig. 1. The circular and square data points used in Fig. 2 correspond to antenna heights of 100 ft and 50 ft, respectively, obtained from [1]. The triangular data points correspond to an antenna height of 300 ft from [3]. The antenna heights are converted to wavelengths at 850 MHz.

Using the distribution of experimental data points in Fig. 2, a linear regression line [4], [5] can be drawn to fit the highest correlation data points (the circled data), for all η in a statistical sense. The measured data will lie below this line with high probability. The linear regression line can now be used to select a value of η for any desired amount of signal decorrelation. From the value of η, the relation of required antenna height and spacing is found. For example, η equals 11 for a correlation of $\rho = 0.7$ as shown from the linear regression line in Fig. 2. This means that a requirement for the cross correlation of two base-station signals not to exceed 0.7 can be satisfied by a value of η as large as 11. (It is desired, of course, for physical design and implementation reasons to keep η as large as possible.) This agrees fairly well with Rhee's and Zysman's conclusion requiring antenna spacings of 6.7λ at a height of 83.5λ ($= 100$ ft) or 3.4λ at a height of 41.7λ, for correlations less than 0.7. A conservative estimate line separated from the linear regression line by 2σ is also shown in Fig. 2 for designing consideration.

II. EFFECT OF ANTENNA ORIENTATION

The extreme correlation data[2] from [3] have been plotted versus η for different angular orientations of two base-station antennas; the resultant plot is shown in Fig. 3. For these data the base-station antennas were pointed at a given angle α shown in Fig. 3, while the measurements were taken by a mobile unit at a distance of approximately 3 mi. From these extreme data, a tendency for increasing correlation value with increasing η has been observed for all angles of antenna orientation. Linear regression curves have again been fitted to the data, one curve for each angle of base-station antenna orientation. The data can be expected to lie below these lines with

---

Manuscript received November 2, 1976; revised January 14, 1977. This paper was presented at the 26th Annual IEEE Vehicular Technology Conference, Washington, DC, March 24–26, 1976.

The author is with Bell Telephone Laboratories, Whippany, NJ 07981.

[1] The Rhee/Zysman data are obtained using omnidirectional antennas; Lee's data are from measurements using directional antennas with 25° azimuth beamwidth.

[2] Extreme correlation data are the highest correlation coefficient data selected from different angular orientations of two base-station antennas.

Reprinted from *IEEE Trans. Veh. Technol.*, vol. VT-25, pp. 290–292, Aug. 1977.

167

VERTICAL POLARIZATION HORIZONTAL SPACING AND
BROADSIDE ORIENTATION FOR THE BASE-STATION ANTENNAS
IN SUBURBAN AREAS - (TRANSMISSION PATH = 3 MILES)

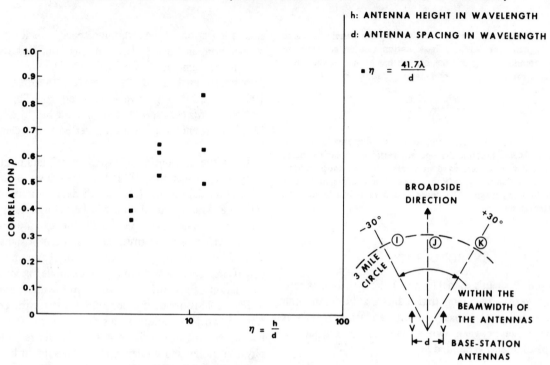

Fig. 1. Correlation versus antenna height and spacing (broadside case)—illustration.

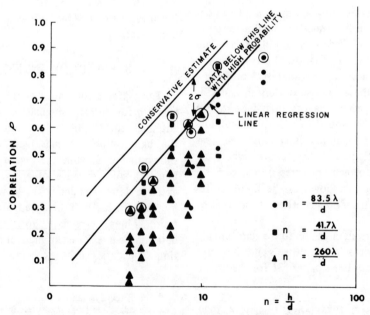

Fig. 2. Correlation versus antenna height and spacing (broadside case)—analysis.

EXTREME DATA OF CORRELATION FOR VERTICAL POLARIZATION HORIZONTAL SPACING BASE-STATION ANTENNAS IN SUBURBAN AREAS - (TRANSMISSION PATH = 3 MILES)

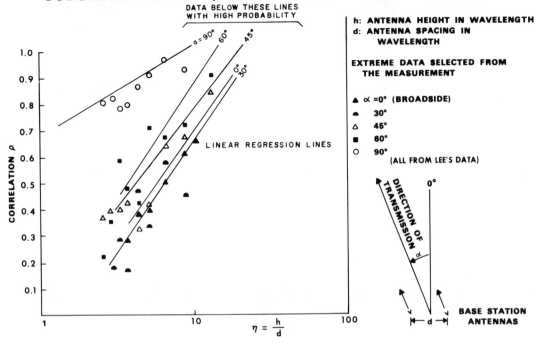

Fig. 3. Correlation versus antenna height and spacing—various angles.

high probability because of the nature of data selected. With a given η, the likelihood of having higher correlation with larger angle of base-station antenna orientation is also shown in Fig. Fig. 3. Note that the linear regression lines for angular orientations of 0° and 30° are close to each other, indicating that no significant difference in correlation will be observed for small displacements from the broadside orientation.

III. LIMITATIONS ON THE USE OF η

When using our analysis, the following points should be considered.

1) In the case of line-of-sight condition, our analysis cannot be applied. See [6] and [7] for more useful information.

2) The base-station antenna heights should be high enough to clear the neighboring scatterers.

3) The antenna beam must cover the area of interest.

4) In this paper, the results only apply to a distance of 2 to 4 mi. As we would expect, there is also a dependence of ρ on the mobile-to-base distance; the larger the distance, the higher the correlation coefficients for a constant base-station antenna separation.

REFERENCES

[1] S. B. Rhee and G. I. Zysman, "Results of Suburban Base-Station Spatial Diversity Measurements on the UHF Band," *IEEE Trans. Communications*, Vol. Com-22, No.-10, p. 1630, October 1974.

[2] W. C. Y. Lee, "Antenna Spacing Requirement for a Mobile Radio Base-Station Diversity," *BSTJ*, Vol. 50, No. 6, July–August 1971, pp. 1859–1874.

[3] —, "Effects on Correlation Between Two Mobile Radio Base-Station Antennas," *IEEE Trans. Communications*, Vol. Com-21, pp. 1214–1223, November 1973.

[4] N. R. Draper and H. Smith, *Applied Regression Analysis*. New York: Wiley, 1966.

[5] B. Ostle, *Statistics in Research*. Ames, IA: Iowa State Univ. Press, 1963.

[6] W. C. Jakes, Jr., and D. O. Reudink, "Comparison of Mobile Radio Transmission at UHF and X-Band," *IEEE Trans. Vehicular Technology*, Vol. VT-16, pp. 10–14, October 1967.

[7] Y. Okumura, E. Ohmori, T. Kawano, and K. Fukuda, "Field Strength and Its Variability in VHF and UHF Land-Mobile Radio Service," *Review of the Electrical Communication Laboratory*, Vol. 16, pp. 825–873, September and October 1968.

Studies of Base-Station Antenna Height Effects on Mobile Radio

WILLIAM C. Y. LEE, MEMBER, IEEE

Abstract—As is well known, a base-station antenna height gain factor of 6 dB/octave has been predicted theoretically for signal path loss over flat ground and has been verified by measured data. However, the 6-dB/octave rule for antenna height effect cannot be used to predict signal strength for terrain contours if the terrain is not flat. A model has been developed for waves propagating over a nonflat ground which allows the antenna height effect to be predicted in different types of actual terrain contours. In the model, the actual terrain profile is classified as one of two different kinds of general terrain types. The relative received power due to the actual terrain path contour is predicted by considering the reflection points of the waves along the path. Experimental data have been used to verify the theoretically estimated results and they show good agreement.

I. INTRODUCTION

AS IS WELL KNOWN, a base-station antenna height gain factor of 6 dB/octave (i.e., doubling the antenna height increases signal level by 6 dB) has been predicted theoretically for path loss over flat ground [1]-[3]. The measurements [4], [5] in flat suburban and urban areas have generally agreed with this fact. It is observed from the measured data collected in hilly areas, however, the 6-dB/octave rule for antenna height effect cannot be used to predict signal strength

for terrain contour if the terrain is not flat. Since the model [6]-[8] used to obtain *6 dB/octave* for the antenna height effect at the base station is generally workable for terrestrial propagations, we have only to check if this model can be applied to a mobile radio environment.

II. DESCRIPTION OF AN EXISTING MODEL FOR FLAT TERRAIN

In this section an existing model [8], [9] used for flat terrestrial propagation is examined for mobile radio reception. Assume that a base-station transmitter and a mobile receiver are separated by a large distance d, and the terrain between the two sites is flat as shown in Fig. 1. Three possible kinds of waves may occur at the mobile receiver: a direct wave, a reflected wave, and a surface wave. The resultant received signal power [8], [9] is then

$$P_r = P_t g_1 g_2 \left(\frac{\lambda}{4\pi d} \right)^2 \quad | \, 1 + \underbrace{\rho e^{j\Delta}}_{\substack{\text{reflected} \\ \text{wave}}} + \underbrace{\eta}_{\substack{\text{surface} \\ \text{wave}}} \, |^2 \qquad (1)$$

where

P_t transmitting power into the antenna,
g_1 gain of the base antenna,

Manuscript received May 5, 1979; revised October 31, 1979. Portions of this paper were presented at the Symposium on Microwave Mobile Communications, Denver, CO, March 22, 1978.

The author was with Bell Laboratories, Inc., Whippany, NJ. He is now with ITT Defense Communications Division, Nutley, NJ 07110. Telephone (201) 284-3373.

Reprinted from *IEEE Trans. Veh. Technol.*, vol. VT-29, pp. 252–260, May 1980.

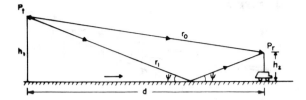

RECEIVED POWER

$$P_r = P_t \, g_1 g_2 \left[\frac{\lambda}{4\pi d}\right]^2 \cdot \left| 1 + \rho e^{j\Delta\psi} + \eta \right|^2$$

ASSUME:
REFLECTION COEFF. $\rho = -1$
PHASE DIFF. $\Delta\psi = \beta(r_1 - r_0) \simeq \dfrac{4\pi h_1 h_2}{\lambda d} \ll 1$

$$P_r = P_t \left(\frac{h_1 h_2}{d^2}\right)^2 g_1 g_2$$

Fig. 1. An existing model on flat terrain.

h_1 height of the base-station antenna,
g_2 gain of the mobile antenna,
h_2 height of the mobile antenna,
d distance between the base station and the mobile antenna,
λ wavelength,
ρ reflection coefficient of the ground,
η the term due to the effect of the surface wave [8], [9] which can be neglected in the mobile radio environment,[1]
Δ phase difference between the direct wave and the reflected wave ($=4\pi h_1 h_2/\lambda d$).

For mobile radio communications, the grazing angle ψ, as shown in Fig. 1, is always small and $\lambda d \gg h_1 h_2$. Hence it is reasonable to assume that

$$\Delta \ll 1$$

and

$$\rho \cong -1. \qquad (2)$$

Under this assumption, (1) becomes

$$P_r \cong P_t g_1 g_2 \left(\frac{h_1 h_2}{d^2}\right)^2 \qquad (3)$$

or, by taking a logarithm on both sides, we obtain

$$P_r \text{ (in dBm)} \cong 10 \log_{10}(g_1 g_2 P_t)$$
$$\underbrace{- 40 \log_{10} d}_{} + \underbrace{20 \log_{10} h_1 + 20 \log_{10} h_2}_{}.$$
$$\qquad\qquad \delta_1 \qquad\qquad \delta_2 \qquad (4)$$

[1] The term is small in the frequency range above 30 MHz and can be neglected above 300 MHz. It is because the earth is not a perfect conductor, some energy is transmitted into the ground and is absorbed proportional to the frequency.

Both δ_1 and δ_2 indicate a 6-dB/octave antenna height gain; received power increases by 6 dB as the antenna height is doubled.

Comparing the measurement data of mobile radio propagation [4] with (4), we have found that the term δ_1 of (4) is fitted, but δ_2 is shown discrepantly. Okumura's data [4] show that only a 3-dB gain is observed by doubling the mobile antenna height in urban and suburban areas. Ott and Plitkins [10] did not observe the noticeable 3-dB/octave antenna height gain at the mobile. Hence the terrestrial propagation model of (4) can only be used to evaluate the base-station antenna height effect over flat ground.

III. A THEORETICAL MODEL FOR NONFLAT TERRAIN

Since natural terrain is not always flat, a model has to be used to cover a nonflat terrain situation. Hence the existing model used in Section II has to be modified in this section.

Assume that a base-station transmitter and a mobile receiver are separated by a large distance d. Between the transmitter and the receiver, a terrain combining level ground with hilly slopes (the slope angle θ is much less than 1 rad) is present in our model, as shown in Fig. 2. There are two types of terrain to be considered:

type A terrain: the mobile antenna is on a slope higher than the base station,
type B terrain: the mobile antenna is on a lower flat ground level.

The parameters d, h_1, and h_2 are already shown in Fig. 1. The parameters D and H shown in Fig. 2 are as follows:

D the length of the flat ground,
H the height difference between the flat ground and the mobile.

In both types A and B, one wave is always reflected on the slope of the hill (Condition 1). Consistent with Snell's Law, the spot at which a reflection of a wave occurs is always close to the top of the hilly slope where the mobile unit of type A or the base-station antenna of type B is located. A second reflected wave, however, may or may not exist, depending on the length of flat ground and the antenna height (Condition 2). Here we have to distinguish between the antenna height and the effective antenna height. The antenna height, h_1 or h_2 shown in Fig. 2, is the actual height above the local ground. The effective antenna height h_1' or h_2' defined in this paper is the height referenced to the extended ground plane where the reflection point occurs as shown in Fig. 3. In the past, the effective antenna height was defined differently by different authors [4], [9]. The effective antenna height stated in this paper has a relation uniquely associated with the reflection mechanism. Consider the following two conditions.

Condition 1: Only one reflection wave can be generated.
For type A:

$$D < D_1 = \frac{dh_1}{h_1 + h_2 + H} \qquad \text{(see Appendix).} \qquad (5)$$

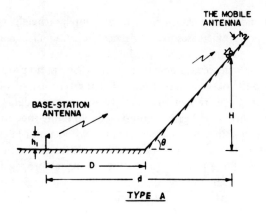

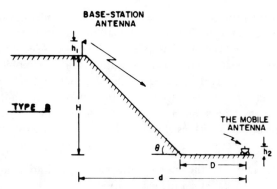

Fig. 2.   Two types of nonflat terrain.

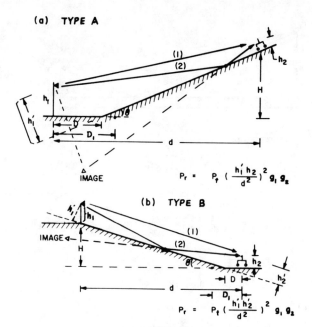

Fig. 3.   Condition 1: one reflected wave can occur.

in which h_1' and h_2' are effective antenna heights.

Condition 2: A second reflected wave can occur.

For type A:

$$D > D_1 = \frac{dh_1}{H + h_1 + h_2}. \tag{10}$$

For type B:

$$D > D_1 = \frac{dh_2}{H + h_1 + h_2}. \tag{11}$$

The Appendix explains (10) and (11). Under the condition of (10) for type A or (11) for type B, the mobile receiver may receive three waves, one direct wave and two reflected waves, as shown in Fig. 4. The received power at the mobile unit can be estimated.

A. Based on the Existing Model, Described in Section II

Over a nonflat terrain three possible waves, one direct and two reflected waves received, can be summed up as follows:

$$P_r = P_t g_1 g_2 \underbrace{\frac{\lambda^2}{(4\pi d)^2}}_{\substack{\text{free-space} \\ \text{transmission} \\ \text{formula}}} |1 + \rho_1 e^{j\Delta_1} + \rho_2 e^{j\Delta_2}|^2 \tag{12}$$

where the parameters P_t, g_1, and g_2 are shown in Fig. 1 and

ρ_1, ρ_2 reflection coefficients of the ground depend on the angle of incidence (when the angle of incidence is very small, $\rho \to -1$ independent of the polarization [3]);

For type B:

$$D < D_1 = \frac{dh_2}{h_1 + h_2 + H} \qquad \text{(see Appendix)}. \tag{6}$$

The mobile receiver is assumed to receiver only two waves, one direct wave and one reflected wave, as shown in Fig. 3 for both types. In type A, an effective antenna height h_1' (shown in Fig. 3(a)) replaces the antenna height h_1 at the base station based on the model shown in Fig. 1:

$$h_1' \cong h_1 + \frac{DH}{d - D} \tag{7a}$$

$$h_2' \cong h_2. \tag{7b}$$

In type B, an effective antenna height h_2' replaces the antenna height h_2 at the mobile unit (shown in Fig. 3(b)):

$$h_2' \cong h_2 + \frac{DH}{d - D} \tag{8a}$$

$$h_1' \cong h_1 \cos \theta. \tag{8b}$$

We can apply the path loss formula over a flat ground shown in (3) to the above two types of terrain contour to yield

$$P_r = \frac{P_t g_1 g_2}{d^4} h_1'^2 h_2'^2 \tag{9}$$

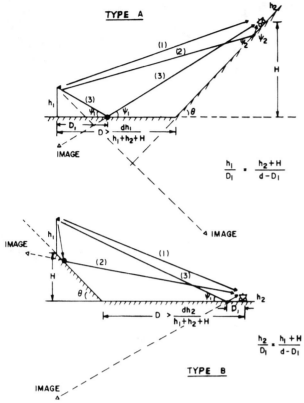

Fig. 4.   Condition 2: two reflection waves can occur.

Δ_1, Δ_2 phase differences between the reflected and the direct paths as the waves propagate from the transmitting antenna to the receiving antenna.

For $d \gg h_1 \cdot (H + h_2)$, the grazing angle (angle of incidence) is very small, and the phase differences Δ_1 and Δ_2 are also small. Reflection coefficients ρ_1 and ρ_2 then become -1, and the following approximations can be made:

$$\sin \Delta_i \cong \Delta_i$$

$$\cos \Delta_i \cong 1 - \frac{\Delta_i^2}{2}$$

where $i = 1$, 2. Substituting these approximations into (12), we obtain

$$|1 - e^{j\Delta_1} - e^{j\Delta_2}|^2 = 3 + 2 \cos (\Delta_1 - \Delta_2)$$
$$- 2 (\cos \Delta_1 + \cos \Delta_2)$$
$$\cong 1 + 2\Delta_1 \Delta_2. \tag{13}$$

Substituting (13) into (12), we obtain

$$P_r = P_t g_1 g_2 \left(\frac{\lambda^2}{(4\pi d)^2} \right) (1 + 2\Delta_1 \Delta_2).$$
$$\cong P_t g_1 g_2 \frac{\lambda^2}{(4\pi d)^2}. \tag{14}$$

As (14) indicates, if a second reflected wave is generated ((10) for type A and (11) for type B), the received power is inversely proportional to d^2. It is the same as if it is received from free-space transmission. Also, the antenna height is out of the picture, as shown in (14). However, the measured data [4] show that the received signal obtained from the mobile unit is always less than that from the free-space propagation. Besides, the effect of changing the base-station antenna height strongly appears in the measured data. Hence the result from (14) cannot be applied to mobile radio propagation over a nonflat terrain.

B. A New Approach

Since the existing model cannot be applied to mobile radio propagation over nonflat terrain, especially when two reflected waves are expected, a new approach is described as follows. Three waves, one direct and two reflected, are summed up in a more general form than in (10), such as

$$P_r = P_0 \mid \alpha_0 - \alpha_1 e^{j\Delta_1} - \alpha_2 e^{j\Delta_2} \mid^2 \tag{15}$$

where

P_0 = free-space transmission formula

$$= P_t g_1 g_2 \frac{\lambda^2}{(4\pi d)^2}. \tag{16}$$

Let α_0, α_1, α_2 be additional attenuation factors due to land-to-mobile propagation compared to land-to-land free-space propagation. α_0 is the attenuation of a direct wave. The two reflected waves, one which has a reflection point close to the mobile contributes mostly to specular reflection with an attenuation α_1 and the other which has its reflection point away from the mobile contributes mostly to diffuse scattering with its attenuation α_2 [11]. Since the diffuse scattering has little directivity, the energy received by the diffuse scattering is much smaller than that by the specular reflection, we may assume that

$$\alpha_1 \gg \alpha_2. \tag{17}$$

Also from the assumption of (2), $\alpha_0 \cong \alpha_1$. Then (15) becomes

$$P_r \cong \alpha_0 P_0 \mid 1 - e^{j\Delta_1} \mid^2$$
$$\cong \alpha_0 P_t g_1 g_2 \left(\frac{h_1' h_2'}{d^2} \right)^2 \tag{18}$$

where h_1' and h_2' are the effective antenna heights which can be related to the antenna heights h_1 and h_2 as illustrated in (5) or (6). Equations (18) and (9) are identical. It means that, if there are two reflected waves, only one reflected wave whose reflection point is closer to the mobile contributes most significantly. The tangential plane for this reflection point near the mobile is used to estimate the effective antenna height as shown in Fig. 5 for each of two terrain types, type A and type B.

FOR **TYPE A**

$$P_r = a_o \frac{P_t \, g_1 \, g_2}{d^4} \cdot h_2^2 \cdot \left(h_1 + \frac{DH}{d-D}\right)^2$$

FOR **TYPE B**

$$P_r = a_o \frac{P_t \, g_1 \, g}{d^4} \cdot (h_1 + H)^2 \cdot h_2^2$$

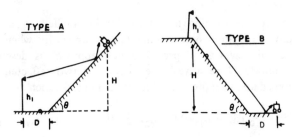

Fig. 5.   Estimate of effective antenna heights.

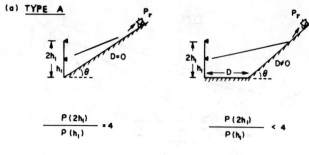

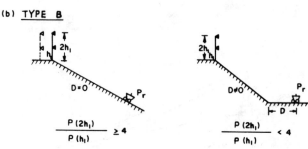

Fig. 6.   Effect on antenna height gain factor.

IV. PREDICTION OF ANTENNA HEIGHT EFFECT FROM THE THEORETICAL MODEL

The signal change due to antenna height change does not depend upon the actual antenna height above the local ground level though the actual antenna height is easy to visualize. Rather, it depends on the effective antenna height determined by the terrain contour between the mobile and the base. There is no linear relationship between the actual antenna height and the effective antenna height. Doubling the actual base-station antenna height, therefore, does not necessarily change the signal levels by 6 dB. Four examples shown in Fig. 6 (assume that the slope angle θ is small, say less than $10°$) will demonstrate this fact. The effective antenna heights of two antennas are first obtained based on the location of the base station as shown in Fig. 6.

1) Type A Terrain, D = 0: The power increased due to the change of antenna height is

$$\Delta P = \frac{P(2h_1)}{P(h_1)} = \frac{P(h_1'')}{P(h_1')} = \left(\frac{h_1''}{h_1'}\right)^2 = \left(\frac{2h_1}{h_1}\right)^2 = 4$$

where h_1'' is the increased effective antenna height at the base.

2) Type A Terrain, D ≠ 0: The power increased due to the change of antenna height is

$$\Delta P = \frac{P(2h_1)}{P(h_1)} = \frac{P(h_1'')}{P(h_1')} = \left(\frac{h_1''}{h_1'}\right)^2 < 4.$$

3) Type B Terrain, D = 0: The power increased due to the change of antenna height is

$$\Delta P = \frac{P(2h_1)}{P(h_1)} = \left(\frac{h_1''}{h_1'}\right)^2 \geqslant 4.$$

4) Type B Terrain, D ≠ 0: The power increased due to the change of antenna height is

$$\Delta P = \frac{P(2h_1)}{P(h_1)} = \left(\frac{h_1''}{h_1'}\right)^2 < 4.$$

From the above examples we have demonstrated that doubling the base-station antenna height may not necessarily increase the signal level by 6 dB, sometimes more sometimes less, dependent upon the effective antenna height at the given site. Hence the 6-dB/octave antenna height rule cannot be applied in the hilly area.

V. COMPARISON OF THEORY WITH EXPERIMENTAL RESULTS

Data at Whippany, NJ, Area

Since Caples [5] made the suburban (Whippany area) measurements with base antenna elevations at 60, 80, and 100 ft above ground and frequency at 821 MHz, we compared the results predicted from the model with Caples' unpublished measured data. Though it is very hard to find a particular contour of the terrain to match all of our models, we found some contours of type A. The six points marked in alphabetical order on Fig. 7 are the sites used for comparison. For demonstration, Fig. 8 shows a contour in the Whippany area which has met a condition of having three waves, i.e., $D > dh_1/(H + h_1 + h_2)$. The signal received by the mobile

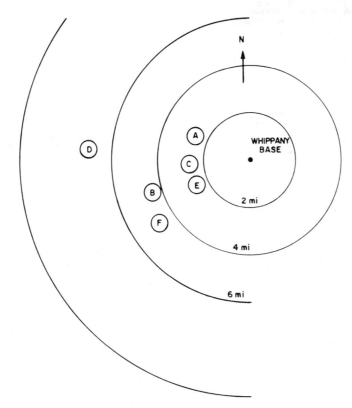

Fig. 7.   Sites used in the Whippany, NJ, area.

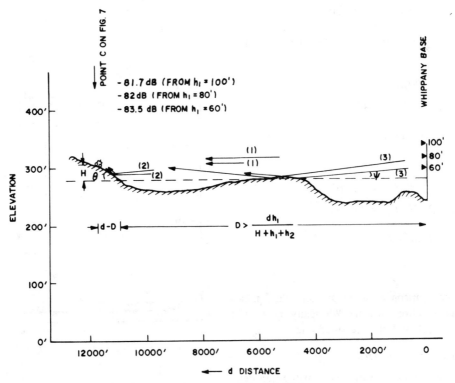

Fig. 8.   A terrain contour of site C in Whippany area.

175

LOCATION	ANT. HEIGHT $(h_1+\Delta h)$ / ANT HEIGHT h_1	ΔP PREDICTED RESULTS (dB)	ΔP MEASURED RESULTS (dB)
A	80'/60'	3.5	4
A	100'/60'	6	5.5
B	80'/60'	0	0
B	100'/60'	0	0
C	80'/60'	1.1	1.5
C	100'/60'	1.1	1.8
D	80'/60'	3.2	3
D	100'/60'	5	4.3
E	80'/60'	0	1
E	100'/60'	0	1
F	80'/60'	0	1
F	100'/60'	0	1

Fig. 9. A list of comparisons between predicted and measured results (Whippany area).

unit from each base-station antenna height h_1 is based on its effective height h_1' in which for

$$h_1 = 100 \text{ ft} \qquad h_1' = 380 \text{ ft}$$

$$h_1 = 80 \text{ ft} \qquad h_1' = 360 \text{ ft}$$

$$h_1 = 60 \text{ ft} \qquad h_1' = 340 \text{ ft}.$$

Hence, by applying (16), we may calculate the relative gains received from the base-station antenna with three different antenna heights and compare those with the measured data as follows:

$$\Delta P = \frac{P_r(h_1 = 80 \text{ ft})}{P_r(h_1 = 60 \text{ ft})} = \frac{P_r(h_1' = 360 \text{ ft})}{P_r(h_1' = 340 \text{ ft})}$$

$$\cong 1.06 \sim 0.5 \text{ dB (predicted)}$$

$$1.5 \text{ dB (measured)}$$

$$\Delta P = \frac{P_r(h_1 = 100 \text{ ft})}{P_r(h_1 = 60 \text{ ft})} = \frac{P_r(h_1' = 380 \text{ ft})}{P_r(h_1' = 340 \text{ ft})}$$

$$\cong 1.11 \sim 1 \text{ dB (predicted)}$$

$$1.7 \text{ dB (measured)}.$$

Fig. 9 is a list of comparison between predicted and measured results for six locations in the Whippany area. The predicted results agree well with the measured ones.

Data in the Camden-Philadelphia Area

Kelly [12] has done some measurements in the Camden-Philadelphia area. Fig. 10 indicates the sites in that area in which the measured data were collected. The data used here

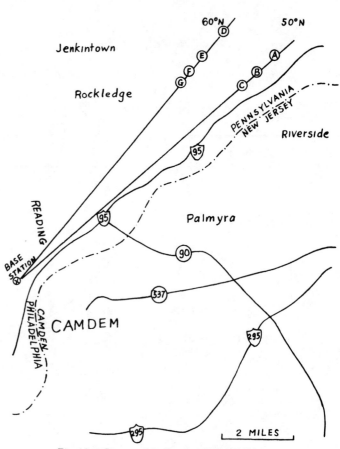

Fig. 10. Sites used in Camden-Philadelphia area.

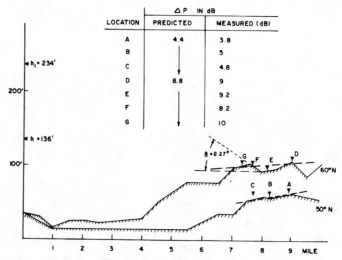

LOCATION	ΔP IN dB PREDICTED	MEASURED (dB)
A	4.4	3.8
B		5
C		4.8
D	8.8	9
E		9.2
F		8.2
G		10

Fig. 11. Measured data from Camden-Philadelphia area.

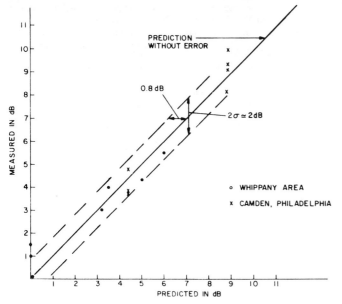

Fig. 12. Indication of errors in prediction.

specified two types of terrain profile that the received wave would be affected by the terrain. From the types of terrain we have found the following.

1) The relative received power can only be predicted by using the effective base-station antenna height which is measured from the plane on which the reflection point occurs.

2) Only one direct wave and one reflected wave (if two, the one closest to the mobile is used) are used to predict the relative received power.

3) The experimental data shown here agree well with the prediction.

4) Doubling the antenna height may not necessarily increase the signal level by 6 dB over nonflat ground, sometimes more sometimes less, dependent upon the effective antenna height.

were those recorded from two base-station antennas at different heights, 136 ft and 234 ft above sea level, respectively. To compare the data with the prediction, we picked data in the direction of 50°N and 60°N, as shown in Fig. 11. The terrain profile in these two directions fits our model as can be seen in Fig. 11.

We picked three data points A, B, C, in the direction of 50°N and four points D, E, F, G, in the direction of 60°N. The ratio of two receiving powers obtained from two different antenna heights, ΔP in decibels, for each location is listed in Fig. 11. The differences of ΔP between the predicted and measurement results are small. The reason for using only two slopes to represent those points is that the general terrain is flat as one slope angle shows in the figure. The reader should not be confused with the drawing which uses two different scales on x and y axes, respectively.

VI. ERRORS IN PREDICTION

Since there are differences between the predicted values and the measured ones, we have to know the deviation of the differences. First, we plot the points with predicted values at the x axis and the measured values at the y axis, shown in Fig. 12. The 45° line is the line of prediction without error. The dotted points are from the Whippany area and the cross points are from the Camden-Philadelphia area. Most of them are close to the line of prediction without error. The mean value of all the data is right on the line of prediction without error. The variation of the predicted value is 0.8 dB from the measured one.

VII. CONCLUSIONS AND SUMMARY

We summarize some theoretical results in Section III. The model we use here can explain a lot of phenomena since the ground is not always flat. From a hilly area we have

APPENDIX

CONDITION OF HAVING A REFLECTED WAVE FROM A FLAT GROUND

According to Snell's Law, the incident angle equals the reflected angle. At a site of reflection D_1 (see Fig. 2)

$$\frac{h_1}{D_1} = \frac{h_2 + H}{D - D_1}, \qquad \text{for type A}$$

or

$$D_1 = \frac{h_1 d}{H + h_1 + h_2}$$

and

$$\frac{h_2}{D_1} = \frac{h_1 + H}{d - D_1}, \qquad \text{for type B}$$

or

$$D_1 = \frac{h_2 d}{H + h_1 + h_2}.$$

Therefore when $D > D_1$, there always exists a reflected wave.

ACKNOWLEDGMENT

The author would like to thank Bell Laboratories, Inc., for letting him publish this paper. The stimulation from this paper had led the author to further develop a new mobile radio propagation model before he left Bell Laboratories.

REFERENCES

[1] P. David and J. Voge, *Propagation of Waves.* Oxford, England: Pergamon, 1969, p. 59.

[2] Propagation of the National Defense Research Committee, *Radio Wave Propagation.* New York: Academic, 1949, p. 386.

[3] W. C. Jakes, Jr., *et al., Microwave Mobile Communication.* New York: Wiley, 1974, p. 83.

[4] Y. Okmura, E. Ohmori, T. Kawano, and K. Fukuda, "Field strength and its variability in VHF and UHF land mobile service," *Rev. Elec. Comm. Lab.*, vol. 16, pp. 825–973, Sept.–Oct. 1968.

[5] E. Caples, private communication.

[6] K. A. Norton, "The calculation of ground wave field intensity over a finitely conducting spherical earth," *Proc. IRE*, vol. 29, p. 63, Dec. 1941.

[7] K. Bullington, "Radio propagation at frequencies above 30 megacycles," *Proc. IRE*, vol. 35, p. 1122, Oct. 1947.

[8] ——, "Radio propagation fundamentals," *Bell Syst. Tech. J.*, vol. 36, p. 593, May 1957.

[9] ——, "Radio propagation for vehicular communications," *IEEE Trans. Veh. Technol.*, vol. VT-26, pp. 295–308, Nov. 1977.

[10] G. D. Ott and A. Plitkins, "Urban path-loss characteristics at 820 MHz," *IEEE Trans. Veh. Technol.*, vol. VT-27, pp. 189–197, Nov. 1978.

[11] P. Beckman and A. Spizzichino, Eds. *The Scattering of Electromagnetic Waves from Rough Surface.* New York: Pergamon, 1963, p. 241.

[12] K. K. Kelly, II, "Flat suburban area propagation at 820 MHz," *IEEE Trans. Veh. Technol.*, vol. VT-27, pp. 198–204, Nov. 1978.

Microwave Propagation Measurements for Mobile Digital Radio Application

DONALD L. NIELSON, MEMBER, IEEE

Abstract—Measurements over a variety of urban and terrain conditions were made using a spread-spectrum waveform centered at 1370 MHz. Chip rates of 10 and 20 MHz were used, giving high time-delay resolution. The transmitter end of the measurement link was elevated and fixed while the receiver was mobile. A detailed analysis of the multipath structure was made for various terrain conditions. This included distributions of the number and spacing of individual multipath components as a function of amplitude threshold and also distribution of total delay. Thresholds are referenced to both average signal level and the maximum level in each pulse interval. Some instances of spatial variation of the received signal are also presented.

I. INTRODUCTION

A. Purpose

THE INTRODUCTION of digital radio communications into the urban environment requires knowledge of the limitations that such an environment imposes on a communications signal. Understanding of the attenuation, distortion, and noise chracteristics is necessary to design a radio system that will work successfully under a wide range of conditions. The purpose of this paper is to describe the radio environment at 1370 MHz for urban, surburban, and rural areas, on the basis of data derived from a measurement program conducted in support of a proposed land mobile digital radio system design. Although the measurement was conducted at a specific frequency, much of this description clearly will apply to frequencies hundreds of megahertz around the measurement frequency. Previous measurements relevant to this subject have been made by Young and Lacy [1], Cox [2], and Turin [3].

B. General Approach

The basic approach to this channel description is to define propagation characteristics in terms of the channel impulse response and the power spectral density and autocorrelation functions of narrowband signals in both time and space. Wideband impulsive noise data were also taken, but space does not permit their inclusion here; a description of them is available [4]. In the measurement experiment, noise was characterized as a summation of nonoverlapping impulses whose bandwidth exceeds that of any receiver employed. When it had been

Manuscript received February 16, 1978; revised April 21, 1978. This work was supported in part by the Defense Advanced Research Projects Agency under Contract No. DAHC15-73-C-0187. This paper was originally presented the IEEE Electronics and Aerospace Systems Convention (EASCON-77), Arlington, VA, September 26-28, 1977.
The author is with SRI International, 333 Ravenswood Avenue, Menlo Park, CA 94025, Telephone (415) 326-6200.

shown that the noise was wideband, the weight and delay distributions of the impulses were measured.

II. DETAILS OF THE PROPAGATION MEASUREMENT EXPERIMENT

A. General

Propagation measurements were divided into wide-band and narrow-band. The wide-band data were used to measure the channel impulse response; the narrow-band data described the temporal and spatial variability of the received signal. It became obvious early in the experiment that a better overall estimate of impulse response could be obtained by taking wide-band data with the receiver in motion rather than with the receiver fixed. When in motion, the receiver samples many independent transmission paths, provided that a correct spatial sampling rate is selected.

The transmitting and receiving systems is described in the Appendix. The receiver was mounted in a measurement van, and the transmitter, horn antenna, and mast were mounted in a pickup truck. Thus both ends of the measurement link were movable. The transmitter was typically placed at high elevations, and the receiver was moved through a variety of urban to rural environments.

B. Terrain Classification

To classify the received data by terrain type, several categories were defined according to the degree of urbanization the receiver witnessed.

Terrain Categorization	Characteristics
A: Dense urban	> Ten-story buildings
B: Moderate urban	< Ten-story buildings
C: Geographically limited urban	Cities with a small, isolated urban cluster
D: Suburban	Residential, one- and two-story buildings
E: Rural	Few structures

Wide-band data were collected in each of these environments and processed off line for impulse response parameters. Fig. 1 shows the transmitter and associated receiver locations used in the data collection effort. As shown later, the impulse response is not easily categorized by degree of urbanization.

Reprinted from *IEEE Trans. Veh. Technol.*, vol. VT-27, pp. 117–131, Aug. 1978.

179

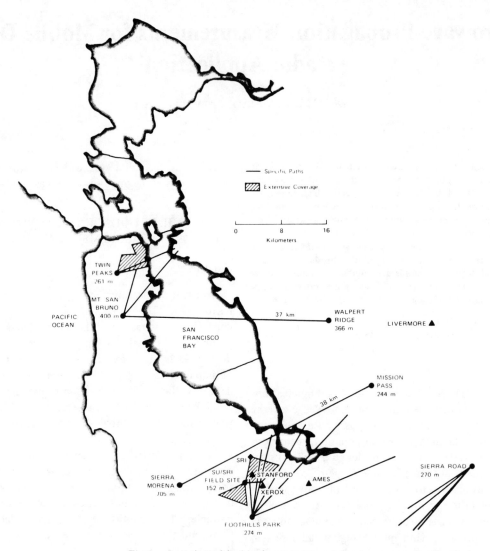

Fig. 1. Locations visited in the measurement program.

C. Data Format for Impulse Response (Wide-Band) Measurements

The data-collection instrumentation was controlled by an Interdata-70 minicomputer. In the case of wide-band propagation measurements, up to 200 received pulses could be recorded in one data record. The transmission of a 127-chip maximal-length pseudorandom sequence at rates of 10 or 20 megachips enabled a wide-band, high-resolution measurement of multipath. Eight-bit digital sampling at 100-MHz rate was accomplished by using a transient digitizer whose memory was transferred onto magnetic tape through the minicomputer where calibration occurred.

The time-delay resolution of the system is illustrated in Fig. 2 for the 20-megachip rate. This waveform is in the normal digitized format produced by the off-line program. The second pulse is a contiguous transmitted pulse rather than multipath. An example of the inability to resolve some multipath components taken with the receiver in motion in downtown San Jose, California, is shown in Fig. 3. Some pulse data were taken while the van was stationary, but nearly all the data presented here were taken when the van was moving.

The digitally recorded multipath waveforms were used to perform two types of processing: one that computed the various multipath descriptors at amplitude levels referenced to the mean signal level and a second that gave the likelihood of multipath at levels referenced to the peak signal level. An explanation of the first type of processing is shown in Fig. 4. This particular time-delay waveform taken in downtown San Francisco is the average of 100 received pulses and is shown with linear time and amplitude scales. Overdrawn on the trace are various scaled descriptors used to characterize the multipath distortion.

The first calculational problem was to distinguish between the samples that were signal and those that were noise. For this purpose, the trigger of a transient digitizer was set approximately one microsecond *ahead* of the leading edge of the signal. Thus the first 50 samples could be used as a noise window from which the mean and standard deviation of the noise were calculated. All sample values greater than the mean plus $2\sigma_n$ were then considered signal, and all values below that signal threshold were disregarded. After the signal threshold had been determined, the signal mean and the standard devia-

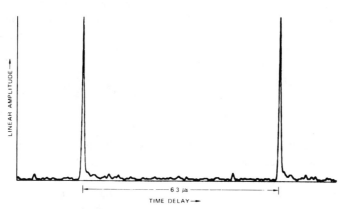

Fig. 2. Back-to-back tests indicating resolution of the 20-megachip signal after off-line processing.

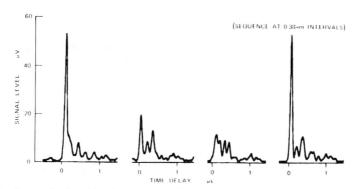

Fig. 3. Example of unresolved multipath components from data taken in San Jose. Sequence at 0.38-m intervals.

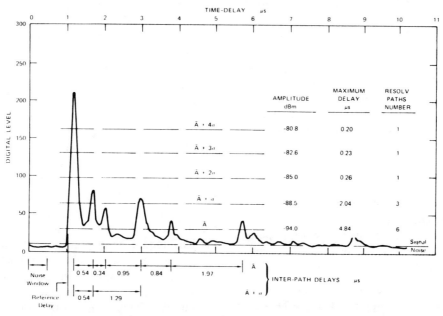

Fig. 4. Multipath scaling nomenclature referenced to average signal level.

tion were calculated by using each of the next 580 samples that exceeded that threshold. Five signal amplitude thresholds were then computed at even one-sigma increments (see Fig. 4). As a final preparation for computing the multipath descriptors, a reference delay was set at the first sample value past the point where the signal first exceeded its mean value.

Having made these preliminary calculations, we then computed five descriptors for each received pulse. Each of these parameters, described below, characterizes the multipath properties of the received signal.

Maximum Width Caused by Multipath: The maximum width at a given amplitude threshold is defined as the time from the reference delay to the last downward crossing of that threshold. Notice that this definition exaggerates the value somewhat by not considering the time difference from first to last crossing of a threshold. This convention, however, departs from the more exact portrayal only when the peak amplitude of the pulse waveform is not near the minimum delay. Since individual multipath records fluctuate substantially with space (and in some cases with time), the larger, more pessimistic number was believed to be more appropriate for communication system design. (Estimates of the delay between first-to-last crossings at thresholds referenced to the peak amplitude are discussed in a later section.) Probability densities of the maximum width, given as a function of amplitude threshold, were computed for individual data runs for aggregate terrain classifications. In the example of Fig. 4, the maximum delay at the $\bar{A} + \sigma$ level (-88.5-dBm equivalent CW input) is 2.0 μs.

For typical match-filter systems, the maximum delay is one of the most important descriptors affecting the channel coherent bandwidth and thereby the selection of signaling rate or signaling bandwidth. Rates substantially greater than half the inverse of the maximum delay result in signaling errors if the delayed component is of significant amplitude relative to the maximum.

Number of Resolvable Multipath Components: Knowing the number of multipath components as a function of amplitude, one can estimate the locking potential for bit synchronization systems. To explore this parameter, the meaning of a resolvable signal component must be defined. First, the sample values considered must have been declared signal and not noise. Then the peak of a resolvable multipath component is defined as one of the following:

- a point on the waveform higher in amplitude than the points adjacent to it;
- the center point of a set of equal-amplitude points higher than the points on either side;
- the center of two or more adjacent equal-amplitude points in an otherwise increasing or decreasing segment of the waveform (i.e., a point of inflection).

The number of resolvable paths for a given threshold is the number identified *above* that threshold. Thus the mean level of Fig. 4 has six resolvable components associated with it, even though strictly speaking the averaged signal shown resolves only four. The likelihood of a given number of resolvable paths is based on the percentage of received pulse waveforms containing that given number of peaks above the specified

threshold. The 3-dB post-detection bandwidth of the receiver was 9 MHz.

Time-Delay Interval Between Multipath Components: When the signal peaks or points of inflection and hence the resolvable multipath components have been located, it is possible to measure the distribution of delays between consecutive peaks within a bracketed one-sigma amplitude range. Intervals were accumulated in bins of 0.1-μs duration. The probability was computed by dividing the number in each amplitude/interval bin by the total number of *intervals* found within that one-sigma amplitude range for all pulses considered. The interpath delays in Fig. 4 are measurable only for threshold $\bar{A}$ and $\bar{A} + \sigma$. The time-delay interval between components describes the jitter in delay that might be experienced when such components fade.

Time-Delay Spread: As used here, time spread is twice the root of the second central moment of the received voltage waveform. That is, time spread is

$$2\sigma_\tau = 2\left[\frac{\sum A_i(\tau - \bar{\tau})^2}{\sum A_i}\right]^{1/2}$$

where

$$\bar{\tau} = \frac{\sum A_i \tau_i}{\sum A_i}$$

and A_i and τ_i are the voltage level and the relative delay of the ith sample. Only signal samples are used, however.

Time spread is one-number representation of the time-delay width of a received pulse waveform. It gives an indication of the potential for intersymbol interference and is a reasonable measure of spread largely under conditions where appreciable spread exists. Very narrow, impulsive waveforms with one or two *closely spaced* rays are not well described by this method [4].

Situations of particularly low multipath are usually limited to rural or residential locations, or instances in which both terminals are elevated high above potential reflectors.

Peak-Related Multipath Processing: Because of the contemplated use of peak finders in the synchronizers of some digital receivers, probably the most useful form of off-line processing of the wide-band data for multipath is that referred to the peak of each received pulse. In this study, we again inventoried all peaks (as defined above) on each received waveform according to their amplitude and time delay. We then computed the likelihood of finding the peak of another multipath component within certain amplitude-time-delay cells. To explore a wide range of multipath situations, only data from records collected while the receiver was in motion were used. The basis for this calculation was the percentage of records (received pulse waveforms) for which a peak lies in a given 40-ns slot at a given amplitude below the maximum peak. The slots ranged from 3 μs before to about 6 μs following the time delay of the maximum. Calculations were repeated for every 2 dB below the maximum down to and including -20 dB.

D. Data Format for Narrow-Band Measurements

Several narrow-band signal measurements were necessary to complement the impulse response data just described. Generally, the reasons for such measurements are

- to estimate the importance of time variability;
- to estimate the importance of spatial variability;
- to measure received power accurately.

The relevance of time variability in the 1370-MHz channel is largely limited to street level operation of a mobile terminal. If the terminal is stationary, the time variability arises from moving vehicles and the associated multipath environment; the time variability is defined by a combination of the spatial variability of the signal and receiver velocity [1], [5]. A knowledge of spatial variability also is relevant to space-diversity reception. The measurement of received signal level is needed for path-loss calculations.

The output for the narrow-band measurements consists of the following principal data formats:

- power spectral density with terminals fixed;
- power spectral density of spatial variations for both signal amplitude and phase;
- spatial autocorrelation functions of signal amplitude and phase.

Power Spectral Density as a Measurement of Time Variability: The measurement test equipment was designed to coherently detect a received narrow-band waveform. This narrow-band output, in the form of synchronously detected quadrature signals, was digitized over a 2.1-s interval using 1024 samples. A conventional FFT was taken on the complex signal; then a power spectral density was calculated. Windowing was imposed on all transforms not used in computing autocorrelation functions.

Doppler shifts observed in the land mobile environment were not expected to be sufficient to spread energy in frequency over any but the smallest fraction of the anticipated modulation bandwidth. There was the possibility, however, that time-varying cancellation of important multipath components could lead to error from time to time. Total cancellation requires exactly two components that have near-equal amplitude and whose relative phase varies. Such cases are rare in the urban environment.

Power Spectral Density as a Measure of Spatial Variability: Some of the more important results gained from the narrow-band measurements were those relating to spatial variability. These results are important particularly for their implications for spatial diversity antenna systems. Analytical forms for power spectra and correlation functions for simple antenna and propagation situations have been derived in the literature [5].

Spatial frequency is analogous to wave frequency. To obtain spectra of spatial frequency, we simply operated the mobile van in the narrow-band coherent-detector mode while driving at a known and constant velocity. The variation of the complex signal in space was thereby recorded. Spatial frequency is obtained from the Doppler-produced shift of the various multipath components by dividing that shift by the van velocity.

The spectrum is therefore a function of the direction, but not the magnitude, of the receiver velocity vector. The spatial frequency is band-limited to values equal to or less than the inverse free-space wavelength of 4.56 m^{-1} at 1370 MHz. The spectra illustrates this bound. Since the correlation functions of both magnitude and phase are obtainable with a coherent system, information concerning both pre- and post-detection combining can be derived. The results are valid only for the direction traveled.

Autocorrelation Functions of Magnitude and Phase: The autocorrelation functions were calculated separately for signal magnitude and phase, both of which were derived from the quadrature waveform. Two transforms were taken: one a 1024-point transform over the full set of data points and one a 1024-point transform over half the data. These transforms were then multiplied, and an inverse transform was taken to yield the autocorrelation function over space corresponding to half the recorded distance or 4.7 m.

III. MEASUREMENT RESULTS AND DISCUSSION

A. Propagation: General

The original terrain classification was intended to particularize future propagation models for various digital mobile radio links, but our results do not support such a discrimination. In many instances, it is difficult to distinguish between data taken in the heart of high-rise San Francisco and those taken in downtown Palo Alto, a city with few tall buildings. It appears that even the most modest urbanization can produce multipath distortion not unlike that in large urban areas such as San Francisco. We specifically illustrate this point later.

Even though similarities are found across various degrees of urbanization, there are also unquestionable differences in the extremes of terrain classification. As one would expect, flat rural countryside, and to a lesser degree residential areas, produced little multipath distortion to the links monitored. When multipath occurred, it was normally single, discrete reflections from large, sometimes identifiable objects. In contrast, when the receiver was not visible to the transmitter, many multipath components contributed to the received energy.

Several characteristics were common to the active channel measurements. First the transmitter was invariably elevated with respect to the receiver. Since the transmitter was in a vehicle, this usually meant locating the transmitter on hilltops overlooking the region of interest. The transmitter locations and elevations are noted in Fig. 1. Although it was not apparent in the beginning, we came to appreciate the value of recording impulse responses while the van was in motion. Because the correlation distances in some cases were less than a few feet, it was thus possible to substantially increase the number of independent samples. The actual distance traveled in recording one group was determined by the total number of recorded pulses. The variation of from 25 to 200 recorded pulses per group resulted in corresponding variations in total street distances of about 9 to 76 m when the van traveled at the normal speed of 10 miles per hour. This rate corresponds to about one sample every 0.38 m.

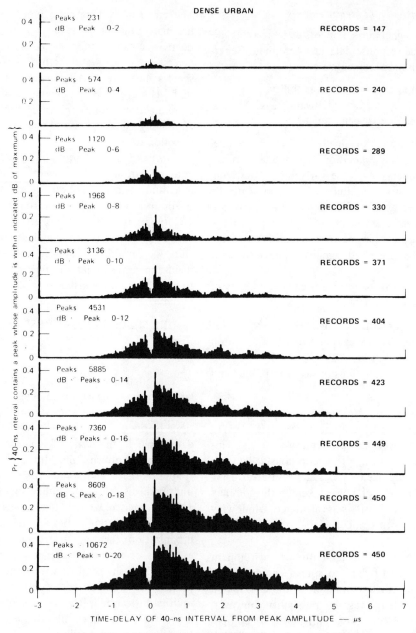

Fig. 5. Peak-referenced multipath distributions—dense urban.

We first discuss the results of the impulse measurements in terms of the parameters mentioned earlier.

B. Results of Channel Impulse Measurements

The following results are arranged by observed parameter and by terrain category.

1) Peak-Related Multipath: One way to describe the impact of multipath distortion on a digital system is to state the likelihood that a certain multipath component will lie within a certain amplitude-time-delay cell. In this instance, the cell is defined as being measured relative to the peak amplitude and delay of the strongest component. If all components other than the maximum are relatively weak, the multipath is of no consequence regardless of its delay. Conversely, a large multi-

path component must lie relatively close to the maximum peak (less than about one-half the signaling-element spacing) if relatively few communications errors are to result.

Figs. 5, 6, and 7 show the likelihood of such multipath occurrence for three terrain categories representing various degrees of urbanization. Each figure gives the probability of the peak of a multipath component lying within a specified amplitude of the maximum component and within a given time delay. The amplitude of the multipath component with respect to the peak value is decreased in 2-dB steps up to 20 dB. The time-delay increments of 40 ns are slightly less than the resolution of the measurement system. Thus if there were more than one multipath component per 40-ns increment on any record, it would not be resolved. (We have shown earlier that not all multipath was resolved by our approximately

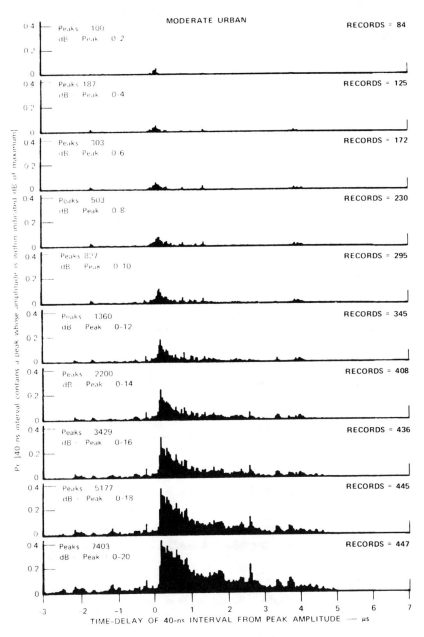

Fig. 6.   Peak-referenced multipath distributions—moderate urban.

9-MHz post detection bandwidth.) The ordinate shown therefore could be defined as the probability of at least one multipath component being present. The gap in the data near zero delay is caused by the time-delay resolution limit of the measurement system.

Data represented in Fig. 5 were calculated from 450 received pulses taken from six data runs in the financial district of San Francisco. The existence of negative delays indicates that the leading edge does not always have the highest amplitude--in particular for these data, the peak is likely to be about one-fourth the way through the total multipath return. As an example of the use of these plots, one could say that the chance of a multipath component less than 20 dB down occurring at a delay of 1 μs ($\pm$ 20 ns) is about 0.25. The number of peaks indicated on the left of each amplitude increment is the total

number of resolved multipath components within the indicated amplitude range of the maximum. The RECORDS on the right is the number of separate pulse waveforms containing at least one of the peaks plotted. Thus within 20 dB of the maximum, about 20 to 25 components exist (10672/450) on the average. This reduces to less than 10 within 10 dB.

Data from the other urban categories are shown in Figs. 6 and 7. Fig. 6 is from relatively homogeneous areas with buildings of from three to nine stories. About two-thirds of the records were made along Mission Street, between Second and Fourth, in San Francisco. On the other hand, Fig. 7 represents cities with a relatively limited downtown area--in particular, San Jose and Palo Alto. Fig. 8 illustrates data taken in low foothills in which the receiver was not within line of site of the transmitter much of the time.

185

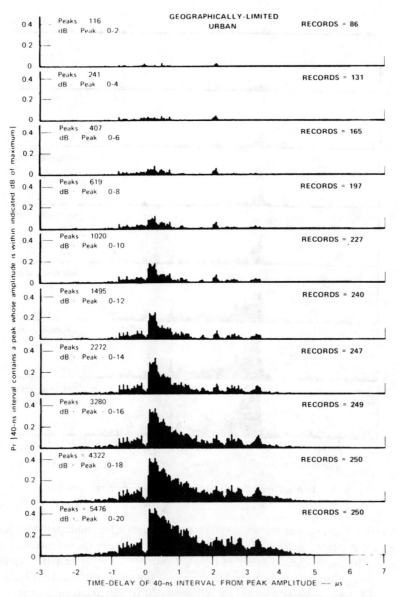

Fig. 7. Peak-referenced multipath distributions—geographically limited urban.

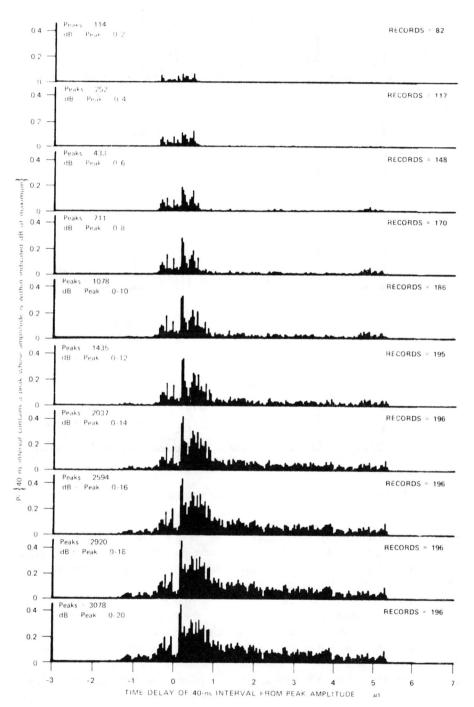

Fig. 8.   Peak-referenced multipath distributions—rural hilly terrain.

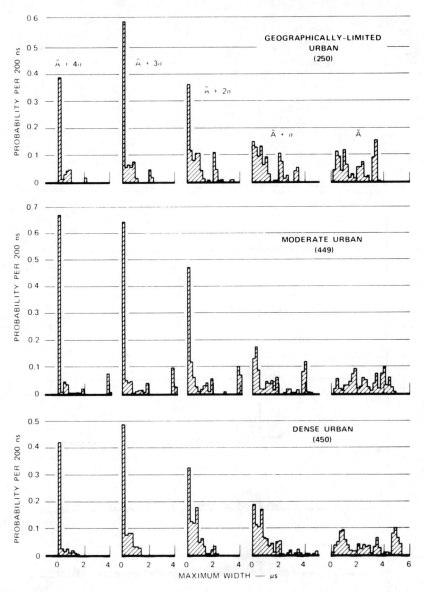

Fig. 9.   Probability densities of maximum delay at average value–referenced thresholds.

In a comparison of the dense urban data with those in Figs. 6 and 7, several significant similarities become apparent despite terrain differences. First, the rates of decrease in probability with an increase in delay are similar, even though the sample sizes are somewhat different. The probabilities at zero delay are also similar among the three cases shown, as are the average number of peaks per record at lower amplitudes. Differences are in the location of the maximum value and in the number of components contributing at the higher levels. The sample sizes are admittedly inadequate to carry the intercomparison further.

The decreases to zero probability in about 5 μs is similar to results given by Turin, *et al.* [3] and quoted by Gans [5]. Since 5 μs translates to about 5000-ft excess path length, and since the likelihood of multipath in the vicinity of the transmitter in each case is extremely small, the reflections appear to have come from objects no further from the receiver than about one-half mile. The important higher-amplitude returns are, of course, from objects much nearer.

We now examine the same impulse data. This time, however, these data are referenced to the average value of the received signal and to four one-sigma amplitude increments above the average.

2) Maximum Pulsewidth Distortion Caused by Multipath: On the basis of the scaling technique illustrated in Fig. 4 and the same raw data used in the previous section, the maximum width of received pulses is presented in Fig. 9 for the various thresholds and terrain categories indicated. The total number of pulses used for each density is shown in parentheses, and histograms were constructed by using bin widths of 200 ns. Some probability densities do not integrate to unity at the highest thresholds, since the signal did not cross all levels on each pulse.

The data show that delays beyond 5 to 6 μs are unlikely and that there are no substantial differences in the various degrees of urbanization in the limited data sets examined. The observed maximum delays are in agreement with those found in other work [3].

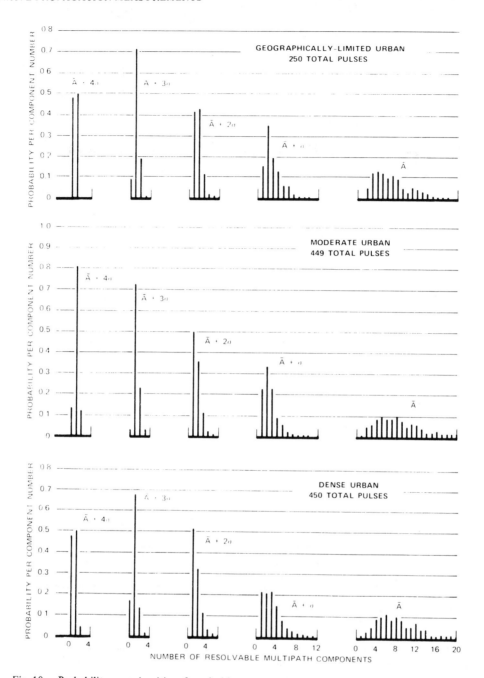

Fig. 10.   Probability mass densities of resolvable components at average value—referenced thresholds.

3) *Number of Resolvable Multipath Components:* In Section II, we have defined the notion of a resolvable multipath component. Fig. 10 illustrates the number of these components observed at or above various thresholds for three terrain categories. Notice that the probability mass functions in some instances show nonzero probabilities for no components at all. These particular values are the probability that the particular thresholds were not crossed. All components in a given record were counted, without regard to the delay at which they occurred. The largest number of components, indicated at the threshold of the average, are consistent with the average peaks per record shown at the lower amplitude levels of Figs. 5–7. As before, little difference among terrain categories appears.

4) *Time-Delay Interval Between Multipath Components:*

The time-delay interval between consecutive, resolvable multipath components is given in Fig. 11. Notice that the only statistical consistency appears in the bottom two amplitude levels. The upper levels are not sufficiently crossed to provide enough samples. In a comparison of the various terrain categories, differences appear only in the "smoothness" of the distributions as level is increased. The dense urban has fewer line-of-site high-amplitude rays, but has more intervals per record. Notice that all "smooth" distributions resemble one another. The average delay from the $\bar{A}$ and $\bar{A} + \sigma$ densities is about 0.2 μs. Were the arrivals Poisson distributed, this mean divided into the 5-μs interval for a corresponding graph in Fig. 9 should yield 25 as the mean number of paths in 5 μs. The actual mean at level $\bar{A}$ is more like 8 paths.

189

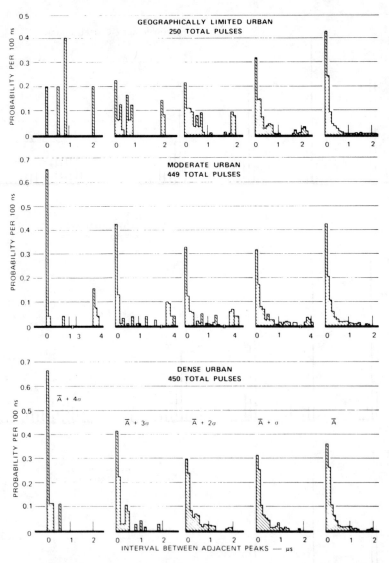

Fig. 11. Probability densities of intercomponent delay at average-value referenced thresholds.

5) *Time-Delay Spread:* The root of the second central moment was computed for each of the received pulse records of the data sets shown earlier. The results are given in Fig. 12. Since this parameter is subject to misinterpretation at low signal-to-noise ratios, two precautions were taken:

- the universal consideration that only samples above the noise plus two sigma are signal;
- all cases used showed a greater than 20-dB signal-to-noise ratio, with the exception of 20 percent of the limited urban terrain category which was about 16 dB.

The values of spread near 3 μs are from signals delayed about that amount. No reason for the bimodal distributions can be suggested other than an inadequate sample size. The 99th percentile of the moderate urban category is about 3.6 μs.

6) *A Case of Isolated Moving Reflectors:* A characteristic of even isolated and flat terrain is that reflectors in the vicinity of the receiver may result in significant multipath components. An example of one such case is illustrated in Fig. 13, where

the measurement van was parked in flat terrain, near a freeway, and distant from the transmitter. These conditions caused time-varying reflections from the passing trucks and buses (not cars) over a small section of roadway where specular reflection was possible.

C. Time and Spatial Variability

Virtually all conditions of time variation in urban and suburban channels are caused by automobiles or aircraft. The effect of such moving reflectors on communication depends on their proximity, their cross section for reflections, and their vector velocity. A group of spectral densities was computed from data taken in suburban Palo Alto about 100 ft from a four-lane thoroughfare, El Camino Real. The root of the second central moment calculations of Doppler spread for these data does not exceed 6 Hz. Although situations could be imagined in which a somewhat greater spread could result, none were observed in about 50 such records. Thus the Doppler spread is probably negligible for most applications.

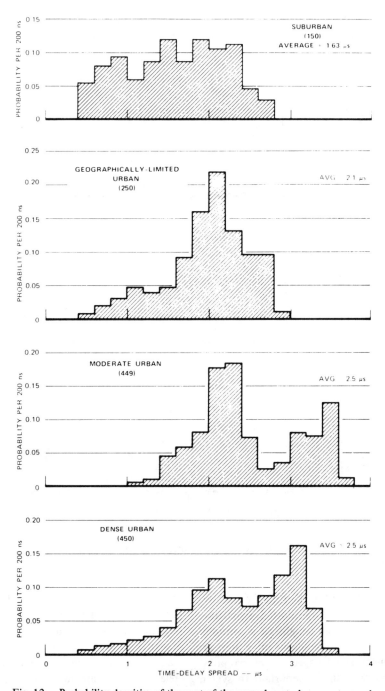

Fig. 12.   Probability densities of the root of the second-central-moment spread.

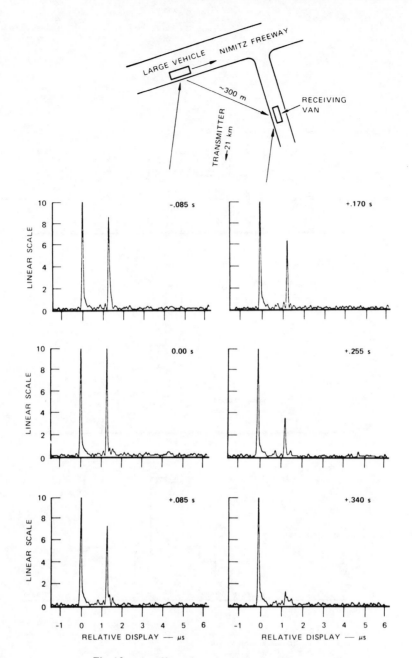

Fig. 13. An effect of moving isolated reflectors.

Spatial variation in signal level, other than that caused by spatial divergence, is the result of the transmitted signal traveling via multiple routes of different lengths to a common point. More concisely, it is the consequence of a nonzero complex (amplitude and phase) angular spectrum at that point. The nature of this variability is highly important to system performance whenever the location of a single receiving antenna cannot be continuously optimized. The multiple paths result in reinforcements and cancellations in space that can either cause pronounced fading on moving receivers or adversely affect the performance of an indiscriminantly located fixed system.

We have not been comprehensive in our approach to this measurement in the sense of developing statistics. Instead, we illustrate in Fig. 14 some typical results for varying terrain conditions. The examples contain the following descriptors: a power spectral density on spatial frequency, a spatial autocorrelation function of the magnitude of the received signal, and a spatial autocorrelation function of phase. Whereas the first can be used to estimate Doppler spread under motion, the correlation functions relate to receiving systems that employ spatial diversity. One can see that, over distances typically available in a car or truck, little decorrelation of the signal magnitude appears. On the other hand, the phase uniformly drops to zero correlation within one-half wavelength.

APPENDIX

The measurement system consisted of a transmitter and a receiver that were capable of operating on two different chip

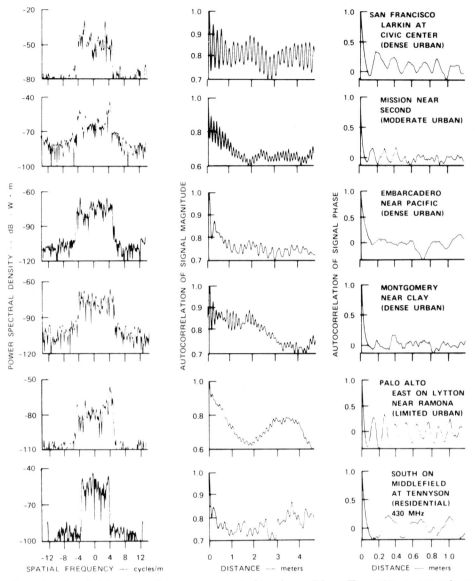

Fig. 14. Examples of spatial frequency data over a wide set of terrain conditions. (Transmitter was on twin peaks except for Palo Alto; frequency was 1370 MHz except as indicated.)

rates or running CW. The general radio characteristics were the following.

Transmitter	
Frequency	1370 MHz
Horn antenna gain	13 dBi
Chip rate	10, 20 Mchips/s
Power	5W
Stability	10^{-11}/s.

Receiver	
Bandwidth (postdetection)	9 MHz
Noise figure	10 dB
Omni antenna gain	7.5 dBi
Wideband matched filters-SAWDs	
100-Hz BW quadrature detector	

Signal-processing equipment associated with the receiver consisted of a transient digitizer capable of storing 2000 eight-bit samples at rates up to 100 MHz. This unit was used on all wide-band signals plus noise sampling. The two 100-Hz narrow-band quadrature channels were simultaneously A/D converted at 488 samples per second each. Both types of data were calibrated in a minicomputer and logged onto magnetic tape for further off-line processing.

REFERENCES

[1] W. Young and L. Lacy, "Echoes in transmission at 450 megacycles from land-to-car radio unity," in *Proc. IRE,* vol. 38, pp. 255–258, Mar. 1950.

[2] D. Cox and R. Leck, "Distributions of multipath delay spread and average excess delay for 910-MHz urban mobile radio paths," *IEEE Trans. Antennas Propagat.,* vol. AP-23, no. 2, pp. 206–213, Mar. 1975.

[3] G. L. Turin *et al.,* "A statistical model of urban multipath propagation," *IEEE Trans. Veh. Technol.,* VT-21, no. 1, pp. 1–9, Feb. 1972.

[4] D. Nielson, "Microwave propagation and noise measurements for mobile digital radio application," SRI Project 2325, ARPA Contract DAHC15-73-C-0187, SRI International, Menlo Park, CA, Jan. 1975.

[5] M. J. Gans, "A power-spectral theory of propagation in the mobile radio environment," *IEEE Trans. Veh. Technol.,* vol. VT-21, no. 1, pp. 27–38, Feb. 1972.

Part II
Mobile Data Communications

A UHF Channel Simulator for Digital Mobile Radio

EDGAR L. CAPLES, MEMBER. IEEE. KHALIL E. MASSAD, AND TIMOTHY R. MINOR

Abstract—A device to simulate the channel propagation characteristics of the ground mobile environment at UHF has been designed, built, and characterized. This device provides a flexible, easily changed set of simulated channel characteristics, which allows the performance of a mobile radio unit to be evaluated in the laboratory under controlled conditions. The channel simulator was designed to simulate mobile platform speeds up to 675 mi/h and multipath components having differential delays approaching 10 μs. The channel simulator can provide up to four easily selectable, independently fading, multipath components, having calculated time delay spreads of up to 3.5 μs. The adjustable fading bandwidths and the exceptional long delays were implemented using the relative new signal processing technologies of charged-coupled devices and surface wave devices. Envelope statistics such as fading distributions and level crossing rates produced by the channel simulator show excellent agreement with theoretical prediction and documented experimental data.

I. INTRODUCTION

AS PART of the Packet Radio System Development Program, a device to simulate the radio channel propagation characteristics of the ground mobile environment at UHF has been developed. The ground mobile radio channel can experience severe fading and multipath effects. The mobile radio channel simulator allows the performance of the packet radio unit to be characterized in the laboratory under a controlled environment. This provides a very cost-effective approach to design optimization.

This paper describes the design and performance of the mobile radio channel simulator. The design goals of the simulator were based upon accepted theoretical work and experimental observations. The design was also motivated by the desire to meet or exceed typical worst case fading and multipath characteristics associated with the environments in which the packet radio may be applied. The simulator is capable of generating up to four multipath signal components, all having the same fading bandwidth but independent Rayleigh statistics. The maximum fading bandwidth is 1800 Hz, corresponding to a simulated platform speed of 675 mi/h at 1780 MHz. The maximum time spread between multipath components is 9.3 μs, resulting in a time delay spread factor of more than 3.5 μs.

The use of relatively new signal processing devices eased the way to a versatile implementation of the mobile radio channel simulator. Signal fading rates over continuous ranges were achieved through the use of charged-coupled devices to realize

Manuscript received August 7, 1979; revised January 10, 1980. This work was supported by the Defense Advanced Research Projects Agency as part of the Packet Radio System Development Program under Contract DAHC15-73-C-0192.

The authors are with Rockwell International, Collins Radio Group, Communications Systems Division, Richardson, TX 75081. Telephone (214)966-5869, (214)996-5637, and (214)996-7658, respectively.

the Doppler spectrum shaping filters. The bandwidths of the shaping filters can be changed simply by varying the sampling rate of the charged-coupled device transversal filter structure. All Doppler spectrum shaping filters are driven from a common clock, thus allowing the several multipath signal components to have the same fading bandwidth. A second signal processing device, the surface acoustic wave (SAW) delay line, allowed the long relative time delays of the multipath components to be implemented in a straightforward manner. A SAW delay line having six taps was designed and fabricated specifically for the simulator. Because of the low propagation velocity of acoustic waves on the surface of the piezoelectric crystal, lithium niobate, the 9.3-μs of delay can be achieved on about 7.6 cm of substrate.

The mobile radio channel simulator accepts a wide-band modulated intermediate frequency (IF) input near 300 MHz and superimposes the desired channel impulse response on the communications signal which emerges at RF (1780 MHz) for the Packet Radio. Thus the simulator has been designed to be easily reconfigured to test other UHF digital radio systems.

II. UHF MOBILE RADIO CHANNEL DESCRIPTION

The UHF radio channel is, in general, characterized by multiple signal paths between the transmitter and the receiver. This is particularly true when both the transmitter and receiver antennas are sited near the ground. The multiple signal paths arise from buildings, terrain, and other structures in the vicinity of the receiver which scatter the signal energy. The multiple reflected signals add vectorially to form a quasi-stationary standing wave pattern with nulls occurring roughly at half-wavelengths of the RF frequency. In addition to the deep fades a mobile receiver experiences when operating in this environment, the multiple signals arrive at the receiver with relative time delays that are directly proportional to the differences in the propagation path lengths.

The envelope distribution of the signal thus described has been shown both analytically and experimentally to approximate the Rayleigh probability distribution when observed over a few tens of wavelengths [1], [2]. The rate at which the envelope fades is directly proportional to the speed of the mobile receiver. Analytically, this observation manifests itself as a Doppler frequency shift associated with each signal component. The resulting signal then has a Doppler frequency spectrum from which the envelope fading rate may be determined.

The spread in relative time delays of the signal components comprising the received signal is perhaps the most important radio channel characteristic affecting the design and performance of digital communications systems. Excessive time delay causes rapid decorrelation of the received signal statistics, frequency selective fading, and intersymbol interference. These

Reprinted from *IEEE Trans. Veh. Technol.*, vol. VT-29, pp. 281–289, May 1980.

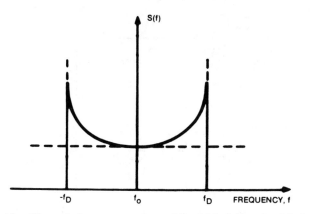

Fig. 1.   Theoretical power spectrum of Rayleigh fading signal (using omnidirectional antenna).

two characteristics, envelope fading and excess time delay, are described more precisely in the following sections.

A. Rayleigh Fading and Doppler Shift

Consider an unmodulated carrier being detected by a mobile receiver. Each signal component arrives at the receiver via different angles relative to the receiver velocity vector and thus each signal component experiences a Doppler shift that is related to the receiver speed and arrival angle according to

$$f_i = \frac{v}{\lambda} \cos \alpha_i = f_D \cos \alpha_i \qquad (1)$$

where v is the receiver speed, λ is the free-space carrier wavelength, α_i is the relative arrival angle of the ith component, and f_D is the maximum Doppler shift.

Due to the Doppler effect, the single frequency carrier results in multiple signals at the receiver having comparable amplitudes, random phases, and relative frequency shifts confined to the Doppler spread about the carrier frequency. The theoretical received signal spectrum is shown in Fig. 1. The above description of the received signal conforms to Rice's model for narrow-band Gaussian noise [3]. From Rice's work the received signal may be expressed as

$$S = x(t) \cos w_c t - y(t) \sin w_c t = R \cos (w_c t + \theta) \qquad (2)$$

where $x(t)$ and $y(t)$ are independent Gaussian processes and can be written as

$$x(t) = \sum A_i \cos (w_i t + \phi_i) \qquad (3)$$

$$y(t) = \sum A_i \sin (w_i t + \phi_i)$$

where A_i, w_i, and ϕ_i are the amplitude, frequency, and phase, respectively, of the ith sinusoid. The envelope and phase of the received signal become

$$R = \sqrt{x^2 + y^2}$$

$$\theta = \tan^{-1} y/x. \qquad (4)$$

Since x and y are independent Gaussian random variables, the distribution on R is Rayleigh and the distribution on θ is uniform over the interval 0 to 2π.

For a single frequency transmitted signal, the fading rate may be defined as the average rate of excursions of the received envelope across its rms level. For a Rayleigh distributed signal, the fading rate is related to the maximum Doppler shift as follows [1]:

$$N_{rms} = \frac{\sqrt{2\pi}}{e} f_D. \qquad (5)$$

A more general expression may be written for the level crossing rate which is the average rate a given level is crossed:

$$N_R = \sqrt{2\pi} f_D \rho e^{-\rho^2} \qquad (6)$$

where $\rho = R/R_{rms}$.

The Rayleigh fading model is supported very well by experimental work. Nielson's [2] measurements in the San Francisco Bay area represent some of the more recent experimental work on mobile propagation. Fig. 2, published by Nielson, shows the measured Doppler spectrum of an unmodulated carrier at 1370 MHz. The abscissa is normalized to cycles/meter; if multiplied by the receiver speed in meters/second, the Doppler frequency is obtained.

B. Excess Multipath Time Delay

The two parameters most often used as statistical descriptors of the multipath channel are the average time delay and the delay spread. Given the time delay profile of the multipath channel which may be as shown in Fig. 3, the average time delay and the delay spread may be calculated to determine the potential for symbol distortion and intersymbol interference. If $P(\tau)$ is the time delay profile, its first moment represents the average time delay, and the square root of its second central moment is defined as the delay spread. The average time delay and the delay spread can be expressed as

$$E(\tau) = \bar{\tau} = \frac{\int_{-\infty}^{\infty} \tau P(\tau)\, d\tau}{\int_{-\infty}^{\infty} P(\tau)\, d\tau} \qquad (7)$$

$$\sigma_s = \sqrt{E(\tau - \bar{\tau})^2} = \left[\frac{\int_{-\infty}^{\infty} (\tau - \bar{\tau})^2 P(\tau)\, d\tau}{\int_{-\infty}^{\infty} P(\tau)\, d\tau} \right]^{1/2}$$

The distribution of the time delay profile has been observed to be generally exponential; however, the actual shape of $P(\tau)$ is reported to have relatively little impact on communication system performance as compared to the value of the time delay spread [1]. Reduced power in signal components of longer delays is to be expected since the longer delays usually mean additional path attenuation which accounts for the exponential

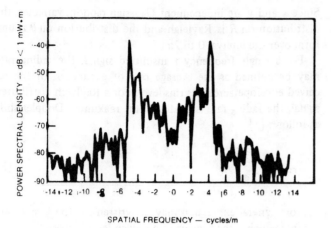

Fig. 2. Measured Doppler spectrum at 1370 MHz.

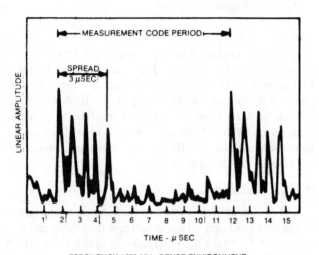

Fig. 3. Baseband multipath signal output of correlation receiver (10 μs symbol duration).

rolloff of the time delay profile. It has been observed, however, that the signal component transversing the minimum distance path is not always the strongest [2].

For urban environments time delay spreads greater than 3 μs have been measured. The results of Nielson's [2] measurements in the San Francisco Bay area indicate time delay spreads of up to 3.5 μs. A time delay spread of 3 μs or more implies that significant power exists beyond 5 μs in the time delay profile, which further indicates that symbol rates greater than 200 K symbols/s may exhibit significant error rates.

III. CHANNEL SIMULATOR DESIGN

The mobile channel simulator is designed to be a convenient test instrument for evaluating the performance of the Packet Radio in the presence of fading and multipath effects. Thus it is capable of generating a fading signal with four multipath components, selectable excess delay, independently adjustable component amplitudes, and an adjustable fading bandwidth.

A. Functional Description

A functional block diagram of the simulator appears in Fig. 4. A surface acoustic wave device (SAWD) delay line produces

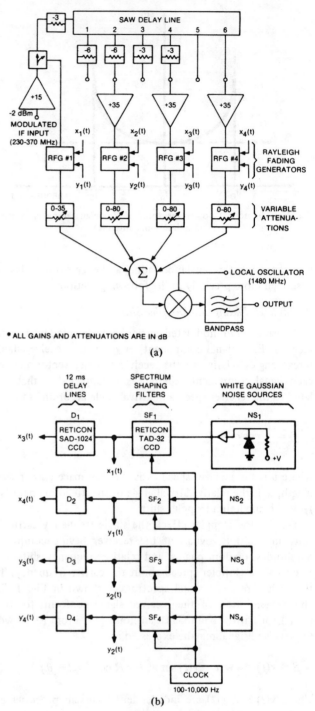

Fig. 4. Mobile channel simulator.

six delayed components of the incident signal, of which three may be selected. Four Rayleigh fading generators impose independent fading characteristics on the incident signal and the three delayed components. The amplitudes of the four fading signals are independently adjustable with variable attenuators. The Doppler fade bandwidth may be varied from 15 to 1800 Hz by changing the clock frequency to the spectrum shaping filters in Fig. 4(b). At the design frequency of 1780 MHz, this simulates vehicle speeds ranging from 6 to 675 mi/h.

The simulator requires an input signal in the 230–370 MHz range, which corresponds to the IF passband of the Packet

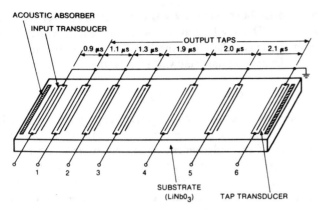

Fig. 5.   SAW delay line.

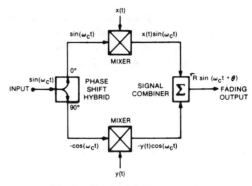

Fig. 6.   Rayleigh fading generator.

Radio. The channel simulation is performed at the IF frequency to permit the application of SAWD technology, which could not be utilized at the Packet Radio output frequency in the 1710–1850 MHz band. The bandwidth of the SAWD delay line is 140 MHz, which is the primary limiting factor on the RF bandwidth of the simulator. The SAWD, which has physical dimensions of 2.5 × 7.6 × 0.95 cm, achieves a delay time equal to that of a 3-km length of coaxial cable.

The SAWD is functionally depicted in Fig. 5. SAW's are excited on a piezoelectric substrate (lithium niobate) by the input transducer. These waves travel down the substrate and are detected at each of the tap transducers. The signal detected at a particular tap is delayed with respect to the input signal, by the amount of time required for the surface wave to propagate from the input transducer to the tap transducer. The delay time is proportional to the length of the propagation path. The delays range from 0.9 μs at tap 1 to 9.3 μs at tap 6.

A uniform signal level between the various taps of the SAWD is not attainable. SAWD's are in general rather lossy; 32 dB of signal attenuation is experienced at tap 6 with respect to the input. Although the majority of this loss occurs in the transducers, some loss occurs in the wave propagation on the substrate. The propagation loss increases as the lengths of the propagation path increase. As a result of the different lengths of the propagation paths to the various taps, the relative signal level between taps does vary as much as 7 dB. As shown in Fig. 4, external fixed attenuators were selected for the outputs of taps 1–4, which attenuate these signals to the approximate level of the signals at taps 5 and 6.

The output signals of the three SAWD taps selected are applied to the inputs of Rayleigh fading generators 2–4 (RFG 2, RFG 3, RFG 4) after amplification to the nominal input signal level required by the generators. Independent fading characteristics are applied to the four signal components by the four Rayleigh fading generators of Fig. 4. The amplitudes of each of the signal components may be independently adjusted with the four variable attenuators at the output of the fading generators.

The four signal components are summed, after the attenuators, and the resulting multipath fading signal is translated up to the Packet Radio frequency band of 1710–1850 MHz. A multipath delay profile, an example of which is presented in Fig. 3, is created by the channel simulator.

Although the channel simulator of Fig. 4 is tailored to the Packet Radio, the concepts are applicable to mobile channel simulation in other UHF frequency bands. The simulator, for instance, could be operated in another band by simply changing the frequency of the local oscillator input to the simulator.

B. Rayleigh Fading Generator

The basic Rayleigh fading generator design is depicted in Fig. 6. Independent band-limited Gaussian noise processes are added in the phase quadrature to produce the Rayleigh fading signal [1], [4]. The Gaussian noise processes are obtained from noisy zener diodes (1N4105) operated near cutoff. The noise power spectrum is approximately flat from 0 to 200 kHz. A spectrum, which approximates the theoretical fading spectrum of Fig. 1, is obtained through the filtering of the white Gaussian noise. Transversal shaping filters are realized with charged-coupled devices (CCD). The passband of the filters may be varied, to simulate Doppler fading bandwidths of 15–1800 Hz, by changing the clock frequency to the CCD's. A detailed description of the design and implementation of the CCD shaping filters is provided in Section III-C.

Four Rayleigh fading generators were implemented as shown in Fig. 4(a), to provide four multipath components which fade independently. Since each Rayleigh fading generator requires two independent narrow-band noise processes, a total of eight Gaussian noise sources and CCD shaping filters appear to be required.

The shaping filters require a significant amount of hardware and physical space. For this reason it is desirable to reduce the number of shaping filters required. The design shown in Fig. 4 utilizes only four noise sources and four shaping filters. The shaping filter outputs, x_1, y_1, x_2, and y_2, are then delayed by 12 ms to obtain four additional noise processes, x_3, x_4, y_3, and y_4, which are uncorrelated to the original noise processes. The delay lines are also implemented with CCD's but are considerably less complex and require less space than the CCD shaping filters.

The 12-ms delay of x_3 with respect to x_1, for instance, serves to decorrelate x_1 and x_3. A calculation to estimate the correlation coefficient of x_1 and x_3 was performed by approximating the power spectrum, of x_1 and x_3 with the flat spectrum, $S_w(f)$ of band-limited white noise across the simulated Doppler fading bandwidth $\hat{f}_D$. The estimated cross-correlation function of x_1 and x_3 is [5]

$$R_w(T) = N \frac{\sin(2\pi \hat{f}_D T)}{2\pi \hat{f}_D T} \tag{8}$$

where N is the total noise power which is equal to the variance σ_x^2 of x_1 (and x_3). T is the delay time between x_1 and x_3. The correlation coefficient $\rho_w(T)$ of x_3 with respect to x_1 is

$$\rho_w(T) = \frac{R_w(T)}{\sigma_x^2} = \frac{\sin(2\pi \hat{f}_D T)}{2\pi \hat{f}_D T} \tag{9}$$

For the 12-ms delay implemented in the simulator, the correlation coefficient magnitude is <0.2 for $\hat{f}_D > 35$ Hz. However, the minimum Doppler fading bandwidth of the simulator is $\hat{f}_D = 15$ Hz, for which $\rho_w(T) = 0.8$, which indicates strong correlation of x_1 and x_3. Referring to Fig. 4, one of the two narrow-band noise sources, x_1 and y_1, utilized by the first fading generator (RFG 1), is totally independent of one of the noise sources utilized in each of the other three fading generators. This further decorrelates the fading characteristics of the four fading components of the simulated multipath signal.

Each of the four CCD delay lines of Fig. 4(b) is implemented with a 1024-cell CCD. The CCD is clocked at the rate of $f_c = 8.5$ kHz. The analog input signal to the CCD is sampled at the clock rate. The minimum Nyquist sampling rate [5], f_N, which will guarantee that an analog signal can be totally reconstructed at the delay line output, is $f_N \geqslant 2B$, where B is the input signal. At the CCD sample rate of $f_c = 8.5$ kHz, the Nyquist condition is satisfied when $B = \hat{f}_D < 8.5$ kHz/2, or the Doppler fading bandwidth $\hat{f}_D$ of the simulator must be less than 4250 Hz. Since the maximum fading bandwidth to be simulated is 1800 Hz, the sampling rate is always at least a factor of two greater than the minimum allowable sampling rate. This factor of two or greater margin allows the analog signal to be reconstructed with a relatively simple low-pass filter. The total delay T of the CCD delay is $T = n_c/f_c$, where n_c is the total number of cells and f_c is the clock rate. The delay is approximately 12 ms for the 1024-cell CCD delay line clocked at 8.5 kHz.

The CCD delay line could be clocked with the same variable frequency clock utilized by the shaping filters. Since this clock frequency is proportional to the simulated fading bandwidth, longer delays would be realized in the CCD delay lines at the lower fading bandwidths, and the Nyquist sampling criteria would also be satisfied for all fading bandwidths. The longer delays would further decorrelate the outputs of the four Rayleigh fading generators at the lower fading bandwidths. However, unless the cutoff frequency of the active filter at the delay line output is also varied, the delayed output signals would not sufficiently smooth across the entire range of fading bandwidths. The added complexity of switchable active filters

in the delay board circuitry was not desired, and for this reason the CCD delay lines are clocked at a fixed frequency. As a result, some correlation of the Rayleigh fading generators occurs at Doppler fading bandwidths of less than 35 Hz.

C. Transversal Shaping Filter Design

Simulation of the fading spectrum appropriate to mobile radio communication is obtained by properly shaping the spectrum of the independent noise sources. The spectrum of the Doppler spread $S(f)$ depicted in Fig. 1 is simulated by passing the output of each Gaussian noise source through a shaping filter whose frequency response approximates the spectrum of the Doppler spread.

To generate a Rayleigh fading signal, several methods are available for realizing the spectrum shaping filter. These methods include using RC filters, active filters, or transversal finite impulse response (FIR) filters. Each method has its advantages and disadvantages. However, to simulate mobile UHF radio channel characteristics, the FIR filter approach was selected. The advantage of using a transversal FIR filter is its capability to provide continuous simulated vehicle speeds. Variable vehicle speeds are obtained by changing the shaping filter bandwidth which changes the simulated Doppler spread. The ability to easily change the bandwidth in an FIR filter eliminates the need to construct several switch-in RC or active shaping filters, each having a prescribed bandwidth. However, a variable clock driver is required for the FIR filter. The clock speed must be proportional to the desired vehicle velocity and must satisfy the following relationship derived in Section IV:

$$0.16 f_{SF} = \hat{f}_D = \frac{V}{\lambda} \tag{10}$$

where f_{SF} is the clocking rate of the FIR filter, $\hat{f}_D$ is the maximum Doppler shift, V is the vehicle velocity, and λ is the signal wavelength. To illustrate the application of (10), consider simulating a 1.8-GHz RF signal ($\lambda = 0.1576$ m) with vehicle velocity $V = 50$ mi/h $= 22.35$ m/s. This will require a clock rate $f_{SF} = 886.3$ Hz.

A block diagram description of the shaping filter is given in Fig. 7. The shaping filter utilizes a CCD, tap weighting resistors, and a summer. It was determined that a 32-tap CCD device would meet the filter specifications and minimize the amount of hardware required.

The value of the tap weights $h(n)$ are computed using the filter design algorithm given in [6]. The computer simulated response of a 32-tap filter using this algorithm is given in Fig. 8. The filter response of Fig. 8 presents a stopband attenuation of -36 dB and a transition region slope of 120 dB/octave. Additional improvement of the transition region and stopband attenuation can be achieved at the cost of increasing the number of taps required and the amount of hardware used. For example, doubling the number of taps provides -44-dB stopband attenuation and a transition region slope of 180 dB/octave.

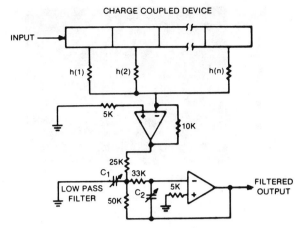

Fig. 7. Transversal shaping filter circuit.

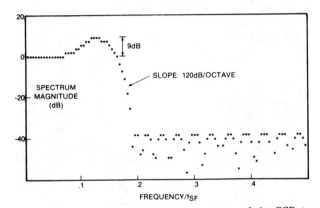

Fig. 8. Computer generated frequency response of the CCD transversal shaping filter.

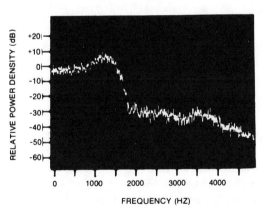

Fig. 9. Power spectrum at shaping filter output.

The transversal shaping filter design was breadboarded and tested for performance evaluation. Fig. 9 depicts the performance of the transversal shaping filter hardware. The spectrum shown was examined with an HP3580A spectrum analyzer at a simulated fading bandwitdh of 1800 Hz. The filter spectrum in Fig. 9 has a stopband attenuation of −30 dB and a transition region slope of 100 dB/octave. This represents an adequate performance level for shaping the Gaussian noise sources.

In the channel simulator design, an active low-pass filter was used to convert the discrete signal back to analog and to minimize the effect of clock pulses appearing at the output of the shaping filter. The circuit used for implementing the active low-pass filter is given in Fig. 7. In order to adapt to the Doppler bandwidth variation of the shaping filter, the active low-pass filter is designed to provide four bandwidths: 30, 125, 375, and 1800 Hz. This is achieved by switching in two capacitors for every bandwidth using switching diodes.

IV. SIMULATOR PERFORMANCE

The performance of the Rayleigh fading generators was evaluated by comparing the envelope statistics of the simulated fading signal with those of the theoretical Rayleigh signal. Specifically, the cumulative probability distribution and level crossing rate distribution of the simulated envelope were compared with the desired theoretical distributions. The cumulative probability distribution is composed of the probabilities, for various levels, that the signal envelope will exceed those levels, at any instant of time. A level crossing rate is defined, for measurement purposes, as the average number of times that the signal envelope crosses a particular level, in a positive-going direction, during a 1-s time interval. The level crossing rate distribution is composed of the crossing rates for various levels.

A. Measurement Technique

The simulated Doppler fading bandwidth $\hat{f}_D$ may be determined by equating the moments of the theoretical and simulated spectrums [4]. The theoretical power spectrum of the fading signal shown in Fig. 1 can be expressed as [1]

$$S(f) = \begin{cases} \dfrac{E^2}{2\pi f_D} \left[1 - (f/f_D)^2\right]^{1/2}, & f \leqslant f_D \\ 0, & f > f_D \end{cases} \quad (11)$$

where E is the rms value of the signal envelope. Let b_n denote the nth moment of the theoretical spectrum $S(f)$. Then,

$$b_n \triangleq (2\pi)^n \int_0^\infty S(f) f^n \, df. \quad (12)$$

By substituting the theoretical spectrum $S(f)$ from (11) into (12), the theoretical fading bandwidth f_D may be expressed as

$$f_D = \frac{1}{2\pi} \sqrt{\frac{2b_2}{b_0}}. \quad (13)$$

The simulated fading spectrum $\hat{S}(f)$ obtained from a spectrum analyzer may be integrated with graphical techniques to obtain the moments of $\hat{S}(f)$. The simulated fading bandwidth $\hat{f}_D$ may then be computed as follows:

$$\hat{f}_D = \frac{1}{2\pi} \sqrt{\frac{2\hat{b}_2}{\hat{b}_0}}. \quad (14)$$

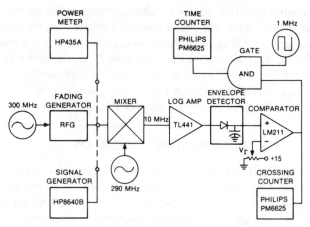

Fig. 10.   Envelope statistics measurement system.

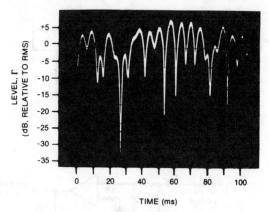

Fig. 11.   Signal envelope from Rayleigh fading generator ($\hat{f}_D = 160$ Hz).

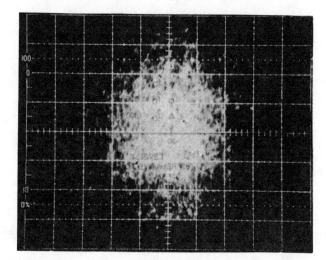

Fig. 12.   Polar plot of in-phase and quadrature noise sources after shaping ($\hat{f}_D = 160$ Hz).

The bandwidth of $\hat{S}(f)$ is varied by changing the clock frequency f_{SF} to the CCD shaping filters, as explained in Section III. The calculation of (14) was performed at a single clock frequency of $f_{SF_1} = 1$ kHz and the simulated fading bandwidth calculated was $f_{D_1} = 163$ Hz. Assuming that the relative shape of $\hat{S}(f)$ remains approximately constant as f_{SF} is varied, then $\hat{f}_D$ will be directly proportional to f_{SF} and may be expressed as follows:

$$\hat{f}_D \cong 0.16 f_{SF}. \tag{15}$$

The probability and crossing rate distributions were determined with the measurement system which is outlined in Fig. 10. Logarithmic signal compression is utilized to permit accurate measurements over a dynamic range of more than 50 dB.

The level crossing rate $N(\Gamma)$ is determined by counting the average number of positive pulses $n_s(T)$ that occur at the comparator output during the time period T. The average crossing rate is expressed as follows:

$$N(\Gamma) = \lim_{T \to \infty} \left. \frac{n_s(T)}{T} \right|_\Gamma \tag{16}$$

where Γ is the particular envelope level for which the crossing rate is being measured. $\dot{N}(\Gamma)$ is the normalized level crossing rate,

$$\dot{N}(\Gamma) = N(\Gamma)/\hat{f}_D \tag{17}$$

where $\hat{f}_D$ is the simulated Doppler bandwidth. The level crossing rates are normalized to allow direct comparison of data obtained at various fading bandwidths.

The comparator output is further utilized to determine the probability that the signal envelope will exceed the level Γ at any instant. A time base frequency $f_c = 1$ MHz is activated only if the comparator output is high. The time base is disabled when this output is low. Let $n_c(T)$ denote the number of time base pulses which occur during the time period T. The average fraction of time, for which Γ is exceeded, $F(\Gamma)$,

can be expressed as follows:

$$F(\Gamma) = \lim_{T \to \infty} \left. \frac{n_c(T)}{f_c T} \right|_\Gamma \tag{18}$$

For an ergodic process, $F(\Gamma)$ is also the probability that the signal envelope will exceed the level Γ. The RF level Γ can be related to dc level V_Γ (see Fig. 10) by applying a continuous wave (CW) input of peak amplitude Γ to the measurement system and measuring the dc level at the envelope detector output.

B. Performance

The manner in which the envelope of the simulated fading signal fluctuates can be observed in Fig. 11. This is a photograph of the log compressed signal envelope from one of the Rayleigh fading generators as it appears on an oscilliscope with a storage display.

The results of a qualitative check for uniformity of the phase distribution of the fading signal are shown in Fig. 12. The figure is a time-exposure photograph of the oscilliscope display obtained by letting the in-phase and quadrature channel Gaussian noise processes, $x(t)$ and $y(t)$ in Fig. 6, control the horizontal and vertical deflections, respectively, of the oscilliscope.

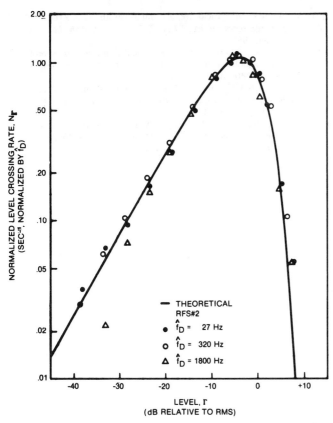

Fig. 13. Level crossing rate distribution of simulated envelope ($\hat{f}_D$ = 27, 320, 1800 Hz).

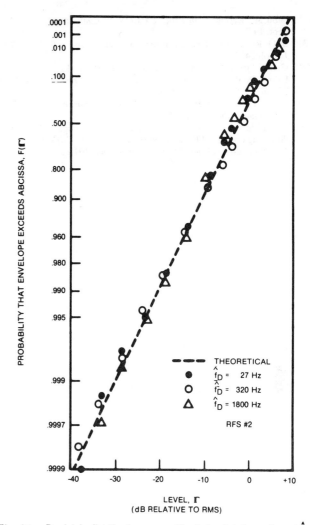

Fig. 14. Rayleigh distribution curve fit of simulated envelope ($\hat{f}_D$ = 27, 320, 1800 Hz).

Since the noise processes control deflections with 90° relative orientation, the resulting display is equivalent to a polar plot of the randomly varying phasor at the output of a Rayleigh fading generator. The uniform intensity of the display, at any fixed radius about the origin, indicates a relatively uniform phase distribution.

The measured level crossing rate distributions for one of the Rayleigh fading generators, at $\hat{f}_D$ = 27, 320, and 1800 Hz, are compared to the theoretical curve in Fig. 13. The level crossing rates were normalized by the fading bandwidth $\hat{f}_D$ to allow direct comparison of data for various fading bandwidths. The envelope level Γ is in decibels relative to the rms envelope level.

The cumulative probability distributions of the signal envelope from one of the fading generators at $\hat{f}_D$ = 27, 320, and 1800 Hz are compared to the theoretical Rayleigh curve in Fig. 14. These fading bandwidths correspond to vehicle speeds of 10, 120, and 675 mi/h at the Packet Radio output frequency of 1780 MHz.

The agreement between the envelope statistics of the simulated fading waveforms and the theoretical fading waveforms, as shown in Figs. 13 and 14, is very good. At $\hat{f}_D$ = 27 Hz and 320 Hz, the measured data deviate less than 2 dB from the theoretical curves for levels down to 38 dB below the rms value of the fading envelope. The fading generator performance at $\hat{f}_D$ = 1800 Hz is somewhat degraded, but the measured data are still within 3 dB of the theoretical curves for levels down to 28 dB below the rms value of the fading envelope.

V. SUMMARY

The design and performance of a flexible UHF mobile radio channel simulator has been described. The design incorporates CCD's for implementing the Doppler spectrum shaping filters and a SAW delay line for realizing the 9-μs of signal delay. The statistics of the simulated signal envelope have been measured and were found to be in close agreement with theoretical predictions and experimental observations.

VI. ACKNOWLEDGMENT

The authors wish to thank R. K. Marston for the many stimulating discussions, and J. R. Logue for his assistance in the experimental work. The efforts of J. C. Aukland and Dr. D. Penunuri of the Electronic Devices Division, Rockwell International, Anaheim, CA, in the design and fabrication of the SAWD delay line are also gratefully acknowledged.

REFERENCES

[1] W. C. Jakes, Ed., *Microwave Mobile Communication*. New York: Wiley, 1974.
[2] D. Nielson, "Microwave propagation measurements for mobile digital

radio applications," in *Proc. EASCON 77 Conf.*, pp. 14-2A–14-2L, Sept. 1977.

[3] S. O. Rice, "Mathematical analysis of random noise," *Bell Syst. Tech. J.*, vol. 24, 1945.

[4] G. A. Arrendondo, W. H. Chriss, and E. H. Walker, "A multipath fading simulator for mobile radio," *IEEE Trans. Commun.*, vol. COM-21, pp. 1325–1328, Nov. 1973.

[5] M. Schwartz, W. R. Bennett, and S. Stein, *Communications Systems and Techniques.*   New York: McGraw-Hill, 1966.

[6] J. McClellan, T. Parks, and L. Rabiner, "A computer program for designing optimum FIR linear phase digital filters," *IEEE Trans. Audio Electroacoust.*, vol. AU-21, pp. 506–526, Dec. 1973.

[7] Y. Okmura *et al.*, "Field strength and its variability in VHF and UHF land-mobile radio service," *Rev. Tokyo Elect. Comm. Lab.*, vol. 16, Sept.–Oct. 1968.

[8] D. C. Cox, "Multipath delay spread and path loss correlation for 910 MHz urban mobile radio propagation," *IEEE Trans. Veh. Technol.*, vol. VT-26, pp. 340–344, Nov. 1977.

[9] ——, "910 MHz urban mobile radio propagation: Multipath characteristics in New York City," *IEEE Trans. Commun.*, vol. COM-21, pp. 1188–1194, Nov. 1973.

[10] J. D. Ralphs and F. M. E. Sladen, "An HF channel simulator using a new Rayleigh fading method," *Radio Electron. Eng.*, vol. 46, pp. 579–587, Dec. 1976.

Characteristics of a Digital Mobile Radio Channel

TOR AULIN, MEMBER, IEEE

Abstract—A field test has been made in order to better understand the digital mobile radio channel. At the mobile receiver (450 MHz, 1200 bits/s) recordings were made of the digital signal and the field strength. These recordings were later analyzed by a computer. Some existing models for digital channels have been tested. Theoretically motivated probability density functions for the fading envelope have also been considered. A new model for the digital channel is proposed. This model is a memoryless binary symmetric channel (BSC) with field strength dependent crossover error probability. This model fits very well to the recorded data.

I. INTRODUCTION

THE CHARACTERIZATION of a digital mobile radio channel is very complex, involving such factors as the environment of the receiver, the speed of the vehicle, the carrier frequency and modulation system used, just to mention a few. The aim of the present report is to investigate different ways of modeling the digital errors for such a channel at a comparatively low data rate (1200 bits/s). This model involves the instantaneous field strength as a parameter. Other models are given in [21]–[29].

A field test has been made in order to get material for characterization of the abovementioned channel. An ordinary FM-radiotelephone system (5 W, 450 MHz) provided with frequency shift keying (FSK) datamodems (1200 bits/s) was used. A vehicle carrying the receiver was moving through the urban parts of the city Malmö in the southwest of Sweden, and a fixed transmitter was located 20 m above the ground in the northern part of the city of Lund. The data was collected in a moderately urban area with high probability of receiving a line-of-sight path. The size of the measurement area could not be classified as either small or large.

In the vehicle, recordings were made of the output from the modem and the field strength at the receiving antenna. These recordings were later digitized and stored on computer magnetic tape. A total of three recordings was made at different occasions, each one of them lasting for approximately 20 min. The vehicle followed the same route every time.

Previous models [1]–[12] for digital channels with memory concerning distributional and correlational properties have been tested, and a new one involving the field strength is proposed. This new model fits very well to the data and is easily handled analytically. The memory is referred to the analog channel, and the digital channel is described by a time-varying binary symmetric channel (BSC). The digital channel is time-varying in the sense that the crossover probability of the BSC

is a deterministic function of the field strength, a function determined by the detector used.

Essentially, four types of probability density functions (pdf's) for the field strength are theoretically motivated from a multipath viewpoint and therefore tested, but none of these pdf's gives a good fit to the data. The cause to this could be that the field strength process is not stationary, an assumption which seems plausible for a mobile radio channel. Another reason might be that the chosen test area cannot be considered as either large or small.

The correlational properties of the field strength are also investigated, indicating a very long memory. This correlation is originally spatial, but since the vehicle is mobile the correlation can be expressed either as a function of distance separation or time separation.

II. THE DATA

The omnidirectional vertical transmitting antenna was placed on the roof of the Electrical Engineering Department in Lund, and the receiver was located in a vehicle moving around in the urban parts of Malmö. The receiving antenna was also omnidirectional and vertical, and the speed of the vehicle varied between 0 and 50 km/h.

The terrain between the two cities is very flat, almost without trees, and the house on which the transmitting antenna was located is situated on the top of a flat hill, approximately 75 m higher than the ground in Malmö. The distance from ground to transmitting antenna was 20 m, and the distance between receiver and transmitter varied between 18 and 22 km. In Malmö, the houses are mostly 3–6 story buildings, and sometimes the vehicle passed places with houses just on one side of the street, sometimes parks.

The binary data source was a pseudorandom noise (PRN) sequence of length 511 according to CCITT [14], 1200 bits/s, periodically repeated (see Fig. 1). This binary data was fed to the FSK-modem connected to the voice-band input of the FM station. The modem operated around 1700 Hz with the frequency shift specified by CCITT [15] for the general telephone network. Carrier frequency was 450 MHz.

The signal from the receiving antenna was frequency demodulated (Fig. 2), to obtain the FSK-signal from the voice-band output and then fed into the modem, giving an analog signal corresponding to the transmitted data. It should be noted that the receiver operates asynchronously.

The so-called squelch signal (Fig. 2) and the analog data signal were simultaneously recorded on an FM tape recorder. A speech signal for comments was also recorded. The squelch signal is obtained by high-pass filtering, rectification, and low-pass filtering the voice-band output from the FM station. When a carrier is present (modulated or not), the noise from

Manuscript received September 5, 1978; revised July 17, 1980 and October 9, 1980. This paper was presented at the Radio Scientific Conference, Royal Institute of Technology, Stockholm, Sweden, March 29–31, 1978.

The author is with Telecommunication Theory, University of Lund, Fack, S-220 07 Lund, Sweden. Telephone 046/107 000.

Reprinted from *IEEE Trans. Veh. Technol.*, vol. VT-30, pp. 45–53, May 1981.

205

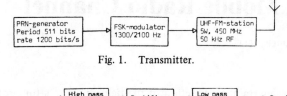

Fig. 1.   Transmitter.

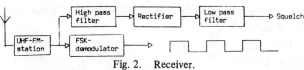

Fig. 2.   Receiver.

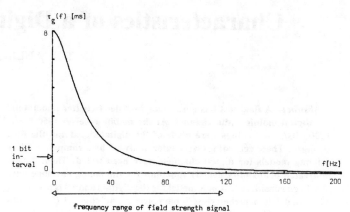

Fig. 3.   Group delay for squelch low-pass filter.

the high-pass filter is supressed. This gives a zero squelch signal. If no carrier is present, noise from the high-pass filter output is not suppressed, thus giving a nonzero squelch signal. As the squelch signal is the rms value of the noise from the high-pass filter output, it is possible to achieve the carrier power or equivlently the field strength from this signal. The squelch signal can be calibrated to give the field strength in decibels.

Of course, the low-pass filter introduces delay, and the computed group delay for this filter is shown in Fig. 3. From this figure it can be concluded that the delay introduced by the filter is far from constant in the frequency range of the field strength signal. The delay varies from 0.5 to 10 bit intervals. Furthermore, a filtered version (not only delayed) of the real field strength signal is observed.

Using a two-channel A/D converter, the two signals from the FM recorder were fed into a digital computer. Since the analog data signal is not synchronized, bit synchronization and detection is done in the computer. This is done in real time by sampling each bit interval of the data signal many times, adding these samples, and comparing them to a threshold. The resulting data is packed in one word for each bit, giving information about the field strength, the transmitted binary data, and whether it was correctly detected or not. A total of approximately 5×10^6 bit intervals were detected and stored.

Examples of recordings at different occasions can be seen in Fig. 4. A large constant added to the field strength signal indicates digital error in this plot.

III. THE DIGITAL CHANNEL

Referring the modems and UHF-FM stations to the channel, the digital channel (Fig. 5) is achieved. As we know what was fed into the digital channel, this can be compared (addition mod-2) to what comes out from it, thus giving the error sequence (Fig. 6) characterizing this channel.

The error sequence is also binary, a one denoting digital error and a zero denoting no digital error. However, the error sequence is more easily handled through its so-called gap lengths (Fig. 7). By a gap length is meant the number of zeros between adjacent ones in the binary error sequence, and it is clear that the digital channel can also be described by the gap length process $\{g_i\}$. In the example of Fig. 7, $g_1 = 3$, $g_2 = 1$, $g_3 = 2$, $g_4 = 0$, and $g_5 = 4$.

A. Gap Length Distributions

It is natural to test whether the digital channel is a memory-less BSC or not. Denoting the crossover probability by p, we

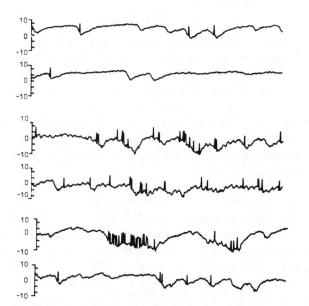

Fig. 4.   Field strength recordings in decibels at different occasions. 511 bit intervals/row.

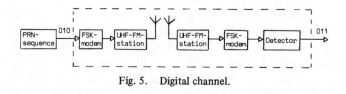

Fig. 5.   Digital channel.

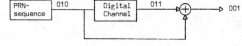

Fig. 6.   Error sequence.

$$\ldots 0\,0\,1\,\underbrace{0\,0\,0}_{g_1}\,1\,\underbrace{0}_{g_2}\,1\,\underbrace{0\,0}_{g_3}\,1\,\underset{\underset{g_4}{\uparrow}}{1}\,\underbrace{0\,0\,0\,0}_{g_5}\,1\,0\,0\,\ldots$$

Fig. 7.   Gap lengths.

would then have

$$P(g = i) = (1 - p)^i \cdot p$$

$$P(g \geqslant n) = \sum_{i=n}^{\infty} P(g = i) = (1 - p)^n \qquad (1)$$

where $P(g \geqslant n)$ denotes the probability that gap length is bigger than or equal to the integer n. Taking the logarithm we get

$$\log [P(g \geqslant n)] = n \cdot \log (1 - p) \qquad (2)$$

and a plot of $\log [P(g \geqslant n)]$ versus n should give a straight line.

Suggestions have been made [3], [4], [10], [12] that the gap length is Pareto distributed, i.e.,

$$P(g \geqslant n) = (n + 1)^{-\alpha}, \qquad n = 0, 1, 2, \cdots \qquad (3)$$

or, equivalently,

$$\log [P(g \geqslant n)] = -\alpha \log (n + 1), \qquad n = 0, 1, 2, \cdots \qquad (4)$$

and a plot of $\log [P(g \geqslant n)]$ versus $\log (n + 1)$ is a straight line.

From the collected digital data the gap length distribution has been estimated, here denoted $\hat{P}(g \geqslant n)$. This estimate can be seen in Fig. 8, where it is plotted linear and logarithmic versus n and also logarithmic versus $\log (n + 1)$.

It is easily seen that the estimated gap length distribution does not yield a straight line in Figs. 8(b) or (c), and the models are thus rejected. For small gaps, however, the Pareto distribution is a good candidate, but even though the curve in Fig. 8(b) is a straight line for big gaps, its asymptote does not cross the origin as it should for a BSC.

B. Gap Length Correlations

A renewal process is a point process, where some event has the property of cutting the memory of the process, i.e., the process starts from the beginning again. (For an exact definition, see [16].) This kind of process has been proposed [1], [2], [5], [6], [8], [11], [12] for the error sequence from a digital telephone channel with memory. The recurrent (memory-cutting) event is a bit error, i.e., a one in the error process. Looking at gap lengths, this means that the process $\{g_i\}$ is uncorrelated and thus characterized by this distribution. Distributions like the one of Fig. 8 can of course be used.

This model of a digital channel with memory has been generalized, by adapting a Markov chain model for the gap lengths [7], [9]. Adjacent gap lengths are now correlated, but also gap lengths of larger distance. Distributions like the one estimated here can be achieved with this model.

The first model can be easily tested and the second investigated by partitioning the gap lengths into nonoverlapping groups and observing the number of transitions between groups. The renewal process model is tested by first-order transitions, i.e., transitions between consecutive gap lengths, and the correlational properties of the Markov chain model are investigated by higher order transitions.

The null hypothesis is that the a_i (defined in Table I) are independent, and the chi-squared test for independence in an $l \times l$ contingency table is used [13]. Transition tables for first- and second-order gap length group transitions have been estimated, but also transitions of order three. These can be seen in Table I.

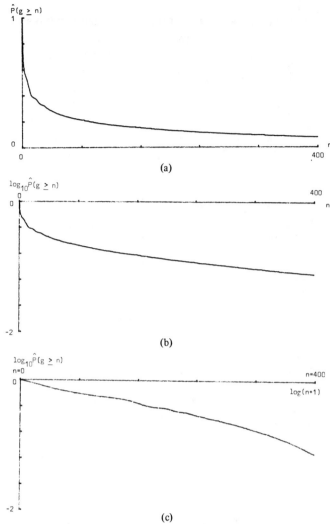

Fig. 8. (a) $\hat{P}(g \geqslant n)$ versus n. (b) $\log_{10} \hat{P}(g \geqslant n)$ versus n. (c) $\log_{10} \hat{P}(g \geqslant n)$ versus $\log (n + 1)$.

The group limits were chosen so that an approximately equal number of gap lengths fell into each group, thereby assuring a reliable test quantity

$$t = \sum_{k,j} \frac{(n_{kj} - n \cdot \hat{p}_k \cdot \hat{p}_j)^2}{n \hat{p}_k \hat{p}_j} \qquad (5)$$

where n_{kj} is the number of transitions from group number k to group number j, n is the total number of transitions and

$$\hat{p}_k = \frac{n_k}{n} \qquad n_k = \sum_j n_{kj}. \qquad (6)$$

t is an approximate chi-square variate with $(l - 1)^2$ degrees of freedom, where l is the number of groups. The following values of t were found:

first order $\quad t = 1735.64; \Pr (\chi_{49}^2 > t) \ll 10^{-5}$

second order $\quad t = 1573.26; \Pr (\chi_{49}^2 > t) \ll 10^{-5}$

third order $\quad t = 1529.63; \Pr (\chi_{49}^2 > t) \ll 10^{-5}$

and this is very strong evidence against independence.

TABLE I
ESTIMATED TRANSITION TABLES AND PROBABILITIES

A. FIRST ORDER

	a_1	a_2	a_3	a_4	a_5	a_6	a_7	a_8		a_1	a_2	a_3	a_4	a_5	a_6	a_7	a_8
a_1	723	321	311	310	240	285	419	417	a_1	.24	.11	.10	.10	.08	.09	.14	.14
a_2	313	131	143	106	58	89	114	81	a_2	.30	.13	.14	.10	.06	.09	.11	.08
a_3	342	129	137	96	64	90	95	107	a_3	.32	.12	.13	.09	.06	.08	.09	.10
a_4	270	112	97	73	94	68	88	63	a_4	.31	.13	.11	.08	.11	.08	.10	.07
a_5	247	56	53	92	133	99	82	49	a_5	.30	.07	.07	.11	.16	.12	.10	.06
a_6	342	80	96	64	102	159	167	128	a_6	.30	.07	.08	.06	.09	.14	.15	.11
a_7	400	103	131	67	70	211	359	300	a_7	.24	.06	.08	.04	.04	.13	.22	.18
a_8	388	103	93	57	50	137	316	809	a_8	.20	.05	.05	.03	.03	.07	.16	.41

B. SECOND ORDER

	a_1	a_2	a_3	a_4	a_5	a_6	a_7	a_8		a_1	a_2	a_3	a_4	a_5	a_6	a_7	a_8
a_1	847	306	309	270	230	308	386	370	a_1	.28	.10	.10	.09	.07	.10	.13	.12
a_2	300	115	121	101	77	97	129	95	a_2	.29	.11	.12	.10	.07	.09	.12	.09
a_3	324	114	144	77	68	94	132	108	a_3	.31	.11	.14	.07	.06	.09	.12	.10
a_4	260	98	91	100	112	70	77	57	a_4	.30	.11	.11	.12	.13	.08	.09	.07
a_5	237	82	72	105	105	95	71	44	a_5	.29	.10	.09	.13	.13	.12	.09	.05
a_6	308	93	87	77	100	152	181	142	a_6	.27	.08	.08	.07	.09	.13	.16	.12
a_7	372	124	135	78	80	193	327	332	a_7	.23	.08	.08	.05	.05	.12	.20	.20
a_8	379	103	102	57	39	129	338	805	a_8	.19	.05	.05	.03	.02	.07	.17	.41

C. THIRD ORDER

	a_1	a_2	a_3	a_4	a_5	a_6	a_7	a_8		a_1	a_2	a_3	a_4	a_5	a_6	a_7	a_8
a_1	844	331	308	275	235	285	365	383	a_1	.28	.11	.10	.09	.08	.09	.12	.13
a_2	319	109	117	100	80	90	119	101	a_2	.31	.11	.11	.10	.08	.09	.11	.10
a_3	292	108	155	80	79	95	155	97	a_3	.28	.10	.15	.08	.07	.09	.15	.09
a_4	273	89	79	123	89	67	81	64	a_4	.32	.10	.09	.14	.10	.08	.09	.07
a_5	241	76	79	98	106	83	75	53	a_5	.30	.09	.10	.12	.13	.10	.09	.07
a_6	290	95	78	77	99	182	185	132	a_6	.25	.08	.07	.07	.09	.16	.16	.12
a_7	376	124	139	66	74	189	331	342	a_7	.23	.08	.08	.04	.05	.12	.20	.21
a_8	389	103	106	46	49	147	330	781	a_8	.20	.05	.05	.02	.03	.09	.17	.40

D. GROUP LIMITS

a_1	a_2	a_3	a_4	a_5	a_6	a_7	a_8
$0 \leq g < 1$	$1 \leq g < 2$	$2 \leq g < 5$	$5 \leq g < 10$	$10 \leq g < 23$	$23 \leq g < 64$	$64 \leq g < 228$	$228 \leq g$

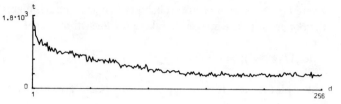

Fig. 9. Test quantity t versus transition order d.

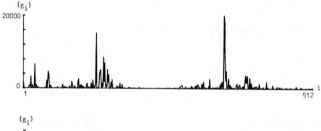

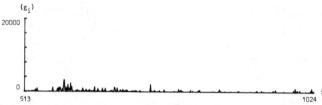

Fig. 10. Observed consecutive gap lengths (horizontal axis shows index number).

Furthermore, the correlational properties indicate that the process is not of the renewal type, but the Markov chain gap model can be fitted to the observed process.

IV. THE ANALOG CHANNEL

A. The Field Strength pdf

From all the collected data, the pdf of the field strength[1] was estimated (Fig. 11). From the figure it is seen that the pdf is very roughly in the domain $2 < F < 8$ [dB]. The cause for this is that the vehicle was sometimes standing still, waiting for a green light. In this situation the field strength is almost constant, a "constant" that is different in different locations, so the pdf is a mixture of a continuous and discrete pdf.

There are essentially four types of pdf's motivated from a theoretical point of view [17]. The underlying physical reason is multipath propagation. These four pdf's have been tested, i.e., it has been tested that

1) $F = 20 \cdot \log_{10} (F'/k)$ where $F' \in$ Rayleigh (b), i.e.,

$$f_{F'}(x) = \begin{cases} \dfrac{x}{b^2} e^{-x^2/2b^2}, & x \geq 0 \\ 0, & \text{elsewhere;} \end{cases} \qquad (7)$$

2) $F = 20 \cdot \log_{10}(F'/k)$ where $F' \in$ Rice (a, b), i.e.,

$$f_{F'}(x) = \begin{cases} \dfrac{x}{b^2} e^{-(x^2+a^2)/2b^2} I_0\left(\dfrac{ax}{b^2}\right), & x \geq 0 \\ 0, & \text{elsewhere} \end{cases} \qquad (8)$$

It is observed that the test quantity becomes smaller and smaller as the transition order is increased. Choosing, e.g., significance level 0.05 percent, one can ask at what transition order significance is lost. Since $\Pr(\chi_{49}^2 > 1.8) < 0.05$ percent, this occurs for the transition order giving a test quantity less than 1.8.

A plot of the test quantity versus transition order can be seen in Fig. 9. Obviously, the test quantity never becomes smaller than 1.8 for transition orders less than 257, so there is very strong evidence against independence between gap lengths separated by 255 gap lengths. The reason for this is probably that when transmission is bad, many short correlated gaps are produced.

C. Remarks

Of course, the correlational properties of the gap length process are best described by the autocorrelation function $E\{g_i \cdot g_{i+j}\}$, but as can be seen from Fig. 10, where a sequence of consecutive gap lengths is plotted, this process is with high probability not stationary. This means that it is not adequate to estimate this function from any single realization of the process, and this is why the method has been chosen.

It is concluded that neither the exponential BSC nor the Pareto distribution fits the estimated gap length distribution.

[1] The field strength in decibels is known only added with an unknown constant. This is caused by unknown antenna gain for receiver and transmitter.

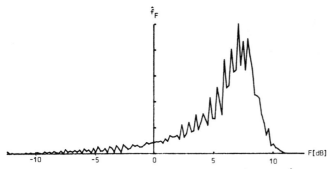

Fig. 11. Estimated pdf for field strength F in decibels, $\hat{f}_F$.

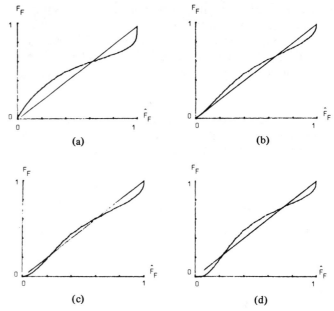

Fig. 12. Straight line test. (a) Rayleigh. (b) Rice. (c) Nakagami. (d) Lognormal.

and $I_0(\cdot)$ is the 0th-order modified Bessel function;

3) $F = 20 \cdot \log_{10} (F'/k)$ where $F' \in$ Nakagami (a, b), i.e.,

$$f_{F'}(x) = \begin{cases} \dfrac{2}{\Gamma(a)} \left(\dfrac{a}{b^2}\right)^a x^{2a-1} e^{-ax^2/b^2}, & x \geq 0, a \geq 1/2 \\ 0, & \text{elsewhere;} \end{cases} \tag{9}$$

4) $F \in N(m, \sigma^2)$, i.e.,

$$f_F(x) = \frac{1}{\sqrt{2\pi\sigma^2}} e^{-(x-m)^2/2\sigma^2}. \tag{10}$$

In (7)–(10) k denotes an unknown constant, whose value does not need to be known to perform the test.

The test quantity was chosen as the squared error between estimated and hypothesized distribution function, i.e.,

$$t = \sum_i (F_F(x_i) - \hat{F}_F(x_i))^2 \tag{11}$$

where $F_F(\cdot)$ denotes hypothesized and $\hat{F}_F(\cdot)$ denotes estimated distribution function.

Since the parameters of the theoretical distribution functions can be varied, giving different test quantities, they were chosen to give the minimum possible test quantity in each of the four cases. The values of the parameters and test quantity were found to be

1) $\left(\dfrac{b}{k}\right)^2 = 2.70, \quad t = 0.92 \qquad$ (Rayleigh)

2) $\dfrac{a}{k} = 1.82, \dfrac{b}{k} = 0.8, \quad t = 0.17 \qquad$ (Rice)

3) $a = 2.45; \left(\dfrac{b}{k}\right)^2 = 4.65; \quad t = 0.12 \qquad$ (Nakagami)

4) $m = 5.77; \quad \sigma = 2.82; \quad t = 0.25 \qquad$ (lognormal).

Apparently, the Nakagami distribution gives the least test quantity and thus the best fit. How good this fit is can easily be seen by plotting the theoretical distribution function versus the estimated. If the two coincide, the result is a straight line. Plots of this kind are shown in Fig. 12, and it is seen that the curve is far from the straight line in all four cases.

The reason for this bad fit could be that the parameters of the underlying pdf vary in time in a stochastic way, so that the resulting pdf is a mixed pdf, i.e.,

$$f_F(x) = \iint f_F(x|a, b) \cdot f_{a,b}(a, b) \, da \, db \tag{12}$$

where $f_{a,b}(\cdot, \cdot)$ is the pdf for the parameters. However, this has not yet been investigated. Note that this time variation originally stems from a spatial variation and a mobile vehicle.

Another reason might be as follows. The well-accepted model for multipath fading in urban areas is that field strengths are Rayleigh or Rice distributed over local areas (the local being defined as an area extending to several hundred wavelengths). It is Rice if there is a line-of-sight path, and Rayleigh if not. It is lognormal over large areas; the transition from local to global distributions is explained by nonstationarities of the channel [17]. So, nonstationarities of the channel should give rise to good fit to the lognormal distribution, since they indicate an approach to the global statistics. The analysis, however, does not confirm this and shows the best fit to be Nakagami.

Since the measurement environment is best represented as moderately urban, there is a high probability of receiving a line-of-sight path. Turin [20] shows that for such a medium the probability of receiving a line-of-sight path is about 0.7, as compared to a dense urban area where it is only 0.2-0.3. The fact that the data is strongly non-Rayleigh supports this. The variation in the terrain is probably not large enough to let the data approach global statistics, so the measurement area may be approximated by only a few different local areas, while many more local statistics are needed to combine to give global statistics. This idea is supported by the fact that the field strength process was stationary over a period of 42.5 s. Assuming an average speed of 40 km/h for the vehicle, this corresponds to 472 m or 708 wavelengths. In heavily built-up areas, the field strength process can become grossly nonstationary over such a distance. The high correlation in the process also shows that statistics of the channel does not change rapidly, i.e., it is more or less stationary over a large distance.

If the above is true, then it explains why the data give good fit to Nakagami. This distribution, with appropriate choice of its parameters, well approximates the Rice distribution. The fact that Rice distribution is the second best for the data, further supports this. Although the Nakagami and Rice are the best among the four considered distributions, they fall short of giving adequate fit to the data. This is probably because not one but several local areas were used.

B. The Field Strength Correlation

Letting $\{F_i\}$ denote the sampled field strength process (in decibels), an estimate for $E\{F_i \cdot F_{i+j}\} = r_F(j)$ has been computed by

$$\hat{r}_F(j) = \frac{1}{N} \sum_{k=1}^{N-j} F_k \cdot F_{k+j} \tag{13}$$

for sections of the recordings containing N samples. This autocorrelation-function has been normalized to give

$$\hat{\rho}_F(j) = \frac{\hat{r}_F(j) - \hat{m}^2}{\hat{r}_F(0) - \hat{m}^2} \tag{14}$$

where

$$\hat{m} = \frac{1}{N} \sum_{k=1}^{N} F_k. \tag{15}$$

Two of these estimates can be seen in Fig. 13. N was chosen to be 51100 corresponding to 42.5 s in real time. The field strength process was selected where it seemed to be rather stationary over the used sections. As can be seen from Fig. 13 there is significant memory in the process. It seems believable that this memory should govern memory in the digital process, since this latter process is highly affected by the former.

When the vehicle was standing still, the field strength process was found to be constant, which should give rise to a constant autocorrelation function. Since the speed of the vehicle was not recorded, it is not known for the estimates of Fig. 13, but looking at the fade rate for the two used data sets, the vehicle was probably moving faster in (a) than in (b). This suggests that the memory in the field strength process should be shorter when the vehicle moves faster and vice versa. This idea is visualized in Fig. 14. Note that since the correlation originally is spatial, plots can also be made with spatial separation on the horizontal axis. These plots will look the same for all speeds.

V. A MODEL OF DIGITAL ERRORS BASED ON FIELD STRENGTH MEASUREMENTS

One of the aims of this work has been to find a model for the digital error process, where the field strength process is involved. The first model in mind was a generalization of Gilbert's model for digital channels with memory [1] (see Fig. 15). This figure illustrates a Markov chain with two states, each state representing a BSC with crossover probability p.

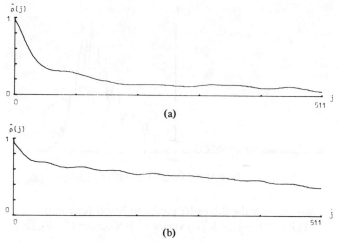

Fig. 13. Estimated correlation function for field strength (in decibels). (a) High fade rate. (b) Low fade rate.

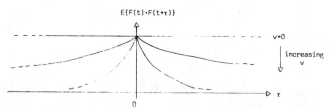

Fig. 14. Hypothesized behavior of $E\{F(t) \cdot F(t + \tau)\}$ at different vehicle speeds v.

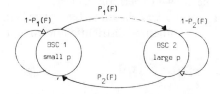

Fig. 15. Markov model for digital channel involving field strength. BSC crossover probability p.

One of the BSC's is a bad digital channel with high probability of error, and the other one is good, having a small probability of error. This is Gilbert's model [1].

The transition probabilities are deterministic functions of field strength F. $P_1(F)$ should be a decreasing function of F since when F is large, the probability of entering the bad state should be small, and when F is small the probability of entering the bad state should be large. Similar arguments suggest that $P_2(F)$ should be an increasing function of F. This is depicted in Fig. 16. It can be observed that this Markov chain is time-varying and thus difficult to handle analytically. Therefore, the model is further generalized, and the aim is to get an analytically simple model.

The generalization is done in two steps, by first introducing more states (see Fig. 17). The number of states (BSC's) is now N, and by $P_{ij}(F)$ is meant the field strength dependent transition probability from state i to state j. It is assumed that $p_1 < p_2 < \cdots < p_N$. Now, how should these $P_{ij}(F)$ look? The field strength can be partitioned into N intervals according to Fig. 18.

It seems reasonable that when the field strength is in interval A_k, $1 \leq k \leq N$, the probability of entering state BSCk is large. This should be true *for all states* that the process is

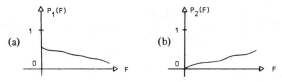

Fig. 16. Possible field strength dependent transition probabilities. (a) $P_1(F)$. (b) $P_2(F)$.

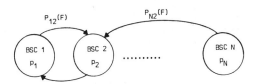

Fig. 17. Generalized Markov chain model.

Fig. 18. Partitioning field strength.

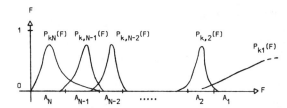

Fig. 19. Typical look of $P_{k,j}(F)$ functions. $k, j = 1, 2, \cdots, N$.

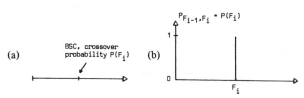

Fig. 20. (a) States in infinite Markov chain. (b) Transition probability functions.

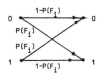

Fig. 21. Time-varying BSC.

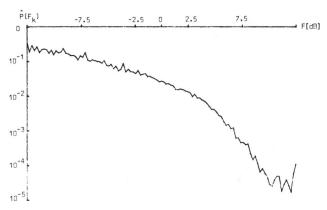

Fig. 22. Estimate of $P(F)$.

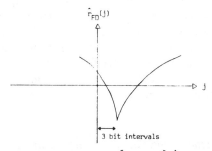

Fig. 23. Estimate of $E\{F_i \cdot D_{i+j}\}, \hat{r}_{FD}(j)$.

leaving. The typical look of the $P_{ij}(F)$ functions can be seen in Fig. 19.

Now, letting N approach infinity, the $P_{ij}(F)$ functions become narrower and narrower, and the finite number of states becomes a continuum of states. The result can be seen in Fig. 20. F_i denotes field strength in bit interval i and so on.

Now, the process is entering a specific state, a BSC with crossover probability $P(F_i)$ in the ith bit interval regardless of the previous state. This means that Markov dependence is lost, and the digital channel can be modeled as Fig. 21 shows, a time-varying BSC. All memory of the digital channel is now referred to the field strength process. It can be concluded that the characteristics of the digital channel, using this model, are determined by the statistical properties of the field strength process, and the function $P(F)$, determined by the detector.

A. Distributional Properties of the P(F) Channel

From the collected data, the $P(F)$ can be estimated. This has been done by counting the number of samples falling into a field strength interval $[F_k, F_{k+1})$, $k = 0, 1, \cdots$, and also by counting the number of digital errors in this interval e_k. Using relative frequencies

$$\hat{P}(F_k) = \frac{e_k}{\# \text{ samples in } [F_k, F_{k+1}]} . \tag{16}$$

This yields a $P(F)$ function shown in Fig. 22.

A few words should be said about $\hat{P}(F_k)$, since they are important in the sequel. As was mentioned in Section II, the squelch signal is low-pass filtered before observation, thereby frequency dependent delay is introduced. This means that the digital samples are sometimes connected with a wrong (and filtered) sample of the field strength signal.

A way of finding the mean delay between field strength signal and digital signal is to estimate the cross correlation between these two signals. This function $E\{F_i \cdot D_{i+j}\} = r_{FD}(j)$, where F_i denotes field strength and D_i digital error signal, should have minimum for $j =$ mean delay, since D_i is only 0 or 1, and field strength should be low when $D_i = 1$.

This cross correlation was estimated, and it looked typically as shown in Fig. 23. The mean delay was found to be

three bit intervals. A delay of three bit intervals was used for estimating the $\hat{P}(F_k)$ function, and the above discussion indicates that this estimate perhaps is not so good. This should be kept in mind in the sequel.

The $P(F)$ channel has been simulated by observing the field strength in each bit interval and generating a digital error randomly with probability $\hat{P}(F_k)$. From the resulting binary error process the gap length distribution $P(g \geqslant n)$ has been estimated (see Fig. 24).

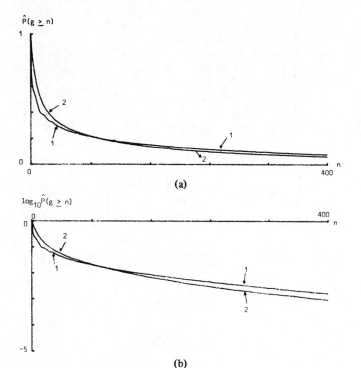

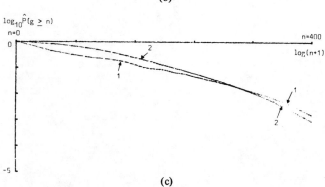

Fig. 24. (a) $\hat{P}(g \geqslant n)$ versus n. (b) $\log_{10} \hat{P}(g \geqslant n)$ versus n. (c) $\log_{10} \hat{P}(g \geqslant n)$ versus $\log (n + 1)$. 1: observed gaps. 2: simulated gaps.

TABLE II
FROM SIMULATED GAP LENGTHS ESTIMATED TRANSITION TABLES AND PROBABILITIES

A. FIRST ORDER

	a_1	a_2	a_3	a_4	a_5	a_6	a_7	a_8		a_1	a_2	a_3	a_4	a_5	a_6	a_7	a_8
a_1	660	659	379	409	300	235	170	115	a_1	.23	.23	.13	.14	.10	.08	.06	.04
a_2	590	620	408	437	393	272	224	130	a_2	.19	.20	.13	.14	.13	.09	.07	.04
a_3	386	374	271	329	277	238	168	111	a_3	.18	.17	.13	.15	.13	.11	.8	.05
a_4	479	405	277	371	373	330	275	173	a_4	.17	.15	.14	.14	.12	.10	.06	
a_5	337	378	285	382	393	397	336	220	a_5	.12	.14	.10	.14	.14	.15	.12	.08
a_6	215	280	226	332	438	471	440	275	a_6	.08	.10	.08	.12	.16	.18	.16	.10
a_7	160	227	178	259	323	466	583	517	a_7	.06	.08	.07	.10	.12	.17	.21	.19
a_8	99	131	130	164	231	269	517	1156	a_8	.04	.05	.05	.06	.09	.10	.19	.43

B. SECOND ORDER

	a_1	a_2	a_3	a_4	a_5	a_6	a_7	a_8		a_1	a_2	a_3	a_4	a_5	a_6	a_7	a_8
a_1	579	574	355	433	369	266	213	138	a_1	.20	.20	.12	.15	.13	.09	.07	.05
a_2	610	566	360	403	394	317	251	173	a_2	.20	.18	.12	.13	.13	.10	.08	.06
a_3	384	389	244	284	248	248	214	143	a_3	.18	.18	.11	.13	.12	.12	.10	.07
a_4	399	457	291	388	371	339	258	180	a_4	.15	.17	.11	.13	.12	.13	.10	.07
a_5	364	407	303	380	377	368	338	191	a_5	.13	.15	.11	.14	.14	.13	.12	.07
a_6	259	299	251	336	382	414	445	292	a_6	.10	.11	.09	.13	.14	.15	.17	.11
a_7	199	217	222	266	351	443	544	471	a_7	.07	.08	.06	.10	.13	.16	.20	.17
a_8	133	165	128	193	236	283	449	1109	a_8	.05	.06	.05	.07	.09	.10	.17	.41

C. THIRD ORDER

	a_1	a_2	a_3	a_4	a_5	a_6	a_7	a_8		a_1	a_2	a_3	a_4	a_5	a_6	a_7	a_8
a_1	589	555	367	377	377	266	230	166	a_1	.20	.19	.13	.13	.13	.09	.08	.06
a_2	565	578	344	411	375	334	256	211	a_2	.18	.19	.11	.13	.12	.11	.08	.07
a_3	347	388	254	298	266	251	223	127	a_3	.16	.19	.12	.14	.12	.12	.10	.06
a_4	386	408	293	366	413	343	275	199	a_4	.14	.15	.11	.14	.15	.13	.10	.07
a_5	387	365	288	368	388	374	317	241	a_5	.14	.13	.11	.13	.14	.14	.12	.09
a_6	268	316	260	385	374	409	401	265	a_6	.10	.12	.10	.14	.14	.15	.15	.10
a_7	239	272	192	271	305	425	551	458	a_7	.09	.10	.07	.10	.11	.16	.20	.17
a_8	146	192	156	207	230	276	459	1029	a_8	.05	.07	.06	.08	.09	.10	.17	.38

D. GROUP LIMITS

a_1	a_2	a_3	a_4
$0 \leq g < 2$	$2 \leq g < 5$	$5 \leq g < 8$	$8 \leq g < 14$

a_5	a_6	a_7	a_8
$14 \leq g < 27$	$27 \leq g < 61$	$61 \leq g < 182$	$182 \leq g$

In Fig. 24, the estimated gap length distributions from Section III-A are also replotted for comparison. Apparently the $P(F)$ channel gives approximately the same gap length distribution as the real channel. The $P(F)$ channel has a tendency of generating more short gaps and fewer long gaps than the real channel, but the cause for this could be that the function $\hat{P}(F_k)$ is not a good estimate. Furthermore, the simulated errors are simulated from a filtered and delayed version of the real field strength signal.

B. Correlational Properties of the P(F) Channel

An identical test to the one in Section III-B has been performed for the gap lengths simulated through the $P(F)$ channel. The result can be seen in Table II.

The test quantities were found to be

first order $t = 4994.26$

second order $t = 3810.15$

third order $t = 3095.63$

and $\Pr (\chi_{49}^2 > t) \ll 10^{-5}$ for all three cases thus giving very good significance against independence. As in Section III-B, at what transition order significance is lost, is now investigated, i.e, when t first becomes smaller than 1.8 (see Fig. 25). For transition orders less than 257, the test quantity again never becomes smaller than 1.8, and the same conclusions as in Secton III-B can be drawn. It can also be noted that Figs. 9 and 25 look almost the same, indicating that the correlation is reaching very far within the simulated error process.

C. Remarks

Just as in Section III-B the gap length process is probably not stationary, which can be seen in Fig. 26, and consequently it is impossible to estimate $E\{g_i \cdot g_{i+j}\}$ to describe gap length correlation.

VI. CONCLUSION

Theoretically motivated models for the distribution and spatial correlation of the field strength could not be successfully applied to the corresponding measured quantity. This was also the case for the digital bit error process. The reason

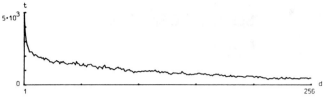

Fig. 25.   Test quantity t versus transition order d.

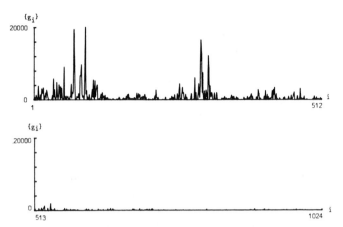

Fig. 26.   Through $P(F)$-channel simulated consecutive gap lengths.

for this bad fit could be that the chosen test areas cannot be described as densely urban, moderately urban, suburban, rural, etc. The best classification should be moderately urban, but there are exceptions. Thus it should be noted that the presented model and numerical results are not applicable to all types of urban areas. Propagation characteristics are grossly different in different kinds of areas [18]-[20]. It is believed that measurements made over a larger area will fit well to previous models for the field strength.

A time-varying BSC with crossover probability $P(F)$ gives reasonable fit between model and data. It can be concluded that the fading characterizes the digital properties of the channel. Therefore, the field strength process should be studied more, concerning stationarity, correlation, spectrum, etc.

ACKNOWLEDGMENT

The author wishes to thank the reviewer for valuable comments, significantly improving the standard of the present work.

REFERENCES

[1]   E. N. Gilbert, "Capacity of a burst-noise channel," *Bell Syst. Tech. J.*, vol. 39, pp. 1253–1265, Sept. 1960.
[2]   A. A. Alexander, R. M. Gryb, and D. W. Nast, "Capabilities of the telephone network for data transmission," *Bell Syst. Tech. J.*, vol. 39, pp. 431–476, May 1960.
[3]   S. M. Sussman, "Analysis of the Pareto model for error statistics on telephone circuits," *IEEE Trans. Commun.*, pp. 213–221, June 1963.
[4]   J. M. Berger and B. Mandelbrot, "A new model for error clustering in telephone circuits," *IBM J. Res. Develop.*, vol. 7, pp. 224–236, July 1963.
[5]   E. O. Elliott, "A model of the switched telephone network for data communications," *Bell Syst. Tech. J.*, pp. 89–109, Jan. 1965.
[6]   B. D. Fritchman, "A binary channel characterization using partitioned Markov chains," *IEEE Trans. Inform. Theory*, pp. 221–227, Apr. 1967.
[7]   A. H. Haddad, S. Tsai, B. Goldberg, and G. C. Ranieri, "Markov gap models for real communication channels," *IEEE Trans. Commun.*, pp. 1189–1197, Nov. 1975.
[8]   J. P. A. Adoul, "Error intervals and cluster density in channel modeling," *IEEE Trans. Inform. Theory*, pp. 125–129, Jan. 1974.
[9]   R. T. Chien, A. H. Haddad, B. Goldberg, and E. Moyes, "An analytical error model for real channels," in *Proc. IEEE Int. Conf. Communications*, 1972, pp. 15.7–15.12.
[10] P. A. W. Lewis and D. R. Cox, "A statistical analysis of telephone circuit error data," *IEEE Trans. Commun.*, pp. 382–389, Aug. 1966.
[11] M. Muntner and J. K. Wolf, "Predicted performance of error-control techniques over real channels," *IEEE Trans. Inform. Theory*, pp. 640–650, Sept. 1968.
[12] J. P. Adoul, B. D. Fritchman, and L. N. Kanal, "A critical statistic for channels with memory," *IEEE Trans. Inform. Theory*, pp. 133–141, Jan. 1972.
[13] P. Billingsley, *Statistical Inference for Markov Processes*. Chicago, IL: Univ. of Chicago Press, 1961.
[14] CCITT v. 52, vol. VIII, White Book.
[15] CCITT v. 23, vol. VIII, White Book.
[16] W. Feller, *An Introduction to Probability Theory and Its Applications*. New York: Wiley, 1957, 1968.
[17] H. Suzuki, "A statistical model for urban radio propagation," *IEEE Trans. Commun.*, pp. 673–680, July 1977.
[18] W. R. Young and L. Y. Lacy, "Echoes in transmission at 450 megacycles from land-to-car radio units," *Proc. IRE*, vol. 38, pp. 255–258, Mar. 1950.
[19] H. F. Schmid, "A prediction model for multipath propagation of pulse signals at VHF and UHF over irregular terrain," *IEEE Trans. Antennas Propagat.*, vol. AP-18, pp. 253–258, Mar. 1970.
[20] G. L. Turin *et al.*, "A statistical model of urban multipath propagation," *IEEE Trans. Veh. Technol.*, vol. VT-21, pp. 1–9, Feb. 1972.
[21] ——, "Simulation of urban vehicle monitoring systems," *IEEE Trans. Veh. Technol.*, vol. VT-21, pp. 9–16, Feb. 1972.
[22] H. Hashemi, "Simulation of the urban radio propagation channel," Doctoral dissertation, Univ. of California, Berkeley, 1977. See also *Proc. 1977 Nat. Telecomm. Conf.*, paper 38-1.
[23] D. C. Cox, "Delay Doppler characteristics of multipath propagation at 910 MHz in a suburban mobile radio environment," *IEEE Trans. Antennas Propagat.*, vol. AP-20, pp. 625–635, Sept. 1972.
[24] ——, "Time and frequency domain characterization of multipath propagation at 910 MHz in a suburban mobile radio environment," *Radio Sci.*, Dec. 1972.
[25] ——, "910 MHz urban mobile radio propagation: Multipath characteristics in New York City," *IEEE Trans. Veh. Technol.*, vol. VT-22, pp. 104–110, Nov. 1973; *IEEE Trans. Commun.*, vol. COM-21, pp. 1188–1194, Nov. 1973.
[26] D. C. Cox and R. P. Leck, "Distributions of multipath spread and average excess delay for 910 MHz urban mobile radio paths," *IEEE Trans. Antennas Propagat.*, vol. AP-23, pp. 206–213, Mar. 1975.
[27] D. C. Cox, "Multipath delay spread and path loss correlation for 910 MHz urban mobile radio propagation," *IEEE Trans. Veh. Technol.*, vol. VT-26, pp. 340–344, Nov. 1977.
[28] D. C. Cox and R. P. Leck, "Correlation bandwidth and delay spread multipath propagation statistics for 910 MHz urban mobile radio channels," *IEEE Trans. Commun.*, vol. COM-23, pp. 1271–1280, Nov. 1975.
[29] D. L. Nielson, "Microwave propagation for mobile digital radio application," *IEEE Trans. Veh. Technol.*, vol. VT-27, pp. 117–132, Aug. 1978.

Error Rate Predictions and Measurements in the Mobile Radio Data Channel

RICHARD C. FRENCH

Abstract—A method of predicting the loss in error performance in mobile radio data transmission is given in which the variation in local mean signal level (shadowing) is included as well as fading. Also, the density function of the received signal envelope is found for the case of fading and shadowing. Field measurements are reported of error rates at VHF and UHF due to vehicle ignition noise, and the distribution of errors is plotted.

I. INTRODUCTION

DATA TRANSMISSION in civil land mobile radio is becoming more important with the introduction of sophisticated systems like digital paging, mobile automatic telephony, vehicle mounted data terminals, etc. In order to design these systems with the best trade-offs between performance, message capacity, and cost the designer must know the error performance of the channel. For example, in mobile automatic telephony, subscriber telephone numbers and control signals must be sent to and from the mobile unit to the fixed site. Suitable error control coding must be applied to these messages with sufficient redundancy to ensure a high probability of establishing a call and avoiding wrong numbers and other failures; too much redundancy will reduce the system capacity unnecessarily. The starting point for these system calculations is a reliable prediction of the channel error performance.

In mobile data communication, extensive errors are caused by variations in the received signal envelope which reduce the signal to near the level at which errors are caused by front end noise. There are also many errors caused by ignition noise from the vehicles in the street, including the user's vehicle unless it has been carefully suppressed.

There are two aspects to the variation in the received signal envelope as the vehicle moves along the street. The first is a rapid fluctuation in the signal envelope called fading; this is caused by multipath propagation leading to wave interference which results in sharp peaks and nulls as the waves add and cancel. The second is shadowing which gives rise to much slower changes in signal level caused by changes in topography such as street width, building height, hills, etc.

Quite simple propagation models [1], [2], [3] can be used to predict the signal level at the vehicle as a function of range, aerial height, difference in ground level, etc. It will be shown that the bit error rate (BER) in mobile data communication can be predicted from this signal level by introducing the

Manuscript received November 20, 1977; revised March 28, 1978.
The author is with Philips Research Laboratories, Redhill, Surrey RH1 5HA, England, Telephone Horley 5544.

fading and shadowing suffered by the signal, and the front end noise performance of the data modem.

Montgomery [6] has given an analytic solution for the performance of "perfect" demodulators in a channel degraded by fading only. The method to be described here starts from the measured performance of the data modem in the laboratory and uses numerical integration methods to find the degradation due to fading and then goes on to consider the effect of shadowing.

Electrical noise is radiated from the ignition systems of normal production vehicles at a level which causes data transmission errors at ranges of tens of meters. Complete suppression of the user's vehicle is possible at reasonable cost, although the noise level tends to increase as the vehicle ages; however there is little expectation that all vehicles on the road will have their ignition circuits completely suppressed in the future. Data systems must therefore be designed which tolerate ignition noise errors, and consequently a reliable prediction of the number of errors to be expected is needed. To meet this need, a series of measurements of ignition noise error rates was made and is reported here.

II. ERROR PERFORMANCE WITH RAYLEIGH FADING

Multipath propagation has been shown to give rise to Rayleigh fading in most urban and many suburban locations, which means that the received signal envelope has a Rayleigh distribution [1], [2], [3]. However, the signal envelope s (see Nomenclature) only has a Rayleigh distribution if it is first normalised to the local mean signal level $\bar{s}$ averaged over a distance (typically 50 m), which is long compared with the distance between fades (about $\lambda/2$) but short compared with the size of topographical features. Consequently, the probability of signal envelope s occurring, with local mean signal level $\bar{s}$, is given by the Rayleigh density function

$$P(s \mid \bar{s}) = \frac{\pi s}{2\bar{s}^2} \exp\left[-\frac{\pi s^2}{4\bar{s}^2} \right]. \tag{1}$$

Data transmission errors occur in a multipath situation because the received signal envelope fades momentarily to near the front end noise level of the radio receiver. To find the error performance with fading, we must first find the performance with steady signals and then introduce the variation in the signal envelope. The error rate of a data modem operating in baseband can usually be predicted [4], but when the data signal is modulated on an RF carrier and passed through a

Reprinted from *IEEE Trans. Veh. Technol.*, vol. VT-27, pp. 110–116, Aug. 1978.

214

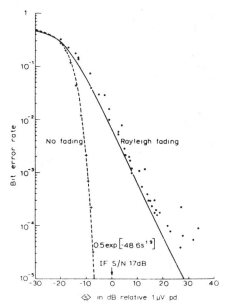

Fig. 1.   Error performance at 165 MHz, 4800 b/s direct FM.

practical receiver the prediction is much more difficult. For this reason the steady signal error performance has been bench measured and then approximated by an exponential function of the form

$$p_e(s) = 0.5 \exp(-Qs^R) \qquad (2)$$

using curve fitting techniques. A typical example of the accuracy of this curve fitting process is shown by the dashed curve in Fig. 1 for a VHF radio (165 MHz) with direct frequency modulation on the RF carrier at 4800 b/s with a deviation of 2.4 kHz and a channel spacing of 12.5 kHz. The function

$$p_e(s) = 0.5 \exp(-48.6s^{1.9}) \qquad (3)$$

is a close approximation to the measured points shown as crosses in the figure. The error probability falls very steeply as the signal envelope increases, and at 1 μV, where the IF S/N ratio is 17 dB, the error probability is too small to measure.

Equation (3) gives the probability of error at signal envelope s and (1) gives the probability of that signal level occurring; consequently, by combining (1) and (3) we have the probability of error in a Rayleigh fading situation (assuming the signal does not vary significantly during a bit):

$$p_e(\bar{s}) = \int_0^\infty p_e(s) P(s \mid \bar{s}) \, ds \qquad (4)$$

$$= \frac{\pi}{4\bar{s}^2} \int_0^\infty s \exp[-Qs^R] \exp\left[-\frac{\pi s^2}{4\bar{s}^2}\right] ds. \qquad (5)$$

This integral can only be evaluated analytically for $R = 2$, but in practice values of R range from 0.27 to 3.1. Consequently, the integral is evaluated numerically on a digital computer.

The range of integration can be reduced to 0–0.5 since $P_e(s) \rightarrow 0$ for $s > 0.5$, for the cases considered. The prediction is given in terms of the received signal level rather than IF S/N ratio since signal level is the basic parameter in mobile radio, particularly when ignition noise is considered.

The predicted error performance with Rayleigh fading found from numerical integration of (5) is shown in Fig. 1 for the VHF direct FM example. The fading has significantly degraded the performance; to achieve an error performance of 10^{-3}, for example, the local mean signal level must be about 17 dB higher with fading present. The error probability has an assynmtotic slope of a decade per 10 dB.

Also shown in Fig. 1 are a number of measured points. Each point is the BER averaged over a seven minute period (2M bits at 4800 b/s) measured in the field on a mobile moving in a Rayleigh fading situation, with ignition noise errors excluded by an attenuator in the receiving aerial. It should be noted that nearly all the measured points show a higher BER than the prediction; the prediction is clearly optimistic. The excess error rate was not caused by ignition noise, which was excluded by the aerial attenuator, or by cochannel interference (the channel was monitored and found to be empty). The higher error rates measured in practice are thought to be caused by variation in the local mean signal level resulting from shadowing as the vehicle moved past buildings, etc. It was therefore decided to include the local mean variation in the prediction to determine its effect.

III. SIGNAL DISTRIBUTION WITH FADING AND MEAN LEVEL VARIATIONS

The first step in finding the error performance with both fading and mean level variations is to find the received signal envelope distribution. The Rayleigh fading of the received signal relative to the local mean has been discussed; we must now consider the variation in the local mean that results from shadowing of the radio signal by large buildings, hills, etc. As the vehicle moves throughout an area at roughly constant distance from the transmitter, the local mean signal level, averaged over let us say 45 m, is found [1], [2] to vary lognormally. That is the local mean expressed in dB, $\bar{s}_d$ is normally distributed about an area mean, m_d equal to the mean of the variable $\bar{s}_d$. Consequently, the density function of the local mean is

$$P(\bar{s}_d) = \frac{1}{\sqrt{2\pi\sigma^2}} \exp\left[\frac{-(\bar{s}_d - m_d)^2}{2\sigma^2}\right] \qquad (6)$$

where σ is the standard deviation (in dB) of the local mean, quoted as 6 dB in London [1] and as 8 to 12 dB in cities in the USA and Japan [2].

It should be noted that the area mean is defined as the mean of the variable $\bar{S}_d$ and is the area mean predicted [2] in propagation models from histograms of excess path loss constructed from measured local mean levels expressed in dB.

We must combine (6) with the density function of the signal envelope for the case of Rayleigh fading about the local mean $\bar{s}_d$ given in (1). In (6) the local mean is expressed in dB, whereas in (1) it is in linear form; however we can use (1) because

$$P(s \mid \bar{s}_d) = P(s \mid \bar{s}). \tag{7}$$

The density function of the signal envelope with Rayleigh fading and lognormal variation in the local mean is given by

$$P(s) = \int_{-\infty}^{\infty} P(s \mid \bar{s}_d) P(\bar{s}_d) \, d\bar{s}_d \tag{8}$$

$$= \sqrt{\frac{\pi}{8\sigma^2}} \int_{-\infty}^{\infty} \frac{s}{\bar{s}^2} \exp\left[-\frac{\pi s^2}{4\bar{s}^2}\right]$$

$$\cdot \exp\left[-\frac{(\bar{s}_d - m_d)^2}{2\sigma^2}\right] d\bar{s}_d \tag{9}$$

replacing $\bar{s}$ with $10^{\bar{s}_d/20}$ (from $\bar{s}_d = 20 \log_{10}\bar{s}$):

$$P(s) = \sqrt{\frac{\pi}{8\sigma^2}} \int_{-\infty}^{\infty} \frac{s}{10^{\bar{s}_d/10}} \exp\left[-\frac{\pi s^2}{4 . 10^{\bar{s}_d/10}}\right]$$

$$\cdot \exp\left[-\frac{(\bar{s}_d - m_d)^2}{2\sigma^2}\right] d\bar{s}_d. \tag{10}$$

The integral in (10) was evaluated numerically, with the infinite limits of integration reduced to $\pm 2.5 \, \sigma$. The density function of the signal is shown in Fig. 2 for a range of values of the standard deviation σ. When the standard deviation is reduced to zero, the lognormal variation in the mean is excluded and the density function should become the Rayleigh function. With $\sigma = 0.01$ dB (zero makes the integral indeterminate), the function is indeed the Rayleigh function. With σ equal to 6, 12, and 24 dB the density function develops a sharper peak which occurs at progressively lower signal amplitudes. This is because the signal density function with the lognormal variation of the local mean is built up from many Rayleigh density functions with a range of mean levels. When the mean is low the density function is tall and narrow; when the mean is high the density function is short and broad. The sum of these has a peak at low amplitudes and a broad plateau at high levels. Fig. 3 shows the distribution of the signal envelope with fading and shadowing.

IV. ERROR PERFORMANCE WITH FADING AND MEAN LEVEL VARIATIONS

To find the error probability $p_e(m_d)$ in the practical case of Rayleigh fading about a lognormally distributed local mean, we have to take the probability of error $p_e(s)$ at steady signal envelope, s given in (2), and the probability $P(s)$ of that signal level occurring in an environment with fading and shadowing

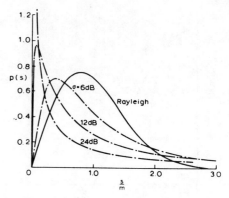

Fig. 2. PDF of signal envelope with fading and shadowing.

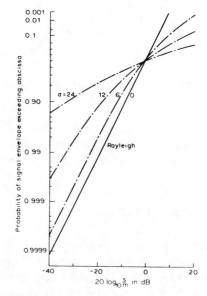

Fig. 3. Distribution of signal envelope with fading and shadowing.

as given in (10). Assuming the signal level remains constant during one bit, the error probability is

$$p_e(m_d) = \int_0^{\infty} p_e(s) P(s) \, ds \tag{11}$$

$$= \int_0^{\infty} 0.5 \exp\left[-Qs^R\right] \sqrt{\frac{\pi}{8\sigma^2}} \int_{-\infty}^{\infty} \frac{s}{10^{\bar{s}_d/10}}$$

$$\cdot \exp\left[-\frac{\pi s^2}{4 . 10^{\bar{s}_d/10}}\right]$$

$$\cdot \exp\left[-\frac{(\bar{s}_d - m_d)^2}{2\sigma^2}\right] d\bar{s}_d \, ds. \tag{12}$$

The double integral was evaluated numerically, and the probability of error is plotted in Fig. 4 as a function of m_d for values of σ between 0 and 12 dB. With σ set very small, the error probability is the same as for the Rayleigh fading case shown in Fig. 1, as it should be. When the standard deviation in the lognormal distribution is set to 6 dB, the error performance

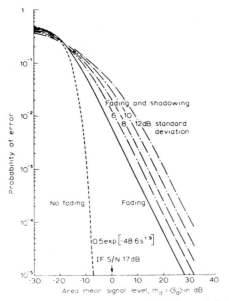

Fig. 4. Predicted error performance with fading and shadowing.

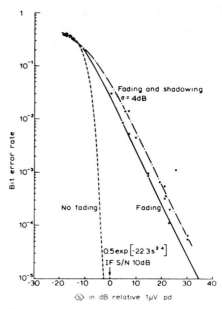

Fig. 5. Error performance in London at 462 MHz, 4800 b/s.

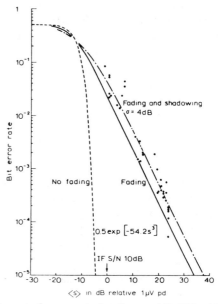

Fig. 6. Error performance in London at 462 MHz, 1200 b/s PSK subcarrier.

is degraded by about 4 dB and is further reduced as the standard deviation is increased. When $\sigma = 12$ dB, the error performance is degraded by nearly 13 dB. The error probability curves are similar in shape to the Rayleigh fading case and show the same assymtote of a decade drop in error probability for a 10-dB rise in area mean signal level.

At low bit rates the signal level varies during the period of a bit, and the bit error rate will be lower than predicted by (12). The dependence of BER on bit rate is treated in [9]. The prediction is given as a function of m_d because m_d is invariant to changes in σ and is directly proportional to the transmitter power even when σ is varied. Consequently, a degradation of 4 dB in m_d due to the introduction of shadowing with $\sigma = 6$ dB in a Rayleigh fading situation could in principle be offset by a 4-dB increase in transmitter power; m_d is also the parameter given by propagation models.

The measured error performance given in Fig. 1 is worse than the Rayleigh prediction by 4 dB in $\langle s \rangle$ where $\langle \cdot \rangle$ denotes mean value. This $\langle s \rangle$, which is the mean value of the signal envelope during a measurement over about 1 km, should not be confused with m_d. It is a property of the lognormal distribution that

$$20 \log_{10} \langle s \rangle = m_d + \frac{\sigma^2}{8.686}. \qquad (13)$$

For example, with $\sigma = 6$ dB the loss in performance has been shown to be 4 dB in m_d; from (13) this is equivalent to a loss of 8 dB in $\langle s \rangle$.

A similar prediction has been made by Hansen and Meno [7] who approximate the modem error performance with a constant error probability of 0.5 up to the receiver error threshold, and then zero probability above. This approximation gives a very pessimistic prediction of error performance showing a 17 dB loss at a BER of 10^{-2} with fading, compared with only 10 dB in Fig. 1 or in [8]. Also, the prediction for fading and shadowing is pessimistic by a similar amount; how-

ever, the degradation caused by introducing shadowing in a fading situation agrees well with the prediction given here. With $\sigma = 6$ dB and a BER of 10^{-2}, Hansen shows a loss of 8 dB in $\langle s \rangle$ in his Fig. 2 which agrees with the 4-dB loss in m_d given here.

Figs. 5 and 6 show the results of error measurements previously made in London at 465 MHz using direct frequency modulation of the RF carrier at 4800 b/s, and using 1200 b/s PSK subcarrier modulation, both with 2.4 kHz deviation. In both figures the prediction for Rayleigh fading is shown and is optomistic, and the prediction with shadowing, $\sigma = 4$ dB is given and is a rough fit to the measured points. The shadowing prediction has been converted to correctly place the curve for the variable $\langle s \rangle$. The 4-dB standard deviation is low for London, but is consistent with the fact that when measurement routes

217

in London were chosen, the ones with a small variation in local mean were selected. The London measurements are not offered as a demonstration of the prediction; there are too few measurements in too small an area, but they are consistent with it.

It should be noted that the prediction involving the variation in local mean gives the average BER, not the BER for a particular message which might only last for a second or so and would be received at a constant local mean level.

V. ERRORS CAUSED BY IGNITION NOISE

Earlier measurements [5] made in London at UHF have shown that ignition noise is a major source of errors, contributing about 20 percent of the errors recorded at 4800 b/s. In order to study the ignition noise errors alone, the variations in the received signal level were eliminated by generating the RF data signal with a signal generator in the vehicle and feeding it direct to the receiver [5]. The base station was turned off, but the receiving aerial was still connected to the receiver so that ignition noise from the street contaminated the steady signal from the signal generator.

Fig. 7 shows a plot of BER due to ignition noise at VHF, at 4800 b/s direct FM (deviation 2.4 kHz). Each point is the average BER in a seven-minute measurement with the vehicle moving around a one-way road system where a continuous stream of traffic is usual. There is a much greater variation in the BER with ignition noise errors alone than with fading errors. The measured points can be approximated by the exponential function

$$p_e(s) = 0.5 \exp(-4.12s^{-0.35}) \qquad (14)$$

as shown in Fig. 7. Note that ignition noise can cause a significant number of errors even with received signal levels of 20 or 30 dB. Comparison with Fig. 1 shows that at the high bit rate of 4800 b/s there are about equal numbers of errors due to fading and ignition noise, i.e., a BER of 10^{-3} at a 10-dB signal level in both cases.

The ignition noise error measurements were made with a steady signal level and the question arises, what error rate would have been measured had the signal suffered fading and shadowing, but with the ignition noise as the only source of errors. The prediction can be made in the same way as before using (12), with the values for Q and R found by fitting an exponential to the steady signal ignition noise error measurements, as in (14). The result is shown in Fig. 7, where it can be seen that fading degrades the performance by some 6 dB and shadowing ($\sigma = 6$ dB) loses a further 3 dB. The degradation caused by fading is far less than with front end noise, but is not insignificant and should be taken into account in predicting the BER in a system.

The BER due to ignition noise at 1200 and 300 b/s with direct FM at 165 MHz is shown in Figs. 8 and 9. The plotted points are again average BERs measured with a steady signal level generated in the measurement vehicle. Best fit exponential curves show that 1200 b/s data is 6 dB less sensitive to ignition

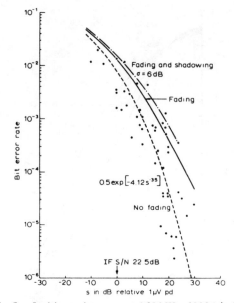
Fig. 7. Ignition noise errors at 165 MHz, 4800 b/s direct FM.

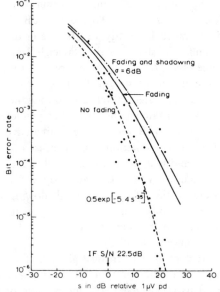
Fig. 8. Ignition noise errors at 165 MHz, 1200 b/s direct FM.

noise than 4800 b/s, and 300 b/s data shows an improvement of 18 dB. The predicted error performance due to ignition noise alone, with Rayleigh fading and with a lognormal mean level variation are also shown in the figures.

Similar ignition noise measurements were made at 4800 b/s at UHF at 462 MHz, and the results are plotted in Fig. 10 with the best fit exponential and the predictions for signal level variations. Comparison with Fig. 7 (4800 b/s at VHF) shows very little difference in the number of ignition noise errors in the two bands. The cases are not completely equivalent, however, because at UHF the deviation is ±4.8 kHz, twice that at VHF and the bit rate is the same, even though the channel bandwidth is twice as great and could have supported a bit rate of 9600 b/s.

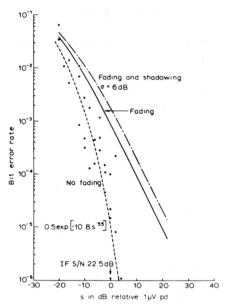

Fig. 9.   Ignition noise errors at 165 Mhz, 300 b/s direct FM.

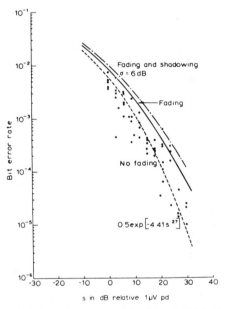

Fig. 10.   Itnition noise errors at 462 MHz, 4800 b/s direct FM.

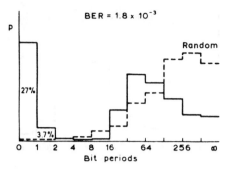

Fig. 11.   Histogram of intervals between errors, 165 MHz 4800 b/s.

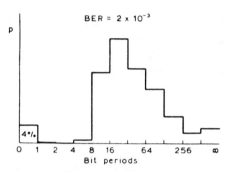

Fig. 12.   Histogram of intervals between errors, 165 MHz 1200 b/s.

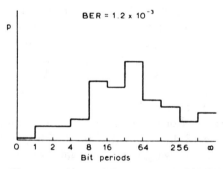

Fig. 13.   Histogram of intervals between errors, 165 MHz 300 b/s.

A. Distribution of Ignition Noise Errors

Ignition noise is in the form of intense short duration impulses which are lengthened by the impulse response of the receiver IF filter to a duration of the order of 0.1 ms. This is short enough for only a single bit in the data transmission to be affected at all but the highest bit rates that can be used in the channel. However, if the IF filter response "rings" substantially, then bursts of errors will occur which will increase the total number of errors a little and will also affect the choice of error control coding.

In the field measurements that have been made, a digital cassette recorder has been used to record the error pattern in the received data signal [5]. The tapes, which consist of a bit by bit record of the occurrence of errors, are replayed into a computer for analysis. This approach permits the distribution of the errors to be studied rather than simply counting the number of errors. The ignition noise records were analyzed by compiling an histogram of the interval (in bit periods) between errors. For easier display the categories used in the histogram are logarithmic, permitting the whole range of intervals to be seen without loss of detail in the region of a few bits where bursts of errors might be seen. At 4800 b/s at VHF, Fig. 11 shows that 27 percent of the errors occurred immediately following the previous error with a further 3.7 percent of errors in the next bit period. This shows a greater occurrence of short bursts of errors than occurs in the case of random errors, which is also shown in Fig. 11 for comparison. At 1200 b/s only 4 percent of errors follow on a previous error (Fig. 12), and at 300 b/s the occurrence of errors in the following bit position is no greater than for random errors (Fig. 13).

219

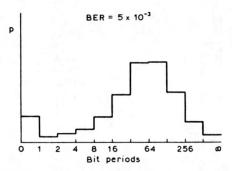

Fig. 14. Histogram of intervals between errors, 462 MHz 4800 b/s.

Fig. 14 shows the histogram for 4800 b/s at UHF where only a small number of two bit bursts of errors occurs. Ignition noise errors at both UHF and VHF are therefore isolated events at all but the highest rates the channel can support with binary signaling.

VI. CONCLUSIONS

A technique has been presented for predicting the error performance of a mobile radio data system as a function of the area mean level m_d which can itself be predicted using straightforward propagation models. The starting point was the laboratory measured steady signal error performance, which is then approximated by an exponential function. An equation for the error probability with fading and shadowing was derived and evaluated using numerical integration.

The loss in error performance due to Rayleigh fading was shown to be 18 dB at a BER of 10^{-3} with a further loss of 4 dB due to shadowing, with a standard deviation of 6 dB. At a standard deviation of 12 dB the further loss is 13 dB, i.e., a total loss of 31 dB.

The probability density function of the received signal for the case of Rayleigh fading and lognormal variations in the local mean was derived and shown to have a sharper peak at a lower signal level than the Rayleigh density function.

Ignition noise error measurements at VHF, 4800 b/s showed a poor performance (BER of 10^{-3}), which improved by 6 dB at a bit rate of 1200 b/s and by 18 dB at 300 b/s. At UHF, 4800 b/s, the error rate is very similar to VHF.

Histograms have been given of the interval between ignition noise errors which show that errors occur singly, except at the highest bit rates where a small proportion of two or three bit error bursts occur.

NOMENCLATURE

s	Amplitude of received signal envelope in μ volts pd.
s_d	$= 20 \log_{10} s$.
$\langle \cdot \rangle$	Mean of $\cdot$.
$\langle s \rangle$	Mean of s over the length of a field measurement.
$\bar{s}$	Local mean of s (over a distance of approximately 50 m).
$\bar{s}_d$	$= 20 \log_{10} \bar{s}$.
m_d	Area mean $= \langle \bar{s}_d \rangle$.
m	Such that $m_d = 20 \log_{10} m$.
σ	Standard deviation in dB of the normal distribution of $\bar{s}_d$.
$P(s \mid \bar{s})$	pdf of s given $\bar{s}$.
$P(\bar{s}_d)$	pdf of $\bar{s}_d$.
$P(s)$	pdf of s with fading and shadowing.
Q, R	Measured constants concerning modem performance.
p_e	Probability of bit error.
$p_e(s)$	p_e at constant envelope s.
$p_e(\bar{s})$	p_e with Rayleigh fading about local mean $\bar{s}$.
$p_e(m_d)$	p_e with fading and shadowing and area mean m_d.

ACKNOWLEDGMENT

I should like to acknowledge the contribution made to this work by my colleagues, P. J. Mabey, R. Wells, T. W. F. Whiter, and K. J. Wheatley.

REFERENCES

[1] R. C. French, "Radio Propagation in London at 462 MHz," *Radio and Electronic Engineer,* vol. 46, pp. 333–336, July 1976.
[2] W. C. Jakes, Ed., *Microwave Mobile Communications.* New York: John Wiley & Sons, 1974, pp. 79–131.
[3] Y. Okumura, *et al.,* "Field Strength and Its Variability in VHF and UHF Land Mobile Radio Services," *Rev. Elect. Comm. Lab.,* vol. 16, p. 825, Sept.–Oct. 1968.
[4] R. C. French, "Error Performance of PSK and FFSK Subcarrier Data Demodulators," *Radio and Electronic Engineer,* vol. 46, pp. 543–548, Nov. 1976.
[5] R. C. French, "Mobile Radio Data Transmission in the Urban Environment," *IEEE Intl. Conf. on Communications,* 1976, pp. 27-15, 27-20.
[6] G. F. Montgomery, "A Comparison of Amplitude and Angle Modulation for Narrowband Communication of Binary Codes Messages in Fluctuation Noise," in *Proc. IRE,* vol. 42, pp. 447–454, Feb. 1954.
[7] F. Hansen and F. I. Meno, "Mobile Fading–Rayleigh and Lognormal Superimposed," *IEEE Trans. on Vehicular Technol.,* vol. VT-26, pp. 332–335, Nov. 1977.
[8] M. Schwartz, W. R. Bennett, and S. Stein, *Communication Systems and Techniques.* New York: McGraw-Hill Book Co., 1966.
[9] R. C. French, "Error Performance in Mobile Radio Data Transmission in the Urban Environment," *Nachrichten Technische Zeitschrift,* vol. 31, pp. 200–203, Mar. 1978.

Burst Error Performance Encountered in Digital Land Mobile Radio Channel

KOITI OTANI, KAZUHIRO DAIKOKU, AND HIDEAKI OMORI

Abstract—Burst error characteristics are studied by using a Rayleigh and Nakagami–Rice fading simulator. Burst error length distribution estimated with fade duration is described. Thus burst length shortening by means of dual frequency diversity is a promising candidate in order to introduce safely forward error correction (FEC) coding into digital land mobile communication systems.

I. INTRODUCTION

EVEN FOR land mobile communication systems, digital processing has been required to serve data transmission, to attain communication privacy, etc. In land mobile radio channels, the transmission quality of the digital signal may be severely impaired with rapid and deep fading induced from multipath propagation [1], [2]. A supplementary technique, whose most prospective candidate may be forward error correction (FEC) coding [3], is required to restore the impairment. In designing a high speed digital transmission system with FEC coding, it is necessary to determine statistical characteristics of burst error as accurately as possible. However there have been few reports which deal with and reveal them.

In this paper, burst error characteristics are experimentally revealed and statistically clarified [4], [5]. A simple and useful definition for burst errors is first described. Then a real time measurement method is proposed. A typical land mobile propagation environment in the VHF or UHF region is simulated with the Rayleigh or the Nakagami–Rice fading simulator [6]. The experimental results indicate that the cumulative distribution of burst error length is approximately governed by the log-normal distribution and that considerable long-range burst error exists. If FEC coding is safely introduced, an auxiliary technique is required to convert the error patterns. Here, a "dual frequency diversity technique" [7]–[10] is introduced to shorten burst error length. It is experimentally revealed that the dual frequency diversity technique is effective.

II. BURST ERRORS IN LAND MOBILE RADIO CHANNELS

A. Definition of Burst Error

A typical example of burst errors occurring in a Rayleigh fading environment is shown in Fig. 1. It is easily found that a burst error region can be defined as a region of consecutive

Manuscript received February 10, 1981; revised June 10, 1981. Part of this paper was presented at the International Conference on Communications, Seattle, WA, June 8-12, 1980.

The authors are with Yokosuka Electrical Communication Laboratory, Nippon Telegraph and Telephone Public Corporation, P.O. Box No. 8, Yokosuka-shi, Kanagawa-Ken, 238 Japan.

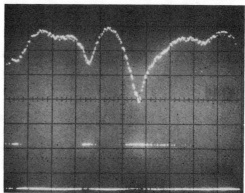

Fig. 1. Typical example of burst error occurring in Rayleigh fading environment. Upper trace is received signal envelope. Lower trace is error pulses. Fading pitch f_D = 10 Hz. Transmission rate f_b = 16 kbits/s, CNR γ_0 = 20 dB.

Fig. 2. Burst error definition, where "0" represents correct bit and "1" represents error bit.

bit stream between two successive error-free regions. Burst error definition is explained in Fig. 2. The run length of an error-free region must be longer than the specific value. In this experiment 50 bits are adopted for the specific value. A burst error region that begins with an error bit may contain some correct bits whose run lengths are shorter than 50 bits. A burst interval which is composed of consecutive error-free bits is also defined as a region between the two burst error regions.

B. Real Time Measurement Method

The implementation of burst error detector is depicted in Fig. 3. Error bits are detected by comparing regenerated and reference data. The burst error detector inspects the above-mentioned specific error-free run length. Detected burst errors are converted into pulse widths proportional to burst error length, which are measured by a time-interval counter. As the real time processing burst error detector is fabricated with simple random logic circuits, its high speed property is easily assured using transistor–transistor logic (TTL) or equivalent.

III. ESTIMATION OF BURST ERROR LENGTH DISTRIBUTION

It has been reported in [5] that the average burst error length $\bar{N}$ in a minimum shift keying (MSK) differential detec-

Reprinted from *IEEE Trans. Veh. Technol.*, vol. VT-30, pp. 156–160, Nov. 1981.

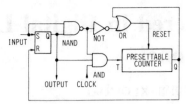

Fig. 3. Configuration of burst error detector.

tion scheme can be accurately estimated as

$$\bar{N} = 1/\{\alpha\gamma_0 f_D T \sqrt{2\pi \ln (1 + 1/\alpha\gamma_0)}\},$$

which agrees well with the experimental result. Here, α, γ_0, f_D, T, and f_b are degradation factor, average carrier-to-noise ratio (CNR), fading rate, $1/f_b$, and transmission rate, respectively.

Next a burst error length distribution will be discussed. The fade duration distribution is not given analytically, because the "level crossing problem" has not been solved yet [11]. But the empirical fade duration distribution in the Rayleigh fading can be given as [12],

$$p(t) = \frac{1}{\sigma t \sqrt{2\pi}} \exp [-\{\ln (t/t_m)\}^2/2\sigma^2],$$

where t_m and σ are median and standard deviation of fade duration, respectively.

Then the burst error length distribution can be estimated as

$$P(N \leqslant x N_m) = \int_0^{x t_m} p(t) \, dt = 1 - \frac{1}{2} \text{ erfc } \{\ln x/(\sigma\sqrt{2})\},$$

where N_m is the median of burst error length and

$$\text{erfc } (x) = \frac{2}{\sqrt{\pi}} \int_x^\infty \exp (-t^2) \, dt.$$

As is governed by log-normal distribution, $\bar{N}$ is given as

$$\bar{N} = N_m \exp (\sigma^2/2).$$

IV. EXPERIMENTAL PROCEDURE

The MSK modulation method is introduced and the differential detection method is used to demodulate the MSK signal. The radio frequency (RF) is 880 MHz. A maximal-length 511 bits pseudorandom noise sequence, whose clock frequency is 16 kbits/s, is fed into the MSK modulator. The receiver is a triple conversion type (70 MHz, 10.7 MHz, and 455 kHz). The main filtering for both waveform shaping and noise suppression is carried out at the 10.7 MHz second intermediate frequency (IF) crystal filter possessing nearly the Gaussian bandpass property. Configurations of transmitter and receiver are shown in Fig. 4.

Two simulation systems are used to analyze burst error characteristics in this experiment. One is the simulation-setup for the Rayleigh or the Nakagami–Rice fading channel, as shown in Fig. 5. Another is for dual frequency diversity, as shown in Fig. 6.

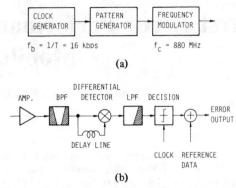

(a)

(b)

Fig. 4. Configuration. (a) Transmitter. (b) Receiver.

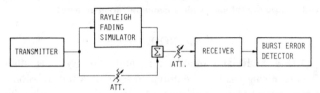

Fig. 5. Simulation setup for burst error measurement in Nakagami–Rice fading channel.

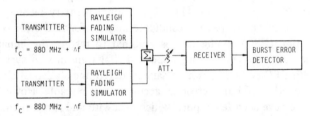

Fig. 6. Simulation setup for burst error measurement in "dual frequency diversity." Two fading simulators, with no cross correlation and equal loss, are installed.

Average burst error lengths are obtained as a function of f_D, when burst error lengths are evaluated from fade duration, as is mentioned in the previous section. For simplicity, f_D is chosen as 10 Hz in the present experiment. When RF is 880 MHz, $f_D = 10$ Hz is equivalent to 12.3 km/h vehicular speed in Rayleigh fading. Experiments are divided into three cases.

Case 1–Burst Errors in Rayleigh Fading Channel: Burst error lengths, burst interval lengths, and burst interval lengths, occurring after the burst error with the specific length are measured in Rayleigh fading channel by using the experimental setup shown in Fig. 5, where the line of sight component must be omitted.

Case 2–Burst Errors in Nakagami–Rice Fading Channel: Burst error lengths are measured with the parameter of power ratio for the line of sight component to multipath component (LMR) by using the experimental setup shown in Fig. 5.

Case 3–Burst Errors when Dual Frequency Diversity Is Adopted: Burst length shortening through dual frequency diversity is examined by using the experimental setup shown in Fig. 6. In this case two radio frequencies, which are modulated by the same baseband signal, are introduced; one is 880 MHz $- \Delta f$ and the other is 880 MHz $+ \Delta f$. The difference between the two is $2\Delta f$. The modulated signals are transmitted simultaneously. The receiver is the same as that for Cases 1 and 2. Burst error lengths are measured only in the Rayleigh fading channel.

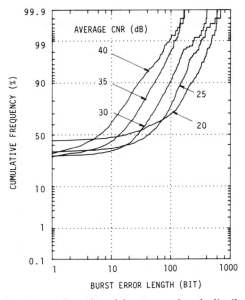

Fig. 7. Experimental results of burst error length distribution as a function of average CNR.

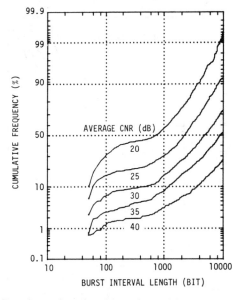

Fig. 9. Experimental results of burst interval length distribution as a function of average CNR.

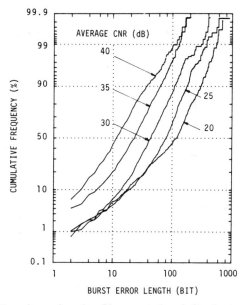

Fig. 8. Experimental results of burst error length distribution obtained by omitting one-bit errors.

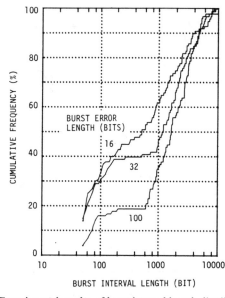

Fig. 10. Experimental results of burst interval length distribution after burst error with specific value.

V. EXPERIMENTAL RESULTS AND DISCUSSION

Case 1–Burst Errors in Rayleigh Fading Channel: Introduction of log-normal scale is effective to depict experimental results. The cumulative distribution of burst error length in the Rayleigh fading channel is shown in Fig. 7. It is indicated that one-bit errors occupy a large percentage of the errors. When one-bit errors are omitted, the cumulative distribution tends toward the log-normal distribution, as shown in Fig. 8. The burst error length distribution, as mentioned in Case 3, can be estimated by using the fade duration that is also expressed by the log-normal distribution. The value of σ calculated from Fig. 7 is approximately 1.5, which agrees well with that of the fade duration reported in [13]. Therefore, it is verified that the estimation is effective.

The cumulative burst interval distribution, which is useful to design FEC coding, is shown in Fig. 9. When the average CNR is lower, the burst interval becomes shorter. The cumulative distribution of burst interval after a burst error with a specific length is depicted in Fig. 10. It is concluded, from Figs. 9 and 10, that the burst interval is insufficient for the guard space of FEC coding, and that a supplementary technique is required to shorten burst error lengths.

Case 2–Burst Errors in Nakagami–Rice Fading Channel: The cumulative distribution of burst error length is shown with the parameter of average received CNR in Fig. 11, and with the parameter of LMR in Fig. 12. As LMR becomes larger, burst error length becomes short. There still remain many burst errors with relative long burst lengths, even in the Nakagami–

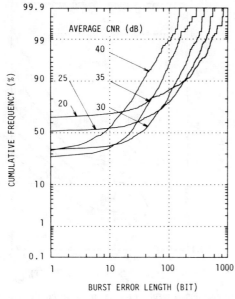

Fig. 11. Experimental results of burst error length distribution in the Nakagami–Rice fading channel as a function of average CNR, when LMR = 3 dB.

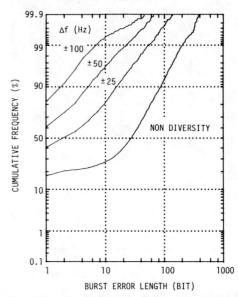

Fig. 13. Experimental results of burst error length distribution as a function of offset frequency Δf, when average CNR is 30 dB.

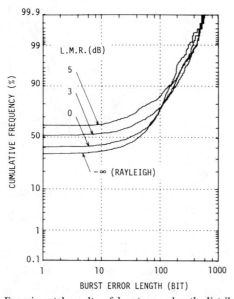

Fig. 12. Experimental results of burst error length distribution as a function of LMR, when average CNR is 25 dB.

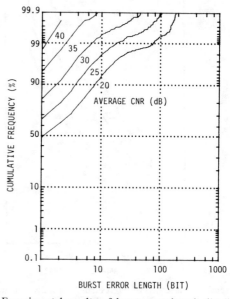

Fig. 14. Experimental results of burst error length distribution as a function of average CNR, when offset frequency $\Delta f = \pm 100$ Hz.

Rice fading channel, where the line of sight component is expected.

Case 3–Burst Errors when Dual Frequency Diversity Is Adopted: The cumulative distribution of burst error length with the parameter of Δf is shown in Fig. 13., when the CNR is kept at 30 dB on the average. Fig. 13 indicates that the burst error lengths for the dual frequency diversity are also governed by the log-normal distribution. The fading induced by the diversity is superimposed on the Rayleigh fading [8]. The fading period and pitch are dependent on Δf. The frequency diversity makes it possible to shorten burst error lengths significantly.

The cumulative burst error length distribution is also shown as a function of CNR in Fig. 14, when $\Delta f = \pm 100$ Hz. The

values of CNR ranging from 20 dB to 40 dB, cover bit error rates from 10^{-2} to 10^{-4}, which are required to maintain high quality voice transmission in VHF or UHF digital land mobile radio channels, even in the Rayleigh fading environment. The experimental results indicate that the dual frequency diversity technique makes it possible to safely introduce FEC coding into the land mobile radio systems.

Consider FEC convolutional coding whose code rate, correctable burst error length, and guard space are r, b, and g, respectively. When the dual frequency diversity is introduced, Δf must be less than $f_b/2g$. If Δf cannot satisfy the condition, the "burst shortening effect" might be reduced. The Δf value must be as small as possible, because efficient spectrum use is always required. Then, it is necessary to decide Δf, considering both correction efficiency and the above condition. When the Iwadare code [14], as an example, is introduced, $r = 1/2$, $b = 16$, and $g = 51$. Thus, the lower bound of correction can be estimated as 99.6 percent from Fig. 13, where Δf and average CNR are ±100 Hz and 30 dB, respectively. Improvement in bit error rates is expected when the present code is used [15]. This is the reason why burst detecting error-free run length is set at 50 bits in this experiment.

VI. CONCLUSION

It is clarified that if the one-bit error may be omitted, the distribution of burst error length can be estimated by the fade duration and that the distribution is governed by the lognormal one, whose standard deviation is approximately 1.5. In the land mobile fading channel, there exist not only relatively long-range bursts but also relatively short-range error-free runs. Consequently it is impractical to apply directly FEC coding into land mobile communication systems. Therefore some auxiliary techniques are needed to shorten the error bursts. It was experimentally determined that the dual frequency diversity is effective to shorten error bursts. The conclusion obtained through the present study is applicable for newly developed Gaussian filtered MSK [16], which makes it possible to realize 16 kbits/s bit rates in a 25-kHz channel.

ACKNOWLEDGMENT

Thanks are expressed to Mr. K. Izumi and Dr. S. Seki of NTT for encouragement and guidance. The authors are also grateful to Dr. M. Ishizuka of Tokyo University, and Dr. K. Hirade of NTT for many helpful suggestions.

REFERENCES

[1] Y. Okumura et al., "Field strength and its variability in VHF and UHF land mobile radio services," Rev. Elec. Commun. Lab., vol. 16, pp.825–873, Sept.–Oct. 1968.

[2] W. C. Jakes, Ed., Microwave Mobile Communications. New York: Wiley, 1974.

[3] W. W. Peterson nd E. J. Weldon, Jr., Error Correcting Codes, 2nd ed., Cambridge, MA: M.I.T., 1972.

[4] H. Omori and K. Otani, "Burst error characteristics of digital land mobile radio," Int. Conf. Commun., Conf. Rec., vol. 1, 24-2, June 1980.

[5] K. Otani and H. Omori, "Distribution of burst error lengths in Rayleigh fading radio channels," Electron. Lett., vol.16, pp.889–891, Nov. 1980.

[6] K. Hirade et al., "Fading simulator for land mobile radio communications," Trans. IECE Japan, vol. 58-B, pp. 449–456, Sept. 1975 [in Japanese].

[7] M. Komura et al., "New radio paging system and its propagation characteristics," IEEE Trans. Veh. Technol., vol.VT-26, pp.362–366, Nov. 1977.

[8] T. Hattori and K. Hirade, "Multitransmitter digital signal transmission by using offset frequency strategy in a land mobile telephone system," IEEE Trans. Veh. Technol., vol. VT-27, pp.231–238, Nov. 1978.

[9] G. A. Arredondo, "Analysis of radio paging errors in multi-transmitter mobile systems," IEEE Trans. Commun. vol.COM-21, pp.1310–1318, Nov. 1978.

[10] R. C. French, "Common channel multi-transmitter data systems," Radio Electron. Eng., vol.50, pp.439–446, Sept. 1980.

[11] I. F. Lindsey, "Level-crossing problems for random processes," IEEE Trans. Inform. Theory, vol.IT-19, pp.295–315, May 1973.

[12] A. Vigant, "Number and duration of fades at 6 and 4 GHz," Bell Syst. Tech. J., vol. 50, pp. 815–841, Mar. 1971.

[13] O. Sasaki and T. Akiyama, "Characteristics of fadeout and fade speed in microwave circuits," Rev. Elec. Comm. Lab., vol.25, pp.445–457 1976.

[14] Y. Iwadare, "On type-B1 burst-error-correcting convolutional codes," IEEE Trans. Inform, Theory, vol.IT-14, pp.577–583, July 1968.

[15] K. Hirade, H. Omori, and K. Otani, unpublished.

[16] K. Murota and K. Hirade, "GMSK modulation for digital mobile radio telephony," IEEE Trans. Commun., vol. COM-29, pp.1044–1050, July 1981.

Calculation of Error Probability for MSK and OQPSK Systems Operating in a Fading Multipath Environment

DONALD R. HUMMELS, MEMBER, IEEE, AND FREDERICK W. RATCLIFFE, STUDENT MEMBER, IEEE

Abstract—A technique is given for determining the error-rate performance of a class of digital communication systems operating with fading multipath interference. The approach uses a truncated series to represent the fading process and takes into account the effects of intersymbol interference caused by linear filtering in the receiver or channel. Application of the method to the cases of minimum shift keyed (MSK) and offset quadriphase shift key (OQPSK) systems reveals a slight performance advantage for MSK.

I. INTRODUCTION

THE OBJECTIVE of this paper is to present a method for analyzing the performance of a digital communication system operating in a fading multipath environment. This problem is of considerable practical interest because multipath transmissions are fairly common when either the transmitter or the receiver is operating mobile in an urban region. Previous work in the area [1]–[5] includes both experimental and analytical efforts. In the latter category, the work of Kwon and Shehadeh [1] for frequency shift keyed (FSK) systems and that of Ma *et al.* [2] for Rayleigh fast-fading channels is significant. In this paper methods are given for finding the error-rate performance of a fairly broad class of commonly used systems operating with fading multipath interference. The methods developed are then applied to find the performance of minimum shift keyed (MSK) and offset quadriphase shift keyed (OQPSK) systems.

II. THE MULTIPATH MODEL

The system under consideration is shown in Fig. 1. The system input is a binary message sequence having symbols that are equally likely and statistically independent. The bit time is T s. Each T_s s the transmitter puts out a waveform from the set $\{s_i(t)\}_{i=1}^M$. Since there are M waveforms in the set, each transmission carries $\log_2 M$ bits of information and $T_s = T \log_2 M$. Although the waveforms normally have finite duration, they are assumed to be at least approximately bandpass with center frequency ω_c rad/s. They are not restricted to have duration T_s s. The sequence of transmissions output by the digital modulator is the desired or direct signal and is given by

$$s_d(t) = \sum_{n=-\infty}^{\infty} s_n(t - nT_s) \tag{1}$$

Manuscript received January 28, 1981; revised March 31, 1981. This work was supported by the Government Electronics Division, Motorola, Inc., Scottsdale, AZ.

The authors are with the Department of Electrical Engineering, Kansas State University, Manhattan, KS 66506.

where the nth transmission is taken from the signal set in accordance with the modulation scheme. A multipath or reflected signal $s_r(t)$ is added during transmission. The reflected signal is assumed to be delayed in time by t_d s relative to the direct signal and to have Rayleigh amplitude and uniform phase distributions. The possibility of a Doppler shift ω_d rad/s, due to relative motion between transmitter and receiver is also included in the model. The direct signal $s_d(t)$ and the reflected signal $s_r(t)$ are summed and passed through a bandpass filter with impulse reponse $h_c(t)$ representing any liner filtering that takes place in the channel. The effects of intersymbol interference caused by the band-limiting in the channel are thereby taken into account. The output of the channel filter is combined with additive white Gaussian noise $w(t)$, and the resulting sum serves as input to the receiver. For all cases of interest here, the receiver can be modeled as a linear filter with impulse response $h_r(t)$ followed by a product detector and a zonal low-pass filter to eliminate sum frequency terms. A sample r taken at time t_0 is the decision variable.

Equivalent Low-Pass Model

An equivalent low-pass model for the system just described is given in Fig. 2. It is developed using conventional complex envelope notation described elsewhere [6]. The digital modulator is represented by a pulse shaping filter with impulse response $\tilde{p}(t)$ driven by a complex data sequence $\tilde{a}(t)$ given by

$$\tilde{a}(t) = \sum_{n=-\infty}^{\infty} a_n e^{j\omega_c n T_s} \delta(t - nT_s) \tag{2}$$

where ω_c is the carrier frequency and

$$a_n = A_n e^{j\theta_n} \tag{3}$$

is the complex data symbol representing the signal amplitude and phase for the nth transmission. Through suitable choice of the data symbols a_n and the pulse shaping filter impulse response $\tilde{p}(t)$, one can represent most commonly used modulation schemes. The appropriate selections for MSK and OQPSK are given in Table I.

The output of the pulse-shaping filter is the complex envelope of the direct signal and is given by

$$\tilde{s}_d(t) = \sum_{n=-\infty}^{\infty} a_n e^{j\omega_c n T_s} \tilde{p}(t - nT_s). \tag{4}$$

Reprinted from *IEEE Trans. Veh. Technol.*, vol. VT-30, pp. 112–120, Aug. 1981.

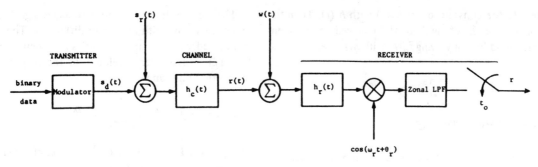

Fig. 1. System model.

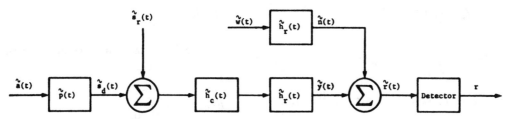

Fig. 2. Equivalent low-pass model.

TABLE I
PULSE SHAPING FUNCTIONS FOR OQPSK AND MSK

MODULATION	DATA		A_i	θ_i	$\tilde{p}(t)$
OQPSK	n even	1	1	0	$A, 0 \leqslant t \leqslant 2T$
		0	1	π	0, elsewhere
	n odd	1	1	$\pi/2$	
		0	1	$3\pi/2$	
MSK		1	1	0	$-j(A/2\Delta\omega) \sin \Delta\omega t, 0 \leqslant t \leqslant 2T$
		0	-1	0	0, elsewhere

The complex envelope of the reflected signal is obtained by modifying $\tilde{s}_d(t)$ accordingly, viz.

$$\tilde{s}_r(t) = R(t)e^{j\phi(t)} \sum_{n=-\infty}^{\infty} a_n e^{j\omega_c n T_s}$$

$$\cdot e^{-j[(\omega_c + \omega_d)t_d - \omega_d t]} \tilde{p}(t - nT_s - t_d) \qquad (5)$$

where t_d is the delay of the reflected signal relative to the direct signal, ω_d is the Doppler shift in rad/s of the reflected signal, $R(t)$ is a Rayleigh amplitude process and $\phi(t)$ represents the uniform phase variations of the reflected signal.

The complex envelopes of the direct and reflected signals are summed and passed through equivalent low-pass channel and receiving filters to yield $\tilde{y}(t)$, the complex envelope of the received signal plus multipath. This signal is added to an equivalent low-pass representation $\tilde{n}(t)$ of the received noise to form the complex envelope $\tilde{r}(t)$ of the signal delivered to the product detector. It is readily shown that a sample r taken at time t_0 at the product detector output is related to the complex envelope $\tilde{r}(t)$ by

$$r = \tfrac{1}{2} \operatorname{Re} \{\tilde{r}(t)e^{j[(\omega_c - \omega_r)t - \theta_r]}\}. \qquad (6)$$

III. CALCULATION OF $P[e]$

Numerical evaluation of the error rate is facilitated by employing series representations for both the signal pulse-shaping function and the fading process. First consider the direct signal $\tilde{s}_d(t)$ as given in (4) and expand the pulse shaping function $\tilde{p}(t)$ in a Fourier series using a periodic extension of $\tilde{p}(t)$ having a period P, somewhat longer than the effective memory of the channel and receiver filters. For convenience we require that the period be a multiple of the bit time, i.e., let $P = kT$ where k is an integer selected such that kT is greater than the effective duration of the receiving system response $h_r(t)$. Then over the time interval of interest a good approximation for $\tilde{p}(t)$ is

$$\tilde{p}(t) \cong \sum_{m=-\infty}^{\infty} c_m e^{jm\omega_0 t} \qquad (7)$$

where c_m is the Fourier coefficient and $\omega_0 = 2\pi/kT$. Using this series approximation (4) leads to

$$\tilde{s}_d(t) = \sum_{n=-\infty}^{\infty} \sum_{m=-\infty}^{\infty} a_n c_m e^{-jn\omega_c T_s} e^{-jnm\omega_0 T_s} e^{jm\omega_0 t}. \qquad (8)$$

227

Let $\tilde{h}(t)$ denote the convolution of $\tilde{h}_c(t)$ with $\tilde{h}_r(t)$. Then the contribution of the direct signal to the received complex envelope $\tilde{r}(t)$ is found by convolving $\tilde{s}_d(t)$ with $\tilde{h}(t)$, i.e.,

$$\tilde{y}_d(t) = \int_{-\infty}^{\infty} \tilde{h}(t-\tau) \sum_{n=-\infty}^{\infty} a_n c_m e^{-jn\omega_c T_s}$$

$$\cdot e^{-jnm\omega_0 T_s} e^{jm\omega_0 \tau} \, d\tau. \tag{9}$$

Interchanging the order of integration and summation yields

$$\tilde{y}_d(t) = \sum_{n=-\infty}^{\infty} \sum_{m=-\infty}^{\infty} a_n c_m e^{-jn\omega_c T_s}$$

$$\cdot e^{-jnm\omega_0 T_s} \int_{-\infty}^{\infty} \tilde{h}(t-\tau) e^{jm\omega_0 \tau} \, d\tau. \tag{10}$$

By making the change of variables $u = t - \tau$, the integral in (10) becomes

$$\int_{-\infty}^{\infty} h(u) e^{-jm\omega_0 u} \, du \, e^{jm\omega_0 t} = \tilde{H}(m\omega_0) e^{jm\omega_0 t}.$$

Thus the preceding reduces to

$$\tilde{y}_d(t) = \sum_{n=-\infty}^{\infty} \sum_{m=-\infty}^{\infty} a_n c_m \tilde{H}(m\omega_0) e^{-jn\omega_c T_s}$$

$$\cdot e^{-jnm\omega_0 T_s} e^{jm\omega_0 t}. \tag{11}$$

Note that $\tilde{H}(m\omega_0)$ is the equivalent low-pass transfer function of the channel and receiver filters combined and can be obtained from

$$\tilde{H}(m\omega_0) = \tilde{H}_c(m\omega_0) \tilde{H}_r(m\omega_0). \tag{12}$$

Aside from the infinite sums in the expression for $\tilde{y}_d(t)$ given in (11), the result is a convenient form for numerical purposes. As a practical matter, it is perfectly reasonable to truncate both series. Since any real transmitter operates within an assigned channel bandwidth, the Fourier series expression of $\tilde{p}(t)$ can be restricted accordingly. As for the transmission index n, unless the channel has an extremely long memory only a few transmissions will contribute to the signal at any given time. If as is assumed in the arguments that follow, the transmission of interest corresponds to $n = 0$, it is appropriate to restrict n to the range $[-N, 1]$ where N is a positive integer such that NT_s exceeds the effective duration of $\tilde{h}(t)$. The term for $n = 1$ is included because in OQPSK and MSK systems this "future" transmission can interfere with the decision on the symbol sent at $t = 0$. The resulting expression for $\tilde{y}_d(t)$ valid for $0 \leqslant t \leqslant 2T_s$ is

$$\tilde{y}_d(t) = \sum_{n=-N}^{1} a_n \sum_{m=-M}^{M} c_m \tilde{H}(m\omega_0)$$

$$\cdot e^{-j(n\omega_c + nm\omega_0) T_s} e^{jm\omega_0 t}. \tag{13}$$

The contribution $\tilde{y}_r(t)$ of the reflected signal to $\tilde{r}(t)$ is found in a similar way, with one major difference. The fading process is modeled with the aid of a series representation described in [1], [7] and further developed in the Appendix where it is shown that one can write

$$\xi(t) = R(t) e^{j\phi(t)} \cong \sum_{k=-K}^{K} b_k e^{j\lambda_k t}. \tag{14}$$

The process $\xi(t)$ given in (14) is a complex Gaussian process with correlation function

$$R_\xi(\tau) = \sum_{k=-K}^{K} R_k e^{j\lambda_k \tau} \tag{15}$$

where the b_k are zero-mean complex Gaussian random variables with covariances

$$E\{b_k, b_l\} = \begin{cases} R_k, & l = k \\ 0, & l \neq k \end{cases}. \tag{16}$$

If the fading process $\xi(t)$ is taken as having the power spectrum

$$S_\xi(f) = \begin{cases} \psi_0/2, & |f| \leqslant B_r \\ 0, & \text{elsewhere}. \end{cases} \tag{17}$$

where B_r denotes the bandwidth of the fading process, then the variances R_k and frequencies λ_k may be conveniently determined from a $2K + 1$ Gauss quadrature rule (GQR) for the uniform weighting function on the interval $[-1, 1]$. The procedure is described in the Appendix.

Using the series representation of (14) in (5) and following the procedures used for the direct signal yields the reflected component of $\tilde{r}(t)$ as

$$\tilde{y}_r(t) \cong \sum_{n=-N}^{1} a_n \sum_{k=-K}^{K} b_k \sum_{m=-M}^{M} c_m \tilde{H}(m\omega_0 + \omega_d + \lambda_k)$$

$$\cdot e^{-j(n\omega_c + nm\omega_0) T_s} e^{-j(\omega_c + \omega_d + m\omega_0) t_d}$$

$$\cdot e^{j(m\omega_0 + \omega_d + \lambda_k) t} \tag{18}$$

valid for $0 \leqslant t \leqslant 2T_s$. The envelope $\tilde{r}(t)$ at the detector input is the sum of three terms, i.e.,

$$\tilde{r}(t) = \tilde{y}_d(t) + \tilde{y}_r(t) + \tilde{n}(t). \tag{19}$$

The decision variable r corresponding to a sample time t_0 in $[0, 2T_s]$ is therefore

$$r = \tfrac{1}{2} \operatorname{Re}\{\tilde{y}_d(t) e^{j(\Delta\omega t_0 - \theta_r)}\} + \tfrac{1}{2} \operatorname{Re}\{\tilde{y}_r(t) e^{j(\Delta\omega t_0 - \theta_r)}\}$$

$$+ \tfrac{1}{2} \operatorname{Re}\{\tilde{n}(t) e^{j(\Delta\omega t_0 - \theta_r)}\} \tag{20}$$

where $\Delta\omega = \omega_c - \omega_r$. The notation is simplified by defining the constants

$$G_{dn} \triangleq \sum_{m=-M}^{M} c_m \tilde{H}(m\omega_0) e^{-j(n\omega_c + nm\omega_0) T_s}$$

$$\cdot e^{j(m\omega_0 + \Delta\omega) t_0} e^{-j\theta_r} \tag{21}$$

$$G_{rnk} \triangleq \sum_{m=-M}^{M} c_m \tilde{H}(m\omega_0 + \omega_d + \lambda_k) e^{-j(n\omega_c + nm\omega_0)T_s}$$
$$\cdot e^{-j(\omega_c + \omega_d + m\omega_0)t_d} e^{j(m\omega_0 + \Delta\omega + \omega_d + \lambda_k)t_0} e^{-j\theta_r}. \tag{22}$$

If the noise term in (20) is represented by defining the random variable n as

$$n \triangleq \mathrm{Re}\{\tilde{n}(t) e^{j(\Delta\omega t_0 - \theta_r)}\} \tag{23}$$

then the decision variable r may be written in the more compact form

$$r = \tfrac{1}{2}\,\mathrm{Re}\{G_{d0}a_0\} + \tfrac{1}{2}\,\mathrm{Re}\left\{\sum_{\substack{n=-N \\ n\neq 0}}^{1} G_{dn}a_n\right\}$$
$$+ \tfrac{1}{2}\,\mathrm{Re}\left\{\sum_{n=-N}^{1} a_n \sum_{k=-K}^{K} G_{rnk}b_k\right\} + \tfrac{1}{2}\,n. \tag{24}$$

As written in (24), the various contributions to the sample r are easily identified. The first term corresponds to the desired signal; the second is the intersymbol interference caused by linear filtering; the thrid term is a result of the multipath interference; and the final term is produced by the additive Gaussian noise at the receiver input. Also, note that n as defined in (23) is a Gaussian random variable with variance given by $R_n(0)$ where $R_n(\tau)$ is the autocorrelation function of the noise process $n(t)$ at the output of the receiver filter. If the white noise at the receiver input has the power spectrum $S_w(f) = N_0/2$, then

$$\sigma_n^2 \triangleq R_n(0) = N_0 B \tag{25}$$

where B is the receiver noise bandwidth and is given by

$$B = \int_{-\infty}^{\infty} |\tilde{H}_r(f)|^2 \, df. \tag{26}$$

For the problems of interest the decision rule is

decide 1
$$r \underset{<}{\overset{>}{=}} 0 \,. \tag{27}$$
decide 0

In addition, the symbol set is symmetric so that $P[e] = P[e\,|\,a_0]$. Let a_0 corresponding to a zero sent be selected. The error probability is then given by $P[r > 0]$. An equivalent expression can be obtained by dropping the factor 1/2 and normalizing r by the signal term. That is let

$$r' = 1 + \gamma_d(D) + \mathrm{Re}\left\{\sum_{k=-K}^{K} \gamma_{rk}(D)b_k\right\} + \eta \tag{28}$$

where D is used to denote a specific transmission sequence $a_{-N}, \cdots, a_{-1}, a_0, a_1$. Specifically let

$$\gamma_d(D) = \frac{\left\{\mathrm{Re}\,\displaystyle\sum_{\substack{n=-N \\ n\neq 0}}^{1} G_{dn}a_n\right\}}{\mathrm{Re}\{G_{d0}a_0\}} \tag{29}$$

$$\gamma_{kr}(D) = \frac{\displaystyle\sum_{n=-N}^{1} G_{rnk}a_n}{\mathrm{Re}\{G_{d0}a_0\}} \tag{30}$$

and

$$\eta = \frac{n}{\mathrm{Re}\{G_{d0}a_0\}}. \tag{31}$$

The Gaussian random variable η is zero mean and has variance

$$\sigma_\eta^2 = \frac{N_0 B}{(\mathrm{Re}\{G_{d0}a_0\})^2}. \tag{32}$$

Note that because the signal component $\mathrm{Re}\{G_{d0}a_0\}$ corresponding to the transmission of a data zero is a negative number, the error probability is now found by calculating $P[r' < 0]$. The calculation is simplified by writing r' in an all real format, viz.

$$r' = 1 + \gamma_d(D) + \sum_{k=-K}^{K} \gamma_{rk_r}(D)b_{k_r}$$
$$- \sum_{k=-K}^{k} \gamma_{rk_i}(D)b_{k_i} + \eta \tag{33}$$

where the subscripts r and i denote real and imaginary parts, respectively. Now define the random variable ψ by

$$\psi = \sum_{k=-K}^{K} \gamma_{rk_r}(D)b_{k_r} - \sum_{k=-K}^{K} \gamma_{rk_i}(D)b_{k_i} + \eta. \tag{34}$$

For a given data sequence D, ψ is a weighted sum of zero-mean Gaussian random variables and hence is a zero-mean Gaussian random variable. If the variance of ψ is known, the conditional error probability $P[e\,|\,a_0, D]$ is readily calculated as

$$P[e\,|\,a_0, D] = P[r' < 0\,|\,D] = Q\left\{\frac{1 + \lambda_d(D)}{\sigma_\psi}\right\} \tag{35}$$

where

$$Q(\alpha) = \int_{-\infty}^{\infty} \frac{1}{\sqrt{2\pi}} e^{-\beta^2/2} \, d\beta. \tag{36}$$

Determining the variance of ψ is straightforward because of the nice properties of the random variables b_k in the series

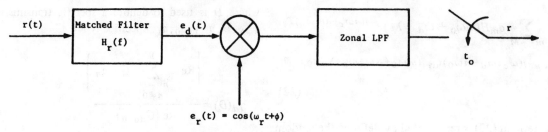

Fig. 3.   Matched filter receiver.

representation of the fading process. They are zero-mean statistically independent complex Gaussian random variables. In addition, the real and imaginary part b_{k_r} and b_{k_i} are statistically independent and have equal variances. The variance of ψ is found by summing the variances of the terms involved and is readily shown to be (see the Appendix)

$$\sigma_\psi^2 = \frac{\sum_{k=-K}^{K} |\gamma_{rk}(D)|^2 r_k}{4(P_d/P_r)} + \sigma_\eta^2 \qquad (37)$$

where P_d/P_r is the ratio of the power in the direct signal to that of the multipath interference.

Finally, the unconditional error probability is obtained by averaging (35) over all significant data sequences, i.e.,

$$P[e] = \sum_{\text{all } D} P[D] Q\left(\frac{1 + \gamma_d(D)}{\sigma \psi}\right). \qquad (38)$$

The calculation implied by the form given in (38) is sometimes called the direct enumeration method. Others have used bounding methods to evaluate similar forms in order to reduce computer execution time. We have not found this to be necessary for practical problems involving linear band-limiting channels. All of the results in the next section were obtained on a minicomputer operating with 32K of core memory. Execution times were generally less than 2 min.

IV. APPLICATIONS TO MSK AND OQPSK

The expressions developed herein have been used to evaluate the performance of MSK and OQPSK systems operating over multipath channels. In carrying out the evaluation, it was assumed in each case that a matched filter receiver of the form shown in Fig. 3 was used.

MSK Results

Before the calculation can be completed, it is necessary to specify system transfer functions and key parameters. The data symbols and pulse shaping filter for MSK have already been given in Table I. The equivalent low-pass transfer function of the MSK matched filter is readily shown to be

$$\tilde{H}_r(f) = -jA \frac{\cos(2\pi fT)}{8\pi^2 (f^2 - \Delta f^2)} e^{-2\pi fT}. \qquad (39)$$

For an MSK system, the carrier frequency and the detector reference frequency always differ by an amount $1/4T$ Hz. The detector reference phase was taken as $\phi = 0$, and a sampling

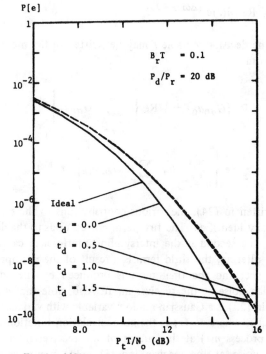

Fig. 4.   MSK error probability, delay time varied.

instant $t_0 = 2T$ was selected for best performance. Note that $T_s = T$ for MSK. The results for MSK are shown in Figs. 4–6 where in each case the probability of error is graphed versus $P_t T/N_0$ over a range of indicated system parameters. For convenience in presenting the results, some parameters have been normalized. The multipath delay t_d is given in bit times and the fading rate is taken as $B_r T$.

OQPSK Results

For the case of OQPSK the equivalent low-pass transfer function of the receiver matched filter is

$$\tilde{H}_r(f) = AT \frac{\sin(2\pi fT)}{(2\pi fT)} e^{-j2\pi fT}. \qquad (40)$$

The detector reference phase and sampling instant were set at $\phi = 0$ and $t_0 = 2T$ as for the case of MSK but in this case the detector reference frequency and carrier frequency are the same. The results for OQPSK are illustrated in Figs. 7–9.

Remarks

Examination of the results indicates that both MSK and OQPSK systems are sensitive to multipath interference and exhibit noticeable performance degradation with multipath interference at 20 dB below the desired signal. There is a slight

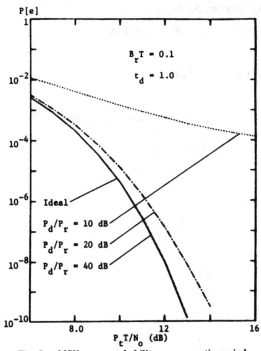

Fig. 5.   MSK error probability, power ratio varied.

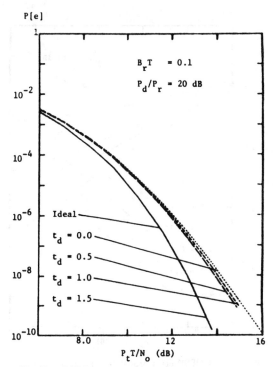

Fig. 7.   OQPSK error probability, delay time varied.

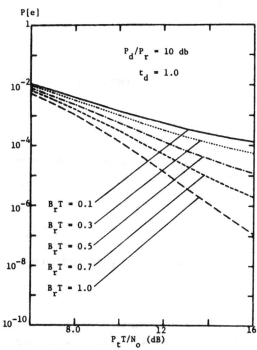

Fig. 6.   MSK error probability, fading rate varied.

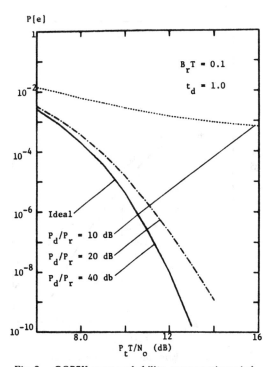

Fig. 8.   OQPSK error probability, power ratio varied.

advantage for MSK which is more apparent in the direct comparison given in Fig. 10 but the difference is not great. It is evident from Figs. 4–7 that the influence of multipath delay time is slight in either case. This is not surprising since the scattering medium imparts a uniform phase variation on the multipath signal. The effects of fading rate are revealed in Figs. 6 and 9 where it is apparent that slow fading ($B_r T = 0.1$) is significantly more degrading than fast fading.

V. CONCLUSION

A procedure has been developed for determining the influence of a fading multipath on the error rate performance of a digital communication system. The model used is adaptable to a variety of digital modulation schemes and takes into account the effects of intersymbol interference produced by band-limiting in the channel or the receiver. The form of the result is such that it is possible to use measured system response functions as well as ideal transfer functions when computing performance. The procedure has been used to compare the performance of MSK and OQPSK systems operating in a fading multipath environment. The results show a slight advantage for MSK.

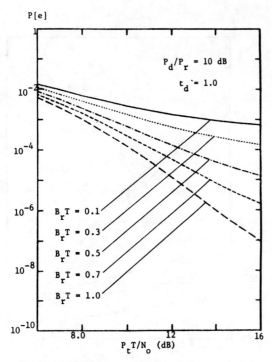

Fig. 9. OQPSK error probability, fading rate varied.

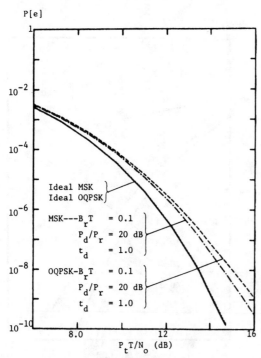

Fig. 10. Error probability comparisons.

APPENDIX

MODELING THE FADING PROCESS

The expressions developed herein for numerical evaluation of error rate utilize a truncated series representation to represent the fading process $\xi(t) = R(t)e^{j\phi(t)}$. The representation is developed from a representation described in Yaglom [7].

The Approximating Process

Consider the process defined by

$$\xi_a(t) \triangleq \sum_{k=-K}^{K} b_k e^{j\lambda_k t} \tag{A1}$$

where the b_k are zero-mean random variables with

$$E\{b_k b_l^*\} = \begin{cases} R_k, & l=k \\ 0, & l \neq k \end{cases} \tag{A2}$$

and the λ_k are constants.

It is relatively easy to show that the process $\xi_a(t)$ is stationary with correlation function

$$R_{\xi_a}(\tau) = \sum_{k=-K}^{K} R_k e^{j\lambda_k \tau}. \tag{A3}$$

Let us further stipulate that the b_k are complex Gaussian random variables with real and imaginary parts b_{k_r} and b_{k_i}, respectively. Also let b_{k_r} and b_{k_i} be statistically independent with equal variances

$$E\{b_{k_r}^2\} = E\{b_{k_i}^2\} = \frac{R_k}{2}. \tag{A4}$$

It may be verified that these restrictions ensure that $\xi_a(t)$ is a complex Gaussian process with

$$\xi_a(t) = \xi_{a_r}(t) + j\xi_{a_i}(t) \tag{A5}$$

where $\xi_{a_r}(t)$ and $\xi_{a_i}(t)$ are zero-mean statistically independent Gaussian processes with variances

$$E\{\xi_{a_r}^2(t)\} = E\{\xi_{a_i}^2(t)\} = \tfrac{1}{2} R_{\xi_a}(0). \tag{A6}$$

The Fading Process

The customary Rayleigh fading process is given by

$$\xi(t) = R(t)e^{j\phi(t)} \tag{A7}$$

where the envelope variations are determined by the Rayleigh process $R(t)$ and the phase variations are determined by the uniform process $\phi(t)$. Like $\xi_a(t)$, $\xi(t)$ is also a complex Gaussian process

$$\xi(t) = \xi_r(t) + j\xi_i(t) \tag{A8}$$

where

$$\xi_r(t) = R(t)\cos[\phi(t)] \tag{A9}$$

and

$$\xi_i(t) = R(t)\sin[\phi(t)]. \tag{A10}$$

Furthermore, it is easy to show that $\xi_r(t)$ and $\xi_i(f)$ are zero-mean statistically independent Gaussian processes with equal variances given by

$$E\{\xi_r{}^2(t)\} = E\{\xi_i{}^2(t)\} = \tfrac{1}{2} R_\xi(0). \tag{A11}$$

Clearly, the process $\xi_a(t)$ will be a useful representation for $\xi(t)$ if the correlation function $R_{\xi_a}(\tau)$ can be made to match $R_\xi(\tau)$.

Selection of the Process Parameters

The set of parameters $\{R_k, \lambda_k\}$ for the process $\xi_a(t)$ are selected so that $R_{\xi_a}(\tau)$ becomes a good approximation to $R_\xi(\tau)$. The approximation improves with increasing K but only a few terms are needed for small values of τ. The procedure makes use of Gauss quadrature methods discussed previously [1]. Let the fading process $\xi(t)$ have a power spectrum given by

$$S_\xi(f) = \begin{cases} \psi_0/2, & |f| \leqslant B_r \\ 0, & |f| > B_r \end{cases} \tag{A12}$$

where ψ_0 is a constant and B_r denotes the bandwidth of the fading process. If B_r is much less than the bit rate, we have slow fading, and B_r much larger than the bit rate corresponds to fast fading. The correlation function of the fading process is given by the transform relation

$$R_\xi(\tau) = \int_{-B_r}^{B_r} \frac{\psi_0}{2} \cos(2\pi f\tau)\, df \tag{A13}$$

making the change of variables $f = B_r \nu$ allows (A13) to be written as

$$R_\xi(\tau) = \frac{\psi_0 B_r}{2} \int_{-1}^{1} \cos(2\pi B_r \nu \tau)\, d\nu. \tag{A14}$$

Let (r_k, ν_k) be a $2K + 1$ point Gauss quadrature rule (GQR) with respect to the unit weighting function $[-1, 1]$. A good approximation to the integral in (A14) which improves with increasing K is given by GQR methods as

$$R_\xi(\tau) \cong \frac{\psi_0 B_r}{2} \sum_{k=-K}^{K} r_k \cos(2\pi B_r \nu_k \tau). \tag{A15}$$

Define

$$R_k \triangleq \frac{\psi_0 B_r r_k}{2} \tag{A16}$$

and

$$\lambda_k \triangleq 2\pi B_r \nu_k. \tag{A17}$$

Then (A15) takes the form

$$R_\xi(\tau) \cong \sum_{k=-K}^{K} R_k \cos(\lambda_k \tau). \tag{A18}$$

A convenient symmetry of a GQR with respect to $[-1, 1]$ is that for each pair (r_k, ν_k) in the rule, the pair $(r_k, -\nu_k)$ is also in the rule. Thus an exactly equivalent representation of (A18) is

$$R_\xi(\tau) \cong \sum_{k=-K}^{K} R_k e^{j\lambda_k \tau}. \tag{A19}$$

Comparison of (A19) with (A1), (A2) reveals that when the $\{R_k, \lambda_k\}$ are determined via the GQR procedures just described, the process $R_a(t)$ will be a good representation for the fading process $\xi(t)$ if K is sufficiently large. The nature of the approximation given in (A19) is such that it compares well with the actual correlation function with only a few terms if τ is small. The memory of the system under analysis thus dictates the number of terms required for a useful representation.

Ratio of Signal Power to Multipath Power

Recall that the direct signal is related to its complex envelope by

$$s_d(t) = \text{Re}\,\{\tilde{s}_d(t)e^{j\omega_c t}\}.$$

The power in $s_d(t)$ is related to that of its complex envelope by

$$P_d = E\{s_d{}^2(t)\} = \tfrac{1}{2} E\{|\tilde{s}_d(t)|^2\}. \tag{A20}$$

In a similar way, the reflected signal may be written as

$$s_r(t) = \text{Re}\,\{\xi(t)e^{-j[(\omega_c + \omega_d)t_d - \omega_d t]}\tilde{s}_d(t-t_d)e^{j\omega_c t}\}. \tag{A21}$$

The power in the reflected signal is readily determined by making use of the fact that the signaling process is stationary and independent of the fading process. One obtains

$$P_r = E\{s_r{}^2(t)\} = \tfrac{1}{2}E\{|\xi(t)|^2\}E\{|\tilde{s}_d(t)|^2\} \tag{A22}$$

or

$$P_r = \tfrac{1}{2} R_\xi(0)E\{|\tilde{s}_d(t)|^2\}. \tag{A23}$$

Since $R_\xi(0) = \psi_0 B_r$, comparing (A23) with (A20) yields the useful result

$$\frac{P_d}{P_r} = \frac{1}{R_\xi(0)} = \frac{1}{\psi_0 B_r}. \tag{A24}$$

In carrying out a series of calculations, one generally begins by specifying the ratio P_d/P_r and the bandwidth of the fading process B_r. This information together with the tabulated GQR is sufficient to determine the required variances R_k and frequencies λ_k. Taking (A16) together with (A24) leads to

$$R_k = \frac{r_k}{2(P_d/P_r)} \tag{A25}$$

where R_k is the variance of the complex Gaussian b_k. Since the real and imaginary parts of b_k are independent with equal variances, it follows that

$$E\{b_{k_r}{}^2\} = E\{b_{k_i}{}^2\} = \frac{r_k}{4(P_d/P_r)}, \tag{A26}$$

a result required in the preceeding error rate calculation.

REFERENCES

[1] S. Y. Kwon and N. M. Shehadeh, "Noncoherent detection of FSK signals in the presence of multipath fading," *IEEE Trans. Commun.*, vol. COM-26, no. 1, pp. 164–168, Jan. 1978.

[2] H. H. Ma, N. M. Shehadeh, and J. C. Vanelli, "Effects of intersymbol interference on a Rayleigh fast-fading channel," *IEEE Trans. Commun.*, vol. COM-28, no. 1, pp. 128–131, Jan. 1980.

[3] M. T. Ma, M. Nesenbergs, and R. H. Ott, "Performance estimate for coherent PSK with random intersymbol interference due to time-varying scatter," *Conf. Rec. 1973 IEEE Int. Conf. Communications*, vol. 2, no. 43, New York, June 11–13.

[4] R. H. Ott, M. C. Thompson, Jr., E. J. Violette, and K. C. Allen, "Experimental and theoretical assessment of multipath effects and on QPSK," *IEEE Trans. Commun.*, vol. COM-26, no. 10, pp. 1475–1477, Oct. 1978.

[5] R. C. French, "Error rate predictions and measurements in the mobile radio data channel," *IEEE Trans. Veh. Technol.*, vol. VT-27, no. 3, pp. 110–116, Aug. 1978.

[6] M. Schwartz, W. R. Bennett, and S. Stein, *Communication Systems and Techniques*. New York: McGraw-Hill, 1966.

[7] A. M. Yagolm, *Stationary Random Functions*, translated by R. A. Silverman, Englewood Cliffs, NJ: Prentice-Hall, 1962.

Transmission of Digital Data over a Rayleigh Fading Channel

M. R. KARIM, MEMBER, IEEE

Abstract—**In a microwave mobile telecommunications system, a digital message must be transmitted several times to overcome the effects of Rayleigh fades that characterize this channel, and thus ensure a high probability that the message is received error-free. Obviously, there are many different transmission schemes that may be suitable for this channel. We present an analytic approach to an evaluation of their comparative performance in terms of the probability of a transmission failure, and provide a basis for the design of an efficient scheme. In the first part, we present some fade statistics that have been used in our analysis. Next, we derive upper bounds on the probability of the transmission failure for three different schemes. The actual failure rates as determined in an experimental simulation are then shown for those schemes that our theoretical study predicts to be acceptable. It is shown that an efficient scheme for the Rayleigh fading channel is the block-protected one in which a message is transmitted four times, each transmission 4-ms long and spaced 4-ms apart. The spacing is obtained by interleaving a similar transmission of another message. The receiver discards a transmission if it fails the parity checks.**

INTRODUCTION

IT IS WELL-KNOWN that the FM signal strength received at the antenna of a moving vehicle in a microwave mobile telecommunication system varies randomly with a Rayleigh distribution [4]. When the signal falls below its statistical mean, a fade occurs that causes any digital data transmitted over the carrier to be corrupted with a noise burst. The length of these bursts depends, of course, on the duration of the fade, which in turn is a function of the fade level, the vehicle speed, and the frequency of the carrier. As the vehicle speed decreases, the average fade duration for the same fade level increases. Thus, at smaller vehicle speeds, even though the fades and hence the error bursts occur less frequently, the effect on the data transmission would be more deleterious [5]. For instance, at 850 MHz and at 12 mph, the signal goes into a −15 dB fade at the rate of approximately six times a second. The probability that the duration of this fade is at least 8 ms is about 0.2. Thus, assuming a 10-kHz data rate, a block of 80 or more bits of data would be corrupted with noise once every 160 ms with a probability of 0.2 when the vehicle speed is 12 mi/h and the noise level is 15 dB below the mean value of the signal. In fact, the severity of these fades makes it virtually impossible to use such simple schemes as automatic request for retransmission.

Various schemes for data transmission through an atmospheric burst error channel have been suggested by Jayant [1], [2] in terms of the time statistics of the error bursts. An error control technique for data communication through a burst-error channel is described by Horstein in [3]. Obviously, there are many other transmission schemes that can be considered for this Rayleigh fading channel. In this paper, we present a technique for evaluating their comparative performance in terms of their failure rates, and provide a basis for the design of an effective transmission scheme. More specifically, for every scheme studied, we derive an upper bound on the probability of transmission failure in terms of the fade statistics. The analysis shows that the bound is a function of the duration of a complete message sequence, the number of transmissions of the message and the spacing, if any, between successive transmissions, which can then be chosen to minimize the failure rate. Although these bounds are generally much higher than the actual failure rates, as we shall see later in this paper, they furnish an important theoretical basis for comparing the different schemes.

The organization of the paper is as follows. In the first part, we present some fade statistics that have been used in the subsequent analysis. Since no theoretical expressions for them are known to exist in the literature, they have been determined by experimentation. In the second part of the paper, we derive the upper bounds on the probability of transmission failure for a few different schemes. Finally, the actual failure rates as determined in an experimental simulation are shown for those schemes that our theoretical studies predict to be acceptable.

ALGEBRAIC CODES FOR ENCODING DIGITAL MESSAGES

All messages should be encoded in some error-correcting codes so that the receiver can determine if a particular message block has been corrupted with noise bursts. Bose–Chaudhuri–Hocquenghen (BCH) codes [7] seem to be attractive, because owing to their cyclic nature, they can be rather simply implemented at both ends of the channel. Moreover, if we decide only to detect the errors but not correct them, then by choosing the proper length of the code, it is possible to detect at least one error with a high probability. In our analysis, we assume that errors are detected only without attempting to make any correction.

TIME STATISTICS USED IN THE ANALYSIS

The number of fades in any interval or the sum of the widths of fades that appear in a given interval is a random variable. A knowledge of their distributions is necessary for

Manuscript received May 6, 1981; revised August 20, 1981.
The author is with Bell Laboratories, Inc., 1 Whippany Road, Whippany, NJ 07981.

Reprinted from *IEEE Trans. Veh. Technol.*, vol. VT-31, pp. 1–6, Feb. 1982.

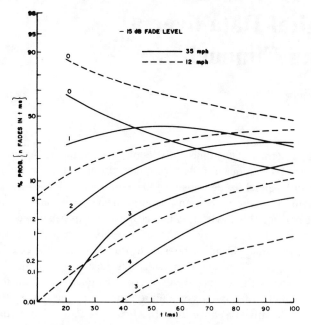

Fig. 1. Distribution of the number of fades occurring in a time window of width t for a Rayleigh fading channel.

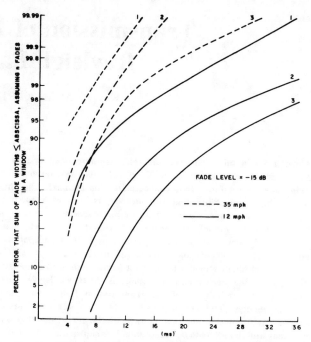

Fig. 2. Conditional distribution of the sum of fade widths assuming that n fades occur in a time window t-ms wide.

our analysis. Since their exact theoretical expressions do not exist in the literature [5], they have been obtained by experimentation using a Rayleigh fading simulator [9] and a computer. All fades considered here are 15 dB or more below the statistical mean of the carrier envelope. The reason for restricting our study to such fades stems from the fact that an acceptable microwave mobile telecommunications service requires the long-term radio frequency (RF) signal-to-noise ratio to be 15 dB. Thus, fades of less than 15 dB have minimal influence on error rates. Fig. 1 shows the probability $P(n)$ that there are n fades in an interval t as a function of t for $n = 0, \cdots, 4$ and for two different vehicle speeds. Notice that although we have avoided using explicitly such random variables as the interfade interval or the fade repetition period, their statistics are implicit in $P(n)$.

Fig. 2 is a plot of the probability distribution function of the sum w_n of the fade widths assuming that n fades have occurred in any time slot. In the figure, three values of n and two vehicle speeds have been used. Thus, the dashed curve marked 1 in Fig. 2 gives the conditional probability that at 35 mi/h the fade width exceeds the abscissa assuming that only one fade occurs in any time window. Similarly, at 12 mi/h, the conditional probability that the sum of the fade widths exceeds the abscissa assuming two fades in a time window is shown by the solid curve marked 2. It should be noted that these conditional distributions do not depend on the width of the window in which n fades have occurred. In the determination of these fade statistics, a large number of contiguous time windows, all of the same width, are considered. As we start timing each of these windows, we also monitor the RF signal. The width of a fade in any window is then measured from the instant it is encountered in that window, as indicated by the signal being at least 15 dB below the average value, even though it may already have started in a preceding window.

ANALYSIS OF FAILURE RATES

Many different transmission schemes can be devised for the Rayleigh fading channel. For any scheme, the probability P_e of the transmission failure is given by the expression

$$P_e = \sum_{n=1}^{\infty} P(n) \times \Pr \left\{ \begin{array}{c} \text{failure of the} \\ \text{scheme assuming } n \text{ fades} \end{array} \right\},$$

where, as before, $P(n)$ is the probability that there are n fades in the interval that a complete message sequence occupies. We intend to use an approximation to this relation, and derive an upper bound on the probability of transmission failure for a few schemes that seem to be attractive for our fading channel. The schemes that we will consider involve transmitting a message four or five times without any feedback from the receiver. Furthermore, we will assume that for a scheme to be practically feasible, each transmission should be around 2-12 ms long. Since the mean velocity of a vehicle in a typical urban area for mobile communications is about 11 mph [8], we will derive the bounds at 12 mi/h which is the lowest of the velocities that can be simulated on our Rayleigh fading simulator. At this velocity, if the complete message sequence consists of five transmissions, and extends over an interval of 80 ms, then from Fig. 1 we have $P(1) = 0.37$, $P(2) = 0.07$ and $P(3) = 0.0036$. Since $P(3)$ is very small compared to $P(2)$, one can ignore the terms in (1) containing $P(3)$, $P(4)$, etc., and approximate P_e by

$$P_e \approx P(1) \Pr \{\text{failure of the scheme assuming one fade}\}$$
$$+ P(2) \Pr \{\text{failure of the scheme assuming two fades}\}. \quad (1)$$

Notice that the less the duration of the complete message

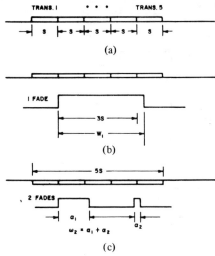

Fig. 3. Digital data transmission Scheme 1 and its failure mechanism due to one or two fades. (a) Scheme involving five transmissions. (b) Orientation of the single fade of width w_1 with respect to the message transmissions causing all five of them to be in the fade. (c) Two fades, one of width α_1 and the other α_2, are oriented with respect to the five transmissions such that all five of them are in fades. Here, w_2 is the sum of the fade widths assuming that there are two fades in the time window $5s$. In this case, the scheme fails only if $w_2 > s$.

sequence, the better this approximation. For example, if the entire message sequence occupies only 20 ms, $P(1) = 0.125$, $P(2) = 0.00075$, and $P(3) \approx 0$. Thus, our approximation (1) is valid if the vehicle speed is 12 mi/h, and the duration of the complete message sequence does not exceed about 80 ms. Using this relation we now proceed to derive the bounds on the probability of the transmission failure for the following schemes.

SCHEME 1

Here, each message block of length s is repeated five times consecutively. As each transmission of the message is received, the decoder at the receiving end examines the message for errors. If any errors are detected, the receiver discards that transmission and waits for the next one.

Fig. 3(a) shows the five transmissions of a message, each s ms long, the complete message thus occupying $5s$ ms. Following the reasoning stated before, we assume $5s$ to be such that the probability for more than two fades to occur in $5s$ is negligibly small. Thus, assuming that there is only one fade in $5s$ and that w_1 is the width of that fade, a necessary condition that all five transmissions of the message are corrupted with that fade is that $w_1 > 3s$. In that case, the fade must be oriented with respect to the five transmissions as in Fig. 3(b).

If, on the other hand, there are two fades in $5s$, the transmission scheme can fail only if $w_2 > s$, where w_2 is the sum of the fade-widths assuming that there are two fades in $5s$. If w_2 were equal to s and yet all five transmissions were corrupted with the two fades, then the latter must be oriented with respect to the message transmissions as in Fig. 3(c). Clearly, the contrived situation depicted in that figure is an extreme case, useful only for deriving an upper bound, and not the exact error rates. Thus, the probability that none of the

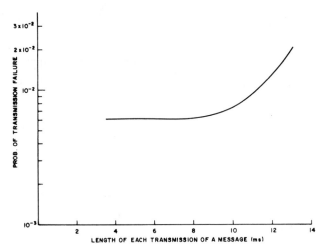

Fig. 4. Computed bounds on the probability of the transmission failure of Scheme 1 at 12 mi/h and -15 dB fade, as a function of the length of each transmission of a message.

five transmissions is received error-free as a result of either one or two fades in $5s$ is bounded by

$$P_e \leq P(1)\,\text{Pr}\,\{w_1 > 3s\} + P(2)\,\text{Pr}\,\{w_2 > s\}, \qquad (2)$$

where w_1 and w_2 have the meanings as stated before, and $P(1)$ and $P(2)$ are the probabilities that there are, respectively, one and two fades in $5s$. For any value of s, P_e can be computed numerically using the graphs of Figs. 1 and 2. It is then possible to minimize P_e by varying s. The computed values of P_e for five transmissions are plotted in Fig. 4 for a few values of s. The velocity, as stated before, is 12 mi/h.

SCHEME 2

The reason for the unacceptably high failure rate of Scheme 1 lies in the fact that at 12 mi/h there is a high probability that a single fade will be wide enough to corrupt all transmissions. Since the average fade duration at this vehicle speed is comparable to any reasonable value of s, and even larger at lower speeds, one way to guarantee that at least one transmission is received error-free is to increase the number of transmissions at the cost of reducing the system throughput. Alternately, one can lengthen each transmission, but then at high data rates, it may not be possible to do so from the viewpoint of the system implementation. An equivalent approach to counteract the effect of long fades is to provide a space between any two adjacent transmissions and then insert one or more different messages in those spaces. The receiver examines each transmission in exactly the same way as before.

The scheme, depicted in Fig. 5(a), uses four transmissions of a message, each s ms long and separated s' ms by similar transmissions of another message or messages. For practical purposes, $s' \geq s$.

Each message now extends over an interval $(4s + 3s')$. Assuming that there is only one fade in this interval, it can affect all transmissions only if $w_1 > (2s + 3s')$ as shown in Fig. 5(b).

Fig. 5(c) illustrates how two fades in the interval $4s + 3s'$ can corrupt all four transmissions of a message. Here for the

237

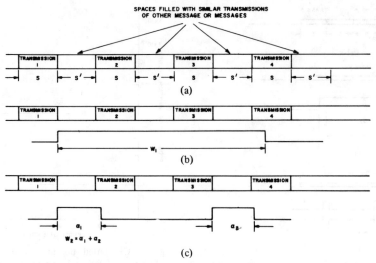

Fig. 5. Block-protected Scheme 2 and the failure mechanism due to one or two fades. (a) The scheme involving four transmissions with spacing s' between adjacent ones. Each s' is filled with another message or messages. (b) A single fade of width w_1 is so oriented with respect to the four transmissions that all of them are affected. Here $w_1 > (2s + 3s')$. (c) Two fades, one of width α_1 and the other of width α_2, are so oriented as to corrupt all four transmissions. Here, for the scheme to fail, the sum w_2 of the widths of the two fades must exceed $2s'$.

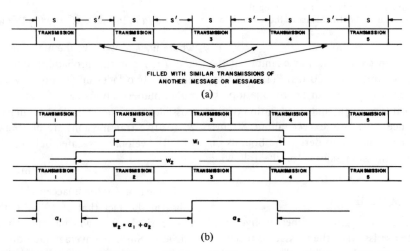

Fig. 6. Bit-protected Scheme 3 and its failure mechanism. (a) Scheme involving five transmissions. Here, each transmission is s-ms long and spaced s'-ms apart. The receiver takes a three-out-of-five majority vote on a bit-by-bit basis. (b) Single fade of width w_1 such that $w_1 > 2(s + s')$ or $w_1 > (3s' + 2s)$ is so oriented as to cause the transmission failure. Since we are only concerned with an upper bound, we take $w_1 > 2(s + s')$ for the scheme to fail. (c) There are now two fades in $(4s' + 5s)$ oriented such that the scheme fails. Here again the scheme may fail only if $w_2 > 2s + s'$ or $w_2 > 2s' + s$. Thus, for the upper bound to be valid, $w_2 > \min (2s + s', 2s' + s)$.

scheme to fail, the sum w_2 of the two fades must exceed $2s'$. Thus, the probability that none of the four transmissions will be received error-free is

$$P_e \leqslant P(1) \Pr \{w_1 > (2s + 3s')\} + P(2) \Pr \{w_2 > 2s\}, \quad (3)$$

where w_1 and w_2 have the same meanings as in (1). Using Figs. 1 and 2 for $P(1)$, $P(2)$ and the conditional probability distribution, P_e is computed as a function of s' for two different values of s and shown in Fig. 7.

SCHEME 3

This scheme employs five transmissions of an encoded message interleaved with an equal number of transmissions of another message. After receiving all five transmissions, the receiver takes a majority vote on a bit-by-bit basis. In other words, the receiver interprets a bit to be zero if the corresponding bit in three or more transmissions is zero; otherwise, it takes the bit to be one.

Fig. 6(a) shows this scheme. Proceeding in exactly the same manner as before, one can show that the probability that the scheme will fail as a result of one or two fades is bounded by

$$P_e \leqslant P(1) \Pr \{w_1 > 2(s + s')\} + P(2) \Pr \{w_2 > (2s + s')\}. \quad (4)$$

The computed values of P_e are shown in Fig. 7 as a function of s' for two values of s.

DISCUSSION OF THE BOUNDS DERIVED

Some general conclusions can be drawn from the computed bounds shown in Figs. 4 and 7. In Scheme 1 using five contiguous transmissions of a message, the upper bound on the

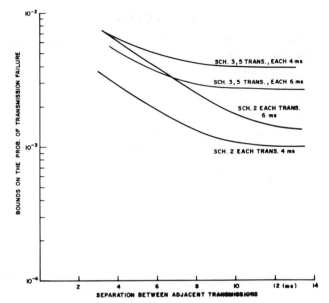

Fig. 7. Computed bounds on the probability of a transmission failure of Schemes 2 and 3 as a function of separation between any two successive transmission.

probability of transmission failure remains virtually constant as s is increased from 4 ms to 8 ms and then increases for higher values of s. The reason is that as s increases, the failure rate due to a single fade decreases, but at the same time, the probability of two fades occurring increases rather rapidly, thereby offsetting any gains due to an increased s. Since the larger value of s reduces the system throughput, a reasonable value is 4 ms for this scheme.

Scheme 3, on the other hand, exhibits a diminishing failure rate with increasing spacing s' between successive transmissions until it is 12 ms. If the length of each transmission of a message is increased from 4 ms to 6 ms, the failure rate seems to improve. Thus, in this scheme, a good choice seems to be $s = 6$ ms, with a spacing of 12 ms between successive transmissions. It should be observed, however, that a larger value of s requires a larger memory at the receiving end. Moreover, the implementation of this scheme is rather complex. Comparing Schemes 1 and 3, the probability of the transmission failure for Scheme 3 is lower than that for Scheme 1 even at such slow vehicle speeds as 12 mi/h, and also results in a much higher system throughput by allowing the intervening spaces between the adjacent transmissions to be filled with similar transmissions of another message. Thus, at the expense of implemental complexity, Scheme 3 seems to be more attractive than Scheme 1.

Comparing all three schemes together, Scheme 2 is the best. It not only retains the simplicity of implementation of Scheme 1, but also leads to a higher system throughput than either of the other two by requiring only four transmissions instead of five. Here, the failure rate decreases as the spacing s' between successive transmissions is increased until $s' = 12$ ms. Beyond this value of s', the error rate increases. If the length s of each transmission is increased from 4 ms to 6 ms, the error rate increases. Thus $s = 4$ ms seems to be an optimum choice of the message length. Although the error rate for $s' = 4$ ms is not as good as for $s' = 8$ or 12 ms, practical considerations dictate a choice of $s' = 4$ ms when $s = 4$ ms, that even though not quite optimal gives much better results than Scheme 1 or 3. Notice that Schemes 2 and 3 provide almost identical word error rates if each transmission is 6-ms long and spaced 6-ms apart. Keeping the same value of s, larger spacings result in a much better error rate for Scheme 2 then for Scheme 3. If $s' < 6$ ms, Scheme 3 is better, but then with $s = 6$ ms, $s' < 6$ ms is not a practically feasible scheme.

The analysis presented here remains valid for velocities less than 12 mi/h where the effects of the Rayleigh fades are more serious. In such cases, it is sufficient to consider only one fade. Obviously, at lower speeds Scheme 2 is much better than Scheme 3, since it requires only one transmission to be error-free.

MEASURED WORD ERROR RATE

From the previous considerations, it is obvious that Schemes 2 and 3 are attractive for a fading channel with characteristics of Figs. 1 and 2. In view of this, the actual error rates for these two schemes were measured in the laboratory for different values of the spacing between successive transmissions of a message, keeping the length of each transmission 4 ms and at different velocities. These are shown in Fig. 8.

To see how good our bounds are, we will compare Fig. 7 with the measured error rates of Fig. 8 valid for 12 mph. It should be noticed that for the bit-protected Scheme 3, involving 5 transmissions, each 4 ms long, the computed bounds are not much higher than the actual error rates for 4-12 ms of intertransmission spacing s'. For example, with $s' = 4$ ms, the bound for this scheme is 6.4×10^{-3} whereas the actual failure rate at 12 mph is 6.2×10^{-3}. For $s' = 8$ ms, the bound is 4.2×10^{-3} as against 3.3×10^{-3} for the actual error rate. Thus, for this scheme, the bound seems to be rather tight.

For Scheme 2 involving four transmissions, each 4 ms long, the difference between the upper bound and the actual failure rate is not so great for relatively smaller values of s'. For instance, with $s' = 4$ ms, the upper bound is 2.6×10^{-3} whereas the actual failure rate is 1.4×10^{-3}. However, as the spacing increases, the relative difference between them continues to increase. For example, if $s' = 8$ ms, they are respectively 1.6×10^{-3} and 4.7×10^{-4} at 12 mi/h.

Referring again to Fig. 8, we notice that Scheme 2, as predicted in our analysis, provides much better error rates for all values of s' and at all velocities ranging from 12 mi/h to 55 mi/h. Notice that with $s = 4$ ms and $s' = 4$ ms, the error rate in Scheme 3 decreases as the velocity increases from 12 mi/h to 20 mi/h to 35 mi/h. The reason is that at a low vehicle speed, there is a high probability of the occurrence of a single fade corrupting three or more transmissions. Thus, taking a three-out-of-five majority vote on the received data does not help at low vehicle speeds. However, as the speed increases, the average width of a fade decreases thereby reducing the failure rate. For Scheme 2, on the other hand, the error rate first decreases and then increases as the speed is increased from 25 mi/h to 55 mi/h, but always remains significantly lower than for Scheme 3. Although not shown in the figure, at speeds as high as 100 mi/h, the error rate for Scheme 2 is also lower.

239

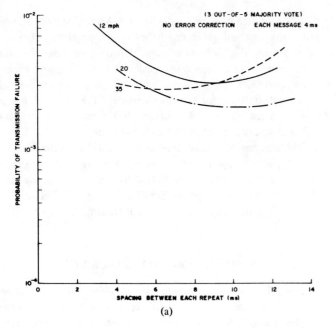

(a)

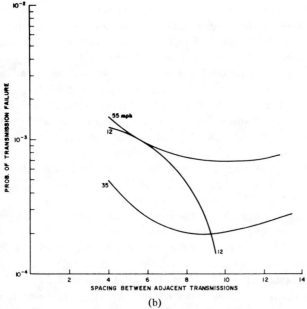

(b)

Fig. 8. Measured probability of the transmission failure of Schemes 2 and 3 as a function of the spacing between two successive transmissions with the vehicle speed as a parameter. (a) Scheme 3 involving five transmissions. The receiver interprets a bit to be one or zero based on a three-out-of-five majority vote. (b) Scheme 2 involving four transmissions. In both cases, each transmission is 4-ms long. No error correction has been used. The fade level is −15 dB.

CONCLUSION

We have presented a technique for comparing different schemes for transmitting digital data over a fading channel. Our study shows that of all the schemes considered, Scheme 2 involving four transmissions of a message, each 4-ms long and spaced 4-ms apart by similar transmissions of another message, provides the lowest probability of the transmission failure and at the same time leads to the highest system throughput. Moreover, this scheme is also much simpler to implement at the receiver end than Scheme 3.

ACKNOWLEDGMENT

The author wishes to thank W. C. Y. Lee for his many valuable suggestions throughout this research and careful reviews of the paper. Many of the ideas described here evolved during hours of discussions with him. Grateful thanks are also due to N. S. Jayant for his many suggestions and constructive criticisms to which the paper owes its general form.

REFERENCES

[1] N. S. Jayant, "Data communication through the atmospheric burst error channel," *IEEE Trans. Commun. Technol.*, vol. COM-15, pp. 383–389, June 1967.

[2] ——, "An erasure scheme for atmospheric noise burst interference," *Proc. IEEE*, (Letters), pp. 1943–1944, vol. 54, Dec. 1966.

[3] M. Horstein, "Efficient communication through burst error channels by means of error detection," *IEEE Trans. Commun. Technol.*, vol. COM-14, pp. 117–126, Apr. 1966.

[4] W. C. Jakes, Jr., Ed., *Microwave Mobile Communications*. New York: Wiley, 1974.

[5] G. A. Arredondo and J. I. Smith, "Voice and data transmission in a mobile radio channel," *IEEE Trans. Veh. Technol.*, vol. VT-26, pp. 88–93, Feb. 1977.

[6] V. Hackenburg, B. D. Holm, and J. I. Smith, "Data signaling functions for a cellular mobile telephone system," *IEEE Trans. Veh. Technol.*, vol. VT-26, pp. 82–88, Feb. 1977.

[7] S. Lin, *An Introduction to Error-Correcting Codes*. Englewood Cliffs, NJ: Prentice Hall, 1970, chs. 4 and 6.

[8] A. Plitkins, private communication.

[9] G. A. Arredondo, W. H. Chriss, and E. H. Walker, "A multipath fading simulator for mobile radio," *IEEE Trans. Commun.*, vol. COM-21, pp. 1325–1328, Nov. 1973.

Part III
Mobile Communications Above 800 MHz

800-MHz Band Land Mobile Telephone
System—Overall View

SADAO ITO AND YASUSHI MATSUZAKA

Abstract—The 800-MHz band land mobile telephone system which is going into service in Tokyo and other major cities is described. This system is characterized by 1) an ordered array of cells which allows each radio channel to be reused by spacing at an appropriate coordination distance in a wide service area (cellular system), 2) development of a new higher frequency band, and 3) a fully automatic exchange system integrated with the ordinary telephone network. Field tests have been carried out in the Tokyo metropolitan area since 1975 and have now been brought to a successful completion.

I. INTRODUCTION

DEVELOPMENT research on a 400-MHz band land mobile radio telephone system was completed by ECL in 1967 for service in the metropolitan areas and in the surrounding cities. However, this sytem was considered to be too small in its capacity to accommodate customers who request subscription to this system because of a shortage of radio channels. Therefore, this system has been used only for emergency communication.

In Japan, with some 30 million vehicles registered, mobile radio telephone systems for the public have not been put into commercial use as yet, even though demands for the ability to make telephone calls while moving are strong.

In order to cope with the increased latent demand for mobile telephone services and to realize a nation-wide system in the near future, a new system with a capacity of up to about ten times greater than that of the above system, and with a wide area service facility has been studied since 1967.

The aims of this study are

1) to establish an automatic exchange technique for nation-wide mobile services;
2) to increase the system capacity, namely, the total number and area density of subscribers accommodated in the service;
3) to develop a new higher frequency band;
4) efficient utilization of radio frequency spectrum by

   a) an appropriate regional arrangement of base radio stations with a rather small area of coverage (radio zones) and reuse of the same radio frequency with approprite coordination distance,
   b) an increase in the number of channels commonly used by each mobile station in a radio zone, and
   c) narrowed occupation bandwidth of radio channels.

Manuscript received June 7, 1978. Reprinted with permission from the *Review of the Electrical Communication Laboratories*, vol. 25, nos. 11-12, November-December, 1977.

The authors are with Nippon Telegraph and Telephone Public Corporation, 1-2356, Take, Yokosuka-shi, Kanagawa-ken 238-03, Japan.

II. BASIC TECHNIQUES FOR MOBILE RADIO TELEPHONE SYSTEM

A. Basic Composition of Mobile Communication Network

A land mobile radio telephone network integrated with the ordinary fixed telephone network is shown in Fig. 1. In general, to cover a widespread service area, the service area is divided into small radio zones. Each radio zone has a mobile base station (MBS) which can communicate with mobile units (MU) within the zone. A set of radio channels is assigned to each MBS.

In order to carry out various control and switching functions, some MBS's are accommodated in a mobile control station (MCS) and a mobile telephone switching center (MTC). These control centers correspond to a toll center (TC) in an ordinary telephone network. The operation of the mobile communication network is described later.

B. Radio Propagation

In mobile radio communication, propagation paths are time varying because of the motion of mobile stations. Especially in land mobile radios, the received signal is attenuated and severely fluctuated by effects of terrain and environmental clutter.

To clarify the propagation characteristics and to establish the design practice for land mobile radio systems, detailed propagation tests were carried out in the frequency band ranging from VHF (200 MHz) to UHF (453, 922, 1310, 1430, and 1920 MHz) on 14 mobile test routes around the city of Tokyo, for a wide variety of natural terrain and environmental clutter [1].

The analyses have led to a practical method of predicting field strengths using a set of charts. The method covers a frequency range of 150-2000 MHz, propagation path lengths of 1-100 km, and base station antenna heights of 30-1000 m. In this method, the field strength on an arbitrary radio path can be estimated by making corrections on the reference median value, which is the median value on a quasi-smooth urban terrain. Correction factors for terrain and clutter effects are obtained from charts. The margin for an arbitrary location probability can be determined by the use of simple charts. The estimated results are in good agreement with measured values.

In conducting this research, a number of mobile observation cars were used to measure electric field intensities received over a widespread area, including both urban and rural districts. The research is continuing, and the efficiency has been raised by mounting data processors on observation vehicles. For mobile communication experiments, a bus has been remodeled for measurements even while mobile. This

Reprinted from *IEEE Trans. Veh. Technol.*, vol. VT-27, pp. 205–211, Nov. 1978.

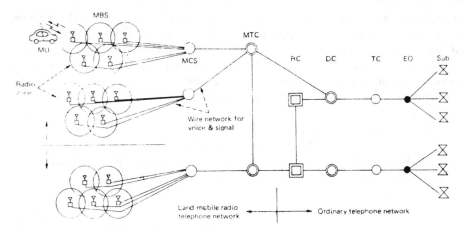

Fig. 1.   Land mobile communication network configuration.

Fig. 2.   Test vehicle.

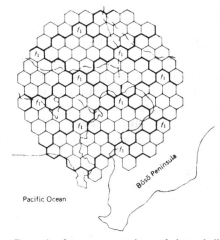

Fig. 3.   Example of zone construction and channel allocation
(12 primary group zones).

bus is equipped with an ac 100-V 6kVA power generator, a radio transmitter, and other measuring instruments, as well as a rack housing an electonic computer. This vehicle also admits seven people for conducting experiments. (Fig. 2).

The electronic computer mounted in this bus has a 16-kW memory capacity and withstands vibrations and shocks when mobile. The computer can perform complicated and versatile data analysis as well as statistical processing, including fluctuations in electrical fields, S/N information, and signal reliability, with the results displayed in the form of charts and graphs. These experimental results have offered good guidance toward the developing system in the 800-MHz band.

C. Efficient Radio Frequency Spectrum Utilization

The following techniques have been studied for efficient radio frequency spectrum utilization to accommodate as many mobile radio subscribers as possible in the given bandwidth: 1) arrangement of base radio stations to produce the appropriate radio zone size and repetitive use of radio channels; 2) increase in the number of radio channels commonly used in each radio zone; and 3) narrow radio channel occupation bandwidth.

1) Radio Zone Planning and Radio Channel Assignment: The basic question of radio zone arrangement has been studied for a model of uniform terrain features and traffic density [2]. To cover a broad service area, the entire area is divided into a lattice of hexagonal zones, as shown in Fig. 3. A number of radio channels are assigned to each zone.

For efficient use of the limited spectrum, the same radio channels are repetitively used, taking cochannel interference into account, to change the desired-to-undesired signal ratio (D/U). Fig. 4 shows that the required number of radio channels decreases with decreasing zone radius for a given number of

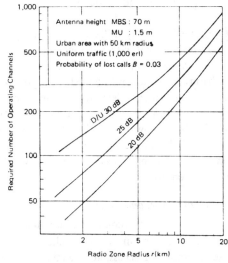

Fig. 4.   Example showing relation between required number of operating channels and radio zone radius.

subscribers. However, it should be noted that the advantage of a small-zone structure may be reduced by nonuniformity of terrain condition and traffic density within a service area.

2) Multichannel Tuning in Mobile Units: The frequency spectrum utilization efficiency is increased if a mobile unit can access any idle radio channel out of a large number of radio channels assigned to the radio zone in question and if these channels can be commonly used by a large group of mobile units. For this purpose, it is necessary for a mobile unit to be capable of tuning to any of the assigned radio channels.

The number of subscribers accommodated in a radio zone for a specified probability of lost calls may be given by Erlang's formula as a function of the number of usable radio channels. The customer handling capacity increases rapidly as the number of usable channels increases. To accommodate large numbers of subscribers in a service area with high traffic density, more than 500 channels would be necessary in a mobile unit. For example, an estimate shows that about 1000 channels are necessary in the Tokyo area. This large number of channels necessitates the use of a radio frequency synthesizer using digital techniques.

3) Modulation System: A theoretical study of interference characteristics was made for various types of modulation, such as FM, PM, AM, and SSB. The result was confirmed experimentally [3]. By combining this result with distant station interference statistics derived from propagation characteristics, the cochannel station separation has been determined.

From these values, the modulation systems were compared from the frequency utilization viewpoint. For example, the frequency utility of an SSB system with a channel separation of 5-kHz is estimated to be about twice that of a narrow-band PM with 25-kHz separation. This improvement is less than that expected from the narrow occupation bandwidth because the necessary number of repetitive zones is largely due to a higher D/U requirement. Hence, the number of accessible channels for mobile units should be increased for the SSB system. In addition, an application of the SSB system in higher frequency bands causes such difficulties as an increase in transmitting power, complicated modulator-demodulator circuits, and degradation of the regenerated carrier due to multipath propagation.

Considering the frequency utilization and the present state of the art, narrow-band PM with a channel separation of about 25 kHz seems the most appropriate. To keep the PM system occupation bandwidth narrow, high stability of the master crystal oscillator and high selectivity of the receiver are required. An opinion test has shown that an overall frequency tolerance of 5 kHz is allowable in PM systems with a channel separation of 25 kHz. Frequency stability of a master oscillator within 2 ppm has been accomplished at 800 MHz with temperature compensation.

D. Signaling, Controlling, and Switching System

1) Digital Signal Transmission Rate: Broad-area service and a small-zone structure require intricate channel controls, and the increased number of accessible channels in mobile equipment makes searching for an idle channel more difficult.

Taking into account the available transmission frequency bandwidth in mobile communication, the plausible digital signal transmission rate is of the order of several hundred bits/s, which may be sufficient to control several tens of voice channels in mobile telephony and to accommodate about 100 000 subscribers in digital radio paging.

2) Control Channel Reliability Improvement: Signal error in the mobile radio channel may result in loss of control and inability to establish a traffic (speech) channel between mobile

and base stations. Several methods are used to improve control and/or traffic channel reliability.

Methods which could improve control channel reliability are diversity, error correcting coding, repeated control signal transmission, and compelled techniques, e.g., recycle (ARQ) and repeat back techniques.

Another technique for control channel reliability improvement involves introducing the new control channel frequency allocation plan in a small cell system. There are two typical control channel frequency allocation methods. One is called the small control zone method. That is, different control channel frequencies may be allocated corresponding to the cell; each constituent cell of a repeating group for traffic channel is provided with different radio frequency control channels. The other method is called the multiple control zone method, which is adapted in the mobile system.

Control channel frequencies may be allocated based on the large cell system concept, but traffic channel frequencies are based on the small cell system concept. In a small cell system, it is advantageous to use the same base station, antenna, and equipment for control channels as well as for traffic channels. A few cells whose number is determined from the system design objectives are provided by the same radio frequency control channel. The same control signal is simultaneously transmitted through this same control channel from each base station. By adopting this technique, control signal transmission reliability within the cells will be improved because the radio signal will be received by a space diversity effect.

In the mobile radio telephone system, the above mentioned improvement methods have been adapted, and necessary reliability improvement has been made.

3) Location Registration and Switching: In the case of a system where the base station calls a mobile station using registered location information, a mobile or base station detects the change of calling zone, and the new location is registered. Location information is stored in the memory of a mobile telephone switching center to which the mobile station belongs. When a mobile station is called, the zone for selective calling is determined by read out of the memory. Hence, the switching control functions require the use of information in the memories of remote stations.

For a change in radio zones during a conversation, tracking exchange is needed. This is described later.

III. SYSTEM OUTLINE

A. Radio Frequency Band

The 800-MHz frequency band is planned to be used where a wide bandwidth necessary for a high capacity system seems to be obtainable. A 25-kHz frequency spacing is allocated between adjacent radio channels. System design objectives are shown in Table I.

B. Radio Channel and Zoning Plans

The service area is divided into many cells. A number of voice channels are assigned to each zone, corresponding to traffic densities. If cells are reduced in size, cochannel reuse distance can be proportionately smaller, and each channel can

TABLE I
SYSTEM DESIGN OBJECTIVES

	Item	800 MHz System
Communication System	Speech connection	Full duplex
	Speech quality	Articulation >80%
	Incompleted connection	3/100
	Exchange	Fully automatic direct pushbutton dialing
Radio System	Radio zone	Urban: Small (5 km radius) Rural: Large (10 km radius)
	Radio frequency	800 MHz band
	Number of subscribers	100,000
	Bandwidth	25 MHz × 2
	RF channel spacing	25 kHz
	Number of channels	500 CH × 2
	Number of mobile equipment accessible channels	About 500 CH (Digital frequency synthesizer)
	Modulation	Narrow band PM
	Frequency stability	2×10^{-6}
	Transmitter power	Base station 25 W Mobile station 5 W
Exchange and Control System	Tracking exchange	Speech channel switching initiated by S/N monitoring at base station
	Regional calling	Determined by location registration
	Signaling in radio section	Digital signaling in paging and access channel Digital & tone signaling in speech channel
	Selective calling	Waiting on a paging channel
	Speech channel selection	Assigned by MCS through an access channel

provide many voice paths in a service area. As described above, for any given spectrum allocation and service area, the system capacity may be increased by decreasing the size of each cell, but as cell size decreases, system costs increase. The optimum cell size in an urban area is about 5 km in radius, from the viewpoint of interrelated factors of frequency utilization, radio propagation, and equipment conditions at 800 MHz. The radius can be expanded to about 10 km in a rural area, according to propagation and traffic conditions. A 15-voice-channel set structure is required in order to avoid cochannel interference.

C. System Block Diagrams

Fig. 5 is a system block diagram. Calls to and from the ordinary telephone network are processed through the MTC, which also has an interface with the mobile and the base station control equipment at the MCS. The MTC switches calls between the trunks to the land line and the access lines to the MBS. The MCS controls the base stations equipment and sets up a radio channel between the mobile units and the MBS. The MBS includes not only the radio apparatus but also the logic circuit providing receiver and transmitter selection.

D. Control and Switching

Control channels are used to provide information needed for the various stages of call set up and control. The control channels are listed below.

1) Two-way paging channel to process land to mobile requests for service: This processing includes a locating step to determine in which cell the mobile is located, and a voice-channel assignment sequence to steer the mobile call on an idle voice channel.

2) Two-way access channel to process the random mobile to land requests for service: This processing includes a lock-out sequence to prevent double seizures, a locating step, and a voice-channel assignment sequence.

Four-channel channel-sets are required in order to achieve the same sort of channel reuse for these control channels as for the voice channels. In the control channel frequency allocation used, each cell in a calling are a consisting of 10-16 cells, is assigned under several hundred Hz offset in the same radio frequency. By adopting this strategy, highly reliable control signal transmission has been attained. The mobile unit automatically scans the set of paging channels and locks to the one which appears to have the greatest signal strength and is waiting for a selective calling signal. The small cell structure results in an increase in the probability of mobile units crossing a cell boundary. In this case, a new voice channel reassignment is necessary. Reassignment is accomplished as follows. The MBS detects S/N deterioration from the voice channel and requests the MCS for a tracking exchange. The MCS orders S/N checked by the supervisory receiver (SRx) for neighboring cells and the original one. The MCS selects a new cell and a new voice channel after comparing the signals from the MBS's and assigns a new channel to the mobile unit. It orders a switchover to the new access line between MTC and the new cell. To provide a nationwide service for a widely roaming mobile unit, it is necessary to memorize a mobile unit location at MTC (home memory office). Each MBS in the same calling area bears a unique identification (calling area sign) and broadcasts it along with the stream of paging data. Then, each mobile set holds it in memory. When a new identification is received, the mobile automatically registers in its home memory office the location information for the calling mobile unit.

The zone construction concept in the mobile telephone radio system is shown in Fig. 6.

IV. EQUIPMENT OUTLINE

A. Radio Base Station and Control Station Equipment

1) Base Station Antenna Arrangement: The base station antenna system is arranged so as to accommodate numerous radio channels at one base station. Two types of high gain omnidirectional antennas, such as a tower-top mounted

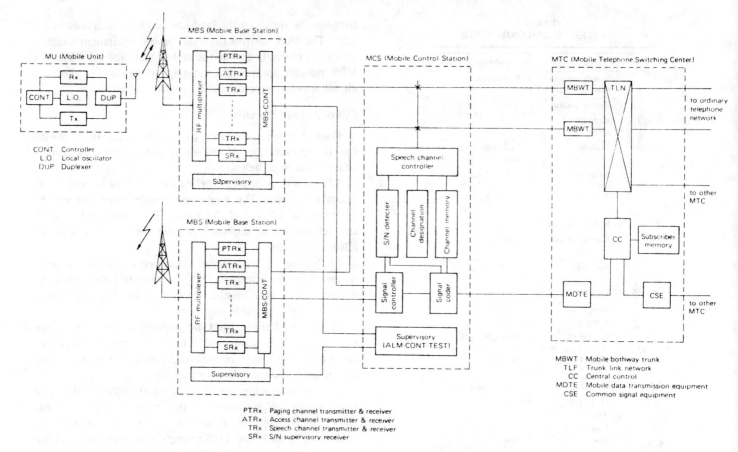

PTRx : Paging channel transmitter & receiver
ATRx : Access channel transmitter & receiver
TRx : Speech channel transmitter & receiver
SRx : S/N supervisory receiver

Fig. 5.   High-capacity land mobile radio telephone system network configuration.

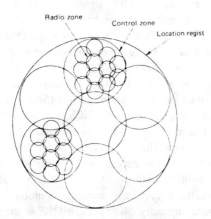

Fig. 6.   Zone construction concept in mobile radio telephone system.

antenna and a tower-side mounted antenna, are used. The antenna multiplexer employs circulators, high-Q cavity resonators and junction boxes for the transmitter side, and a double common amplifier for the receiver side.

2) Base Station Transmitter and Receiver: The base station transmitter is designed for conventional 25-W output power. Four compact transmitter sets are installed in one bay by a plug-in structure.

Four kinds of receivers, such as Rx for a speech channel, PRx for a paging channel, ARx for an access channel, and SRx for tracking exchange purposes, are used. A stand-by set is used for each paging channel transmitter and receiver, and for each access channel transmitter and receiver to allow automatic changeover when a regular set has trouble.

3) Base Station Control Unit (MBS-CONT): The base

station control unit, equipped in the base stations and located between the radio equipment (transmitters and receivers) and the mobile control unit in the mobile control station, relays and converts control signals received from the mobile equipment and/or the mobile control station.

4) Mobile Control Equipment (MCE): The mobile and base station control equipment installed in the mobile control station and composed of bay-type equipment has the following radio channel control functions for each base station and mobile unit:

1) sending paging signals,
2) access channel and voice channel designation,
3) voice channel tracking exchange control, and
4) dialing signal conversion from mobile unit.

5) Supervisory Equipment (MSU): The supervisory system has overall channel test and monitoring functions, as well as remote control and supervision of the base station facilities. The attended station equipment in the maintenance office is composed of three bay type devices, a control desk, and a keyboard printer. The unattended station equipment in the base stations is a bay-type device and contains a test transceiver for channel test and monitoring.

B. Mobile Radio Telephone Switching Center Equipment

The standard D10 Electronic Switching System, equipped with signaling devices, and designed to transmit and receive signals to and from MCS, is used in the MTC.

The D10 ESS performs the following functions by stored program control:

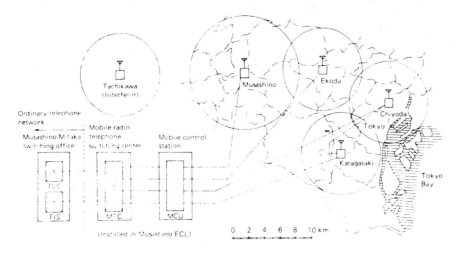

Fig. 7. Field test configuration (Tokyo metropolitan area and suburbs).

1) connection between mobile telephone and an ordinary telephone,

2) charging mobile subscribers,

3) switching for tracking exchange,

4) location registration, and

5) paging in the registered location information.

The mobile subscriber's information is stored in a special MTC, and is referred to from other offices processing mobile calls. Common channel signaling circuits are used for information transmission (Remote file access).

C. Mobile Unit

The mobile telephone equipment consists of an antenna, a transceiver unit including logic circuits, and a telephone unit which can be accessed to hundreds of different radio channels under the control of the MCS. The multichannel mobile unit can be realized by introducing the digital frequency synthesizer technique to produce tunable frequencies with high stability for the narrowed bandwidth. The dial in handset is adopted to provide handy small size and light weight, so that the operational functions are facilitated.

Though the simplified telephone unit is useful for reliability and economy, operational options (additional telephone unit, dial illumination, etc.) are prepared for customer demands.

V. FIELD TEST RESULTS

A. Outline

Four base stations are sited in the center of the Tokyo metropolitan area and at the Electrical Communication Laboratory in Musashino City. Another is sited in the suburbs of Tokyo. Equipment and electronic switches employed in MCS and MTC are also installed at ECL. The mobile radio telephone network extends to Musashino-Mitaka telephone office and to the ordinary telephone network. Fig. 7 shows the field test network configuration. Circles indicate the coverage area for each base station at the center.

B. Results

Major test program results are summarized as follows.

1) Mobile radio propagation characteristic measurements in urban and suburban areas, in the 800-MHz band, had taken many things into consideration, such as building height, street width, and terrain features. It was confirmed that the 800-MHz band can successfully be used for land mobile services.

2) Preliminary site selection determination for the service area confirmed designed tolerance determined by the field strength measurement.

3) The error rate performance of high-speed digital stream for signaling which is provided for setup and completion of calls to and from a number of mobile units was measured under Rayleigh type fading. It was confirmed that digital signaling reliability is satisfactory.

4) The debugging of call control flow between the mobile unit and the base station was completed.

5) D-10 ESS was modified, and with added functions for the mobile telephone switching system such as billing, mobile location memory, tracking exchange, etc., it performed satisfactorily.

6) The voice-circuit quality of an FM voice channel in the presence of rapid and severe fading, such as when a car is moving, was evaluated by means of a listener's subjective test. Sound articulation for more than 80 percent in the service area is secured. The field tests mentioned above have been carried out, using vehicular test facilities.

VI. CONCLUSION

Based on results of previously mentioned field tests, a high-capacity mobile telephone system in the 800-MHz band has satisfied design objectives. This system involves various advanced techniques which are usable for many other mobile communication systems.

Commercial use of the system will start in 1979. It is foreseen to have a considerable impact on the communication industry as well as social activities of the country.

REFERENCES

[1] Y. Okumura *et al.*, "Field strength and its variability in VHF and UHF land mobile radio service," *Rev. Elec. Commun. Lab.*, NTT, Japan, vol. 16, pp. 825–873, Sept./Oct. 1968.

[2] K. Araki, "Fundamental problems of nation-wide mobile radio telephone system," *Elec. Commun. Lab. Tech. Jour.*, NTT, Japan, vol. 16, pp. 843–865, May 1967.

[3] Int. Radio Consultive Committee, Final Meeting, Geneva, Switzerland, Doc. XIII/149, 1969.

Radio Link Design of Cellular Land Mobile Communication Systems

MASAHARU HATA, MEMBER, IEEE, KOTA KINOSHITA, MEMBER, IEEE, AND KENKICHI HIRADE, MEMBER, IEEE

Abstract—**A procedure for a radio link design of cellular land mobile radio systems is discussed. The relation between the prescribed total outage and the necessary margins for thermal noise and co-channel interference is first derived. It is then shown that the respective margins can be calculated separately. A simple and useful procedure for determining transmitter power and co-channel reuse distance is presented in concrete flowchart form. Based on this procedure, an example of a radio link design for a digital mobile telephone system is shown.**

I. INTRODUCTION

IN A TYPICAL VHF/UHF land mobile radio environment, the transmitted wave is affected not only by multipath fading but also by shadowing. These severe fluctuations make it difficult to maintain the required transmission quality within the whole cell. In the mobile radio link design, the probability of fade below the required threshold level prescribed on the basis of the transmission quality in the multipath fading environment must be taken into consideration. This degradation due to shadowing is defined as an outage [1]-[4].

The fundamental parameters of a mobile radio link design are transmitter power, or cell radius, and co-channel reuse distance. These parameters are determined under the prescribed conditions for the transmission quality and the allow-

able outage. In order to determine these parameters, it is necessary to take into account thermal noise and co-channel interference, since the transmission quality is strongly dependent on these factors. Therefore, the allowable outages must be allotted and prescribed for both factors. While many studies of the mobile radio link design have been reported [5]-[9], there are few reports dealing with the design procedure that take into account both thermal noise and co-channel interference [2]-[4].

In this paper, it is first shown that the necessary margins for these factors can be calculated separately, and a simple and useful procedure for determining the transmitter power and co-channel reuse distance is then derived in concrete flowchart form. Following this procedure, a radio link design of a digital mobile radio system is shown as an example.

II. PROPAGATION MODEL

Land mobile radio propagation characteristics have been studied by numerous people [10]-[13]. Based on their results, land mobile radio propagation in the VHF/UHF band is characterized by three aspects: Rayleigh fading, lognormal shadowing, and path loss.

When the received signal is measured over the distance of a few tens of wavelengths, the received signal envelope shows rapid and deep fluctuations about the local mean with vehicle movement. These fluctuations are caused by multipath propagation and vehicle movement. The distribution of the signal

Manuscript received May 27, 1981; revised September 20, 1981.

The authors are with the Yokosuka Electrical Communication Laboratory, Nippon Telegraph and Telephone Public Corporation, 1-2356, Take, Yokosuka-shi, Kanagawa-ken, 238-03 Japan.

Reprinted from *IEEE Trans. Veh. Technol.*, vol. VT-31, pp. 25-31, Feb. 1982.

envelope can be approximated by the Rayleigh distribution, i.e., the received signal shows Rayleigh fading.

The local mean varies siowly within a small area considered to be at a constant distance from the transmitting base station. This relatively slow variation of the local mean is caused by shadowing effects, and is shown to be lognormally distributed. This is the so-called lognormal shadowing, and the probability density function (PDF) of local mean X is represented as

$$p(X) = \frac{1}{\sqrt{2\pi}\sigma X} e^{-1/2\sigma^2 \ln^2(X/X_m)}, \tag{1}$$

where σ is the standard deviation, whose value in decibels is empirically shown as $5 \sim 7$ dB[1] in a typical urban area, and X_m is the area mean.

Letting the distance between the base station and a moving vehicle be r, the area mean X_m is given by

$$X_m = X_m(r) = A \cdot r^{-\alpha}, \tag{2}$$

where A and α are the propagation constants, and the value of α is about $3 \sim 4$ in a typical urban area.

A radio link should be designed based on the mobile radio propagation characteristics described above. In the following discussion, the required transmission quality is prescribed on the basis of the transmission performance in the simple Rayleigh fading environment without shadowing. The outage is taken as the fraction of the service area over which the prescribed transmission quality cannot be maintained because of shadowing effects.

III. OUTAGE AND MARGIN

Thermal noise and co-channel interference are two main factors affecting the transmission quality. The outage which takes these two factors into account can be derived as follows.

To simplify the discussion, let us assume that there exists only one interfering base station as shown in Fig. 1. Let X and Y be the local means of the desired and undesired signals, respectively. Assuming that X and Y are subjected to mutually independent lognormal shadowing, the joint PDF of X and Y is given by

$$p(X, Y) = \frac{1}{2\pi\sigma^2 XY} e^{-1/2\sigma^2 \{\ln^2(X/X_m) + \ln^2(Y/Y_m)\}}, \tag{3}$$

where $X_m = X_m(r)$ and $Y_m = Y_m(r)$ are the area means of X and Y, respectively. Letting the local means of carrier-to-noise ratio (CNR), and carrier-to-interference ratio (CIR) be Γ and Λ, respectively, and by changing the variables in (3) such that $X = \Gamma$ and $X/Y = \Lambda$, the joint PDF of Γ and Λ is given by

$$p(\Gamma, \Lambda) = \frac{1}{2\pi\sigma^2 \Gamma\Lambda} e^{-1/2\sigma^2 \{\ln^2(\Gamma/\Gamma_m) + \ln^2(\Lambda/\Lambda_m \cdot \Gamma_m/\Gamma)\}}, \tag{4}$$

[1] Letting the standard deviation in decibels be expressed as σ_0, the relation between σ_0 and σ is given by $\sigma_0 = 10 \cdot \sigma \cdot \log_{10} e$.

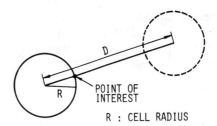

Fig. 1. Co-channel reuse model.

where $\Gamma_m = \Gamma_m(r)$ and $\Lambda_m = \Lambda_m(r)$ are the area means of CNR and CIR, respectively.

For the threshold levels Γ_{th} and Λ_{th} prescribed from the required transmission quality, the probability that $\Gamma \leq \Gamma_{th}$ or $\Lambda \leq \Lambda_{th}$ is expressed as

$$P_r[\Gamma \leq \Gamma_{th} \quad \text{or} \quad \Lambda \leq \Lambda_{th}]$$
$$= P_r[\Gamma \leq \Gamma_{th}] + P_r[\Lambda \leq \Lambda_{th}]$$
$$- P_r[\Gamma \leq \Gamma_{th} \quad \text{and} \quad \Lambda \leq \Lambda_{th}], \tag{5}$$

where

$$P_r[\Gamma \leq \Gamma_{th}] = \int_0^{\Gamma_{th}} \int_0^{\infty} p(\Gamma, \Lambda) \, d\Gamma \, d\Lambda, \tag{6}$$

$$P_r[\Lambda \leq \Lambda_{th}] = \int_0^{\infty} \int_0^{\Lambda_{th}} p(\Gamma, \Lambda) \, d\Gamma \, d\Lambda, \tag{7}$$

$$P_r[\Gamma \leq \Gamma_{th} \quad \text{and} \quad \Lambda \leq \Lambda_{th}]$$
$$= \int_0^{\Gamma_{th}} \int_0^{\Lambda_{th}} p(\Gamma, \Lambda) \, d\Gamma \, d\Lambda. \tag{8}$$

Substituting (4) into (6)-(8), and after making some modifications, (5) becomes

$$P_r[\Gamma \leq \Gamma_{th} \quad \text{or} \quad \Lambda \leq \Lambda_{th}]$$
$$= \frac{1}{2} \text{erfc} \left\{ \frac{\ln(\Gamma_m/\Gamma_{th})}{\sqrt{2}\sigma} \right\} + \frac{1}{2} \text{erfc} \left\{ \frac{\ln(\Lambda_m/\Lambda_{th})}{\sqrt{2}\sigma} \right\}$$
$$- \frac{1}{2\sqrt{\pi}} \int_{-\infty}^{\frac{\ln(\Gamma_{th}/\Gamma_m)}{\sqrt{2}\sigma}} e^{-t^2} \text{erfc} \left\{ t + \frac{\ln(\Lambda_m/\Lambda_{th})}{\sqrt{2}\sigma} \right\}, \tag{9}$$

where erfc $(\cdot)$ is the complementary error function defined as

$$\text{erfc}(x) = \frac{2}{\sqrt{\pi}} \int_x^{\infty} e^{-t^2} \, dt.$$

Equation (9) indicates that the outage which takes into account thermal noise and co-channel interference is a function of the necessary margins for CNR and CIR, i.e., Γ_m/Γ_{th} and Λ_m/Λ_{th}. In other words, (9) gives the necessary area means of CNR and CIR Γ_m and Λ_m for the threshold levels Γ_{th} and Λ_{th}, and the allowable outage $P_r[\Gamma \leqslant \Gamma_{th} \text{ or } \Lambda \leqslant \Lambda_{th}] = F_f$.

Fig. 2 shows the necessary margins of CNR and CIR computed from (9), where the dashed lines are the asymptotes. The lines parallel to the horizontal axis give the CIR margins when the CNR margin is infinite, and the lines parallel to the vertical axis give the CNR margins when the CIR margin is infinite. From this figure, the following conclusions can be drawn.

1) Allotment of the outage for thermal noise and co-channel interference can be made according to system scale or system grade. For example, when the total allowable outage is 10 percent, it is possible to make a link design for the point A which gives priority to thermal noise, or for the point B which gives priority to co-channel interference. The former link design is suitable for realizing larger cell systems or low power transmitter power systems, while the latter one is applicable for smaller cell high capacity systems.

2) When the outage is allotted separately for the respective factors, the necessary margins for CNR and CIR can be calculated separately. For example, assuming that the total prescribed outage is 5 percent, and that 1 percent is allotted for thermal noise and 4 percent for co-channel interference, the necessary margins for CNR and CIR are determined from the point marked by the star in this figure. As the point lies a little above the 5 percent curve, this design requires a slightly larger margin for the prescribed outage. The same relation generally holds for other allotted values. Therefore, this design always falls on the side of ensured safety.

IV. RADIO LINK DESIGN

Based on the relationship between outage and margin derived above, the transmitter power, or the cell radius, and the co-channel reuse distance, both of which are the fundamental parameters of a mobile radio link design, can easily be determined.

The threshold values for the local mean of CNR Γ_{th} and the local mean of CIR Λ_{th} are assumed to be prescribed separately on the basis of the transmission performance in the simple Rayleigh fading environment without lognormal shadowing. The allowable outage for thermal noise and co-channel interference can be determined separately for the prescribed transmission quality. Thus, the transmitter power and the co-channel reuse distance can be determined as follows.

A. Determination of Transmitter Power

Let F_f^1 be the outage at some point on the cell fringe as shown in Fig. 1. The relation between F_f^1 and the necessary margin for CNR Γ_m/Γ_{th} is given by

$$F_f^1 = P_r[\Gamma \leqslant \Gamma_{th}]$$
$$= \int_0^{\Gamma_{th}} \frac{1}{\sqrt{2\pi}\sigma\Gamma} e^{-1/2\sigma^2 \ln^2 (\Gamma/\Gamma_m)} d\Gamma$$
$$= \frac{1}{2} \operatorname{erfc}\left\{ \frac{\ln (\Gamma_m/\Gamma_{th})}{\sqrt{2}\sigma} \right\}. \tag{10}$$

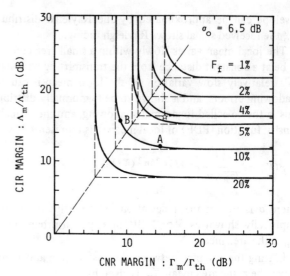

Fig. 2.   Necessary margins for CNR and CIR.

The results thus determined are shown in Fig. 3. As Γ_m is a function of the distance between the base station and a moving vehicle, Γ_m/Γ_{th} represents the minimum margin of CNR at some point on the cell fringe.

In planning the system, the outage must be prescribed within the whole cell. Therefore, it is necessary to make clear the relation between the outage at the cell fringe and the outage within the whole cell. Using (2), the outage within the whole cell F_a^1 can be calculated as

$$F_a^1 = \frac{1}{\pi R^2} \int_0^R F_f^1 2\pi r \, dr$$
$$= \frac{1}{2} \operatorname{erfc}(X_0) - \frac{1}{2} e^{(2X_0 Y_0 + Y_0^2)} \operatorname{erfc}(X_0 + Y_0), \tag{11}$$

where

$$X_0 \equiv \frac{\ln (\Gamma_m(R)/\Gamma_{th})}{\sqrt{2}\sigma} \quad \text{and} \quad Y_0 \equiv \frac{\sqrt{2}\sigma}{\alpha}. \tag{12}$$

The first term of (11) is equal to the outage at the cell fringe given by (10), and the second term is the correction term. The numerical results obtained by (11) are shown in Fig. 4. This figure shows that the radio link can be designed based on the outage at the cell fringe. Consequently, the necessary margin for CNR can easily be calculated by (10).

The required area mean of CNR Γ_m is then given as the sum of Γ_{th} (dB) and margin Γ_m/Γ_{th} (dB) corresponding to the outage F_f^1. When the path loss L_p, which is related to the cell radius, and the receiver noise power kTB_iN_f are given, the transmitter power P_t can be calculated by

$$P_t = (\Gamma_m \cdot kTB_i N_f \cdot L_p)/(G_t \cdot G_r), \tag{13}$$

where G_t and G_r are the antenna gains including line losses at the transmitter and receiver, respectively. Fig. 5 shows a flowchart for the procedure to determine the transmitter power.

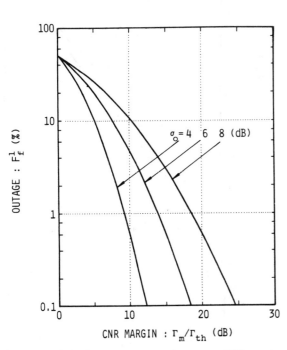

Fig. 3.   Relation between outage and necessary CNR margin.

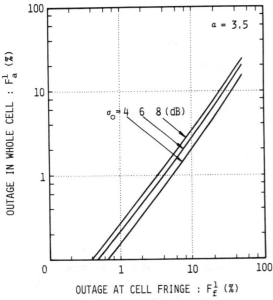

Fig. 4.   Relation between $F_f{}^1$ and $F_a{}^1$.

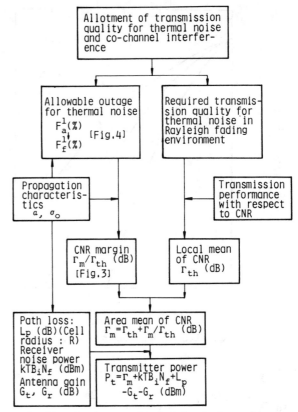

Fig. 5.   Flowchart for procedure to determine transmitter power.

B. Determination of Co-Channel Reuse Distance

Let us assume that there exists only one interfering base station, and that the desired and undesired signals are not correlated. Then, the PDF of the local mean CIR Λ becomes

$$p(\Lambda) = \frac{1}{2\sqrt{\pi}\sigma\Lambda} e^{-1/4\sigma^2 \ln^2 (\Lambda/\Lambda_m)}. \tag{14}$$

Letting $F_f{}^2$ be the outage at the cell fringe, the relation between outage $F_f{}^2$ and the necessary margin for CIR Λ_m/Λ_{th} can be calculated by

$$
\begin{aligned}
F_f{}^2 &= P_r[\Lambda \leqslant \Lambda_{th}] \\
&= \int_0^{\Lambda_{th}} \frac{1}{2\sqrt{\pi}\sigma\Lambda} e^{-1/4\sigma^2 \ln^2 (\Lambda/\Lambda_m)} \, d\Lambda \\
&= \tfrac{1}{2} \operatorname{erfc}\left\{ \frac{\ln (\Lambda_m/\Lambda_{th})}{2\sigma} \right\}.
\end{aligned}
\tag{15}
$$

The results are shown in Fig. 6.

The relation between the outage at the cell fringe and the outage within the whole cell $F_a{}^2$ can be calculated by

$$
\begin{aligned}
F_a{}^2 &= \frac{1}{\pi R^2} \int_0^R F_f{}^2 2\pi r \, dr \\
&\doteqdot \tfrac{1}{2} \operatorname{erfc}(X_0{}') - \tfrac{1}{2} e^{(2X_0{}'Y_0{}' + Y_0{}'^2)} \operatorname{erfc}(X_0{}' + Y_0{}'),
\end{aligned}
\tag{16}
$$

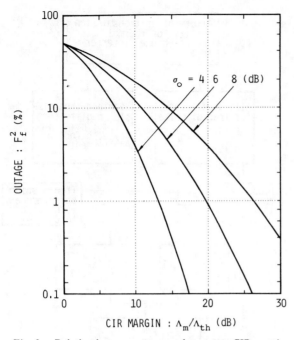

Fig. 6.   Relation between outage and necessary CIR margin.

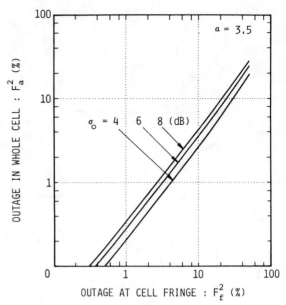

Fig. 7.   Relation between $F_f{}^2$ and $F_a{}^2$.

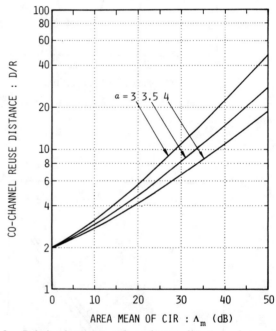

Fig. 8.   Relation between co-channel reuse distance and area mean of CIR.

where

$$X_0' \equiv \frac{\ln (\Lambda_m(R)/\Lambda_{th})}{2\sigma} \quad \text{and} \quad Y_0' \equiv \frac{2\sigma}{\alpha}. \qquad (17)$$

In this calculation, Λ_m, $\Lambda_{th} \gg 1$ is assumed. The first term of (16) is equal to (15), and the second term is the correction term. The numerical results of (16) are shown in Fig. 7.

From (2), the area mean of CIR Λ_m at the worst point shown in Fig. 1 is given by

$$\Lambda_m = \left(\frac{R}{D-R}\right)^{-\alpha} \equiv \Lambda_m(R). \qquad (18)$$

This can be rewritten as

$$D/R = 1 + \Lambda_m(R)^{1/\alpha}, \qquad (19)$$

and the results obtained are shown in Fig. 8. The ratio D/R is the minimum co-channel reuse distance normalized by the cell radius, because $\Lambda_m(R)$ is given by the sum of Λ_{th} (dB) and the minimum margin Λ_m/Λ_{th} (dB), which corresponds to the fixed outage $F_f{}^2$. Fig. 9 shows a flowchart for the procedure to determine the co-channel reuse distance.

In the above calculation, it is assumed that the desired and undesired signals are subjected to mutually independent lognormal shadowing. In practical mobile radio propagation, shadowing may, however, be partially correlated, because the shadowing is caused by buildings or the terrain near the vehicle. The PDF of the local mean of CIR, taking the correlation into account, can be derived as

$$p(\Lambda) = \frac{1}{2\sqrt{\pi}\sigma\sqrt{1-\rho}\,\Lambda} e^{-(1/4\sigma^2(1-\rho))\ln^2(\Lambda/\Lambda_m)} \qquad (20)$$

where ρ is the correlation coefficient. The results are shown in Fig. 10. Comparing (14) with (20), it is found that the correlation effect is equivalent to decreasing the standard deviation from σ to $\sigma\sqrt{1-\rho}$. Therefore, it can be concluded that Fig. 6 presents the worst case interference probability.

C. Example of a Mobile Radio Link Design

According to procedure described above, let us determine the transmitter power and the co-channel reuse distance for a digital mobile radio link.

The following conditions are assumed.

1) The frequency band of the system is 900 MHz, and the cell radius is $R = 3$ km. Standard deviation of the lognormal

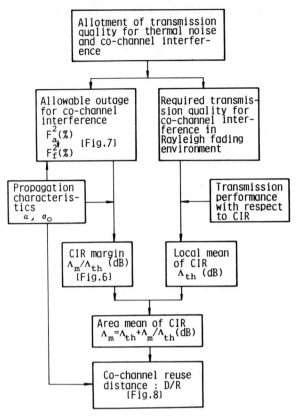

Fig. 9. Flowchart for procedure to determine co-channel reuse distance.

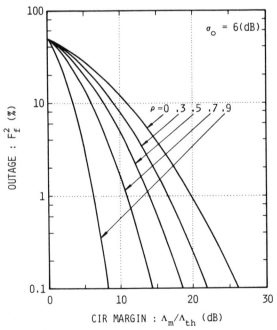

Fig. 10. Correlation effect on the relation between outage and CIR margin.

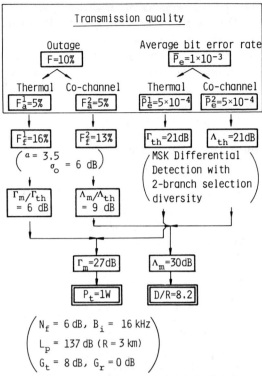

Fig. 11. An example of digital mobile radio link design.

is adopted as the modulation-demodulation scheme. The necessary transmission bandwidth is $B_i = 16$ kHz for the bit rate of 16 kb/s. The two-branch selection diversity technique is also applied.

Fig. 11 shows the procedure of the calculation according to the flowcharts shown in Figs. 5 and 9. The transmission performance is based on the theoretical performance [14] taking into account a 2 dB degradation. The path loss is based on the empirical formula [15]. From this procedure, the transmitter power and co-channel reuse distance are determined as $P_t = 1$ W and $D/R = 8.2$, respectively.

V. CONCLUDING REMARKS

The relation between outage and the necessary margins has been derived by taking into account both thermal noise and co-channel interference. The results show that the necessary margins for thermal noise and co-channel interference can be calculated separately. A simple and useful procedure for determining the transmitter power and the co-channel reuse distance is presented in concrete flowchart form. The procedure can be applied to not only digital but also analog mobile radio link designs.

To realize a more accurate transmitter power design, it is necessary to take other degradation factors, for example, man-made noise or terrain factors, into account. These factors should be treated as additional margin or path loss. In a cellular system, it is also necessary to make the degisn of the co-channel reuse distance more accurate because of the presence of multiple interfering base stations. Considering that the design falls on the safety side, this accuracy can be realized by adding 8 dB, which corresponds to six interfering base stations, to the area mean of CIR calculated by this procedure.

shadowing is $\sigma_0 = 6$ dB, and the propagation constant is $\alpha = 3.5$.

2) An average bit error rate of $\overline{P}_e = 1 \times 10^{-3}$ and an outage of $F_a = 10$ percent are required, and these values are allotted equally for thermal noise and co-channel interference.

3) Minimum-shift keying (MSK) with differential detection

As shown in the example of the mobile radio link design, the space diversity effect which mitigates the Rayleigh fading, can be taken as that of decreasing the required local mean of CNR and CIR. On the other hand, the site diversity effect, which is obtained by the hand-off technique and is effective for mitigating the shadowing, can be taken as that of decreasing the necessary margins of CNR and CIR.

Verification with an actual system is necessary to make the procedure discussed here more accurate. An experiment for this purpose is now being planned.

ACKNOWLEDGMENT

We wish to thank Dr. K. Miyauchi, Director of the Integrated Transmission System Development Division, and Dr. S. Seki, Chief of the Mobile Communication Equipment Section for their helpful discussions.

REFERENCES

[1] W. C. Jakes, Jr., *Microwave Mobile Communications.* New York: Wiley, 1974, pp. 377–386.
[2] N. Yoshikawa and T. Nomura, "On the design of a small zone land mobile radio system in UHF band," *IEEE Trans. Veh. Technol.*, vol. VT-25, pp. 57–67, Aug. 1976.
[3] T. Kamata, M. Sakamoto, and K. Fukuzumi, "800 MHz band land mobile telephone radio system," *Rev. Elec. Commun. Lab.*, vol. 25, pp. 1157–1171, Nov./Dec. 1977.
[4] V. H. MacDonald, "Advanced mobile phone service: The cellular concept," *Bell Syst. Tech. J.*, vol. 58, pp. 15–41, Jan. 1979.
[5] K. Araki, "Fundamental problems of nationwide mobile radio-telephone system," *Rev. Elec. Commun. Lab.*, vol. 16, pp. 357–373, May/Jun. 1968.
[6] R. C. French, "The effect of fading and shadowing on channel reuse in mobile radio," *IEEE Trans. Veh. Technol.*, vol. VT-28, pp. 171–181, Aug. 1979.
[7] F. Hansen and F. I. Meno, "Mobile fading-Rayleigh and lognormal superimposed," *IEEE Trans. Veh. Technol.*, vol. VT-26, pp. 332–335, Nov. 1977.
[8] W. Gosling, "A simple mathematical model of co-channel and adjacent channel interference in land mobile radio," *Radio Electron. Eng.*, vol. 48, pp. 619–622, Dec. 1978.
[9] L. Lundquist and M. M. Peritsky, "Co-channel interference rejection in a mobile radio space diversity system," *IEEE Trans. Veh. Technol.*, vol. VT-20, pp. 68–75, Aug. 1971.
[10] W. C. Jakes, Jr. and D. O. Reudink, "Comparison of mobile radio transmission at UHF and X-bands," *IEEE Trans. Veh. Technol.*, vol. VT-16, pp. 10–14, Oct. 1967.
[11] Y. Okumura, *et al.*, "Field strength and its variability in UHF and VHF land mobile radio service," *Rev. Elec. Commun. Lab.*, vol. 16, pp. 825–873, Sept./Oct. 1968.
[12] H. W. Nylund, "Characteristics of small area signal fading on a mobile circuit in the 150 MHz band," *IEEE Trans. Veh. Technol.*, vol. VT-17, pp. 24–30, Oct. 1968.
[13] D. O. Reudink, "Properties of mobile radio propagation above 400 MHz," *IEEE Trans. Veh. Technol.*, vol. VT-23, pp. 143–160, Nov. 1974.
[14] F. Adachi, "Postdetection selection diversity effects in a digital FM land mobile radio with discriminator and differential detections," *Trans. IECE Japan*, vol. 63-B, pp. 759–766, Aug. 1980.
[15] M. Hata, "Empirical formula for propagation loss in land mobile radio services," *IEEE Trans. Veh. Technol.*, vol. VT-29, pp. 317–325, Aug. 1980.

Vehicle Location in Angular Sectors Based on Signal Strength

SANG-BIN RHEE, MEMBER, IEEE

Abstract–The results of field measurements carried out in center city Philadelphia and in the Whippany/Morristown, NJ suburban area to assess the accuracy of a vehicle location technique at 820 MHz based on signal strength comparison are described. Six co-sited directional antennas, each covering a $60°$ angular sector in azimuth, were used to detect the signal transmitted by the mobile. The angular location of the vehicle was determined by comparing the signal strengths received "simultaneously" through the directional antennas. The measured vehicle location was then compared against the true location of the vehicle at the time of the measurement to generate statistics on location accuracy. An estimate is made on the expected improvements in the locating accuracy when three co-sited directional antennas are used, each of which provides coverage for a $120°$ sector in the horizontal plane. Also described are the effects of signal sample "integration time" and antenna beam shaping on the accuracy of the position estimate. The measurement results presented put a bound on the expected range of accuracies in the signal-strength-based "angle-of-arrival" vehicle location technique.

I. INTRODUCTION

IN MANY of the proposed cellular mobile telephone systems, a capability to determine the angular direction of mobile units from a given land site within a particular service area is desirable for the efficient utilization of the frequency spectrum. In such systems, a given service area is partitioned into many cells. Frequency channels are assigned to each cell in such a manner as to permit their regular reuse and to avoid interference between cochannel cells. Since the frequency reuse distance of a channel is determined by the level of interference, the primary purpose of vehicle locating is to prevent mobile units from using frequency channels far from their assigned cells, where they may not only encounter but also cause interference.

A number of different vehicle location techniques [1] have been under consideration in the past, including schemes which use "angle-of-arrival" and "time-of-arrival" information. The angle-of-arrival technique is based upon the mobile transmitter signal strengths received by a cluster of co-sited directional antennas covering $360°$ of the azimuth plane. A simple algorithm associates vehicle location in angular sectors with the directional antenna receiving the largest signal level. The time-of-arrival technique utilizes the measured time delay information between the land-transmitted signal and that signal transponded back to the land site by the mobile. Alternatively, both angle-

of-arrival and time-of-arrival information may be combined in some appropriate algorithm to locate the mobile.

This paper deals solely with experimental results obtained using the angle-of-arrival technique. The measurements were first performed in Philadelphia center city and then repeated in the suburban Morristown/Whippany, NJ area to compare location accuracies in different mobile environments.

The antenna heights in both experiments were kept at approximately 100 ft above the local ground level to simulate a practical cell-site antenna height. The signal sample "integration time" and its effects on the vehicle location accuracy are discussed in this paper. Effects of antenna beam shaping on the location accuracy are also included in the discussion of the measurement results.

II. TEST CONFIGURATION

A six co-sited corner reflector antenna system, as shown in Fig. 1, was set up at the land site to receive the signal from the mobile transmitter. Each corner reflector used a single half-wave dipole as the exciter element. The gain of the antenna was 8 dB above a half-wave dipole at the beam center. The six corner reflector antennas were positioned in such a manner that each antenna illuminated a $60°$ sector. In addition to these corner reflector antennas, the antenna mast supported one collinear array omnidirectional antenna having 6-dB gain above a half-wave dipole. The omnidirectional antenna was used as a reference to compare measured signal differences between the directional and the omnidirectional antennas. Fig. 2 shows the antenna arrangements at the top of a 50-ft mast. Radiation patterns of the omnidirectional and directional antennas, as measured at the antenna range, are given in Figs. 3 and 4.

The six corner reflector antennas and one omnidirectional antenna were connected to two receivers at the land site, as shown in Fig. 5. Receiver 1 was connected to the omnidirectional antenna, and receiver 2 was shared by the six directional antennas. The signals received by each directional antenna were sampled through a single-pole six-throw switch controlled by the on-board computer in the Mobile Communications Laboratory (MCL), which functioned as a stationary data recording machine for this experiment. The switch position, triggered by a pulse generator, was changed at a 1-kHz rate for this measurement. At each switch position, a set of three measurements was made: the first measurement sampled the directional antenna signal strength, the second sampled the omnidirectional antenna signal strength, and the third sampled the relative sig-

Manuscript received July 7, 1978. A portion of this paper was presented orally at the Microwave Mobile Symposium, Boulder CO, March 1973.

The author is with Bell Laboratories, Whippany, NJ 07981. Telephone: (201) 386-6796.

Reprinted from *IEEE Trans. Veh. Technol.*, vol. VT-27, pp. 244–258, Nov. 1978.

255

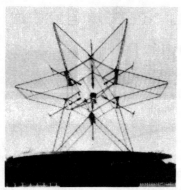

Fig. 1. Cluster of six corner reflector antennas (top view).

Fig. 2. Omnidirectional collinear array antenna and a cluster of six directional antennas on a 50-ft mast.

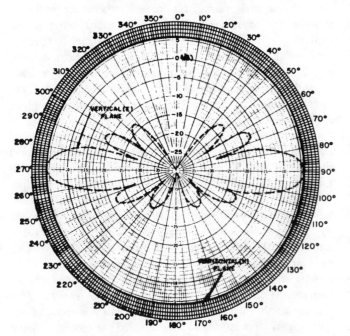

Fig. 3. Omnidirectional land site antenna radiation patterns (0 dB corresponds to the reference half-wave dipole gain).

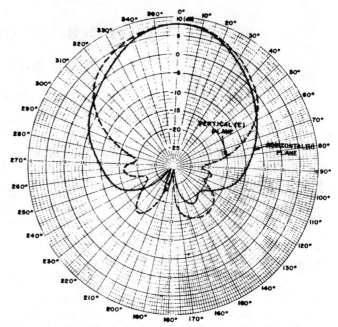

Fig. 4. Corner reflector antenna radiation patterns (0 dB corresponds to the reference half-wave dipole gain).

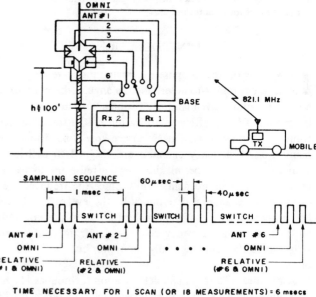

Fig. 5. Experimental configuration for vehicle location measurements.

nal strength between the directional and omnidirectional antennas. The data analysis discussed in this paper, however, treats only the data sampled on the six directional antennas.

III. MEASUREMENT AREA

For the Philadelphia urban measurements, the land site was established at the intersection of 17th and Lombard Streets. The Bell Telephone Company of Pennsylvania central office, the "Pennypacker Building", at this location was used to house a 50-ft antenna mast and the omnidirectional and directional antenna cluster. The roof height of the building, which is 54 ft above the street level, and the 50-ft antenna mast on the top of the roof, resulted in an antenna height of 104 ft above the local ground level.

The surrounding region, as viewed from the Pennypacker rooftop, is shown in Fig. 6. Center city, where most of the tall buildings are concentrated, is located to the north of the Pennypacker site by approximately ½ to ¾ mi. Relatively open areas exist in all other directions except for a few isolated buildings which are taller than the land site antenna height. In the immediate vicinity of the land site, the building heights are generally 20–30 ft lower than the Pennypacker rooftop, making the receiving antenna height at least 70–80 ft higher than the heights of the neighboring buildings.

For the Morristown/Whippany, NJ suburban area measurements, the land site was established at the Bell Laboratories, Whippany, NJ location. A 100-ft antenna mast was used to support the antenna cluster. The general characteristics of the surrounding environment are "typically suburban." Within the measurement area, most of the buildings are residential in nature, seldom exceeding two to three stories in height. The terrain elevations, however, varied between 200 ft and 800–900 ft above sea level. The largest "city" included in the measurement area was Morristown, NJ, about 4 mi away from the receiver site.

IV. ANTENNA ORIENTATION AND MEASUREMENT COURSE

During the experiment, the transmitting mobile traveled along preselected measurement courses. These measurement courses were selected based upon the distance from the land site and the terrain features between the land site and the mobile vehicle. The measurement courses for the Philadelphia urban measurements are shown in Fig. 7. Two different antenna orientations were needed in the measurements: an angular displacement of 30° between the two orientations resulted in the interchanging of the antenna beam center and the boundaries for two orientations. The initial orientation of the six directional antennas is superimposed on Fig. 7. Four "circumferential" runs (measurement courses A, B, C, and D) were used to circumscribe the land site at radial distances of approximately ½, 1, 1½, and 2 mi, respectively. Additionally, six "radial" runs were specifically selected to study vehicle location statistics when the mobile travels along antenna beam boundaries (such as courses F and H) or exclusively within the center of one antenna beam (such as E, I, and G). Measurements along the same nine measurement courses (A through I) were repeated with the antenna cluster rotated by 30°, interchanging the directions of antenna beam centers and boundaries from the initial antenna orientation. The measurement course associated with the second antenna orientation is distinguished here from the first by "prime" notation, i.e., measurement courses A', B', etc. Fig. 8 shows the second antenna orientation superimposed on the measurement courses A' through J'. For the second set of measurements, a new measurement course, run J' on Vine Street, was added because of its unique features: the western half of Vine Street is a depressed highway simulating an open-top waveguide. The urban Philadelphia measurement area was contained within approximately a 2½ mi radius circle centered

Fig. 6. Views from "Pennypacker" land site rooftop, corner of 17th and Lombard Streets.

at the Pennypacker land site and bounded by Girard St. to the north, Oregon St. to the south, Front St. to the east, and Schuylkill Expressway to the west. This area included all of the high-rise Philadelphia center city area.

The antenna orientation and the measurement courses for the suburban area are shown in Fig. 9. The measurement courses are all of the "circumferential" type, and extend out to approximately 6 mi from the land site located at BTL, Whippany. Only a single antenna orientation was used for the suburban measurements. Radial runs were excluded in the suburban tests due to the limited availability of "radial" streets.

V. DATA AVERAGING

As discussed in Section II and shown in Fig. 5, the transmitted signal from the mobile was sampled at a 3-kHz rate at the land site through one omnidirectional and six directional antennas. At each of six switch positions, three separate measurements were made. A 2048-word data buffer was used in the MCL computer memory to combine 112 complete scans, 18 measurements for each scan, with 32 words for data identification to form "records" of the data. For the analysis discussed herein, the 112 signal samples contained in one record for each of the six directional antennas were individually averaged. These averages, referred to as "one record averages" are compared statistically to determine the mobile transmitter location. Since the signal was sampled at a 3-kHz rate, it takes 672 ms to fill the 2016 data word buffer. The vehicle location statistics discussed in this paper, therefore, are based upon signal strength samples averaged over 672 ms.

Parts of the measurement data from both the Philadelphia and Morristown/Whippany tests were selected for further study to assess the vehicle location accuracy in terms of signal sample "integration time." Data taken from measurement courses A, from both the urban and suburban tests, were used to compare the vehicle location accuracies when the location decisions were made based upon the signal strength averages obtained

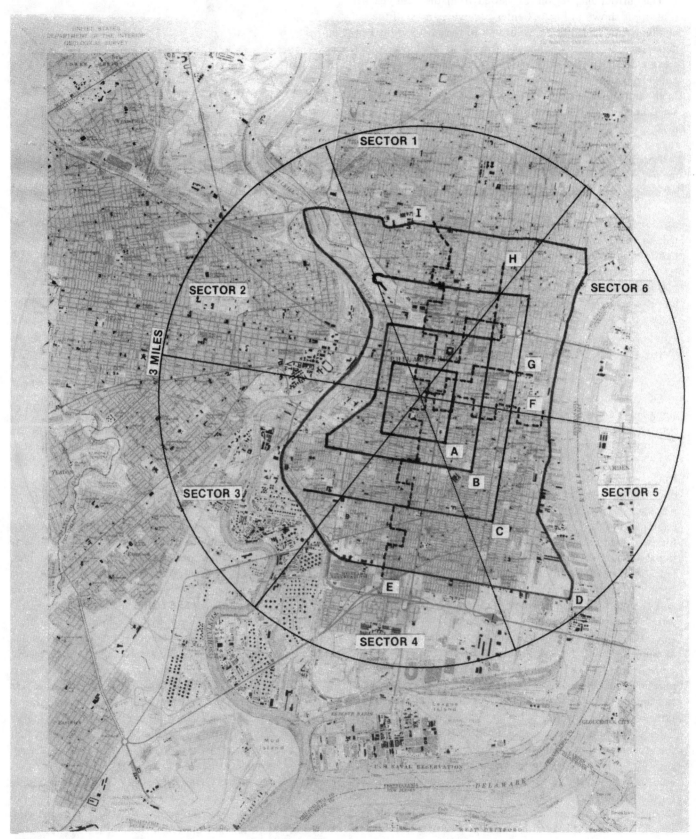

Fig. 7.   Measurement courses A through I superimposed on antenna orientation (Philadelphia).

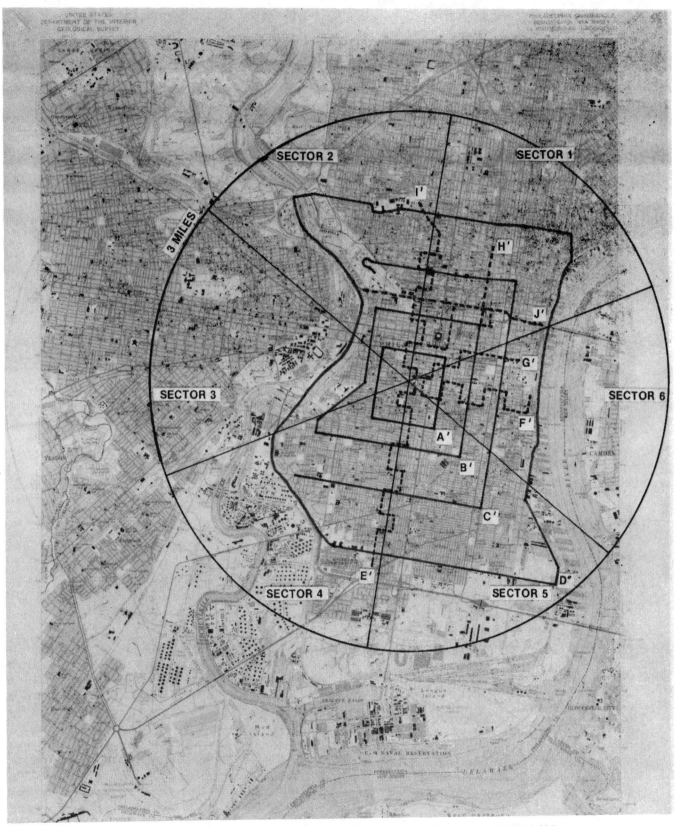

Fig. 8.   Measurement courses A′ through J′ superimposed on antenna orientation (Philadelphia).

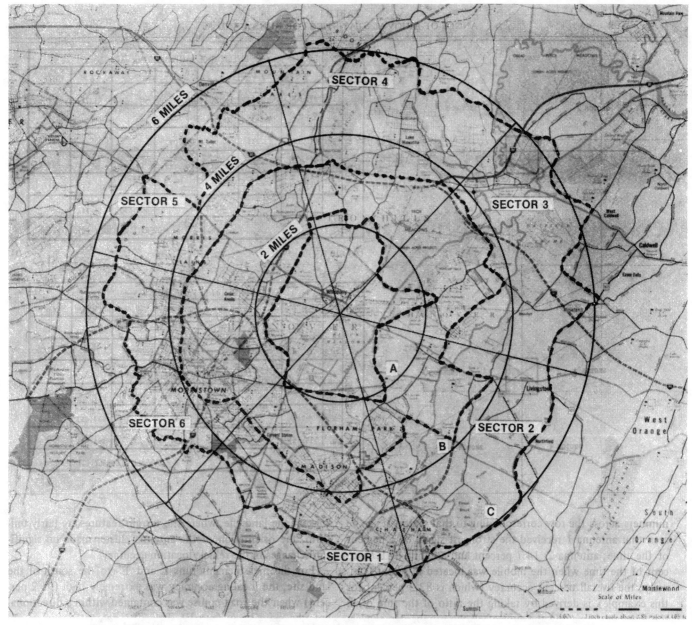

Fig. 9.   Measurement courses A through C and antenna orientation (Whippany/Morristown suburban area).

from one scan (6 ms), 5 scans (30 ms), 10 scans (60 ms), and finally 112 scans (672 ms). These results are reported in Section VII.

VI. MEASUREMENT RESULTS

All of the measurement results are presented in a form which compares the direction from which the maximum signal is received at the land site with the actual directional orientation of the transmitting vehicle relative to the land site. The true location of the vehicle is monitored through an on-board distance logging system. The relative cumulative distance traveled, "major markers"[1], and a voice communications link between

---

[1] "Major markers" are associated with landmarks along the measurement course, such as street intersections.

the mobile transmitter and the land site serve to pinpoint the vehicle's true location. For each prescribed measurement course, the number of correct vehicle location decisions are compared with the total number of decisions made on that run. A correct decision is one where the maximum average signal (averaged over a number of instantaneous samples) is received by the directional antenna whose 60° sector contains the true location of the mobile transmitter. Table I illustrates such a selection process.

Table I (A) shows the results of the urban Philadelphia run A. The six antenna positions are listed in the top row and the true vehicle location sectors are listed in the left hand column. To obtain the percentages given in parentheses, which denote the time each antenna received the strongest signal while the transmitting vehicle was located in a given sector, we read the

260

TABLE I
ANGLE-OF-ARRIVAL STATISTICS FOR RUNS A AND A'

ANT. # / SECTOR	DIRECTION OF MAXIMUM SIGNAL						TOTAL
	1	2	3	4	5	6	
1	193 (83.5%)	34 (14.7%)	-	-	-	4 (1.7%)	231
2	2 (1.3%)	152 (96.8%)	3 (1.9%)	-	-	-	157
3	1 (0.2%)	14 (3.2%)	394 (90.6%)	26 (6.0%)	-	-	435
4	-	-	7 (2.8%)	243 (95.7%)	4 (1.6%)	-	254
5	-	-	-	40 (11.0%)	318 (87.8%)	4 (1.1%)	362
6	164 (35.7%)	-	-	-	35 (7.6%)	261 (56.7%)	460
						OVERALL ACCURACY (%)	82.2%

(A) run A

ANT. # / SECTOR	DIRECTION OF MAXIMUM SIGNAL						TOTAL
	1	2	3	4	5	6	
1	232 (41.7%)	248 (44.5%)	-	-	-	77 (13.8%)	557
2	10 (5.1%)	121 (61.4%)	66 (33.5%)	-	-	-	197
3	-	-	163 (97.6%)	4 (2.4%)	-	-	167
4	-	-	1	242 (96.0%)	9 (3.6%)	-	252
5	-	-	-	-	169 (72.8%)	63 (27.2%)	232
6	37 (16.1%)	-	-	-	-	193 (83.9%)	230
						OVERALL ACCURACY (%)	68.5%

(B) run A'

numbers across the row corresponding to that sector. It can be seen that antenna 1 received the strongest signal 83.5 percent of the time; antenna 2, 14.7 percent and antenna 6, 1.7 percent of the time when the mobile was located in sector 1. Finally, the overall percent accuracy (which is 82.2 percent for this example), is derived by taking the ratio of the sum of all the diagonal terms and the sum of all the numbers in the last column.

Tables I–IX each contain two parts. Part (A) shows the results of measurements with the directional antennas in one orientation, and part (B) for the same measurement course with the directional antenna cluster rotated by 30°. A direct comparison can be made between these pairs of tables to assess the effects of antenna orientation with respect to street features on the locating accuracy. Table X contains only one part. Run J' along Vine Street was implemented only with the second antenna orientation. Table XI represents composite locating accuracy and was obtained by adding all the numbers in the squares represented by a given row and column from each of the previous nine tables and assigning the resultant number to the corresponding square in Table XI. The overall accuracies of 78.3 percent from Table XI (A) and 71.6 percent from Table XI (B) indicate that the overall location accuracy did not change significantly with antenna orientation. However, it becomes apparent that for the measurement courses A and B, which pass through the dense high-rise center city area north of the receiver site, the antenna orientation makes a significant difference in the vehicle locating accuracy. To the south and

west of the land site, where the terrain features are fairly uniform, the orientation of the antenna cluster made no significant changes in the vehicle location accuracy.

For the measurement runs E and E' to the south of the land site, the locating accuracy was extremely high (95.2 percent) when the road course was contained within a directional antenna main beam (run E). The 70.3 percent accuracy observed for run E' indicates that, although a mobile is in a "clean" environment, the expected location accuracy is low near the two-antenna beam crossover due to the practical limitations associated with antenna alignment accuracy. When the mobile was in a "hostile" center city environment, such as runs H and H', the location accuracies were not significantly affected by the antenna beam orientation. The percent accuracies for runs H and H' were about the same, although the road course for run H was in the center of the directional antenna beam and the road course for run H' was at the edge of the antenna beam. A similar observation can be made for runs F/F' and I/I'.

For run G/G', a clear advantage was observed when the measurement course was contained within the center of the antenna beam. As expected, for the measurement run J', where the mobile traveled on a "depressed" highway on Vine Street (sector 2), the location accuracy was indeed extremely poor (40.3 percent). It was obvious that the strongest signals received at the land site were the result of reflections independent of the mobile's true position.

It can be concluded from the above observations that in a

TABLE II
ANGLE-OF-ARRIVAL STATISTICS FOR RUNS B AND B'

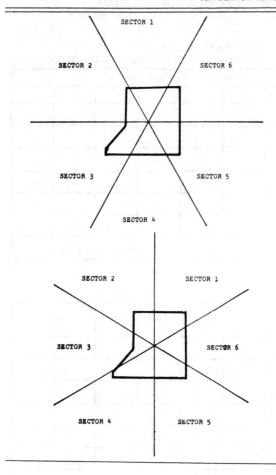

SECTOR	1	2	3	4	5	6	TOTAL
1	531 (74.4%)	155 (21.7%)	-	-	-	28 (3.9%)	714
2	7 (1.3%)	537 (98.5%)	1 (0.2%)	-	-	-	545
3	-	104 (12.4%)	722 (86.4%)	10 (1.2%)	-	-	836
4	3 (0.7%)	-	19 (4.4%)	384 (89.7%)	22 (5.1%)	-	428
5	-	-	102 (8.6%)	982 (82.5%)	106 (8.9%)		1190
6	35 (3.3%)	4 (0.4%)	-	52 (4.9%)	148 (14.0%)	816 (77.3%)	1055

Columns 1–6 under heading DIRECTION OF MAXIMUM SIGNAL (ANT. #). Rows under TRUE VEHICLE LOCATION.

OVERALL ACCURACY (%) 83.3%

(A) run B

SECTOR	1	2	3	4	5	6	TOTAL
1	375 (67.6%)	90 (16.2%)	1	-	7 (1.3%)	82 (14.7%)	555
2	3 (1.0%)	150 (47.9%)	160 (51.1%)	-	-	-	313
3	-	3 (1.1%)	270 (98.5%)	1	-	-	274
4	-	-	24 (6.7%)	323 (90.7%)	9 (2.5%)	-	356
5	21 (4.3%)	15 (3.1%)	8 (1.6%)	1	410 (83.7%)	35 (7.1%)	490
6	68 (15.7%)	-	-	-	61 (14.1%)	305 (70.3%)	434

OVERALL ACCURACY (%) 75.7%

(B) run B'

TABLE III
ANGLE-OF-ARRIVAL STATISTICS FOR RUNS C AND C'

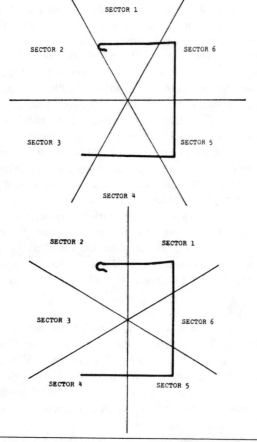

SECTOR	1	2	3	4	5	6	TOTAL
1	462 (42.7%)	442 (40.9%)	40 (3.7%)	-	15 (1.4%)	122 (11.3%)	1081
2	-	-	-	-	-	-	-
3	-	-	158 (98.8%)	2 (1.2%)	-	-	160
4	-	-	15 (2.1%)	706 (97.2%)	5 (0.7%)	-	726
5	-	-	-	77 (7.0%)	1004 (91.6%)	15 (1.4%)	1096
6	21 (3.0%)	-	-	5 (0.7%)	125 (18.1%)	541 (78.2%)	692

OVERALL ACCURACY (%) 76.5%

(A) run C

SECTOR	1	2	3	4	5	6	TOTAL
1	321 (49.1%)	86 (13.1%)	37 (5.7%)	-	69 (10.6%)	141 (21.6%)	654
2	48 (13.5%)	76 (21.4%)	217 (61.1%)	14 (3.9%)	-	-	355
3	-	-	-	-	-	-	-
4	-	-	2 (0.4%)	494 (92.5%)	38 (7.1%)	-	534
5	44 (3.9%)	2 (0.2%)	-	-	1018 (90.4%)	62 (5.5%)	1126
6	33 (6.4%)	-	-	-	21 (4.0%)	465 (89.5%)	519

OVERALL ACCURACY (%) 74.5%

(B) run C'

TABLE IV
ANGLE-OF-ARRIVAL STATISTICS FOR RUNS D AND D'

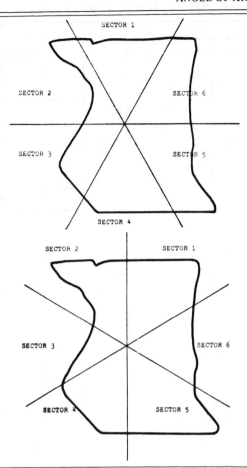

ANT. # SECTOR		DIRECTION OF MAXIMUM SIGNAL						TOTAL
		1	2	3	4	5	6	
TRUE VEHICLE LOCATION	1	570 (49.8%)	208 (18.2%)	41 (3.6%)	3 (0.3%)	49 (4.3%)	273 (23.9%)	1144
	2	131 (18.2%)	507 (70.6%)	42 (5.8%)	13 (1.8%)	-	25 (3.5%)	718
	3	-	11 (5.1%)	204 (94.9%)	-	-	-	215
	4	-	-	59 (7.1%)	739 (89.3%)	29 (3.5%)	1 (0.1%)	828
	5	-	-	-	3 (0.4%)	748 (98.9%)	5 (0.7%)	756
	6	274 (14.1%)	71 (3.7%)	1 (0.1%)	27 (1.4%)	466 (24.0%)	1100 (56.7%)	1939
						OVERALL ACCURACY (%)		69.1%

(A) run D

ANT. # SECTOR		DIRECTION OF MAXIMUM SIGNAL						TOTAL
		1	2	3	4	5	6	
TRUE VEHICLE LOCATION	1	24 (11.8%)	-	-	-	7 (3.4%)	173 (84.8%)	204
	2	269 (19.6%)	540 (39.4%)	481 (35.1%)	61 (4.5%)	5 (0.4%)	16 (1.2%)	1372
	3	-	-	275 (86.8%)	42 (13.2%)	-	-	317
	4	-	2 (0.4%)	-	423 (84.6%)	75 (15.0%)	-	500
	5	13 (1.7%)	10 (1.3%)	-	10 (1.3%)	633 (84.2%)	86 (11.4%)	752
	6	1 (0.2%)	-	-	-	2 (0.4%)	491 (99.4%)	494
						OVERALL ACCURACY (%)		65.6%

(B) run D'

TABLE V
ANGLE-OF-ARRIVAL STATISTICS FOR RUNS E AND E'

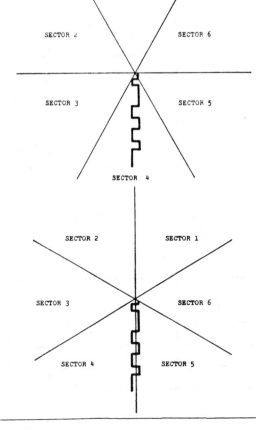

ANT. # SECTOR		DIRECTION OF MAXIMUM SIGNAL						TOTAL
		1	2	3	4	5	6	
TRUE VEHICLE LOCATION	1	-	-	-	-	-	-	-
	2	-	-	-	-	-	-	-
	3	-	-	-	-	-	-	-
	4	28 (1.5%)	5 (0.4%)	39 (2.1%)	1743 (96.0%)	-	-	1815
	5	-	-	-	19 (24.1%)	60 (76.0%)	-	79
	6	-	-	-	-	-	-	-
						OVERALL ACCURACY (%)		95.2%

(A) run E

ANT. # SECTOR		DIRECTION OF MAXIMUM SIGNAL						TOTAL
		1	2	3	4	5	6	
TRUE VEHICLE LOCATION	1	-	-	-	-	-	-	-
	2	-	-	-	-	-	-	-
	3	-	-	-	-	-	-	-
	4	2 (0.4%)	16 (2.9%)	-	278 (49.7%)	263 (47.0%)	-	559
	5	3 (0.3%)	102 (11.5%)	-	43 (4.8%)	739 (83.3%)	-	887
	6	-	-	-	-	-	-	-
						OVERALL ACCURACY (%)		70.4%

(B) run E'

263

TABLE VI
ANGLE-OF-ARRIVAL STATISTICS FOR RUNS F AND F′

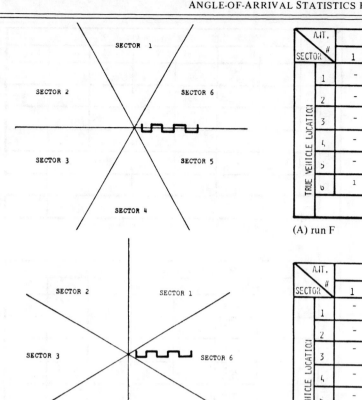

SECTOR # \ ANT #	DIRECTION OF MAXIMUM SIGNAL						
	1	2	3	4	5	6	TOTAL
TRUE VEHICLE LOCATION 1	-	-	-	-	-	-	-
2	-	-	-	-	-	-	-
3	-	-	-	-	-	-	-
4	-	-	-	-	-	-	-
5	-	-	30 (3.4%)	-	770 (88.2%)	73 (8.4%)	873
6	1	-	-	-	170 (24.8%)	514 (75.0%)	685
OVERALL ACCURACY (%)							82.4%

(A) run F

SECTOR # \ ANT #	DIRECTION OF MAXIMUM SIGNAL						
	1	2	3	4	5	6	TOTAL
TRUE VEHICLE LOCATION 1	-	-	-	-	-	-	-
2	-	-	-	-	-	-	-
3	-	-	-	-	-	-	-
4	-	-	-	-	-	-	-
5	-	-	-	-	-	-	-
6	108 (7.9%)	-	19 (1.4%)	-	10 (0.8%)	1222 (89.8%)	1359
OVERALL ACCURACY (%)							89.8%

(B) run F′

TABLE VII
ANGLE-OF-ARRIVAL STATISTICS FOR RUNS G AND G′

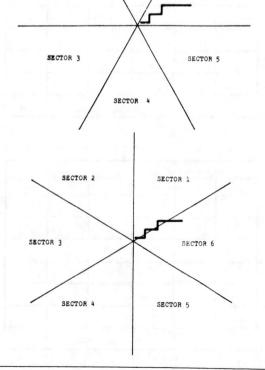

SECTOR # \ ANT #	DIRECTION OF MAXIMUM SIGNAL						
	1	2	3	4	5	6	TOTAL
TRUE VEHICLE LOCATION 1	-	-	-	-	-	-	-
2	-	-	-	-	-	-	-
3	-	-	-	-	-	-	-
4	-	-	-	-	-	-	-
5	-	-	-	-	-	-	-
6	170 (16.9%)	-	-	-	10 (1.0%)	826 (82.1%)	1006
OVERALL ACCURACY (%)							82.1%

(A) run G

SECTOR # \ ANT #	DIRECTION OF MAXIMUM SIGNAL						
	1	2	3	4	5	6	TOTAL
TRUE VEHICLE LOCATION 1	391 (51.6%)	7 (0.9%)	-	-	50 (6.6%)	310 (40.9%)	758
2	-	-	-	-	-	-	-
3	-	-	-	-	-	-	-
4	-	-	-	-	-	-	-
5	-	-	-	-	-	-	-
6	221 (35.0%)	-	-	-	45 (7.1%)	365 (57.8%)	631
OVERALL ACCURACY (%)							54.4%

(B) run G′

TABLE VIII
ANGLE-OF-ARRIVAL STATISTICS FOR RUNS H AND H'

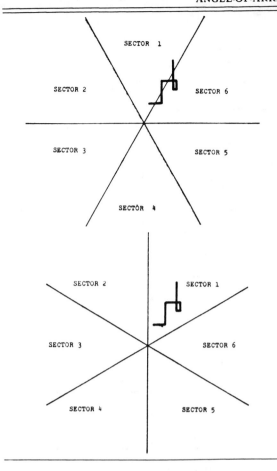

SECTOR \ A.I.T. #	DIRECTION OF MAXIMUM SIGNAL						TOTAL
	1	2	3	4	5	6	
1	604 (65.9%)	-	-	-	-	312 (34.1%)	916
2	-	-	-	-	-	-	-
3	-	-	-	-	-	-	-
4	-	-	-	-	-	-	-
5	-	-	-	-	-	-	-
6	100 (10.9%)	-	-	-	-	818 (89.1%)	918
						OVERALL ACCURACY (%)	77.5%

(TRUE VEHICLE LOCATION)

(A) run H

SECTOR \ A.I.T. #	DIRECTION OF MAXIMUM SIGNAL						TOTAL
	1	2	3	4	5	6	
1	1269 (76.8%)	71 (4.3%)	9 (0.5%)	-	37 (2.2%)	266 (16.1%)	1652
2	-	-	-	-	-	-	-
3	-	-	-	-	-	-	-
4	-	-	-	-	-	-	-
5	-	-	-	-	-	-	-
6	-	-	-	-	-	-	-
						OVERALL ACCURACY (%)	76.8%

(TRUE VEHICLE LOCATION)

(B) run H'

TABLE IX
ANGLE-OF-ARRIVAL STATISTICS FOR RUNS I AND I'

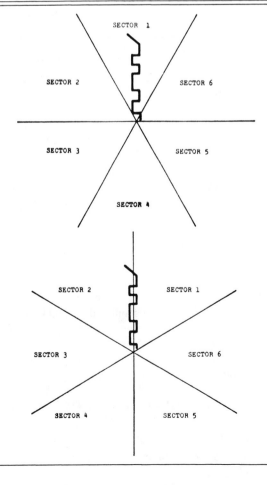

SECTOR \ A.I.T. #	DIRECTION OF MAXIMUM SIGNAL						TOTAL
	1	2	3	4	5	6	
1	1370 (72.2%)	461 (24.3%)	3 (0.2%)	-	14 (0.7%)	49 (2.6%)	1897
2	-	-	-	-	-	-	-
3	-	-	-	-	-	-	-
4	-	-	-	-	-	-	-
5	-	-	-	-	-	-	-
6	52 (41.9%)	-	-	-	6 (4.8%)	66 (53.2%)	124
						OVERALL ACCURACY (%)	71.1%

(TRUE VEHICLE LOCATION)

(A) run I

SECTOR \ A.I.T. #	DIRECTION OF MAXIMUM SIGNAL						TOTAL
	1	2	3	4	5	6	
1	576 (77.7%)	154 (20.8%)	7 (0.9%)	-	-	4 (0.5%)	741
2	77 (9.2%)	608 (72.6%)	137 (16.4%)	1 (0.4%)	-	14 (1.7%)	837
3	-	-	-	-	-	-	-
4	-	-	-	-	-	-	-
5	-	-	-	-	-	-	-
6	-	-	-	-	-	-	-
						OVERALL ACCURACY (%)	75.0%

(TRUE VEHICLE LOCATION)

(B) run I'

TABLE X
ANGLE-OF-ARRIVAL STATISTICS FOR RUN J'

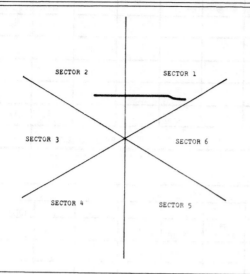

		DIRECTION OF MAXIMUM SIGNAL						
AIT # / SECTOR		1	2	3	4	5	6	TOTAL
TRUE VEHICLE LOCATION	1	535 (69.8%)	46 (6.0%)	42 (5.5%)	-	10 (1.3%)	134 (17.5%)	767
	2	-	54 (40.3%)	80 (59.7%)	-	-	-	134
	3	-	-	-	-	-	-	-
	4	-	-	-	-	-	-	-
	5	-	-	-	-	-	-	-
	6	-	-	-	-	-	-	-
							OVERALL ACCURACY (%)	65.4%

TABLE XI
ANGLE-OF-ARRIVAL STATISTICS–COMPOSITE RESULTS

		DIRECTION OF MAXIMUM SIGNAL						
AIT # / SECTOR		1	2	3	4	5	6	TOTAL
TRUE VEHICLE LOCATION	1	3730 (62.3%)	1300 (21.7%)	84 (1.4%)	3 (0.1%)	78 (1.3%)	788 (13.1%)	5983
	2	140 (9.9%)	1196 (84.2%)	46 (3.2%)	13 (0.9%)	-	25 (1.8%)	1420
	3	1 (0.1%)	129 (7.8%)	1478 (89.8%)	38 (2.3%)	-	-	1646
	4	31 (0.8%)	5 (0.1%)	139 (3.4%)	3816 (94.2%)	60 (1.5%)	1	4051
	5	-	-	30 (0.7%)	241 (5.5%)	3882 (89.1%)	203 (4.7%)	4356
	6	817 (11.9%)	75 (1.1%)	1	84 (1.2%)	960 (14.0%)	4942 (71.8%)	6879
							OVERALL ACCURACY (%)	78.3%

(A) composite results runs A–I

		DIRECTION OF MAXIMUM SIGNAL						
AIT # / SECTOR		1	2	3	4	5	6	TOTAL
TRUE VEHICLE LOCATION	1	3733 (63.3%)	702 (11.9%)	96 (1.6%)	-	180 (3.1%)	1147 (20.1%)	5888
	2	407 (12.7%)	1549 (48.3%)	1141 (35.6%)	76 (2.4%)	5 (0.2%)	30 (0.9%)	3208
	3	-	3 (0.4%)	708 (93.4%)	47 (6.2%)	-	-	759
	4	2 (0.1%)	18 (0.8%)	27 (1.2%)	1760 (80.0%)	394 (17.9%)	-	2201
	5	81 (2.3%)	129 (3.7%)	8 (0.2%)	54 (1.5%)	2969 (85.1%)	246 (7.1%)	3487
	6	468 (12.8%)	-	19 (0.5%)	-	139 (3.8%)	3041 (82.9%)	3667
							OVERALL ACCURACY (%)	71.6%

(B) composite results runs A'–J'

relatively "clean" and open environment, where most location errors are due to the small difference in the antenna gain at beam crossover, an ideal "fan-shaped" antenna beam pattern can improve the location accuracy. However, in an hostile environment, where "error signals" are distributed throughout the adjacent sectors, antenna beam shaping will not help significantly to improve the location accuracy.

Similar results for the suburban Morristown/Whippany measurements are presented in Table XII. The location accuracies for all measurement runs were better than 95 percent. The overall accuracy of almost 97 percent indicates a high degree of reliability for angular vehicle locating by this technique in a typical suburban area.

It is evident from Tables I–XII that if the measurement area were divided into larger angular sectors, the location "accuracies" would be improved. For example, if two adjacent antenna beams were combined to create a three-lobe antenna system, each lobe providing coverage for a 120° sector, some of the decisions interpreted as "wrong" decisions in Tables I–XII in the six-lobe system would now be correct in the three-lobe locating system. When the mobile is in sector 1, for instance, and the strongest signal is received by antenna #2, the location decision is still correct if antennas #1 and #2 are combined to provide coverage for the 120° sector represented by the individual sectors #1 and #2 in the foregoing tables. In this way, the 6-by-6 array of numbers can be rearranged into a 3-by-3 array to simulate the performance of a three-lobe antenna experiment. When Table XI (A) and (B) are reevaluated by combining sectors (and antennas) 1 and 2, 3 and 4, and 5 and 6, the simulated three-lobe antenna system performance indicates an improvement in overall locating accuracy from 78.3 percent to 89.7 percent for the combined results of runs A through I (Table XI (A)) and from 71.6 percent to 79.7 percent for runs A' through J' (Table XI (B)). A similar analysis of the suburban test results indicates that a simulated three-lobe locating system provides a slight improvement in accuracy over the six-lobe test results: 96.6 percent to 98.9 percent. Actual measurements with a three-lobe antenna system were subsequently performed in Philadelphia, confirming this finding.

VII. EFFECTS OF SIGNAL SAMPLE INTEGRATION TIME

As discussed in Section V, the signal samples taken once every 6 ms through each directional antenna at the land site

TABLE XII
ANGLE-OF-ARRIVAL STATISTICS—SUBURBAN RESULTS

(A) run A

ANT. # SECTOR (TRUE VEHICLE LOCATION)	DIRECTION OF MAXIMUM SIGNAL 1	2	3	4	5	6	TOTAL
1	411 (97.2%)	4	–	–	–	8	423
2	–	530 (100%)	–	–	–	–	530
3	–	14	689 (99.0%)	–	–	–	703
4	–	–	31	791 (95.4%)	7	–	829
5	–	–	–	1	491 (95.7%)	21	513
6	9	–	–	–	2	437 (97.5%)	448
OVERALL ACCURACY (%)							97.7%

(B) run B

ANT. # SECTOR (TRUE VEHICLE LOCATION)	DIRECTION OF MAXIMUM SIGNAL 1	2	3	4	5	6	TOTAL
1	972 (96.4%)	22	–	–	–	14	1008
2	–	835 (100%)	–	–	–	–	835
3	–	–	857 (100%)	–	–	–	857
4	–	–	26	615 (94.8%)	8	–	649
5	–	–	–	11	618 (98.2%)	–	629
6	–	–	–	–	134	1052 (88.7%)	1186
OVERALL ACCURACY (%)							95.8%

(C) run C

ANT. # SECTOR (TRUE VEHICLE LOCATION)	DIRECTION OF MAXIMUM SIGNAL 1	2	3	4	5	6	TOTAL
1	1085 (93.9%)	34	–	–	–	37	1156
2	10	1135 (93.9%)	64	–	–	–	1209
3	–	30	1775 (98.3%)	–	–	–	1805
4	–	–	146	1972 (93.0%)	3	–	2121
5	–	–	–	1	2272 (99.6%)	7	2280
6	4	–	–	–	10	2156 (99.4%)	2170
OVERALL ACCURACY (%)							96.8%

(D) composite results

ANT. # SECTOR (TRUE VEHICLE LOCATION)	DIRECTION OF MAXIMUM SIGNAL 1	2	3	4	5	6	TOTAL
1	2468 (95.4%)	60	–	–	–	59	2587
2	10	2500 (97.1%)	64	–	–	–	2574
3	–	44	3321 (98.7%)	–	–	–	3365
4	–	–	203	3378 (93.9%)	18	–	3599
5	–	–	–	13	3381 (98.8%)	28	3422
6	13	–	–	–	146	3645 (95.8%)	3804
OVERALL ACCURACY (%)							96.6%

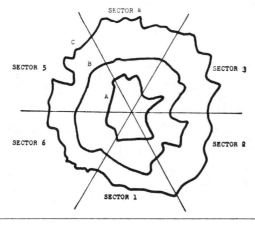

were integrated over a period of 672 ms (112 scans) to produce the vehicle location statistics discussed above. To ascertain the effects of the signal sample integration time on the overall vehicle location accuracy, data from two measurement courses, one urban and the other suburban, were selected for a detailed comparison.

The vehicle location decisions were made, first, based upon a single measurement through each of the directional antennas every 672 ms. Next, five consecutive measurement samples, 6 ms apart, taken through each of the directional antennas were averaged every 672 ms and then compared to make the vehicle location decision. The sample integration time was then increased to ten samples, again 6 ms separation between samples from each directional antenna averaged every 672 ms and used to make the location decision. The one, five, and ten scan-averaged location statistics were then compared against the 112 scan-averaged results for measurement runs A from both the urban and suburban tests.

The results of the sample integration time study are summarized in Tables XIII and XIV. Table XIII contains the urban measurement results and Table XIV shows the results from the suburban tests. Although the percent accuracy increases monotonically with increase in the sample integration time, it is clear from these tables that no drastic improvement in location accuracy is obtained when the number of scans is increased from one to 112. However, from Tables XIII and XIV, it can be concluded that maximum improvement is realized when the integration time is increased from one to five scans.

TABLE XIII
EFFECTS OF SAMPLE INTEGRATION TIME (RUN A) URBAN MEASUREMENT RESULTS

(A) 1 scan (6 ms)

SECTOR \ ANT.#	1	2	3	4	5	6	TOTAL
1	174 (75.3%)	36 (15.6%)	-	-	-	21 (9.1%)	231
2	10 (6.4%)	134 (85.4%)	13 (8.3%)	-	-	-	157
3	5 (1.2%)	48 (11.0%)	349 (80.2%)	33 (7.6%)	-	-	435
4	-	-	17 (6.7%)	213 (83.9%)	24 (9.4%)	-	254
5	2 (0.6%)	1 (0.2%)	-	62 (17.1%)	282 (77.9%)	15 (4.1%)	362
6	171 (32.2%)	4 (0.9%)	-	-	65 (14.1%)	220 (47.8%)	460

% ACCURACY 72.3%

(B) 5 scans (30 ms)

SECTOR \ ANT.#	1	2	3	4	5	6	TOTAL
1	177 (76.6%)	34 (14.7%)	-	-	-	20 (8.7%)	231
2	4 (2.5%)	140 (89.2%)	13 (8.3%)	-	-	-	157
3	2 (0.5%)	37 (8.5%)	364 (83.7%)	32 (7.4%)	-	-	435
4	-	-	13 (5.1%)	224 (88.2%)	17 (6.7%)	-	254
5	-	-	-	60 (16.6%)	294 (81.2%)	7 (1.9%)	362
6	164 (35.6%)	-	-	-	56 (12.2%)	240 (52.2%)	460

% ACCURACY 75.8%

(C) 10 scans (60 ms)

SECTOR \ ANT.#	1	2	3	4	5	6	TOTAL
1	184 (79.7%)	33 (14.3%)	-	-	-	(6.1%)	231
2	6 (3.8%)	143 (91.1%)	8 (5.1%)	-	-	-	157
3	1 (0.2%)	29 (6.7%)	376 (86.4%)	29 (6.7%)	-	-	435
4	-	-	9 (3.5%)	228 (89.8%)	17 (6.7%)	-	254
5	-	-	-	53 (14.6%)	305 (84.3%)	4 (1.1%)	362
6	159 (34.6%)	-	-	1 (0.2%)	51 (11.1%)	249 (54.1%)	460

% ACCURACY 78.20%

(D) 112 scans (672 ms)

SECTOR \ ANT.#	1	2	3	4	5	6	TOTAL
1	193 (83.5%)	34 (14.7%)	-	-	-	4 (1.7%)	231
2	2 (1.3%)	152 (96.8%)	3 (1.9%)	-	-	-	157
3	(0.2%)	(3.2%)	(90.6%)	(6.0%)	-	-	435
4	-	-	7 (2.8%)	243 (95.7%)	4 (1.6%)	-	254
5	-	-	-	40 (11.0%)	318 (87.8%)	4 (1.1%)	362
6	164 (35.7%)	-	-	-	35 (7.6%)	261 (56.7%)	460

% ACCURACY 82.2%

TABLE XIV
EFFECTS OF SAMPLE INTEGRATION TIME (RUN A) SUBURBAN RESULTS

(A) 1 scan (6 ms)

SECTOR \ ANT.#	1	2	3	4	5	6	TOTAL
1	369 (87.2%)	10 (2.4%)	-	-	-	44 (10.4%)	423
2	27 (5.1%)	489 (92.3%)	14 (2.6%)	-	-	-	530
3	-	28 (4.0%)	653 (92.9%)	22 (3.1%)	-	-	703
4	-	2 (0.2%)	62 (7.5%)	738 (89.0%)	27 (3.3%)	-	829
5	-	-	-	39 (7.6%)	439 (85.4%)	36 (7.0%)	514
6	38 (8.5%)	3 (0.7%)	-	-	35 (7.8%)	371 (83.0%)	447

% ACCURACY 88.8%

(B) 5 scans (30 ms)

SECTOR \ ANT.#	1	2	3	4	5	6	TOTAL
1	397 (93.9%)	5 (1.1%)	-	-	-	(5.0%)	423
2	5 (1.0%)	517 (97.5%)	8 (1.5%)	-	-	-	530
3	-	13 (1.8%)	676 (96.2%)	14 (2.0%)	-	-	703
4	-	-	34 (4.1%)	772 (93.1%)	23 (2.8%)	-	829
5	-	-	-	18	467 (90.9%)	29 (5.6%)	514
6	20 (4.5%)	1 (0.2%)	-	-	21 (4.7%)	405 (90.6%)	447

% ACCURACY 93.8%

(C) 10 scans (60 ms)

SECTOR \ ANT.#	1	2	3	4	5	6	TOTAL
1	404 (95.5%)	3 (0.7%)	-	-	-	16 (3.8%)	423
2	-	524 (98.9%)	6 (1.1%)	-	-	-	530
3	-	14 (2.0%)	680 (96.7%)	9 (1.3%)	-	-	703
4	-	-	30 (3.5%)	783 (94.5%)	16 (2.0%)	-	829
5	-	-	-	14 (2.7%)	478 (93.0%)	22 (4.3%)	514
6	16 (3.6%)	1 (0.2%)	-	-	11 (2.5%)	419 (93.7%)	447

% ACCURACY 95.4%

(D) 112 scans (672 ms)

SECTOR \ ANT.#	1	2	3	4	5	6	TOTAL
1	411 (97.2%)	4 (0.9%)	-	-	-	8 (1.9%)	423
2	-	530 (100%)	-	-	-	-	530
3	-	14 (2.0%)	689 (98.0%)	-	-	-	703
4	-	-	31 (3.7%)	791 (95.4%)	7 (0.9%)	-	829
5	-	-	-	1 (0.2%)	491 (95.7%)	21 (4.1%)	513
6	9 (2.0%)	-	-	-	2 (0.5%)	437 (97.5%)	448

% ACCURACY 97.2%

XIII. SUMMARY AND CONCLUSIONS

Signal-strength based angle-of-arrival vehicle location measurement results have been presented. Experimental results from both heavily built-up urban areas and a typical suburban area are presented for comparison. The signal sample integration time and its effect on the location decision accuracy have been evaluated. From these analyses the following conclusions can be drawn.

1) Angle-of-arrival vehicle locating accuracy is affected substantially by high (compared with land site antenna elevations) man-made structures. In the Philadelphia measurements, to the south of the land site where the building heights are generally low (see Fig. 6), the location accuracy is generally in the 90 percent range. However, to the north of the land site, where the tall buildings are concentrated, the accuracy is generally in the 60 to 70 percent range.

2) There is no obvious relationship between the locating accuracy and the distance from the land site receiver to transmitting mobile. In other words, the location accuracy does not appear to depend upon the absolute signal strength so long as the signals can be distinguished from noise. For example, location accuracies from runs A, B, C, and D of the urban region and runs A, B, and C of the suburban area do not decrease monotonically.

3) Location errors do not necessarily occur only near the beam boundaries. In heavily "shadowed" areas, locating errors can occur with equal probability even if the vehicle is near beam center. In this case, directional antenna beam shaping to increase the locating accuracy would be futile.

4) The directional orientation is not likely to contribute significantly to the overall vehicle location accuracies in the sub-urban area. However, in the urban area, lower error rate can result if the antennas are oriented to include the concentration of high-rise buildings within one directional antenna coverage area.

5) Sample integration time beyond five scans (30 ms) is not likely to contribute significantly to the overall locating accuracy.

6) Overall locating accuracies of 70–80 percent can be expected in heavily built-up urban areas. A much higher accuracy, of the order of 95–98 percent, can be expected in a typical suburban area. The location accuracies in the urban area are expected to increase to the 80- to 90-percent range with a three-lobe antenna locating system.

ACKNOWLEDGMENT

The author would like to acknowledge the efforts of S. F. Carnes, L. F. Smith, and G. F. Walls who devoted many weeks to gather the data discussed in this paper. Data reduction related to the sample integration time was performed by K. L. Steigerwalt. Thanks are also due to G. C. DiPiazza and A. Plitkins for their constant encouragement during the course of this work.

REFERENCES

[1] *IEEE Trans. Veh. Technol.*, Special Issue on Automatic Vehicle Monitoring, vol. VT-26, Feb. 1977. Although this issue contains mostly articles related to the automatic vehicle monitoring (AVM) – or "pinpoint" location of vehicles – for applications in the areas of fleet operation and dispatch services, the article by S. H. Roth covers the history of vehicle location with numerous references.

A Periodic Switching Diversity Technique for a Digital FM Land Mobile Radio

F. ADACHI, T. HATTORI, MEMBER, IEEE, K. HIRADE, AND T. KAMATA

Abstract—A simple and efficient diversity technique is proposed for use in a digital FM land mobile radio communication system. This technique receives two RF signals periodically by switching two antenna branches at a rate moderately higher than the bit rate. The improved bit error rate (BER) performance resulting from the use of diversity is shown to be the effect of transforming the probability density function of the signal energy per bit to noise power density ratio to a sharper distribution. Laboratory simulation test results show that in a Manchester-coded frequency-shift keying (FSK) system with a bit rate of 600 bit/s and a frequency deviation of ±5 kHz, the diversity gain at an average BER of 1×10^{-3} is about 10 dB for an optimum switching rate of about 2 kHz. This diversity improvement is also verified by the field test performed in a suburban area.

I. INTRODUCTION

IN LAND MOBILE radio communication systems, signal transmission between a base station and a mobile unit is usually performed not only by a direct line-of-sight route, but also via multiple random paths because of reflection, scattering, and diffraction. Thus in the case of UHF or microwave land mobile radio, rapid and deep fading phenomenon will occur on

the received signals at both stations as the mobile unit moves through an interference field made of many waves which arrive with different amplitudes and phases. This fading phenomenon is generally called multipath fading or Rayleigh fading. A received signal suffering such fading phenomenon has a Rayleigh distributed envelope and a uniformly distributed phase [1]-[3].

In a Rayleigh fading environment, signal transmission performance is greatly degraded. Diversity reception is one of the most useful techniques to reduce the influence of such fading on signal transmission performance [4], [5]. Many diversity techniques for land mobile radio have been proposed and researched. Most of them adopt a method which combines the RF signals on the different diversity branches suffering uncorrelated Rayleigh fadings. Typical combining methods are selection, maximal ratio, and equal gain [6], [7]. Switching diversity using a single receiver is a kind of selection combining diversity technique with an advantage for mobile radio use because of equipment simplification and cost economy [8], [9].

This paper proposes a more simplified switching diversity technique to be used in a digital FM land mobile radio. This technique adopts a simple method which receives two RF signals periodically by switching two antenna branches at a rate moderately higher than the bit rate. In Section II, the background for such a concept is given, and it is shown that the cause of diversity effect on the bit error rate (BER)

Manuscript received May 12, 1976; revised April 27, 1978. A part of this paper was originally presented at the Twenty-Sixth Annual Conference of the IEEE Vehicular Technology Group, March 24–26, 1976, Washington, DC.

The authors are with the Mobile Communications Section, Electrical Communication Laboratories, Nippon Telegraph and Telephone Public Corporation, 1-2356, Take, Yokosuka-shi, Kanagawa-ken, 238-03, JAPAN.

Reprinted from *IEEE Trans. Veh. Technol.*, vol. VT-27, pp. 211–219, Nov. 1978.

performance is due to transforming the probability density function (pdf) of the signal energy per bit to noise power density ratio to a sharper distribution. Section III analyzes the diversity improvement on the BER performance. In Section IV, the laboratory simulation test results for a Manchester-coded frequency-shift keying (FSK) system with limiter-discriminator detection are described. For the bit rate of 600 bit/s and frequency deviation of ±5 kHz, an optimum switching rate is about 2 kHz. In such a case, the diversity gain at the average BER of 1×10^{-3} is about 10 dB. Section V deals with a field test performed in a suburban area. It is proved that the experimental system demonstrates diversity action in a real fading environment.

II. BACKGROUND

Two of the authors have clarified the effect of mobile speed on the BER performance in a Manchester-coded FSK system with limiter-discriminator detection in the 900 MHz band by the laboratory simulation test [10].

The fading simulator used in the experiment is able to generate Rayleigh fading [11]. The fading rate, i.e., the maximum Doppler frequency f_D $(=v/\lambda)$, corresponding to mobile speed v and carrier wavelength λ, is variable from 0 Hz to 10 kHz. Fig. 1 shows the effect of the fading rate on the BER performance of a Manchester-coded FSK system with a bit rate of $f_b = 600$ bit/s and a frequency deviation of $\Delta f_d = \pm 5$ kHz. In this measurement, the predetection IF filter's 3-dB bandwidth is $B_{if} = 16$ kHz and the postdetection baseband filter's 3-dB bandwidth is $B_0 = 626$ Hz.

From the above laboratory simulation test results, it is found that the average BER performance is closely related to the fading rate, i.e., mobile speed. There exists an optimum value of $f_D \approx 1.5$ kHz in the fading rate corresponding to a fictitious speed of $v \approx 1250$ km/h. The optimum value is not closely dependent on the average signal level.

It is well known that total error probability P_e of an FSK system with limiter-discriminator detection in a Rayleigh fading environment is given by [12]

$$P_e = P_1 + P_2 + P_3 \tag{1}$$

where P_1 is average BER due to Rayleigh envelope fading, P_2 is average BER due to random FM noise, and P_3 is average BER due to time delay spread.

In the above case, average BER P_3 due to time delay spread is negligible because the bit rate of $f_b = 600$ bit/s is negligibly small in comparison with the coherent bandwidth of $B = 250$ kHz.[1]

In an FSK system with limiter-discriminator detection, the average BER P_2 due to random FM noise is given by [12]

$$P_2 = \frac{1}{2}\left[1 - \sqrt{2}\left(\frac{\Delta f_d}{f_D}\right)\left\{ 1 + 2\left(\frac{\Delta f_d}{f_D}\right)^2\right\}^{-1/2} \right]. \tag{2}$$

This result indicates that P_2 is smaller than 5×10^{-3} unless

---

[1] This is a typical value measured by Cox in an urban area such as New York [13].

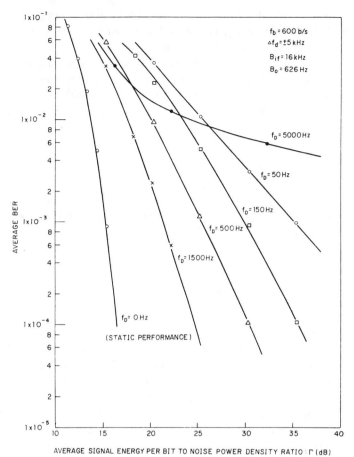

Fig. 1. Effect of fading rate on average BER performance.

$(\Delta f_d/f_D)$ becomes smaller than 5.0. However, the measured BER P_2 is much smaller than 5×10^{-5} because of the low-pass filtering effect.

The average BER P_1 due to Rayleigh envelope fading is obtained by averaging the static BER performance over the fading dynamic range. The static BER performance can be approximately represented as the following relation [12]:

$$P_e(\gamma) \approx \tfrac{1}{2}e^{-\alpha\gamma}, \tag{3}$$

where γ is signal energy per bit to noise power density ratio and α is a constant parameter determined from the bit rate, frequency deviation, and predetection IF filter bandwidth. Therefore, P_1 is given by

$$P_1 = \int_0^\infty P_e(\gamma)p(\gamma)\,d\gamma \approx \int_0^\infty \tfrac{1}{2}e^{-\alpha\gamma}p(\gamma)\,d\gamma \tag{4}$$

where $p(\gamma)$ is the probability density function (pdf) of γ. As the noise power density N_0 is constant, the pdf of $\gamma = E_b/N_0$ is equal to that of signal energy E_b during one time slot $T = 1/f_b$. Signal energy E_b is given by

$$E_b = \int_0^T e^2(t)\,dt \tag{5}$$

where $e(t)$ is the Rayleigh fading signal. Because $e(t)$ can be mathematically represented as a narrow-band Gaussian process [3], the pdf of E_b, i.e., γ, is determined from the Gaussian process autocorrelation function $\psi(\tau)$ [14].

For the quasi-stationary case, where the fading rate f_D is much lower than the bit rate f_b, the averaging time T becomes much shorter than the decorrelation time[2] of $e(t)$. Then, the pdf of γ is approximately given by the well-known exponential distribution

$$p(\gamma) = \frac{1}{\Gamma} e^{-(\gamma/\Gamma)} \qquad (6)$$

where Γ is the average signal energy per bit to noise power density ratio. Therefore, P_1 is given by

$$P_1 = \frac{1}{2(\alpha\Gamma + 1)} \approx \frac{1}{2\alpha\Gamma}. \qquad (7)$$

This indicates that P_1 is independent of the fading rate.

However, the above result is not true for the nonquasi-stationary case, where the fading rate is not negligibly small in comparison with the bit rate. For such a nonquasi-stationary case, the pdf of γ is not given by (6), but becomes a sharper distribution with small variance [14]. The shape of its pdf resembles that of Gamma or Erlang's distribution. This result means that the fading dynamic range of γ can be reduced. Therefore, the average BER P_1 due to Rayleigh envelope fading can be reduced by an increase in fading rate. This improvement effect comes from integrating the received signal power over one time slot T, which is not much shorter than the decorrelation time of $e(t)$. Then, the average BER performance can be improved as the fading rate increases.

But, if the fading rate becomes excessively high, the average BER P_2 due to random FM noise, which is given by (2), will dominate. This implies that there exists an optimum value in the fading rate, i.e., mobile speed, for BER performance improvement.

Thus it is concluded that the same improvement effect may be obtained by using a technique that would transform the pdf of γ to a sharper distribution. One of the equivalent techniques is to receive two RF signals periodically by switching two antenna branches at a rate moderately higher than the bit rate. This is a new switching diversity technique in that it does not possess a level detector. A block diagram of the receiver using this periodic switching diversity technique is shown in Fig. 2. The diversity effect on the BER performance is analyzed in the following section.

III. DIVERSITY EFFECT ON BER PERFORMANCE

In the receiver model shown in Fig. 2, let us assume that both of the RF signals received by the respective antennas are multipath fading waves with a Rayleigh distributed envelope

---

[2] The decorrelation time is related to the autocorrelation function $\Psi(\tau)$ by the requirement that for any time greater than the decorrelation time, the magnitude of the normalized autocorrelation function must be much less than 1.

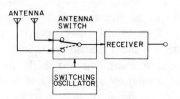

Fig. 2.   Block diagram of periodic switching diversity technique.

and a uniformly distributed phase. Furthermore, the two average received signal powers are equal to each other and the fading rate is much lower than the bit rate.

For the quasi-stationary case, where the switching rate is much lower than the bit rate, the receiver input during one time slot is mostly either of the two RF signals received by the respective antennas. Therefore, it is equally probable that the signal energy per bit to noise power density ratio γ becomes either of the γ_1 and γ_2. Considering that the pdf of γ_1 and γ_2 are given by respectively,

$$\begin{cases} p(\gamma_1) = \dfrac{1}{\Gamma} e^{-(\gamma_1/\Gamma)} \\[2mm] p(\gamma_2) = \dfrac{1}{\Gamma} e^{-(\gamma_2/\Gamma)}, \end{cases} \qquad (8)$$

the pdf of γ is given by

$$p(\gamma) = \tfrac{1}{2}p_1(\gamma) + \tfrac{1}{2}p_2(\gamma) = \frac{1}{\Gamma} e^{-(\gamma/\Gamma)}, \qquad (9)$$

where Γ is the average signal energy per bit to noise power density ratio on each diversity branch. This means that the pdf of γ is identical with the pdf of γ_1 and γ_2, corresponding to the nondiversity case. In this case, the average BER P_1 due to Rayleigh envelope fading is also given by equation (7), and the diversity effect is not obtained.

For the nonquasi-stationary case, where the switching rate is much higher than the bit rate, the two RF signals are periodically switched and combined during one time slot. In this case, the signal energy during one time slot becomes one half of the sum of the respective signal energies. Therefore, γ is given by

$$\gamma = \tfrac{1}{2}(\gamma_1 + \gamma_2). \qquad (10)$$

Considering that the pdf of γ_1 and γ_2 are given by equation (8), respectively, the pdf of γ is given by [4]

$$p(\gamma) = \frac{1}{\Gamma|k|} \left[e^{-\{2\gamma/\Gamma(1+|k|)\}} - e^{-\{2\gamma/\Gamma(1-|k|)\}} \right] \qquad (11)$$

where k denotes the complex fading correlation between the two fading signals. The above equation corresponds to that of the well-known maximal-ratio combining diversity technique with a signal energy per bit to noise power density ratio of $\Gamma/2$ in each diversity branch. Consequently, the average BER

P_1 due to Rayleigh envelope fading is given by

$$P_1 = \int_0^\infty P_e(\gamma) p(\gamma) \, d\gamma$$

$$= \frac{1}{2\Gamma|k|} \left[\frac{1}{\alpha + \{2/\Gamma(1 + |k|)\}} - \frac{1}{\alpha + \{2/\Gamma(1 - |k|)\}} \right]$$

$$\approx \frac{1}{\alpha^2 \Gamma^2 (1 - |k|^2)}. \tag{12}$$

For the intermediate case between the quasi-stationary case and the nonquasi-stationary case, where the switching rate is nearly equal to the bit rate, the average BER P_1 due to Rayleigh envelope fading should be represented as the intermediate form between (7) and (12).

For the nonquasi-stationary case, where the switching rate becomes excessively high, the switching noise should appear at the discriminator output, just as the random FM noise did when the fading rate was increased. Though the random FM noise is a random process, this switching noise is a deterministic process because the switching operation is periodic. Therefore, the switching noise can be removed by a low-pass filter with a lower cutoff frequency than the switching rate.

On the other hand, when one takes the receiver input from one of the antenna branches and gates the received signal on and off periodically at a rate much higher than the bit rate, the signal energy per bit to noise power density ratio γ is given by

$$\gamma = \gamma_1/2. \tag{13}$$

Then, the pdf of γ is given by

$$p(\gamma) = \frac{2}{\Gamma} e^{-(2\gamma/\Gamma)}. \tag{14}$$

In this case, the average BER P_1 due to Rayleigh envelope fading is given by replacing Γ with $\Gamma/2$ in (7). Therefore, the same diversity effect is not obtained.

The feasibility of the periodic switching diversity technique is verified by the following laboratory simulation and field tests.

IV. LABORATORY SIMULATION TEST

A. Simulation Test System

A block diagram of the laboratory simulation test system is shown in Fig. 3.

A pseudonoise (PN) sequence with a bit rate of $f_b = 600$ bit/s and a repetition period of $N = 2^9 - 1 = 511$ bits is used as a test pattern signal. The transmitter consists of an encoder and a 900 MHz band FM modulator. The encoder includes a sum-logic circuit and a code converter. The sum-logic circuit differentially encodes the transmitting test pattern signal to simplify the timing recovery circuit used in the receiver. The code converter transforms a nonreturn to zero (NRZ) type signal into a Manchester-coded type signal to suppress the

direct current component. The Manchester-coded signal is fed to the 900 MHz band FM modulator generating a Manchester-coded FSK signal, which is equivalent to an NRZ binary FSK signal with a bit rate of 1200 bit/s. In this case, frequency deviation Δf_d is variable, and the transmitting band is not restricted.

The Manchester-coded FSK signal is transmitted to the receiver through a multipath fading simulator [11] with two branches. The multipath fading simulator provides two fading signals, each having a Rayleigh distributed envelope and a uniformly distributed phase. The fading rate f_D is variable from 0 Hz to 10 kHz. The envelope correlation ρ between the two fading signal envelopes is also variable from 0 to 1.

The receiver consists of an RF switch unit, an FM receiver, and a decoder. The RF switch unit consists of a p-i-n diode switch and an astable multivibrator with adjustable free-running frequency. The FM receiver is a conventional double-conversion type using a limiter–discriminator. Its total noise figure is $N_F = 9.8$ dB. Two Butterworth crystal filters are used as the first and second IF filters of this FM receiver. Overall 3-dB predetection bandwidth is $B_{if} = 16$ kHz. The decoder is composed of a baseband filter, a timing recovery circuit, a decision circuit, and a difference-logic circuit. The baseband filter is a Gaussian type active filter with 3-dB bandwidth of $B_0 = 626$ Hz. The baseband Gaussian filter is used for low-pass filtering of the discriminator output. The timing recovery circuit is composed of a digital phase-locked loop. The recovered timing error is smaller than ±9 degrees. Using recovered timing, the low-pass filtered output is decided upon as "0" or "1" and regenerated by the decision circuit.

After being differentially decoded by the difference-logic circuit, the regenerated output is fed to the error rate counter for the BER measurement.

B. Test Results

In the following simulation test, the average signal energy per bit to noise power density ratios on the respective diversity branches are equal to each other, $\Gamma_1 = \Gamma_2 = \Gamma$. The fading rate is set equal to $f_D = 40$ Hz, corresponding to a typical mobile speed of $v = 48$ km/h = 30 mi/h for the 900-MHz band. The measured BER is the average of several BER measurements. Each measurement takes about 3 minutes, so that several hundred signal fades may occur in each measurement. Other parameters are

1) switching rate f_s;
2) frequency deviation Δf_d;
3) envelope correlation ρ.

Fig. 4 shows the measured average BER performance with the switching rate as a parameter for $\Delta f_d = \pm 5$ kHz and $\rho = 0$. As was expected, the test results indicate that the average BER performance is markedly improved by setting the switching rate to an optimum value. With an optimum setting, the received average signal level necessary for the average BER of 1×10^{-3} is reduced by about 10 dB relative to the signal level of a nondiversity case. This reduced quantity corresponds to the diversity gain of this system.

Fig. 5 shows the measured average BER versus switching

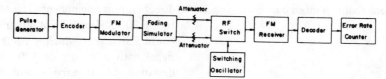

(a) Overall block diagram of experimental simulation test system

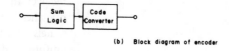

(b) Block diagram of encoder

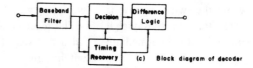

(c) Block diagram of decoder

Fig. 3. Block diagram of experimental simulation test system.

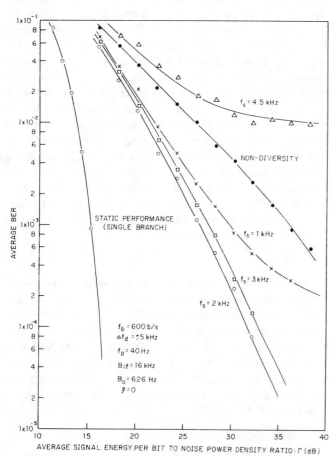

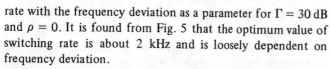

Fig. 4. Effect of switching rate on average BER performance.

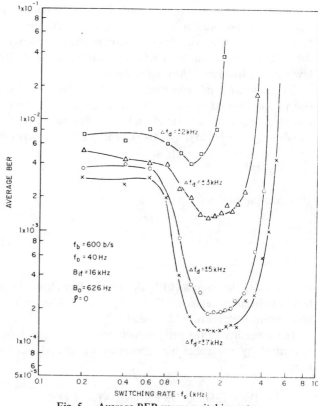

Fig. 5. Average BER versus switching rate.

rate with the frequency deviation as a parameter for $\Gamma = 30$ dB and $\rho = 0$. It is found from Fig. 5 that the optimum value of switching rate is about 2 kHz and is loosely dependent on frequency deviation.

Fig. 6 shows the measured average BER performance with the envelope correlation ρ as a parameter for $\Delta f_d = \pm 5$ kHz and $f_s = 2$ kHz. The results indicate that the improvement effect is reduced by only about 2 dB, unless the envelope correlation exceeds $\rho = 0.8$.

C. Discussion

The simulation test results surely show that the average BER performance can be improved by increasing the switching rate, but is degraded at an excessively high switching rate. Therefore, it is found that there exists an optimum value in the switching rate.

The reason why the average BER performance is degraded at an excessively high switching rate is believed to be caused by the following. When the switching rate is excessively high, the spectrum of the combined receiver input is so spread that signal distortion is caused by IF filter band restriction. As-

274

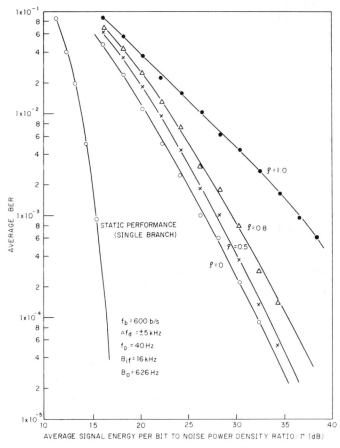

Fig. 6.   Effect of correlation on average BER performance.

suming that the IF filter bandwidth is wide enough for the signal transmission, the average BER performance will not be degraded by the signal distortion. However, it will be degraded in turn by the excessively increased noise power. Therefore, there exists an optimum value in the switching rate.

The constant parameter α, included in (3), is found to be $\alpha \approx 0.2$ from experimental data on static BER performance for a bit rate of $f_b = 600$ bit/s, frequency deviation of $\Delta f_d = \pm 5$ kHz, and predetection IF filter bandwidth of $B_{if} = 16$ kHz. Since differential encoding is used in the simulation test, the measured average BER should be approximately given by $2 \times P_1$, where P_1 is given by (7) or (12). Thus the average BERs for the nondiversity case and the periodic switching diversity case with a very high switching rate are given by 5×10^{-3} and 1×10^{-4}, respectively, at an average signal energy per bit to noise power density ratio of $\Gamma = 30$ dB. As shown in Fig. 4, the simulation test results for the nondiversity case and for the diversity case with $f_s = 2$ kHz agree well with the above calculated values. The influence of correlation causes the diversity gain to be decreased by 3.5 dB for $|k|^2 = 0.8$ from (12). Considering that the envelope correlation ρ between the two fading signals is approximately given by $\rho \approx |k|^2$ [4], the simulation test results shown in Fig. 6 agree with the calculated values.

V. FIELD TEST

The field test was performed in a suburban area in order to verify the feasibility of the periodic switching diversity system in a real fading environment. In this test, a Manchester-coded FSK system with a bit rate of $f_b = 600$ bit/s and a frequency deviation of $\Delta f_d = \pm 5$ kHz was used. The switching rate was set as an optimum value of $f_s = 2$ kHz.

A. Field Test System

The block diagrams of the base and mobile station systems are shown in Figs. 7 and 8, respectively.

The base station is located on the top of Yokosuka Electrical Communication Laboratory about 160 m above the test area. The transmitter has an output power of 5 watts. The transmitter output is passed through an RF attenuator and is radiated from a base station antenna which is an 8-element Yagi antenna having a gain of 10 dB over a dipole. The RF attenuator is used to vary the received signal strength at the mobile receiver. The test pattern signal and the encoder used in the field test are identical with those used in the laboratory simulation test. The carrier frequency is 880,000 MHz.

The mobile station is in a van. Two $\lambda/4$ whip antennas are located on the ground plain above the van roof. The antenna arrangement is square to the direction of vehicle movement. Antenna spacing is variable from 3 cm to 64 cm, i.e., from 0.09λ to 2λ. A power divider is inserted in each diversity branch for the envelope measurement of fading signals and the BER measurement with and without diversity. An antenna switch unit is operated by an astable multivibrator with an optimum switching rate of 2 kHz. The FM receiver and the decoder are identical with those used in the laboratory simulation test. The decoder output is fed to an error detector to measure the average BER.

In the error detector, an exclusive-or gate compares the decoder output with a reference PN sequence generated locally by recovering the frame synchronization from the decoder output. Thus a bit error pulse occurs whenever any bit of the decoder output is different from the reference PN sequence. The outputs of the field strength measuring receivers and the error detectors are recorded in an FM tape recorder for later processing.

B. Statistical Characteristics of Field Strength

The field test area is the Kurihama area characterized by a small scale factory district, at a distance of about 3 km from the base station shown in Fig. 9. The test is made along a street, which is about 2 km around and is approximately orthogonal to a radial line of the direction between the transmitter and the receiver, at a constant moving speed of about 30 km/h.

By the measurement of the fading statistical characteristics on the received signal, it is found that the received signal envelope follows closely to the Rayleigh distribution locally and its local average follows closely to the lognormal distribution with a standard deviation of $\sigma = 3.7$ dB. The median value of the local average is 34 dBμ, i.e., the median value Γ_m of the local average Γ of the signal energy per bit to noise power density ratio is $\Gamma_m = 54.5$ dB, when the attenuation of the base station RF attenuator is 0 dB.

Fig. 10 shows the measured envelope correlation versus antenna spacing. The plotted value is the average of several

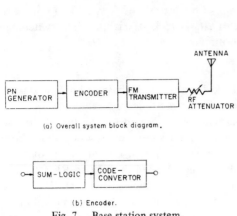

(a) Overall system block diagram.

(b) Encoder.

Fig. 7. Base station system.

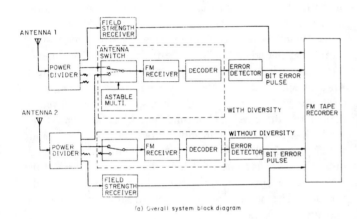

(a) Overall system block diagram

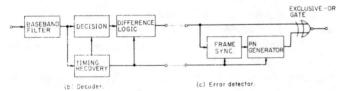

(b) Decoder.   (c) Error detector.

Fig. 8. Mobile station system.

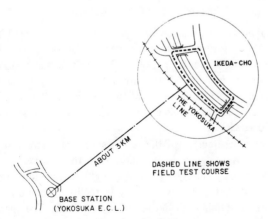

Fig. 9. Map showing field test area.

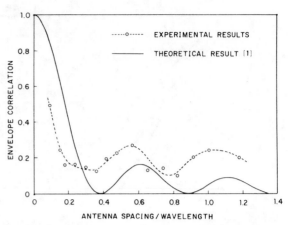

Fig. 10. Envelope correlation versus antenna spacing.

measurements. Each measurement takes 2 seconds so that each measuring distance may be about 50 wavelengths. The shape of the curves is roughly similar to the theoretically predicted one [1] without being a close fit at any point.

C. Measured Average BER Performance

The average BER is computed by counting the total number of the bit error pulses and dividing by the total number of the transmitted bits. Each measurement takes about 30 minutes, so a test signal composed of 1 080 000 bits is transmitted.

The measured average BER performances with and without diversity are shown in Fig. 11. In this case, the antenna spacing is 2 λ, so the envelope correlation is nearly zero. The test results verify that the use of the periodic switching diversity can surely reduce the received average signal level necessary for an average BER of 1×10^{-2} or 1×10^{-3} by about 5 or 10 dB, respectively, relative to that without diversity.

The influence of antenna spacing on the diversity improvement is shown in Fig. 12 for $\Gamma_m = 29.5$ dB. The diversity improvement is degraded only at an antenna spacing of 0.09 λ.

D. Discussion

From the measurement of the fading statistical characteristics, it is found that the received signal envelope follows closely to the Rayleigh distribution locally and its local average follows closely to the lognormal distribution with a standard deviation of $\sigma = 3.7$ dB. Therefore, the pdf of the local average Γ of the received signal energy per bit to noise power density ratio is given by

$$p(\Gamma)d\Gamma = \frac{1}{\sqrt{2\pi}\sigma} e^{-\frac{(10 \log \Gamma - 10 \log \Gamma_m)^2}{2\sigma^2}} d(10 \log \Gamma) \quad (15)$$

where Γ_m is the median value of Γ. The local averages of the two fading signals received by the respective diversity antennas can be assumed to vary coincidentally since the antenna spacing is about less than a few wavelengths. Thus the average BER $P_1{}^*$ including the effect of the lognormal distribution of Γ is obtained by averaging the local average BER P_1 in the Rayleigh fading with constant average power, which is given in (7) or (12), over $p(\Gamma)$. The average BER $P_1{}^*$ with and without diver-

276

sity are given by, respectively,

$$P_1{}^* = \int_0^\infty P_1(\Gamma)p(\Gamma)\,d\Gamma$$

$$\approx \frac{2}{\alpha^2(1-|k|^2)}\int_0^\infty \Gamma^{-2}p(\Gamma)\,d\Gamma$$

$$= \frac{2}{\alpha^2(1-|k|^2)\Gamma_m{}^2}e^{\left\{\frac{\sqrt{2}\,\ln 10}{10}\sigma\right\}^2} \tag{16}$$

$$P_1{}^* \approx \frac{1}{2\alpha\Gamma}e^{\frac{1}{4}\left\{\frac{\sqrt{2}\,\ln 10}{10}\sigma\right\}^2} \tag{17}$$

Since the differential encoding is used, the measured average BER should be approximately equal to $2 \times P_1{}^*$. The constant parameter α is about 0.2 as shown in Section IV. Thus the average BER with and without diversity are about 4.3×10^{-4} and 7.1×10^{-3}, respectively, when $\Gamma_m = 30$ dB. As shown in Fig. 11, the field test results agree well with the above calculated values.

The measured envelope correlation between two fading signals is about 0.5 for an antenna spacing of 0.09 λ as shown in Fig. 10. Since the envelope correlation is approximately equal to $|k|^2$ [4], an antenna spacing of 0.09 λ causes the value of the average BER to be increased by two times as much from (12). The field test results shown in Fig. 12 agree with the above result.

VI. CONCLUSION

This paper describes a simple switching diversity technique to receive two RF signals periodically by switching two antenna branches at a rate moderately higher than the bit rate.

After the background for the concept was described, the cause of diversity effect was explained as being due to transforming the probability density function of signal energy per bit to noise power density ratio to a sharper distribution with smaller variance. Then, the feasibility of this periodic switching diversity technique was verified by the laboratory simulation and field tests.

Although a similar diversity effect can also be obtained for co-channel interference performance, adjacent-channel interference performance may not be improved since periodic switching would tend to cause spectrum foldover into the desired channel band. This is a potential problem which is an area for further study.

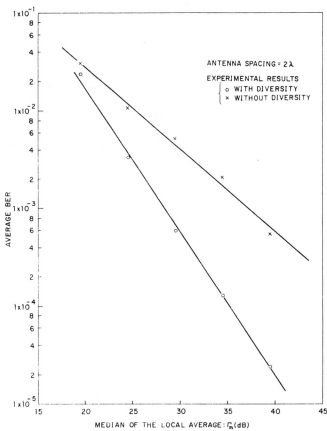

Fig. 11.   Average BER versus median of the local average.

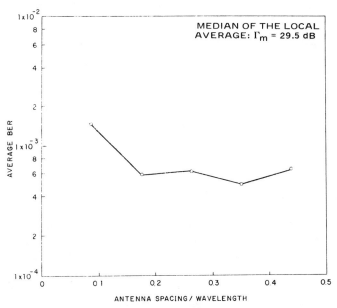

Fig. 12.   Average BER versus antenna spacing.

ACKNOWLEDGMENT

The authors wish to thank Mr. S. Ito, Chief of the Mobile Radio Communication System Section, for his helpful guidance.

REFERENCES

[1]   R. H. Clarke, "A Statistical Theory of Mobile Radio Reception," *Bell System Tech. J.*, Vol. 47, pp. 957–1000, July–Aug. 1968.

[2] Y. Okumura, E. Ohmori, T. Kawano, and K. Fukuda, "Field Strength and its Variability in VHF and UHF Land Mobile Service," *Rev. Elec. Comm. Lab.*, Vol. 16, pp. 825–873, Sept.–Oct. 1968.

[3] M. J. Gans. "A Power-Spectral Theory of Propagation in the Mobile Radio Environment," *IEEE Trans. Veh. Technol.*, Vol. VT-21, pp. 27–38, Feb. 1972.

[4] M. Schwartz, W. R. Bennett, and S. Stein, *Communication Systems and Techniques,* McGraw-Hill Inc., New York, 1965, ch. 10 and 11.

[5] W. C. Jakes, Jr., *Microwave Mobile Communications,* John Wiley and Sons Inc., New York, 1974, ch. 5 and 6.

[6] —, "A Comparison of Specific Space Diversity Techniques for Reduction of Fast Fading in UHF Mobile Radio Systems," *IEEE Trans. Veh. Technol.*, Vol. VT-20, pp. 81–92, Nov. 1971.

[7] J. D. Parsons, M. Henze, P. A. Ratlif, and M. J. Withers, "Diversity Techniques for Mobile Radio Reception," *The Radio and Electronic Engineer,* Vol. 45, pp. 357–367, July 1975.

[8] A. J. Rustako, Jr., Y. S. Yeh, and R. R. Murray, "Performance of Feedback and Switch Space Diversity 900 MHz FM Mobile Radio Systems with Rayleigh Fading," *IEEE Trans. Commun. Technol.*, Vol. COM-21, pp. 1257–1268, Nov. 1973.

[9] W. E. Shortall, "A Switched Diversity Receiving System for Mobile Radio," *IEEE Trans. Commun. Technol.*, Vol. COM-21, pp. 1269–1275, Nov. 1973.

[10] T. Hattori and K. Hirade, "Offset Diversity Effect in Multi-Station Paging System," Rep. of Comm. Sys. Conf., CS-97, IECE of Japan, Oct. 1974.

[11] K. Hirade, K. Abe, T. Hanazawa, and F. Adachi, "Fading Simulator for Land Mobile Radio Communication," *Trans. IECE of Japan,* Vol. 58-B, pp. 449–456, Sept. 1975.

[12] Ibid. [5], pp. 230–240.

[13] D. C. Cox, "Time and Frequency Domain Characteristics of Multipath Propagation at 910 MHz in a Suburban Mobile Radio Environment," *Radio Science,* Vol. 7, pp. 1069–1077, Dec. 1972.

[14] M. I. Schwartz, "Distribution of the Time-Average Power of a Gaussian Process," *IEEE Trans. Inform. Theory,* Vol. IT-16, pp. 17–26, Jan. 1970.

Periodic Switching Diversity Effect on Co-Channel Interference Performance of a Digital FM Land Mobile Radio

FUMIYUKI ADACHI

Abstract—The effect of periodic switching diversity on the bit error rate (BER) performance of a binary frequency-shift keying (FSK) system in the presence of co-channel interference is described. The distribution of the signal-to-interference energy ratio per bit presented to the FM detector is found and the diversity effect on the BER performance in a Rayleigh fading environment is analyzed. The diversity effect on the BER performance in a Manchester-coded FSK system with limiter-discriminator detection is verified by laboratory simulation tests using a Rayleigh fading simulator.

I. INTRODUCTION

IN UHF OR microwave land mobile radio communication systems, the same carrier frequency is reused in different radio zones for efficient frequency utilization. Since the signal transmission is usually performed via multiple propagation paths, both desired and interfering signals are subject to Rayleigh fading with vehicle movement [1], [2]. In the presence of fading, the desired signal may fade below the received interfering signal with a high probability, so that the signal transmission performance is severely degraded.

It is well known that diversity techniques are able to improve the co-channel interference performance in a fading signal environment. Many diversity techniques have been proposed and researched [3], [4]. A simple and efficient diversity technique suitable for a digital FM land mobile radio using a binary FSK system with limiter-discriminator detection has been proposed, and its diversity effect on the bit error rate (BER) performance in a Rayleigh fading signal environment has been verified [5]. This technique receives two RF signals periodically by switching two antenna branches at a rate moderately higher than the bit rate (see Fig. 1).

This paper describes the periodic switching diversity effect on the BER performance of a binary frequency-shift keying (FSK) system in the presence of co-channel interference. The distribution of the signal-to-interference energy ratio per bit (SIR) presented to the FM detector is found, and the diversity effect on the BER performance in the presence of co-channel interference is analyzed. Its diversity effect in a Manchester-coded FSK system with limiter-discriminator detection is verified by laboratory simulation tests.

Manuscript received January 3, 1978; revised May 2, 1978.
The author is with the Mobile Communications Section, Electrical Communication Laboratories, Nippon Telegraph and Telephone Public Corporation, 1-2356. Take, Yokosuka-shi, Kanagawa-Ken, 238-03, Japan.

II. DIVERSITY EFFECT ON THE BER PERFORMANCE IN THE PRESENCE OF CO-CHANNEL INTERFERENCE

A. Distribution of SIR

The periodic switching diversity strategy is to switch between two RF waves received by the different antenna branches periodically at a rate moderately higher than the bit rate of the binary FSK signal (see Fig. 1). The diversity can change the statistics of the SIR presented to the FM detector. The analysis used in [5] can be also applied to provide the probability density function (pdf) of the SIR.

Let us assume that a single interferer exists and that both desired and interfering signals exhibit mutually independent slow Rayleigh fadings. When the switching rate is much higher than the bit rate, two RF waves received by the respective diversity antennas are periodically switched and combined in a bit interval. Thus the signal energy ϵ_s and the interference energy ϵ_i in a bit interval, presented to the FM detector, become one half of the sum of the corresponding energies on the respective diversity branches, respectively. We obtain

$$\epsilon_s = \epsilon_{s1} + \epsilon_{s2}$$
$$\epsilon_i = \epsilon_{i1} + \epsilon_{i2} \qquad (1)$$

where ϵ_{sn} and ϵ_{in} are the signal energy and the interference energy, in a bit interval, on the nth branch ($n = 1, 2$), respectively. Following the result in [5], the joint pdf of ϵ_s and ϵ_i, $p(\epsilon_s, \epsilon_i)$, is given by

$$p(\epsilon_s, \epsilon_i) = \frac{1}{E_s E_i |k|^2} [e^{-\{2\epsilon_s/E_s(1+|k|)\}}$$
$$- e^{-\{2\epsilon_s/E_s(1-|k|)\}}]$$
$$\cdot [e^{-\{2\epsilon_i/E_i(1+|k|)\}} - e^{-\{2\epsilon_i/E_i(1-|k|)\}}] \quad (2)$$

where E_s and E_i are the average signal energy and the average interference energy on each branch, respectively, and k is the complex fading correlation coefficient between the two diversity branches. The complex fading correlation coefficient is related to the envelope correlation coefficient ρ. ρ is very nearly equal to $|k|^2$ [2]. Therefore, defining the SIR presented to the FM detector as $\lambda = \epsilon_s/\epsilon_i$, the pdf of λ, $p(\lambda)$, is easily

Reprinted from *IEEE Trans. Veh. Technol.*, vol. VT-27, pp. 220–223, Nov. 1978.

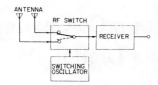

Fig. 1. Periodic switching diversity.

derived from (2):

$$p(\lambda) = \frac{\Lambda}{4|k|^2}\{2(1+|k|^2)(\Lambda+\lambda)^{-2}$$

$$- (1-|k|^2)^2[\{\Lambda(1-|k|)+\lambda(1+|k|)\}^{-1}$$

$$+ \{\Lambda(1+|k|)+\lambda(1-|k|)\}^{-1}]\} \qquad (3)$$

where $\Lambda = E_s/E_i$ is the average SIR on each branch.

B. BER Performance

With one crucial but not unreasonable assumption, a deceptively simple form may be obtained for the BER performance on the basis of the FM capture effect. Let us assume the following. No error can occur as long as the signal energy ϵ_s presented to the FM detector does not fade below the interference energy ϵ_i presented to the FM detector, i.e., $\lambda \geq 1$. If ϵ_s fades below ϵ_i, i.e., $\lambda < 1$, errors occur with probability $1/2$. Let us denote the BER by $P_e(\Lambda)$ when the average SIR on each branch is Λ. From the above assumption, the BER is equal to one half of the cumulative probability at $\lambda = 1$:

$$P_e(\Lambda) = \frac{1}{2}\int_0^1 p(\lambda)d\lambda. \qquad (4)$$

Substituting (3) into (4), we obtain

$$P_e(\Lambda) = \frac{3\Lambda+1+|k|^2(\Lambda-1)}{2(\Lambda+1)\{(\Lambda+1)^2-|k|^2(\Lambda-1)^2\}}. \qquad (5)$$

For $k = 1$, (5) reduces to the BER without diversity:

$$P_e(\Lambda) = \frac{1}{2}\cdot\frac{1}{(\Lambda+1)}. \qquad (6)$$

Comparing (5) with (6), it is found that the periodic switching diversity can improve the co-channel interference performance.

C. Comparison

We compare the periodic switching diversity with the well-known selection and maximal-ratio combinings with uncorrelated two branch signals. There are several methods of instrumenting the selection and maximal-ratio combiners [4]. For the selection combiner, we consider two methods: the total-power method, which selects the branch with the larger total-power (desired signal power plus interference power), and the desired-signal-power method, which selects the branch with the larger desired signal power. For the maximal-ratio combiner, we also consider two methods: the perfect-pilot

method, which adjusts the branch gains to be equal to the complex conjugate of the desired signal pilot phasor, and the separate-pilot method, which adjusts the branch gains to be equal to the complex conjugate of the sum of the desired signal pilot phasor and the interferer pilot phasor.

Bond and Meyer [6] have derived the probability distribution of the SIR λ for the selection combining using the total-power method. The probability distributions of λ for the selection combining using the desired signal power method and for the maximal-ratio combining are derived in [7]. Remember that the BER $P_e(\Lambda)$ is equal to one half of the cumulative probability at $\lambda = 1$ as shown in (4). For the selection combining, we obtain

$$P_e(\Lambda) = \frac{1}{2}\cdot\frac{13\Lambda+3}{(\Lambda+1)(\Lambda+3)(3\Lambda+1)},$$

for the total-power method (7)

and

$$P_e(\Lambda) = \frac{1}{(\Lambda+1)(\Lambda+2)},$$

for the desired-signal-power method. (8)

For the maximal-ratio combining, we obtain

$$P_e(\Lambda) = \frac{1}{2}\cdot\frac{1}{(\Lambda+1)^2}, \quad \text{for the perfect-pilot method} \qquad (9)$$

and

$$P_e(\Lambda) = \frac{1}{2}\cdot\frac{3\Lambda+1}{(\Lambda+1)^3}, \quad \text{for the separate-pilot method.}$$

$$(10)$$

By comparing (5) with (7)–(10), it is found that the performance of the periodic switching diversity is just the same as that of the maximal-ratio combining using the separate-pilot method. Equations (5)–(10) are plotted in Fig. 2.

III. EXPERIMENTAL PROCEDURE

A block-diagram of the laboratory simulation test system is shown in Fig. 3.

A. Transmitter

Both desired and interfering modulating signals are mutually independent 511-bit pseudonoise (PN) sequences with a bit rate of $f_b = 600$ bit/s. In an each encoder, after being differentially encoded, the above PN sequence is transformed into a Manchester-coded data signal. Then each 900-MHz band carrier is frequency modulated with the Manchester-coded data signal, resulting in a Manchester-coded FSK signal equivalent to a nonreturn to zero (NRZ) binary FSK signal with a bit rate of 1200 bit/s.

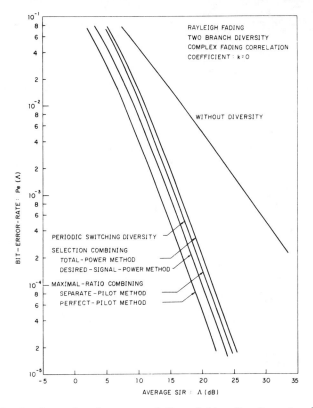

Fig. 2. Comparison between periodic switching diversity and well-known selection and maximal-ratio combinings.

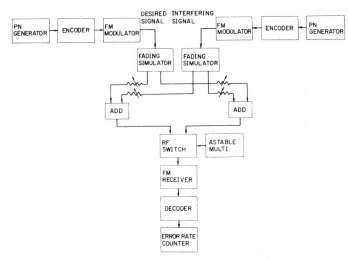

Fig. 3. Laboratory simulation test system.

The carrier frequency separation between the desired signal and interfering signal is set to zero so that an ideal co-channel situation may be studied.

B. Fading Simulation

The two FSK signals are fed to the Rayleigh fading simulators [8], respectively. Each fading simulator provides two transmission paths to simulate the correlation which two fading signals may have at the diversity antennas. The envelope correlation coefficient ρ is variable from 0 to 1 so that the influence of correlation on the diversity effect may be measured. The envelope correlations in the respective fading simulators are chosen to be equal to each other. The fading of the desired signal is independent of that of the interfering signal.

C. Receiver

The receiver consists of an RF switch unit, an FM receiver, and a decoder. The RF switch unit consists of a p-i-n diode switch and an astable multivibrator with adjustable free running frequency. The FM receiver is a conventional double conversion type using a limiter-discriminator. Two Butterworth crystal filters are used as the first and second IF filters of this FM receiver. Overall 3-dB predetection bandwidth is 16 kHz.

The decoder is composed of a postdetection filter, a timing recovery circuit, decision circuit, and a difference-logic circuit. The post detection filter is a Gaussian-type active filter with 3-dB bandwidth of 626 Hz. The timing recovery circuit is composed of a digital phase-locked loop with timing error smaller than ±9 degrees. The postdetection filter output is decided upon as "mark" or "space" by the decision circuit. After being differentially decoded by the difference-logic circuit, the BER is measured by the error rate counter.

IV. EXPERIMENTAL RESULTS AND DISCUSSION

The BER performance was measured for a typical vehicle speed of 48 km/h, and the average carrier-to-noise ratio (CNR) on each diversity branch of 45 dB. In the following measurements, the SIR on the two diversity branches were equal to each other, and the frequency deviation of the desired signal Δf_s, and that of the interfering signal Δf_i, were chosen as $\Delta f_s = \Delta f_i = \pm 5$ kHz.

A. Optimum Switching Rate

Fig. 4 shows the measured BER as a function of the switching rate f_s for the envelope correlation of $\rho = 0$. The results indicate that the measured BER decreases, then increases again as the switching rate increases to an excessively high switching rate. Therefore, there exists an optimum value in the switching rate. A possible explanation for the BER increase at high switching rate is as follows [5]: when the switching rate is excessively high, the spectrum of the IF filter input is so spread that the signal distortion is caused by IF filter band restriction. Thus in the following measurements the switching rate was chosen to be the optimum value of $f_s = 2$ kHz.

B. Measured BER Performance

Fig. 5 shows the measured BER performance with the envelope correlation coefficient ρ as a parameter. Although differential encoding is used in the laboratory simulation test, each measured BER value should be equal to the theoretical value predicted in Section II because we assume that errors occur with probability 1/2 when the signal energy fades below the interference energy. For comparison, the theoretical BER performances are plotted as solid curves. Reasonably good agreement is obtained.

V. CONCLUSION

This paper describes the improvement made by periodic switching diversity on the co-channel interference performance of a binary FSK system with limiter-discriminator detection and Rayleigh fading. The distribution of the SIR presented to

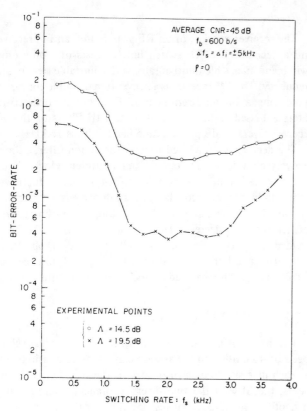

Fig. 4. Bit error rate versus switching rate with average SIR as parameter.

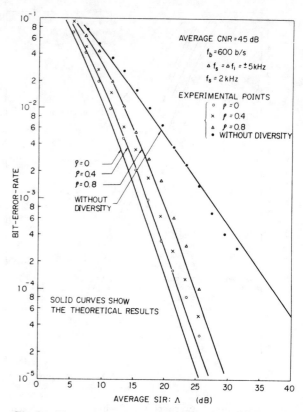

Fig. 5. Bit error rate versus average SIR with ρ as parameter.

the FM detector is found and the diversity effect on the BER performance in a Rayleigh fading environment is analyzed. The experimental verification by the laboratory simulation tests is also presented.

The ability to combat the co-channel interference has been surely verified. However, the adjacent-channel interference performance may be degraded because periodically switching the RF stage would tend to cause the adjacent-channel spectrum to fold over into the desired channel band unless adjacent-channel selectivity is provided before switching.

ACKNOWLEDGMENT

The author wishes to thank Mr. S. Ito, Chief of Mobile Radio Communication System Section and Mr. K. Hirade, Staff Engineer of Mobile Radio Communication Equipment Section for their useful discussions.

REFERENCES

[1] Y. Okumura, E. Ohmori, T. Kawano, and K. Fukuda, "Field Strength and its Variability in VHF and UHF Land Mobile Service," *Rev. Elec. Comm. Lab.,* vol. 16, pp. 825–873, Sept.–Oct. 1968.

[2] R. H. Clarke, "A Statistical Theory of Mobile Radio Reception," *Bell Sys. Tech. J.,* vol. 47, pp. 957–1000, July–Aug. 1968.

[3] J. D. Parsons, M. Henze, P. A. Ratliff, and M. J. Withers, "Diversity Techniques for Mobile Radio Reception," *The Radio and Electronic Engineer,* vol. 45, pp. 357–367, July 1975.

[4] W. C. Jakes, Jr., *Microwave Mobile Communications,* John Wiley and Sons Inc., New York, 1974, ch. 5 and ch. 6.

[5] F. Adachi, T. Hattori, K. Hirade, and T. Kamata, "A Periodic Switching Diversity Technique for a Digital FM Land Mobile Radio," *IEEE Tran. Veh. Technol.,* vol. VT-27, no. 4, pp. 000-000, Nov. 1978.

[6] F. E. Bond and H. F. Meyer, "The Effect of Fading on Communication Circuits Subject to Interference," *Proc. IRE,* vol. 45, pp. 636–642, May 1957.

[7] Ibid. [4], pp. 362–377.

[8] K. Hirade, K. Abe, T. Hanazawa, and F. Adachi, "Fading Simulator for Land Mobile Radio Communication," *Trans. IECE of Japan,* vol. 58-B, pp. 449–456, Sept. 1975.

Mobile Radio Performance for a Two-Branch Equal-Gain Combining Receiver with Correlated Signals at the Land Site

WILLIAM C. Y. LEE, MEMBER, IEEE

Abstract—It has generally been accepted that in a two-branch diversity receiver a near maximum diversity advantage is realized when the cross correlation between the two branches is less than 0.7. Based on this figure, space diversity reception at the mobile presents little problem since the antenna separation distances that achieve this amount of decorrelation in the mobile environment are very small (<20 cm at 850 MHz). However, the space diversity antenna separation requirement at the land site necessary to achieve the same amount of signal decorrelation is in the range of 10 wavelengths or more at antenna elevations of 150 ft or greater. Therefore, a comprehensive characterization of the effect of changing the cross correlation between the two received signals at the land site is important to effective system design. The performance of the two-branch equal-gain diversity system as a function of the cross-correlation between the two received signals from the diversity antennas is described. The cumulative probability distributions, level crossing rates, and duration of fades from a two-branch equal-gain combined diversity signal with variable correlation between the two branches are described also.

I. INTRODUCTION

IN MOBILE communications, diversity reception can be used to mitigate the effects of multipath fading. Space diversity reception is particularly attractive from the implementatation standpoint, and a two-branch space diversity arrangement appears to be a practical cost/performance compromise. The diversity advantage that is realized with such an arrangement is a function of both the type of diversity circuit which is employed and the degree of decorrelation between the two-branch received signals. It has generally been accepted that a near maximum diversity advantage will be realized when the cross correlation between the two branches is less than 0.7 [1]. Based on this figure, space diversity reception at the mobile presents little problem since the antenna separation distances that achieve this amount of decorrelation in the mobile environment are very small (<20 cm at 850 MHz). However, the space diversity antenna separation requirement at the land site necessary to achieve the same amount of signal decorrelation is in the range of 10 wavelengths or more at antenna elevations of 150 ft or greater [2], [3]. Therefore, a comprehensive characterization of the effect of changing the cross correlation between the two received signals at the land site is important to effective system design.

This paper describes the performance of the two-branch equal-gain diversity system as a function of the cross correlation between the two received signals from the diversity antennas. The cumulative probability distributions, level crossing rates, and duration of fades for a two-branch equal-gain combined diversity signal with variable correlation between the two branches are described.

II. CUMULATIVE PROBABILITY DISTRIBUTION FOR A TWO-BRANCH EQUAL-GAIN DIVERSITY SIGNAL

In [4], the probability density function for a voltage combined two-branch diversity signal ϵ is expressed in terms of the eigenvalues of its normalized correlation matrix. By substituting these eigenvalues into the probability density function and then performing the integration, we obtain

$$P(\epsilon \leqslant \psi) \approx 1 + \frac{(1 - \sqrt{\rho})e^{-aA^2} - (1 + \sqrt{\rho})e^{-bA^2}}{2\sqrt{\rho}}, \quad (1)$$

where ρ is the normalized correlation coefficient between the two signals,

$$a = \frac{g_2}{2(1 - \sqrt{\rho})}, \quad (2a)$$

$$b = \frac{g_2}{2(1 + \sqrt{\rho})}, \quad (2b)$$

$$g_2 = \begin{cases} 1.135, & \text{for } \rho < 1 \\ 1, & \text{for } \rho = 1, \end{cases} \quad (2c)[1]$$

and

$$A = \frac{\psi}{\nu} = \frac{\psi}{\text{rms of a single branch}}. \quad (2d)$$

Manuscript received January 27, 1978; revised May 19, 1978. This paper was presented at the 27th Annual Vehicular Technology Conference, Orlando, FL, March 16–18, 1977.

The author is with Bell Laboratories, Whippany, NJ 07981. Telephone: (201) 386-4922.

[1] The value of g_2 given in this paper is preferable to the value of g_2 suggested by [7] which applies for the case of low values of x and $\rho = 0$ only.

Reprinted from *IEEE Trans. Veh. Technol.*, vol. VT-27, pp. 239–243, Nov. 1978.

Equation (1) is an approximation. The constant g_2 is obtained by graphically comparing (1) with the exact solution which can be integrated numerically from the joint probability density function of two signal envelopes [5].

The cumulative distribution of (1) can be expressed in terms of the instantaneous two-branch combined carrier-to-noise ratio (CNR) γ as follows: The relation between the instantaneous combined voltage ϵ of the two-branch received signal and the instantaneous combined CNR γ is defined as [6]

$$\gamma = \frac{\epsilon^2}{2N}, \qquad (3)$$

where N is the mean-squared noise envelope of a single branch. Also, the average CNR for a single branch signal Γ can be expressed in terms of the rms of a single branch as

$$\Gamma = \frac{\nu^2}{N}. \qquad (4)$$

Combining (3) and (4) we obtain the following relation

$$\frac{\gamma \,(2 \text{ branches})}{\Gamma \,(\text{single branch})} = \frac{1}{2}\left(\frac{\epsilon}{\nu}\right)^2. \qquad (5)$$

The cumulative distribution of (1) then becomes

$$P(\gamma \leqslant x) \approx 1 + \frac{(1-\sqrt{\rho})e^{-2ax/\Gamma} - (1+\sqrt{\rho})e^{-2bx/\Gamma}}{2\sqrt{\rho}}. \qquad (6)$$

$P(\gamma \leqslant x)$ is plotted in Fig. 1 in terms of the normalized two-branch combined C, x/Γ. Fig. 1 shows how the diversity advantage of the two-branch equal-gain combined signal varies as a function of the cross correlation between the two branches. For example, the percentage of time the signal amplitude is below $x/\Gamma = -15$ dB for a single channel is 3 percent, but for two-branch diversity with $\rho = 0.7$ this percentage reduces to 0.2 percent.

Equation (6) agrees with the exact solution very well, especially below $x/\Gamma = -10$ dB where the error is negligible. In the neighborhood of $x/\Gamma = 0$ dB, the error is about 0.3 dB.

III. LEVEL CROSSING RATE FOR A TWO-BRANCH EQUAL-GAIN DIVERSITY SIGNAL

From [8], the average level crossing rate $\bar{n}(\epsilon = \psi)$ of the two-branch combined signal ϵ for any level ψ is shown to be

$$\bar{n}(\epsilon) = \int_0^\infty \dot{\epsilon} \rho(\epsilon, \dot{\epsilon}) \, d\dot{\epsilon}, \qquad (7)$$

where $\dot{\epsilon}$ is the derivative of ϵ. The joint probability density function $p(\epsilon, \dot{\epsilon})$ can be expressed as

$$p(\epsilon, \dot{\epsilon}) = \int_0^\epsilon p(R_1, R_2 = \epsilon - R_1, \dot{\epsilon}) \, dR_1 \qquad (8)$$

since $\epsilon = R_1 + R_2$, and R_1 and R_2 are the signal envelopes of two branches. In order to obtain (8), we first find the joint characteristic function $\Phi(w_1, w_2, w_3)$ of the joint probability

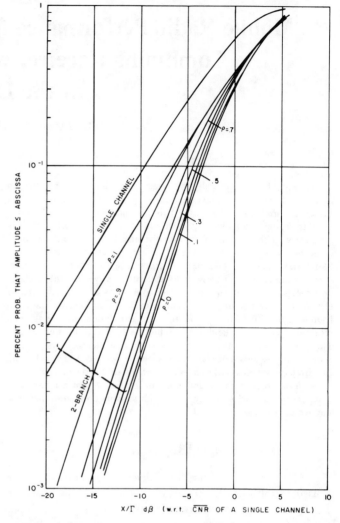

Fig. 1.   Cumulative probability distribution of a two-branch equal-gain combining signal.

density function of the random variables R_1, R_2, and $\dot{\epsilon}$ as

$$\Phi(w_1, w_2, w_3) = E[\exp{(j(w_1 R_1 + w_2 R_2 + w_2 R_2}$$
$$+ w_3 \dot{\epsilon}))] \qquad (9)$$

based on the theoretical model described in [2] and assuming a uniform distribution of vehicle angular orientation. Then $p(R_1, R_2, \dot{\epsilon})$ is the inverse Fourier transformation of the function Φ. Inserting $p(\epsilon, \dot{\epsilon})$, which is obtained from (8), into (7) and letting $r_1 = R_1/\nu$ and $r_2 = R_2/\nu$, the following result is obtained from Appendix I:

$$\bar{n}(\epsilon = \psi) = \frac{\beta V}{\sqrt{2\pi}} \cdot \frac{1}{(2\pi)^2} \cdot \sqrt{\frac{2}{\pi}} \exp - \left(\frac{A^2}{1-\rho}\right)$$

$$\cdot \int_0^A \int_0^\infty -\frac{1}{y^2}\left(\frac{2r_1(r_1 - A)}{1-\rho}\right)$$

$$\cdot \exp\left[-\left(\frac{2r_1(r_1 - A)}{1-\rho} + y^2\right)\right]$$

$$\cdot I_0\left[\left(\frac{2r_1(r_1 - A)}{1-\rho} + y^2\right)\sqrt{\rho}\right] dy \, dr_1 \quad (10a)$$

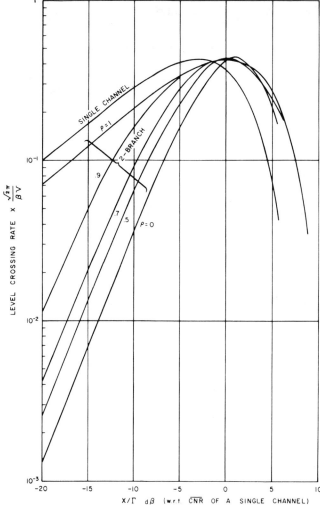

Fig. 2. Level crossing rate of a two-branch equal-gain combining signal.

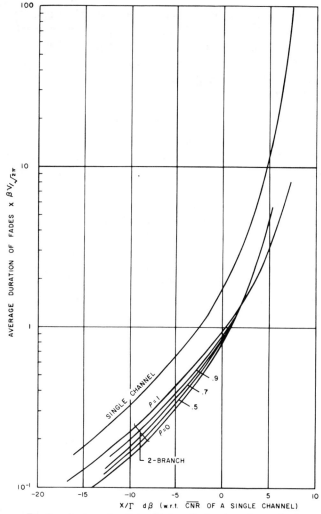

Fig. 3. Average duration of fades of a two-branch equal-gain combining signal.

where I_0 is the zero-order modified Bessel function of the first kind. The integrals of (10a) can be solved numerically since the integrand involving the parameter y diminishes very quickly as y increases. In (10a) ρ is the normalized cross-correlation coefficient, and V is the velocity. For a given ρ, the land-site antenna separation depends on whether the incoming signal is normal (broadside) or in-line to the axis of two land-site antennas [2]. Hence the level crossing rate depends on the land-site antenna separation, the speed of the vehicle, and the voltage ratio A. Substituting (5) into (10a), the average level crossing rate is expressed in terms of the normalized two-branch combined CNR x/Γ. The average level crossing rate $\overline{n}(\gamma = x)$ then becomes

$$\overline{n}(\gamma = x) = \left(\frac{\beta V}{\sqrt{2\pi}}\right) \cdot \frac{1}{(2\pi)^2} \cdot \sqrt{\frac{2}{\pi}} \exp\left(-\frac{2x/\Gamma}{1-\rho}\right)$$

$$\cdot \int_0^{\sqrt{2x/\Gamma}} \int_0^\infty -\frac{1}{y^2} \left(\frac{2r_1(r_1 - \sqrt{2x/\Gamma})}{1-\rho}\right)$$

$$\cdot \exp\left[-\left(\frac{2r_1(r_1 - \sqrt{2x/\Gamma})}{1-\rho} + y^2\right)\right]$$

$$\cdot I_0\left[\left(\frac{2r_1(r_1 - \sqrt{2x/\Gamma})}{1-\rho} + y^2\right)\sqrt{\rho}\right] dy \, dr_1 \quad (10b)$$

and is plotted in Fig. 2. The level crossing rate shown in Fig. 2 is normalized by the vehicle speed and the transmitting frequency. At $x/\Gamma = -15$ dB, the level crossing rate is different by about one order of magnitude between a single-channel signal and a two-branch diversity signal with $\rho = 0.7$.

IV. AVERAGE DURATION OF FADES FOR A TWO-BRANCH EQUAL-GAIN DIVERSITY SIGNAL

From Rice's paper [9], the average fade duration $\overline{t}(\gamma = x)$ at any carrier-to-noise ratio x of the two-branch combined signal can be expressed as

$$\overline{t}(\gamma = x) = \frac{P(\gamma \leqslant x)}{\overline{n}(\gamma = x)}. \quad (11)$$

Since $P(\gamma \leqslant x)$ is given by (6) and $\overline{n}(\gamma = x)$ can be found from (10b), (11) is readily obtained. However, (6) is an approximate solution and will therefore introduce errors in (11). Fortunately, the exact solution of $\overline{t}(\gamma = x)$ can be obtained for the case of $\rho = 0$ and 1. As shown in Fig. 3, the region of the average duration of fades for $0 \leqslant \rho \leqslant 1$ is therefore considerably narrowed. Hence, $\overline{t}$ can be obtained with reasonable accuracy by using the value of $\overline{t}$ at $x/\Gamma = -10$ dB (where the error in $P(\gamma \leqslant x)$ is small) and connecting these values to the common point at $x/\Gamma = +2$ dB. The average duration of fades is also normalized by the vehicle speed and the transmitting frequency. As shown in Fig. 3, decreasing the cross correlation shortens the average fade duration for any CNR below $x/\Gamma = 2$ dB. At $x/\Gamma = -15$ dB, the average fade duration of a single-channel signal is twice as long as it is for a two-branch diversity signal with $\rho = 0.7$.

V. CONCLUSION

This paper has described the performance of a two-branch equal-gain combining receiver with correlated mobile radio signals at the land site. We have obtained approximate solutions for the cumulative probability distribution and the average duration of fades, and a numerically integrated solution for the level-crossing rate for this particular system. All the figures are a function of ρ only. At the land site the values of ρ will be different not only due to the antenna separation but also due to the orientation of the land-site antennas with respect to the incoming signal. References [1]–[3] have described how to obtain the values of ρ in detail. With a given ρ, curves 1–3 can be used to describe the received signal performance.

APPENDIX I

THE DERIVATION OF EQUATION (10a)

The characteristic function of (9) is

$$\Phi(\omega_1, \omega_2, \omega_3) = E[e^{j(\omega_1 R_1 + \omega_2 R_2 + \omega_3 \dot{\epsilon})}]$$

$$= E[e^{j(\omega_1 R_1 + \omega_2 R_2) + j\omega_3(\dot{x}_1 \cos \eta_1 + \dot{y}_1 \sin \eta_1 + \dot{x}_2 \cos \eta_2 + \dot{y}_2 \sin \eta_2)}] \quad \text{(A1)}$$

$$\Phi(\omega_1, \omega_2, \omega_3) = \int_0^\infty \int_0^\infty e^{j(\omega_1 R_1 + \omega_2 R_2)}$$

$$\cdot \int_0^{2\pi} \int_0^{2\pi} \overbrace{\int\int\int\int}^{\infty}_{-\infty} e^{j\omega_3(\dot{x}_1 \cos \eta_1 + \dot{y}_1 \sin \eta_1 + \dot{x}_2 \cos \eta_2 + \dot{y}_2 \sin \eta_2)}$$

$$\cdot p(x_1, y_1, x_2, y_2) \cdot p(\dot{x}_1, \dot{y}_1, \dot{x}_2, \dot{y}_2) \, d\dot{x}_1 \, d\dot{y}_1 \, d\dot{x}_2 \, d\dot{y}_2 \, d\eta_1 \, d\eta_2 \, dR_1 \, dR_2. \quad \text{(A4)}$$

where the complex form of a single branch signal is

$$g_i = x_i + jy_i = R_i e^{j\eta_i},$$

its envelope is

$$R_i = \sqrt{x_i^2 + y_i^2},$$

and the derivative of its envelope is

$$\dot{R}_i = \dot{x}_i \cos \eta_i + \dot{y}_i \sin \eta_i.$$

The probability density function of $\{x_i, y_i\}$ and $\{\dot{x}_i, \dot{y}_i\}$ can be calculated from a theoretical model in [2]:

$$p(\{x_i, y_i\}, \{\dot{x}_i, \dot{y}_i\}) = p(\{x_i, y_i\}), p(\{\dot{x}_i, \dot{y}_i\}), \quad \text{(A2)}$$

where x_i, y_i, $\dot{x}_i$, and $\dot{y}_i$ are Gaussian. Then

$$p(\dot{x}_1, \dot{y}_1, \dot{x}_2, \dot{y}_2) = \frac{1}{4\pi^2 \, |\Lambda'|^{1/2}} \cdot \exp \left\{ -\frac{1}{2 \, |\Lambda'|^{1/2}} \right.$$

$$\cdot [\sigma_{\dot{x}}^2(\dot{x}_1^2 + \dot{y}_1^2 + \dot{x}_2^2 + \dot{y}_2^2)$$

$$- 2R_{c'}(\dot{x}_1 \dot{x}_2 + \dot{y}_1 \dot{y}_2)$$

$$\left. - 2R_{cs'}(\dot{x}_1 \dot{y}_2 - \dot{y}_1 \dot{x}_2)] \right\}, \quad \text{(A3)}$$

where

$$|\Lambda'| = |\sigma_{\dot{x}}^4 - R_{c'}^2 - R_{cs'}^2| = \frac{(\beta V)^2}{2} |\Lambda|$$

$$\sigma_{\dot{x}}^2 = \frac{(\beta V)^2}{2} \sigma_x^2$$

$$R_{c'} = \frac{(\beta V)^2}{2} R_c \qquad |\Lambda| = \sigma_x^4 [1 - \rho^2]$$

$$R_{cs'} = \frac{(\beta V)^2}{2} R_{cs}.$$

From (A1)

After integrating six integrals over dx_1, dy_1, $d\dot{x}_2$, $d\dot{y}_2$, $d\eta_1$, and $d\eta_2$, (A4) becomes

$$\Phi(\omega_1, \omega_2, \omega_3) = \int\int_0^\infty e^{j(\omega_1 R_1 + \omega_2 R_2)} R_1 R_2 \frac{1}{|\Lambda|^{1/2}}$$

$$\cdot \exp \left[-\frac{\sigma_x^2}{2 \, |\Lambda|^{1/2}} (R_1^2 + R_2^2) \right]$$

$$\cdot \exp \left[-\frac{\omega_3^2 (\beta V)^2}{2} \sigma_x^2 \right]$$

$$\cdot I_0 \left[\left(\frac{R_1 R_2}{|\Lambda|^{1/2}} - \omega_3^2 \frac{(\beta V)^2}{2} \right) \right.$$

$$\left. \cdot [R_c^2 + R_{cs}^2]^{1/2} \right] dR_1 \, dR_2. \quad \text{(A5)}$$

The probability density can be obtained from (A5) as

$$p(R_1, R_2, \dot{\epsilon}) = \frac{1}{(2\pi)^3} \iiint \Phi(\omega_1, \omega_2, \omega_3)$$

$$\cdot e^{-j(\omega_1 R_1 + \omega_2 R_2 + \omega_3 \dot{\epsilon})} d\omega_1 \, d\omega_2 \, d\omega_3$$

$$= \frac{1}{(2\pi)^3} \int_{-\infty}^{\infty} e^{-j\omega_3 \dot{\epsilon}} R_1 R_2 \frac{1}{|\Lambda|^{1/2}}$$

$$\cdot \exp\left[-\frac{\sigma_x^2}{2|\Lambda|^{1/2}} (R_1^2 + R_2^2) \right]$$

$$\cdot \exp\left[-\frac{\omega_3^2 (\beta V)^2}{2} \sigma_x^2 \right]$$

$$\cdot I_0 \left[\left(\frac{R_1 R_2}{|\Lambda|^{1/2}} - \omega_3^2 \frac{(\beta V)^2}{2} \right) \right.$$

$$\left. \cdot [R_c^2 + R_{cs}^2]^{1/2} \right] d\omega_3. \tag{A6}$$

Since $p(\epsilon, \dot{\epsilon})$ is expressed in (8) as

$$p(\epsilon, \dot{\epsilon}) = \int_0^{\epsilon} p(R_1, R_2 = \epsilon - R_1, \dot{\epsilon}) \, dR_1,$$

by inserting (8) in (7), the average level crossing rate becomes

$$\bar{n}(\epsilon = \psi) = \int_0^{\infty} \dot{\epsilon} p(\epsilon, \dot{\epsilon}) \, d\dot{\epsilon}$$

$$= \frac{1}{2\pi^3} \int_0^{\psi} \int_0^{\infty} -\frac{1}{\omega_3^2} \frac{R_1(\epsilon - R_1)}{\sigma_x^4(1-\rho)}$$

$$\cdot \exp\left[-\frac{\sigma_x^2}{2\sigma_x^4(1-\rho)} (2R_1^2 + \epsilon^2 - 2R_1\epsilon) \right]$$

$$\cdot \exp\left[-\omega_3^2 \frac{(\beta V)^2}{2} \sigma_x^2 \right] \cdot I_0 \left[\left(\frac{R_1(\epsilon - R_1)}{\sigma_x^4(1-\rho)} \right. \right.$$

$$\left. \left. -\omega_3^2 \frac{(\beta V)^2}{2} \right) \rho \right] d\omega_3 \, dR_1. \tag{A7}$$

Simplifying (A7) results in (10a).

REFERENCES

[1] W. C. Y. Lee, "Antenna spacing requirement for a mobile radio base-station diversity, *Bell Syst. Tech. J.,* vol. 50, pp. 1859–1876, July-Aug., 1971.

[2] W. C. Y. Lee, "Effects on correlation between two mobile radio base-station antennas," *IEEE Trans. Commun.,* vol. Com-21, pp. 1214–1224, Nov. 1973.

[3] S. B. Rhee and G. I. Zysman, "Results of suburban base-station spatial diversity measurements in the UHF band," *IEEE Trans. Commun.,* vol. Com-22, p. 1630, Oct. 1974.

[4] W. C. Y. Lee, "A study of the antenna array configuration of an M-Branch diversity combining mobile radio receiver," *IEEE Trans. Veh. Technol.,* vol. VT-20, pp. 93–104, Nov. 1971.

[5] M. Schwartz, W. R. Bennett and S. Stein, *Communication Systems and Techniques.* New York: McGraw-Hill, 1966, p. 469.

[6] M. Schwartz, W. R. Bennett and S. Stein, *ibid.,* p. 453.

[7] M. Schwartz, W. R. Bennett and S. Stein, *ibid.,* p. 457.

[8] S. O. Rice, "Mathematical analysis of random noise," *Bell Syst. Tech. J.,* vol. 24, p. 53, Jan. 1945.

[9] S. O. Rice, "Distribution of the duration of fades in radio transmission," *Bell Syst. Tech. J.,* vol. 37, p.109, Jan. 1948.

Multitransmitter Digital Signal Transmission by Using Offset Frequency Strategy in a Land–Mobile Telephone System

TAKESHI HATTORI, MEMBER, IEEE, AND KENKICHI HIRADE

Abstract—In a high-capacity land-mobile telephone system which employs a small zone technique, it is advantageous to provide control channels separate from voice channels. We first review two control channel allocation methods: the individual control zone system and the multiple control zone system. From the viewpoints of efficient frequency utilization and reliable call processing, the multiple control zone system is shown to be preferable. It is experimentally verified that an offset carrier frequency strategy is well suited to the realization of this system. Simulation test results are presented which determine the design parameters. Offset carrier frequency allocation methods concerning three types of fundamental zone configuration are derived. The carrier frequency synchronization and the phase adjustment of the modulation signals are investigated for the actual system construction.

I. INTRODUCTION

IN A HIGH-CAPACITY mobile telephone system, the small zone technique is usually chosen for efficient frequency utilization and increased capacity [1], [2]. In such a system, several tens of voice channels are assigned to each small zone according to the traffic condition. Furthermore, it is necessary to provide control channels separate from the voice channels

Manuscript received January 17, 1978; revised May 1, 1978.
The authors are with the Mobile Communication Section, Electrical Communication Laboratories, Nippon Telegraph and Telephone Public Corporation, 1-2356 Take, Yokosuka-shi, Kanagawa-ken 238-03, Japan.

for efficient call processing. This paper describes a multitransmitter digital control signal transmission technique using an offset carrier frequency strategy, which is well suited to such a control channel [3]-[6].

In Section II, we review the control channel allocation methods and show that a multiple control zone system in which one control channel common to multiple radio zones is assigned, is more suitable than an individual control zone system in which different control channels are assigned to different radio zones. Section III describes the technical problems encountered in realizing the multiple control zone system. Factors which degrade signal transmission are also considered. In Section IV, we describe the experimental simulation test system which was constructed to clarify the realization of the multiple control zone system using the offset frequency strategy and to determine the system parameters. Section V summarizes the simulation test results. We devote Section VI to obtaining the carrier frequency allocation method for the three types of fundamental zone configurations. The allowable carrier frequency drift corresponding to each zone configuration is also presented. Finally, in Section VII, the phase synchronization of the modulating signals is dealt with after first investigating the performance of baseband and carrier transmission links between the control station and each base station.

Reprinted from *IEEE Trans. Veh. Technol.*, vol. VT-27, pp. 231–238, Nov. 1978.

II. CONTROL CHANNEL ALLOCATION METHOD

There are two distinct methods of control channel allocation. One method is to allocate different radio frequency channels for each of the radio zones (individual control zone system, Fig. 1(a)), and the other is to allocate the identical radio frequency channel for a group of adjacent radio zones whose number is determined from the system design objective (multiple control zone system, Fig. 1(b)). These adjacent radio zones are considered as a control zone.

Let us compare the above two methods from the viewpoints of reliable call processing and efficient frequency utilization. When a mobile moves from one control zone to another, it is necessary to search and lock up a new control channel. It is a difficult task to search and lock up a new control channel quickly and reliably due to the multipath fading which is usually encountered in the mobile radio channel. Since the call processing is impossible during the actual searching time, any call generated during that time is lost. Therefore, the occurrence rate of such an event must be minimized. Moreover, the number of control channels should be as small as possible from system design considerations. From these viewpoints, the multiple control zone system is more advantageous than the individual control zone system.

III. MULTITRANSMITTER SIGNAL TRANSMISSION

In this section, we will describe the technical problems and the degradation factors effecting the multiple control zone system realization.

In the multiple control zone system, each base station which belongs to the same control zone transmits the same RF signal simultaneously. Therefore, the mobile unit in the overlapped area receives several RF signals transmitted from adjacent base stations, while in the inner area of each zone it receives one RF signal transmitted from the corresponding base station. This means that the signal transmission performance in the overlapped area depends strongly upon the carrier frequency differences among the base station transmitters and the modulating signal phase differences. Since it is impractical to synchronize the carrier frequencies of different base station transmitters at the 900-MHz band, the beat interference due to their carrier frequency differences is unavoidable.

Let us now consider the channel characteristics of the mobile reception in the overlapped area. In this case, we assume and overlapped area between two adjacent radio zones. Furthermore, we assume that the mobile unit is moving at a typical constant speed of $v = 48$ km/h. As the signal transmission from each base station to the mobile unit is usually accomplished via multiple random paths, a multipath fading phenomenon occurs on each of the RF signals. Such a multipath phenomenon is represented as a multipath wave having a Rayleigh distributed envelope and a uniformly distributed phase. Therefore, in our system model, a mobile unit receives a combined wave of two Rayleigh fading waves with an interference beat frequency as shown in Fig. 2.

In the case where frequency-shift keying (FSK) is used as the modulation method, it will be experimentally shown that the timing of each RF signal transmission should be synchro-

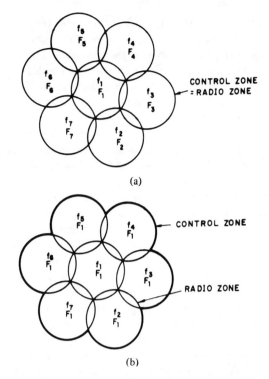

(a)

(b)

Fig. 1. Control channel frequency allocation methods. (a) Individual control zone system. (b) Multiple control zone system. (f_i ··· voice channel frequency, F_i ··· control channel frequency).

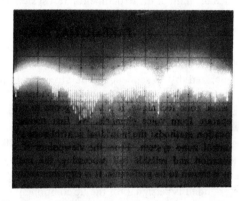

Fig. 2. Envelope of combined wave received by a mobile unit under fading environment. V: 25 dB/div, H: 10 ms/div, fading rate: $f_D = 40$ Hz, carrier frequency offset: $\Delta f = 1$ kHz.

nized as closely as possible, but the carrier frequency of each transmitter should be set according to a certain offset allocation. In particular, when the center frequencies are set under an optimum offset allocation, the signal transmission performance under a multipath fading environment can be markedly improved. It is very difficult to analyze this improvement effect rigorously, especially when the limiter-discriminator is used as the detection scheme for the FSK signal. However, the improvement of such an offset strategy is considered to be due to the same cause as in the case of energy detection [7].

In the practical zone configuration, more than three radio zones are required to cover the entire service area. Furthermore, it is necessary to satisfy the prescribed frequency offset relation in the carrier frequencies of any two adjacent base station transmitters. The midfrequency between the two carrier frequencies is not always located at the center frequency of the transmission band. Therefore, the midfrequency offset from the center frequency is one of the important factors degrading signal transmission, particularly when we consider the carrier frequency allocation and the frequency drift of the mobile unit local oscillator, as shown in Fig. 3.

In our experimental setup, the following three system parameters are assumed to be previously determined from the system design of the high-capacity mobile telephone system [2]. First, a Manchester-coded FSK system with a limiter-discriminator is assumed to be used because of a common utilization of the narrow-band FM transceiver for the voice transmission. Second, the bit-rate of the control signal transmission is $f_b = 300$ bits/s. This is determined from the traffic conditions. Third, the receiver's predetection bandwidth is $B_{if} = 16$ kHz, which is determined from voice transmission conditions. The other parameters needed to specify the signal transmission performance are carrier frequency offset, frequency deviation, midfrequency offset, baseband signal phase difference, cross correlation coefficient of the received signal envelopes, and receiver input level.

In the following two sections, we describe the experimental test system and then present the test results with the various influencing factors as parameters.

IV. EXPERIMENTAL SIMULATION TEST SYSTEM

The block diagram of the experimental test system is shown in Fig. 4. In this system, a Manchester-coded FSK system with a limiter-discriminator is used as the modulation-demodulation method. A pseudo-noise (PN) sequence with the bit-rate of $f_b = 300$ bits/s and a repetition-period of $M = 2^9 - 1 = 511$ bits is generated by a sequence generator and is fed to an encoder as a test pattern signal.

The encoder consists of a sum-logic circuit and a code-converter. The sum-logic circuit is used for differentially encoding the transmitting test pattern for the simplification of the timing-recovery circuit used in the decoder. The code-converter is used for transforming an NRZ-type signal into a Manchester-coded type signal for the dc component supression. This signal is divided into two branches, one of which is fed to a phase shifter in order to measure the degradation of signal transmission due to the phase difference between the modulation signals. These digital signals are fed to the FM modulators with one carrier frequency being offset relative to the other by a certain value. Thus the two Manchester-coded FSK signals are generated in the 900-MHz band. The two FSK signals are fed to the Rayleigh fading simulator [8] which was designed to simulate the signal received by a mobile unit with an omnidirectional antenna at a given speed through the multipath environment. In this simulator, two fading waves are generated, and the cross correlation as well as the fading rate are variable.

Then, the two fading waves generated by the simulator are combined and fed into the receiver. The receiver consists of an FM receiver and a decoder. The FM receiver is a conventional double conversion type using a limiter-discriminator and its total noise-figure is $N_F = 9.8$ dB. Both the first and the second IF filters of the FM receiver are the Butterworth-type filters. The overall predetection 3-dB-down bandwidth is $B_{if} = 16$

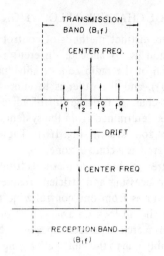

Fig. 3. Relationship between transmission band and reception band in presence of local oscillator frequency drift.

kHz. The decoder is composed of a baseband filter, a timing-recovery circuit, a decision circuit, and a difference-logic circuit. The baseband filter is a Gaussian-type active filter with a 3-dB-down bandwidth of $B_0 = 313$ Hz. The baseband filter is used for low-pass filtering of the discriminator output. The timing-recovery circuit is made of a digital phase-locked loop, and the recovered timing error is small, less than ±9°. Using the recovered timing, the low-pass-filtered output is assigned as a "0" or "1" and regenerated by the decision circuit. After being differentially decoded by the difference-logic circuit, the regenerated output is fed to the error-rate counter for measuring the bit-error-rate (BER) performance.

The fading rate is $f_D = 40$ Hz, which corresponds to a typical vehicular velocity of $v = 48$ km/h at the 900-MHz. The other parameters of the experimental simulation tests are as follows:

a) carrier frequency offset $\Delta f = 0 - 5$ (kHz),
b) frequency deveation $\Delta f_d = \pm2 - \pm8$ (kHz),
c) mid-frequency offset $\Delta f_c = 0 - \pm6$ (kHz),
d) median value of receiver input level E_{i1}, E_{i2} (dBµ),
e) cross correlation coefficient $\rho = 0, 0.4, 0.8, 1.0$, and
f) phase difference between the modulating signals $\Delta\theta = 0 - 90°$.

V. EXPERIMENTAL TEST RESULTS

Let us now describe the experimental simulation test results for the purpose of determining system design parameters. The experimental simulation tests were performed at the bit-rate of $f_b = 300$ bits/s, and the fading rate of $f_D = 40$ Hz.

Fig. 5 shows the average BER performance with the carrier frequency offset as a parameter. The other parameters are $\Delta f_d = \pm3$ kHz, $E_{i1} = E_{i2}$, $\rho = 0$, and $\Delta\theta = 0°$. From these experimental test results, the following observations can be made.

a) Compared to single-channel reception, two channels with an optimum carrier frequency offset result in a marked reduction in the required carrier-to-noise-ratio (CNR) for a given value of BER. The reduced values for the BER's of 1×10^{-2} and 1×10^{-3} are 8.0 dB and 14.0 dB, respectively.

b) The slope of the BER curve in the case of the optimum

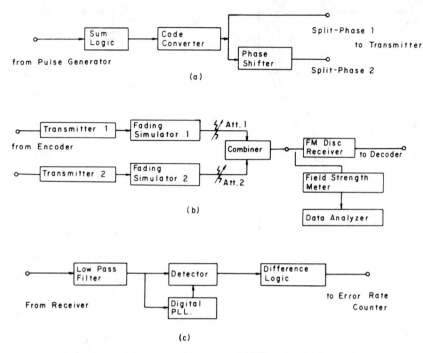

Fig. 4.   Block diagram of experimental dual transmitter system. (a) Encoder. (b) Transmitter to receiver. (c) Decoder.

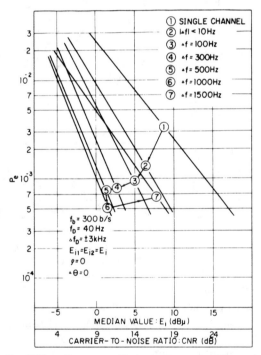

Fig. 5.   BER performance with carrier frequency offset Δf as a parameter.

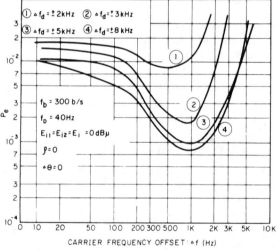

Fig. 6.   BER versus carrier frequency offset with frequency deviation Δf_d as a parameter.

carrier frequency offset is steeper than that of single-channel reception. The necessary change in signal strength so as to reduce a given BER by one-tenth is 5 dB, while it is as much as 10 dB in single-channel reception.

c) The BER performance with two channels and any value of frequency offset is always better than that of single-channel reception. This means that the carrier frequency offset always brings some improvement in the BER performance.

Fig. 6 shows the average BER versus frequency offset with the frequency deviation as a variable parameter. From these experimental test results, the following observations can be made.

d) There exists an optimum value of the carrier frequency offset which minimizes the BER, and the optimum value depends very little upon the frequency deviation. The value is about $\Delta f = 1$ kHz for the case of the frequency deviation being larger than ±3 kHz. It is necessary to set the frequency deviation greater than ±3 kHz in order to obtain marked improvement.

e) It is found that the average BER performance degrades as the frequency offset departs from the optimum value. The maximum values of frequency offset, for which the BER value is twice as much as that of the optimum case, are $\Delta f_{max} = 1.7$, 2.2, and 2.5 kHz corresponding to $\Delta f_d = ±3$, ±5, and ±8 kHz, respectively. The minimum value is $\Delta f_{min} = 0.3$ kHz, regardless of frequency deviation.

Fig. 7 shows the average BER performance versus the offset

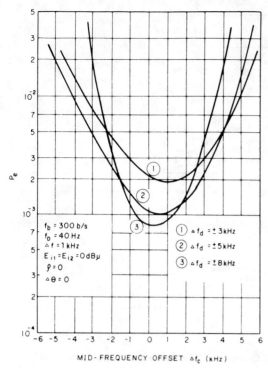

Fig. 7. BER performance versus the offset of the mid-frequency between two carriers relative to the band center frequency.

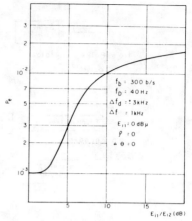

Fig. 8. BER performance versus E_{i1}/E_{i2}.

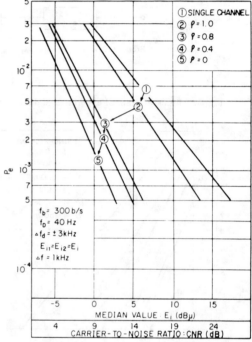

Fig. 9. Effect of cross correlation on error rate performance.

of the midfrequency between the two carriers relative to the center frequency of transmission band. From these test results, the following observation is made.

f) The average BER degrades as the midfrequency offset increases, and the degradation rate depends upon the frequency deviation. Considering that more than three carrier frequencies are required in the frequency allocation and that the frequency drift of the local oscilator of the mobile unit is about $\pm 2 - \pm 3$ kHz at the 900-MHz band, the frequency deviation must be set to $\Delta f_d = \pm 3 - \pm 5$ kHz. In this case, six carrier frequencies can be allocated without a degradation twice as much as the optimum value.

Let us now consider the case of $E_{i1} = E_{i2}$. Fig. 8 shows the average BER versus E_{i1}/E_{i2} when $E_{i1} = 0$ dBμ and E_{i1} is a variable. The other parameters are $\Delta f_d = \pm 3$ kHz, $\Delta f = 1$ kHz, $\rho = 0$, and $\Delta \theta = 0$. The experimental test results indicate the following.

g) The improvement gradually decreases as E_{i1}/E_{i2} increases. The BER, when $E_{i1}/E_{i2} \to \infty$, approaches that of a single-channel reception. However, there is always an improvement unless $E_{i1}/E_{i2} \geqslant 5$ dB. Considering that the area where E_{i1}/E_{i2} becomes large may be located not in the overlapped region between the adjacent radio zones but in the inner region of each radio zone, and that the received input level in such an inner region is large enough to give a low average BER without using the offset strategy, the signal transmission performance is in a good balance for the whole service area.

Fig. 9 shows the average BER performance with the cross correlation coefficient as a parameter. The experimental test results indicate the following.

h) The improvement effect decreases as the cross correlation coefficient approaches $\rho = 1.0$. The degradation values in the required CNR for the BER of 1×10^{-3} are 0, 2.0, 3.1, and

10.0 dB corresponding to $\rho = 0, 0.4, 0.8$, and 1.0, respectively. Therefore, it is found that the improvement effect is reduced by about 3 dB unless $\rho \geqslant 0.8$.

Considering that the two adjacent base stations are far enough apart to give $\rho \ll 1.0$ in the practical radio zone configuration, the degradation due to the cross correlation need not be taken into account.

Fig. 10 shows the average BER versus the phase difference between the modulating signals. In this experiment, the other parameters are $\Delta f_d = \pm 3$ kHz, $\Delta f = 1$ kHz, $E_{i1} = E_{i2} = 0$ dBμ, and $\rho = 0$. From this experimental test result, the following observation can be made.

i) The maximum allowable value of phase difference for which the BER value is twice as much as that of $\Delta \theta = 0$ is about $\Delta \theta_{max} = 70°$.

VI. CARRIER FREQUENCY ALLOCATION METHOD

Considering that more than three radio zones are required to cover the entire service area, it is necessary to derive a carrier

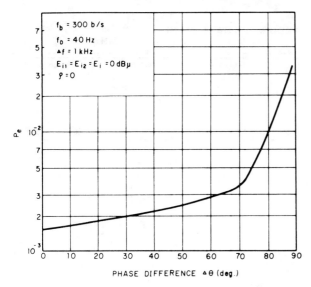

Fig. 10. Effect of modulation signal phase difference on BER performance

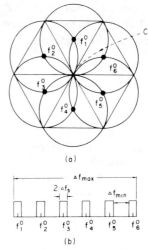

Fig. 11. Triangular zone configuration and its carrier frequency allocation. (a) Zone configuration. (b) Carrier frequency allocation.

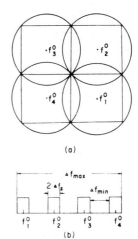

Fig. 12. Rectangular zone configuration and its carrier frequency allocation. (a) Zone configuration. (b) Carrier frequency allocation.

frequency allocation method for the adjacent base station transmitters. The allocation method will be derived for three kinds of fundamental zone configurations: the triangular, rectangular, and hexagonal zone configurations, which are shown in Figs. 11, 12, and 13, respectively. Any other practical irregular zone configuration may be composed of these fundamental zone configurations.

A. Triangular Zone Configuration

The triangular zone configuration is shown in Fig. 11(a), where each circle represents a unit radio zone. It is found that there exists an extreme point such as point C in the figure, which is covered by six adjacent radio zones. Therefore, it is necessary to consider the combining effect of the six transmitted waves.

Let us denote the nominal values and the practical values of the six base station transmitter frequencies by f_i^0 and f_i, $(i = 1, 2, \cdots 6)$, respectively. Letting the allowable carrier frequency drift be Δf_s, the following relation between f_i^0 and f_i must hold:

$$|f_i^0 - f_i| \leqslant \Delta f_s, \qquad \text{for } i = 1, 2, \cdots 6. \tag{1}$$

On the other hand, it has been previously described in the comment e) that there exists the maximum value of Δf_{max} and the minimum value of Δf_{min} in the carrier frequency offset for which the BER value is less than twice the optimum value. Therefore, any two of the six practical carrier frequencies must satisfy the following relation:

$$\Delta f_{min} \leqslant |f_i - f_j| \leqslant \Delta f_{max}, \qquad \text{for } i, j = i, 2, \cdots 6, i \neq j. \tag{2}$$

Accordingly, from (1), (2), and Fig. 11(b), it is found that the following relation is obtained:

$$\Delta f_{max} = 12 \cdot \Delta f_s + 5 \cdot \Delta f_{min}. \tag{3}$$

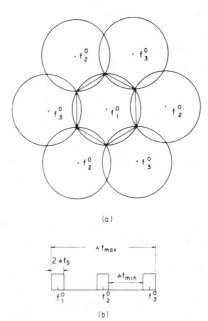

Fig. 13. Hexagonal zone configuration and its carrier frequency allocation. (a) Zone configuration. (b) Carrier frequency allocation.

Therefore, the nominal values of the six carrier frequencies may be allocated at the frequency points shown in Fig. 11(b). The relation between the nominal carrier frequencies f_{i+1}^0 and f_i^0 is given by

$$f_{i+1}^0 = f_i^0 + (\Delta f_{max} + \Delta f_{min})/6. \qquad (4)$$

B. Rectangular Zone Configuration

Fig. 12 shows the rectangular zone configuration and its carrier frequency allocation method. In this zone configuration, the following relations corresponding to the above derived (3) and (4) are easily obtained:

$$\Delta f_{max} = 8 \cdot \Delta f_s + 3 \cdot \Delta f_{min}, \qquad (5)$$

$$f_{i+1}^0 = f_i^0 + (\Delta f_{max} + \Delta f_{min})/4. \qquad (6)$$

C. Hexagonal Zone Configuration

Fig. 13 shows the hexagonal zone configuration and its carrier frequency allocation method. In this zone configuration, the following relations are easily obtained:

$$\Delta f_{max} = 6 \cdot \Delta f_s + 2 \cdot \Delta f_{min}, \qquad (7)$$

$$f_{i+1}^0 = f_i^0 + (\Delta f_{max} + \Delta f_{min})/3. \qquad (8)$$

VII. PRACTICAL SYSTEM DESIGN

In order to realize a practical system of multitransmitter digital signal transmission system using a carrier frequency offset strategy, it is necessary to construct the carrier frequency synchronizer and the modulation signal phase synchronizer. Let us now consider the system design of these synchronizers.

A. Carrier Frequency Synchronizer

Considering that the maximum allowable values of the carrier frequency drift Δf_s corresponding to the three fundamental zone configurations are respectively given by (3), (5), and (7) and that the maximum values Δf_{max} and the minimum values Δf_{min} of the carrier frequency offset are experimentally determined as indicated in the comment e), the values of Δf_s are as shown in Table I. When the carrier frequency is selected in the 900-MHz band, the required values of the relative frequency stability are also shown in Table I. In particular, when the frequency deviation is set as $\Delta f_d = \pm 5$ kHz and the hexagonal zone configuration is adopted, the required relative frequency stability is about $\pm 3.0 \times 10^{-7}$ (0.3 ppm), which may be realized by the use of the precision controlled free-running oscillators. Therefore, the carrier frequency synchronizer is composed of an independent synchronizing system which is well suited to the practical system construction.

B. Modulating Signal Phase Synchronizer

Since the time delays occurring in the transmission line from the control station to each of the base stations are dif-

TABLE I
MAXIMUM ALLOWABLE FREQUENCY DRIFT AND RELATIVE STABILITY AT 900 MHZ

Δf_d	Triangular Zone		Rectangular Zone		Hexagonal Zone	
	Drift (Hz)	Stability ($\times 10^{-7}$)	Drift (Hz)	Stability ($\times 10^{-7}$)	Drift (Hz)	Stability ($\times 10^{-7}$)
3 kHz	17	0.19	100	1.1	183	2.0
5 kHz	58	0.65	163	1.8	267	3.0

TABLE II
TRANSMISSION LINE PERFORMANCE

	Baseband Trans. Line				Carrier Trans. Line		
	0.9mm Ø		0.65 mm Ø		Micro-wave	Coaxial Cable	Non-loading
Phase Delay Performance (deg./kHz·km)	NL	L	NL	L			
	5.53	26.94	7.50	27.0	1.19	1.26	2.05
Delay Time of Channel Modem (msec/pair)					1.5	1.5	1.5
Total Phase Delay (deg.)	29.3	80.8	40.3	81.0	198	200	224
	for 10 km				for 100 km		

ferent, it is necessary to equalize all of the time delays to that of the maximum. In this case, the maximum allowable modulation signal phase difference is about $70°$, as described in comment i).

Let us now investigate the absolute value of the time delay. Considering that the radius of such a service area as the Tokyo metropolitan area is about 50 km, the maximum transmission line length is assumed to be about 100 km. Therefore, the baseband transmission line and the carrier transmission lines will both be used. The former is used when the transmission line is less than 10 km and the latter is used where the line is larger than 10 km. Since the transmission delay characteristics are given in Table II for the respective transmission lines, the maximum phase delays of the modulation signal are also given in Table II. Therefore, it is concluded that the required maximum value of the variable phase shift is about $300°$. The variable phase shifter required to compensate for such a phase difference may be easily realized by the use of a shift register. Since the annual phase change is estimated to be about $0.01°/100$ km in microwave or coaxial cable and $0.3°/10$ km in wire line, it is not necessary to adopt automatic compensation.

VIII. CONCLUSION

It has been shown that a multitransmitter simulcast digital signal transmission technique using a carrier frequency offset strategy is useful for a multiple control zone system realization. It has also been shown that the carrier frequency synchronizer and the modulation signal phase synchronizer can be easily constructed for the actual mobile telephone system. This technique may be widely applied not only to the mobile telephone system but also to other digital mobile communication systems.

ACKNOWLEDGMENT

The authors wish to thank S. Ito and M. Kohmura for their helpful guidance.

REFERENCES

[1] R. E. Fisher, "A description of the Bell system HCMTS cellsite radio and control hardware," in *Conf. Rec. 27th Annu. Conf. IEEE Veh. Technol.*, Mar. 16–18, 1977, pp. 166–167.

[2] S. Ito and Y. Matsuzaka, "800 MHz band land mobile telephone system overall view," *IEEE Trans. Veh. Technol.*, this issue, pp. 000–000.

[3] G. A. Arredondo, "Analysis of radio paging errors in multi-transmitter mobile systems" *IEEE Trans. Veh. Technol.*, vol. VT-22 no. 4, pp. 226–234, Nov. 1973.

[4] T. Hattori and K. Hirade, "Offset diversity effect in multi-station paging system," Rep. Comm. Sys. Conf., CS 74-97, IECE of Japan, 1974.

[5] M. Kohmura *et al.*, "Error rate performance improvement of selective calling signal transmission in mobile radio." Rep. of Comm. Sys. Conf., CS 74-124, IECE of Japan, 1974.

[6] G. P. Schleicher, "Design for system reliability in personal radio paging," *IEEE Trans. Veh. Technol.*, vol. VT-25, no. 1, pp. 13–19, Feb. 1976.

[7] T. Hattori, K. Hirade, and F. Adachi, unpublished.

[8] K. Hirade *et al.*, "Fading simulator for land mobile radio communication," IECE of Jap. Trans. on B, vol. 58-B, no. 9, pp. 449–459, 1975.

Advanced Mobile Phone Service

FRANKLIN H. BLECHER, FELLOW, IEEE

Abstract—The advanced mobile phone service (AMPS) system, an FM cellular radio system in the final stages of development, is described. A brief description of the system is followed by a discussion of the control algorithms which are basic to its operation. Finally, a status report is presented on the Chicago developmental system (an operational cellular system) and the cellular test bed in Newark, NJ (a field laboratory used to evaluate the radio performance of FM cellular systems with cells as small as 1.4-mi radius).

INTRODUCTION

THE advanced mobile phone service (AMPS) system was to satisfy the following objectives:

1) nationwide service,
2) efficient use of allocated frequency spectrum,
3) service quality approaching the wireline network,
4) technical and economic capability of operating in service areas as small as thousands of users and as large as hundreds of thousands of users.

It is evident from the fourth objective that, not only must a high-capacity mobile system be capable of serving large numbers of subscribers, but the capital investment and operating expense per user must be reasonable. In the case of FM systems, more than half of the investment is in the mobile telephone set. Consequently, considerable effort was expended to minimize the cost of the mobile set by appropriately allocating requirements between mobile and land-based equipment. The AMPS system exploits three technologies: 1) a stored program control central computer and switching system, 2) large-scale integrated custom circuits, and 3) microprocessors. Without the availability of these technologies, AMPS would not have been economically viable [1].

SYSTEM OVERVIEW

Fig. 1 shows a simplified diagram of the system plan. The allocated 40-mHz frequency spectrum is divided into 666 duplex radio channels, providing about 96 channels per cell for the seven-cell cluster frequency reuse pattern. Cell sites (base stations) are located at alternate corners of the hexagonal cells. The cell sites contain radio, control, voice frequency processing and maintenance equipment, as well as a complement of transmitting and receiving antennas. The cell sites are interconnected with the Mobile Telecommunications Switching Office (MTSO) by means of wireline

transmission facilities. Each voice radio at the cell site is connected to the MTSO via a voice frequency trunk. In addition, 2400-bit/s data links between the MTSO and each of the cell sites are used for the transmission of digital control signals.

In a mature AMPS system[1] such as shown in Fig. 1, directional antennas are employed with an RF beamwidth of 120°. Consequently, each cell site has three directional antennas for transmission and three pairs of receiving directional antennas in order to provide 360° of coverage. A maximum of 32 radio channels can be assigned to each directional antenna. The use of directional rather than omnidirectional antennas provides a 4–5 dB signal-to-interference advantage and makes a seven-cell cluster frequency reuse pattern possible [2].

As a mobile in the calling state moves about the service area, a "location" measurement is made every few seconds by the serving cell site. This measurement determines if the currently serving directional antenna should continue in this role or if the mobile should be "handed-off" to another directional antenna associated with the same cell site or to another cell site. By this means, the mobile is insured a satisfactory signal-to-interference ratio over essentially the entire service area. Obviously, good system control is of major importance to the successful operation of an FM cellular system.

AMPS SYSTEM CONTROL

Call Setup

Every cell site has at least one setup radio channel which is used for paging and access. The term paging describes the process of determining if a mobile is available to receive a given incoming call. The term access is the complementary function of starting a mobile-originated call or responding to a paging signal. Fig. 2 shows a simplified diagram of the radio communication paths between a mobile, cell site, and MTSO. A mobile in the on-hook state (idle condition) automatically tunes to the strongest setup channel. The forward setup channel contains a continuous synchronous stream of digital signals. Included in these signals are paging messages which contain the binary equivalent of the mobile unit's telephone number. When paging is not needed, the cell site adds "filler text" to preserve the synchronous format. Another message called the "overhead word" is transmitted periodically as part of the paging data and includes 1) the identification of

---

Manuscript received July 14, 1979; revised November 1, 1979. This paper was presented at MIDCON'78, Dallas, TX, December 12–14.

The author is with Bell Laboratories, Room 3F326, Whippany, NJ 07981. Telephone (201) 386–4056.

[1] An AMPS system is said to be mature when all cell sites are located at alternate corners of the hexagonal cells and employ directional antennas. In a so-called start-up system, the cell sites are located at the center of the cells and employ omnidirectional antennas.

Reprinted from *IEEE Trans. Veh. Technol.*, vol. VT-29, pp. 238–244, May 1980.

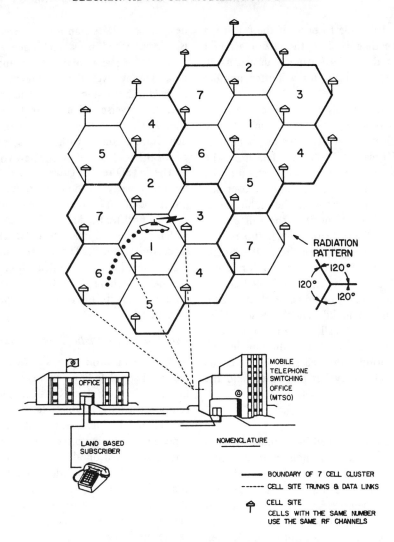

Fig. 1.   System plan.

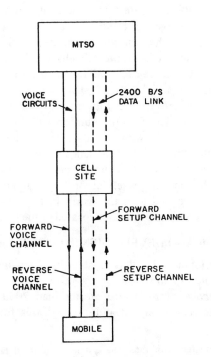

Fig. 2.   Communication paths between mobile, cell site, and MTSO.

the mobile service area (permits automatic roaming), 2) the number of setup channels to be scanned, and 3) information necessary for the mobile to identify the access channels when paging and access functions do not share the same channels (mature system).

Land-Originated Call

When a mobile determines that it is being paged, it responds by trying to seize the reverse setup channel (mobile-to-cell site).[2] Since all mobiles in the vicinity of a particular cell site compete for the same reverse setup channel, several techniques are used to minimize collisions. First, every 11th bit in the forward setup channel is a busy/idle bit indicating the status of the reverse setup channel. Second, the mobile transmits a seizure message on the reverse setup channel, called a "seizure precursor," which tells the system with which cell site the mobile is attempting to communicate. Third, after a mobile sends its precursor, it opens a "window" in time in which it expects to see the busy/idle bits in the

---

[2] The reverse setup channel operates independently of the forward setup channel and transmits isolated bursts of digital signals.

297

forward setup channel go from idle to busy. If the transition does not occur within the time window, the seizure attempt is immediately aborted. If the initial seizure is unsuccessful, the mobile is permitted to try again for a limited number of times.

When the mobile does successfully seize the reverse setup channel, in the case of a page response, it transmits to the cell site its mobile identification number. This information is then relayed to the MTSO via the 2400-bit/s data link. The MTSO assigns the mobile an idle voice channel, and the channel assignment is transmitted to the mobile over the forward setup channel (cell site-to-mobile). The mobile tunes to the assigned voice channel and notifies the cell site of this fact by looping back to the cell site a 6-kHz supervisory audio tone (SAT), transmitted by the cell site to the mobile over the forward voice channel. When confirmation is received at the MTSO, the MTSO commands the serving cell site to transmit a data message over the forward voice channel activating an alerting device in the mobile telephone set. When the mobile subscriber answers the call, a change in state of a 10-kHz signaling tone (ST) transmitted by the mobile over the reverse voice channel notifies the cell site, and thus the MTSO, that the called mobile party has responded, and the call can proceed.

Mobile-Originated Call

A mobile-originated call is established in a similar manner. The mobile subscriber dials the desired phone number into a register in the mobile set. The call setup is not started until the subscriber presses a "send" button.[3] The mobile then attempts to seize the reverse setup channel as discussed previously, and to transmit its own identification number as well as the number of the called party. This information is then relayed by the cell site to the MTSO which assigns an idle voice channel and establishes voice communication with the mobile. The MTSO completes the call through the wire-line network using standard digit outpulsing techniques. Communication between subscribers takes place when the called party answers.

Handoffs

A key feature of cellular systems is the ability to handoff a mobile unit from one directional antenna to another associated with the same cell site or to another cell site. In AMPS, location information is gathered by the serving cell site, as well as by surrounding cell sites. This information is transmitted to the MTSO over the various cell-site landline data links. The MTSO decides whether a handoff is necessary and, if it is, selects an idle voice channel associated either with another directional antenna of the currently serving cell site or another cell site. The MTSO directs the cell site associated with the new voice channel to turn on the appropriate transmitter and to transmit SAT.

The MTSO directs the currently serving cell site to inform the mobile unit, via the forward voice channel, to tune to the new channel. Data transmission over the forward voice channel is accomplished by a technique known as blank-and-burst. The voice signal is blanked for about 50 ms and a burst of data is sent over the talking path. The mobile unit, after receiving the handoff command, sends a brief burst of ST over the reverse voice channel to the currently serving cell site. The mobile then turns off its transmitter, tunes to the new voice channel, turns on its transmitter again, and transponds the SAT found on the new voice channel.

The MTSO reconfigures the switching network, connecting the other party to the new serving antenna. On receiving the transponded SAT, the cell site associated with the new serving antenna notifies the MTSO. The MTSO identifies the reception of ST on the old channel and SAT on the new channel as a successful handoff. The entire handoff process takes about 0.2 s including the blank-and-burst period and the mobile channel switching time. It has been found that the handoff does not significantly degrade the quality of voice transmission.

Data Format for Radio Transmission

A difficult problem associated with data transmission is the rapid signal fading experienced by the mobile as it travels through the complex RF signal patterns. To combat burst errors caused by Rayleigh fading, all data words are encoded and repeated several times at the source, and a bit-by-bit three-out-of-five majority vote is taken at the data receivers. The coding used on all radio channels is the Bose–Chandhuri–Hocquenghem (BCH) code (40, 28) in the forward direction and (48, 36) in the reverse direction (see Fig. 2). Figs. 3, 4, and 5 show the data format used for the forward setup channel, the reverse setup channel, and the voice channels (forward and reverse), respectively.

The combination of 1) message repeats to combat burst errors and 2) the BCH coding for single bit error correction plus capability for detecting additional errors provides an acceptable message error rate and an extremely low falsing rate [3], [4].[4] The data are transmitted at the highest rate possible consistent with the RF channel bandwidth. A 10-kbit/s rate was chosen for AMPS, yielding a maximum information throughout of about 1200 bits/s.

With reference to the forward setup channel, a mobile with an even identification number will look at the "A" word and a mobile with an odd identification number will look at the "B" word. This data format has the advantage of increasing the time between message repeats and thus reduces the deleterious effect of Rayleigh fades. The subnumerals associated with the words in Figs. 3–5 correspond to the order in which they are repeated in the message.

THE CHICAGO DEVELOPMENTAL CELLULAR SYSTEM

A developmental cellular system has been installed in the Chicago metropolitan area and consists of ten cell sites providing service over an area greater than 2000 mi^2. Fig. 6 shows the cell-site layout and coverage area for the system.

---

[3] This is called preorigination dialing and has as one advantage a conservation of air-time usage.

[4] Undetected error rate. The system disregards data messages with more than one error.

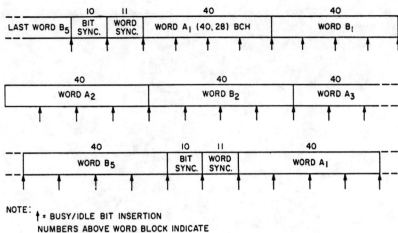

NOTE:

↑ = BUSY/IDLE BIT INSERTION

NUMBERS ABOVE WORD BLOCK INDICATE
NUMBER OF BITS PER WORD.

BIT SYNC. = 1010····010

WORD SYNC. = 11100010010

Fig. 3.   Data format for forward setup channel.

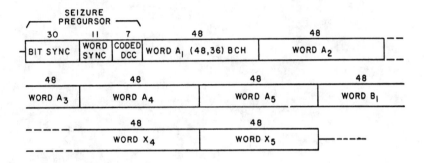

NOTE:

X = A, B, C, D, OR E

BIT SYNC. = 1010····010

WORD SYNC. = 11100010010

DCC = DIGITAL COLOR CODE

Fig. 4.   Data format for reverse setup channel.

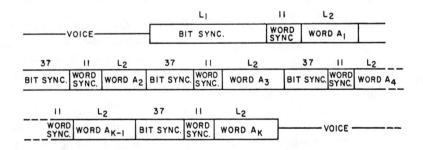

NOTE:

	FORWARD	REVERSE
L₁ =	100	101
L₂ =	40	48
K =	11	5

BIT SYNC. = 1010·······010

WORD SYNC. = 11100010010

ON THE REVERSE CHANNEL, A
SECOND MESSAGE (B) MAY
FOLLOW WORD A_K

Fig. 5.   Data format for forward and reverse voice channels.

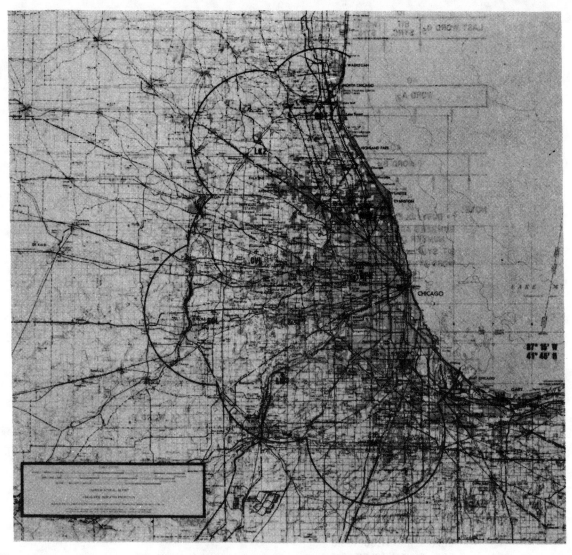

Fig. 6.   Developmental cellular system in Chicago Metropolitan area.

The location of each of the ten cell sites is indicated by a cross and a three-letter abbreviation for the name of the cell site. The MTSO located in Oak Park, IL, is indicated by a circle. This is a so-called "start-up" system and differs from a mature system principally in that cell sites are located at the centers of the cells and employ omnidirectional antennas.[5] This system configuration minimizes land equipment investment at start-up and, in addition, permits planned growth into a mature system. Each of the ten cell sites is connected to the MTSO which employs an ESS #1 processor and switch. Overall system control is provided by the processor in the MTSO.

Given below are the objectives of the AMPS developmental cellular system:

1) validate the system hardware/software design;
2) demonstrate the ability to operate and maintain a cellular system with normal craftspeople support;
3) explore the market for this service more fully and characterize the users.

A six-month technical trial of the system (called the "equipment test") was carried out during the period July 1978 to December 1978. Approximately 90 Bell System employees used the system during the equipment test. On December 20, 1978, a market trial with paying customers was initiated by Illinois Bell Telephone Company (this is called the "service test"). Prospective business customers for this service are selected in accordance with statistically valid sampling techniques in order to verify the results of market research previously carried out. It is anticipated that about 1400 subscribers will be using the trial system by the end of 1979.

[5] A start-up system with omnidirectional antennas requires a reuse factor of 12 cells. In comparison, a mature system uses directional antennas which cause substantially less interference outside of the 120° sector which the front lobe illuminates and thus, in general, makes possible a reuse factor of seven cells.

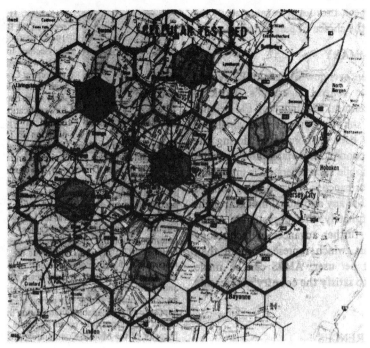

Fig. 7.   Layout of CTB in Newark, NJ.

Each mobile subscriber has a mobile telephone set mounted in his car with the following features [5], [6]:

- RF power output: 10 W;
- frequency coverage: transmitter band is 825–845 mHz, contains 666 channels spaced 30 kHz apart, receiver band is 870 to 890 mHz;
- RF channel switching: settling time after switch between two channels is less than 40 ms;
- modulation: angle-modulated RF signals;
- diversity: switched;
- voice frequency processing: 2:1 syllabic compandor;
- dialing: preorigination push button dialing, called address stored in register in the mobile set until user presses "send" button;
- logic control: call setup and handoffs completely automatic.

The system has operated very well in terms of both call control and quality of voice frequency transmission. Call setup and handoff algorithms have been thoroughly exercised and found to be satisfactory. It should be noted that even though a start-up system uses relatively large cells (8–10 mi radius), the control algorithms are essentially the same as used in a mature system with small cells (1–2 mi radius). It is not surprising, therefore, that it has been found in the cellular test bed (described in the next section) that the same control algorithms work quite well in 1–2 mi radius cells.

The radio coverage of the system has been carefully measured using a well-equipped mobile laboratory, and it has been found that, under algorithmic handoff control, there are no serious holes in the coverage pattern. The quality of voice communication is good, approaching that of the wireline network.

THE CELLULAR TEST BED

The cellular test bed (CTB) is essentially a field laboratory installed in and around Newark, NJ. The objective of the CTB program is to demonstrate the feasibility of AMPS design parameters for both a start-up system (noise-limited operation) and a mature small-cell system (interference-limited operation). The CTB consists of three main cell sites defining a 1.4-mi radius hexagonal cell, six interferer sites surrounding the main cell sites (representing essentially the maximum interference in a seven-cell cluster system), and a central control and monitor system. The cell sites are equipped with a complement of both omnidirectional and directional antennas. A well-equipped mobile communication laboratory is used to make system measurements, and a special laboratory facility has been provided for rapid processing of CTB data.

Fig. 7 shows a map of the layout of the CTB. The three main cell sites are located within the three small circles associated with the center hexagonal cell. The six interferer cell sites are located within the six cells which use the same channel frequencies as the center cell.

It was recognized early in the AMPS program that it was dangerous to extrapolate radio data measured in relatively large cells (8- or 4-mi radius) down to small cells (1 or 2 mi). Consequently, the CTB is basically a small-cell system, but with appropriate power scaling can simulate large-cell systems as well. The CTB uses essentially the same control algorithms as used in the service test system.

The control algorithms, radio coverage, and voice quality in both a noise-limited start-up system and an interference-

301

limited mature system have been thoroughly evaluated in the CTB, and the results support the choice of parameters used.

SUMMARY

This paper has presented an overview of the AMPS system development emphasizing the control algorithms. Work to date has demonstrated the technical feasibility of FM cellular systems for both large-cell start-up systems and small-cell mature systems. It has also been demonstrated during the service test that AMPS is economically viable and provides very satisfactory service to mobile subscribers. It is improtant to note that the system performance is realized using today's technology and does not require any additional breakthroughs in new system concepts. Fortunately, the subsystem in AMPS which will profit most from further advances in technology is the mobile telephone unit, which represents more than half of the total investment per user. AMPS can be made available early in the 1980's to satisfy the country's increasing mobile telephone needs.

REFERENCES

[1] *Bell Syst. Tech. J.*, Jan. 1979; a comprehensive description of the AMPS system.
[2] V. H. MacDonald, "The cellular concept," *Bell Syst. Tech. J.*, pp. 15–41, Jan. 1979.
[3] Z. C. Fluhr and P. T. Porter, "Control architecture," *Bell Syst. Tech. J.*, pp. 43–69, Jan. 1979.
[4] G. A. Arredondo, J. C. Feggeler, and J. I. Smith, "Voice and data transmission," *Bell Syst. Tech. J.*, pp. 97–122, Jan. 1979.
[5] R. E. Fisher, "A subscriber set for the equipment test," *Bell Syst. Tech. J.*, pp. 123–143, Jan. 1979.
[6] J. T. Walker, "Service test mobile telephone control unit," *Bell Syst. Tech. J.*, pp. 145–152, Jan. 1979.

Advanced Mobile Phone Service:

Voice and Data Transmission

By G. A. ARREDONDO, J. C. FEGGELER, and J. I. SMITH

(Manuscript received July 28, 1978)

Use of the AMPS (Advanced Mobile Phone Service) microwave channel, operating in the 800- to 900-MHz band, creates unique problems in addition to those connected with conventional land communications. Because the channel characteristics are not fixed, they present design challenges and impairments that must be dealt with to protect mobile telephone users from experiencing excessive variabilities in voice transmission quality and in control and signaling reliability. This paper describes the radio transmission features of the AMPS system, emphasizing the processing and control techniques designed to deal with the dynamic nature of the mobile radio channel.

I. INTRODUCTION

Transmission of voice and digital control information over the AMPS microwave radio channel in the 800- to 900-MHz frequency range presents significantly different problems than those encountered in conventional land communication systems. Unlike wire-line systems, the channel characteristics are never fixed, but vary with movement of the vehicle and changes in its surroundings. These dynamics give rise to a formidable set of design challenges since the character of the radio channel can change dramatically during a single call as the vehicle moves through the service area and is "handed off" to successive cell sites. Although these channel variations will occur, the radio transmission parameters, and consequently the voice and data transmission functions, have been designed to prevent the user as much as possible from experiencing corresponding changes in voice quality and in control and signaling reliability.

This paper examines the relationship between the impairments produced by the channel and the characteristics of the transmitted waveform. In particular, a consideration of the constraints affecting

the performance of processors for voice and data transmission will provide the rationale for design selections in these areas. A feature of the system is the use of syllabic companding in the voice processor to control the modulation process in the presence of speech variability and also to enable the system to operate effectively in the presence of channel impairments. The technique chosen to transmit signaling data between the cell sites and the mobiles is described in detail. This technique incorporates a self-clocked modulating waveform and contains considerable redundancy to ensure reliable transmission over the mobile telephone channel.

Section II begins with a description of the radio channel. This channel is highly variable—no single set of rules covers all cases—and no attempt is made to qualify every statement with exceptions. However, the main features of the environment at 850 MHz that affect the design are presented, and impairments relevant to the cellular radio environment are outlined.

Baseband performance specifically related to mobile radio is discussed in Section III, along with the modulation methods and signal processing used in the system. Finally, Sections IV and V present an overview of the voice and data transmission methods chosen for AMPS.

II. THE AMPS MICROWAVE CHANNEL

2.1 Multipath propagation

Measurements[1-6] made by Bell Laboratories in Philadelphia, New York City, Whippany and Newark, N. J., and by others elsewhere confirm that a moving vehicle in an urban environment seldom has a direct line-of-sight path to the land transmitter. The propagation path contains many obstacles in the form of buildings and other structures, hills, and also other vehicles. Because there is no unique propagation path between transmitter and receiver, the instantaneous field strength at the mobile and base receivers exhibits a highly variable structure. The measurements show that the main propagation features in the radio environment are (i) multipath due to scatter or reflections from buildings and other obstructions most often within a few hundred feet of the vehicle, and (ii) shadowing of the direct line-of-sight path by intervening features of the terrain.

The received signal at the mobile is the net result of many waves that arrive via multiple paths formed by diffraction and scattering. The amplitude, phase, and angle of arrival of these waves are random, and the short-term statistics of the resultant signal envelope fluctuations over local geographic areas approximate a Rayleigh distribution. Figure 1 shows a typical envelope of the received signal at a moving antenna measured along a short distance of travel. The so-called Rayleigh signal fades occur approximately one-half wavelength apart because of plane wave interference.[2] At carrier frequencies near 850

Reprinted with permission from *Bell Syst. Tech. J.*, vol. 58, pp. 97–122, Jan. 1979.
Copyright © 1979, AT&T.

THE BELL SYSTEM TECHNICAL JOURNAL, JANUARY 1979

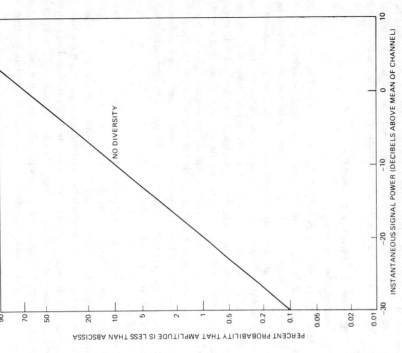

Fig. 2—Amplitude distribution function.

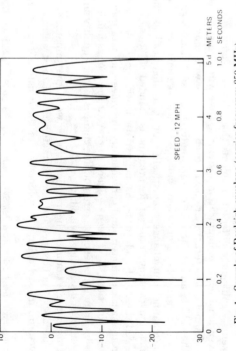

Fig. 1—Sample of Rayleigh envelope (carrier frequency 850 MHz).

MHz, independent fades are about 7 inches apart. As the mobile receiver moves through the radio interference pattern, it is therefore subjected to frequent fades. By reciprocity, the base station receiver tuned to a different frequency experiences the same sort of fades, although not at exactly the same time. These Rayleigh fades place the most severe limits on the quality of voice and data transmission at UHF.

Signal envelope fades into noise and interference can cause severe degradation in voice and data transmission. Let us look in greater detail at the representation of the multipath fading pattern given in Fig. 1, starting with the amplitude distribution.

Figure 2 shows the probability distribution function of the received instantaneous signal power normalized to its mean value.[2] The statistics of the fades are such that 10 percent of the time the signal will be 10 dB below its local mean, 1 percent of the time 20 dB below the mean, etc., where mean is defined in the figure as the mean received signal power. The plot in Fig. 1 is in decibels below this mean. Since vehicle motion induces signal fades via the multipath interference pattern, both the fading rate and fade duration depend on vehicle velocity.[2,7] Figure 3 is a plot, with velocity a parameter, of the rate of level crossing downward through a given level relative to the local mean. At 850 MHz, the rate of crossing a level 10 dB below the local mean happens to be numerically equal to the vehicle speed in miles per hour. Thus, at 20 mph, there will be a fade crossing the −10 dB level an average of 20 times per second. Related to the crossing rate is the average time the fading signal spends below a given level, i.e the

fade duration. The fade duration is inversely proportional to vehicle speed. At 20 mph, the average fade duration below −10 dB is 5 ms, as may be seen in Fig. 4.

In addition to the rapid Rayleigh fluctuations, there are also slower variations due to shadowing by local terrain features. Changes in the local mean-received signal power occur as the vehicle moves. The changes observed in local mean are slow only if compared to the Rayleigh fades, since 5-dB changes in mean signal level in less than 100 feet of vehicle travel are typical. A consistent result observed for these variations is that they have nearly a normal distribution for the received signal level measured in decibels—often referred to as a log-normal distribution. The variance of this log-normal distribution lies between 6 and 10 dB, with the larger variances generally found in heavily built-up urban areas.

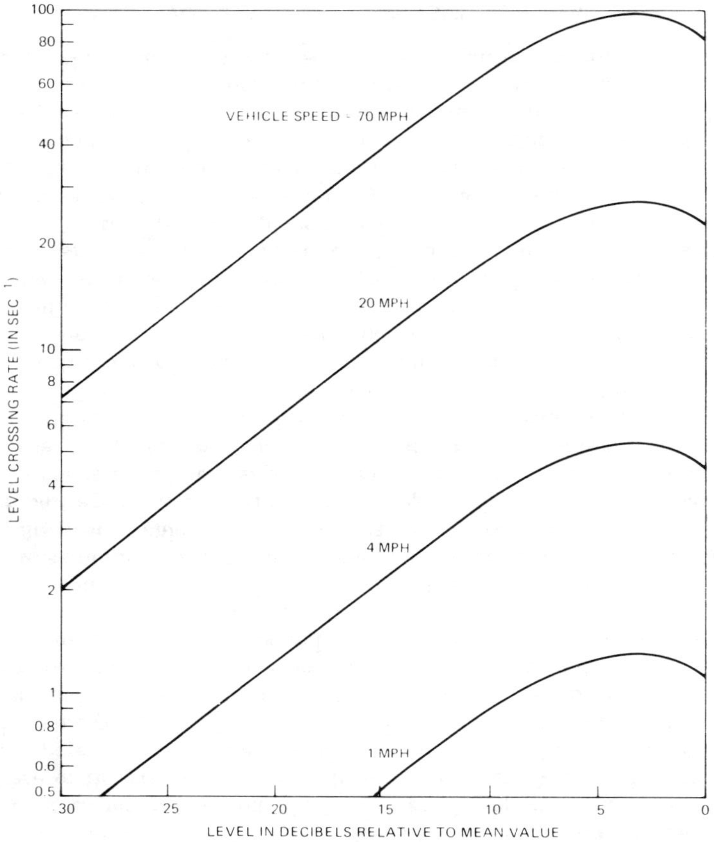

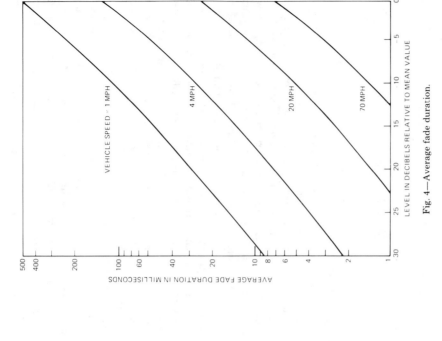

Fig. 3—Level crossing rate.

Fig. 4—Average fade duration.

The delay distribution associated with multipath propagation has also been directly measured.[4,8] Since the resultant received signal is the superposition of signals which arrive via many paths, a spread in channel delay is observed. Measurements have shown that the received signals have a spread in delay which can be of the order of 3.5 microseconds in urban areas. The delay distortion which can result from this phenomenon provides limitations on the maximum signal bandwidth that can be transmitted over the channel. The delay spread-related coherence bandwidth[4,8,9] is defined as the bandwidth within which fading has a 0.9 or greater correlation. This bandwidth is usually >40 kHz in urban areas and >250 kHz in most surburban areas, so that frequency selective fading due to delay spread will not significantly

impair transmission performance over the narrowband 30-kHz channels used in the AMPS system.

As the vehicle moves through the fading signal pattern, interruptions of voice modulation or losses of bits in data transmission occur when noise or interference captures the FM receiver during signal fades. The high rate of occurrence of deep fades, particularly those associated with multipath and shown in Fig. 1, provides the major source of transmission impairments in AMPS. While the use of linear modulation such as AM is conceptually possible, the rate of change and depth of fades that can occur at UHF have not permitted satisfactory transmission quality to be attained in this environment with those techniques. Frequency modulation—the approach used in AMPS—avoids the direct effect of these loss variations on information transmission. For this reason, frequency modulation has been selected for transmitting both

VOICE AND DATA TRANSMISSION   305

THE BELL SYSTEM TECHNICAL JOURNAL, JANUARY 1979

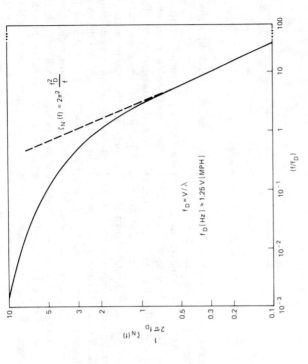

Fig. 5—Power spectrum of random FM.

speech and the binary data associated with system control functions, and it is in the context of FM with discriminator detection that transmission impairments will be discussed.

2.2 Impairments

The fading signal described in the preceding section will be received in the presence of various sources of impairments including receiver Gaussian noise, random FM, system-generated interference, and man-made environmental noise.

At high carrier-to-receiver thermal noise ratios, the FM receiver is "captured" by the signal, and the conversion to baseband produces a noise component with approximately a Gaussian probability density for the instantaneous voltage and the usual parabolic power spectrum characteristic of discriminator detection.[10] In addition to this "pseudo-Gaussian" noise is the so-called "click" noise[10] that results from capture of the receiver by noise. This impairment occurs with high probability if the instantaneous noise level exceeds the IF signal amplitude, as it often does near the bottom of signal fades. During these intervals, the phase of the composite IF waveform can change by 2π radians in a time period commensurate with the reciprocal of the IF bandwidth. This change causes the discriminator to present an impulse to the baseband processor, with the result that the click noise power spectrum is approximately flat in the voice bandwidth after the FM discriminator. Clicks furnish a major baseband noise component, and arrive in bursts which are time-correlated with RF signal fades.

The same multipath phenomenon that produces Rayleigh fading creates another impairment, referred to as random FM.[2] Random FM results from vehicle motion, and is due to time variation in the composite phase angle of the multipath signal at the antenna terminals. It provides an additional error component in the discriminator response. The power spectrum at baseband of random FM is a monotonically decreasing function of frequency (Fig. 5). Because of the waveform parameters and processing used in AMPS, random FM represents primarily a lower bound on baseband impairments for voice transmission when other noise and interference sources are removed. It is not a significant factor in AMPS data transmission.

The co-channel interference that results from channels reused in a mature small-cell system creates additional impairments. As discussed in Ref. 11, the system employs frequency reuse. More than one user can share the same channel frequency if they are far enough apart, but since their separation distance is finite, channel reuse generates a form of co-channel interference. The level and distribution of this interference depend on the frequency reuse pattern, and this has been balanced against system cost and performance objectives. Other factors include the implementation specifics, such as antenna height, directiv-

ity, system handoff and control algorithms, siting requirements, and the channel assignment plan.

During the short-duration Rayleigh fades of the signal envelope caused by vehicle motion, the FM receiver can be captured by interference. The result is a burst of interfering voice modulation which is unintelligible because of the short duration of the fades (Fig. 4). In voice transmission, the relative amplitude of the baseband interference during the burst is dependent on the relative amplitudes of the instantaneous frequency deviation of the interfering and desired voice signals.

In addition, since the signal carrier and the co-channel-interferer carrier will usually be offset (because of oscillator tolerances) by a difference frequency that can fall within the receiver voice bandwidth, a detected difference frequency is sometimes audible as a "wobbling tone." For fading channels, this tone is audible at average carrier-to-interference ratios as high as 30 dB.

An associated side effect of co-channel interference, with offset-carriers, is the creation of additional click-line impairments that affect both voice and data transmission. The presence of a frequency offset increases the rate of occurrence of 2π phase steps due to carrier interference. The amplitude of the resulting interference clicks is generally less than those discussed earlier, since phase changes occur more slowly than those produced by receiver noise. The rate of phase change for the interference clicks depends primarily on the carrier offset frequency rather than on the RF bandwidth.

Environmental noise provides another source of potential impairment to AMPS transmission. Automotive ignition systems are major noise sources in this category, but others include neon lights, electrical machinery, and arc welding systems. In contrast with receiver Gaussian noise, environmental noise is often nonstationary and impulsive. The intensity of environmental noise is a strong function of local traffic conditions, and can vary from insignificance (many rural and suburban areas) to levels which can completely dominate other sources of noise and interference (intense urban "rush-hour" traffic).

Data have been collected in the central cell region of the Cellular Test Bed[12] in Newark, N.J. to characterize the "impulse" noise environment in a typical urban area. For example, Fig. 6 gives the probability distribution function of the peak power level referred to the antenna terminals (using a 28-kHz predetection filter) produced by impulse-noise in urban Newark. Data for this figure were obtained by first screening the data base to determine the maximum impulse noise level in each half-second data record, and then using these largest values to form the "bounding" distribution function of Fig. 6.

In the AMPS frequency band, the time-density of the impulses is relatively low, so that the ratio of peak to average power is very large.

This is illustrated in Fig. 7, which contains two 1-second noise traces obtained from the Cellular Test Bed. The bottom trace contains post-IF filter noise data obtained by periodically sampling the composite receiver and impulse noise environment. The average noise power implied by this trace is about −120 dBm. The top trace contains only the largest value achieved by the composite noise process between successive points obtained for the bottom trace. For this example, the ratio of peak-to-average power is about 45 dB.

The non-Gaussian nature of this form of noise leads to baseband impairment characteristics different from those generated by receiver noise. The impairment tends to be a repetitive string of pulses, with pulse amplitude dependent on the relative amplitude of the "impulses" and RF signal, as well as the bandwidth and impulse response of the predetection filter. The baseband impairment power is proportional to the pulse rate. To place in perspective the relative importance of environmental noise and receiver Gaussian noise, current results indicate that environmental noise is primarily an urban consideration, and the impact on voice transmission will be more important than its effect on AMPS data transmission. The effect of environmental noise on signaling performance is low because the arrival rates of the noise impulses are low compared with the signaling data rates. Signaling is also aided in this respect by the redundancy used in data coding (Section V).

III. TRANSMISSION

In many FM systems, the capture of the receiver by the signal of interest at modest values (10 dB) of IF S/N or S/I ratio provides an important mechanism for enhancing baseband performance when RF impairments are present. The capture phenomenon is not as dramatic in suppressing impairments in the AMPS system as it is in broadcast nonvehicular FM systems because of the severity and rapidity of the signal fades on the mobile channel. These fades create transitory situations during which the RF signal no longer dominates noise or interference. The resulting loss of signal capture introduces impairments into the baseband response that can be orders of magnitude higher than those experienced with nonfading channels operating at the same average RF signal level. The severity of these impairments will not be uniform over the coverage region of AMPS, but will tend to follow the trends in signal and interference strength dictated by propagation considerations (path loss dependence and shadow fading).

The AMPS system employs both spatial diversity signal reception techniques and specialized designs for the voice and data transmission functions to prevent as much as possible the user from experiencing the effects of channel impairments.

THE BELL SYSTEM TECHNICAL JOURNAL, JANUARY 1979

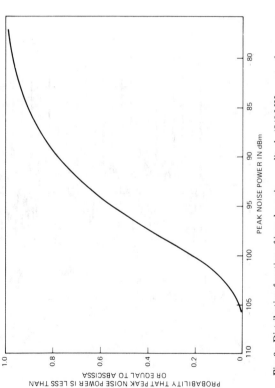

Fig. 6—Distribution function of impulse noise amplitude (848 MHz center frequency, 28 kHz bandwidth).

VOICE AND DATA TRANSMISSION

3.1 Channel spacing

In the AMPS system, RF transmission channels are spaced by 30 kHz. This spacing is achieved by limiting to 12 kHz the peak-frequency deviation generated by modulating voice signals, and by applying an RF frequency assignment plan that does not permit the use of adjacent channels in the same cell.[11]

The frequency spacing of RF voice channels is an important system parameter, as it affects both performance and cost. The voice-channel spacing selected for AMPS reflects a consideration of each of these factors.

For practical reasons, the RF channels cannot be bandlimited prior to transmission from either the cell site or the mobile transmitter. Hence, the potential for transmission impairments that can result from adjacent channel interference is a major consideration.

The peak frequency deviation and baseband spectrum of the modulating signal determine the spectral occupancy of the radiated FM waveform. Adjacent channel interference resulting from "splatter," of this waveform into neighboring channels is influenced by the spacing of the RF channels, the adjacent channel response of the receiver predetection filter, and the geographic separation of adjacent voice channels.

Impairments resulting from adjacent channel interference can be reduced by increasing the frequency spacing of the voice channels. This approach, however, will also reduce the total number of RF channels available for use in the system. A reduction in the number of available channels increases the rate at which cell-splitting must occur in order that the user population be served without excessive facility-blocking. Thus, on the average, fewer users will be served by each cell-site, and an increase in costs will result.

The performance factors related to channel spacing have been investigated in the laboratory by using a Rayleigh Channel Simulator[13] to test transmission in the various impairment environments. Laboratory data were used to quantify performance sensitivities and tradeoffs. The impairment environments included Gaussian receiver noise, man-made impulse noise, co-channel and adjacent channel interference, random FM, and frequency synthesizer noise. In addition, field data from the Cellular Test Bed have been used to corroborate the laboratory models and results obtained with them.

The results of these tests and also the results of cost-analysis studies were used to establish the channel spacing and waveform parameters that are used in AMPS.

3.2 Diversity

The high rate of occurrence of deep fades, particularly those associated with multipath and represented in Fig. 1, can be reduced by the

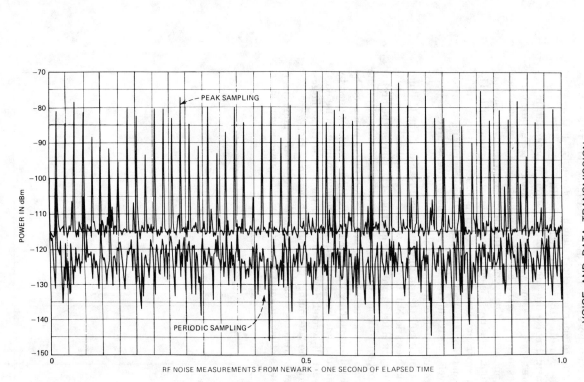

Fig. 7—Environmental noise trace.

use of spatial diversity.[2] One class of systems using spatial diversity employs signals from two or more antennas that are co-phased and added prior to detection (equal-gain or "Granlund" diversity). Alternatively, the antenna which gives the highest S/N ratio could be selected for signal reception (selection diversity), or outputs of multiple antennas could be switched to a single receiver using a control algorithm that is driven by the detection of signal fades (switched diversity). Spatial diversity can significantly improve transmission performance because of the small probability that all antennas, if spaced a half wavelength or more apart, will simultaneously experience a signal fade. As an illustration, the distribution function for the composite envelope resulting from two-branch, equal-gain, diversity combining is compared with that of a single branch receiver in Fig. 8. With two branches,

the probability of fades 10 dB below the mean signal strength decreases to 0.8 percent from the 10-percent probability obtained without diversity. At 18-dB average carrier-to-receiver noise ratio, the resulting improvement in voiceband S/N ratio is about 12 dB.

This substantial improvement is not obtained without cost, however. Equal-gain and selection diversity each require simultaneous dual-channel reception for each diversity branch, including separate antennas and RF units, IF strips, etc., up to the point of the diversity combination. "Switched" diversity requires less duplication of equipment, so it costs less than the others, but it also does not work as well.[2] In AMPS, current plans are to use equal-gain or selection diversity at the cell sites, where the cost is shared by many users, and to use "switched" diversity in the mobile units.

IV. VOICE PROCESSING

4.1 Considerations

Control of the system RF characteristics, which affect the level of noise and interference impairments in the detected voiceband signal, involves considerations such as effective radiated power, cell radius, and the frequency reuse factor.[11] Since practical considerations restrict the flexibility of this type of control, other techniques, in addition to receiver diversity, have been investigated. In AMPS, speech signal processing has provided a relatively economical degree of freedom for substantially improving the quality of service.

In addition to RF considerations discussed earlier, studies[14] have shown that considerable variability exists in talker volumes and in the corresponding amplitude of electrical signals generated by different talkers using telephone microphones. The average signal power at baseband in the FM receiver is proportional to the mean-squared frequency deviation, f^2_{rms}, produced in the transmitter modulator. To maximize performance in the presence of impairments, it is important that f^2_{rms} be controlled. In AMPS, the rms frequency deviation for the "nominal" talker is set at 2 kHz.

Previous studies[14] suggest that, in the absence of some type of modulation control, talker and microphone variability will result in a log-normal distribution for f^2_{rms}, with a standard deviation of about 5 dB. Speech from "weak" talkers will suffer a degradation in receiver-voiceband, signal-to-impairment ratio directly proportional to the reduction in f^2_{rms}. This reduction directly affects perceived transmission quality, producing a commensurate reduction in the subjective rating of channel quality. At the opposite extreme, speech from "loud" talkers is impaired through excessive "clipping" distortion in the transmitter. (Amplitude clipping is used in the transmit processor to limit the peak-instantaneous frequency-deviation associated with the transmitted waveform so that adjacent-channel interference effects can be con-

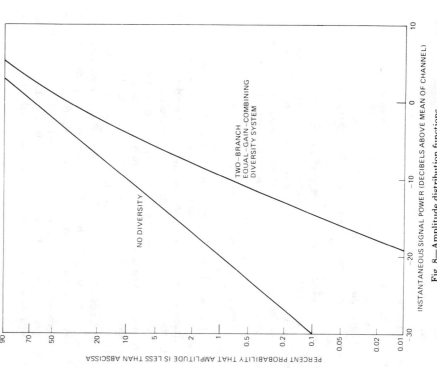

Fig. 8—Amplitude distribution functions.

VOICE AND DATA TRANSMISSION

trolled.) The baseband processing selected for AMPS provides a means of reducing the effect of variability in volume levels on impairment and distortion performance.

4.2 Description

Figure 9 is a block diagram of the voice processing circuitry. The use of filtering and amplitude limiting in the transmit processor, to control spectrum splatter into adjacent channels (and filtering in the receiver to control the effects of noise), follows typical design procedures for FM systems. The use of differentiator pre-emphasis and integrator de-emphasis to improve performance in the presence of channel impairments is also consistent with standard design approaches. A difference in this application is that, instead of suppressing noise relative to speech as in most FM systems (where the noise characteristics are different from those of the AMPS), de-emphasis here primarily shapes the spectrum of the major noise component (the "clicks") so that it is similar to, and generally subjectively masked by, the presence of speech.[15]

The compandor has been found to provide important improvements in AMPS voice transmission quality. It controls the effect of speech level variability on clipping distortion and frequency deviation generated by the modulator, and also improves the subjective quality of the channel when it is operating in the presence of impairments.

Compandors have been used in wire-line telephone circuits to improve performance over relatively noisy paths and also to reduce crosstalk problems. Their use in AM radio systems has been previously considered, but uncertainties in the path loss between transmitter and receiver for various links have forced the use of special channels dedicated to providing control information for the receiver. For analog FM transmission, however, path loss variation (or its equivalent) is far less of a problem than for AM transmission. Thus, use of the compandor in the AMPS system does not require complex special control channels.

The syllabic compandor is made up of a matched compressor-expandor pair with carefully controlled time constants. Both are variable gain devices, with gain control as illustrated in Fig. 10 and nominal input-output characteristics as shown in Fig. 11. The signal-dependent "gain" of the compressor is matched by a complementary signal-dependent "loss" of the expandor so that speech may be transmitted without perceptible distortion and level changes. This matching is achieved by balancing and stabilizing the operating point of each of the devices, and insuring that each has the proper time constant for gain control.

The compandor in this application uses attack and recovery times[16,17] of 3 and 13.5 ms, respectively, which are the CCITT-recommended nominal values. Achieving these values requires smoothing the output of a half-wave rectifier with a low-pass filter having a 20-ms R-C time constant. Although the selected values for the attack and recovery times reflect a compromise between low-frequency distortion and intersyllabic noise-quieting,[17] they serve a dual purpose in mobile telephony. The compressor reduces, by the companding law, the variability in clipping distortion and rms frequency deviation associated with the distribution of speech volumes to which the system will be exposed. The most common companding law for wire-line systems is nominally 2:1, which provides a reduction in the output-level variation by a factor of 2 (in dB) over that of the compressor's input

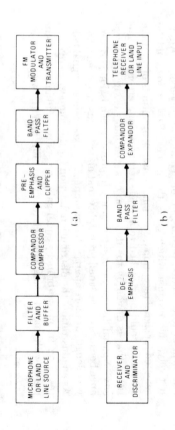

Fig. 9—AMPS audio processor. (a) Transmit processor. (b) Receive processor.

VOICE AND DATA TRANSMISSION

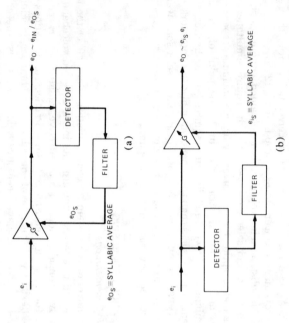

Fig. 10—Compandor operation. (a) 2:1 compressor. (b) 2:1 expandor.

THE BELL SYSTEM TECHNICAL JOURNAL, JANUARY 1979

waveform. The compressor's response time is sufficiently slow so that it does not respond to level changes that occur significantly faster than the 20-ms R-C time constant, but restricts primarily the slower syllabic variations. Hence, the compressor does not significantly affect the speech-crest factor and spectral content.

The bandpass filter which precedes the compressor serves to band-limit speech signals so that out-of-band speech energy does not influence the gain of the compressor or affect the inband loss of the amplitude limiter.

The receiver expandor not only removes transmitter predistortion created by the compandor compressor, but also suppresses receiver noise and interference relative to speech signals, thereby quieting the receiver. For low-level impairments whose average level varies slowly with respect to the expandor response time (such as random FM, Gaussian noise, and the co-channel carrier-offset "wobbling tone"), the expandor output signal-to-impairment ratio (in decibels) is improved by a factor that approaches the companding law. This is the typical quieting mechanism for wire-line systems.

The second way in which the audio impairments of mobile radio are suppressed is through the finite response time of the expandor. The expandor is normally in a high-loss state in the absence of an applied audio signal. Thermal noise clicks present in the receiver-audio-filter response may be larger in amplitude than levels corresponding to

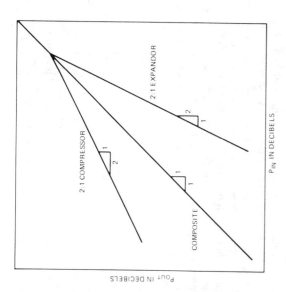

Fig. 11—Input/output characteristic of compandor.

nominal talkers. However, individual clicks at the input to the audio receiver last only about 0.3 ms and lack sufficient energy in the loss control bandwidth to cause the expandor to change from its high-loss state fast enough to respond to them.[18] Since expandor-loss control is achieved through integration of the received baseband signal by means of a low-pass filter with a time constant of 20 ms, the expandor will not be fully driven from its high-loss state by burst of clicks or co-channel interference lasting less than about 20 ms. This inertia in the expandor response results from the CCITT attack-time standard, which is made large enough to prevent excessive voice distortion at low frequencies due to compandor action. For mobile telephone operation, this specification serves a dual purpose by inhibiting the expandor response to bursts of clicks and interference.

Because of the above attributes, the expandor is a very effective suppressor of radio impairments at the receiver, especially in the absence of voice-signal modulation. The quieting is also subjectively evident between syllables and during natural pauses in speech. In addition, noise that is dominated by short-term speech power tends to be masked by speech. This, in conjunction with receiver quieting during the absence of speech, enables the 2:1 compandor/de-emphasis combination to provide a very effective subjective improvement in transmission quality in the presence of radio impairments. The nature and severity of the channel impairments, as discussed, create an acute need for such improvements.

The use of a higher companding law, such as 4:1, to magnify the transmission control and quieting performance of the 2:1 compandor planned for the AMPS system was also considered. Increasing the companding law beyond 2:1 can introduce additional voice transmission impairments[15] because of the impact of the processing between the compressor and expandor on the overall net loss of the compandor. Power removed from the speech signal by filtering and amplitude limiting (necessary functions for noise and RF spectrum control) can introduce commensurate syllabic-level variations in the speech signal leaving the receive-audio processor because of the multiplicative effect of the compandor. Limiting the companding law to 2:1 effectively eliminates this distortion mechanism, while still offering most of the subjective performance benefits of higher companding laws when channel impairments are present.

V. DATA TRANSMISSION

5.1 Purpose

Mobile units in the AMPS system respond to orders received from the cell sites, which are in turn controlled via data links from a Mobile Telecommunications Switching Office (MTSO).[11,19] All phases of the

For AMPS, a biphase (Manchester), bit-encoding format was adopted. Each logic 1 is encoded as a 0, 1 and each logic 0 as a 1, 0, and the peak frequency deviation chosen to minimize the bit error probability on the fading channel is ±8 kHz for an RF predetection bandwidth of approximately 30 kHz. The envelope of the Manchester-encoded baseband spectrum for a random bit stream, and the resulting RF spectrum, are shown in Figs. 12 and 13. While this coding doubles the effective transmission rate, it does provide several advantages.

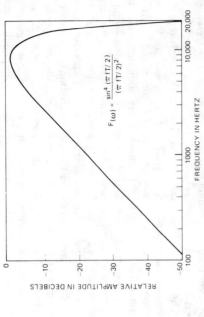

$$F(\omega) = \frac{\sin^4(\pi fT/2)}{(\pi fT/2)^2}$$

Fig. 12—Power spectrum of Manchester coded data (information rate = 10 kb/s).

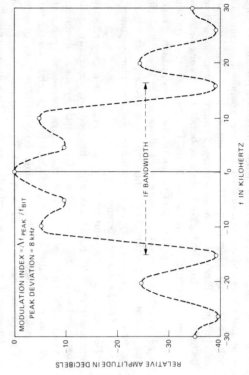

Fig. 13—RF spectrum of FSK signal.

mobile call, including call setup, handoff between cell sites, and call disconnect require data signaling over the radio channel. On this channel, there are two categories[20] of signaling messages—those sent within a continuous stream of bits and those sent as discontinuous bursts. In the first category are mobile pages, system status reports, and various overhead function messages incorporated within a continuous digital stream transmitted over dedicated "paging" channels from the cell site to the mobiles. The second category includes call release and cell-site handoff orders sent to the mobile on the voice channel, and requests sent to the cell site on the appropriate "access" channel by the mobile for access to the system.

The paging message for a mobile consists principally of the mobile telephone number of the vehicle being paged plus some overhead bits as described elsewhere in this issue.[20] To the 28 message bits required for a page, 12 additional bits are appended for parity protection, and the encoded message is transmitted at a 10-kb/s rate. An active mobile tunes to the strongest paging channel in its assigned set and monitors the messages received while awaiting its own telephone number. From these messages the mobile can derive instruction pertaining to system access and eventual voice channel assignments.

The transmission rate for mobile access transmissions to the cell site and handoff commands from the cell site to mobile is also 10 kb/s, but these messages are not sent as part of a continuous data stream. To obtain synchronization of the discontinuous message transmission at the mobile or cell site receiver, these transmissions have a synchronization prefix attached that uses an alternating 1010..."dotting" sequence. This sequence, which is recognized as a 5-kHz tone, initializes the phase of a clock that is subsequently updated in a phase-locked loop. The message following the synchronization prefix consists of a burst of 10-kb/s data lasting approximately 100 ms. This message supplies the information necessary to accomplish the discontinuous signaling functions. For all data functions (continuous paging, discontinuous signaling requests for service, handoff, and call disconnect), the messages are automatically repeated to provide five voting detections for each bit. The message repeats are stored and summed (majority voted) at the receiver.

5.2 Carrier modulation

All methods of digital transmission over radio channels are applicable to mobile radio. The method chosen for AMPS uses direct-binary frequency-shift-keying (FSK) of the carrier with discriminator detection. Binary data can be transmitted with FSK modulation up to a rate approximately equal to the IF bandwidth, but for any bit rate an optimum peak deviation exists that minimizes the bit error probability.

rate of 10 kb/s. Error bursts of about 10 bits occur 10 times a second, a rate that is the average rate of occurrence of 15 dB fades at 20 mph. Note, however, that longer bursts of 50 bits or more occur every second. The reason for this is that fades below −15 dB have a high probability that they will be of long duration. That is, although the average fade duration of −15 dB fades is about 2.5 ms, durations five times this average are not at all unlikely. The error-burst distribution on a log plot (Fig. 14) is a straight line because the fade-width distribution (Fig. 15) follows an exponential law.

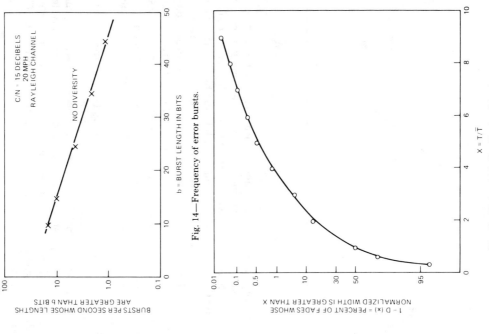

Fig. 14—Frequency of error bursts.

Fig. 15—Fade width distribution function.

Because of the biphase coding of the 10-kb/s data stream, the peak of the power spectrum for data transmission is well above the voice-band. This separation is an advantage in a system transmitting both voice and signaling data on the same channel. Synchronization of the receiver to the data stream is also aided by the ever-present biphase bit transitions which exist independently of the code transmission being sent. Furthermore, since the spectrum of biphase coding has no zero frequency component, the desired binary FM waveform can be implemented with a phase modulator preceded by an integrator. The maximum modulator phase shift required is the shift over one bit interval (±0.8 radian), which is within the capability of the phase modulator used for voice signals.

For data transmission as for voice, attention must be focused on the short-term signal-envelope variations (the Rayleigh fades), since for both modulation systems operating at carrier-to-noise or carrier-to-interference ratios of interest, the error performance is dominated by the fading character of the channel. The bit-error probability when the instantaneous carrier envelope is 15 dB above the noise level is, for noncoherent FSK, less than 10^{-7}. However, when the channel is subjected to Rayleigh fading at a 15-dB average carrier-to-noise ratio, the bit-error probability is approximately 3 percent. Thus, most errors occur during deep fades of the signal into noise or co-channel interference as the vehicle moves through the multipath interference pattern.

These errors occur in dense bursts associated with the duration of individual signal fades. Furthermore, the bit-error probability is substantially independent of data rate until bit lengths approach the average fade duration. That is, integration over the bit interval cannot improve the error rate unless integration times are at least on the order of the average fade duration. Consequently, data rates should be either very low (200 Hz) or as high as the channel bandwidth allows. Time delay spread, which has no measurable effect on voice transmission, does affect the faster data modulation. The spread in time delay observed[4,8] results in an irreducible bit error rate for digital transmission that is independent of the noise level. This rate, which is of the order of 10^{-2} or less, is due to FM distortions at baseband created by the delayed echoes at the receiver input. The effect of these echoes on message error rate is negligible because of the large amount of redundancy employed in the system to cope with the more severe effects of signal envelope fades into noise and interference.

The bit-error rate is essentially one-half during fades into noise or interference, and error-burst frequency and duration are related to the speed-dependent fade interval and fade-duration distributions. Figure 14 shows the frequency of error bursts of a given length for a 15-dB average carrier-to-receiver noise ratio. The data shown in this figure were obtained at 20 mph, where the average duration of a fade 15 dB below the mean signal level is approximately 25 bits for a transmission

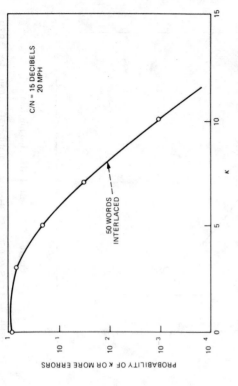

Fig. 17—Error rate distribution for a 100-bit word with bit interlace.

5.3 Channel encoding

The virtual certainty that bits in long blocks will be lost for any practical mobile environment places constraints on the type of coding that can be used. Figure 16 illustrates why simple forward-error correction is not practical. To transmit 100 message bits in a fading channel with a message error rate of 2 percent at 15-dB average carrier-to-noise ratio requires a decoder capable of correcting 25 or more errors. One might consider massive interleaving of bits, which will reduce the number of message bits "trapped" by a given fade. Figure 17 shows the results of this on code detection performance. With a 50-bit spacing between each code bit (i.e., 50 words were interleaved to reduce error bursts), the error rate remaining after six error corrections in a 100-bit word is still approximately 5 percent. The effectiveness of bit interleaving in the mobile channel is limited by the high probability of long fades.

The radio channels do not lend themselves to a request for repeat and retransmission when an error is detected. Instead, each message is automatically repeated and the repeats summed to decrease the effective bit-error rate.

Each repetition is encoded with a cyclic redundancy check and the sum word is error-corrected. The usual trade-off is possible between the number of errors corrected and the number of errors detected. A single error correction on the summed message results in a performance comparable to the performance of land data links, and it has the advantage that implementation at the mobile is simple. For both the continuous paging function and the discontinuous functions of handoff on the land-to-mobile link, a 40-bit shortened BCH code (distance 5)

was chosen.[20] For the access and vertical services function on the mobile-to-land link, a 48-bit message using the same BCH code was chosen. Each message is given a total of five suitably spaced transmissions, and the five words are summed with bit-by-bit majority voting.* The one-error correction capability results in a word error rate of 2×10^{-3} at 15 dB. Because the probability is high that a given fade will create multiple errors, the spacing of the word-repeats is an important parameter related to the vehicle speed. For the data shown in Figs. 18 and 19, the spacing between corresponding bits in adjacent repetitions is 10 ms (or 100 bits), and is representative of the message formats of the AMPS system.

Message repetition with majority voting and single-error correction has proved to be a simple way to supply reliable signaling over the mobile telephone channel. The redundancy inherent in this approach and the self-clocking nature of the Manchester modulating waveform are the basis of the data transmission technique used to provide the signaling and control information essential to the operation of the system.

VI. CONCLUSION

The characteristics of the urban radio channel in the 800- to 900-MHz band have strongly influenced the design of the voice and data transmission systems in the AMPS system. The dynamic nature of the channel leads to extremely large fluctuations in the transmission

* The land-to-mobile discontinuous message is repeated 11 times, but only 5 of these repeats are loaded. The extra redundancy assures reception of the 5.

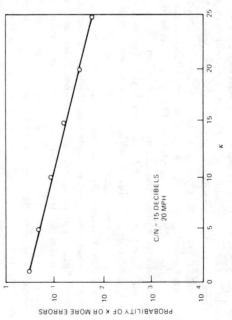

Fig. 16—Error rate distribution for single transmission of a 100-bit word.

VOICE AND DATA TRANSMISSION

discussed in Ref. 12. These tests have not only given considerable insight to aid in selection of transmission models and objectives, but also supplied the means by which the design performance could be validated in the field environment.

REFERENCES

1. R. H. Clark, "A Statistical Theory of Mobile Radio Reception," B.S.T.J., 37, No. 6 (July–August 1968), pp. 957–1000.
2. W. C. Jakes, ed. *Microwave Mobile Communications*, New York: John Wiley, 1974.
3. Y. Okumura, E. Ohmori, T. Kawano, and K. Fukuda, "Field Strength and its Variability in VHF and UHF Land-Mobile Radio Service," Rev. Elec. Comm. Lab., 16 (September 1968), pp. 825–873.
4. D. C. Cox and R. P. Leck, "Distribution of Multipath Delay Spread and Average Excess Delay for the 900 MHz Urban Mobile Radio Path," IEEE Trans. Anten. Prop., AP-23 (March 1975), pp. 206–213.
5. W. Rae Young, "Comparison of Mobile Radio Transmission at 150, 4500, 900, and 3700 MC," B.S.T.J., 31, No. 6 (November 1952), pp. 1068–1085.
6. G. L. Turin et al., "A Statistical Model of Urban Multipath Propagation," IEEE Trans. Veh. Tech., UT-21, No. 1 (February 1972), pp. 1–9.
7. G. A. Arredondo and J. I. Smith, "Voice and Data Transmission in a Mobile Radio Channel at 850 MHz," IEEE Trans. Veh. Tech., VT-26, No. 1 (February 1977).
8. D. C. Cox and R. P. Leck, "Correlation Bandwidth and Delay Spread Multipath Propagation Statistics for 910 MHz Urban Mobile Radio Channels," IEEE Trans. Commun., COM-23 (November 1957), pp. 1271–1280.
9. C. C. Bailey and J. C. Lindenlaub, "Further Results Concerning the Effect of Frequency-Selective Fading on Differentially Coherent Matched Filter Receivers," IEEE Trans. Comm. Sys., COM-16 (October 1968), pp. 749–751.
10. S. O. Rice, "Noise in FM Receivers," Proceeding of the Symposium of Time Series Analysis, M. Rosenblatt, ed., New York: John Wiley, 1963, Ch 25.
11. V. H. MacDonald, "AMPS: The Cellular Concept," B.S.T.J., this issue, pp. 15–41.
12. G. C. DiPiazza, A. Plitkins, G. I. Zysman, "AMPS: The Cellular Test Bed," B.S.T.J., this issue, pp. 215–248.
13. G. A. Arredondo et al., "A Multipath Fading Simulator for Mobile Radio," IEEE Trans. Veh. Tech., VT-22 (November 1973), pp. 241–244.
14. K. L. McAdoo, "Speech Volumes on Bell System Circuits—1960 Survey," B.S.T.J., 42, No. 7 (September 1963) pp. 1999–2012.
15. G. A. Arredondo and J. C. Feggeler, "The Impact of the Unique Mobile Radio Channel on Information Transmission," 1977 NEC Conference Record, pp. 178–179.
16. R. O. Carter, "Theory of Syllabic Compandors," Proceedings of the IEEE, 111, No. 3 (March 1964), pp. 503–515.
17. R. Toumani, U. S. Patent 3919654, issued November 11, 1975.
18. J. C. Feggeler, "Experiments with Companding in Mobile Telephony," 1976 ICC Conference Record, II, pp. 27–5 to 27–10.
19. V. Hackenburg, B. D. Holm, and J. I. Smith, "Data Signaling Functions for a Cellular Mobile Telephone System," IEEE Trans. Veh. Tech., VT-26, No. 1 (February 1977).
20. Z. C. Fluhr and P. T. Porter, "AMPS: Control Architecture," B.S.T.J., this issue, pp. 43–69.

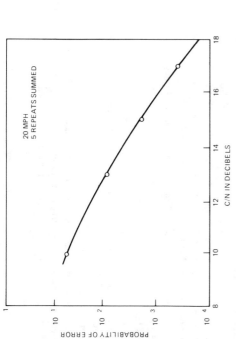

Fig. 18—Error rate for (40,28) code (carrier frequency 850 MHz).

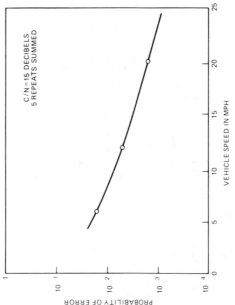

Fig. 19—Error rate vs vehicle speed for a (40,28) code.

environment not only from call to call, but also during individual calls. Since the potential impact of this variability is great, processing precautions have been taken in the AMPS system to prevent the user from experiencing corresponding variabilities in voice transmission quality and control reliability. The techniques themselves have undergone extensive testing, both in a controlled laboratory environment in which the radio channel is simulated and also in an experimental cell site at Whippany, N. J. Testing has also been carried out in the field as part of the Cellular Test Bed experiments in Newark, N. J. as

VOICE AND DATA TRANSMISSION

Advanced Mobile Phone Service:

Cell-Site Hardware

By N. EHRLICH, R. E. FISHER, and T. K. WINGARD

(Manuscript received August 1, 1978)

The hardware facilities of the AMPS cell site connect the mobile radio customer to the land telephone network and perform actions necessary for RF radiation, reception, and distribution; voice and data communications and processing; equipment testing, control, and reconfiguration; and call setup, supervision, and termination. Cell-site operational control is achieved partially through wired logic and partially through programmable controllers. This paper describes the cell-site functional groups, their physical characteristics and design, and the ways they interface with the rest of the AMPS system.

I. INTRODUCTION

In the AMPS system, the interface between the land telephone network and the radio paths to the mobiles occurs at the cell sites. In addition to performing functions needed for trunk termination and for radio transmission and reception, the cell site handles many semiautonomous functions under the general direction of the Mobile Telephone Switching Office (MTSO). Figure 1 is a block diagram of the major AMPS subsystems.

Cell sites have facilities to:

(*i*) Provide RF radiation, reception, and distribution.
(*ii*) Provide data communications with the MTSO and mobiles.
(*iii*) Locate mobiles.
(*iv*) Perform remotely ordered equipment testing.
(*v*) Perform equipment control and reconfiguration functions.
(*vi*) Perform voice-processing functions.
(*vii*) Perform call setup, call supervision, and call termination functions.

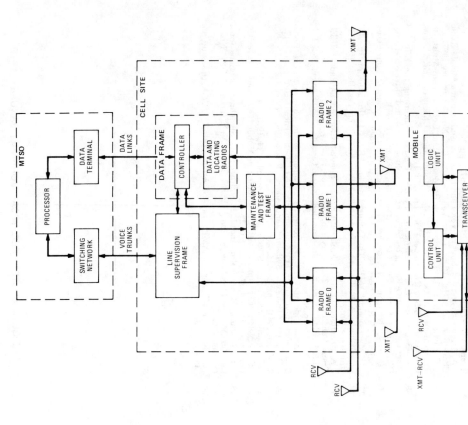

Fig. 1—AMPS major subsystems.

(*viii*) Handoff or receive from another cell site any mobile which has moved out of the normal service area of the cell site carrying the call.

Cell-site operations are controlled partially by wired logic and partially by programmable controllers. Control functions are redundant and can be reconfigured as needed to overcome a localized failure. A battery plant assures maintenance of service in case of commercial power outage. Facilities dependent upon traffic requirements in each cell coverage area are modular so that additional units may be installed as needed to match busy-hour traffic levels. This will ensure that plant investment can grow sensibly as a function of anticipated revenues.

THE BELL SYSTEM TECHNICAL JOURNAL, JANUARY 1979

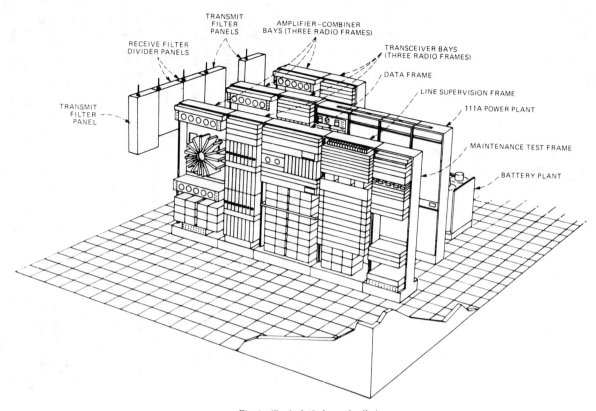

TRANSMIT
FILTER
PANELS

RECEIVE FILTER
DIVIDER PANELS

AMPLIFIER—COMBINER
BAYS (THREE RADIO FRAMES)

TRANSMIT
FILTER
PANEL

TRANSCEIVER BAYS
(THREE RADIO FRAMES)

DATA FRAME

LINE SUPERVISION FRAME

111A POWER PLANT

MAINTENANCE TEST FRAME

BATTERY PLANT

Fig. 2—Typical 48 channel cell-site.

Figure 2 is an isometric view of a typical cell site with a capacity of 48 voice channels. The precise number of frames at each site is a function of the voice channel requirements for that site. There are four frame codes, and the smallest size cell site requires one of each code. Each radio frame has a maximum capacity of 16 radios. When the number of voice radios grows beyond 16, another radio frame must be added. Each line supervision frame (LSF) can handle 48 voice channels and, when this number is exceeded, another LSF is added. A single data frame (DF) and a single maintenance test frame (MTF) are necessary regardless of the number of voice radios in the cell site. The maximum size of a cell site is 144 voice radios, which would require a total of 14 frames: nine radio frames, three line supervision frames, one data frame, and one maintenance test frame.* The discussion in this paper of the functional design of the cell site parallels the organization of these frames.

Section II describes the data frame, which serves as the master control center for the cell site. Section III describes the line supervision frame, which interfaces the four-wire voice trunks (originating at the MTSO) with the cell-site voice-radio transceivers. Section IV describes the radio frame, which is composed of two bays. Section V describes the maintenance and test frame, which gives the cell site the ability—through the use of another programmable controller—to test for troubles in the radio and audio equipment. Section VI describes the power system. Section VII describes the physical design of a cell site.

II. DATA FRAME

The data frame (see Figs. 3 and 4) contains the equipment for major cell-site control functions, which include communication with the MTSO, control of voice and data communication with mobiles, and communication with the controller in the maintenance test frame. Communication between controllers is necessary for requesting performance of specific tests and for receiving results. The DF contains both hardwired logic and programmable controllers. Only one set of hardwired logic and one controller is needed per cell site regardless of the number of voice radios. Because of the critical functions performed in the DF, redundancy of all subassemblies is provided to assure continuation of service in the presence of a failure. The DF can reconfigure itself under the direction of the MTSO, which maintains service by permitting any malfunctioning subassembly to be replaced with an off-line redundant unit.

The data frame (see Fig. 4) contains five major subsystems:

---

* In addition to these transmission and control frames, four additional WE 111A power system frames and an associated battery system are required for the maximum size cell site.

CELL-SITE HARDWARE

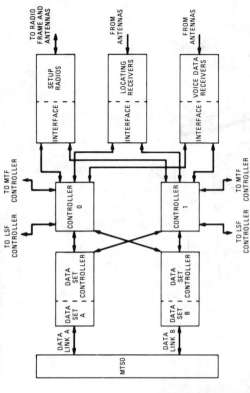

Fig. 4—Data frame block diagram.

(i) Land data links, described in Section 2.1.
(ii) Controllers described in Section 2.2.
(iii) Setup radio communication, described in Section 2.3.
(iv) Locating radios, described in Section 2.4.
(v) Voice-channel data communications, described in Section 2.5.

2.1 Land data links

Data communication between the MTSO and each cell site takes place over two redundant data links connecting Western Electric 201D data sets at each termination. The 201D data set operates at a 2.4-kb/s rate and supplies TTL level outputs so that no buffering is required between it and the DF logic. The data set controller converts the 32-bit serial messages into 16-bit parallel words for transfer to the controllers. The 201D also can configure itself for loop-around testing under remote control of the MTSO. This feature is essential for maintenance because the cell sites will normally be unmanned. The data sets and the data set interfaces also operate in the reverse direction to take and transmit data from the controllers to the MTSO.

2.2 Controllers

The controller of the data frame (see Fig. 5) consists of a PROCON, a writable store unit (WSU), a parity generator and checker, and a data bus to connect the PROCON to the numerous peripherals with which it must communicate. All units are provided redundantly to assure continuation of service in the presence of failure.

The PROCON is a small general-purpose programmable controller,

Fig. 3—Data frame.

① INTERCONNECTION PANEL
② COAXIAL INTERCON. PANEL
③ RF SWITCH UNIT
④ SYNTHESIZER PANEL
⑤ RADIO SHELF
⑥ DIVIDER SHELF
⑦ MAINTENANCE PANEL
⑧ PROCON PANEL
⑨ WRITABLE PROGRAM STORE PANEL
⑩ MAIN CONTROL UNIT
⑪ DATA SET PANEL
⑫ CONVERTER PANEL
⑬ FILTER PANEL

CELL-SITE HARDWARE

Separate control signals from the PROCON indicate the address of the peripheral to be connected to the data bus to receive a particular message. In a similar manner, peripherals are connected to the data bus to allow the controller to read information from a peripheral's output register when the peripheral is acting as a sensor. Parity is added at the source for all data messages placed on the bus and is checked by the unit receiving the message before it is used.

2.3 Setup radio communication

Setup radios, as described in Ref. 1, transmit only data, and are used in the initial phase of "setting up" the call prior to the establishment of a voice path for communication. They are for the general (shared) use of the cell site in communicating with all mobiles within its zone. In addition, the setup radios also transmit overhead messages to assure that idle mobiles within the cell coverage zone are ready and able to communicate should a call be initiated to or from the mobile.

In the forward direction (land to mobile), referred to as the forward setup channel, messages may be either one or two words in length. Each word consists of data bits transmitted serially at a rate of 10 kb/s and encoded before transmission to provide 28 message bits and 12 BCH error detection/correction bits for a total of 40 bits per word. In the reverse setup direction, the mobile transmits—at the same data rate—48-bit words, with 36 of these bits available for message information and 12 bits used for the error detection/correction code. The number of words in the reverse direction vary in number. The number of words needed is transmitted as part of the message information. In each direction, each word is repeated five times to allow a majority voting of the detected word to protect the integrity of the transmission against the effects of noise, multipath fading, and interference. To minimize the effects of noise that comes in bursts, the five repeats of each message in the forward direction are interleaved with similar messages addressed to another mobile. This group of two words, each transmitted five times, is preceded by 10 bits of dotting (alternate ones and zeros) for bit synchronization and 11 bits of Barker Code* for word synchronization (see Fig. 6). The bit-and-word synchronization permits the mobiles to frame the forward setup messages and determines when each word and each sequence of the five-word repeats begin and end. Each mobile will look at only one of the two interleaved sets of words in the message stream, depending on whether the last digit of the mobile's telephone number is odd or even.

An additional bit, called the busy-idle bit, is inserted immediately following the bit sync, the word sync, and every 10 bits of each message word. If the bit is a 1, the reverse setup channel of the particular cell

---

* Barker Code consists of a bit sequence that is highly unlikely to be reproduced by rhythmic or random noise. It is 11100010010.

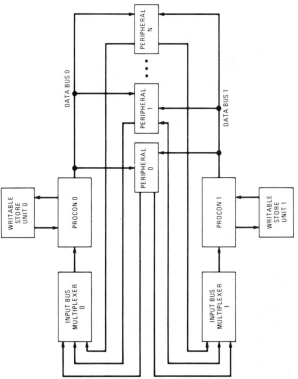

Fig. 5—Data frame controller.

developed at Bell Laboratories, designed to have sequencing and control functions with very high reliability. It is self-checking; an ASW (all seems well) signal indicates the presence or absence of a failure. The redundant PROCON recognizes this indication and reports failure to the MTSO. The MTSO will then use the properly functioning PROCON for further cell-site control and will print out in a maintenance center a request to dispatch a craftsperson to the cell site to correct the problem.

PROCON processes 16-bit parallel data words but uses 24-bit words for program instructions. It contains data manipulation units (DMU), a control unit (CU-16), and program storage units (PSU). The DMU contains instruction decoders, internal registers, logical/arithmetic capability, and peripheral communication logic. The control unit contains program-addressing logic, clock distribution, and fault-detection circuits. Each PSU board contains 2048 (2K) 24-bit words of read-only memory (ROM). The PROCON contains 4000 words of ROM and accesses an additional 4000 24-bit words of random-access memory (RAM) in its associated WSU. This increases its effective program store capacity to 8000 words. The WSU also provides 2000 18-bit words of data memory (DM) for PROCON access. Sixteen bits of each DM word contain data, and the remaining two bits are used for parity.

The PROCON output is linked to a 16-bit data bus, which connects it to all peripherals, both within the DF and in other cell-site frames.

CELL-SITE HARDWARE

during the equipment and service tests will not require more than one set-up transmitter and one spare.

2.4 Locating radios

To maintain signal strength sufficient for good-quality voice and data transmission, each mobile must communicate with an appropriately located cell site within the MSA. When a call is initially set up, locating the appropriate cell site is done by the mobile as it scans all setup channels and selects the one with the highest signal level for use in transmitting the reverse setup messages. After the call has been established, the mobile may move out of the area of sufficient signal strength. It then becomes necessary to route the call through another cell site whose location provides better signal quality to that mobile. Reference 1 describes how the system implements a handoff.

After the handoff event has been completed, the call continues until another handoff is required or until either party terminates the call.

To determine when and if a handoff is necessary, locating measurements are made once every few seconds on each active voice channel. Two techniques for locating are provided in the AMPS systems. The primary method is signal-strength measurement. The alternate method is called phase-ranging and is described in Section III.

Signal measurements for locating are performed by equipment consisting of a locating radio receiver (LRR), a tunable synthesizer, and a locating receiver interface (LRI). There are four LRRS with their associated synthesizers and interface circuit packs per cell site. Three sets are required to handle the busy-hour traffic load. The fourth is a spare to assure maintenance of service by reconfiguration should any of the on-line equipment become defective.

The cell-site controller (Section 2.2) keeps track of all calls which the cell is serving and makes a locating measurement on each call every few seconds. The controller sends, via the data bus to the LRI, a message containing a 10-bit binary number representing the channel code. The LRI then directs the associated synthesizer to tune its local oscillator to the frequency of the selected channel. The LRR develops an output voltage which is a function of the carrier signal quality. After a period of time to allow for settling, this voltage is held fixed by a track-and-hold circuit, while an analog-to-digital converter in the LRI converts the voltage representing an input signal range between −110 and −30 dBm into an 8-bit binary number and places it in the output register. Concurrently, a "Ready Output flag" is set to signal the controller that the measurement is available for readout. Because the controller has stored the channel number for which the measurement request was made, it is unnecessary to include any channel identification in the output word. Only the signal strength value is returned to the controller.

(NOT TO SCALE)

BUSY-IDLE BIT INSERTION (10 MESSAGE BITS BETWEEN SUCCESSIVE BUSY-IDLE BITS)
LOGIC 0 = BUSY
LOGIC 1 = IDLE

A_1 = FIRST OF FIVE REPEATS OF WORD A (40-BIT MESSAGE WORD)
B_1 = FIRST OF FIVE REPEATS OF WORD B (40-BIT MESSAGE WORD)
A_2 = SECOND OF FIVE REPEATS OF WORD A (40-BIT MESSAGE WORD)
B_2 = SECOND OF FIVE REPEATS OF WORD B (40-BIT MESSAGE WORD)
B_5 = FIFTH OF FIVE REPEATS OF WORD B (40-BIT MESSAGE WORD)

Fig. 6—Forward set-up channel message stream. A given logic unit reads only one of the two interleaved messages.

site transmitting the message stream is idle, and any mobile desiring to initiate a call or to respond to a page may transmit. If the bit is a 0, the reverse setup channel is being used by another mobile transmitting a call origination or a page response. A mobile wishing to transmit on that channel must wait a short time interval and monitor the channel again until idle bits are observed.

There is no essential difference between a voice radio and a setup radio, *per se.* In fact, the identical radio equipment codes may be used in either position. The differences in practice between the setup radio and the voice radio are the frequency channel to which each is assigned and the interface circuits that control the operation of the radio.

In the case of the setup radio transmitter, four circuit packs,* three designated as setup transmitter interface and one as setup transmitter controller, take the information from the controller and prepare it in a form appropriate to sending the data message over the setup channel. The three setup transmitter-interface packs behave as one functional unit. They latch and hold the data received from the controller, determine the appropriate time to load this word into a shift register, check the word for parity, inhibit the transmission of a word if parity does not check properly, shift the data out of the register one bit at a time to convert the word from parallel to serial form, and convert the data into Manchester coding.† The setup transmitter controller determines which of the setup radios will be used on line and which will be retained as the redundant spare. The setup transmitter controller has the capability of controlling up to five setup radio transmitters. In the Chicago developmental system, however, the anticipated traffic levels

---

* The physical design of these circuit packages is discussed in Section 7.2.
† See Ref. 2 for a discussion of Manchester coding.

The MTSO considers voice channel signal quality information from the controllers in the serving cell and in adjacent cells. A handoff process is initiated to transfer the mobile as it moves between cells so that it will again be served by the cell site receiving the best signal quality. The process of executing the handoff is described in Ref. 1.

2.5 Voice channel data communications

After a call has been set up, it must be monitored to determine when it is necessary to send various orders to the mobile, such as an order to turn off the mobile's transmitter at the termination of the call, or an order following a user request for one of the optional vertical services. The method of monitoring the call (referred to as call supervision) is discussed in Section III for all features except locating, which has been discussed above. Orders and requests for vertical services must be transmitted so as not to interfere significantly with voice conversations. They are sent in the form of binary data messages over the voice channel by momentarily muting the voice and inserting a binary data sequence, then restoring the audio capability. The data sequence requires approximately a tenth of a second. This technique, called blank-and-burst, is discussed in more detail in Refs. 1 and 2. Below is a brief summary of the method of implementing this technique.

The data messages over the voice channel in the direction from the cell site to the mobile are referred to as forward blank-and-burst. Those from the mobile to the cell site are called reverse blank-and-burst. The forward blank-and-burst order is initiated by the MTSO, which sends an appropriate message over the data link to the controller in the cell site. The controller then sends the required message to the voice transmitter data interface (VTDI), a single function spread over three circuit packs; it also directs the LSF controller to set up the required connection in the LSF between the VTDI and the voice radio channel assigned to the addressed mobile. The VTDI accepts the order from the controller in three successive parallel 16-bit words and converts them into a single 40-bit serial word that is sent at a 10-kb/s rate to the voice radio transmitter via an electronically switched connection in the Line Supervision Frame (LSF). The message format is shown in Fig. 7. The VTDI also precedes the data word with the bit sync and the word sync and repeats this grouping of bit sync, word sync, and the 40-bit data word 11 times before the LSF restores the channel to the voice mode. The use of 11 repeats ensures that there will be a sufficient number of properly received words to permit accurate word decoding by the mobile's logic unit in the noisy or interference-limited environment of AMPS.

If the mobile customer has subscribed to vertical service features, his request for a specific vertical service (such as third-party add-on to a call) must be transmitted as a data word via the blank-and-burst technique. The implementation of blank-and-burst in the reverse direction (mobile to cell site) is somewhat different from that of the forward direction.

The customer initiates his request for vertical service by entering a specific number sequence (including the telephone number of a third party, if applicable) via the TOUCH-TONE® calling pad into a register within the mobile logic unit. Then the customer depresses the SEND button* which is analogous to operating the switch-hook to obtain an operator's attention. The SEND button causes the signalling tone (ST)† to be transmitted over the voice channel for about 0.5 second. The LSF, recognizing that a signaling tone has been detected, operates a relay on the trunk switching unit to put the trunk into the on-hook state. When the MTSO, which monitors the on-hook, off-hook condition of each trunk, detects an on-hook condition of 0.5-second duration, it sends a message to the cell site telling the requesting voice channel to transmit data.

The voice receiver data (VRD) group in the data frame consists of a voice receiver data radio, a tunable frequency synthesizer, two interfacing circuit packs, and a data modem consisting of four circuit packs (clock initialization, clock acquisition system, Barker sequence detector and bit decoder, and majority voter). One VRD group is used for the entire cell site because traffic levels on it are expected to be low and the messages handled are not time-critical. It is backed up by a redundant spare. The working VRD must be tuned, therefore, to the frequency of the channel expecting a reverse blank-and-burst message. Upon receipt of the MTSO message indicating the channel number of a mobile that had "flashed," the PROCON orders the synthesizer associated with the data receiver to tune to the designated channel. When the PROCON detects the "in lock" flag (which indicates tuning is complete); it orders a forward blank-and-burst message to be sent to that mobile directing it to transmit a reverse blank-and-burst message. The mobile then transmits over the voice channel the data message corresponding to the request which the customer had initiated via the TOUCH-TONE calling pad and SEND button.

The reverse blank-and-burst message format is diagrammed in Fig. 7 and consists of 100 bits of "dotting" bit sync (alternate 1s and 0s), 11 bits of word sync (Barker code), and 48 bits of message data, of which 36 are information bits and 12 are error-detecting/correcting bits. This grouping of bit sync, word sync, and message is repeated four more times, for a total of five consecutive transmissions, except that in the last four the bit sync is limited to 37 bits of dotting rather than 100. The Barker sequence detection and bit decoder, the clock initialization,

---

* Other features of the SEND button are discussed in Ref. 3.
† The signaling tone is an out-of-voice-band 10-kHz tone detectable within the LSF. The function of the signaling tone and the operation of the LSF in detecting various states of the call are discussed in Section III.

and the clock acquisition system circuit packs detect the dotting and develop from it a clock signal synchronized with the clock in the mobile to facilitate detection of the Barker code and the data message.

The five transmissions of the message are each delayed within the majority voter shift registers long enough to cause them to enter the bit summing network (voter) in bit synchronism as shown in Fig. 8. As a result, a voted output occurs, one bit at a time, according to the detected value of each bit that occurred on at least three of the five transmissions. This word, made up of majority voted bits, is then converted in an interface circuit pack from a 48-bit serial word to three successive 16-bit parallel words and sent over the data bus to the PROCON. The PROCON tests the BCH error detection/correction coding, reformats the message, and sends the information over the data link to the MTSO. The MTSO performs the necessary actions to comply with the customer's request for a vertical service. The customer's request is received by the MTSO within a second after the "flash" message is received at the cell site.

III. LINE SUPERVISION FRAME

The line supervision frame (LSF), shown in Fig. 9, provides the perchannel audio-level speech-path interface between the MTSO-controlled telephone trunk network and the radio frame that transmits the radio frequency voice communication to and from the mobile unit. In addition to this principal function, the LSF also performs the following system functions:

(i) Enables transmission of forward blank-and-burst data messages by connecting the VTDI circuits to the appropriate voice transmitter.

(ii) Provides line supervision and control through monitoring of the supervisory audio tone (SAT) and the signaling tone.

(iii) Turns transmitters and receivers on and off as requested by the MTSO via the DF according to the level of mobile telephone traffic.

(iv) Provides range measurements on each mobile by measuring the phase delay of the received SAT.

(v) Enables voice channel trunk maintenance tests to be performed by switching trunks into loop-back configurations.

The audio circuits in the LSF are supplied in modules. Thus, a single LSF can support from 1 to 48 separate voice channels. As many as three LSFs can be connected to a single DF, allowing the maximum capacity of a cell site to be 144 voice channels.

The LSF has two functional parts: the voice channel circuits and the frame controller. The voice channel circuits are modular; the quantity supplied varies according to the number of voice trunks terminating in the frame. This number depends on the traffic requirements for the cells, but it cannot exceed 48 in a single LSF. The controller is installed complete, with redundancy, independent of the number of trunks terminating in the frame.

Each voice channel circuit consists of a group of eight printed circuit boards and six jacks used for testing and monitoring the trunk/voice channel circuits and the voice channel circuits/voice radio interfaces.

LEGEND

SYMBOL	FORWARD DIRECTION	REVERSE DIRECTION
K	11 REPEATS	5 REPEATS
L_1	100 BITS	101 BITS
L_2	40 BITS	48 BITS

* IN REVERSE DIRECTION A SECOND MESSAGE (B) MAY FOLLOW WD A_k

† FORWARD DIRECTION IS FROM THE CELL SITE TO THE MOBILE
REVERSE DIRECTION IS FROM THE MOBILE TO THE CELL SITE

Fig. 7—Voice channel data message formats.

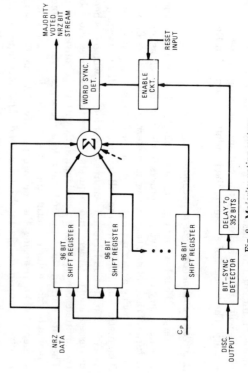

Fig. 8—Majority voting system.

CELL-SITE HARDWARE

3.1 Voice channel circuits

The voice channel circuit performs all the baseband signal processing for a single voice radio. Before the transceiver baseband signals can interface with the telephone network, certain control signals must be added on the transmitter path, and other control signals must be removed from the receiver path. To obtain these control signals, each line circuit has access to several busses carrying both analog and digital information. Each line circuit is permanently wired to the 6-kHz supervisory audio tone (SAT) bus and to the 10-kHz clock bus. Access to the trunk-maintenance bus, serial-data bus, and phase-range bus is controlled by signals from the LSF controller. The state of each line circuit is indicated by a group of status signals that may be read by the LSF controller. The five status signals are: (i) transmitter power on/off, (ii) maintenance relay state (normal or loop-around), (iii) line control logic fade timing, (iv) line control logic timed out, and (v) off-hook. Each line circuit contains a logic circuit that controls dc line supervision on the MTSO-cell-site path and shuts off the cell-site transmitter if mobile-to-cell-site transmission is interrupted for more than 5.5 seconds.

The audio processing section serves to interface the four-wire, voice-grade, telephone trunks with the cell-site transceivers. A syllabic compandor reduces audio noise in the transmission system. The compandor is composed of two sections. A compressor at the transmitting end reduces variations in speech input power levels by a factor of 2 (in decibels). An expandor at the receiving end performs the inverse operation. The loss of the expandor must complement the gain of the compressor so that the end-to-end relative signal levels are unaffected. The overall effect of these circuits provides an improved signal-to-noise ratio for the received speech. Both the mobile and the cell-site audio circuits must contain similar speech compressors and expandors. (See Ref. 2 for a more complete discussion.)

Figure 10 is a block diagram of the audio processing circuits. The PC7 transmit-audio compressor circuit pack contains the compressor half of the compandor circuit. The audio from the voice trunk feeds into the compressor; the compressed audio output feeds into the audio filter. The PC1 transmit-audio filter contains a sharp 300- through 3000-Hz bandpass filter, which band-limits the audio from the compressor. One of the three possible cell-site SAT frequencies* is selected at the SAT cross-connect panel, added at the output of the low-pass filter, and combined with the audio signal in an operational amplifier summing circuit. The output is the composite audio and SAT signal, which is passed through the data/voice switch in the PC2 bit encoder

---

* 5970, 6000, or 6030 Hz.

Fig. 9—Line supervision frame.

1   INTERCONNECTION PANEL

2   TRUNK SWITCHING UNIT PANEL

3   JACK PANEL ASSEMBLY

4   SAT DISTRIBUTION PANEL

5   LSF DISPLAY UNIT

6   LSF CONTROL UNIT

7   VOICE CHANNEL CIRCUIT PANEL

8   CONVERTER PANEL

and data-voice switch to the transmitter in the radio frame when the switch is in normal or voice position.

When the cell site must send short bursts of high-speed data (during the time the mobile is tuned to the voice channel), it uses the blank-and-burst mode. While data are being sent, a framing pulse switches the data-voice switch to the data mode. The framing pulse inhibits the audio, selects for use one of the two redundant data busses, disconnects the voice transmitter from the audio system, and connects it to the signaling system bit encoder. Serial data from the selected data bus are gated into the Manchester encoder. The data and the 10-kHz clock are exclusively NOR-gated to give a Manchester-encoded format. The data then pass through a Bessel shaping-filter, which removes the high-frequency components. The serial data message, Manchester-encoded, is then passed to the transmitter in the radio frame and transmitted to the mobile. See Ref. 5 for more details on data transmission.

Communications in the other direction—from the mobile—are received by the associated voice receiver in the radio frame. These signals contain audio plus the SAT and on occasion the 10-kHz signaling tone (ST). While data in the form of blank and burst messages are also sent from the mobile over the voice channel, those messages are not processed through the voice radios or the line supervision frame. Instead, they are received by the voice data radio receiver in the data frame and processed through its associated modem.

The output of the voice receiver's discriminator is sent to the PC4 receive audio processor, basically a combination bandpass filter and frequency modulation de-emphasis filter. The overall transfer characteristic is a 6-dB/octave slope in the voiceband and a sharp 24-dB/octave fall-off in the region outside the voiceband. The output is fed to the audio expandor circuit. An output ahead of the filter, containing the SAT and the 10-kHz ST, is connected to the SAT and ST detectors, respectively. The audio expandor circuit is mounted on the PC5 line control circuit card. The input to the expandor is from the PC4 receive audio processor circuit pack and the output is connected to the operating company voice trunk.

In addition to the expandor circuit, the PC5 line control circuit contains logic to detect the voice channel status, to control the on/off status of the voice transmitter and receiver, and to transmit status indications to the data frame controller. Voice channel status is developed from the transmitter power array in the LSF controller (see Section 3.3) and from the outputs of the SAT and ST detectors for the following status reports: timing, timed out, off-hook, and transmitter power on. The transmitter is turned off to prevent radiation of power on any channel not in use. Similarly, the receiver is disconnected from

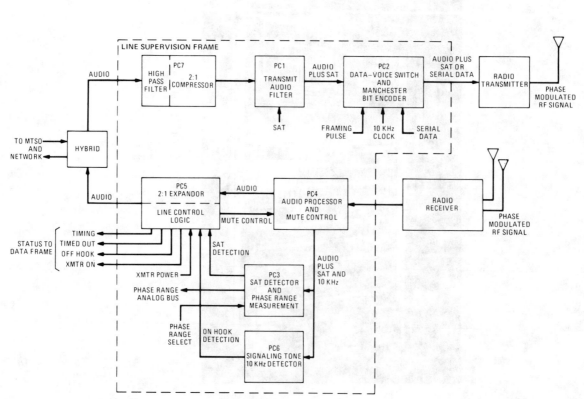

Fig. 10—Audio processing circuit.

the trunk to prevent receiver noise (which is maximum in the absence of a detected carrier) from entering the land line trunk when the receiver channel is unoccupied. The muting circuits to disconnect the receiver from the trunk are located in PC4.

The SAT, which is added to the transmitter baseband signal at the output of the audio bandpass filter, is transponded at the mobile and detected in PC3 of the cell-site receiver signaling system. It monitors the continuity of the cell-site-to-mobile path and furnishes ranging information. The SAT detector output is at logic 1 as long as the correct SAT frequency is detected and the carrier-to-noise ratio is greater than 7 dB. If SAT is not detected, the line control goes into a timing condition. If recovery is not made in 5.5 seconds, the call is considered lost and the circuit will time out and shut off the cell-site transmitter.

A phase-locked loop detector performs an estimate of the distance between the cell site and the mobile by comparing the phase of the transmitted and received SAT signals. The mobile-to-cell-site distance is a linear function of this phase difference. The difference in phase is converted into a dc analog signal, which is connected via the phase-range switch and the phase-range bus to an analog-to-digital converter in the LSF controller.

The mobile may autonomously transmit a 10-kHz signaling tone as part of its disconnect sequence or as an acknowledgment of the receipt of certain orders. The PC6 contains a detector circuit, which is an active 10-kHz (ST) bandpass filter followed by a full-wave rectifier, low-pass filter, and level comparator. The ST output is a logic 1 when the tone is present. It is fed to the PC5 line control circuit. The line control circuit monitors both the SAT and ST logic outputs generated by the tone detectors in the signaling system and uses them to control the dc supervision current (off-hook signal) in the MTSO to cell-site trunk and the transmitter on-off status. When the mobile party disconnects, the mobile sends the 1.1-s, 10-kHz ST. The line control circuit, via control of the trunk switching unit, removes the off-hook signal from the land trunk. The MTSO detects the trunk on-hook transition and sends a blank and burst release order to the mobile to shut off its transmitter.

For maintenance aids, the voice trunks from the MTSO connect to a set of test jacks for each trunk. There are six jacks per trunk:

(i) Transmitter network out: Disconnects the trunk and connects to trunk output.

(ii) Transmitter compressor in: Disconnects the trunk and connects to the audio compressor input.

(iii) Transmitter monitor: Monitors the transmit trunk.

(iv) Receiver network in: Disconnects the trunk and connects to the trunk input.

(v) Receiver out: Disconnects the trunk and connects to audio processor output.

(vi) Receiver monitor: Monitors the receive trunk.

3.2 Trunk switching unit

The trunk switching unit (TSU) consists of the trunk maintenance switch and the loop signaling switch for one trunk. It contains two relays mounted on a printed circuit board. In the normal state, each trunk connects through its TSU to its associated audio processor. The maintenance relay signal from the LSF controller operates the maintenance relay to disconnect the trunk from the audio processors and connect it to the test trunk. A maintenance relay status signal is returned to the LSF controller to indicate that the relay has operated. The off-hook signal from the line control circuit operates the second relay to provide a closure for the loop signal current to operating company equipment.

3.3 Line supervision frame controller

The LSF controller receives data words from the DF cell-site controllers and examines each word to determine the voice circuit to be accessed and the function to be performed. The LSF controller consists entirely of wired logic and contains redundant circuitry, designated side A and side B. Each side may accept data words from either cell-site controller, the choice being determined by the load signal used. Both sides can access any of the voice circuits. A block diagram of one side of the LSF controller is shown in Fig. 11. To avoid complexity, this figure omits all interactions with the redundant side.

The transmitter power control circuit consists of two array access circuit packs, one for each side of the LSF controller, and two transmitter power array circuit packs, which are common to both sides of the controller. The array access circuit pack contains the control to set and reset the selected flip-flop in a 48-element array contained in the two transmitter power array circuit packs. The inputs consist of the radio address, the frame address, and the transmitter-on and transmitter-off signals. The output controls the on/off state of each voice transmitter and is sent to the transmitter via its associated PC5 line control circuit.

The maintenance selector circuit is similar to the power control circuit. It consists of two array access circuit packs, one on each side of the LSF controller, and two maintenance array circuit packs which are common to both sides of the controller. The maintenance array consists of 48 flip-flops that are set or reset by signals from the array access circuits. The outputs go to the 48-trunk switching units to operate the maintenance relays.

The data/voice selector consists of a demultiplexer circuit pack on each side of the LSF controller. Its purpose is to select the voice channel

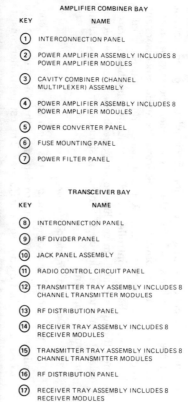

THE BELL SYSTEM TECHNICAL JOURNAL, JANUARY 1979

AMPLIFIER COMBINER BAY

KEY	NAME
①	INTERCONNECTION PANEL
②	POWER AMPLIFIER ASSEMBLY INCLUDES 8 POWER AMPLIFIER MODULES
③	CAVITY COMBINER (CHANNEL MULTIPLEXER) ASSEMBLY
④	POWER AMPLIFIER ASSEMBLY INCLUDES 8 POWER AMPLIFIER MODULES
⑤	POWER CONVERTER PANEL
⑥	FUSE MOUNTING PANEL
⑦	POWER FILTER PANEL

TRANSCEIVER BAY

KEY	NAME
⑧	INTERCONNECTION PANEL
⑨	RF DIVIDER PANEL
⑩	JACK PANEL ASSEMBLY
⑪	RADIO CONTROL CIRCUIT PANEL
⑫	TRANSMITTER TRAY ASSEMBLY INCLUDES 8 CHANNEL TRANSMITTER MODULES
⑬	RF DISTRIBUTION PANEL
⑭	RECEIVER TRAY ASSEMBLY INCLUDES 8 RECEIVER MODULES
⑮	TRANSMITTER TRAY ASSEMBLY INCLUDES 8 CHANNEL TRANSMITTER MODULES
⑯	RF DISTRIBUTION PANEL
⑰	RECEIVER TRAY ASSEMBLY INCLUDES 8 RECEIVER MODULES

Fig. 12—Typical radio frame, equipped with 16 voice channels.

Fig. 11—Line supervision frame controller block diagram.

and control the flow of serial data for the forward blank-and-burst function. The data/voice selector contains an eight-bit register to store the radio address, the frame address, and the VTDI select bit. The VTDI select bit chooses the voice transmitter data interface it will use as the serial data and framing pulse source. The selected serial data are placed on a bus that drives all the bit encoder and data voice switches in the 48 voice circuits. The address output of the register is used to drive the data voice demultiplexer. It is a 1-out-of-48 decoder, which delivers the framing pulse to the selected bit encoder and data voice switch that receive the serial data.

The phase-range selector circuit consists of a phase-range demultiplexer circuit pack in each side of the LSF controller. The phase-range demultiplexer is a 1-out-of-48 decoder, which receives the radio and frame address from the input register and is enabled by the set phase-range switch signal from the operation code decoder. The analog-to-digital converters change the phase-range analog-voltage output of the phase-ranging circuit to an eight-bit binary code, which is transmitted to the cell-site controller.

CELL-SITE HARDWARE

(*i*) A channel-transmitter module (see Fig. 13) produces a 1-watt carrier, which is phase-modulated by voice/SAT or frequency-modulated with 10 kb/s data provided by a transmit channel circuit within the LSF. A 666-channel frequency synthesizer, located within the transmitter module, generates the correct channel frequency, which is also the local oscillator for the companion receiver.

(*ii*) A power-amplifier module (see Fig. 14) boosts the 1-watt angle modulated carrier, from the transmitter module, to 45 watts.

(*iii*) The channel multiplexer combines the 16 45-watt carriers, from the power-amplifier modules, onto one coaxial transmission line, which goes to a transmit antenna.

(*iv*) A channel-receiver module receives a two-branch diversity input derived from the two receiving antennas feeding an array of broadband amplifiers and hybrid power splitters. From these inputs and from a local oscillator signal, derived from the companion transmitter module, the receiver demodulates a baseband voice/SAT or data signal, which is delivered to a receive-channel circuit within the LSF.

A radio frame need not be fully loaded with modules; any number of sets, from 1 to 16, are used depending upon the required channel

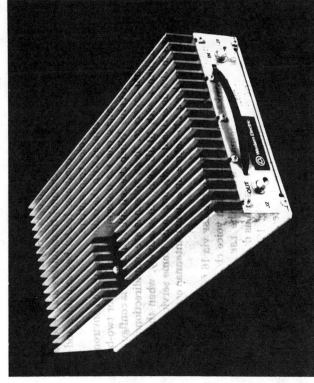

Fig. 14—Typical power amplifier module.

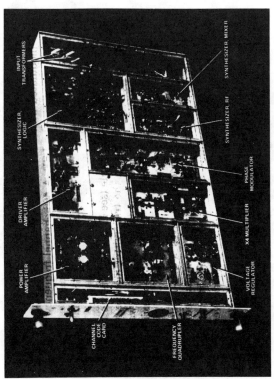

Fig. 13—Typical channel transmitter module unit with covers removed.

IV. RADIO FRAME

4.1 Overview

Figure 12 is a photograph of a 16-channel radio frame.* As stated earlier, each radio frame is composed of two bays. The transceiver (TR) bay contains 16 pairs of voice channel transmitters and receivers. A companion power amplifier/combiner (PA/C) bay amplifies and combines the outputs of the voice transmitters.

The radio frame interfaces with the radio transmission environment through three antennas: one for transmit, the others for two-branch space-diversity receive. When the cell site equipment is configured for omnidirectional coverage, these antennas are omnidirectional (in the azimuthal plane) with 10-dB gain. Alternatively, when the cell site functions in the directional mode, one radio frame services each face (direction) via three 120-degree directional antennas each with 10-dB gain.†

The radio frame interfaces with the LSF via 16 four-wire, balanced bidirectional trunks, one servicing each voice channel. "Transmitter-on" control signals originate within the LSF. Finally, dc power is supplied from the +24 V battery system as described in Section VI.

Each duplex voice channel (see Fig. 12) is served by a "radio" consisting of a set of four modules located within the radio frame.

---

* When more than 16 voice radio channels are required at a cell site, additional radio frames are added.

† Additional antenna gain, easily obtained in the directional mode, is not required.

CELL-SITE HARDWARE

capacity. The channel multiplexer, as presently designed, must provide for all 16 channels; the unused inputs are terminated by 50-ohm loads. A brief design overview of each radio module follows.

4.2 Channel transmitters

Figure 15 is a block diagram of a 16-channel radio frame. The blocks marked TRAN₀ to TRAN₁₅ are 1-watt output, PM voice/SAT or FM data transmitter modules. The channel frequency for each transmitter, situated in the 870- to 890-MHz band, is generated within its self-contained frequency synthesizer. A digital program plug inserted into the front panel of each transmitter module selects the desired channel. Thus, each voice transmitter resides permanently on one selected radio channel.

Figure 16 is a block diagram of the frequency synthesizer, which uses the indirect frequency synthesis method to generate any one of 666 stable carriers upon digital command from 10 parallel binary program lines. Each carrier, at one-quarter the final output frequency, is stable to within ±1 part per million over a 0°C to +40°C temperature range. A relatively unstable, varactor-tuned, voltage-controlled oscil-

lator (VCO) generates the synthesizer output frequency f_0. A portion of the VCO output power enters a mixer, where it is heterodyned against $f_1 = 228.02250$ MHz, which is derived from a quartz crystal-controlled oscillator located within the MTF (see Section V). The output difference frequency $f_1 - f_0$ (between 5.5 and 10.5 MHz) is "divided down" by a selected integer N, in a programmable digital frequency divider. The specific combination of dc voltages on the 10 parallel binary program lines determines the division factor N, which can range between 737 and 1402. A stable 7.500-kHz reference oscillator (f_2) is compared with the divider output frequency $[(f_1 - f_0)/N]$, nominally near 7.5 kHz, in the phase detector. Any phase error is fed back to the VCO in the form of a dc control voltage, keeping the total loop in phase-lock. When in lock, the output frequency is given by $f_0 = f_1 - Nf_2$. Therefore, f_0 will have the same long-term frequency stability as the two stable reference oscillators f_1 and f_2, yet can be varied in integer steps of 7.5 kHz, by assigning different values to N. Since f_0 is in the 217.5- to 222.5-MHz band, which is one-quarter the output frequency, the 7.5-kHz frequency steps are multiplied to 30-kHz steps, the final channel spacing, in a subsequent ×4 frequency multiplier.

As an example of this frequency synthesis process, suppose the transmitter is tuned to channel 134, which is centered at 870.030 MHz. Then

$$f_0 = \frac{870.030}{4} = 217.5075 \text{ MHz},$$

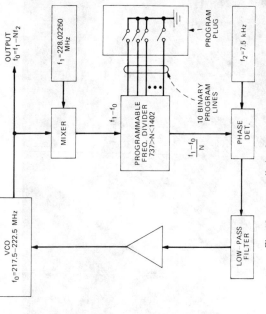

Fig. 16—AMPS cell-site frequency synthesizer.

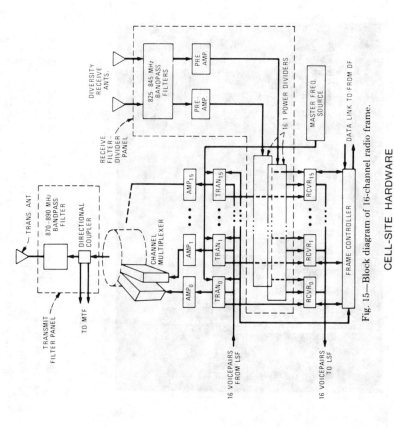

Fig. 15—Block diagram of 16-channel radio frame.

CELL-SITE HARDWARE

and

$$f_1 - f_0 = 10.515 \text{ MHz}.$$

The division ratio is

$$N = \frac{f_1 - f_0}{f_2} = 1402;$$

thus, the frequency divider must be programmed to generate this integer.

The synthesizer output is quite pure. When the output frequency is quadrupled, the resulting audio noise in a 0.3- to 3.0-kHz band (after FM detection, deemphasis, and C-message weighting) is 40-dB below a reference 1-kHz tone with ±8-kHz peak frequency deviation.

Figure 17 shows the transmitter circuits following the frequency synthesizer. Power entering at a specified frequency in the 217.5- to 222.5-MHz band (from the frequency synthesizer) is first split, one portion going to a low-power-transistor frequency quadrupler which generates the 870- to 890-MHz local oscillator (LO) for the companion receiver. Since the LO equals the transmit frequency, the duplex-receive frequency will be 45 MHz lower (or higher) if the first intermediate frequency (IF) of the receiver is 45 MHz. For example, if a specific transmitter is programmed to transmit on channel 134, which is centered at 870.030 MHz, then its companion receiver will receive the duplex channel, located 45 MHz lower at 825.030 MHz.

The other portion of the output power (from the frequency synthesizer) enters the phase modulator, which is a two-stage, varactor-diode, reflection-type circuit. Balanced audio (or data) originating within the LSF modulates the dc bias on the varactor diodes. The modulator provides a peak phase deviation of ±12 radians (after subsequent ×4 multiplication) with less than 5-percent audio distortion.

The resultant phase-modulated carrier enters a four-stage transistor amplifier, where it is boosted to about 3 watts. This power drives a varactor-diode frequency quadrupler. After passing through a ferrite isolator, the quadrupler output appears as a 1-watt phase-modulated carrier in the 870- to 890-MHz transmit band. This output power is delivered to a companion 45-watt power amplifier located in the adjacent power amplifier/combiner frame.

4.3 Power amplifier

In Fig. 15, the blocks marked AMP_0 to AMP_{15} are Class C power amplifier modules, which boost the 1-watt input from a companion transmitter to approximately 45 watts output. The power amplifiers, which consume most of the dc power in a cell site, are designed to be powered directly from the "raw," 24-V battery supply whose voltage can vary between +21 and +28 V, depending upon the battery's state of charge. Thus, a significant cost savings is achieved by avoiding a requirement for voltage regulation of these major loads. All other equipment within the radio frame is powered from regulated (dc-to-dc converter) voltage sources.

4.4 Channel multiplexer

The 45-watt output signal from each power amplifier module is delivered into a channel multiplexer,[5,6] which is an array of 16 cavity resonators each functioning as a narrowband filter feeding a common load, the transmit antenna. The multiplexer combines these 16 signals with a maximum of 3 dB loss per channel. The minimum channel-to-channel isolation is 18 dB. Figure 18 is a photograph of the cavity multiplexer. Note that the cavities are arranged in a radial array about a 16-branch stripline feeder assembly contained within the center section. Power enters each cavity from a coaxial connector (and coupling loop) attached to the back of the cavity. The combined power exits the multiplexer by a coaxial connector connected to a "load point" at the back of the assembly. The coupling to each cavity is determined by an acceptable compromise between transmission loss and off-channel isolation. The length of each stripline to each cavity feedpoint, from the common load point, is approximately ¾ wave-length. To meet the 3-dB loss per channel, the channels are spaced

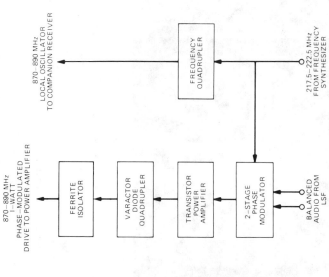

CELL-SITE HARDWARE

Fig. 17—AMPS cell site transmitter modulator and multiplier.

was conceived with a basic modularity of 16 in mind. The transmitter channel multiplexer, though providing low loss, is relatively expensive. Thus, in the receive chain, the 1-to-16 demultiplexer was chosen to be a 16-way broadband hybrid-power splitter which is low in cost but unfortunately inserts a 10 log 16 = 12-dB loss into each receive path.

To recover this loss, a low-noise preamplifier (see Fig. 15) is stationed ahead of the power divider. Composed of two commercially available 25-dB gain low-noise amplifiers "parallel-coupled" via two 3-dB quadrature hybrids, this preamplifier provides redundancy and also reduces by 9 dB the generation of intermodulation spurious signals. The noise figure of this amplifier-hybrid combination is 2.5 dB, and the third-order intermodulation products at the output are greater than 65 dB down from two RF signals which are −35 dBm at the input.

This UHF preamplifier is preceded by an interdigital bandpass filter giving at least 55-dB rejection to signals arriving from the 870- to 890-MHz transmit band. The total system noise figure, measured at the antenna, should not exceed 10-dB.

① STRIPLINE FEEDER
② LOAD POINT

Fig. 18—Sixteen channel multiplexer.

630 kHz, or 21 channel frequencies, apart. Intermodulation is controlled by ferrite isolators, providing 30-dB reverse loss, contained within the output section of each 45-watt power amplifier. With three channels excited, the measured intermodulation products are at least 55 dB down from the desired signals.

4.5 Directional coupler post-transmit filter

The combined 16-channel group leaving the multiplexer (see Figs. 2 and 15) enters a transmit filter panel attached to the wall of the cell-site building. Here the channel group first passes through a dual directional coupler where samples (30 dB down) of the forward and reflected wave are taken. This sampled power feeds via two coaxial cables to the maintenance and test frame (Section V), where appropriate transmitter tests are made and analyzed.

Finally, the channel group passes through a low-loss, 870- to 890-MHz, bandpass filter, where out-of-band harmonics and spurious signals are removed. This interdigital filter is an eight-resonator structure that exhibits an inband loss of about 0.5 dB. The channel group reaches the antenna via a run of 1-⅝ inch o.d. coaxial cable having a loss of about 0.66 dB/100 ft.

The transmitter system is designed to provide a power of at least 10 watts per channel at the transmit antenna.

4.6 Receiver filter/preamplifier/divider

The receive signals from each of the antennas first enter the receive filter-divider panel (see Figs. 2 and 15). The arrangement of radio hardware and signal distribution on both transmit and receive ends

4.7 Receiver

Following the receive-filter preamplifier and 16:1 divider (see Fig. 15) are 16 two-branch diversity receivers labeled RCVR$_0$ to RCVR$_{15}$.

Figure 19 shows a detailed block diagram of the receiver module. The RF receive band is 825 to 845 MHz. The transmit and receive frequencies are separated by 45 MHz, and the frequency synthesized for each transmit channel is used as the first conversion local oscillator frequency in the receiver. The voice receiver noise figure is about 11-dB. A two-resonator 825- to 845-MHz bandpass filter in the feed to each voice-receiver module prevents leakage of LO out of each module into other modules and helps suppress the "half-IF" response in Mixer A. The half-IF response results from the second harmonic of an incoming signal beating against the second harmonic of the mixer's local oscillator signal. For such a response to fall at the IF frequency, the incoming signal must be displaced, in frequency, one-half the IF frequency away from the local oscillator frequency.

In the voice-receiver module, the channel to be detected is first mixed down to 45 MHz in Mixer A, which is a Schottky-diode, single-balanced mixer. The conversion loss is about 6 dB. A PIN diode attenuator, ahead of Mixer A, is driven by an automatic gain control (AGC) bus and provides up to 40-dB of attenuation. This reduces the dynamic range of the signals entering the diversity combiner. A one-stage, 12-dB gain, 45-MHz IF amplifier with a two-resonator, 30-kHz bandwidth, quartz-crystal filter at both its input and output performs preliminary channel filtering.

The 45-MHz first IF is next down-converted to a 1.8-MHz second IF by Mixer B, a balanced FET type, which is driven by a 43.2-MHz

CELL-SITE HARDWARE

originally proposed by Granlund.[8] The complete theory of operation of this system has been described by Halpern[9] and Jakes[10], a simplified explanation is presented in the appendix to this paper.

The practical limitations in the combiner design have resulted in its having a dynamic range of 50 dB. The gain and AGC in the mixer/IF were determined to suit these limitations.

The 400-kHz output signal from the diversity combiner enters a conventional limiter and a "quadrature coil" discriminator, both contained in one integrated-circuit package. The resulting baseband audio/SAT or data are then delivered over a balanced line to a receiver voice channel circuit in the LSF.

V. MAINTENANCE AND TEST FRAME

The MTF (see Fig. 20) contains the oscillators and frequency dividers to generate the master clock signals and the SAT for other equipment in the cell site. It also permits testing of the cell-site radios, the associated RF transmission circuits, and the voice trunks connecting the cell site to the MTSO.

The frame is digitally controlled by the maintenance test frame controller (MTFC), which is operated as a peripheral unit to the cell-site controller located on the DF. The MTFC's main function is to interface the cell-site controller with the various circuits and test instruments on the MTF. There is also a manual capability of loading commands into the MTFC locally, independently of the cell-site controller.

The MTF makes it possible to monitor the functioning of the cell site under the overall direction of the MTSO. When a local failure occurs, the MTF furnishes the information necessary to "maintenance busy" a faulty voice channel, or to reconfigure active and redundant circuits for maintaining service while a craftsperson goes to the cell site to replace the faulty unit.

5.1 Oscillator section

The master oscillator set generates a high-frequency reference (228.02250 MHz) and a low-frequency reference (7.500 kHz) for all the frequency synthesizers in the cell site (see Section 4.2). The 228-MHz oscillator is crystal-controlled and enclosed in a temperature-controlled oven. It has a frequency stability of ±1 part per million per year. The frequency is distributed via coaxial cable to all radios in the radio frames and in the DF, and to the test synthesizer within the MTF. Thus, individual precise frequency sources for each of the radios are not required.

The 7.5-kHz clock signal is derived from a separate oven-controlled, 10-MHz oscillator, whose frequency is first divided by 4000 to 2.5 kHz

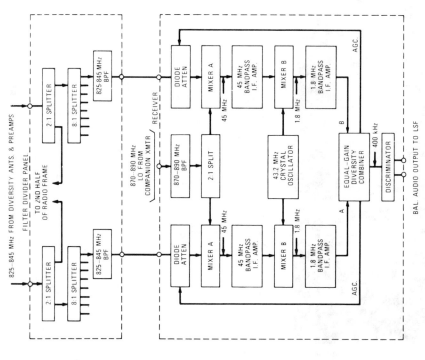

Fig. 19—AMPS cell-site voice receiver block diagram.

crystal-controlled second local oscillator. A 1.8-MHz IF amplifier with a two-resonator, 30-kHz bandwidth, L-C (inductor-capacitor) filter at both input and output performs final channel filtering. The combined gain of the second mixer and 1.8-MHz IF amplifier is about 43 dB, which is adjustable. The overall frequency response of the voice receiver is essentially eight-pole* (eight-resonator), with four poles resulting from the 45-MHz quartz-crystal filters and four poles from the L-C double-tuned circuits in the 1.8-MHz section of the IF amplifier.

The second IF frequency was made as low as the first IF image rejection would permit to simplify the design of the diversity combiner. The two-branch, equal-gain diversity combiner uses a technique

---

* Eight poles appear in the low-pass prototype of this eight-resonator filter.

and then multiplied by 3. The signal is then distributed to the radios in a way similar to the 228-MHz clock signal distribution. The divider chain is tapped at 1 MHz for the PROCON clock and at 10 kHz for the serial data clock. A redundant master oscillator set will also be switched into operation automatically in the event of a lost output signal or a gross frequency change.

Three SAT frequencies—available at 5.97, 6.00, and 6.03 kHz—are each derived from a separate oscillator and distributed to the audio-processing circuits in the LSF. The 22-Hz (nominal) clock is generated by dividing the 10-kHz data clock by 456 to obtain 21.93 Hz and then sent to the LSF for use in fade time-out measurements. All clocks are redundant and can be tested by the counter within the MTF.

5.2 Test equipment

The MTF radio test equipment consists of a test receiver tunable to any transmitter channel and a test generator tunable to any receiver channel. A test frequency synthesizer for channel tuning and a test audio processor, in conjunction with the test radios, furnish controlled simulation of a mobile transceiver. There are also a digital voltmeter and a counter, both remotely controllable, and a standard 1-milliwatt, 1000-Hz reference oscillator. These units can isolate a trouble condition in the cell site, via remote control from the MTSO, to a single radio transmitting or receiving channel (or group of channels). The channel can then be shut down and a craftsperson sent to replace or repair any faulty unit of the channel.

The test receiver measures the appropriate signals to compute the following parameters of each transmitter channel for comparison against specified maintenance limits:

(*i*) Incident power to the antenna.
(*ii*) Reflected power from the antenna.
(*iii*) Transmitter frequency.
(*iv*) Transmitter deviation.
(*v*) Modulation quality (SINAD*).

The test generator injects known signals to allow measurement of the following parameters for each dual-diversity receiving channel:

(*i*) Sensitivity (noise quieting with a low-level RF input).
(*ii*) Audio output quality at an RF input above threshold.

5.3 Maintenance and test frame controller

Much of the equipment in the MTF is used to facilitate remote testing of the cell-site radios, the master oscillator equipment, and the interconnecting trunks. The MTFC serves as the digital control interface

Fig. 20—Maintenance and test frame.

1. INTERCONNECTION PANEL
2. RF PATCH PANEL
3. 228–MHz REFERENCE PANEL
4. REFERENCE CLOCK GENERATOR PANEL
5. SUPERVISORY AUDIBLE TONE GENERATOR PANEL
6. CIRCUIT BREAKER PANEL
7. VOLTMETER PANEL
8. FREQUENCY COUNTER PANEL
9. LAMP AND DISPLAY PANEL
10. WORK SHELF ASSEMBLY
11. MILLIWATT REFERENCE GENERATOR
12. RF TEST UNIT
13. FRAME CONTROLLER
14. POWER CONVERTER PANEL
15. FUSE PANEL
16. POWER FEEDER PANEL

---

*SINAD = $\dfrac{\text{signal} + \text{noise} + \text{distortion}}{\text{noise} + \text{distortion}}$

mined. A frequency counter is connected via a switch to measure a subharmonic of the test-receiver local oscillator (LO/4) and the IF frequency from the test receiver. The counter display may be read locally or transmitted to the MTSO. The transmitter frequency may be calculated as $4 \times (LO/4) + IF$.

Maintenance of the clock systems also requires measurements of the master oscillator distribution bus frequency (228 MHz), the low-frequency group of clocks, and the SAT frequencies. Any such frequency may be individually measured on command from the MTSO.

5.4.2 Other radio measurements

To measure phase deviation, the SAT that is continuously modulating the transmitter channel is measured. The modulated discriminator output of the test receiver is measured locally using the MTF voltmeter. The voltmeter measurements are returned to the MTSO and compared to fixed, predetermined tolerance numbers.

To test whether the receiver sensitivity is within limits, the MTSO, after ascertaining that the channel frequency to be tested is not in use, uses the synthesizer to tune the test generator to the desired receiver frequency. The output of the test generator passes through a variable attenuator and a switch to the directional coupler of either diversity input of the receiver under test. The MTFC switches the attenuator to its higher attenuation position. Noise-quieting of the receiver under test is verified at the MTSO. The output of the test generator is then switched to the other diversity input and the noise-quieting verified again. The two measurements are compared against a stored limit as a go/no-go test for each diversity section of the receiver.

To measure the audio output quality of the receiver, the MTSO applies a standard test tone to modulate the test generator over the voice trunk. The attenuator is switched to its lower attenuation state. The audio output from the receiver under test is verified for presence at the MTSO.

5.4.3 Data radio interface measurements

The test receiver and generator can receive and transmit serial high-speed data. This capability allows simple tests to be performed on the setup radio interfaces and voice radio data interfaces. To check the forward setup channel interface, a special 200-bit serial data message is transmitted via the setup transmitter and its interfaces to the test receiver. The test receiver sends the received data to the MTFC, where it is stored in temporary memory. The controller then does a bit-by-bit comparison of the message with an identical message stored in its program memory and generates an "all-seems-well" message if the two messages check. The reverse setup channel is tested in the same manner except that the roles are changed—i.e., the test generator

between the cell-site controller and the MTF oscillators and test equipment. It also serves as a data interface to the various instruments on the MTF. Since most of these instruments require several seconds to complete their measurements, the MTF does the waiting and raises a flag when a sequence of measurements is completed. This saves tying up the cell-site controller in a long-wait loop.

The MTFC consists of a PROCON and a writable store unit, similar to those in the DF, and a group of logic and modem cards. The PROCON controls the operation of the test equipment in the MTF and formats and transmits the responses to each requested test measurement. It operates under the direct control of the PROCON in the DF which, in turn, is commanded by the MTSO. The logic cards provide the necessary interface buffering, while the modem, test receiver, test generator, and SAT transponder simulate the action of a mobile to permit measurements of (i) the data messages transmitted or received by any radio and (ii) the performance of the SAT detection and phase-range measurement circuits.

A lamp and display panel provides a manual capability to load commands into the MTFC and to observe its bit-and-flag status. This panel can manually reset the MTFC for manual error recovery and system testing.

5.4 Typical test operation

All tests are controlled by the MTSO, which also has to operate on some of the data to arrive at the desired measurement. The following sequences show the test procedures but do not necessarily correspond to specific MTSO test algorithms.

5.4.1 Transmission power and frequency tests

To measure transmitted power, the power from the forward-power coupling ports of the directional couplers is summed and routed via a switch to the mixer input of the test receiver. Power from the reflected-power coupling ports of the directional coupler is summed and connected through a second position of the switch to the mixer input. After determining that the channel frequency to be tested is not in use on any of the antennas, the MTSO uses the test synthesizer to tune the test receiver to the desired frequency and energizes the appropriate transmitter. Transmitter forward or reflected power, depending on the position of the switch, is read by means of a calibrated voltmeter and transmitted to the MTSO. The application of appropriate scale factors permits calculating the power into the antenna, and return loss. These numbers are then compared against stored limits to determine whether performance is satisfactory or faulty.

With the system configured as for the power measurement, the frequency transmitted on the channel under test may also be deter-

transmits a message to the setup receiver and its interfaces where it is received, reformatted, and sent via the controller and the data link to the MTSO for checking. The voice radio data interfaces are checked in a similar fashion.

VI. POWER SYSTEM

In the Chicago developmental trial, the primary power system for each cell site is the Western Electric type 111A. The input to this system is commercial three-phase, four-wire, 208-volt, 60-Hz power. Its output is a nominal +24 volts with a capacity of up to 800 amperes. A J87123 battery plant floats across the rectifier outputs and provides an emergency power source in case of loss of commercial power.

The electronic equipment operates mainly from dc voltages at the levels of +5, ±15, and +24 volts. Commercial 60-Hz ac power is used for cooling fans in the radio and data frames and for the commercial voltmeter and counter in the MTF. An inverter can develop the necessary 110-volt, 60-Hz power from the battery plant during commercial power failure so that system operation and test can continue.

The +24-volt battery supply is distributed to all cell-site frames. The +24-volt loads are powered directly from the nominal +24-volt* battery busses. The +5- and ±15-volt loads derive their power from dc-to-dc converters. The total 24-volt load amounts to 300 amperes for a system with only one radio frame, 430 amperes with two radio frames, and 560 amperes with three radio frames. In all cases, another 100-ampere capacity has been included in the power plant for battery charging. Where the radio frames are not fully loaded with radios, or when all radio transmitters are not operating, these loads will, of course, be less.

VII. PHYSICAL DESIGN

The AMPS cell site is functionally and physically divided into frames of radio control and transmission equipment, a power system, antenna interface equipment connecting the radios to the outside antennas, antennas, cables, and supporting mast and structure. The cell site equipment must be capable of being located in a variety of places. The Chicago developmental system† includes (i) small self-contained buildings with a dedicated antenna mast, (ii) small self-contained buildings adjacent to an existing microwave tower to make maximum use of tower facilities, and (iii) a portion of the top floor of a large downtown central office building.

Rented building space of many types may be necessary for future growth. In addition, designs must consider the visual appearance of

---

* Which can vary between 21 and 28 volts, depending on the battery's state of charge.
† The developmental system layout is described in Ref. 11.

CELL-SITE HARDWARE

buildings; the antenna mast assembly, because of its height, will be especially visible and may draw the attention of local zoning boards.

Since the AMPS is a new service using largely new equipment, there was little to guide design decisions. Thus, there is a need to learn how the equipment will function and how people will use the service. Production will be low in volume for the early years, relative to other telephone equipment. For these reasons, the physical design concept chosen for the Chicago trial equipment sought to fill several objectives. The design had to be flexible to accommodate many anticipated early changes and to make maximum use of existing general-purpose hardware to avoid the expense, time, and tooling necessary to generate a customized equipment technology. The equipment was partitioned into smaller units than will be ultimately optimum so that the system would be more flexible and responsive to changes. This section contains a general physical description of the equipment designed to accommodate these considerations.

The cell-site equipment may be housed either in a dedicated building or in an appropriately located existing building. The approximate floor area required for the trial equipment is 22 by 23 ft with a vacant wall or ceiling required for the placement of antenna interface equipment such as the filter divider panels. The cell sites should take advantage of existing facilities where possible to meet operational and economic objectives.

The outside equipment consists initially of omnidirectional, vertically polarized transmit and receive antennas mounted on a free-standing mast, or other tower. These antennas must be located and installed with particular attention to height and diversity spacing requirements. As the system grows into a directional configuration, the antenna array will also require directional transmit and receive antennas. The antennas are connected to their respective filter panels within the building via coaxial cable feedlines that pass into the building through a cable hatch plate. An effective grounding system is required to minimize voltage potentials generated by lightning. The building and mast must be surrounded by an external ring ground, and the interior of the building must contain another ring ground with all equipment frames and metal cabinets connected to it.

A typical interior equipment layout is shown in Fig. 2. The antenna interface equipment is supported by a wall and located as near as possible to the hatch plate. The radio control and transmission equipment is housed in standard Bell System Electronic Switching System (ESS) frames, 7 ft high, 2 ft, 2 in. or 3 ft, 3 in. wide, and 18 in. deep. The end guards selected are 24 in. deep to protect the equipment wiring. The ESS cable trays on top of the equipment bays are used for frame interconnection paths, and most of the interbay cables are equipped with connectors. The frames are sufficiently modular in design so that

Fig. 21—Backplane wiring showing both local wiring and interpanel cabling.

different channel capacity requirements of the various cell sites can be easily accommodated.

The remaining equipment, which may be considered as support equipment, consists of the power plant, battery stand and batteries, inverter, fuse panel, and air pressurization equipment.

7.1 Technologies

7.1.1 Components

Circuits for the AMPS cell-site equipment use both conventional discrete components (transistors, diodes, capacitors) and silicon integrated circuits (ICs). Analog and digital ICs with 5-volt and 15-volt power are used. Western Electric, commercial, and KS specification dual-in-line packages are employed, with most ICs having 16 pins. For ongoing designs beyond the trial hardware, additional emphasis is expected to be placed on using the highest-reliability devices available at acceptable costs. Many of the radio devices for use in the 900-MHz radio band are technologically new, and the technology is rapidly changing due in part to the considerable interest in this band generated by several new radio services, including AMPS.

7.1.2 Circuit boards

In addition to the conventional printed wiring board design, boards with wire-wrap interconnected socket pins on 1/10-in. centers are used in many of the plug-in logic circuit packages to give maximum flexibility for changes introduced during the trial. These will be replaced by double-sided or multilayer epoxy-glass printed boards on subsequent production of additional systems. Where circuits are replicated many times or high confidence existed that no changes would be made, conventional double-sided printed-wiring boards were chosen to save space and reduce cost.

7.1.3 Backplane wiring

The next level of interconnection is between circuit packs to merge them into panels or groups of panels. The logic boards are connected through the WE 947 backplane connector with an array of wire-wrap pins of 1/8-in. centers. Most of the power wiring is printed on the backplane. Where possible, a ground plane is also printed on the backplane to minimize noise. Most of the panel-level signal wiring for these panels is 30-gauge and is wrapped with an automatic wiring machine. Connections that require twisted pair or twisted-shielded pair for noise or impedance-matching considerations are manually installed after machine wrapping is completed. Figure 21 is a photograph of some of the backplane wiring.

The boards in the analog circuit sections of the frames generally use a lower-density connector, and the wiring between connectors is man-

ually wrapped. RF signals within a frame are routed using 0.141-in. semirigid coaxial cable terminated in SMA or type-N connectors. The semirigid cable minimizes spurious radiation and pickup and provides low signal loss in constrained space.

7.1.4 Frame wiring

The next level of wiring is between panels, or between the top of the frame and panels. For logic and audio signals, this wiring is generally twisted pair or twisted-shielded pair, depending on the sensitivity of the signal and the length of the run. Power wiring from the power modules uses large-gauge wire or laminated bus bars where the amount of current is large and space is limited. Semirigid coaxial cables are used for radio frequency signals.

7.1.5 Interframe cabling

Most wiring between equipment frames is via connectorized cable between interconnection panels at the top of the frames. Standard twisted pair cable is normally used, with twisted-shielded pair being used where extra shielding is required. The RF signals between frames, and between filter panels and frames, are routed on RG-214 coaxial cables fitted with type-N connectors. The filter panels are connected to the antennas with 1-5/8-in. semirigid coaxial cable between the transmitter filter panel and the transmit antennas and 7/8-in. semirigid coaxial cable between the receiver filter panel and the receive antennas.

THE BELL SYSTEM TECHNICAL JOURNAL, JANUARY 1979

CELL-SITE HARDWARE

Fig. 23—PC code circuit package.

7.2 Equipment and apparatus mechanical design

7.2.1 Circuit package mechanical design

The individual circuit packages for the cell-site equipment are all apparatus-coded and are of three general types. The most used are F-coded (a temporary manufacturing code for use during a trial period) packages that use either printed or wire-wrap boards for component interconnection and are fitted to the 946A circuit pack connector (see Fig. 22). These cards are mounted into 80A apparatus housings and connected to 947C backplane connectors. The F-coded circuit packages are used primarily for logic and control circuitry in the data frame and in the controllers of the line supervision and maintenance and test frames. They also contain some analog circuitry associated with the controllers. The main audio and signaling data circuits that are required on an individual channel basis are implemented on seven PC codes. These codes are also mounted in 80A apparatus housings but use gold fingers on 0.060-inch-thick, printed double-sided, epoxy-glass boards fitted directly into a backplane connector to reduce cost relative to the F-code boards (see Fig. 23). The third type of board used primarily for analog circuits is an A-code board also on epoxy glass but

0.090-inch thick, with gold fingers that fit into a 36B apparatus housing containing 905B type connectors (see Fig. 24).

7.2.2 Mechanical design of the radio modules

Radio modules in the data frame perform setup, locating, and signaling functions. Other radio modules in the radio frame perform voice channel functions, a capability which can be increased on a module-per-voice-channel basis. Test radio modules are also housed in the maintenance and test frame, along with the reference frequency equipment. The transmitters, receivers, and synthesizers were designed by Bell Laboratories and manufactured under KS specifications. To maximize early design flexibility and to minimize early tooling costs, a flexible packaging technique using three special extrusions was developed. The radio subassemblies could be developed individually and later packaged together with a minimum of circuit interaction. Figure 13 shows the voice/data transmitter with its covers removed to illustrate the packaging technique. This same general design approach was used for the voice/data transmitters and receivers, the frequency synthesizers, the test radio modules, and the reference frequency leveler amplifiers.

The other major radio module is the power amplifier unit. It is used on an individual radio channel basis and was manufactured to a KS specification (Fig. 14). The heat sink for the power amplifier was specified to be compatible with a forced-air cooling system that is part of the radio frames. Power dissipation requirements and long-life considerations indicated forced-air cooling as the best way to get a cost-effective design for the 900-MHz output-power device.

Fig. 22—F code circuit package.

CELL-SITE HARDWARE

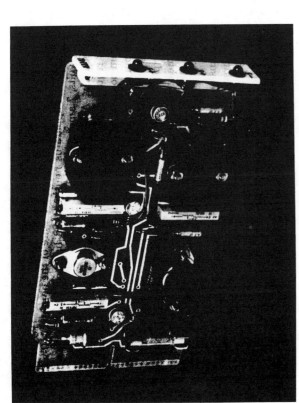

Fig. 24—A code circuit package.

7.2.3 Channel multiplexer

The channel multiplexer (see Fig. 18) is a 16-to-1 RF multiplexer, which uses individually tuned high Q cavities to combine efficiently the RF power from 16 transmitters into a single transmit antenna. The individual cavities must remain physically stable over a wide range of ambient temperature and varying power dissipation. To accomplish this, the cavities are made of invar, a steel formulation with a very small coefficient of thermal expansion. The cavities are plated with at least one-half mil of copper to provide good electrical conduction in the skin region at RF. A final thin layer of gold plate on the copper maintains good conduction at the material joints and ensures a good interface to the cavity interior. A fan cools the combiner, aids its temperature stability, and stabilizes the characteristics of the combiner stripline.

7.2.4 Power units

The primary power for the cell-site equipment is a +24-volt dc reserve power system, described in more detail in Section VI. The 24-volt dc direct current is distributed to each frame and either is used directly, in the case of RF power amplifiers, or is converted to the correct, regulated power needed by each frame. This conversion re-
quires the use of various quantities and combinations of four plug-in codes of dc-to-dc converters. One unit, coded 121A, is of the nominal 50-watt type which occupies only one-half of an apparatus housing, and has an output capacity of 2.3 amperes at −14.7 volts. The other three units—coded 122D, E, and F—are of the nominal 150-watt type, occupy a full apparatus housing, and have outputs of 7 amperes at +14.7 volts, 7 amperes at −14.7 volts, and 17.5 amperes at +5.3 volts, respectively. Although each of these codes was specified to unique AMPS requirements, they are part of a larger standard family of Bell System power converters. The converters of each code within a frame are connected to a common bus. Moreover, at least one extra power unit is provided for redundancy on each bus. In general, the loss of any single power unit will result in an alarm but no loss of service to customers.

7.2.5 Antennas and mast

Transmit and receive antennas for the trial system are high-gain, omnidirectional, and vertically polarized. They are end-supported but are electrically center-fed to minimize antenna-pattern squint-angle change over the frequency band. Two receive antennas per cell site provide diversity and there is one transmit antenna per radio frame (16 radio channels). The antennas are approximately 13 feet long, including the mounting, and are placed in a 2-½-in. diameter fiberglass housing When the system requires directional capability, the omnidirectional antennas will be augmented by directional transmit and receive antennas.

The omnidirectional antennas are typically mounted at the corners of a triangular platform (about 10 feet on a side) at the top of a 150-foot free-standing steel mast, as shown in Fig. 25. Later, the directional antennas will be mounted behind the contoured dielectric covers. There will be two receive antennas (for diversity) and one or two transmit antennas per face. Where an existing structure such as a microwave tower or downtown central office building is used, special mounting arrangements must be engineered for each site. As the system grows and cells are subdivided, the antenna height may be reduced to about 100 feet.

Since the vertical pattern has a half-power beamwidth of about 7 degrees, the omnidirectional antenna has the disadvantage of being susceptible to relatively small angular deflections from vertical. The antenna mast and platform were designed to minimize deflection and cost. The two major sources of deflections are the wind and uneven solar heating of the steel mast. In general, the antenna hardware was designed to meet two wind criteria; (i) system operation within specifications for normally encountered wind conditions, and (ii) survival under extreme but rare conditions such as winds up to 100 mph.[12]

The RF transmission line to the antennas uses semirigid air-filled

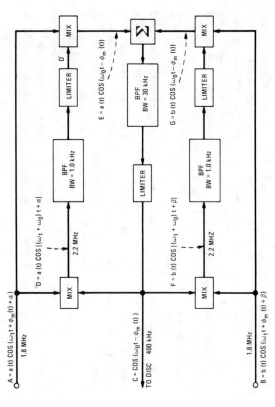

Fig. 26—Two-branch equal-gain diversity combiner.

$$A = a(t) \cos(\omega_1 t + \phi_m(t) + \alpha),$$
$$B = b(t) \cos(\omega_1 t + \phi_m(t) + \beta),$$

where

$a(t)$, $b(t)$ are slowly varying uncorrelated Rayleigh amplitude functions,

$\omega_1 = 2\pi$ (1.8 MHz) = carrier frequency,

$\phi_m(t)$ = the voice phase modulation, and

α, β = slowly varying, random, uncorrelated, carrier phases of channels A and B, respectively.

It is the function of the combiner to co-phase A and B (set $\alpha = \beta$), so that A and B can then be coherently added together. Assume that this regenerative loop is already in operation so that there exists the constant amplitude output signal

$$C = \cos(\omega_0 t - \phi_m(t)),$$

where

$$\omega_0 = 2\pi \ (400 \text{ kHz}) = \text{output signal}.$$

Note that α and β are absent.

The upper left mixer (modulator) takes the product A and C whose upper sideband is

$$D = a(t) \cos[(\omega_1 + \omega_0) t + \alpha].$$

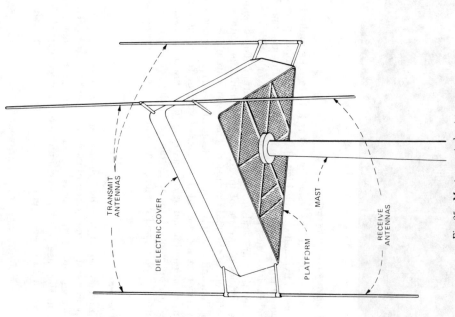

Fig. 25—Mast-mounted antennas.

coaxial cables to keep the RF losses low. The cables are routed inside the mast through a suspended conduit cluster. The conduit allows for cable system growth and ease of replacement if required. The interior mounting provides protection to the cables and significantly improves the visual appearance. An air pressurization system keeps the cables pressurized and dry internally.

APPENDIX

Operating Theory of the Two Branch, Equal Gain, Diversity Combiner

In Figs. 19 and 26, consider the two 1.8-MHz input signals, A and B, which arrive from the two 1.8-mHz IF amplifiers.

CELL-SITE HARDWARE

Note that the voice modulation term $\phi_m(t)$ has been removed, but the random modulation α remains.

The signal D, which is a 2.2-MHz carrier with slowly varying phase modulation, passes through the narrowband filter and limiter, which removes the amplitude term $a(t)$. The subtleties associated with the choice of the filter bandwidth are thoroughly discussed by Halpern[9]. The resulting constant-amplitude signal,

$$D' = \cos[(\omega_1 + \omega_0)t + \alpha],$$

is product-modulated with A in the upper right-hand "mixer." The lower sideband is given by

$$E = a(t)\cos[\omega_0 t - \phi_m(t)].$$

Note that this second modulation process has removed the random phase term α.

By similar reasoning, the signal

$$G = b(t)\cos[\omega_0 t - \phi_m(t)]$$

is generated by the lower regenerative loop. E and G, being phase-coherent, can be summed in a hybrid. This sum passes through a third limiter where the amplitude function is removed, giving the constant amplitude output signal

$$C = \cos[\omega_0 t - \phi_m(t)].$$

REFERENCES

1. Z. C. Fluhr and P. T. Porter, "AMPS: Control Architecture," B.S.T.J., this issue, pp. 43–69.
2. G. A. Arredondo, J. C. Feggeler, and J. I. Smith, "AMPS: Voice and Data Transmission," B.S.T.J., this issue, pp. 97–122.
3. R. E. Fisher, "AMPS: A Subscriber Set for the Equipment Test," B.S.T.J., this issue, pp. 123–143.
4. A. K. Johnson and J. I. Smith, "Radio Frequency Design for a High-Capacity Mobile Telephone System," Nat. Telecommun. Conf. Record (Los Angeles, Cal., December 1977), 1, pp. 16:4-1,2.
5. A. K. Johnson, "Determination of Filter Requirements for a High Capacity Mobile Telephone System Base Station," Symp. Microwave Mobile Commun. Conf. Record (Boulder, Col. September 1974), paper V-4, p. 32.
6. A. K. Johnson, "Computer Simulation of High Capacity Mobile Telephone System 16 Channel Multiplexer," IEEE Veh. Tech. Conf. Record (Orlando, Fla., March 1, 1977), p. 109.
7. K. Kurokawa, "Design Theory of Balanced Transistor Amplifier," B.S.T.J., 44, No. 8 (October 1965), pp. 1675–1698.
8. J. Granlund, "Topic in The Design of Antennas for Scatter," Lincoln Laboratories, Massachusetts Institute of Technology, Technical Report 135, November 1956.
9. S. W. Halpern, "The Theory of Operation of an Equal-Gain Predetection Combiner with Rayleigh Fading Channels," IEEE Trans. Commun., COM-22, No. 8 (August 1974), pp. 1099–1106.
10. W. C. Jakes, Jr., ed., Microwave Mobile Communications, New York: John Wiley, 1974, Ch. 5.
11. D. L. Huff, "AMPS: The Developmental System," B.S.T.J., this issue, pp. 249–269.
12. D. L. Chandler, "Deflection Analysis of Supporting Structures for Antennas to be Used in a Mobile Telephone System," IEEE Trans. Veh. Tech., VT-26, No. 2 (May 1977).

Advanced Mobile Phone Service:

The Cellular Test Bed

By G. C. DI PIAZZA, A. PLITKINS, and G. I. ZYSMAN

(Manuscript received August 1, 1978)

The Cellular Test Bed is a comprehensively instrumented field test laboratory supporting the development and evaluation of the Advanced Mobile Phone Service (AMPS). It consists of three main cell sites and six co-channel interferer sites configured in a small-cell hexagonal grid centered on the Newark, N.J. area. The sites interface with a central control and monitoring facility that incorporates a miniprocessor and related peripherals. A highly instrumented mobile laboratory performs fundamental data-gathering tasks and functions as the system mobile unit. A dedicated analysis facility is used to process and interpret the field-gathered data and simulate alternative operating system algorithms and their effect upon performance.

I. INTRODUCTION

Bell Laboratories is engaged in an ongoing field studies program to characterize the performance of UHF cellular mobile telecommunications systems. This program, designated the Cellular Test Bed (CTB) in its present phase, evolved from fundamental investigations of propagation-related phenomena. The initial thrust of the field studies program was to expand the work of previous investigators in order to generate a modeling of the influences of the environment on UHF signal propagation between a land site and mobile unit. To accomplish this modeling, a specially instrumented vehicle and land transmitting stations were developed and installed in the Whippany, N.J. and metropolitan Philadelphia, Pa. areas to provide UHF signal propagation data. The stations were located in a variety of propagation environments typical of suburban and urban communities so that conclusions drawn from the data are applicable to the broad deployment requirements of a practical cellular system.

Specifically, in the first phase of the field experiments, statistics were generated on UHF path loss as a function of range, propagation environment, and antenna elevation. The tests furnished data to characterize environmental noise and the correlation properties of signals received at the mobile unit from transmitting antennas at widely separated land sites. The results of these early experiments supplied the information necessary to specify system radio-plan parameters affecting radio coverage and frequency reuse.

A second phase of the field program emphasized the evaluation of specific antenna designs, equipment, and radio plan functions basic to the successful operation of high-capacity cellular systems. Field testing included data gathering on polarization and space diversity, vehicle location by signal strength and time delay, antenna gain and directivity, high-speed signaling, and voice transmission. These data have formed the basis for the development of cellular system control algorithms, particularly those related to vehicle location and handoff, and the performance specification of the radio transmission equipment.

The third and current phase of the program is structured to provide system-level evaluation of a broad class of cellular radio plan designs. The field configuration used for this effort, the CTB, consists of three main cell sites and six co-channel interferer sites installed in a small-cell hexagonal grid centered on the metropolitan Newark area. A primary objective of the CTB is the technical demonstration of small-cell interference-limited system operation.

The important features of the CTB test instrumentation and analysis facilities are:

(*i*) The data base is generated in a field environment using all the essential features of a small-cell radio plan configuration.

(*ii*) The instrumentation incorporates data-gathering facilities that permit the generation of a comprehensive, high-resolution data base, which can be used to design and evaluate system control algorithms.

(*iii*) The analysis facilities provide for fast turn-around data validation and fully utilize the field instrumentation capability to develop performance results.

These features ensure that data gathered in the CTB are reliable, reproducible, and statistically consistent with the objectives of each test sequence.

II. CTB OBJECTIVES

Efficient spectrum management of cellular systems such as AMPS requires the effective application of many interrelated system control algorithms. These algorithms are used to process inputs such as received signal measurement data and, on the basis of assumed propagation models, generate control decisions. The algorithm operation was developed and studies were performed using computer simulations that rely upon a statistical modeling of the propagation environment. The corresponding circuit functions were evaluated with hardware simulations of the radio transmission path. The CTB extends laboratory and computer simulation results by characterizing, in the field environment, basic operating sequences of the cellular radio plan and evaluating their influence on the quality of service.

The limited tests performed in the laboratory are extended in the CTB to incorporate hardware, software, and environmental interaction effects that are not well understood or anticipated. Consequently, final confirmation that circuit performance is predictable and proper comes from the live field environment. Similarly, the CTB provides a reference calibration for system-level performance simulations obtained by computer modeling. Computer-generated simulations are inherently well suited to evaluate effects of parameter perturbations and to extend simple system models to more complex configurations; the CTB provides a field reference to establish the validity of the basic models and enables proper interpretations of simulation results derived in modeling more sophisticated system configurations.

The CTB instrumentation, therefore, is designed to provide data on cellular system performance at two extremes of system complexity. The noise-limited system plan is studied in a three cell-site, omnidirectional antenna configuration; the small-cell interference-limited system plan is evaluated under the influence of a complete set of co-channel interferers in a directional antenna configuration. The latter arrangement stresses full frequency reuse, characteristic of the mature form of AMPS.

In both these equipment configurations, CTB data characterize system performance parameters, among which are the distributions of carrier-to-noise ratio (CNR) and carrier-to-interference ratio (CIR) over the cellular coverage region. Since these signal, noise, and interference relationships have a direct correspondence to voice quality and signaling reliability, they provide a first-order measurement of how closely system design objectives are being met.

Evaluations of signaling performance under dynamic field conditions are also of fundamental significance to the successful operation of AMPS. CTB-collected data relate transmission errors to the observed CNR and CIR distributions, to vehicle speed influences, to terrain characteristics, and to man-made noise effects.

Additional system functions tested in the CTB include vehicle-locating algorithms and voice channel handoff among cell sites. The frequency of handoffs, the location within the cell where handoffs occur most often, the improvement in CNR and CIR following handoffs, and the adequacy of locating decisions are all precisely characterized for comparison with results achieved in simulations. Such comparisons provide a reference which serves to qualify and build confidence in system-simulation modeling.

The CTB must furnish performance evaluations which are easily interpreted and which, therefore, minimize the time needed for subsequent analysis at the system level. This capability has been incorporated through the minicomputer/microprocessor technology used to control tests, collect data, and perform preliminary processing. This technology makes it possible to simultaneously meet the seemingly contradictory objectives of rigorous performance characterization and timely engineering-level data interpretation.

III. CONFIGURATION

The Cellular Test Bed site configuration (Fig. 1) has three centrally located cell sites for radio coverage of the Newark, N.J. area, and six

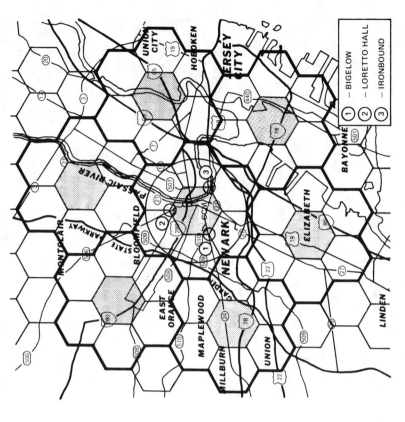

LEGEND:
1 – BIGELOW
2 – LORETTO HALL
3 – IRONBOUND

Fig. 1—Cellular Test Bed site configuration.

located telemetry site via radio link and then sent on to the CCM site via land lines. These radio and land links, in addition to the cell site links, permit essentially all measurement data, including the mobile AMPS radio plan geometries. The sites can be power-controlled to simulate other radio plans. In the directional mode, the central sites provide corner-excited coverage of a single hexagonal cell, 1.4 miles in radius, and partial coverage of the six adjacent cells. In the omnidirectional mode, the same sites provide center excitation of three separate cells.

The six co-channel transmitter sites are located 4.6 cell radii from the central cell. Each CTB co-channel site simulates the interference generated by the three sites serving the particular co-channel cell by means of a power-control algorithm which accounts for antenna directivity and height, terrain, site location, and channel occupancy. The main and co-channel sites interface via voice and data land lines with a Central Control and Monitoring (CCM) facility located in central Newark. The CCM site emulates the algorithmic processing and radio plan control functions of an Electronic Switching System (ESS) in AMPS. It also contains the facilities necessary to acquire and record the collected data base.

The CTB "mobile" (Fig. 2) is a specially instrumented test vehicle designated the Mobile Communications Laboratory (MCL). It is equipped with the transceiver and control facilities necessary to perform the required operating and data-gathering tasks. Data acquired by the MCL are processed, formatted, and transmitted to a centrally

via radio link and then sent on to the CCM site links, in addition to the cell site links, permit essentially all measurement data, including the mobile AMPS radio plan geometries. The sites can be power-controlled to simulate other radio plans. In the directional mode, the central sites, is carried by land lines to the "serving" cell site where it is transmitted for recording at the MCL.

This CTB configuration is sufficiently flexible to test the radio plan and control algorithms for a number of system configurations that are of interest. By means of power control scaling, the CTB simulates various cell sizes and co-channel separation distances to permit evaluation of each stage of AMPS growth and study of other radio plan alternatives.

IV. DATA RECORDING

The design philosophy of the field instrumentation allows flexible use of the field components to emulate both noise and interference-limited system performance. Accordingly, the hardware and software are designed to accommodate the broad spectrum of operational algorithms proposed to control and manage a mature cellular system. To accomplish this, the field configuration incorporates data-gathering and performance-monitoring functions that offer the analyst all the data resolution necessary to quantify the performance of system-level control of each operational event. For example, it is expected that in AMPS a system control algorithm will sample the signal strength received from each off-hook mobile in the service area once every few seconds. So that the Cellular Test Bed can acquire the additional signal strength data necessary to evaluate the effectiveness of such periodic interrogations, capability is incorporated within the MCL and at each cell site to sample signal-strength information once every one-half second. The one-half second interval serves as the basic CTB data-acquisition frame for all data recording.

The cell site data-acquisition system sequentially samples, at a 512-Hz rate, the signal received from the mobile on all eight cell site receive antennas. These samples are averaged by the cell site processor to produce eight one-half second means of the signal strength, based on 64 samples each. Each mean value and the last instantaneous sample contributing to that mean are transferred to the CCM every data frame.

The MCL data acquisition system provides a more comprehensive RF data record since it performs more than 3300 measurements during the equivalent one-half second interval. On the basis of these measurements, the MCL establishes and transmits to the CCM the following radio transmission parameters for each data frame:

  (*i*) Mean received cell site setup channel carrier level from each of the three central cell sites.

Fig. 2—Cellular Test Bed mobile—Mobile Communications Laboratory (MCL).

(ii) Mean received cell site voice channel carrier level from the serving cell site.

(iii) Mean received interferer carrier level from each of the six interferers.

(iv) Mean mobile-received noise.

(v) Peak mobile-received noise histogram.

This microscopic data gathering and recording takes place concurrently with the execution of the system control operational algorithm under test. Similarly, all system status parameters, including those related to mobile-unit performance, are measured and recorded every one-half second. Such a data base enables system-control algorithm performance to be thoroughly evaluated and developed to maturity.

More specifically, the instrumentation data collected in CTB are grouped broadly into four categories which quantitatively characterize (i) radio frequency transmission, (ii) the performance of system control algorithms, (iii) the performance of specific system functions, and (iv) the performance of the data acquisition system; the latter data serve to qualify and aid the interpretation of the other three data categories. The data are further classified according to source: mobile or land-originated. Table I lists representative examples of each data category and identifies its source.

As described below, the data are collected from both instantaneously sampled and real-time processed events. The instrumentation data collected in the CTB include 30 instrumentation words from the MCL and 24 words of data from each cell site. To accomplish this, 102 words of instrumentation data are recorded during each one-half second of real time.

In addition, operational status, self-check results, and data from the

Table I—Representative examples of data categories and sources

Data Category	Source
1. Transmission Data:	
Carrier amplitude	Mobile and land
Average and impulsive noise	Mobile
Co-channel signals	Mobile
Locating signals	Land
2. Algorithm Data:	
Location estimates	Land
Handoff events	Land
Cell site/mobile traffic distribution	Land
3. System Function Data:	
Signaling performance	Mobile
Voice transmission	Mobile
Diversity	Mobile
4. Operational Data:	
Time references	Land and mobile
True vehicle position	Mobile
Control flags	Land
Bookkeeping data	Land and mobile

system control process are added to complete the data package. The full complement of data constitutes a 204-word record of information recorded every one-half second.

V. IMPLEMENTATION

The comprehensive data base described above is obtained from measurements using specially designed land site and mobile data acquisition facilities. Specific equipment designs for these facilities are described below.

5.1 Central cell sites

The radio coverage plans proposed for AMPS require the use of both omnidirectional and directional antennas. Consequently, each of the CTB central cell sites uses 12 antennas (three 6-dB* omnidirectional antennas and nine 8-dB directional antennas) to evaluate the coverage algorithms. An additional omnidirectional antenna is used at each site for test control. The composite antenna array, illustrated in Fig. 3, is

---

* Relative to one-half wavelength dipole reference antenna.

Fig. 3—Cell site antenna array.

supported approximately 100 feet above the local street surface by a free-standing Corten* steel mast at two of the cell sites and by a roof-mounted 50-ft mast at the third site. Each mast has a winch and an internal halyard assembly of three steel cables for raising and lowering the antenna frame from the ground to facilitate antenna and transmission cable servicing.

Two of the three omnidirectional antennas are appropriately spaced for diversity reception of the mobile unit transmission; the third is assigned for cell site transmission. Three directional antennas serve each of the three 120-degree sectors (or faces) surrounding the site. Two directional antennas, appropriately spaced, are used to achieve diversity reception for the face they serve; the third directional antenna is used for cell site transmissions. Figures 4 and 5 illustrate typical radiation patterns of the CTB antennas.

Each antenna in the array is coupled to the cell site equipment through a 150-ft, 5/8-in.-diameter, 50-ohm, semirigid cable having a

---

* Registered trademark of the U.S. Steel Company.

nominal RF transmission loss of 0.03 dB per foot at 850 MHz. The return-loss performance of the antenna, transmission line, and connector assembly is maintained at ≥15 dB.

The four transmit antennas are excited by the cell site configuration shown in Fig. 6. Two independent radios service omnidirectional operation; two additional independent radios service directional operation. Each transmit radio path includes a UHF variable-power amplifier, which can produce up to 10 watts at its corresponding antenna terminals, and the two radios servicing the directional antennas can transmit on any of the three cell site faces—A, B, or C.

The receiver configuration of the three central cell sites, shown in Fig. 7, is more complex. Two receive antennas are used to achieve diversity reception on each radio channel in service and, as in the transmit case, each radio serving the directional antennas can be switched to service any of the three cell site faces. Basic to the cell site operating and data-gathering architecture is the instrumentation receiver, which has been designed to satisfy, concurrently, the operating

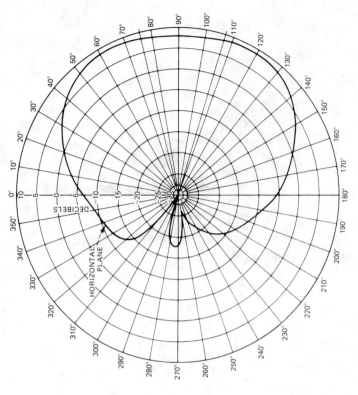

Fig. 5(a)—Azimuthal pattern of 8-dB directional antenna.

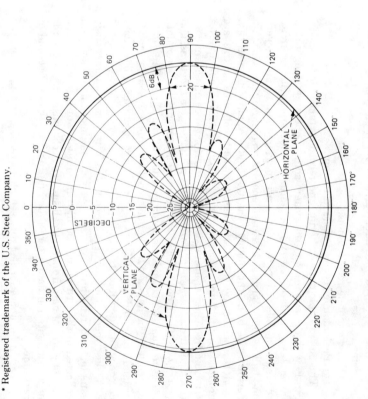

Fig. 4—Vertical pattern of 6-dB omnidirectional antenna.

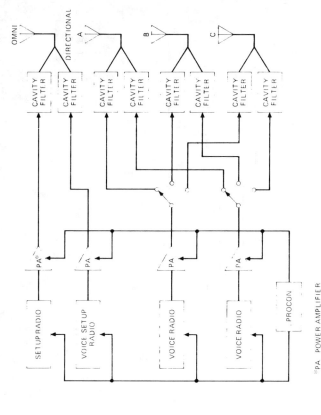

Fig. 6—Cell site transmitter configuration.

*PA POWER AMPLIFIER

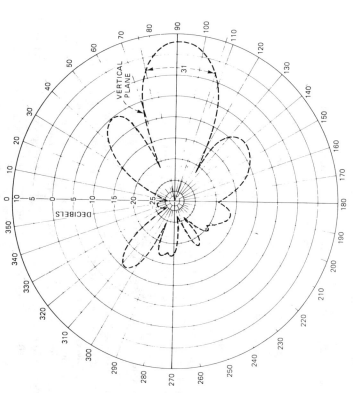

Fig. 5(b)—Vertical pattern of 8-dB directional antenna.

operations requirements, the PROCON at each site can be reprogrammed remotely from the CCM.

5.2 Co-channel sites

Since the co-channel sites need not perform system receive and data-acquisition functions, they have a much simpler transmission architecture than the central cell sites. Figure 8 shows that the interferer architecture includes two cell site radios with transmit functions only. These radios drive power amplifiers whose outputs are attenuated as required and are then hybrid-coupled to an omnidirectional antenna and a directional antenna. The radios can be modulated with either a voice signal originating at the CCM or a data signal supplied by a local signaling subsystem. The equipment control functions are administered by an eight-bit microprocessor that interfaces with the CCM via telephone data lines.

During field evaluation operations, both transmitters are active. One supplies the interference signal at the radio frequency used by the "serving" central cell site. The second transmitter generates a carrier signal at a frequency unique to the particular co-channel site. The MCL, therefore, acquires signal strength data on the composite inter-

algorithm under test and the CTB's data-gathering requirements. At a 512-Hz rate, the receiver switch shown in Fig. 7 electronically sequences through all eight cell site receive antennas. The signal strength from each antenna is sampled to form a one-half second mean, which is calculated by the programmable controller (PROCON) and sent to the CCM site. The CCM requests, receives, and records such information from all three main cell sites every one-half second. All information recorded is tagged to identify the time of the measurements and the particular radio/antenna combination and cell site in use.

As mentioned above, a PROCON is embedded within the control architecture of each central cell site; it responds to command and interrogation messages sent by the CCM via conventional land lines and Western Electric 201 data set facilities. The cell site PROCON is interfaced to peripherals that enable it to perform data acquisition, data processing, and equipment calibration and surveillance functions consistent with cell site evaluation and data-gathering requirements.

To facilitate field modification of both the configuration and test

CELLULAR TEST BED

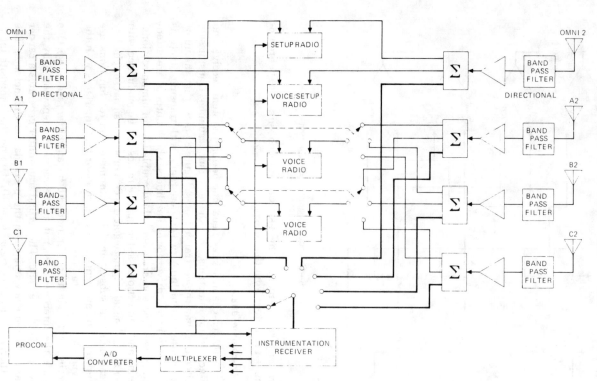

Fig. 7—Cell site receiver configuration.

ference generated by all six co-channel sites and the interference unique to each site.

5.3 Central control and monitoring site

Figure 9 illustrates the system design of the CCM, which is based on an HP 2100 miniprocessor data-acquisition system. Through software, it emulates radio plan control functions performed by an ESS, supervises data gathering and recording, and automatically calibrates and monitors the performance of all the Cellular Test Bed's land-based radio components. The CCM interrogates and instructs the mobile unit via telemetry link and the cell sites via specially conditioned land lines. Operator intervention, if needed, is also available. The cell site control message formats, as in the AMPS design, include seven parity bits to ensure high reliability of data transmission. The CCM software requests data retransmission whenever errors occur. The CCM also contains the calibrated audio facilities necessary to conduct voice quality tests.

5.4 Telemetry site

The telemetry site (TM) incorporates the radio transceiver facilities, which permit the CCM to reliably instruct and interrogate the MCL anywhere within the CTB test probe area. To meet the transmit/receive path reliability requirements of this important radio link, the TM site is centrally located within the probe area and uses a high-gain transmit and diversity-receive antenna system elevated 230 feet above the local street surface. The TM site also incorporates voice communication facilities to administer field test operations.

5.5 Mobile communications laboratory

The interior of the MCL (see Fig. 10) contains radio, logic, miniprocessor, and data-recording facilities. The RF/analog subsystem, which consists of five measurement channels driven by two electronically selectable RF preamplifiers fed from two receive antennas appropriately spaced for diversity reception, is illustrated in Fig. 11. The same antennas and preamplifiers also feed the AMPS mobile radio used to evaluate the performance of the voice and signaling subsystems.

The main measurement receiver uses a computer-controlled agile local oscillator, which mixes the RF signals down to three intermediate frequencies. Each of these frequencies feeds into two highly selective channels that use logarithmic detectors. Two channels (one high-gain, one low-gain) service each IF signal to achieve an instantaneous dynamic range that is linear from −150 to −30 dBm. The two channels are adjusted to maintain a 20-dB overlap centered at −90 dBm. The measurements for calculating real-time average values are selected using either the high-gain measurement or by accepting the low-gain

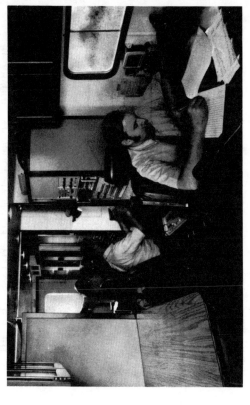

Fig. 10—Mobile Communications Laboratory interior.

Instantaneous data sampled from these receivers are processed to obtain a true incident power by a stored program reference tabulation. This processing translates the output from a 10-bit analog-to-digital converter to a number proportional to the corresponding instantaneous input signal power. The instantaneous signal power samples are summed over one-half second of real-time to calculate average values.

The MCL is also equipped with a gyroscopic-bearing and distance-tracking system so that all system status and measurement information recorded each one-half second are tagged with true vehicle position.

5.6 CTB calibration and performance monitoring

The calibration and performance-monitoring equipment in the CTB's hardware and software designs and the subsequent off-line statistical processing of the measurement data can precisely control and qualify the field experiments to obtain results comparable in resolution and reliability to those achieved in the laboratory. Examples of the calibration and performance monitoring subsystems incorporated within the central and interferer cell sites are shown in Figs. 12 and 13. The MCL uses a similar calibration and monitoring system.

The cell site transmit calibration and monitoring subsystem monitors, via precision coupler and temperature-compensated detection circuits, the RF power incident to and reflected from each antenna/cable assembly (see Fig. 12). The detected voltages, sampled and processed by the PROCON, are sent to the CCM, where they are monitored and recorded (on-line) to insure the integrity of the cell site transmit function.

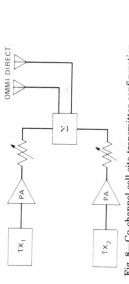

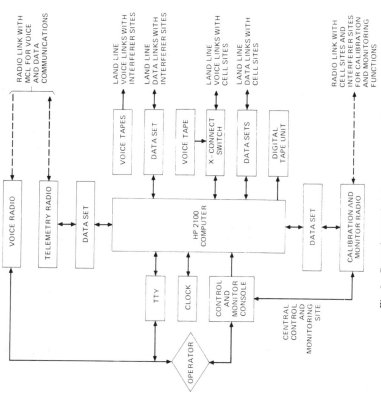

Fig. 8—Co-channel cell site transmitter configuration.

Fig. 9—Central control and monitoring facility.

result if it exceeds a threshold approximately in the middle of the overlap region.

Environmental noise is monitored on one antenna by a single logarithmic detector with a linear range from −150 to −70 dBm. The output of the diversity switch in the mobile radio is measured by an eighth logarithmic detector having a linear range from −120 to −40 dBm, with the useful range extending nearly 10 dB more at each end.

CELLULAR TEST BED

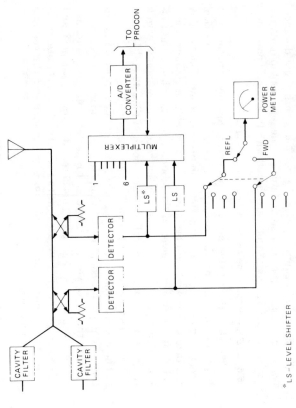

Fig. 12—Cell site transmitter calibration subsystem.

*LS—LEVEL SHIFTER

loss requirements are met. As shown, the test generator subsystem also furnishes the reference signals necessary to establish the FM quieting performance of the AMPS radios. Calibration of the CTB's transmit-and-receive subsystems is maintained within ±½ dB during each field evaluation sequence. The calibrations are performed at least before and after each test sequence and are hardcopied as part of the data package.

VI. CONTROL/RECORDING ARCHITECTURE

This section describes the system control and data-recording structures of the CTB that perform the AMPS emulation and data-acquisition functions. As noted previously, an extensive data base of transmission parameters is established at the CCM every data frame. The algorithmic software module accesses the appropriate cell site transmission data at programmed intervals and makes system control decisions, which are communicated to the cell sites and implemented by the operating system. The following paragraphs discuss the communication, control, measurement, and data-recording aspects of CTB operation.

6.1 CTB data communication

As described earlier, the CTB field experiments are administered through the CCM, which is linked with cell sites by data lines and to

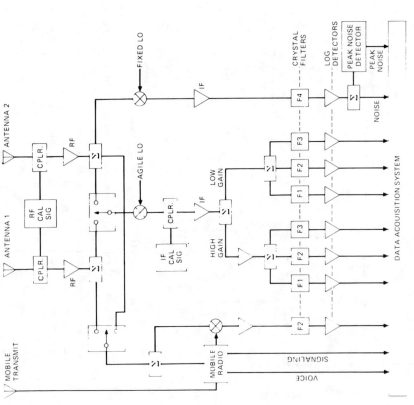

Fig. 11—MCL RF/analog subsystem configuration.

The type of calibration and monitoring subsystem used in the cell site receivers is illustrated in Fig. 13. In practice, the test generator is set, under CCM control, to a reference power level. The CCM then (via land lines and the PROCON) automatically steps a programmable, precision attenuator to supply the input reference signals necessary to calibrate the cell site instrumentation receiver over its entire 80-dB dynamic range. At each reference level, 1000 samples are taken and averaged to generate stored program reference tabulations which, during real-time data acquisition, are used to determine the true instantaneous signal strength incident at the terminals of the receive antenna. The test generator also furnishes a reference signal to each antenna and cable subsystem. The instrumentation receiver monitors the forward and reflected power to ensure that antenna system return-

CELLULAR TEST BED

6.2 System control

The CTB configuration must be properly initialized to start data acquisition. First, the interferer transmitters and the main cell site instrumentation receivers must be tuned to the serving channel. Then the test can start by synchronizing the data-acquisition frames at each cell site and the MCL with the CCM system clock. From that point on, microscopic data measurements at the MCL and cell sites depend on their local clocks. The CCM data-collection subsystem initiates each frame with a "request-for-data" message to the cell sites and the MCL. The data received are checked and formatted by a CCM software module and placed in a buffer for the system-control algorithmic module. This module is coded so that it can access data available to the AMPS control algorithms only at the proper time intervals. The output of the module may request a system reconfiguration, which is accomplished by the CCM with appropriate data-link messages. All system decisions, requests for action, and actions are recorded with the underlying data for later analysis.

6.3 Measurement of RF transmission parameters

Radio transmission parameters are measured at each of the cell sites and at the MCL. Each cell site instrumentation receiver switches sequentially to each of eight RF channels (Fig. 7) for sampling the mobile carrier level as received on each of two omnidirectional and three pairs of directional antennas. The data-sampling rate is 512 Hz, enabling the acquisition system to make 64 measurements per channel each data frame. The samples are processed through a calibration stored-program reference tabulation to generate quantities proportional to the RF signal as received at the antenna terminals. The cell site programmable controller then forms eight averages from these samples every data frame. If we assume an underlying Rayleigh distribution, these averages estimate the local means within a 95-percent confidence interval of approximately 1 dB. These eight averages together with the final eight instantaneous samples form the RF parameter list, which is transmitted to the CCM every data frame and recorded on digital tape in the format shown in Table II.

6.4 MCL activities

The MCL is a highly sophisticated data acquisition facility. As discussed in Section V, its five basic measurement channels are alternately switched to two diversity-receiving antennas. Further, measurements are made on both the high- and low-gain IF channels with the MCL computer selecting the proper value in real-time. Measurements are made on setup, voice, interferer, and noise channels. In addition, the AMPS diversity signal and peak-noise distribution are measured.

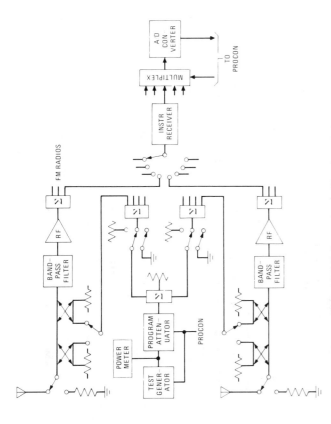

Fig. 13—Cell site receiver calibration subsystem.

the MCL by a full-duplex telemetry channel. These interconnections, together with powerful processing capability at each remote site, form a comprehensive data communications structure.

Basically, three types of messages are used for data communications within this field configuration: First, control messages, such as signaling requests to cell sites, permit the execution of system-level operations. Second, special data acquisition requests and data messages to and from cell sites and the MCL permit the acquisition of data at the MCL. Third, CTB operational-control messages permit the automatic calibration of cell sites, synchronize the data-acquisition frame at each cell site and the MCL, control interferer site power and frequency, and provide status information on the proper performance of the system. The last category of messages allows direct CCM instructions to the mobile logic unit via telemetry link and also permits the MCL and CCM operators to request test pauses.

The land-line messages are transmitted at a rate of 2400 b/s, while the MCL data transfer rate is 1800 b/s. All messages are formatted into 32-bit blocks with seven bits devoted to error control. The data are encoded in a shortened (127, 120) Bose-Chaudhuri-Hocquenghem (BCH) code, which is used in an error-detection mode with retransmission.

CELLULAR TEST BED

Table II—CCM data tape format—frame record

Word	Description
1 to 10	CCM operational data
11 to 14	MCL operational data
	MCL measured data:
15	Serving channel diversity mean signal strength
16	Serving channel mean signal strength
17 to 22	Interferer 1 to 6 mean signal strength
23 to 25	Setup channel mean signal strength—3 cell sites
26	Noise mean
27 to 32	Peak noise histogram
33	Supervisory tone status
34	Serving channel
35	Mobile power status
36	Order
37	Standard deviation on serving channel signal strength
38 to 48	Signaling related data; voice and setup channels
	Cell site measured data:
49 to 65	Mean and instantaneous received signal strength—cell site 1
66 to 68	Reserved
69 to 77	Cell site 1 supervisory tone transmitted power and other status reports
78 to 93	Mean and instantaneous received signal strength—cell site 2
94 to 97	Reserved
98 to 106	Cell site 2 supervisory tone, transmitted power and other status reports
107 to 122	Mean and instantaneous received mobile signal strength—cell site 3
123 to 126	Reserved
127 to 135	Cell site 3 supervisory tone, transmitted power and other status reports
136 to 145	Algorithm requests
146 to 149	Algorithm calculations (e.g., angle-of-arrival data)
150 to 167	Interferer channel and frequency assignments
168 to 204	CCM status flags

Table III—MCL measurement sequence*

Measurement	Parameter
1 to 12†	Setup channel signal strength—3 cell sites
13	Serving channel signal strength—diversity
14	Noise
15	Peak noise
16 to 27†	Interferer 1-3 signal strength
28	Serving channel signal strength—diversity
29	Noise
30	Peak noise
31 to 34†	Serving channel signal strength
35	Serving channel signal strength—diversity
36	Noise
37	Peak noise
38 to 49†	Interferer 4 to 6 signal strength
50	Serving voice channel signal strength
51	Noise
52	Peak noise

* Sixty-four measurement sequences constitute a data frame.
† These samples constitute measurements on both mobile receive antennas and on both low and high gain channels. The proper subset of these samples is selected by software.

The signal-strength data transferred to the CCM and recorded there consist of:

(i) Setup channels (three).
(ii) Interferer channels (six).
(iii) Voice channel.
(iv) AMPS receiver.
(v) Noise.
(vi) Histogram (six levels).
(vii) Standard deviation of voice channel signal power.

6.5 System function and algorithmic data

The MCL with its versatile mobile logic unit monitors the performance of the signaling system. It reports the results of the paging scan, supervisory tone outages, and correctable as well as incorrectable data errors on the voice channel. By reporting to the CCM the state of the AMPS mobile (such as its operating channel), the MCL gives a direct measure of the performance of the AMPS signaling system.

The MCL uses an analog tape recorder to record the voice as received on the AMPS serving channel. Timing and event markers are also recorded on the audio tape to synchronize it with the digital data. This provides a complete record of performance and objective information on the AMPS serving channel.

The cell sites monitor and report to the CCM the status of the supervisory tone present on the serving channel. Also, as described previously, the cell sites report to the CCM the final instantaneous received signal-level measurements on the serving channel.

The AMPS algorithmic-software module, embedded within the CCM

Table III gives the fundamental MCL measurement sequence. As suggested, the sequence has 52 measurements with a data frame consisting of 64 repetitions of this sequence.

The MCL minicomputer processes the instantaneous data to obtain mean power estimates for every data frame. Each setup, voice, and interferer channel power estimate is based on 128 signal-strength samples since the contributions from both mobile diversity antennas are averaged together. Again, with a Rayleigh signal distribution, the averages estimate the mean power within a 95-percent confidence interval of approximately ¾ dB. Peak noise samples, which consist of 256 measurements per frame, are cast into a six-level histogram. The ranges are:

$$- 93 \text{ dBm} < \text{range } 1$$
$$- 97 \text{ dBm} < \text{range } 2 \leq - 93 \text{ dBm}$$
$$-101 \text{ dBm} < \text{range } 3 \leq - 97 \text{ dBm}$$
$$-105 \text{ dBm} < \text{range } 4 \leq -101 \text{ dBm}$$
$$-109 \text{ dBm} < \text{range } 5 \leq -105 \text{ dBm}$$
$$-113 \text{ dBm} < \text{range } 6 \leq -109 \text{ dBm}.$$

The instantaneous measurements are recorded on the digital tape unit at the MCL, while the CCM receives processed data in histogram form.

CELLULAR TEST BED

operating system, accesses the instantaneous data each locating interval. On the basis of these signal samples, it makes handoff decisions, which are then implemented by the CCM operating system. The operating system records on the digital tape algorithmic level calculations, decisions, assignments (such as channel number and mobile power), and the results of their implementation, while the system continues its data-gathering functions.

6.6 Operational data

The operational data recorded in the CTB provide timing and MCL position information. Both the CCM and the MCL are equipped with crystal-controlled clocks supplying timing data with 20-μs resolution. The MCL timing data are transmitted to the CCM on the telemetry channel each data frame. The CCM-generated timing information is also recorded on digital tape. Using the calibrated position tracking system, the MCL's position is monitored each data frame and is known within tens of feet throughout a test.

Clearly, data acquired in the CTB must be reliable (or appropriately marked) to lead to valid performance evaluation. For this reason, on-line data on the state of the CTB are generated and recorded on the CCM digital tape. These data include trouble and status flags as described below.

If properly encoded data are not received at the CCM within the alloted time span (300 ms), a trouble flag is set to mark that event in the recorded data and a trouble report is issued on the CCM system console. An incomplete data package received at the CCM also causes a trouble flag and report. Once a complete error-free data transmission is received, the CCM validation routines examine the cell site signal-strength data for plausibility. If unreasonable measurement values are detected, the CCM sets a corresponding trouble flag.

Finally, the received signal-strength measurements are displayed in real-time on a graphics terminal. The test coordinator can request the display of any signal-strength measurement from each cell site. Unusual behavior in the displayed data is noted and may cause the test to be interrupted.

The AMPS locating-algorithmic program, which is resident within the CCM operating software, uses some of the cell site measured data to make required system handoff decisions. The algorithmic routine examines the aforementioned trouble flags and inhibits decisions when flags are set. If a handoff is deemed necessary, the algorithm requests new cell site and/or face and channel assignments from the operating system. This information is checked for plausibility and then stored and recorded on digital tape. Invalid algorithmic requests cause a trouble report to the system console and set a corresponding trouble

flag in the recorded data. Valid requests cause the operating system to issue the necessary instructions to the cell sites.

The MCL routinely sends the frequency of its AMPS operating channel to the CCM via telemetry. The CCM check routines, after accounting for response delays, compare the reported frequency of the MCL operating channel with that of the algorithm-assigned channel. In case of mismatch, a system reinitialization flag is set and recorded on tape, and a system-recovery process is initiated. The algorithm can also issue a system-restart request when a "lost mobile" condition occurs. This condition sets both the mobile status and the system reinitialization flags. On system reinitialization, the system software verifies the proper operational status of the cell site transmitters and measurement receivers. Improper operation is reported on the system console.

As part of the on-line monitoring system, the cell sites measure and report the RF output power of the transmitter to the CCM. This information is recorded on digital tape and is used on-line to alert the operator in case of a malfunction. The data are also collated and recorded within the 204-word block each data frame.

VII. DATA PROCESSING

The basic objective of the CTB data acquisition and processing tasks is to quantitatively evaluate system performance and to present results in a form suitable for system-level engineering evaluations that will help determine the final AMPS design. Fundamental to such performance evaluations is the capability of generating high-quality results in a form that is easy to interpret. CTB data processing achieves this capability through a combination of "quick-look" status-assessment programs, data-validation programs, various data-reduction routines, special data-collecting and data-organizing techniques, and highly interactive graphic procedures for displaying results.

The quick-look software enables a first-cut, fast-turnaround process for examining the field-collected data, prior to complete processing, to gauge how well the experimental data conform to pretest expectations. These cursory results are used to provide feedback to the data-collection activities, adjust the experimental setup as appropriate, and fine-tune the test configuration to collect data under conditions most suitable to the test objectives.

The data-validation and data-reduction routines convert the raw field data into a form suitable for input to the analysis programs. During this process, certain data are identified for removal from the data base, as necessitated by limitations in CTB field hardware or software. These routines, in combination, perform the translation of bulk-recorded field data into information suitable for the evaluation and evolution of algorithms in subsequent analyses. The analysis and

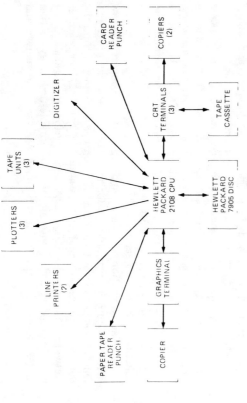

Fig. 14—Data Analysis Laboratory configuration.

display software provides data organization specifically matched to final-performance interpretations. These programs are further enhanced by a capability to reproduce the field experiment in the laboratory. The system-control algorithms can be modified and evaluated in a real-time simulation, which uses the raw field data as its input and develops a new set of performance measures. This latter software has been designed to take full advantage of the high resolution in the instrumentation data collected in the CTB.

The majority of these data-processing functions are performed in a highly interactive, hands-on environment with a dedicated minicomputer. This arrangement permits the flexibility and control essential to the effective utilization of sophisticated programs and engineering judgment in processing the extensive CTB instrumentation data base.

The data recorded in the CTB accumulate at a rate of approximately 25,000 words per minute. The data-processing effort outlined above is necessary, therefore, to convert this serial field data into an effective and manageable data base. The listed processing techniques organize the data into a structured, easily interpreted form. The specific data structure selected for that purpose is based on a geographic grid, which easily accommodates graphic displays of results and aids the final engineering-level performance evaluations.

The data-processing tasks that precede and are basic to generating, managing, and analyzing the CTB data base are enumerated below.

7.1 Data validation

The first data-processing function, preliminary even to data validation, is performed in the field: Calibration references are generated for the instrumentation receivers, signal amplitude samples are real-time averaged, and true vehicle location data are recorded and merged with measurement results. The data are collected at the CCM and written on a common digital tape for further processing in the CTB minicomputer-based facility.

The minicomputer facility (Fig. 14) is used for many preliminary processing functions. First, each field tape is verified by self-checking/ plotting routines. The verification process identifies and isolates equipment and operational software faults that occurred during data acquisition. The validated data are also inspected at this time to flag specific performance characteristics that may prove useful in analysis and interpretation.

Figure 15 shows a typical plot generated during the verification process. The figure includes six distinct types of recorded parameters, described below:

(i) Average power. The data for average power are displayed as a time series, with each one-half-second average value individ-

ually plotted in dBm on a time axis scaled to 100 seconds per inch. (The abscissa is labeled in "record" numbers, where one record corresponds to a one-half-second data frame.) Traces 1 and 2 represent the averages for two of the three CTB cell site signals and trace 3 for the environmental noise data.

(ii) Peak noise. The data for peak noise, plotted as trace 4, represent a weighted mean of the field-recorded threshold counts derived from a peak-detecting circuit. The equivalent average power of the noise peaks is plotted to the same scale as the other power data.

(iii) Normalized signal variance. This variance, trace 5, characterizes the randomness of the transmission path. It is formed by calculating the one-half-second (256-sample) standard deviation for the power distribution and normalizing it to the mean value estimated over the same time period. A value of 1 corresponds to the Rayleigh distribution, while values in the range of 1 to 0 indicate Rician distributions with varying ratios of specular to random components.

(iv) Trace 6 plots vehicle relative motion; its slope indicates speed. A 27.5-mph speed corresponds to a slope running on a diagonal across the page.

(v) Location markers. The "major markers," which are inserted during data collection to provide coordinate references, appear as tick marks at the top of Fig. 15. Location marks and record numbers are used to isolate the data sections of operational faults and remove them from further processing.

(vi) System trouble flags. The system flags, which are inserted by CTB operational software to identify system faults, appear as tick marks at the bottom of Fig. 15.

7.2 Data reduction

Data reduction indiscriminately converts all valid bulk field data to a form suitable for more complete selective processing. In data reduction, the normalized and compressed field-recorded data, which were efficiently packed for transmission over the telemetry link and arranged to expedite live data handling, are converted to engineering units and reformatted for more straightforward manipulation in subsequent statistical calculations.

Also, during data reduction, the field-entered absolute location reference markers are converted into true geodetic coordinates. The "digitized" coordinate data are also validated before further use through a microfilm plot, generated under computer control, which describes the vehicle's route. The microfilm is projected to produce an overlay on an original map trace which has been used to lay out the test route; it thus confirms the validity of the position information. One such route trace generated on the STARE system is shown in Fig. 16. The numbers alongside the marked route denote field-recorded major markers.

Following route validation, field-measured data and digitized coordinate data are consolidated to associate the proper geodetic coordinates with each data entry. The combined data can then be used by higher-level data-processing programs to yield performance interpretations.

7.3 Performance evaluation

The validated, reduced data are organized into a geographically defined grid structure and consolidated to facilitate analysis and inter-

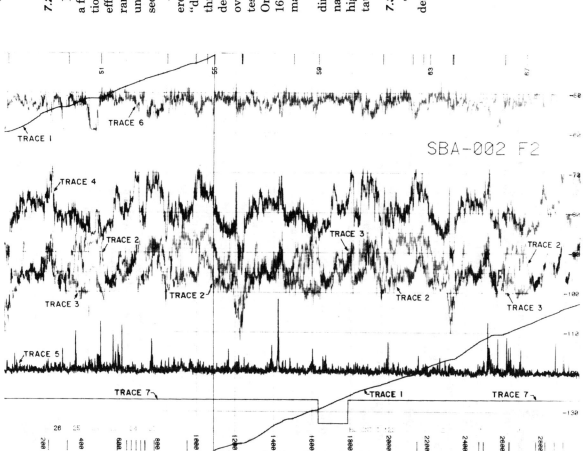

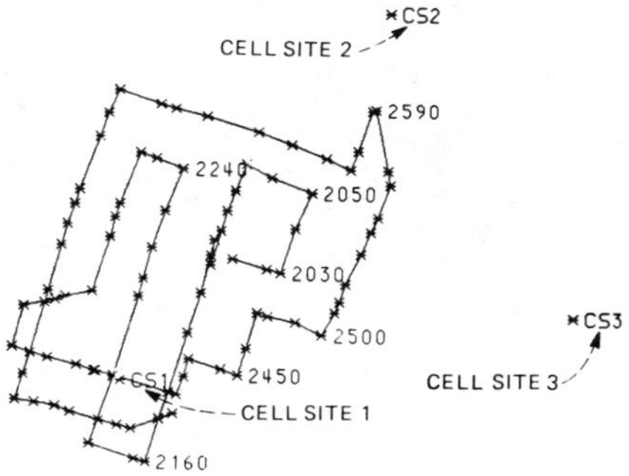

Fig. 16.—Route trace on STARE system.

SBA-002 F2

Fig. 15—Typical verification graph.

CELLULAR TEST BED

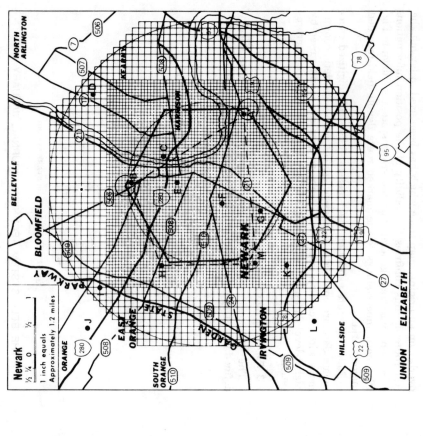

Fig. 17—Small grid binning structure.

Table IV—Information stored by region

16-Bit Words	
1 to 3	Number served by cell site
4 to 9	Number served by cell site face
10 to 12	Number $\bar{S}_s/\bar{N} < (X, X \pm \frac{1}{2})$ dB
13 to 15	Number $\bar{S}_s/\bar{I}+\bar{N} < (Y, Y \pm 2)$ dB
16	Number of handoffs intercell
17	Number of handoffs intracell
18	Number $\bar{S}_m/\bar{N} < X$ dB
19	Number $\bar{S}_m/\bar{I}+\bar{N} < Y$ dB
20	$\sum$ Distance
21 to 23	Number of signaling errors by cell site
24	Number of nonstandard terminations

32-Bit Words	
25	$\sum \bar{S}_s$
26	$\sum (\bar{S}_s)^2$
27	$\sum \bar{N}$
28	$\sum (\bar{N})^2$
29	$\sum \bar{N}_p$
30	$\sum (\bar{N}_p)^2$
31	$\sum \bar{S}_m$
32	$\sum (\bar{S}_m)^2$
33	$\sum \bar{I}$
34	$\sum (\bar{I})^2$
35	$\sum \{\bar{S}_s \cdot \text{Distance}\}$
36	$\sum \{(\bar{S}_s)^2 \cdot \text{Distance}\}$
37	$\sum \{\bar{S}_m \cdot \text{Distance}\}$
38	$\sum \{(\bar{S}_m)^2 \cdot \text{Distance}\}$
39	$\sum \{\bar{I} \cdot \text{Distance}\}$
40	$\sum \{(\bar{I})^2 \cdot \text{Distance}\}$

pretation. For this purpose, data collected in the measurement area of primary interest (a 28-square-mile circular region centered on the main cell) are subdivided into an array based on the MCL's position at the time the measurements were recorded. Such data organization is desirable because it lends itself to a straightforward evaluation of many significant system performance parameters. Handoff locations, signal amplitude distributions, and cell site service zones are typical performance parameters that are most directly described in a spatial representation. The location data supplied by the MCL accurately position the vehicle within tens of feet of its actual location and allow for such a data organization.

The principal area of interest in performance evaluations is circumscribed by the central cell's boundary. This area is subdivided into small square regions of approximately 300 feet on a side (about one city block). The outer area, extending for a distance of one radius beyond the main cell, is subdivided into regions of two different sizes, 300- and 600-ft squares, as shown in Fig. 17. This results in a data-base structure that geographically partitions the 28-square mile measurement area into about 4,500 regions. Each measurement result is identified according to the vehicle's true location at the time the data sample was collected and assigned to the appropriate small region.

The data maintained within the geographically based structure are arranged in a form to allow further processing without format conversions and time-consuming recalculations. These data are stored as accumulated running sums so that combining regions or merging data bases is accomplished by simple addition.

Table IV lists specific CTB data stored in this small-region form. Dividing the data base into 16-bit and 32-bit word formats minimizes the size of the data base while still retaining full data precision. The data in Table IV consist of system algorithm controlled events (entries 1 to 9, 16, 17, 24), propagation measurement results (entries 25 to 40), performance delineators (entries 10 to 15, 18, 19, 21 to 23), and a sum-distance-traveled entry (20). The symbols in the table are defined as follows:

$$\bar{S}_s = \text{mean value of serving signal}$$
$$\bar{S}_m = \text{mean value of maximum signal}$$
$$\bar{N} = \text{mean value of environmental noise}$$
$$\bar{I} = \text{mean value of interfering signal}$$
$$\bar{N}_p = \text{mean value of weighted peak noise}$$
$$X, Y = \text{preset threshold levels.}$$

The "maximum signal" is the maximum of the three cell site signals received by the mobile; it represents the upper bound on system performance as determined by signal amplitude. This upper bound

CELLULAR TEST BED

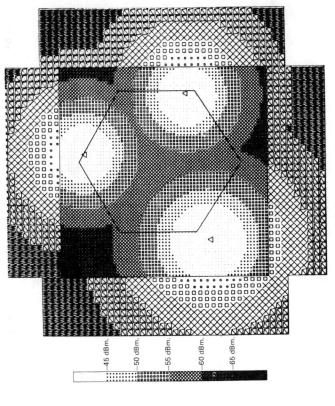

—45 dBm.

—50 dBm.

—55 dBm.

—60 dBm.

—65 dBm.

Fig. 18—Typical shade plot.

serves as a reference point for comparing the results of different algorithms.

Certain system performance evaluations have the greatest significance when displayed in a velocity-independent form. To obtain such results, the data collected while the mobile is stopped or moving slowly must be appropriately weighted. As an example, the one-half-second averaged signal amplitude is not a valid indicator of the mean local field strength at slow speeds. Velocity weighting (entries 35 to 40 of Table IV) preserves the distance dependence in the results while providing unbiased signal mean estimates.

Table V lists some of the results directly available from the data stored for each region. The data include statistical descriptors of signal strength and performance measures expressed as percentages of the total data collected within each region. Such data are available for each of the 4,500 small regions.

Further processing of the preliminary results develops outputs in a form suitable for specific performance evaluations. For these, graphic displays are most useful since they take advantage of the inherent ability of the human eye to sort quickly through large quantities of pattern data. Because of the geographic grid arrangement of data, it is a relatively straightforward task to develop graphic output in the form of "shade plots" of the desired information. In shade plots, the expected range of each variable is divided into a number of bands, each of which is represented by a unique shade of gray and plotted in an x-y grid.

A shade plot using the data generated from propagation rules developed from earlier field measurements is shown in Fig. 18. The algorithm that is used accounts for antenna height and gain (not all equal in this example) and calculates the signal level within each small region for each of the three cell sites with an assumed 10 watts of power delivered to the antenna terminals at each site. The maximum signal strength determined for each region is then plotted. Although this specific example produces a particularly symmetric result because of the idealized assumptions, the utility of this technique is apparent.

Figure 18 is an example of one general category of performance results. Conventional statistical data-processing techniques extend

such shade plot characterizations to specific performance evaluations. In addition, a performance summary is calculated for each measurement run as the data are processed to the small-region form. The results (Table VI) provide a quick-look system-level overview, which can be compared with premeasurement expectations to gauge how the tests are progressing.

7.4 Real-time simulation

The real-time simulation software supplies a field-like operational capability in the data analysis laboratory. Because of the microscopic resolution with which the CTB signals and operations are monitored and recorded by the field instrumentation, field data can be reprocessed in the laboratory much the way they are processed by the system controller at the time of data collection.

In the simulations, the system operating algorithms can be modified easily to study the effects of proposed changes on the resulting system performance. The real-time simulations, operating on the identical instrumentation data used by the system controller in the field, generate outputs that can be used by the same analysis routines used to

Table V—Derived performance results

1. Mean and standard deviation S_s, N, S_m, I, N_p
2. $\overline{S_s/N} < (X, X \pm 2)$ dB (percent*)
3. $\overline{S_s/I + N} < (Y, Y \pm 2)$ dB (percent)
4. $\overline{S_m/N} < X$ dB (percent)
5. $\overline{S_m/I + N} < Y$ dB (percent)
6. Service by cell site (percent)
7. Service by face (percent)
8. Mean and standard deviation S_s', S_m', I' (prime denotes distance weighting)

* All percentages are normalized to total number of ½-second records within each region.

the modifications and guide the choice of alternative solutions. The much more complete and laborious analysis processing is thus by-passed until viable solutions have been isolated. The combination of direct feedback during the simulations plus full analysis of final results assures a high success rate when the proposed solutions finally undergo field evaluation in the live system.

VIII. ACKNOWLEDGMENTS

Most major projects represent the efforts of many people. Such is the case with the Cellular Test Bed. The authors, in documenting the CTB, have merged the contributions of all members of the Mobile Telephone Field Studies Department. Their dedication and hard work are gratefully acknowledged.

process standard field data. In this manner, much of the time and cost penalties associated with field operations can be avoided as various alternative engineering solutions are explored. Once an apparently satisfactory modification is obtained, this result is confirmed through a final "live" evaluation of the new algorithm in the field.

In performing the simulations, the user can select for reprocessing specific data segments that represent spatial or time-based portions of the field-recorded data of particular interest. These data segments can be submitted to an array of algorithm and parameter modifications to test their influence on system performance while the initial system state (serving cell site, antenna, power, etc.) is user-specified or forced to duplicate the configuration that existed at the time the field data were observed. These techniques permit quick-turnaround iterations to isolate observed problems rapidly and to develop proven solutions.

Table VII lists examples of intermediate results that can be calculated and selected for display while the simulations are being performed. The data provide on-line feedback concerning the success of

Table VI—Tabulated performance results

Percent of area included in data base
Total run time
Total distance traveled
Average velocity
Total number of intercell handoffs
Total number of intracell handoffs
Probability of intercell handoff
Probability of intracell handoff
Total number of nonstandard terminations
Total number of signaling errors by cell site
Percent of time mobile was served by face and cell site

Histograms

$\bar{S}_c/N$	5 to 30 dB
$\bar{S}_m/N$	5 to 30 dB
$\dfrac{\bar{S}_c}{\bar{I}+N}$	4 to 29 dB
$\dfrac{\bar{S}_m}{\bar{I}+N}$	4 to 29 dB
$\Delta(\bar{S}_c/N)$	-30 to $+30$ dB
$\Delta\left(\dfrac{\bar{S}_m}{\bar{I}+N}\right)$	-30 to $+30$ dB
Time to first handoff	5 to 90 seconds
Time between subsequent handoffs	5 to 90 seconds

Table VII—Intermediate display options

Total time of run
Number of records processed
Total number of calls processed
Number of handoffs per call
Number of degraded calls
Number of locating data requests from serving and nonserving cell sites
Number of times locating signals are below secondary threshold while average serving signal is above degraded call level
Number of lost mobiles
Number of times trouble flag is set on requested data
Numbers and types of handoffs
Percent of time mobile is served by each cell site (and face)

Advanced Mobile Phone Service:

The Developmental System

By D. L. HUFF

(Manuscript received July 27, 1978)

A developmental AMPS system has been implemented in the urban and suburban areas of Chicago. A Mobile Telecommunications Switching Office at Oak Park, Illinois, controls the ten cell sites used in the system. An Equipment Test, serving approximately 100 mobile users, was initiated in mid-1978. A Service Test, involving approximately 2000 tariffed mobile units, will follow the Equipment Test. This paper describes the developmental system, the activities which were prerequisite to the major system test phases, and the status of the system as of July 1978.

I. INTRODUCTION

In March 1977, the Federal Communications Commission authorized Illinois Bell Telephone (IBT) to construct and operate a developmental AMPS system in the Chicago area. Configured as an AMPS start-up cellular system using large cells and omnidirectional antennas to minimize initial equipment needed, the system was laid out to cover approximately 2100 square miles in the urban and suburban areas of Chicago.

This developmental system has ten cell sites and 136 voice channels controlled by a Mobile Telecommunications Switching Office (MTSO) located at Oak Park, Illinois.

Technical and economic evaluations of the system are being carried out with a two-phase program: an Equipment Test phase, using approximately 100 mobile units assigned to Bell System personnel in the area, began in July 1978; a Service Test phase, with IBT authorized to furnish tariffed mobile service for up to 2500 mobile users, is scheduled to follow the Equipment Test.

Section II of this paper defines the basic objectives of the developmental system.

Section III describes the system that has been implemented, including the cell-site locations and the anticipated coverage area, buildings constructed at nine locations, and a mobile installation and maintenance facility.

Section IV discusses the major activities that were prerequisite to the start of the two evaluation phases. These activities included: the manufacture, installation, and testing of cell-site equipment; the development of various software programs; the construction of buildings to house equipment; the integration of cell sites with the MTSO; and the procurement and installation of mobiles. This section also discusses system test and operation activities.

Section V describes the early preliminary system test and evaluation activity using the MTSO at Oak Park, Illinois, interconnected to experimental cell sites and mobile units in the Oak Park laboratory and in Whippany, New Jersey. Successful tests of basic call processing, using early versions of software designs, have decreased the amount of testing that otherwise would have been necessary as the Chicago system was placed on line.

Section VI describes tools for collecting and processing data from the Chicago system, including the Data Retrieval System (DRS), and the Mobile Telephone Laboratory (MTL) used for radio propagation measurements and system trouble-shooting.

II. DEVELOPMENTAL SYSTEM—PURPOSES AND OBJECTIVES

Most of the principal Bell System objectives for the Chicago AMPS developmental system can be loosely grouped into two categories that relate to the system's two phases of test and evaluation:

    (*i*) Equipment Test objectives
    (*ii*) Service Test objectives.

2.1 Equipment Test objectives:

    (*i*) Complete all system shakedown and debugging activities necessary to assure a high-quality, reliable system during the Service Test period and in subsequent service.

    (*ii*) Test prototype designs of Bell System-supplied components and confirm the suitability of non-Bell System manufacturers' mobile units and cell-site radio equipment.

    (*iii*) Evaluate the basic engineering procedures used to lay out the system and apply experience gained to improve procedures for future systems.

    (*iv*) Verify achievement of objectives for radio serving signal quality, including acceptable location/handoff procedures.

    (*v*) Verify acceptability of system recovery procedures, call processing sequences, and the overall signaling plan.

THE BELL SYSTEM TECHNICAL JOURNAL, JANUARY 1979

357

Reprinted with permission from *Bell Syst. Tech. J.*, vol. 58, pp. 249-269, Jan. 1979.

(*vi*) Demonstrate co-channel operation using two of the 10 cells spaced at the appropriate frequency reuse distance for start-up cellular systems.

2.2 Service Test objectives:

(*i*) Verify quality of service anticipated and engineered for the Chicago developmental system, including voice circuit quality, low blocking rates, and overall technical performance.

(*ii*) Confirm viability and worth of AMPS by demonstrating that the public's needs for mobile telephone communications can be met at a satisfactory cost.

(*iii*) Collect data to support market study activities, including verifying various market research and sales prediction procedures currently being used to determine the future market for AMPS.

(*iv*) Collect data for estimating the average traffic generated per mobile and the geographical distribution of mobile traffic.

(*v*) Determine customer reactions and sensitivities to the basic service; mobile installation, operation, and maintenance procedures; and vertical services.

2.3 Overall developmental system objectives

During the overall test of the developmental cellular system, the objective will be to gain experience in:

(*i*) Engineering and implementing an AMPS system.
(*ii*) Selecting cell site locations.
(*iii*) Installing and testing AMPS equipment.
(*iv*) Operating and maintaining an AMPS system.
(*v*) Interacting with mobile customers and equipment radio suppliers.

III. DEVELOPMENTAL SYSTEM DESCRIPTION

The AMPS developmental system in Chicago has been engineered to represent a typical start-up cellular system. Figure 1 shows the anticipated 2100-square-mile coverage area with the locations of the 10 cell sites indicated by crosses and three-letter codes (explained in Table I).

For the start-up AMPS system, cell-site locations were chosen, where possible, to take advantage of existing high-elevation structures for antenna placement, and to minimize site location deviations from the ideal grid. The use of existing structures reduced the initial system cost and the possibility of potential delays caused by zoning problems. The compromise achieved with this layout required only three new antenna masts to be erected. The remaining seven cell sites have antennas on existing structures. In Fig. 2, the circles represent the

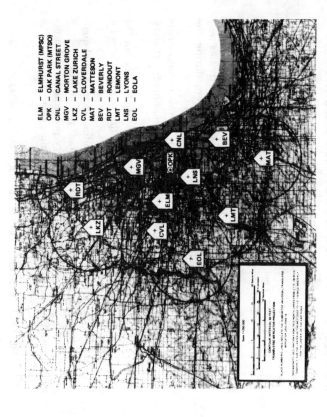

ELM – ELMHURST (MPSC)
OPK – OAK PARK (MTSO)
CNL – CANAL STREET
MGV – MORTON GROVE
LKZ – LAKE ZURICH
CVL – CLOVERDALE
MAT – MATTESON
BEV – BEVERLY
RDT – RONDOUT
LMT – LEMONT
LNS – LYONS
EOL – EOLA

Fig. 1—Chicago service area.

Table I—Developmental system cell-site locations in Illinois and number of duplex voice channels assigned

Cell Site	Voice Channels	Antenna Height (ft)	Address
Beverly (BEV)	16	150	413 W. 105th Street, Chicago
Canal Street (CNL)	26	550	10 South Canal Street, Chicago
Cloverdale (CVL)	15	325	Schmale Road, Cloverdale
Eola (EOL)	8	310	Drehl Road, Eola
Lake Zurich (LKZ)	9	285	U.S. Highway 12, Lake Zurich
Lemont (LMT)	8	250	127th Street, Lemont
Lyons (LNS)	16	150	8542 W. 44th Street, Lyons
Matteson (MAT)	12	260	Vollmer Road, Matteson
Morton Grove (MGV)	18	185	Narragansett Street, Morton Grove
Rondout (RDT)	8	150	Bradley Road, Libertyville Township
	136		

bility (based on certain assumptions about mobile traffic distributions and mobile user characteristics). Table I lists the number of voice channels assigned to each cell site using the current engineering rules. An important objective of the Service Test is an evaluation of these preliminary assumptions of traffic and user characteristics. The experience with AMPS mobile customers will serve as the basis for appropriate modifications to the engineering rules.

Since the nine duplex voice channels of the Lake Zurich cell site are reused in the Matteson cell, only 127 different voice channel frequency pairs are actually assigned to the developmental system, along with 10 setup channel frequency pairs. The required voice and data trunks between the MTSO and each of the cell sites is provided using tariffed private line facilities.

Figure 3 illustrates the floor plan of a typical cell site. The buildings are small—approximately 20 by 30 ft of floor space—with room for the cell-site equipment, power supply system, maintenance and test equipment, and maintenance personnel. Except during maintenance activities, the buildings are unattended. Figure 4 is a photograph of the Rondout cell site, showing the cell site building and the 150-ft monopole. Figure 5 shows the Cloverdale cell site, with the building at the foot of the 325-foot AT&T microwave tower and the antennas mounted on top of the tower.

One of the developmental system objectives discussed in the previous section involves determining customer reaction and sensitivity to installation and maintenance procedures. To avoid excessive customer inconvenience, a dedicated installation and repair facility in Elmhurst is being used in the Chicago developmental system. Termed the Mobile Phone Service Center (MPSC), it also serves as the base location for the Mobile Telephone Laboratory (MTL) and for the IBT craft force who maintain the ten cell sites. Spare parts and test equipment for the cell sites are housed at this location, as well as a small data-processing facility for rapid examination of MTL data. Figure 6 shows an external view of this building, while Fig. 7 is a floor plan showing the internal configuration. There are sufficient installation and repair bays at the center to handle the estimated numbers of customers per month during the Service Test. The size of the craft force and the amount of automated test equipment necessary to verify quickly the proper operation of an installed mobile have been determined based on processing Service Test customers efficiently and without undue inconvenience.

IV. MAJOR ACTIVITIES COMPLETED OR UNDER WAY

4.1 Cell-site equipment manufacture

Twelve complete sets of cell site equipment were assembled at the Western Electric factory in Burlington, North Carolina. Two sets of

THE BELL SYSTEM TECHNICAL JOURNAL, JANUARY 1979

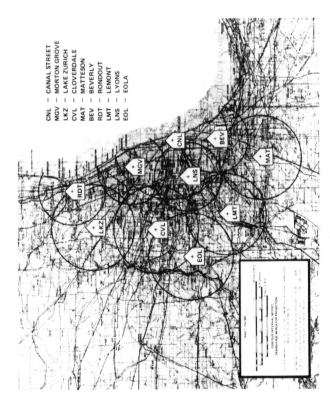

CNL — CANAL STREET
MGV — MORTON GROVE
LKZ — LAKE ZURICH
CVL — CLOVERDALE
MAT — MATTESON
BEV — BEVERLY
RDT — RONDOUT
LMT — LEMONT
LNS — LYONS
EOL — EOLA

Fig. 2—Idealized coverage areas.

expected coverage area of each cell site. Variations in antenna heights and associated antenna cable losses lead to variations in the size of these circles. The circles represent the estimated ideal "36-dBμ contour"* that results from applying empirically derived 900-MHz path-loss and antenna-height advantage equations to the effective radiated power of each site. The idealized smooth contours will not be realized in practice, since propagation from each cell site will not be uniform in all directions.

For all cell sites except Canal Street, new buildings have been constructed to house cell-site equipment. Since the Canal Street location had available surplus floor space, it was the first to have cell-site equipment installed and made operational. The MTSO location at Oak Park, Ill., is indicated by a small circle in Fig. 1. AMPS software testing was carried out at this location, in addition to control of the developmental system as it came on line.

The system will serve approximately 2000 mobile units during the Service Test with an estimated 2-percent busy-hour blocking proba-

---

* On this contour, the approximate signal-to-noise ratio averages 18 dB. Studies have shown that this level of signal strength on the cell boundaries will provide the required overall quality of service for AMPS.

DEVELOPMENTAL SYSTEM

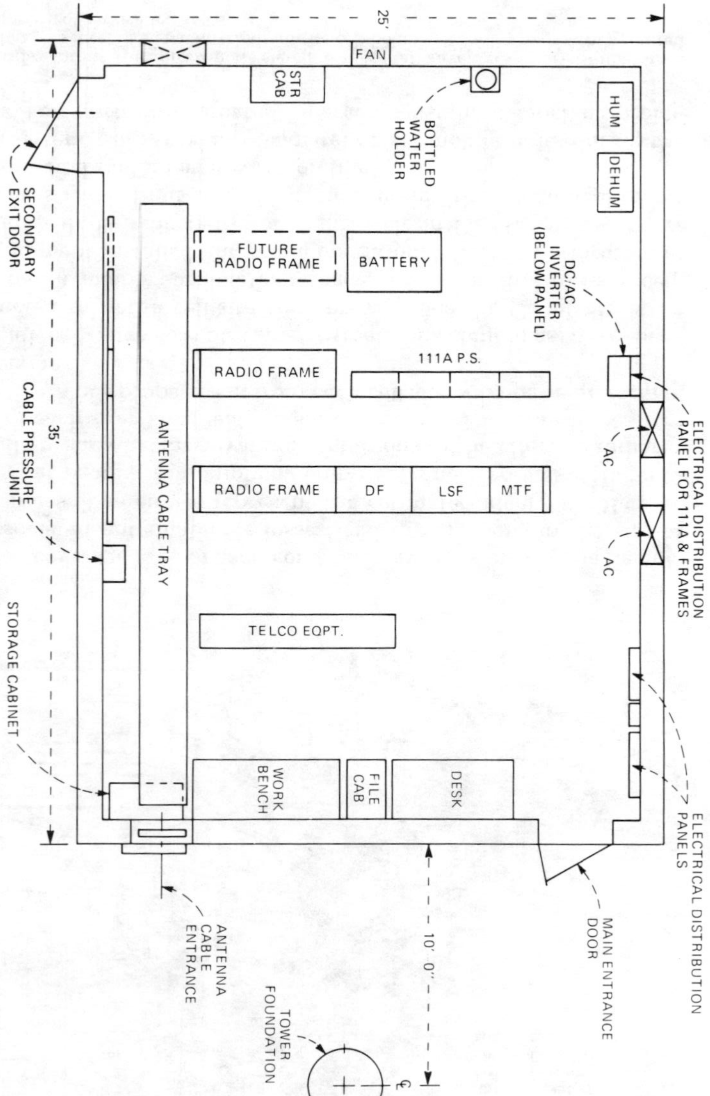

Fig. 4—Rondout cell-site building and mast.

equipment were used for early interface and software debug testing with the No. 1 ESS and mobile unit subsystems; one at the MTSO location at Oak Park, Illinois, and the other at the Bell Laboratories, Whippany, New Jersey, location where the cell site was designed. The remaining 10 sets of cell-site equipment were installed in the developmental system.

All cell sites were thoroughly factory tested before shipment. These tests included computer-driven wiring tests, manual tests, and tests with an HP-21MX minicomputer that thoroughly checked each cell-site

ELECTRICAL DISTRIBUTION PANEL FOR 111A & FRAMES

ELECTRICAL DISTRIBUTION PANELS

MAIN ENTRANCE DOOR

HUM   DEHUM

AC   AC

DC/AC INVERTER (BELOW PANEL)

BOTTLED WATER HOLDER

FAN

STR CAB

BATTERY

FUTURE RADIO FRAME

111A P.S.

RADIO FRAME

RADIO FRAME

DF

LSF

MTF

TELCO EQPT.

DESK

FILE CAB

WORK BENCH

10' 0"

TOWER FOUNDATION

ANTENNA CABLE TRAY

ANTENNA CABLE ENTRANCE

25'

35'

SECONDARY EXIT DOOR

CABLE PRESSURE UNIT

STORAGE CABINET

DEVELOPMENTAL SYSTEM

Fig. 3—Cell-site building layout.

Fig. 6—The Mobile Phone Service Center in Elmhurst, Illinois.

4.2 Software development

The development of the software to be used in the No. 1 ESS MTSO for AMPS control and maintenance in the Chicago developmental system is basically complete.* As new capabilities were developed, they were incorporated into a new issue of the generic program, which was released for testing and debugging using the No. 1 ESS at the Oak Park laboratory. A cell site and four developmental mobiles, which were not part of the developmental system, were connected to the Oak Park No. 1 ESS to aid in the software testing and debugging effort. As each issue of the generic program stabilized, it was used to control the developmental system cell sites that were operational at the time.

Stored-program software has also been developed for the data terminal equipment, the maintenance and test frame equipment, and the data frame in the cell site.

Stored-program software for the logic unit of the Equipment Test mobiles also has been developed. The necessary capability was released incrementally via new programmable read-only memories installed in the logic units in use.

The three companies producing mobiles for the Service Test have developed the software required by their mobiles' designs.

4.3 Building construction

IBT contracted for the construction of the nine new cell site buildings required for the Chicago trial. All were completed by January 1978, except for the Rondout building, which was delayed because of a zoning problem. The mast foundation at the three sites using the 150-ft monopole mast required additional construction activity.

4.4 Cell-site installation, test, and integration

Installers of the Western Electric-Central Region (WE-CR) installed the 111A power plant and other peripheral hardware required for each

AMPS
ANTENNAS

AMPS CELL
SITE BUILDING

Fig. 5—Cloverdale cell site.

frame on a stand-alone basis. Tests of the interconnected frames ("string tests") included manual adjustments and alignments of each site's radio channels. Special software programs were loaded into the data frame programmable controller (PROCON), which executed and tested all the functional capabilities of the cell-site subsystem.

---

* It is anticipated that minor modifications will be made in the software based on experience gained during the Equipment Test.

cell site, as soon as the building became available. IBT craftspeople installed the electronic equipment at each cell site except Canal Street, where WE-CR personnel did this work. IBT craftspeople, supported by Bell Laboratories and Western Electric-Merrimack Valley (WE-MV) installation engineers, also performed the installation testing of the cell sites using handbooks developed by WE-MV.

Installation test procedures included a large number of manual tests and final adjustments of equipment, followed by a rerun of the string test software programs used initially during factory testing. These tests involved 14 programs, each manually loaded into the data frame PROCON via a paper tape reader and a display, debug, and test (DDT) unit. Errors detected in the cell-site hardware were displayed as specific codes on a printer. Another program generated specific orders to, and received specific replies from, a single mobile unit, which was either the Mobile Telephone Laboratory (MTL) or an instrumented mobile-equipped automobile.

Another class of cell-site test used an HP-21MX minicomputer located at the Oak Park facility and patched into the voice and data trunks connecting the cell site to the MTSO. An autonomous cell-site-to-mobile test program was run, using either the MTL or a specially instrumented mobile-equipped automobile as the mobile. This program required the data frame operational software to be in use in the cell site and thus tested all hardware and software subsystems exclusive of the MTSO. All paging data transmission, voice transmission, supervisory, and fade and disconnect functions that take place between the cell site and mobile were tested.

The next step was to integrate the tested cell site and its operational software with the MTSO and its generic software; with the data terminal equipment and its resident software; and with the data- and voice-trunking facilities between the MTSO and the cell site. The integration commenced with the running of a cell-site initialization program called CLSI, part of the MTSO generic software program. This program initializes the data frame operational program and performs basic functional tests that ensure communication between the MTSO and the cell site. Basic simple call processing tests were then run on each voice channel of the cell site, including land-to-mobile and mobile-to-land calls. Finally, the resident cell-site diagnostic programs within the MTSO were employed to detect failed or suspect hardware and to confirm the system's ability to reconfigure cell site redundant equipment. With no major equipment problems apparent, integration of the cell site with the MTSO was considered complete, and it joined the previously integrated cell sites in participating in system operation and shakedown.

4.5 System test activity

As described in more detail in Section V, preliminary functional testing and debugging began in November 1976, with the No. 1 ESS

Fig. 7—Floor plan of Mobile Phone Service Center.

DEVELOPMENTAL SYSTEM

Table II—Examples of system-level tests being conducted

Facilities Used	Purpose	Procedures
MTL, Cell Sites	*Service Area Coverage* Evaluate engineering coverage and service quality.	Measure signal strengths at selected locations in the 2100-square-mile system area.
HP-21 Minicomputer, MTL, Cell Sites	*Voice Channel and Data Channel Signaling* Validate forward blank and burst functions over the voice channel as tested and evaluated by the CTB. Evaluate data transmission over the forward setup channels.	HP-21 generates continuous stream of data messages from a cell site and MTL mobile measure data word error rates at various geographical locations having different propagation characteristics.
	Test and evaluate data transmission over the mobile-to-cell site reverse voice channel and the reverse setup channel.	Reverse setup channel and reverse voice data channel tests use MTL onboard mobiles to transmit large numbers of data messages to a particular cell site. HP-21 records errors that site encounters.
MTSO, MTL, Cell Sites, DRS	*Mobile Control Algorithm* Determine the general performance of the location and handoff algorithms and the resulting ability to control mobile operating frequencies to permit an adequate serving signal and to prevent excessive co-channel interference.	MTL makes a record of the serving cell site and serving signal strength for onboard mobiles and the actual mobile geographic locations. DRS records location and handoff events.
MTSO, Cell Site	*System Reconfiguration* Evaluate ability of generic MTSO diagnostic software to isolate and reconfigure any voice/data trunk group or other redundant equipment group within the data terminal equipment or cell sites.	Simulate equipment failure and note performance of MTSO system integrity programs.
MTL, MTSO, Cell Site, Mobiles	*Cell Site Load Test* Evaluate ability of a cell site to respond to increasing traffic levels.	Computer-driven MTL mobiles plus vehicles equipped with Equipment Test mobiles place heavy traffic through a selected cell site.

interconnected with an experimental cell site and fixed laboratory mobiles, all located in the Oak Park laboratory. Also tested was an experimental cell site at Whippany, New Jersey, controlled by an HP-21MX minicomputer simulating the MTSO control function. The tests at both locations led to the correction of numerous minor design problems that would not otherwise have been discovered until the developmental system testing was well under way.

System test planning was a continuing and evolving activity closely tied to the related activities of collection, processing, and evaluation of data. Planning included identifying required data, generating requirements for specific system tests to obtain the data, defining the data-collection technique, designing specific test plans, converting them to specific operating procedures, and planning the processing and analysis of the data.

System tests planned for the developmental system primarily address the confirmation of overall system performance of a commercially manufactured system, although some evaluation of specific technical functions are also being performed.

Specific tests not requiring the complete system were performed using the earliest available cell sites, while other tests requiring the complete system did not commence until May 1978.

A significant test activity, called partial week service, utilized the MTSO, all integrated cell sites, and all available mobiles operating as a system during weekends commencing in March 1978. This operational activity was very effective in discovering system problems in time for early correction.

Table II contains examples of other system-level tests currently being conducted.

4.6 Mobile procurement and installation activities

Two mobile designs are being used in the developmental system. OKI Electric Industry Company, Ltd., Tokyo, Japan, manufactured 135 mobile transceiver and control units for the Equipment Test phase of the program. In addition, OKI built 135 Bell Laboratories-designed logic units to control the transceivers. Early production models were subjected to exhaustive testing at Bell Laboratories, including environmental tests, and were placed into use in the experimental systems described in Section V. The production units underwent acceptance testing at the Mobile Phone Service Center in Elmhurst, Illinois.

Contracts for developing and producing approximately 2200 mobiles required for the Service Test were placed with OKI; with Motorola, Inc., Schaumburg, Illinois; and with E. F. Johnson, Waseca, Minnesota. These mobiles, to be leased to commercial customers during the Service Test, are manufactured to a specification requiring an integrated transceiver-logic unit and a standard interface between it and the control unit. Extensive testing of early production models of these

mobiles was performed by Bell Laboratories. Delivery of these mobiles to Chicago commenced in November 1978.

A minicomputer-based automatic mobile test set was used for preinstallation testing of the Equipment Test mobiles and the testing of installed units in Bell System personnel's vehicles. Initially used in the mobile test laboratory in Whippany to evaluate early production units, the test set was moved to the Mobile Phone Service Center described in Section III and used to perform acceptance tests of the Equipment Test mobiles. Operating instruction and maintenance handbooks were prepared for this test set, and IBT craftspeople were trained to operate the unit prior to the installation of the first significant quantities of Equipment Test mobiles. A similar test set was developed for use with the Service Test mobiles.

A Cooperative Mobile Supplier Program permits any qualified manufacturer of an AMPS mobile design to participate in the developmental system test. This program creates the potential for future additional competitive suppliers of commercial Bell System-owned or customer-owned mobiles. At present, eight manufacturers have expressed an interest in participating in this program.

4.7 Developmental system schedule

The fabrication and factory testing of cell-site hardware were complete at the end of 1977. Cell-site building construction was likewise complete by year's end, except for the tenth cell site which required relocation because of a zoning disapproval. Cell-site equipment installations, tests, and integrations with the MTSO were completed by late May 1978, with the exception of the last cell site. System shakedown and debugging started in April 1978 and continued throughout the Equipment Test, from July 1978, to the end of the year. The system tests outlined in an earlier section are under way. The Service Test phase will follow the Equipment Test phase. Software development and mobile procurement activities are on schedules that coincide with the support of the Equipment Test and Service Test phases.

V. EXPERIMENTAL SYSTEMS—TEST AND EVALUATION ACTIVITIES

Reference has been made to experimental systems established at the Oak Park and Whippany laboratories for early testing and debugging of an integration of all AMPS subsystems. Early versions of the MTSO generic software were developed and tested with a No. 1 ESS peripheral. The initial tests used a breadboard model of the cell site as the computer peripheral; from November 1976 to June 1978, a production cell site served as the MTSO peripheral. This cell site was connected to fixed nonradiating mobiles through a transmission simulator incorporating a Rayleigh fader. In May 1977, roof-mounted antennas were added at Oak Park to permit live radiation testing to mobile-equipped automobiles operating in the vicinity. A Bell Laboratories experimental FCC license was obtained for this purpose.

A production cell site installed at Whippany was connected to the Oak Park MTSO via leased voice and data trunks in February 1977.

Early system testing and debugging employed a fixed nonradiating mobile in the laboratory, connected to the cell site via a coaxial cable. Roof-mounted antennas were later added to provide a radiating capability, and testing continued under the control of an HP-21 minicomputer simulator of the MTSO, utilizing the Whippany cell site, and a mobile-equipped automobile.

The ability to investigate abnormal system performance caused by a hardware or software design problem at the responsible design location has greatly simplified the logistics of problem investigation and has accelerated problem correction.

The benefits derived from these experimental systems permitted:

(*i*) Ongoing development and early functional integration of the hardware and software subsystems of AMPS.

(*ii*) Development and refinement of procedures and techniques that were required to test and evaluate the developmental system.

(*iii*) Development, validation, and evaluation of installation and test procedures that were used on cell-site and mobile equipment.

(*iv*) Testing and debugging of the MTL system prior to assignment in the developmental system.

(*v*) Early training of technical personnel responsible for operating, maintaining, and testing the developmental system.

(*vi*) Early evaluation of operating, maintenance, and recovery procedures.

(*vii*) Early experience with and refinement of equipment field change procedures, configuration control, and failed unit and spares logistics.

Test activities involving the experimental systems at Oak Park and Whippany diminished as developmental system equipment became more available. The use of these systems has resulted in shorter key activity intervals in the Chicago trial.

VI. DATA COLLECTION AND PROCESSING
6.1 Data collection tools

Three major data collection systems were developed for the Chicago trial: the Data Retrieval System (DRS), the Mobile Telephone Laboratory (MTL), and a telemetry capability in a selectable number of mobile units employed during the Service Test. In addition, a number of less-sophisticated tools were developed, such as specially instrumented mobiles in automobiles. Finally, specific functions of certain test units (such as the HP-21MX minicomputer for autonomous testing and trouble-shooting of cell sites) supply data from the developmental system.

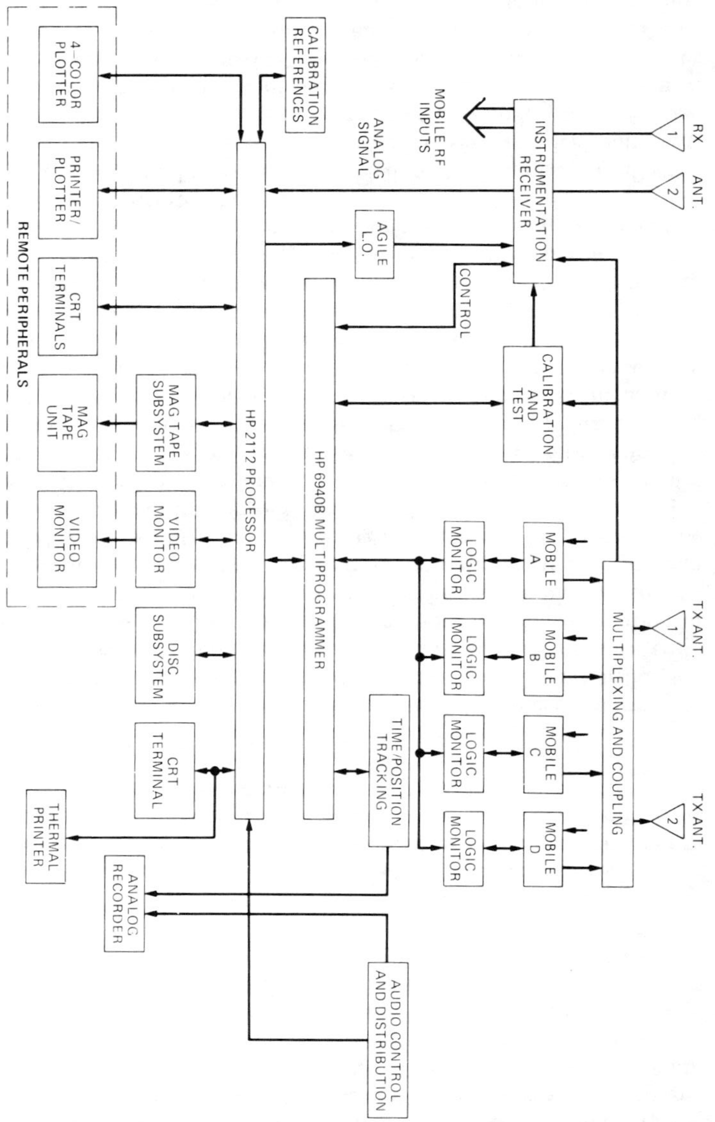

Fig. 8—Mobile Telephone Laboratory—block diagram.

6.1.1 Data Retrieval System

The DRS is a peripheral system that has been added to the No. 1 ESS MTSO to collect data for following the progress of a particular call and the operation of various facets of a given system algorithm, as well as to collect statistical data on many calls. The conversion of recorded DRS data to formats compatible with an HP-21 minicomputer is part of the overall data processing and analysis activity in the developmental system.

6.1.2 Mobile Telephone Laboratory

The second major data collection facility is the Mobile Telephone Laboratory, assigned to the Chicago area on December 1, 1977. The MTL tests and evaluates the system from the mobile's viewpoint and performs system trouble-shooting and system data collection functions. Because AMPS logic is distributed among the MTSO, the cell site's data frame PROCON, and the mobile logic unit, the monitoring and recording of logic activities within the mobile during various stages of a call is necessary to evaluate the performance of the overall system. The MTL performs this task by controlling and monitoring its instrumented on-board mobile units. The MTL is also a calibrated laboratory for measuring signal and noise environments at selected locations in the Chicago coverage area. It also performs testing of cell sites using the on-board minicomputer-controlled mobile units to originate calls automatically with specific time relationships at specific geographical locations.

Figure 8 is a simplified block diagram of the MTL. An onboard HP-21MX minicomputer subsystem controls all major equipment functions. A major subsystem collects signal and noise information from sources within the system using a well-calibrated instrumentation receiver with a wide dynamic range and low noise figure. This measurement receiver is rapidly tuned to the frequencies of interest using an agile local oscillator controlled by the on-board computer. Another subsystem contains four mobile units that can generate traffic under HP minicomputer control, and whose detailed operations can be precisely monitored and recorded for both real-time and off-line analysis.

Test transmitters and receivers on the vehicle provide an autonomous test and calibration capability to ensure that data being collected have not been invalidated by any malfunction of MTL equipment. Finally, a position and timing system permits associating collected data with time, vehicle speed, and vehicle position within the system.

Data-recording peripherals associated with the HP-21MX on-board computer include both magnetic tape and disk equipment and permit real-time on-board data examination using CRT displays, typewriter outputs, and printer outputs.

6.1.3 Mobile unit telemetry

Certain data are desired on the performance of the mobile telephone equipment and, in particular, the interaction of the user with the system during the Service Test phase of the developmental system. For this purpose, a significant number of Service Test mobile units are designed to monitor many of their own actions and telemeter basic information about customer usage characteristics to the MTSO.

Control of the telemetry resides in the MTSO, which indicates to the mobiles whether or not telemetry is to be sent and the interval between transmissions. If telemetry is to be sent, the mobile autonomously initiates telemetry requests at the specified intervals. Upon receiving a request, the MTSO orders the mobile via the setup channel to send its accumulated telemetry information over the reverse setup channel. The DRS retrieves all telemetry data for subsequent analysis.

6.2 Mobile monitor and control units

Figure 9 is a photograph of mobile monitor and control units (MCU) housed in the glove compartment of a special test automobile. Each MCU is a unit of special test equipment electrically connected to the transceiver unit and the logic unit of an Equipment Test mobile telephone installed in the test automobile.

The two MCU units have the following features:

(i) A continuous display of the channel number to which the mobile transceiver is tuned.

(ii) A continuous indication of the received (integrated) signal strength of the mobile unit.

(iii) A provision for switching the mobile unit to a manual operation mode where the mobile is tuned continuously to a channel selected by the vehicle operator. This mode is used for establishing duplex voice communications in preparing for and controlling particular segments of a test involving the vehicle.

(iv) A display of the mobile unit transmitter on-off state.

(v) A continuous display indicating which of the two receive diversity antennas is being used.

(vi) An ability to disconnect the diversity function and to select manually one or the other of the two antennas.

Three such specially equipped test automobiles have been used in the experimental systems at Whippany and at Oak Park and in the Chicago developmental system.

6.3 Data processing plans and facilities

The overall Chicago developmental system data processing program includes the following functional tasks: rapid (quick-look) verification that data were collected as intended; validation that the data truly represent actual system or subsystem performance; manipulation of data to produce outputs for analysis; further manipulation to add certain data to a larger data base; and manipulation of this larger data base to develop results of statistical significance as a function of some parameter, such as time or location.

The requirements for, and the uses of, Chicago developmental system data fall into two separate categories: system troubleshooting and system test and evaluation. System troubleshooting data requirements typically consist of specific test results, such as event listings, plots, and statistics compiled during a particular daily test over a period of time. System test and evaluation activities generally require larger amounts of data, typically collected over longer periods of time and in numerous geographical locations. Although both types of data are needed during the trial period, system troubleshooting is the predominant need for the early time frame, and initial data-processing efforts are concentrated here.

Two data facilities have been assembled for processing data collected in the developmental system. The first of these is a quick-look data-processing facility for MTL data located in the Mobile Phone Service Center building. It consists of additional computer peripherals in a room adjacent to the parked MTL and connected to the MTL computer via umbilical cables. This arrangement permits converting the MTL data collection equipment into a data-processing laboratory to allow preliminary validation of data and decisions on follow-up near-term activities to be based on observed test results. Software programs to

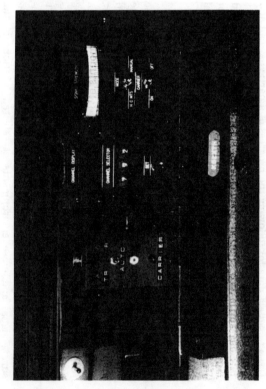

Fig. 9—Mobile monitor and control units.

reduce and manipulate data for this quick-look function have been designed.

The other facility with a data-processing capability built around an HP-21MX minicomputer has been developed at Bell Laboratories, Whippany. Data reduction software processes DRS, HP-21MX, and MTL data collected and validated in Chicago. This system has the ability to merge DRS and MTL data for specific analysis tasks.

VII. CONCLUSION

A sophisticated developmental system for testing AMPS has been installed in Chicago. The investment of the Bell System in this trial is substantial in terms of design, development, and test activities completed and anticipated, and in terms of procurement costs for the MTSO, the cell sites, the mobiles, and the land and buildings required by the system. Successful completion of the Equipment Test and Service Test phases will add considerable technical information to the base of knowledge of cellular systems to be used in establishing standards for the service, as well as providing unique market-related information. The future of AMPS, and of the Chicago developmental system, will depend upon the results of the technical and market tests, as well as upon regulatory actions.

Energy Deposition in Simulated Human Operators of 800-MHz Portable Transmitters

QUIRINO BALZANO, MEMBER, IEEE, OSCAR GARAY, AND FRANCIS R. STEEL, ASSOCIATE MEMBER, IEEE

Abstract−The measured values of energy deposited in simulated human tissue exposed for one minute in the immediate vicinity of 800 MHz portable radio transmitters are presented. The deposited RF energy was evaluated by temperature measurements. The portable radio used in the tests had a 6-W experimental transmitter operating at 840 MHz. Two different antennas were tested for energy deposition: a sleeve dipole and a resonant whip. The two antennas have given substantially different results indicating different field structures near the two radiators. The experiments with flat slabs have shown that the sleeve dipole deposits higher levels of power density than the resonant whip in the near field although the length of the latter radiator is about half the size of the former. The temperature profiles generated by both antennas inside the head of the simulated operator indicate the presence of a "hot spot" about 1 in below the surface of the temporal bone. This phenomenon was not detected previously at lower frequencies. The short antenna exposes the eye of the operator to more intense power deposition than the sleeve dipole. The temperature increases measured during the investigation are so small that no thermal damage to tissue should be caused by normal use of the portable radio.

I. INTRODUCTION

NEW TECHNOLOGIES are rapidly developing for mobile and portable communication systems at 800–900 MHz. In the near future, a large number of operators are expected to be using equipment at these frequencies, recently made available for communication purposes. The 800–900 MHz band is very close to the frequencies used for medical diathermy (918 MHz). Diathermy applicators at 918 MHz are well known for efficiently depositing energy deep into human tissue. This fact may create some concern about the exposure of the head of a portable transmitter operator, because the radio is held close to the mouth in normal use.

Since previous work [1], [2] had shown that E-field probes do not give reliable information about RF exposure near portable radios, expected power deposition levels in operators have been determined by temperature measurements in simulated humans. Two well-known antennas have been used in the measurements of energy deposition. Both types of radiators are expected to be widely used at 800–900 MHz.

At these frequencies, it was found that commercially available field hazard probes do not read high values of power density at a 2-in distance from portables, as they do at lower bands [1]. However, given the large differences between penetrating power in simulated tissue and E-field probe readings detected at 450 MHz, this experimental investigation was

necessary to determine any possible relation between instrument readings and deposition levels. A simple E-field measurement would still be the most attractive way to determine a hazard level, but at 800–900 MHz, this method cannot be used in the near field of a transmitting antenna.

II. SIMULATED OPERATORS

Two different simulated operators have been used to evaluate power deposition near portable transmitters in the 800–900 MHz band. A flat double layer slab of simulated tissue was employed to investigate the deposition properties of the electromagnetic fields in the immediate vicinity of the antenna. This flat phantom, completely analogous to the one used at 450 MHz [1], is a simple structure which gives results rapidly interpretable in terms of power flow at the surface of the "dummy." As mentioned, the flat phantom is used only for the purpose of investigating the EM fields in close proximity of the radio. Relevant data about the possible exposure of an operator are collected by means of a more sophisticated structure. The phantom operator consists of a real human skull stuffed with simulated brain tissue [3], [4].

The skull is supported by a shell of bone mixture approximately 0.3-in thick and 9-in high, shaped to simulate the contour of the neck and shoulders of the operator. The supporting bone structure is filled with simulated muscle tissue [2]. The skull belonged to a young human adult. It is approximately 6-in high, 6-in wide (cranial index approximately 86), and has a maximum diameter of over 8 in. The "dummy" operator is shown in Fig. 1. The phantom is sealed by stretching a very thin rubber membrane (<0.003 in) over the skull and the first 2 in of the neck. A thin layer (<1 mm) of clear epoxy coating could be used to simulate a layer of skin, if the epoxy were mixed with other materials to obtain the proper dielectric constant and conductivity. The need to introduce a layer of skin on the phantom may arise at higher frequencies (e.g., 2500 MHz), but, for tests at the 800–900 MHz band, the present "dummy" is very adequate. Fig. 2 shows a close-up of the phantom before filling with brain material. The picture gives a good idea of the sealing method.

III. EXPERIMENTAL PROGRAM

An experimental portable transmitter of 6-W radiated power at 840 MHz was used throughout the program. The radio case (with batteries) was 8-in long. The power deposition properties of two different antennas have been evaluated: a

Manuscript received January 19, 1978; revised May 2, 1978.
The authors are with the Communications Products Division, Motorola, Inc., 8000 W. Sunrise Blvd., Ft. Lauderdale, FL 33322. Telephone; (305) 473-6000, ext. 2469.

Reprinted from *IEEE Trans. Veh. Technol.*, vol. VT-27, pp. 174–181, Nov. 1978.

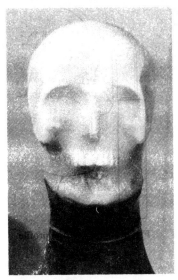

Fig. 1. Head phantom.

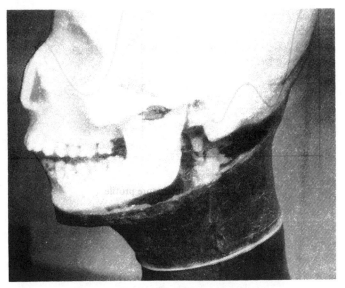

Fig. 2. Head phantom.

quarter wave resonant whip about 3-in long and a sleeve dipole. The sleeve dipole consists of a 2-in section of feeding coaxial sleeve and a 6-in long radiator. The thin section of the sleeve dipole is about 3.5-in long. The head phantom was exposed by holding the radio case in front of its mouth. This position caused the left eyeball of the "dummy" to be aligned with the axis of both antennas. The radio was held at a 0.2-in distance from the mouth of the dummy as shown in Fig. 3. This distance was selected as the best compromise. For greater spacing between radiator and phantom, it is practically impossible to make reliable temperature measurements. At shorter distances, the radio would not be in a position of normal use. In the condition shown in Fig. 3, the left eyeball and frontal lobe of the skull are about 2 in from both antennas. The flat phantom was exposed holding the antennas at 0.35 in and 2 in away from the surface of the slab (see sketches in Fig. 14 and 15). In both models, temperature measurements were performed by penetrating with a thermal probe along the local normal to the surface. The depth of penetration depended upon the temper-

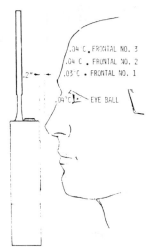

Fig. 3. Temperature profile.

ature readings. At each point of penetration, the temperature versus depth profile was measured with a precision of $\pm 0.01°C$. All exposures were for one min. The experimental method and the instrumentation have been described in a previous work [1].

IV. EXPOSURE OF HEAD PHANTOM

The maximum temperature increases measured using the sleeve dipole antenna are shown in Fig. 3. Frontal point number 1 is 0.75 in above the superciliary arch and is the spot on the left frontal eminence of the skull closest to the antenna. Frontal points 2 and 3 are 1.5 in and 2.25 in above the superciliary arch and follow the normal projection of the antenna axis on the surface of the phantom. The temperature profiles at the four locations of Fig. 3 are shown in Figs. 4 and 5. Fig. 4 indicates that the maximum temperature increase caused by the radio is at the surface of the eye, not deeper in the organ as is the case with plane incident waves [5], [6]. Of great interest is the same peak of the specific absorption rate (SAR in mW/g) at about 1 in below the skull surface detected in all frontal profiles. The curvature of the frontal bone at the points of measurement causes lines normal to the surface to converge at the same spot in the simulated brain tissue. The SAR peaks (sometimes called "hot spots") are probably associated with the "focusing" of EM energy by this curvature of the frontal bone. The maximum measured value of SAR was 2.5 mW/g (Fig. 4(b)). Temperature measurements deeper in the brain tissue, all the way to the center of the skull, have failed to give values above the measurement precision of 0.01°C. The absorption peaks near the center of the brain found by others [7] for plane incident waves using a spherical model of the head and phantoms similar to ours were not detected. This result does not exclude the presence of such peaks, but they might be at levels substantially lower than the "hot spot" shown in Figs. 4 and 5, and are immeasurable with our available instruments and power. At a given frequency, the absorption "mode" (SAR profile) of a body in the immediate vicinity of an RF source is dependent on the radiator geometry and can be completely different from the far field absorption "mode" which is, by definition, source independent (a characteristic of the absorbing body for each direction of incidence

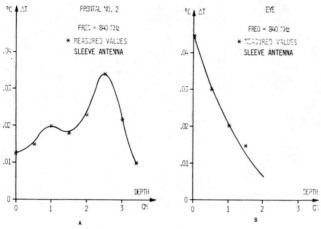

Fig. 4. Temperature profiles.

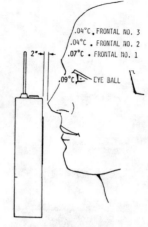

Fig. 6. Temperature profile.

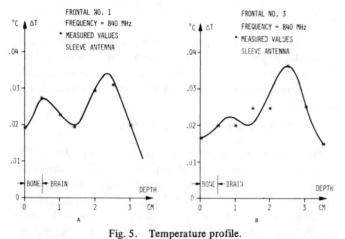

Fig. 5. Temperature profile.

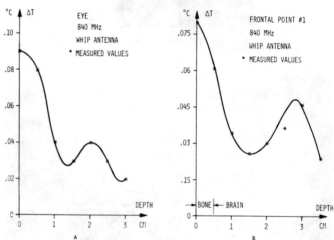

Fig. 7. Temperature profile.

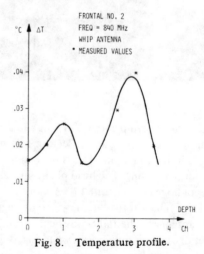

Fig. 8. Temperature profile.

and polarization of the incoming wave). The difference between SAR profiles in the near field with a source change is exhibited by the following results.

Fig. 6 shows the maximum temperature increases detected in the head phantom measured at the same points as in Fig. 3 when a short (3 in length) resonant whip was used. The temperature profiles are given in Figs. 7 and 8. Comparing Fig. 7 with Fig. 4, one can see that the eye is more exposed by the whip than by the sleeve. The whip doubles the peak SAR (5.5 mW/g maximum value) and causes, in addition, a secondary absorption peak at about a 2-cm depth in the simulated eye. At frontal point number 1, there is little deposition in the frontal bone, and the absorption peak is about 3 cm below the surface in the region of point 1. The temperature profile at point 3 due to radiation with the whip is analogous to the one of Fig. 8. As in the previous case, the experimental data indicate the presence of a "hot spot" 3-cm inside the simulated cerebral cortex.

Although the "hot spot" is analogous to the one detected using the sleeve (there is only a slight difference in the depth below the surface), it does not constitute the absolute absorption peak (or maximum SAR), because the surface of the eye and the cerebral tissue below the frontal bone at location 1 absorb more power than the "hot spot" in the simulated cortex. Experimental data indicate that the short whip produces higher SAR's than the sleeve antenna. One may think that the phenomenon is caused by an increase in incident power den-

sity due to smaller size of the antenna. As will be shown shortly, this is not the case. There is actually higher power density in the vicinity of the sleeve than near the whip.

V. EXPOSURE OF THE FLAT PHANTOM

A large number of measurements were performed with the flat phantom, especially for close spacing between antennas and "dummy," because the temperature increases are the largest and give a good insight into the power deposition properties of

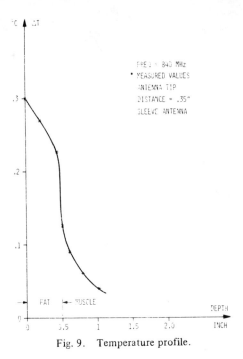

FREQ = 840 MHz
* MEASURED VALUES
ANTENNA TIP
DISTANCE = .35"
SLEEVE ANTENNA

Fig. 9.   Temperature profile.

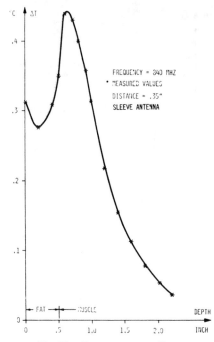

FREQUENCY = 840 MHZ
* MEASURED VALUES
DISTANCE = .35"
SLEEVE ANTENNA

Fig. 10.   Temperature profile.

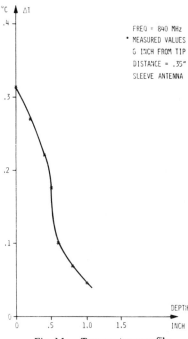

FREQ = 840 MHz
* MEASURED VALUES
0 INCH FROM TIP
DISTANCE = .35"
SLEEVE ANTENNA

Fig. 11.   Temperature profile.

the fields in the immediate vicinity of the radiators. Only the most significant results, characterizing the energy coupling between the antennas and the phantom, are presented. Figs. 9–11 show the temperature profiles for a 0.35-in distance between sleeve dipole and model measured in the phantom at the tip of the antenna (Fig. 9), at the feed point (Fig. 10), and at the end of the fat section of the radiator (Fig. 11). The geometry of the antenna is depicted in the sketch of Fig. 14. At both ends of the radiator, the EM energy is deposited essentially in the surface fatty layers of the "dummy". In Figs. 9 and 11, one can see that there is a negative temperature gradient from the fat into the simulated muscle. The relatively small deposition in the deep tissue can be explained in terms of high impedance fields incident normally at the air/fat interface [1], [2]. At the feed point of the sleeve antenna, the energy deposition is essentially in the muscle tissue near the fat/muscle interface, indicating that the incident fields have a strong component tangent to the surface of the phantom [2].

The power deposition mechanism along the axis of the antenna from the tip to the feed point changes smoothly from essentially fat heating to essentially muscle heating. Figs. 12 and 13 show the transition of the power deposition mechanism. They plot the temperature profile inside the phantom for a 0.35-in distance between antenna and dummy. The measurements were performed at locations directly under the antenna axis at 1- and 2-in distances from the tip in the direction of the feed point. Fig. 12 shows that there is a peak of SAR (peak value approximately 9 mW/g) in the fatty tissue, indicating the presence of a maximum of the *E*-field component incident orthogonally on slab. There is an increase of energy absorption by the muscle tissue moving along the axis of the antenna from the tip (minimum) to the feed point (maximum) as shown in Figs. 9–10 and 12–13. As is clear from the profile of Fig. 13, at a 2-in distance from the tip of the antenna, the maximum temperature increases in the simulated fat and muscle tissue are the same. In the region along the antenna axis between the feed point (3.5 in from the tip of the sleeve) and the point of

Fig. 13, there is an additional increase of energy deposition in the muscle in conjunction with a decrease of energy absorption by the simulated fat. At the feed point, the maximum SAR of the muscle tissue, as determined by the highest temperature increase, is about 26 mW/g.

This value is obviously an underestimate because of the heat exchange across the muscle/fat boundary, as is clear from the curve of Fig. 10. The temperature profiles in the region between the feed point and the end of the sleeve are similar to those of the previous figures, showing that the power deposition along the large diameter section of the antenna is analogous to the one along the small diameter section.

From the temperature measurements, it is possible to plot the distribution of the power density (in mW/cm^2) penetrating

371

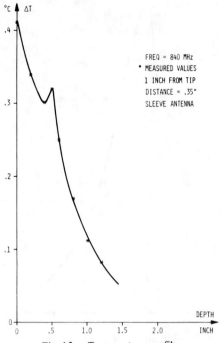

Fig. 12.   Temperature profile.

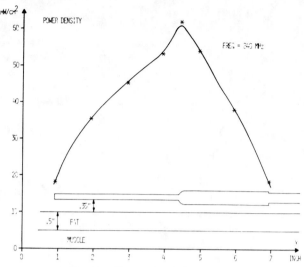

Fig. 14.   Penetrating power density.

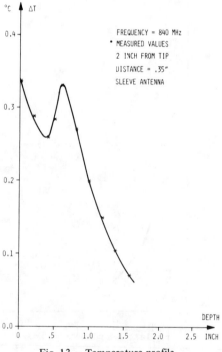

Fig. 13.   Temperature profile.

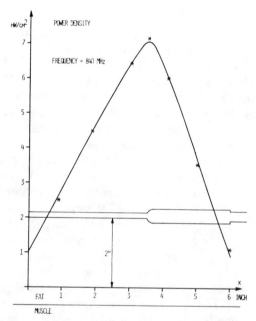

Fig. 15.   Penetrating power density.

the surface of the phantom. Such a curve is shown in Fig. 14 for the exposure at a 0.35 in distance. At such a short distance, there is a small area of the slab, near the feed point of the dipole, exposed to a penetrating density of over 60 mW/cm². The deposited power density distribution falls off very rapidly along the axis of the antenna, and at the tip of this section is 18 mW/cm², about the same value detected at 450 MHz using a whip antenna [2]. An explanation for the near constant value of deposited power density versus frequecy at the tip of λ/4 dipoles was given in a previous paper [8]. The average deposited power density along the axis of tee antenna is about 42 mW/cm². The exposure decreases very rapidly with distance as shown by Fig. 15, plotting the power density penetrating

the dummy for a 2-in distance between phantom and radiator. The peak power density is slightly over 7 mW/cm², and the average is 4 mW/cm². The maximum deposition has decreased by a factor of 9 and the minimum by a factor of 18, showing that the power propagation near the antenna is neither cylindrical nor spherical. The phase fronts are too complicated to be approximated by simple geometric surfaces. In addition, the tissue is in a strong induction field at this distance, forming yet another "coupling" mechanism.

The results of the deposition measurements using the 3-in resonant whip are shown in Figs. 16-19, plotting the temperature profiles at three different points along the antenna axis. The distance between the radiator and phantom is 0.35 in. Figs. 16 and 18 are similar to Figs. 9 and 10, but the levels of the latter plots are higher than those of the former. Comparing Figs. 18 and 10, one finds that the peak SAR in the muscle tissue caused by the short whip is about 22 percent smaller than the one due to the sleeve dipole. Figs. 9 and 16 indicate that the maximum SAR in the fatty tissue caused by the whip is about 25 percent lower than the level caused by the sleeve

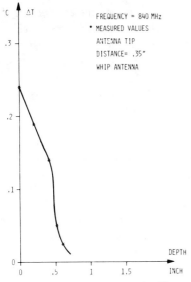

Fig. 16. Temperature profile.

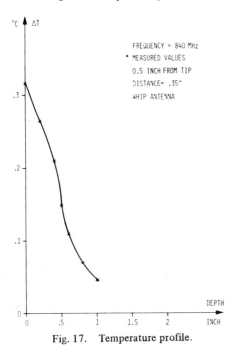

Fig. 17. Temperature profile.

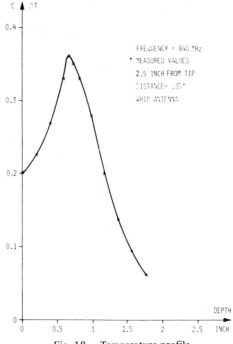

Fig. 18. Temperature profile.

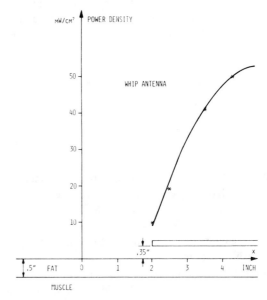

Fig. 19. Penetrating power density.

antenna. Muscle tissue absorption shown in Fig. 16 is much smaller than that found in Fig. 9. No explanation in terms of currents on the whip have been formulated for this occurrance. The difference can be explained only by involving the currents on the radio case. The sleeve dipole has a well-balanced system of current flow, as can be seen from the power deposition plot of Fig. 14. A half-wave (total length) dipole deposits a considerable amount of energy in the muscle tissue near the tip of the antenna, as is clear from Figs. 9 and 11, and from previous work on 450 MHz radios [2]. Figs. 16 and 17 indicate that the current structure on the short resonant whip and its radio case is *not* the one of a resonant half-wave (total length) dipole. As may be expected, the radio case does not act as an infinite ground plane.

Far-field patterns clearly indicate that the whip and the case radiate like a 3/4λ unbalanced dipole, asymmetrically fed. Near the base of the antenna, at a 0.35 in distance, the current on the whip dominates the power deposition mechanism which is completely analogous to the one detected near the feed point of the sleeve. At the tip of the whip, where the local current is very small, the effects of the currents on the radio case are detected as producing locally a wave of impedance higher than that of the energy radiated by a balanced half-wave dipole.

Whatever the mechanism, it is interesting to note that there is a lower power density near the smaller of the two antennas, as shown by the curves in Figs. 19 and 20. Fig. 19, plotting the penetrating power density for a 0.35-in distance between whip and phantom, indicates that the maximum density at the feed point of the antenna is about 53 mW/cm², approximately 17 percent lower than the 62 mW/cm² detected using the sleeve dipole. At the tip of the whip, the penetrating power density is 10 mW/cm², 40 percent less than the value measured at the tip of the sleeve antenna. The average value of the

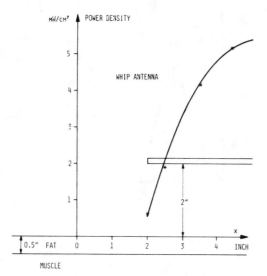

Fig. 20. Penetrating power density.

deposited power density along the axis of the whip is about 35 mW/cm² , or 20 percent less than the average along the axis of the sleeve. The power deposition curve for the 2-in distance shown in Fig. 10 has a shape similar to the one in Fig. 9. The average deposited power density along the antenna axis is approximately 3.5 mW/cm². At the tip of the radiator, power deposition in the muscle tissue was practically nil.

VI. REVIEW OF POWER DEPOSITION DATA: COMPARISON WITH FIELD PROBES

The experimental data collected at 840 MHz using a resonant whip and a sleeve dipole indicate that there is a substantial difference in the power deposition mechanism along the axes of the antennas even for a 2-in spacing, a distance which is normally kept between a source and the field probes used in detecting RF hazards.

As at lower frequencies (450 MHz) [2] the fields near the tip of the radiator deposit power in the surface fatty or bone layers of the simulated tissue. This fact is clear from the temperature profiles in Figs. 7(b), 9, 11, 16, and 17. These fields may be called "high impedance" fields as opposed to the "low impedance" fields near the feed point of the antennas. The latter fields deposit most of their penetrating power in the deeper muscle or brain tissue, as shown by Figs. 10, 13, and 18. The difference is further evidenced by the exposure of the eye of the operator closer to the antennas. Figs. 4(b) and 7(a) show that the base of the whip antenna exposes the simulated eye more than the "high impedance" point of the sleeve dipole. It is clear then that even at frequencies as high as 800–900 MHz, the distance of 2 in from the source does not insure that a near uniform impedance wave front is incident at different points along the structure of the radiator.

One may ask what the readings of power density meters might be in this situation. Power density meters (e.g., the Narda 8310 survey instrument) have E-field sensors and readout power density, calibrated in terms of a plane incident wave (P density $= |E|^2/377$). Since we know that the field impedance is not constant in the present instance, it is interesting to com-

pare the readings of a power meter, normally used in RF hazard surveys, with the power density effectively being absorbed by the flat simulated operator. Tests were performed using the Narda 8310 isotropic probe. The resonant whip is too short to conduct any good measurements of power density along the axis of the antenna. The instrument sensor is protected by a foam ball of 2-in radius, which interferes with the edge of the radio case, making it impossible to probe near the base of the whip.

The results obtained with the sleeve antenna are shown in Fig. 21. The instrument was used as suggested by the manufacturer. The probe handle was orthogonal to the axis of the free-standing antenna, and the anterior pole of the foam sphere covering the sensor was touching the antenna. At each point of measurement, the probe was rotated around its axis of symmetry for maximum reading. As one can see, the instrument readings are practically constant along the axis of the antenna, and their curve bears little relation to the penetrating power density plot. The other feature worthy of notice is the fact that the probe gives a reading close to the maximum power density penetrating the flat phantom.

The incident power density indicated by the instrument is, per se, very misleading. An experimenter with some knowledge of radiation would immediately come to the conclusion that the probe is not sensing power density and thus doubt the significance of the measurements. Only after an "a posteriori" comparison with the penetrating power density determined by thermal measurements can one say that a particular type of field probe (the Narda instrument) at a 2-in distance from the feed point of a particular antenna (the sleeve dipole) gives a reading that is approximately equal to the power density penetrating a flat slab of simulated human tissue. If the Narda probe is positioned in such a fashion that it correctly senses the E-field, the instrument readings shown in Fig. 22 are even more misleading than the results in Fig. 21. The Narda field probe indicates minimum incident power density where there is a maximum exposure. More research must be performed to determine whether a survey probe of the Narda type can be constructed to meaningfully determine exposure near portable radios at 800–900 MHz.

VII. CONCLUSION

This paper has analyzed in detail some features of the near field of 800–900 MHz portable radios. A sleeve dipole and a resonant whip at these frequencies exhibit different field structures. The sleeve is responsible for higher absorbed power densities near the feed point. One could expect the short whip to generate the stronger fields (because of the smaller size), but RF currents on the radio case reduce the near field power density of this radiating system below the levels attained by the sleeve dipole. Both antennas are capable of depositing high levels of power density in small areas around the feed points, if the radiator is held very close (less than 0.5 in) to the operator. If the radio is used properly, positioned as in Fig. 3, but at a 2-in distance from the mouth instead of the 0.2-in shown, the exposure is nearly immeasurable with available thermal probes, indicating that the maximum SAR is less than 0.3 mW/gr,

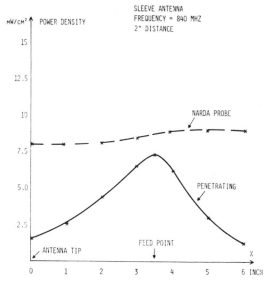

Fig. 21.   Power density along antenna axis.

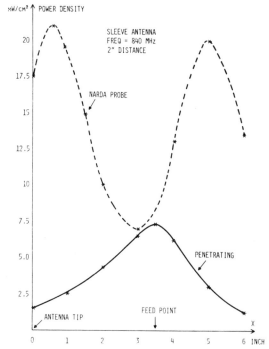

Fig. 22.   Power density along antenna axis.

which is about 10 dB lower than the average free space SAR permitted by current safety standards [9]. For the spacing of Fig. 3, which is so small as to cause harmonic distortion in the radio microphone, the exposure causes only very small temperature increases which probably would not be associated with thermal tissue damage.

Field probes like the Narda 8310 hazard meter do not seem to give a correct indication of locally incident power density on the antenna near fields we have examined. However, at the feed point of the sleeve dipole, the instrument produces a reading close to the value of the power density penetrating a flat slab of simulated human tissue. Additional research is necessary to establish whether field probes can be used to meaningfully measure exposure levels near portable transmitters in the 800-900 MHz frequency band.

REFERENCES

[1] Q. Balzano *et al.*, "Heating of biological tissue in the induction field of portable radio transmitters," *IEEE Trans. Veh. Technol.*, vol. VT-27, pp. 51–56, May 1978.

[2] Q. Balzano *et al.*, "Energy deposition in biological tissue near portable radio transmitters at VHF and UHF," Rec. Twenty-Seventh Ann. Confer. IEEE Vehicular Technology Group, Orlando, FL, pp. 25–39, Mar. 16–18, 1977.

[3] A. W. Guy, "Analyses of electromagnetic fields induced in biological tissue by thermographic studies on equivalent phantom models," *IEEE Trans. Microwave Theory Techn.*, vol. MTT-19, pp. 205–216, Feb. 1971.

[4] A. W. Guy, private communication.

[5] A. W. Guy *et al.*, "Measurement of absorbed power patterns in the heads and eyes of rabbits exposed to typical microwave sources," Proc. 1974 Conf. Precision Electromagnetic Measurements, London, England, pp. 255–257, July 1974.

[6] A. Taflove and M. E. Brodwin, "Computation of the electromagnetic fields and induced temperatures with a model of the microwave-Irradiated human eye," *IEEE Trans. Microwave Theory Tech.*, vol. MTT-23, pp. 888–896, Nov. 1975.

[7] J. C. Lin, "On microwave inducted heating," *IEEE Trans. Microwave Theory Tech.*, vol. MTT-25, pp. 605–613, July 1977.

[8] Q. Balzano *et al.*, "A comparison between the energy deposition in portable radio operators at 900 MHz and 450 MHz," Rec. Twenty-Eighth Annu. Conf. IEEE Vehicular Technology Society, Denver, CO, March 22–24, 1978.

[9] O. P. Gandhi *et al.*, "Deposition of electromagnetic energy in animals and in models of man with and without grounding and reflector effects," *Radio Science*, vol. 12, no. 6(s), pp. 39–48, Nov.-Dec 1977.

Author Index

Subject Index

Editors' Biographies

Dennis Bodson (S'60–M'61–SM'71) was born in Washington, DC, on July 7, 1939. He received the B.E.E. and M.E.E. degrees in electrical engineering from the Catholic University of America, Washington, DC, in 1961 and 1963, respectively, and a Master's degree in public administration from the University of Southern California Washington Center for Public Affairs, Washington, DC, in 1976. He is currently working on his Ph.D. degree in electrical engineering.

During 1963–1966 he served as an officer in the U.S. Air Force at the National Security Agency. From 1966 to 1969 he was with Vitro Laboratories, Atlantic Research Corporation, and the U.S. Army Materiel Command, where he was engaged in research and development and systems engineering. In 1969 he joined the Staff of the National Communications System (NCS), an organization of the Federal government, where he serves in the NCS Office of Technology and Standards, Washington, DC. His prime areas of responsibility are telecommunications technology, electromagnetic pulse, and the development of Federal standards relating to telecommunications in the areas of digital facsimile and video teleconferencing.

Mr. Bodson is a Registered Professional Engineer in Washington, DC, and Virginia, is certified by the National Council of Engineering Examiners, holds an FCC First Class Radiotelephone License, is an Amateur Radio Extra Class Licensee, and is a Fellow of the Radio Club of America. He is currently the Director of Region 2 of the IEEE.

George F. McClure (M'57–SM'75–F'81) received the M.S. degree in engineering from the University of Florida, Gainesville.

He is currently Manager of Electronics Research and Technology at Martin Marietta Orlando Aerospace, Orlando, FL. Earlier, he was responsible for systems design and applications of mobile communications, including mobile telephone and military tactical communications.

Mr. McClure is Editor of the IEEE TRANSACTIONS ON VEHICULAR TECHNOLOGY.

Samuel R. McConoughey (S'48–A'50–M'56–M'67–SM'77) received the B.S.E.E. degree from Iowa State College.

He is presently an Electronics Engineer with the Network Analysis Branch, Common Carrier Bureau of the Federal Communications Commission, Washington, DC. He previously served the FCC as Chief of the Mobile Services Division and as a Supervisory Engineer with the Industrial and Public Safety Rules Division of the Safety and Special Radio Services Bureau. Prior to joining the FCC he served in various engineering and marketing positions at Northrop, LTV, GE, Prodelin, Michigan Wisconsin Pipeline, and AT&T.

Mr. McConoughey is currently President of the IEEE Vehicular Technology Society. He is also a Fellow of the Radio Club of America.